Contents

Contributing Authors

Thomas Alexander
Professor of History, Emeritus, Brigham Young University
Settling the Wasatch Front

Karl Ricks Anderson
Coordinator, Seminaries & Institutes, The Church of Jesus Christ of Latter-day Saints
The Western Reserve

Paul L. Anderson
Curator, Museum of Art, Brigham Young University
Building Meetinghouses

Ronald O. Barney
Archivist and Historian (retired), Church History Department, The Church of Jesus Christ of Latter-day Saints
Church Headquarters

Alexander L. Baugh
Professor of Church History and Doctrine, Brigham Young University
Travels between Ohio and Missouri
Settling Northern Missouri

Richard E. Bennett
Professor of Church History and Doctrine, Brigham Young University
Eastern United States and Canada

Lowell C. Bennion
Professor of Geography, Emeritus, Humboldt State University, Areata, California
Plural Marriage

Barbara Hands Bernauer
Assistant Archivist, Community of Christ
Community of Christ

Susan Easton Black
Professor of Church History and Doctrine, Brigham Young University
The First Year of the Church of Christ
The Mormon Battalion

David F. Boone
Associate Professor of Church History and Doctrine, Brigham Young University
Missionary Work

Jay H. Buckley
Associate Professor of History, Brigham Young University
Exploring Utah

Brian Q. Cannon
Professor of History and Director, Charles Redd Center for Western Studies, Brigham Young University
Settling the Salt Lake Valley

Sean Cannon
Chair, Department of History, Geography, and Political Science, Brigham Young University-Idaho
The Mormon-Missouri War

Lyndia McDowell Carter
Independent scholar, Springville, Utah
Handcart Pioneers
Rescuing the Martin and Willie Companies

Howard A. Christy
Senior Editor (retired), Office of Scholarly Publications, Brigham Young University
Mormon-Indian Relations

Richard O. Cowan
Professor of Church History and Doctrine, Brigham Young University
Temples; Stakes

James A. Davis
Associate Professor of Geography, Brigham Young University
Historical Sites

Jill Mulvay Derr
Senior Research Historian (retired), Church History Department, The Church of Jesus Christ of Latter-day Saints
The Relief Society

W. Randall Dixon
Archivist and Historian (retired), Church History Department, The Church of Jesus Christ of Latter-day Saints
Church Headquarters

John Eldredge
Independent Scholar, Salt Lake City, Utah
Utah War

Jessie L. Embry
Associate Director, Charles Redd Center for Western Studies, Brigham Young University
Specialized Congregations

Donald Enders
Historian (retired), Church History Department, The Church of Jesus Christ of Latter-day Saints
Palmyra & Manchester

Ronald K. Esplin
Managing Editor, Joseph Smith Papers Project, Church History Department, The Church of Jesus Christ of Latter-day Saints
President Brigham Young

Scott C. Esplin
Professor of Church History and Doctrine, Brigham Young University
Church Academies

J. Spencer Fluhman
Assistant Professor of History, Brigham Young University
Origins of Early Church Leaders
The Spiritual Environment of the Restoration

Jeff Fox
Associate Director, Center for Teaching & Learning, Brigham Young University
Political Affiliation

Arnold K. Garr
Professor of Church History and Doctrine, Emeritus, Brigham Young University
Church Academies

Kenneth W. Godfrey
Instructor (retired), Logan Institute of Religion, The Church of Jesus Christ of Latter-day Saints
Conflict in Hancock County

Fernando R. Gomez
President, Mexican Mormon History Museum
Middle America

Cynthia Doxey Green
Independent Scholar, Winston-Salem, North Carolina
Cultural Ambassadors

Mark Grover
Latin American and African Studies Librarian, Harold B. Lee Library, Brigham Young University
Middle America; South America

William G. Hartley
Associate Professor of History, Emeritus, Brigham Young University
Planning the Exodus; The Exodus Begins

Matthew Heiss
Historian, Church History Department, The Church of Jesus Christ of Latter-day Saints
Africa; The Middle East

Clark B. Hinckley
Senior Vice President (retired), Zions Bancorporation
Travels of Gordon B. Hinckley

Gail Geo. Holmes
Independent Scholar, Omaha, Nebraska
The Middle Missouri Valley

Kent P. Jackson
Professor of Ancient Scripture, Brigham Young University
Latter-day Scriptures

G. Wesley Johnson
Professor of Business History, Emeritus, Brigham Young University
The Mormon Outmigration

Marian Ashby Johnson
Partner, Ashby & Johnson History Consultants
The Mormon Outmigration

Edward L. Kimball
Professor of Law, Emeritus, Brigham Young University
Spencer W. Kimball

David Magleby
Professor of Political Science, Brigham Young University
Political Affiliation

James B. Mayfield
Professor Emeritus of Public Administration and Middle East Studies, University of Utah
Welfare and Humanitarian Aid

Kahlile Mehr
Slavic Collection Manager, FamilySearch, The Church of Jesus Christ of Latter-day Saints
Europe

Reid L. Neilson
Managing Director, Church History Department, The Church of Jesus Christ of Latter-day Saints
Asia; Australia and the Pacific

Samuel M. Otterstrom
Associate Professor of Geography, Brigham Young University
Membership Distribution
The Future of the Church

Max H Parkin
Instructor (retired), Salt Lake Institute of Religion, The Church of Jesus Christ of Latter-day Saints
The Settlement of Zion

Keith W. Perkins
Professor of Church History and Doctrine, Emeritus, Brigham Young University
Kirtland, Ohio

Clayne L. Pope
Professor of Economics, Emeritus, Brigham Young University
Economic Development

Larry C. Porter
Professor of Church History and Doctrine, Emeritus, Brigham Young University
The Joseph and Lucy Mack Smith Family
Cradle of the Restoration

Gregory A. Prince
President and CEO, Virion Systems, Inc.
David O. McKay

Daniel Reeves
Charles University, Department of Social Geography and Regional Development
Three American Churches

A. LeGrand Richards
Associate Professor of Education, Brigham Young University
Specialized Congregations

William Russell
Professor Emeritus of Political Science and History, Graceland University
Community of Christ

Steven L. Shields
International Field Ministries, Community of Christ
The Succession Crisis

Kip Sperry
Professor of Church History and Doctrine, Brigham Young University
Genealogy

Mark L. Staker
Senior Researcher, Church History Department, The Church of Jesus Christ of Latter-day Saints
Kirtland, Ohio

Gary Topping
Archivist, The Roman Catholic Diocese of Salt Lake City
The Gentiles

Richard E. Turley Jr.
Assistant Church Historian and Recorder, Church of Jesus Christ of Latter-day Saints
Utah War

Wayne Wahlquist
Professor of Geography, Emeritus, Weber State University
Pioneer Trails

David J. Whittaker
Curator of Western & Mormon Manuscripts (retired), Harold B. Lee Library, Brigham Young University
Early Missions; The Twelve Apostles
Missions of the 19th Century

Fred E. Woods
Professor of Church History and Doctrine, Brigham Young University
Gathering to Zion

Foreword
by Richard Lyman Bushman

THE INTEREST IN ATLASES OF RELIGION begins with the idea of holy land and holy places. Many religions have created sacred geographies based on journeys, significant out-of-the-way sites, and cities that figured in their foundation stories. Judaism, Christianity, and Islam honor Jerusalem, and Islam has added Mecca and Medina as sacred places. Then there are the Red Sea, Sinai, Bethlehem, and Galilee. A rudimentary sacred geography, anchored to these places, resides in the minds of most believers.

Latter-day Saints are no exception. They added a sacred city of their own to the traditional Christian geography, a New Jerusalem in Missouri, where a temple was to be built in America. They lost their city when the local citizens drove them from Jackson County, but the route of their history became sacred. In the course of forming The Church of Jesus Christ of Latter-day Saints, a path was blazed from Sharon, Vermont, through Palmyra, New York, and on to Kirtland, Independence, Far West, and Nauvoo to Salt Lake City. The twentieth-century Church memorialized this route by marking the spots and erecting monuments. The path creates a kind of holy land within America, the path the Saints have trod. Every young Latter-day Saint learns where Joseph Smith was born, where the First Vision took place, and where the Saints moved in pursuit of Zion. The Great Trek from Nauvoo to Utah lives in the Mormon imagination as vividly now as it did a hundred and fifty years ago.

Atlases of religion would seem to be a natural outgrowth of religious geography. To grasp the temporal structure of their faith, the way it emerges from historical events, Latter-day Saints need historical-spatial information. Atlases capture that information, stabilize it, and depict it. With good reason, the official version of Latter-day Saint scriptures includes maps at the back. Maps have been around for a long time, but strangely the first significant atlas, *Historical Atlas of Mormonism*, was not published until 1994, a predecessor to *Mapping Mormonism*. An extensive section on Mormonism in *The New Historical Atlas of Religion in America* (2001) by Edwin Scott Gaustad and Philip L. Barlow (a Latter-day Saint), was a path-breaking contribution, but it was restricted by inclusion in a larger work.

With this new atlas, Latter-day Saint geography finally comes into its own. *Mapping Mormonism: An Atlas of Latter-day Saint History* is far more comprehensive than either of its predecessors. The 1994 atlas featured just 78 two-color maps; the new version offers 240 pages of full-color maps, often two or three on a page. The earlier book had sections on "David O. McKay's Worldwide Journeys," "Distribution of World Membership," and "Missions," but nothing like the 24 pages covering the Church in Asia, Africa, the Middle East, and areas all around the globe. A reader can discover whether or not LDS meetings are held in Kabul and Baghdad (they are) and find out when the Church had a mission in Iran (1975-1978). We can see exactly where the Church is strongest and how fast membership is growing in each country. Some readers may be surprised to learn that the Church was strongest in the early twentieth-century eastern United States in the South, the heartland of the evangelical faiths that have been most critical of the Church. The Southeast also stood out for the high percentage of homegrown Latter-day Saints, as contrasted to Utah-born members, who comprised the membership.

As the use of the word "History" in the title suggests, this atlas maps time as well as space. Using a variety of devices, it recaptures development and growth as well as expansion and movement. There are nearly as many chronological charts and tables as there are maps in its pages. We can learn about the stages of Church growth in Southern California, for example; a graph shows when the rapid growth after World War II abruptly leveled off after 1970.

Mapping Mormonism offers a spatial rendition of the founding story, the well-known and essential historical-spatial basis of Latter-day Saint belief up through the trek to the Great Basin. What is remarkable is how much else is treated cartographically. The growth in genealogical activity is one, along with welfare and humanitarian aid, Church education, Church administration, and Church architecture. This atlas depicts typical chapels and the various standard building plans over the twentieth-century down to the present. The birthplaces of many General Authorities are mapped. By compressing vast amounts of data in a map or a chart, the atlas enables us to grasp a great deal of information in a glance.

The maps and charts also throw light on issues scholars have been arguing about for years. One circular map records all the towns within twenty miles of Palmyra, significant because of the long debate over whether the 1820 revivals occurred right in town or in a nearby village. The book also points out that "almost 90 theories of Book of Mormon geography have been published over the past 170 years," showing that the current debates are anything but new. Ten of the possible Book of Mormon geographies are depicted on two pages in this atlas. On another contested topic, a graph summarizes the much disputed projections of Church growth for the next thirty years. Rodney Stark's extravagant projection of 55,000,000 members by 2040 is indicated with one line, and more modest projections are indicated with seven others. These seven cluster between 22,000,000 and 29,000,000 members by 2040, a more sober estimate than Stark's. Some readers will be interested to learn that in recent years the Seventh-day Adventists have been growing faster and now are more numerous than the Latter-day Saints, although different counting rules make it hard to tell which church is actually larger.

Even Latter-day Saints with a detailed knowledge of Church history will learn something on nearly every page. Information can be found in *Mapping Mormonism* that one would not imagine existed. A map of Salt Lake City shows the gentile-owned churches and businesses from 1860 to 1910 and those owned by Latter-day Saints. Even then, Church establishments clustered in the north and gentiles in the south of the downtown city, much like today. Another map records all the property in Brigham City owned by families practicing polygamy in 1870 compared to the properties of monogamous families. On a row of 28 thumbnail maps of county-by-county votes for president, senators and governor, a reader can watch the conversion of Utah from a predominantly Democratic state in the 1930s to an increasingly Republican stronghold beginning with Dwight D. Eisenhower.

The overall effect of this rich series of maps is to show the extent of the Church's global reach. Joseph Smith had worldwide aspirations from the beginning; missionaries opened a number of foreign lands to the restored gospel before his death, and many countries followed later in the century. Since then have now been added many other worldwide Church functions: wards and stakes, area authorities, humanitarian projects, schools and institutes, microfilming operations, global television, thousands of chapels, and over a hundred temples. General Authorities visit remote places, and so do the seventeen BYU performing arts groups. The Church is beginning to mark significant historical sites outside of the United States, claiming small pieces of various national histories for itself. The new areas in turn are contributing personnel for the missionary corps and the body of General Authorities. All this, this great web of Latter-day Saint relationships now encompassing the globe, is made visible and legible in *Mapping Mormonism.*

Richard Lyman Bushman
New York City
January 31, 2012

Introduction

LATTER-DAY SAINTS are obsessed with their history, as much as or more so than any other religious or cultural group. In Church and at school, Mormons spend as much time studying Church history as each book of scripture, and even academic historical books (such as the recent Joseph Smith Papers series) reach the top of LDS bestseller lists. There are many reasons for this, such as the emphasis on family and genealogy, but the most important reason is likely the fact that what sets Mormonism apart from the rest of Christianity is largely contained in the historical narrative of Joseph Smith.

However, the average Mormon's understanding of Church history is often fraught with error, myth, and incompleteness. Among those not of this faith, the problem is even greater. Each tends to focus on the most positive or negative aspects, respectively, of this history, not catching the larger picture. Each distrusts the assertions of the other. How can we all better understand the remarkable story that has shaped Mormonism into what it is today?

The landmark *Historical Atlas of Mormonism* (1994) showed the value of maps and geography as tools for better understanding the history of this movement. Events happen in space as well as time, so the theories and tools of geography, the study of space and place, are just as useful as history for making sense of why these events happened where, how, and when they did. The map is one of the discipline's most powerful tools for doing this. Maps leverage our innate ability to recognize visual patterns, especially for those of us who consider ourselves "visual thinkers," concisely portraying large volumes of data. One map can contain several thousand pieces of information; in tabular form, they would require several pages, and would be much less engaging and much more difficult to comprehend. The *Historical Atlas* quickly became a standard reference work for Church history, portraying many topics that most people had never seen in map form.

Despite its invaluable contribution, the 1994 *Historical Atlas* has since become dated, especially by continued historical scholarship and by advances in geographic and cartographic technology. BYU Studies and the editors of the original atlas agreed that it was time to update the book. However, we soon recognized an opportunity to completely re-envision the atlas by revisiting the original topics, and exploring new ones. Even for those topics that had changed very little, we completely redesigned the maps. We decided to use this opportunity to accomplish two major goals:

1. To broaden the scope of the atlas, geographically and historically. We now have much greater coverage of the twentieth century up to the present, and we cover the broader Church in regions beyond the headquarters.

2. To use maps and other visual representations to better understand the history of the Church, especially where they can help to clarify common misconceptions and myths.

Conversely, we do not intend this book to be a comprehensive history of the Church or a study of its spiritual doctrines and practices. These topics are important, probably more important than most of the maps herein, but much has been written on them already; we recommend the following as good places to learn the basic doctrine and history of Mormonism:

Daniel H. Ludlow, ed., *Encyclopedia of Mormonism*, New York: Macmillan, 1992 (full text online http://lib.byu.edu/digital/Macmillan/).

Arnold K. Garr, Donald Q. Cannon, Richard O. Cowan, eds., *Encyclopedia of Latter-day Saint History*, Salt Lake City: Deseret Book, 2000.

Richard L. Bushman, *Mormonism: a very short introduction*, New York: Oxford University Press, 2008.

Church Educational System, *Church History in the Fulness of Times*, Salt Lake City: The Church of Jesus Christ of Latter-day Saints, 2003 (full text online http://www.lds.org/manual/church-history-in-the-fulness-of-times-student-manual).

We have also included a brief glossary as an appendix (see p. 242) to define some of the uniquely Mormon terms commonly found in this atlas.

One of the most difficult things about a work like this is to present religious history with an appropriate viewpoint. The miraculous events that the religion claims either happened or they didn't happen, and thus the writers either believe or they do not. Therefore, most books about religion either attempt to promote faith or are antagonistic to it. Writing a book that is interesting and enlightening to believers, critics, and everyone else is challenging. The editors of *Mapping Mormonism* (and most, but not all, of the expert contributors) are believing Latter-day Saints, but we have tried to strike a balanced scholarly perspective. We have endeavored to avoid an overtly religious tone in the written text, and we have not avoided topics that we felt were historically and geographically important but that may not portray the Church or its members in a totally positive light (e.g., polygamy). However, we also avoided an overtly antagonistic tone, along with topics that some might use to try to damage the Church without helping us to better understand it (most of which aren't very geographical topics anyway).

Throughout the process of creating this new atlas, we were often asked how it fit with current trends in publishing and the Internet. Is a reference work or coffee-table book like this passé? The Internet cannot (yet) replicate the visual quality of a printed book, which is so important for such a visual work like this, nor is it as accessible as a book in many ways. That said, there are several advantages of the Internet, and we have created a companion website, mappingmormonism.byu.edu, to complement the book. There one can find digital versions of some of the most popular maps in the atlas, which can be used (within the copyright) for educational and personal purposes. We have also developed MormonPlaces (mappingmormonism.byu.edu/mormonplaces), which lets you see the details about specific places relevant to LDS history (e.g., settlements, events, cemeteries), which are often shown only in a summarized form in the printed atlas. More than this, MormonPlaces is a collaborative scholarship tool, where scholars, descendants, or anyone with interest can share with the community what they know about specific places, building a common database of Mormon historical geography.

We have learned much as we have produced this volume, and we hope readers will find it educational and enlightening. *Mapping Mormonism* is a labor of love and represents years of work by all involved. The editors especially appreciate the contributions of more than fifty contributing authors who lent their expertise to one or more of the topics. We appreciate the help of our assistant cartographers, who as undergraduate students were able to refine their skills while providing valuable scholarly and creative insight. We are also grateful to the staff of BYU Studies who worked tirelessly to work through the final steps of publication.

History and geography are never fully "known," and we are sure that some readers will find errors in the information presented herein or discover new information that supersedes what we have included. If so, let us know and we will be happy to put it on the website.

The Editors
June 2012

Brandon S. Plewe is an assistant professor of Geography at Brigham Young University. After a bachelor's degree in Cartography and Mathematics from Brigham Young University, he earned his master's and PhD degrees from the State University of New York at Buffalo. A cartographer at heart, his career has focused on historical geographic information systems (GIS) and historical cartography, with an emphasis on representing the spatial history of Utah and The Church of Jesus Christ of Latter-Day Saints. He and his wife Jamie have five children.

S. Kent Brown is an emeritus professor of Ancient Scripture at Brigham Yound University and is the former director and associate director of the BYU Jerusalem Center for Near Eastern Studies. He taught at BYU from 1971 to 2008. He is married to the former Gayle Oblad; they are the parents of five children and the grandparents of twenty-five grandchildren.

Donald Q. Cannon is professor emeritus of Church History and Doctrine at Brigham Young University. He received bachelor's and master's degrees from from the University of Utah and a doctorate from Clark University. He has written or edited several books, including Unto Every Nation and The Nauvoo Legion in Illinois. He and Joann McGinnis Cannon are the parents of six children.

Richard H. Jackson received his PhD from Clark University in 1970 in Historical Geography and recently retired after four decades as a professor and administrator in the Geography Department at Brigham Young University. He has written extensively about Mormon settlement and community planning in the American West, and the way that people and place have interacted to create the distinctive geography that characterizes the Mormon West that stretches from Canada to Northern Mexico.

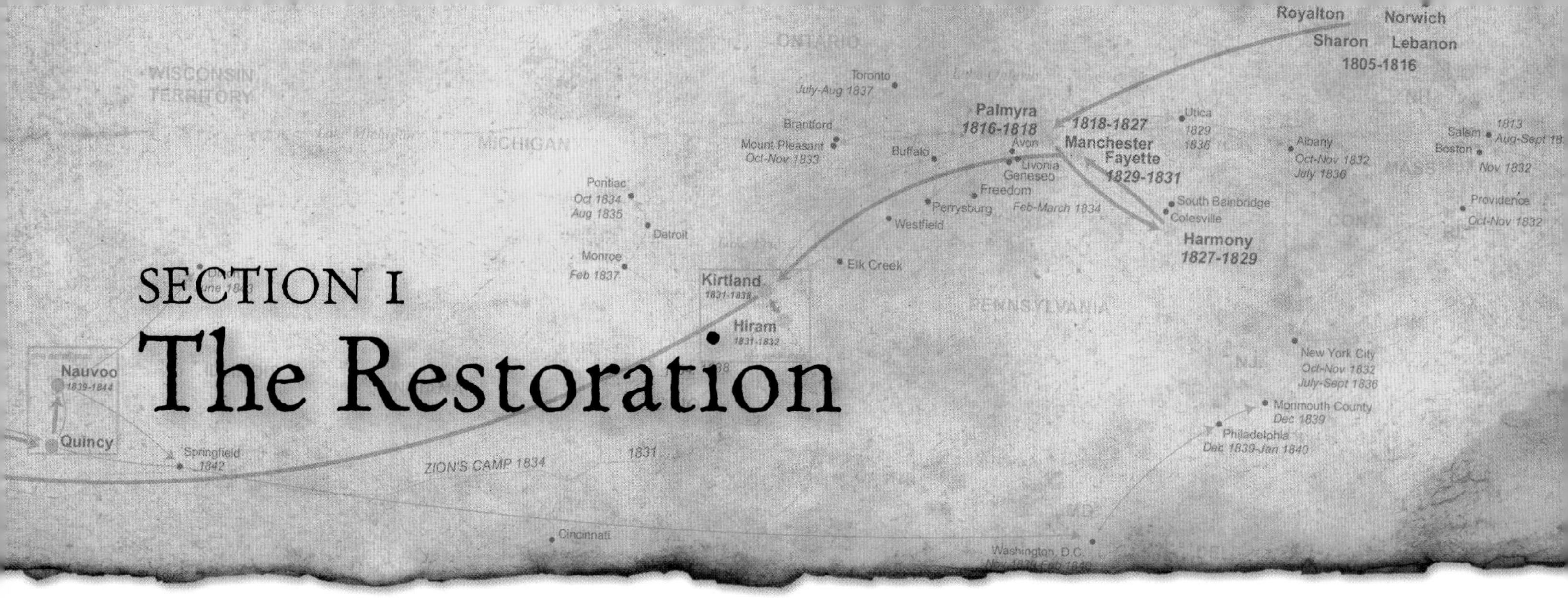

SECTION 1
The Restoration

THE RESTORATION of the Church of Jesus Christ through the Prophet Joseph Smith created a geographic imprint upon which we can still trace the people, places, and events that were fundamental to the Church. The migration of Joseph's ancestors first led them to New England and later to upstate New York as the Erie Canal provided access to better lands to the west. The differing Protestant religious backgrounds of the newly arriving migrants created a social milieu that influenced the spiritual development of Joseph, while the unique geography of the upstate New York area, created by glaciation south of the Great Lakes, contained places that figured centrally in the sacred experiences of the boy prophet.

Following the organization of the Church in 1830, Joseph and new members and officers joined the westward movement of Americans to the Ohio, Mississippi, and Missouri river valleys, where they colonized the fertile land, founded communities, and ultimately came into conflict with other settlers of the region. In less than 15 years the Prophet Joseph and early missionaries crisscrossed the Mississippi–Ohio valley and traveled to the East Coast and Europe in their missionary journeys and in ministering to the congregations of the new faith. The geography they created included numerous farms, towns, two temples, and even the large city of Nauvoo. Within this new geography, sacred events occurred that resonate through the Church of Jesus Christ even today, including the revelation and translation of scriptures that are part of the standard works Church members revere as holy.

1805 | 1810 | 1815 | 1820

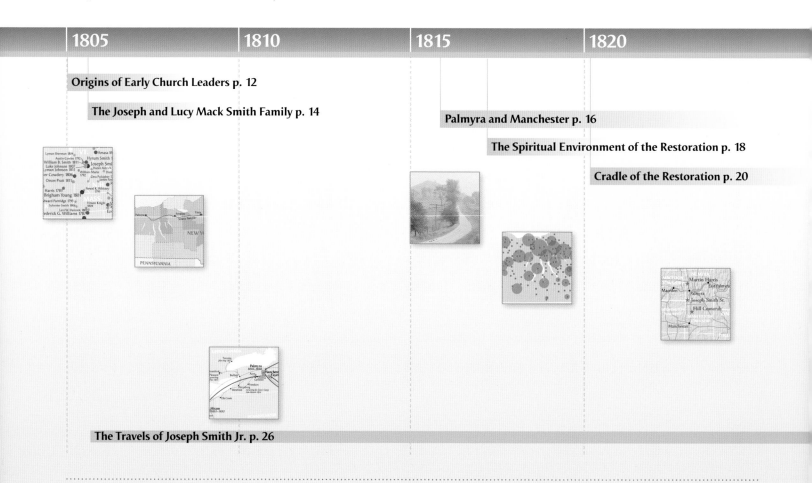

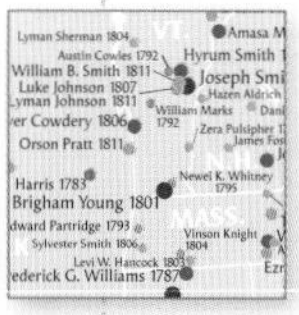

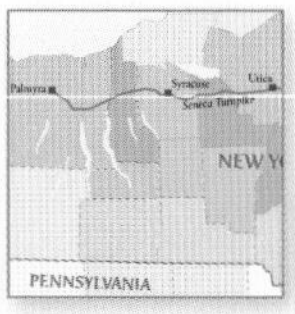

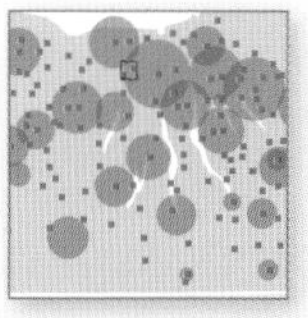

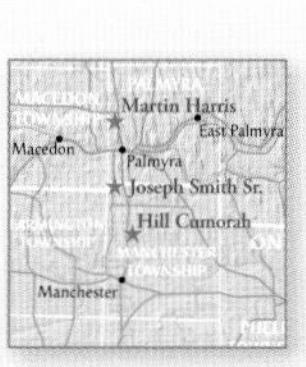

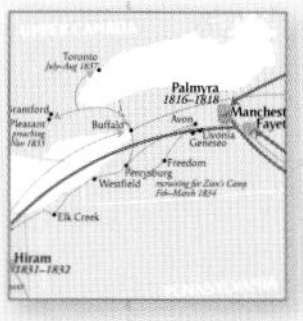

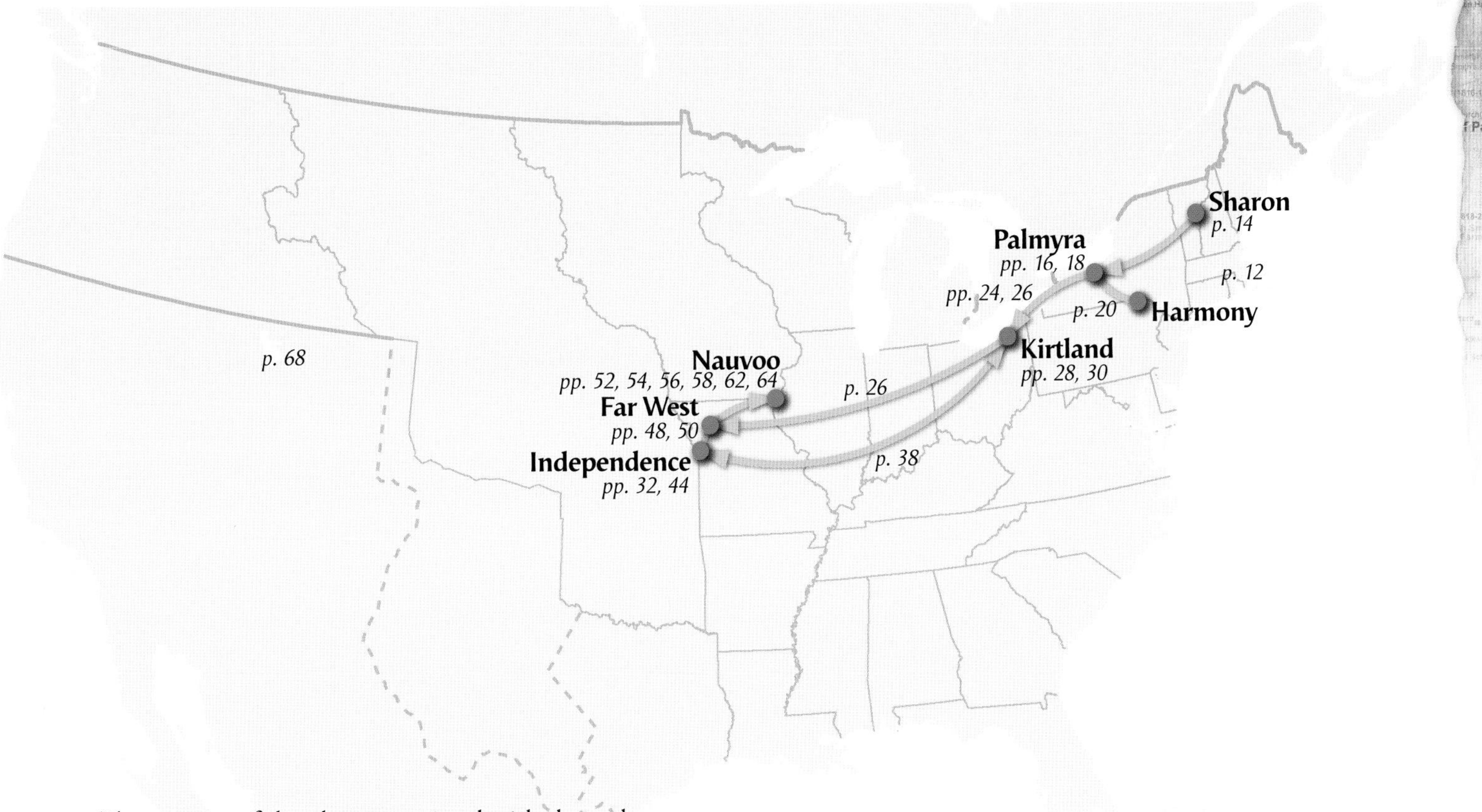

1846 boundaries

The sanctity of the places associated with the early years of the Church is reflected in their current importance. The Church has restored and rebuilt homes or other places where significant events occurred during this time—such as the Prophet Joseph's birthplace, the city of Nauvoo, or the Carthage Jail (see p. 136)—reflecting modern efforts to make the geography and history of the times and places of the Restoration clearly understandable to the modern generation.

1825 | **1830** | **1835** | **1840**

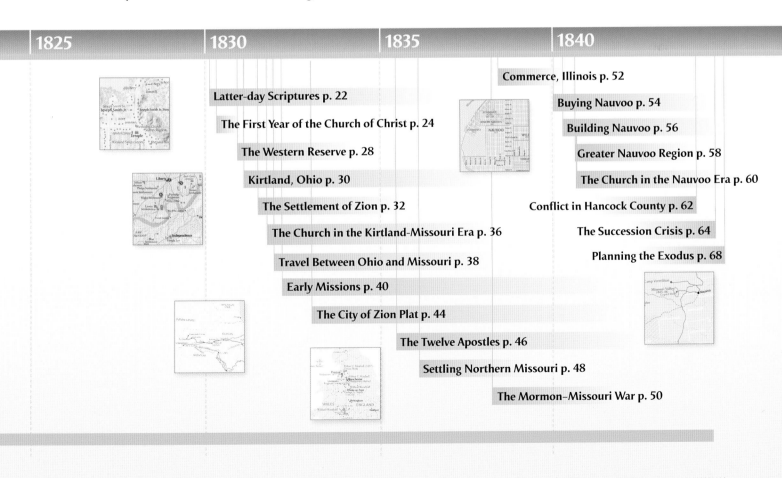

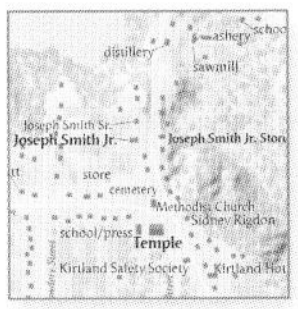
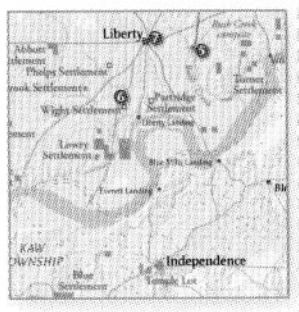

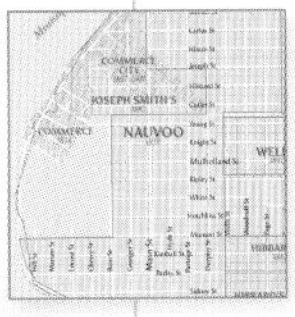
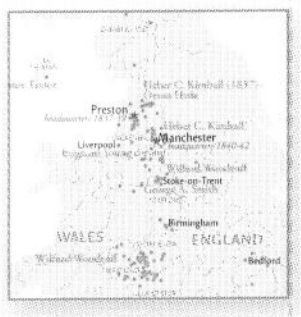

Origins of Early Church Leaders

Prior to 1816

THE CULTURE AND SOCIETY from which the early Latter-day Saints emerged left indelible impressions on the history of The Church of Jesus Christ of Latter-day Saints. Joseph Smith's ancestors and the vast majority of the Church's early leaders were born and lived in the northern United States—nearly 60 percent from New England alone. While the northern states were diverse in their local economies, politics, and religious demography, in the generation before the Church's 1830 organization the section featured a rapidly expanding population, a mobile citizenry, extensive agriculture, industrial development, and widespread adherence to Evangelical Protestantism. The area had its beginnings as distinct English and Dutch colonies, and, by the time of the American Revolution, agricultural communities and a few seaside cities stretched along the Atlantic seaboard. Conflicts with native peoples notwithstanding, white settlement pushed west in an accelerated way following the Revolution. In the early Republic, the population doubled about every two decades, and western migration, fueled by the search for arable land and economic opportunity, pulled settlers away from older communities. Especially after the War of 1812, innovations in transportation and communication expanded economic markets and abetted western migration.

In religion, the northern states bore the stamp of two centuries of colonial religious development. By 1830, they also reflected the upheavals of religious disestablishment, religious diversity, and evangelical revival. Protestants predominated, but in bewildering variety. New England Puritans established "Congregational" churches across Massachusetts, Connecticut, Vermont, New Hampshire, and Maine. Baptists established a foothold in Rhode Island but spread rapidly in the eighteenth and early nineteenth centuries. Quakers founded Pennsylvania but actively recruited German Protestants to the colony. New York, originally a Dutch colony, first supported Dutch Reformed (Calvinist) churches but eventually became the most religiously diverse of the British North American colonies. Scottish Presbyterians came by the thousands in the eighteenth century, establishing strongholds in Pennsylvania, New York, and New Jersey. Methodists came in small numbers until the late 1700s but experienced unparalleled growth in the decades following. Anglicans (known as Episcopalians after the American Revolution) originally predominated in the colonial South but had made inroads into northern communities by the nineteenth century. Catholics had small numbers in the colonies until waves of Irish immigrants helped transform northern cities like Boston and New York. Whereas in 1790 the largest Christian bodies in the United States were, in order, the Congregationalists, Presbyterians, Baptists, and Anglicans, by 1830 the ecclesiastical landscape had been transformed. In that year, the largest in terms of proportionate denominational strength were Baptists (25 percent), Methodists (23.4 percent), Presbyterians (17 percent), and Congregationalists (10.6 percent). At the time of the Church's organization, those denominations featuring broadly evangelical priorities—emphasis on Christian "new birth," Bible preaching, moral rigor, and aggressive evangelism—had come to dominate in the northern United States.

J. Spencer Fluhman

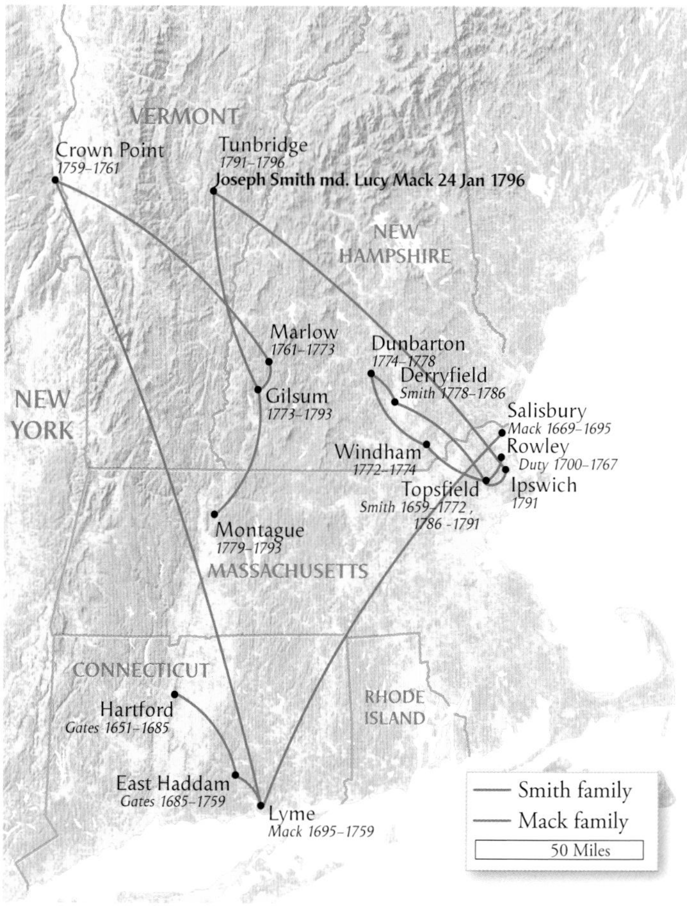

Joseph Smith's Ancestors

The migrations of the Smith and Mack families reflect some of the main themes of New England history before 1830. Solomon Mack, Joseph Smith's maternal grandfather, came of age in Lyme, Connecticut, and spent his teenage years in hard agricultural labor. A veteran of the French and Indian and Revolutionary wars, Mack married Lydia Gates in 1759 and spent most of his adult life in various money-making ventures. After a long series of adventures and disappointments, Mack experienced a Christian conversion late in life. Lydia, who had joined a Congregational church in adulthood, had been the primary religious influence in the lives of the children. The Macks' youngest child, Lucy, met Joseph Smith, son of Asael and Mary Duty Smith on a visit to a brother in Tunbridge, Vermont. The Smiths had lived in Topsfield, Massachusetts, for four generations; but Asael, the youngest of five children and lacking an inheritance in land, left the village in search of a living in early adulthood. After several attempts at farming in eastern Massachusetts and New Hampshire, the Smiths settled in Vermont in 1791. Asael and some of his family, including Joseph Smith Sr., were drawn to Universalism, a liberal Christian movement that emphasized God's reasonableness and the "universal" salvation of the human family. The Joseph and Lucy Smith family also moved several times in search of economic stability (see p. 14) and, like their ancestors, found themselves caught between the Calvinist orthodoxy of New England's traditionally dominant churches and the heterodox doctrines of Universalism.

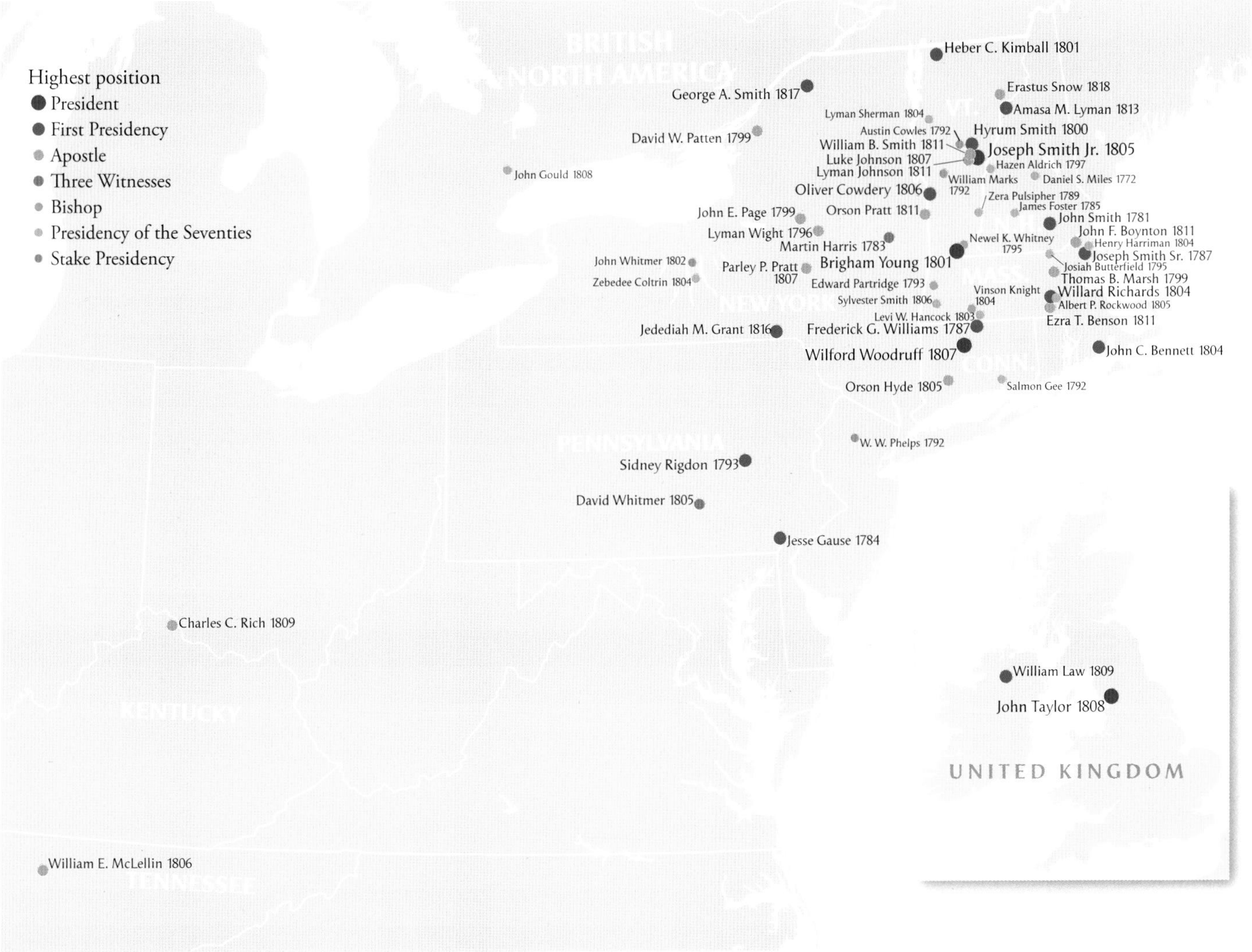

Birthplaces of Early Leaders of The Church of Jesus Christ of Latter-day Saints

Included here are members of the First Presidency, Quorum of Twelve Apostles, First Seven Presidents of the Seventy, Stake Presidencies, Presiding Bishops, and Patriarchs (seventies were not General Authorities until 1976). There is an obvious predominance of leaders from New England and upstate New York; this led to a definite New England culture in the early Church. Of the leaders shown here whose previous religious affiliations are known, fourteen had associated with Methodism, eight with Congregationalism, seven with Alexander Campbell's "restoration" movement (eventually called the "Disciples of Christ"), six with the Baptists, three with Presbyterianism, three with Unitarianism or Universalism, and one each for Anglicanism, Quakerism, Shakerism, and Lutheranism (see p. 18); some leaders had multiple religious affiliations before joining with the Latter-day Saints; others had none.

Significant Events Preceding the Restoration

- **1776** Declaration of Independence signed
- **1783** Treaty of Paris signed, ending Revolutionary War
- **1787** United States Constitution drafted
- **1789** George Washington elected president of the United States
- **1796** John Adams, second president of the U.S.
- **1796** Marriage of Joseph Smith and Lucy Mack
- **1803** Thomas Jefferson, third president of the U.S.
- **1803** United States purchases "Louisiane" territory from France
- **1805** Joseph Smith, Jr. born in Vermont
- **1808** James Madison, fourth president of the United States
- **1812** Outbreak of hostilities between United States and Britain
- **1814** Treaty of Ghent signed, ending War of 1812
- **1814** Steam locomotive invented in England
- **1816** James Monroe, fifth president of the U.S.
- **1824** John Quincy Adams, sixth president of the United States
- **1825** Erie Canal completed in New York
- **1828** Andrew Jackson, seventh president of the United States
- **1828** Twenty-three miles of rail completed on the Baltimore & Ohio Railroad

1775 | 1785 | 1795 | 1805 | 1815 | 1825

The Joseph and Lucy Mack Smith Family

1792–1816

ASAEL AND MARY DUTY SMITH moved their family of eleven children (seven sons and four daughters) in 1791 from Topsfield, Massachusetts, to Tunbridge, Vermont, where Asael had purchased land in what was called the "Tunbridge Gore." By 1795 Asael and his son Jesse had substantial homesteads, and soon another son, Joseph, bought his own property. Joseph met Lucy Mack of Gilsum, New Hampshire, who was visiting her brother in Tunbridge, and the couple were married in 1796. Over the next twenty years, they lived in nine different homes in Vermont and New Hampshire before leaving New England for the New York frontier.

At each locale, Joseph found difficulty in his attempts to support his family. Most notable was his mercantile business in Randolph in 1802 (while renting out the Tunbridge farm), exchanging merchandise for ginseng root, which he crystallized for sale to China, where its reported medicinal properties were in high demand. Unfortunately, he was swindled out of the anticipated proceeds by a Royalton merchant named Stevens, his son, and a shipmaster in New York City. To pay his debts to the Boston merchants who had supplied him, Joseph was forced to sell the Tunbridge farm and the family's personal effects and hand over Lucy's marriage dowry of $1,000. He would be poor for the rest of his life; despite this, Lucy would later recall that the family was generally happy as they worked to eke out a living.

After leaving Randolph, Joseph worked for several years as a tenant farmer, renting land as long as he could (typically until the landlord sold it), then moving on. Joseph Jr., the future Prophet, was born while they were renting land recently purchased by Lucy's father on the border of Sharon and Royalton townships. Here Joseph taught school when not farming in the winter. Lucy would recollect that, through hard work, their "circumstances gradually improved, until we found ourselves quite comfortable again." In fact, while living in West Lebanon, New Hampshire, they were able to enroll Hyrum in a private school in 1811 on the Dartmouth College campus.

During the following winter, "typhus fever" (typhoid) swept the Connecticut River Valley, prostrating and killing thousands. The disease seized the Smith family, affecting all the children. Joseph Jr. also became afflicted with a serious bone infection (osteomyelitis), which required a new and revolutionary surgical procedure by Dr. Nathan Smith, founder of the Dartmouth Medical School. The operation saved Joseph's left leg from amputation by drilling and removing diseased portions of the bone. Young Joseph recuperated for a short time at the home of an uncle in Salem, Massachusetts, a significant trip for a seven-year-old that foreshadowed a lifetime of travel (see p. 26).

In Norwich, Vermont, the family's fiscal condition continued to deteriorate with two years of crop failures (1814 and 1815). The next year, the fate of the Smith family was sealed by forces on the other side of the world. A volcanic eruption in the Dutch East Indies (Indonesia) cooled global temperatures to the point that snow fell at the Smith farm in June 1816. Their crops failed with thousands of others in New England.

Joseph Sr. decided to join a mass emigration to what was hailed as the promised land of western New York. Newspapers of the day advertised lands in New York, Pennsylvania, and Ohio as "well-timbered, well-watered, easily accessible and undeniably fertile—all to be had on long-term payments for only two or three dollars an acre." Joseph made the journey in two to three weeks in the summer of 1816 to look for opportunities in the Palmyra area. The rest of the family soon followed the next winter, setting up a new life in a place that would forever change their destiny.

Larry C. Porter

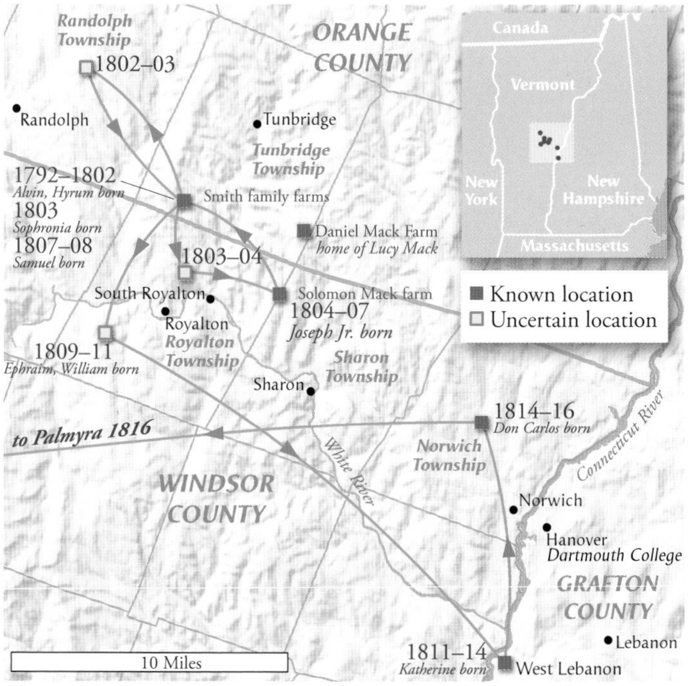

Joseph Smith Sr. and His Family in Vermont

The parents of Joseph Smith and Lucy Mack had settled in the frontier of Vermont and New Hampshire in the early 1790s; it was here that the couple began to raise their family. Due to recurring financial troubles and failed ventures, the growing family was forced to move nine times in twenty years. In most places, Joseph purchased or rented land to farm, except for an attempt at being a merchant in Randolph. Their moves frequently took them back to his parents' land in Tunbridge or her parents' land on the border of Sharon and Royalton. It was while living at the latter that the future prophet Joseph Jr. was born. An epidemic of typhoid hit the family in 1813 during their time in Lebanon, New Hampshire; this led to a serious leg infection in young Joseph, who may have died if not for the latest medical practices being pioneered at nearby Dartmouth College.

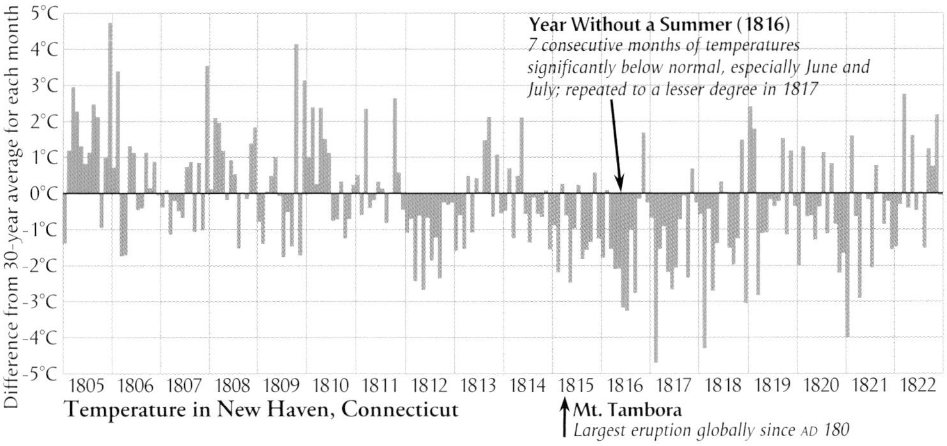

The Year Without A Summer

On April 10–11, 1815, Mount Tambora exploded on the island of Sumbawa, Dutch East Indies (now Indonesia), and ejected approximately 25 cubic miles of debris into the air. Probably the greatest volcanic eruption in the past 1,800 years (greater than Krakatau in 1883), it pushed a layer of ash into the stratosphere that remained aloft for several years. As shown in the graph (which depicts how significantly each month's temperature differs from that month's long-term average in New Haven, Connecticut, the nearest weather station to Vermont at the time), this ash reflected enough sunlight back into space to significantly cool global temperatures for several years, especially the summer of 1816, commonly called "the year without a summer" or "eighteen hundred and froze to death."

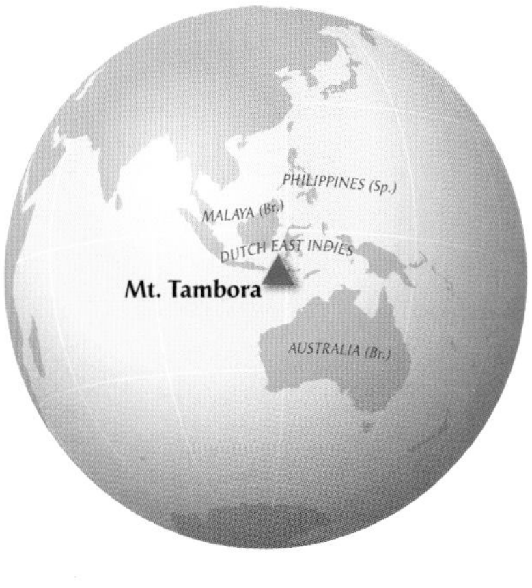

Route of Smith Family

Father Smith's determination to investigate the prospect of land in New York was not uncommon. Western New York was a classic American frontier, full of promise for those brave enough to settle in the wilds. The land had been ceded by the native Six Nations in the 1780s, and by 1801 property throughout western New York was for sale. The area grew rapidly between 1810 and 1820 at the expense of Vermont (in which sixty townships declined in population) and the rest of New England. Emigration reached its peak in the cold years of 1816 and 1817.

The exact route followed by Lucy and her family from Norwich, Vermont, to Palmyra, New York, in the winter of 1816–1817 is not known precisely. They did pass through South Royalton, Vermont, where they had to leave Lucy's mother because of an injury sustained in the overturn of a wagon. Lucy eventually dismissed their teamster Caleb Howard near Utica, New York, after he treated Joseph Jr. poorly then tried to steal her wagon. Their course took them to Syracuse along the Seneca Turnpike, then to Palmyra, where they arrived sometime in the month of January.

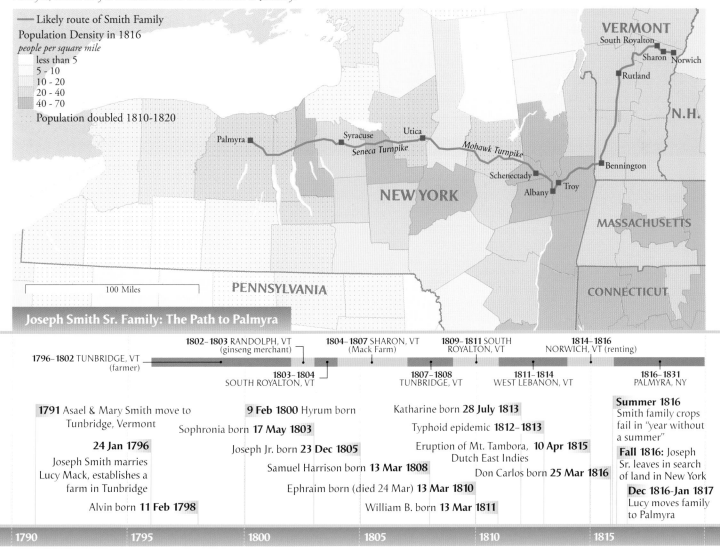

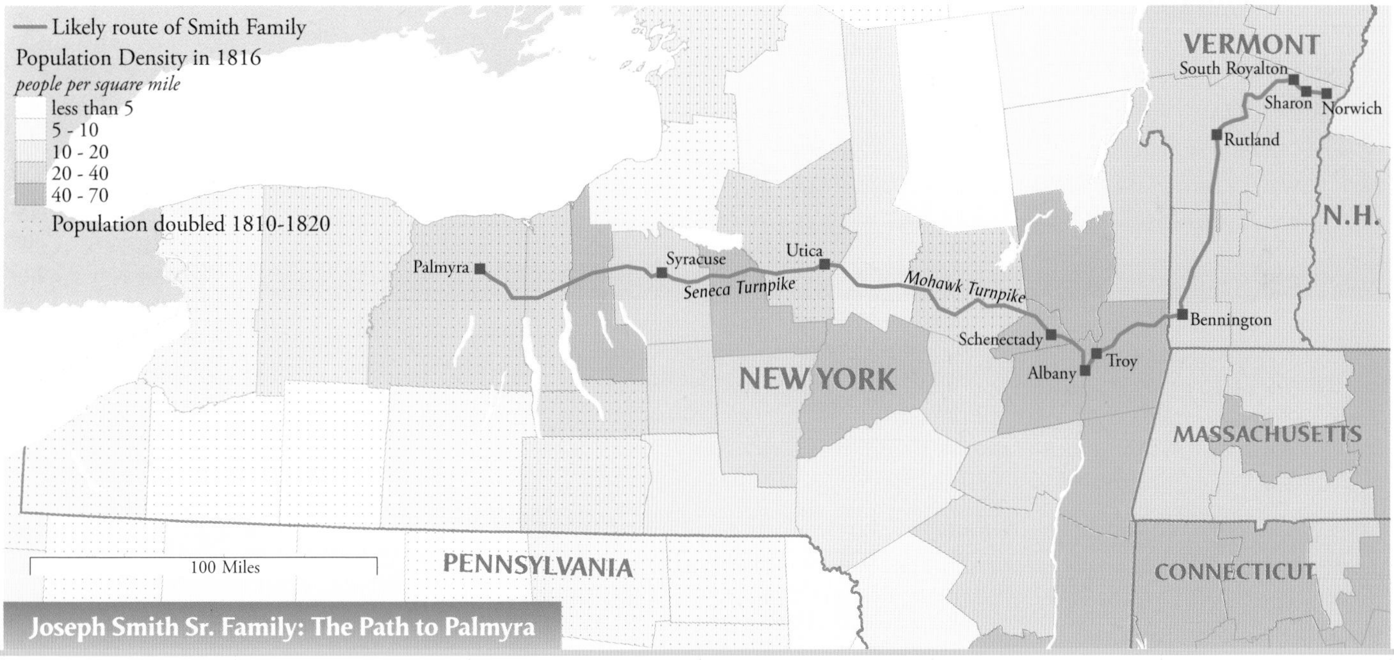

Joseph Smith Sr. Family: The Path to Palmyra

1796–1802 TUNBRIDGE, VT (farmer)
1802–1803 RANDOLPH, VT (ginseng merchant)
1803–1804 SOUTH ROYALTON, VT
1804–1807 SHARON, VT (Mack Farm)
1807–1808 TUNBRIDGE, VT
1809–1811 SOUTH ROYALTON, VT
1811–1814 WEST LEBANON, VT
1814–1816 NORWICH, VT (renting)
1816–1831 PALMYRA, NY

1791 Asael & Mary Smith move to Tunbridge, Vermont

24 Jan 1796 Joseph Smith marries Lucy Mack, establishes a farm in Tunbridge

Alvin born **11 Feb 1798**

9 Feb 1800 Hyrum born

Sophronia born **17 May 1803**

Joseph Jr. born **23 Dec 1805**

Samuel Harrison born **13 Mar 1808**

Ephraim born (died 24 Mar) **13 Mar 1810**

William B. born **13 Mar 1811**

Katharine born **28 July 1813**

Typhoid epidemic **1812–1813**

Eruption of Mt. Tambora, Dutch East Indies **10 Apr 1815**

Don Carlos born **25 Mar 1816**

Summer 1816 Smith family crops fail in "year without a summer"

Fall 1816: Joseph Sr. leaves in search of land in New York

Dec 1816-Jan 1817 Lucy moves family to Palmyra

1790 | 1795 | 1800 | 1805 | 1810 | 1815

Palmyra & Manchester

1816–1830

Soldiers of the American Revolution praised the fertile soil and climate of the "Genesee Country" of western New York, encouraging interest in white settlement. The Phelps and Gorham land syndicate, in 1788, purchased 2,600,000 acres from the Iroquois, surveyed "townships," and began land sales. Farmington Township, including the future Manchester, was the first to be sold, followed soon by Palmyra Township.

The Ganargua River runs through Palmyra Township in a wide, shallow valley. On a ridge above, Palmyra Village (originally called Swift's Landing) took root, initially settled by migrants from southern New England and the Mid-Atlantic States. The elite were merchants, skilled craftsmen, capable farmers, and professionals—educated, some churched and others unchurched. They established the economic, social, and religious basis of Palmyra.

The Joseph Smith family arrived in 1816 and 1817, when 500 to 600 people lived in the village of principally frame and log buildings. The Smiths were northern New Englanders, were penniless, had not owned land for fifteen years, lacked in education, were divided in religion, and clung to antiquated folkways. Vermonters were considered unpolished "rural folk." The Smiths sought to fit into Palmyra culture, and owning property was a major criterion for social acceptance.

They lived two years on West Main Street in a rented house, toiled at day labor, and ran a notions shop at the east end of the village. They then moved two miles south on Stafford Road into a log home within feet of the Manchester town line, doing farming, some coopering (barrel-making), and hiring out as laborers.

In 1820, they purchased 100 acres in Manchester Township for a farm. Five miles south was Manchester Village, named for the famed English industrial city. The village of 300 was located along the swift-moving outlet of Canandaigua Lake. It had advantages for industrial and commercial growth, having a rich hinterland of forest and farms. Milling and manufacturing efforts were initiated but made little progress, and Manchester settled back into a farming mode while Palmyra flourished with the advent of the Erie Canal. That year, 1825, the Smiths lost title to their farm, remained on it four years as renters, then moved away in 1830.

The Smiths were part of both Palmyra and Manchester. In each, they developed a farm, built a house, worked, socialized, attended church, bartered, paid taxes, sent children to school, and then married them off. In the log house, a daughter was born and a son died, but it is Joseph's divine work for which this home and region is remembered by the Latter-day Saints.

Somewhere near the log house, Joseph experienced his 1820 First Vision (see p. 20). In Palmyra Township, the angel Moroni instructed Joseph about the gold plates, the plates were shown to eight witnesses, the printer's copy of the manuscript of the Book of Mormon was produced, Joseph and his family and friends preached, the Book of Mormon was printed, and converts were made. On the Manchester side, the angel returned to instruct Joseph about the ancient record, Joseph obtained it at "the hill," the plates were placed for safekeeping on the farm, and converts were baptized. All of these events were precursors to the organization of the Church of Christ.

Donald Enders

Looking South over the Smith Family Farm

Between 1820 and 1825, the family cleared 60 acres of the 100-acre Manchester land, planted an orchard, created cultivated fields and meadows, dug wells, built a frame home, fenced, and produced 1,000 pounds of maple sugar annually. In the township the farm was above average for size and value per acre, and known for "its good order and industry."

The Palmyra property, 80 acres, was eventually purchased by Hyrum, who partially cleared and fenced it. On it was a cooper's shop, animal shelter, corral, and well. Hyrum had cows and raised corn and beans. He was also taxed for five acres in Manchester. However, the Smiths never finished paying for either property.

The Hill Cumorah

The Hill Cumorah is one of the largest of many drumlins (hills of sediment deposits from the last Ice Age) in the Palmyra area, rising 110 feet from the surrounding plain. It was apparently unnamed when Joseph retrieved the plates from it in 1827. Locals eventually called it Gold Bible Hill, and later Spring Hill, while Church members were calling it Cumorah by 1834, assuming that it was the site of the last great Nephite battle. Originally heavily forested, farmers had cleared it for pasture by the time this photograph was taken in 1907; the Church, after purchasing it in 1923 (see p. 136), has reforested most of the hill.

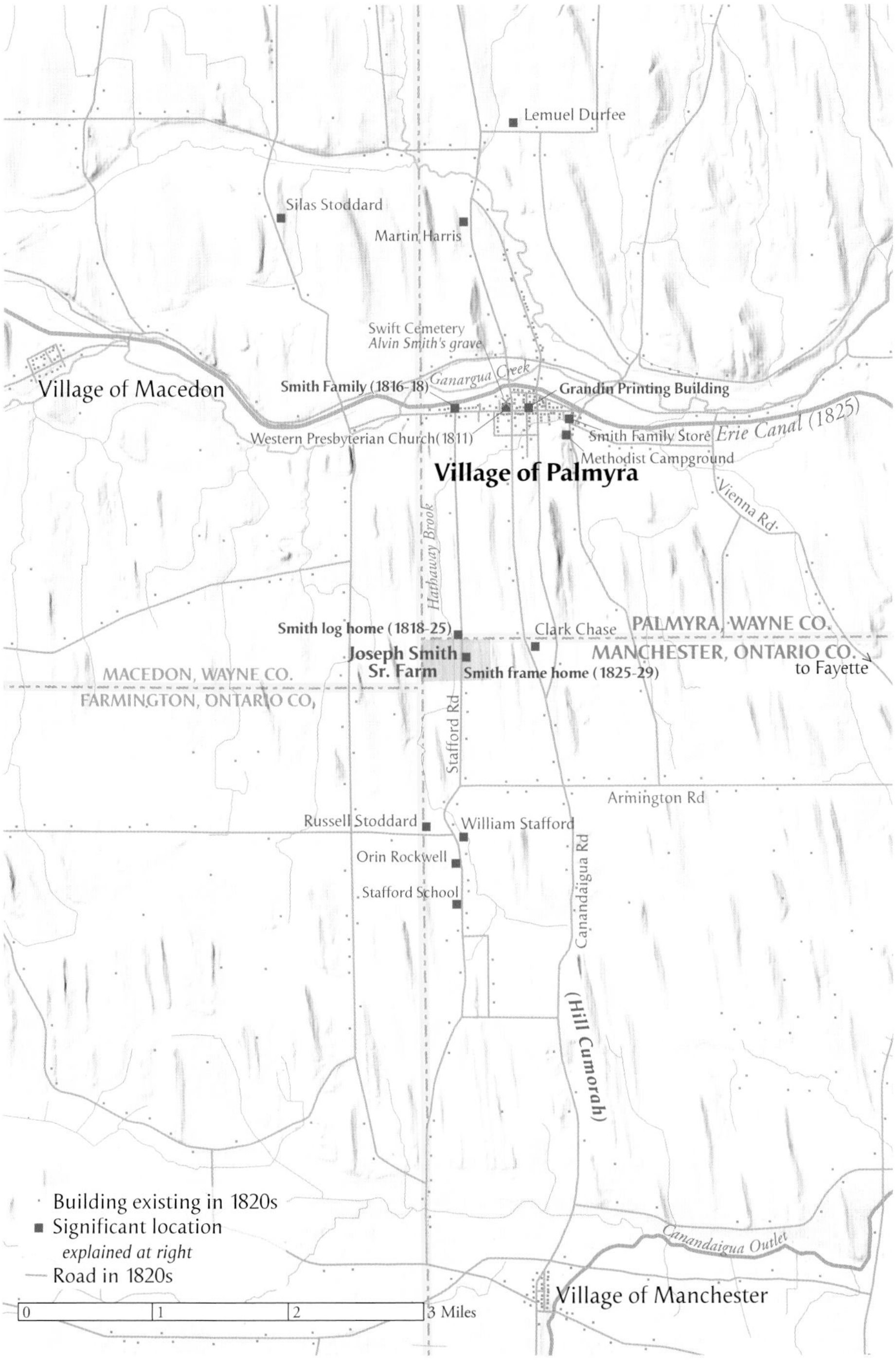

Palmyra and Manchester Townships both contained homes in which the Joseph Smith Sr. family lived, and they had extensive social, religious, and economic dealings in both townships. For example, Hyrum worked, did business, and was a member of the Presbyterian Church, Masonic fraternity, and militia in Palmyra. In Manchester he married Jerusha Barden, taught school, was a school trustee, and did business.

The following locations, shown on the map, were significant to the story of the Restoration:

Lemuel Durfee purchased the Smith farm in 1825 but allowed them to remain as renters.

Silas Stoddard had a son Calvin who was an early convert and married Sophronia Smith.

Martin Harris was one of Joseph's earliest supporters; he mortgaged his farm to pay for the printing of the Book of Mormon.

The **Erie Canal** sparked mobility and economic growth in the towns along its route; Palmyra Village's business district tripled. The Canal made New York "the Empire State," and New York City the nation's harbor.

Alvin Smith was buried in 1823 in a small cemetery in the center of Palmyra.

Egbert B. Grandin established a printing business in a row of brick stores in 1828, where the Book of Mormon was printed.

The **Smith family** rented a house in western Palmyra Village when they first emigrated here.

The **Smith family store** operated for a short time, selling baked goods, root beer, and notions.

The **Western Presbyterian Church** that some of the Smiths joined met in a small church and civic building that no longer stands.

The **Methodist Church** came to Palmyra about 1808, but for many years held camp meetings before a meetinghouse could be built.

The **Smith Cabin**, on the southern border of Palmyra, sat on 80 acres eventually owned by Hyrum.

The **Smith Farm** with its frame home (completed 1824) occupied 100 acres in the extreme northwest corner of Manchester Township.

While working at the farm of **Clark Chase**, Joseph found what he later called the Seer Stone.

Russell Stoddard was a carpenter and mill owner who supplied materials and work to construct the Smith frame home but then tried to obtain the title and evict them.

William Stafford was a prominent farmer in the area who befriended the Smiths.

Orin Rockwell's son Porter was one of young Joseph's best friends, who would remain his loyal protector throughout his life.

Oliver Cowdery was employed as the teacher in the **Stafford School** when he first met the Smith family and heard of the gold plates.

The Spiritual Environment of the Restoration

1790–1830

Joseph Smith came of age in a religious culture characterized by creative energy, remarkable growth, and rapid change. Although some during the American founding era worried that intellectual skepticism and the lack of public funding for churches might cripple Christianity, by 1820 the opposite had proven true. Protestants enjoyed a period of unprecedented expansion, public power, and cultural influence. At the same time, though they could sometimes unite against a common foe such as Roman Catholicism, some of the period's most dramatic religious controversies broke out among Protestants themselves. The Latter-day Saints appeared in this period of Protestant "awakening."

The Protestant Evangelicals enjoyed the most growth, especially the Methodists, Baptists, and Presbyterians. They emphasized an emotional conversion experience and aggressive Bible preaching. The Evangelicals adapted the revival meeting to the realities of the new frontier. The relatively tame revivals in New England in the late 1700s became more energetic as they moved west into New York in the 1820s. Makeshift preaching stands and temporary camp meetings could reach people that established brick-and-mortar churches could not. Also, whereas Christians during the First Great Awakening (1730s–50s) had agreed that ministers should receive a classical education, the preachers of the nineteenth century's Second Great Awakening (1790s–1830s) rejected what they regarded as educational elitism among their more cultured contemporaries. Armed with their Bibles and populist rhetoric, the new evangelists extolled the ability of ordinary people to grasp the Bible's message of salvation.

Their missionary efforts brought them into contact, and often conflict, with one another in newly settled areas. Some Protestants endeavored to cooperate in the "churching" of the new West. For instance, Congregationalists and Presbyterians, similar in their Calvinist theology, formed a Plan of Union agreement in 1801, that they would support each other's ministries and avoid directly competing with one another in new communities. In the end, most western Congregational churches became fully Presbyterian. Such cooperative efforts were challenged, however, in the often-chaotic social atmosphere of upstate New York. Waves of revivalism swept the landscape often enough to famously earn the region the title of "Burned-Over District." Indeed, perhaps the most famous revivalist of the early nineteenth century, Charles G. Finney, launched his renowned career in Rochester in the 1820s and 1830s.

Western New York proved to be a fruitful field for religious innovation: conversion, competition, and controversy kept spiritual energies high for decades. Joining the Evangelicals, some of the more radical religious innovators of the period founded their movements in the state or made it a center of activity. A generation before Joseph Smith's Church of Christ, the Shakers (United Society of Believers in Christ's Second Appearing) had founded several villages in the region. Roughly contemporary with the early Latter-day Saints was John H. Noyes's Oneida community, which rejected traditional marriage and market priorities and helped bolster New York's reputation as a radical religious marketplace. The Spiritualist movement had its beginnings in New York a few years later. Given the pitch of its rhetoric and the significance of its contributions and controversies, historians have returned time and again to early New York as an especially rich place to examine the new nation's religious transformations.

J. Spencer Fluhman

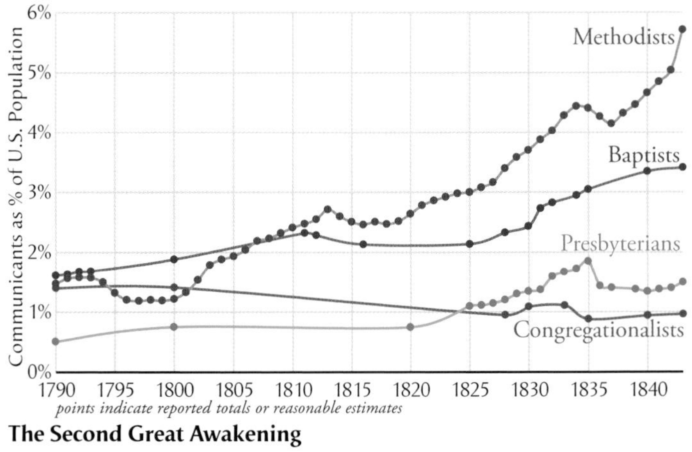

The Second Great Awakening

Though the Congregationalists and Presbyterians had ranked as the nation's largest denominations at the time of the American Revolution, in the early republic the phenomenal growth of the Methodists and Baptists reordered the religious landscape. The Methodists and Baptists proved to be the most enthusiastic supporters of the revivals and were the most effective at adapting them to early national culture and society. Methodist growth was particularly remarkable; whereas they had barely registered on the scale of Christian adherents in 1776, by 1840, Methodists had surpassed all other Protestant groups in membership.

The Second Great Awakening

- **1791** The Bill of Rights guarantees the free exercise of religion
- **late 1790s** Revivals sweep through New England
- **1799-1801** Major revivals in Kentucky
- **1801** Major revival at Yale College
- **1801** Plan of Union between Congregational and Presbyterian churches
- **1810** Pro-revival Cumberland Presbyterian Church splits from anti-revival Presbyterian churches
- **1810** American Board for Foreign Missions formed
- **1816** Methodists found Asbury College
- **1818** Connecticut disestablishes Congregational Church
- **1819** Methodist General Conference held near Palmyra
- **1820** Joseph Smith's First Vision
- **1821** Charles G. Finney holds his first revivals in New York
- **1826** American Home Missionary Society formed
- **1830** Joseph Smith Jr. founds the Church of Christ
- **1831** Wesleyan College founded in Connecticut
- **1832** American Baptist Home Missionary Society formed
- **1833** Massachusetts ends state support of Congregational Church

1790 1800 1810 1820 1830

"An Unusual Excitement on the Subject of Religion"

The spiritual tumult of the early republic touched the Joseph Smith family intimately, as evangelical revivals ignited all around them. There were at least 30 revivals, new churches, and large conferences held within 20 miles of the young teenage Joseph Smith. This competitive atmosphere left him with a profound confusion over religious truth, as evidenced by his various autobiographical accounts. Significantly, the revivals left his own family divided along denominational lines. His mother and some siblings affiliated with the Presbyterians, but his father attended no church for a prolonged period though expressing affinity for both liberal Christian theology and popular visionary culture. By his own account, young Joseph Smith Jr. was attracted to the Methodist revivals, as was Emma Hale, his future wife.

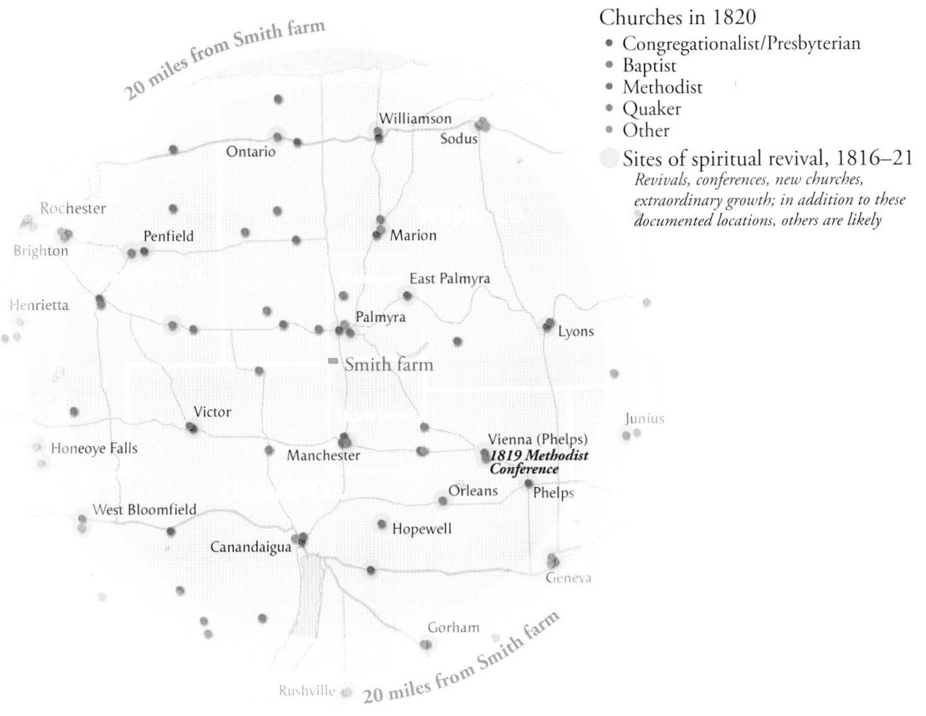

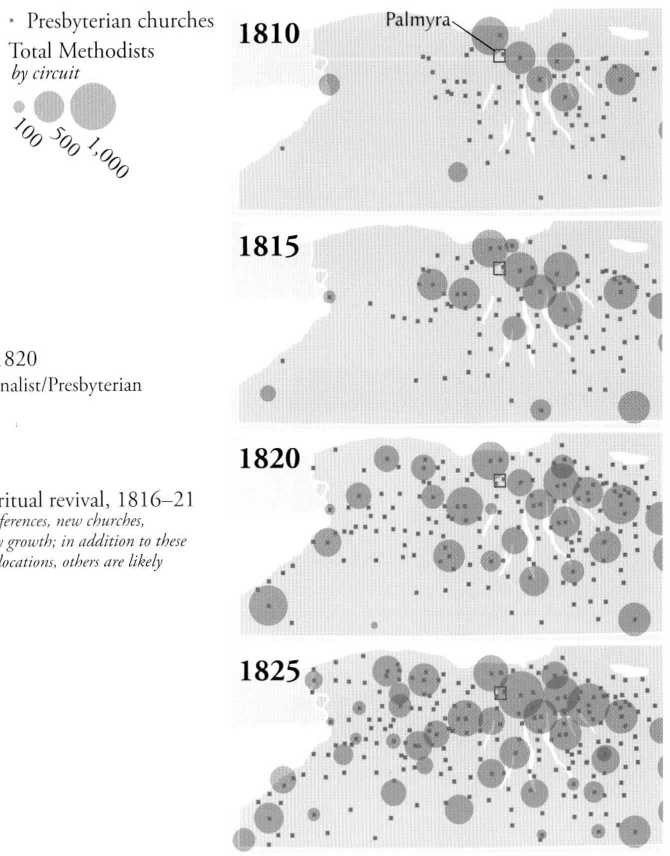

Church Growth in the "Burned-Over District"

Methodists, Presbyterians, and Baptists squared off in upstate New York before 1840. Joseph Smith's many autobiographical references to these groups and to their individual members as his leading antagonists bear out the fact that these groups dominated the region. They could unite against Joseph Smith's fledgling Church, but just as often they disagreed among themselves. Theologically, they disagreed about predestination and free will. Ecclesiastically, they differed over questions of church government. Methodists and Presbyterians argued bitterly with Baptists over the question of infant baptism.

Predominant Religion, 1830

New York, and other "Mid-Atlantic" states generally, were particularly diverse religious regions, at least in terms of Protestant denominations. Whereas New England had long been a solidly Congregationalist area, due in part to the persistence of the legal establishment of Congregational churches in most New England states until after the War of 1812, New York, New Jersey, and Pennsylvania had been culturally and religiously diverse since colonial times. In the early republic, New York and Ohio in particular became hotly contested "marketplaces" of religious innovation and change. Where New England's early nineteenth-century revivalism tended to develop within established congregations, revivals in western New York and Ohio often generated new religious communities altogether.

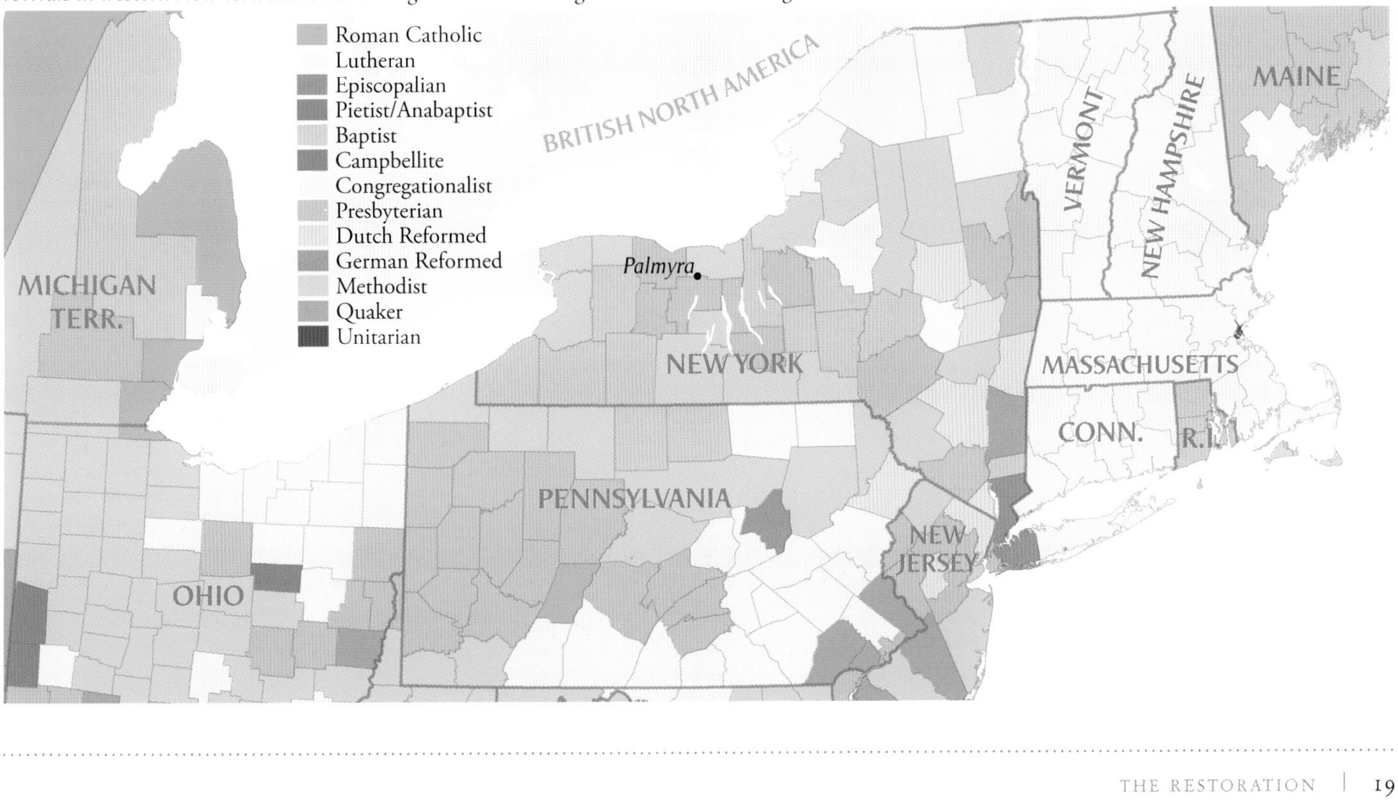

Cradle of the Restoration

1820–1830

During his teen years, **Joseph Smith Jr.** was caught up in the "unusual excitement on the subject of religion," as were many of the other residents of the region (see p. 18). Several of Joseph's family decided to join the Western Presbyterian Church of Palmyra, but he considered it "a scene of great confusion and bad feeling" between the various denominations that resulted in "a strife of words and a contest about opinions." He later reported that in 1820, in answer to his prayer concerning this confusion and his remorse for his own sins, he was visited by God the Father and Jesus Christ and was told that he should join none of the churches but that "the true doctrine—the fullness of the gospel, should, at some future time, be made known to him."

More than three years transpired as Joseph matured, working on the family farm and hiring out for labor in the area. On the night of September 21, 1823, as he prayed in the upstairs loft of the family cabin he shared with his siblings, Joseph stated that he was visited by an angel who identified himself as Moroni, who said that "God had a work for me to do; and that my name should be had for good and evil among all nations, kindreds, and tongues." Joseph was told of a record written on plates of gold that he was to translate and that were deposited in a nearby hill. However, when he attempted to retrieve the plates the next day, thoughts of profit entered his mind, and the angel reappeared, forbidding him to take the plates but directing him to return on the same date each year until he was mature enough to be entrusted with the sacred artifacts.

Over the next several years, Joseph's unique experiences occurred amid the typical experiences of becoming an adult. Joseph traveled, found work, made lifelong friends, fell in love, got married, obtained a home, and started a family. Such experiences drew him to the Susquehanna River valley of southern New York and northern Pennsylvania, 100 miles from Palmyra. Each autumn he returned to the Hill Cumorah to meet with Moroni until he obtained the plates in 1827 at the age of 21.

At the couple's new home in Harmony, Joseph began the work of translation, aided at first by Emma, his wife, then by Palmyra friend Martin Harris, whose visit with scholars in Albany and New York City convinced him of the truthfulness of the work in the spring of 1828. After Harris lost the first 116 pages of the translated manuscript, the work stopped for a year until schoolteacher Oliver Cowdery arrived from Palmyra in the spring of 1829. Joseph and Oliver translated and transcribed the Book of Mormon in three months in Harmony and Fayette, during which time they experienced further angelic visitations from biblical figures to restore the priesthood and to show Oliver, David Whitmer, and a repentant Martin Harris the plates.

After Joseph obtained a copyright to the manuscript in Utica, 5,000 copies of the Book of Mormon were printed by E. B. Grandin in Palmyra (funded by Harris). On April 6, 1830, Joseph's followers gathered from the entire region (at least 20 from Colesville, 15 from Manchester, and 20 from Fayette) to organize a new church, the Church of Christ, as dictated in a recent constitutional revelation (now D&C 20). This ten-year period of restoration has significantly impacted the religious thinking of millions, as the fledgling Church has become a worldwide institution of steadily expanding dimensions.

Larry C. Porter

Movement of Joseph Smith during the Restoration

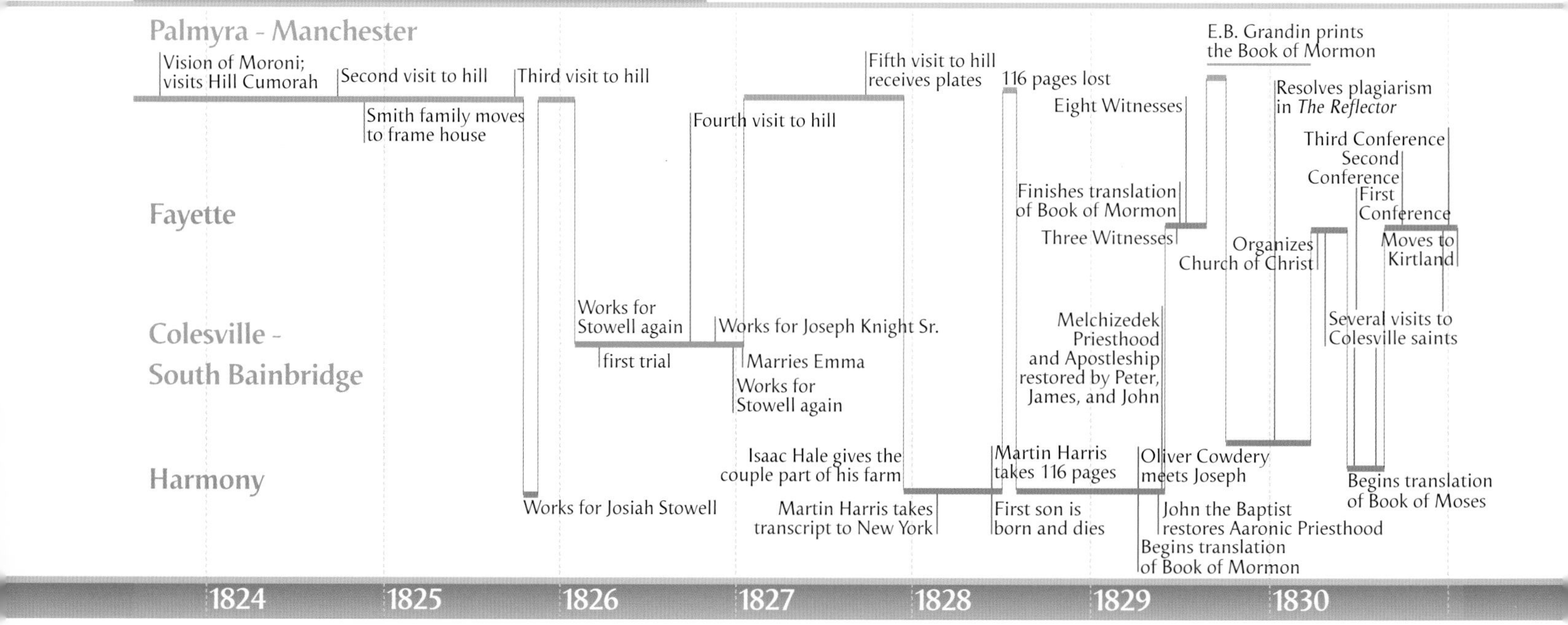

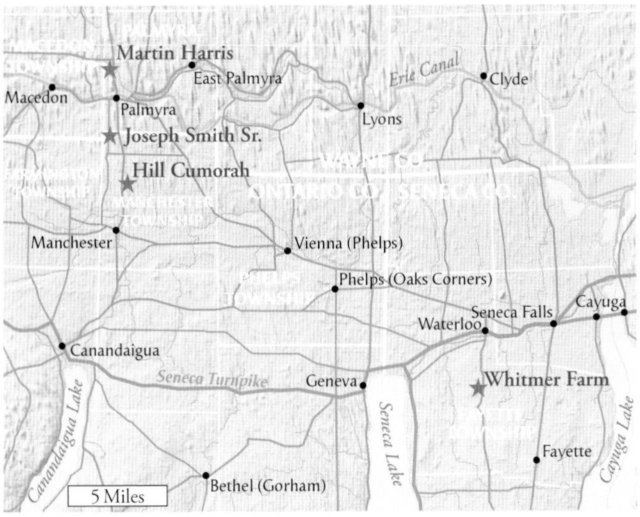

Palmyra, Manchester, and Fayette Townships

Palmyra was a rapidly growing village when the Smith family moved there in 1816–1817 (see p. 14). Even when they moved south, this was still the nearest village. The Book of Mormon was printed on the press of E.B. Grandin in Palmyra (see p. 16), becoming available in March 1830 just before the Church was organized. Although Joseph encountered great opposition to his work, he and his family also found many believers, and a branch was formed in the area in 1830.

Joseph Smith Sr. and his family lived in two homes straddling the border between Palmyra and Manchester townships between 1818 and 1830 (see p. 16). On this land in 1820, Joseph Jr. received his First Vision, and it was in the log house that he was visited by Moroni in 1823. He moved away to work in 1825 but returned in 1827 with his new bride, Emma; during their one-year stay there he obtained the gold plates, but frequent attempts to steal the plates forced them to leave. While staying here in 1829 to oversee the publication of the Book of Mormon, Joseph showed the plates to eight witnesses.

Fayette Township was the home of Peter Whitmer and his family. Early converts to Joseph's message, they welcomed Joseph, Emma, and Oliver Cowdery when persecution heightened to the south. Here Joseph completed the translation of the Book of Mormon, the Three Witnesses received their vision of the plates (July 1829), and the Church was organized in April 1830.

Western New York

Western New York was a rapidly developing frontier between 1820 and 1830, as the woodland was cleared for farms and new towns sprang up. Toll turnpikes and the Erie Canal (completed in 1825) connected the towns. Although his exact route is not always known, Joseph Smith traveled the 100 miles connecting west-central and south-central New York through Ithaca more than 20 times, either by foot or by wagon (the latter often borrowed from friends).

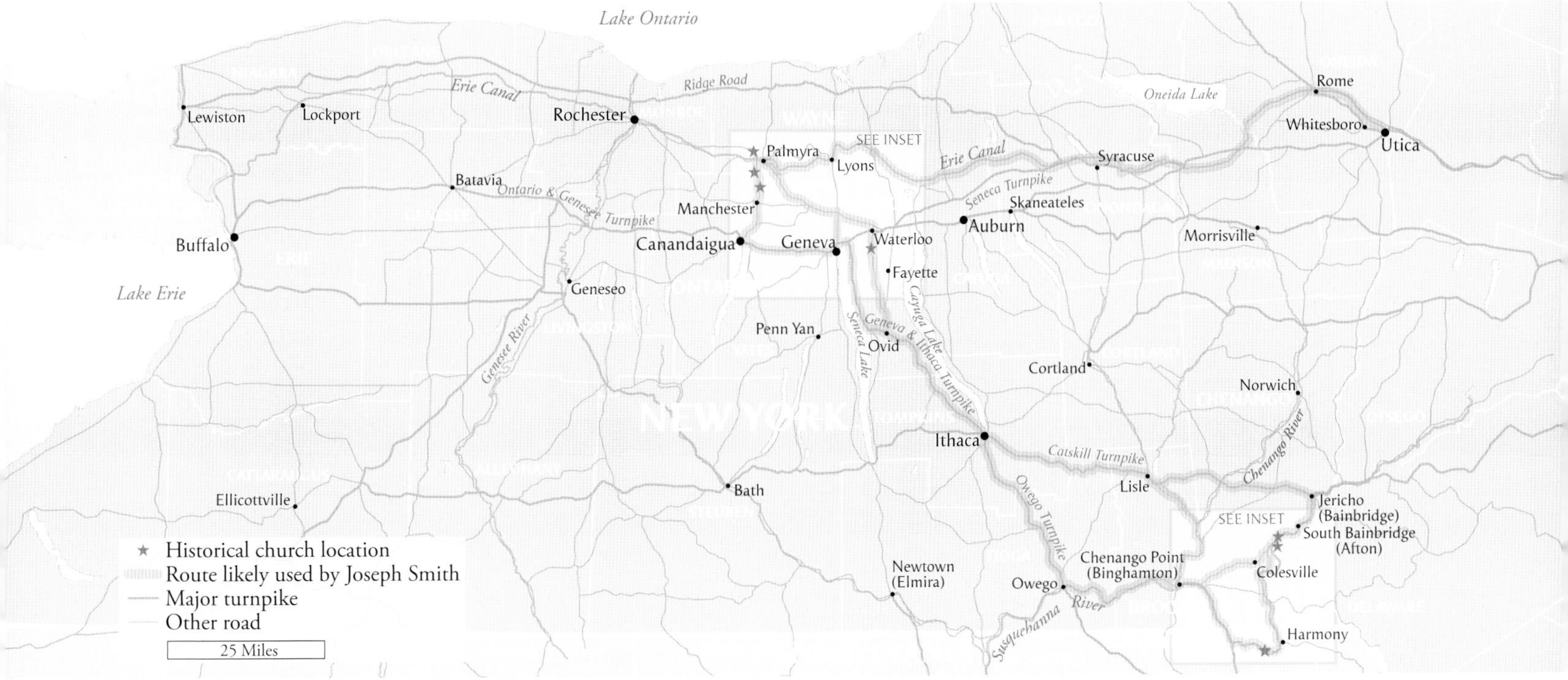

Bainbridge, Colesville, and Harmony Townships

Near the village of South Bainbridge (now Afton) was the home of Josiah Stowell, a well-to-do farmer who hired Joseph Smith and his father to look for a rumored Spanish silver mine in Harmony. Although the search was unproductive, Joseph continued to work at the Stowell farm during 1826 while he courted Emma Hale. The two were married in South Bainbridge in January 1827.

Colesville Township contained the farm of Joseph Knight Sr., who also employed Joseph Smith Jr. in 1826. Knight and his family were quickly converted to Joseph's teachings, often supporting him during the translation as well. Many of their friends also believed, but enough people opposed Joseph that he was taken to court (and acquitted) here at least twice. In June 1829, the Melchizedek Priesthood was restored somewhere between here and Harmony. In 1830, one of the first branches of the newly organized Church of Christ was created at the Knight farm.

Harmony Township (now Oakland) was first visited by Joseph Smith Jr. when he boarded at the home of Isaac Hale while employed by Josiah Stowell searching for a silver mine in early November 1825. Rather than precious metal, Joseph discovered Hale's daughter Emma. Hale never believed Joseph's stories of his visions and opposed their marriage, but he eventually sold Joseph and Emma a portion of his farm along the Susquehanna River. This was their primary residence for most of 1828–30, and here Joseph (with Emma, Martin Harris, and Oliver Cowdery) translated most of the Book of Mormon and received the Aaronic Priesthood in 1829. Joseph and Emma were still residing here in 1830, when Joseph began retranslating the Bible.

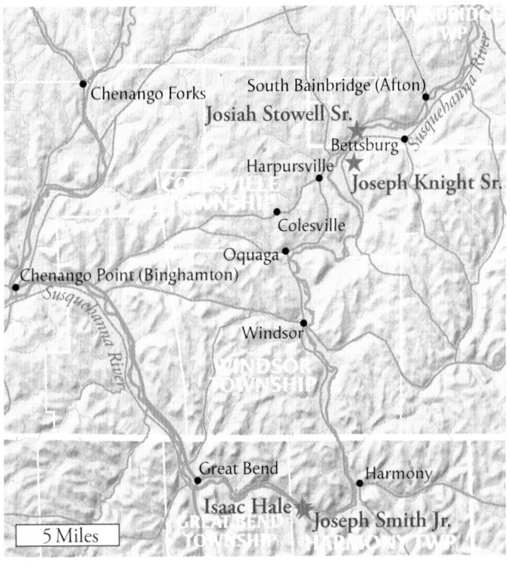

Latter-day Scriptures

1830–present

THE CHURCH OF JESUS CHRIST OF LATTER-DAY SAINTS and its scriptures are linked together in profound ways. The scriptures record the Church's founding events, chronicle its early development, set forth its beliefs, and map out its mission for the future. As Christians, Mormons hold the Bible to be scripture, but they also accept the Book of Mormon as an ancient scripture from the New World. Since its first printing in Palmyra, New York, in March 1830, about 120 million copies have been published. As the Church began to spread throughout the world, the Book of Mormon was translated into the languages of the nations where Latter-day Saints were active. That process continues today, and now the Book of Mormon has been translated and published in over 80 languages.

Because Mormonism enjoys an ongoing revelatory tradition, it is not surprising that it has a growing canon of new revelations accepted as scripture. Joseph Smith began recording revelations as the word of God as early as 1828 and continued throughout his life. In 1833, a collection of these revelations, the Book of Commandments, was in the printing process when a mob destroyed the Church's press; only a few copies were rescued and bound. In 1835, a larger set of revelations was published as the Doctrine and Covenants. As new revelations have been received, new editions have been published, the most recent in 1981. The Pearl of Great Price is a collection of translations and narrations of Joseph Smith, first published in 1851 in Liverpool, England. It and the Doctrine and Covenants have been translated into nearly 60 languages.

Scriptures were published first in Missouri (the Book of Commandments) and then in Ohio and Illinois (the Doctrine and Covenants). From the 1850s to 1870s, Britain became the primary publishing center, due to the availability and cost of printing technology compared to frontier Salt Lake City.

In 1979, the Church published an LDS edition of the King James Version of the Bible, with maps, study helps, footnotes, and cross references keyed to the other LDS scriptures. A comparable Spanish edition was published in 2009. LDS scriptures have also been made available electronically in multiple languages, in DVD format, and on the Internet.

Kent P. Jackson

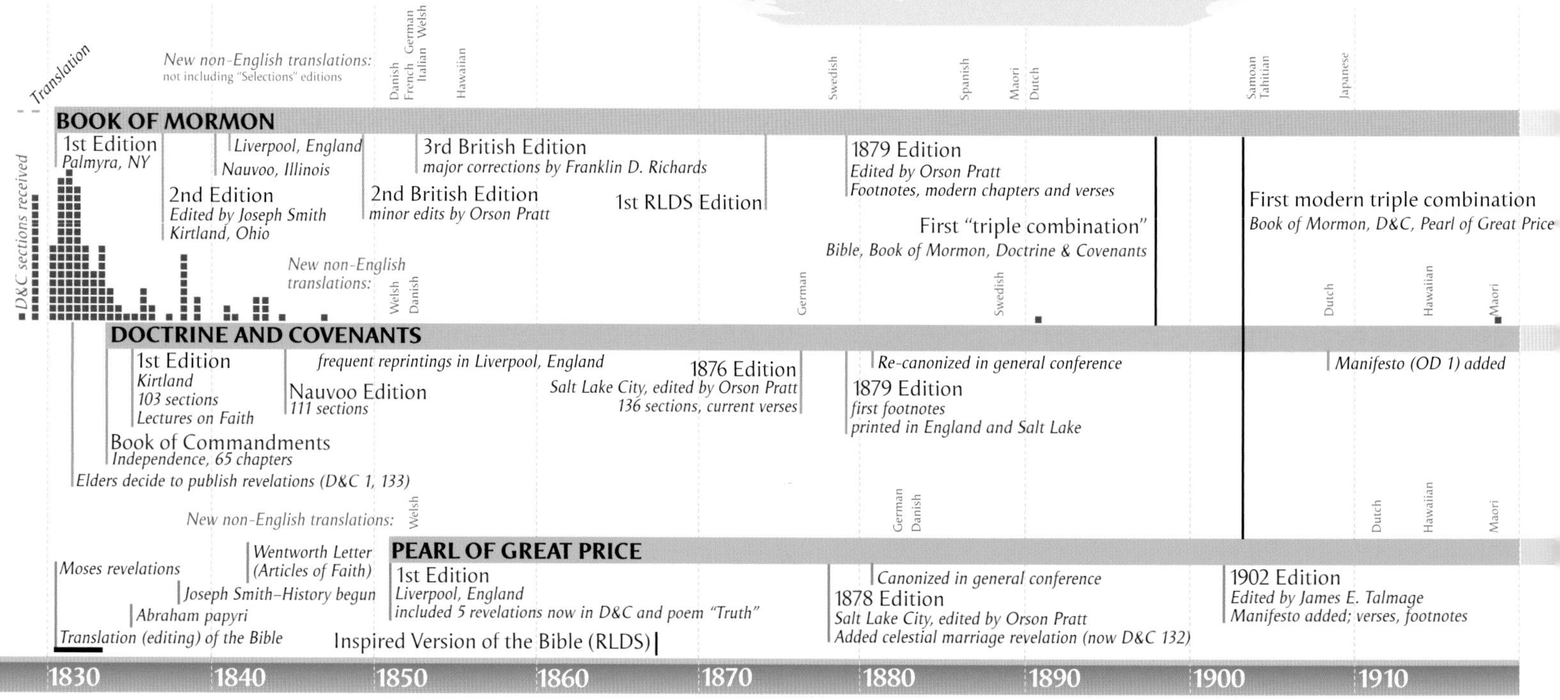

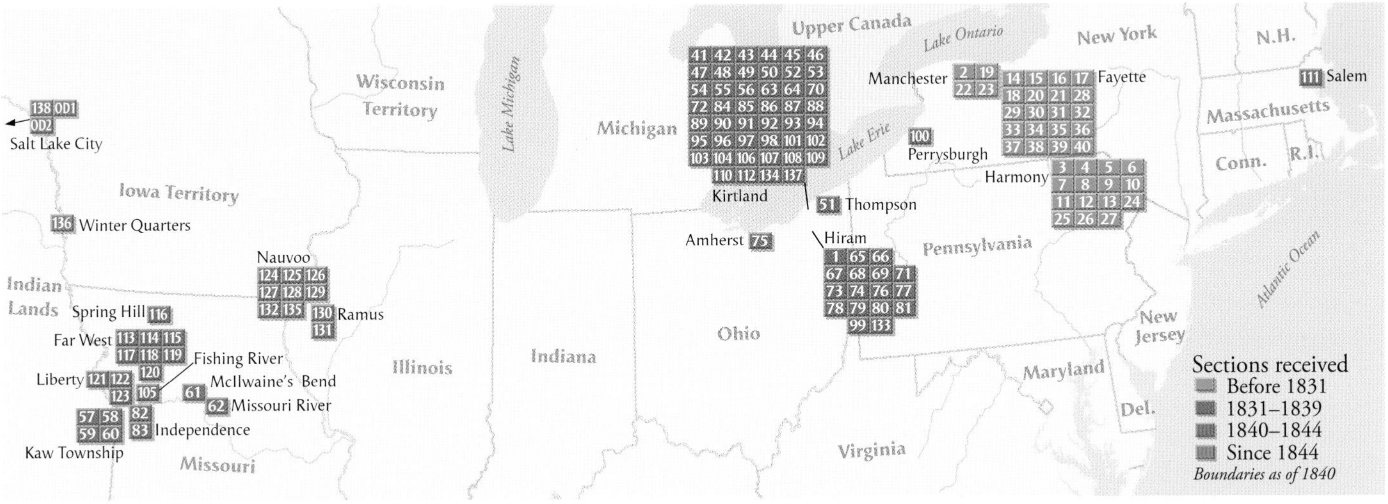

The history of the Doctrine and Covenants mirrors the early history of the Church. The earliest revelations, through 1830, are from the Church's New York–Pennsylvania period. When Joseph Smith and his followers moved to northeast Ohio in 1831, that area became the focal point of the Prophet's revelatory work. Half of the sections in the Doctrine and Covenants were received during Joseph's seven-year stay there, evidence of the rapid development of Church doctrine and practice during that period. Meanwhile, Latter-day Saints began to colonize western Missouri, so during the 1830s, revelations were divided between the two gathering places. Revelations received in western Illinois in the first half of the 1840s reflect the Church's establishment of a new gathering place there, from which the Saints were ultimately driven to the Great Basin in the American West.

◀ **Translating the scriptures** into languages other than English began as soon as the message of Mormonism spread outside of North America and Britain. The early translations followed the establishment of missions. European languages were the earliest, but soon the scriptures were translated into Pacific Island languages and later into the languages of Asia. In early stages of the Church's development in some international areas, selections from the Book of Mormon were printed before a complete publication was warranted. Many translations have been a labor of love by pioneering converts, but most current translations involve a combination of automated and human translating that has greatly increased the pace of the work. More editions continue to be released, focusing on smaller languages in areas recently opened by missionaries, such as rural Asia, Africa, scattered Pacific islands, and indigenous communities in Latin America.

Materials available in primary language
- Nothing available
- Few Church materials (pamphlets, manuals, etc.)
- Selections of the Book of Mormon
- Book of Mormon
- Doctrine and Covenants, Pearl of Great Price, Book of Mormon
- LDS Edition of the Bible and all above
- /// Materials available in secondary language

Czech
Braille Armenian
Portuguese
Tongan
Norwegian
Finnish
Chinese Rarotongan
Korean
Afrikaans
Thai Indonesian
Catalan Icelandic Polish Russian Croatian Fijian
Hindi Vietnamese Kekchi
Arabic Aymara Greek
Hungarian
Spanish-Braille Ilokano
Haitian-Creole Romanian Pangasinan Tagalog Cebuano Ukrainian
Igbo Xhosa Teluga Swahili Hmong Latvian Amharic Estonian Malagasy Armenian Lithuanian Fante Shona Albanian Bulgarian
Chinese-simplified Cambodian Mongolian Kiribati Turkish Slovenian Neo-Melanesian Tswana Zulu Marshallese Yapese Lingala Bislama Tamil Twi Hiligaynon
Serbian Yoruba Urdu Sinhala Guarani *84 Languages*

BOOK OF MORMON

1920 Edition
Significant text corrections by James E. Talmage
New chapter headings, dates, introduction, layout

1981 Triple Combination
Text corrections, new footnotes, maps

Spanish Triple Combination

Retail edition
Doubleday

Earliest Text edition
Royal Skousen

Kirtland Revelation Books
part of Joseph Smith Papers

New maps, photos

Armenian
Czech Spanish
Portuguese
Finnish
Japanese French Tongan Norwegian
Samoan
Italian Tahitian
Korean
Chinese
Thai Indonesian

DOCTRINE AND COVENANTS

1921 Edition
James E. Talmage: Lectures on Faith removed, new layout, footnotes

Sections 137, 138, OD 2 added

Vietnamese Afrikaans Croatian Icelandic
Fijian Polish Kekchi Greek
Arabic English-Braille
Hungarian Russian Spanish-Braille
Cebuano Tagalog Rarotongan Catalan Ilokano
Albanian Bulgarian
Swahili Romanian Ukrainian
Latvian Malagasy Armenian Lithuanian
Haitian Cambodian Mongolian Shona Igbo
Chinese-simplified
58 Languages

Since 1980, the Doctrine and Covenants and the Pearl of Great Price have been translated simultaneously

Swedish
Czech
Armenian
Samoan
Spanish
Portuguese
Norwegian
Finnish Japanese French Tongan
Italian
Korean
Chinese Thai
Tahitian Indonesian

PEARL OF GREAT PRICE

1921 Edition
James E. Talmage: new layout, index

two revelations as insert (future D&C 137, 138)

LDS edition KJV Bible
Footnotes, topical guide, dictionary, maps, JST

LDS edition Spanish Bible

1920 | 1930 | 1940 | 1950 | 1960 | 1970 | 1980 | 1990 | 2000

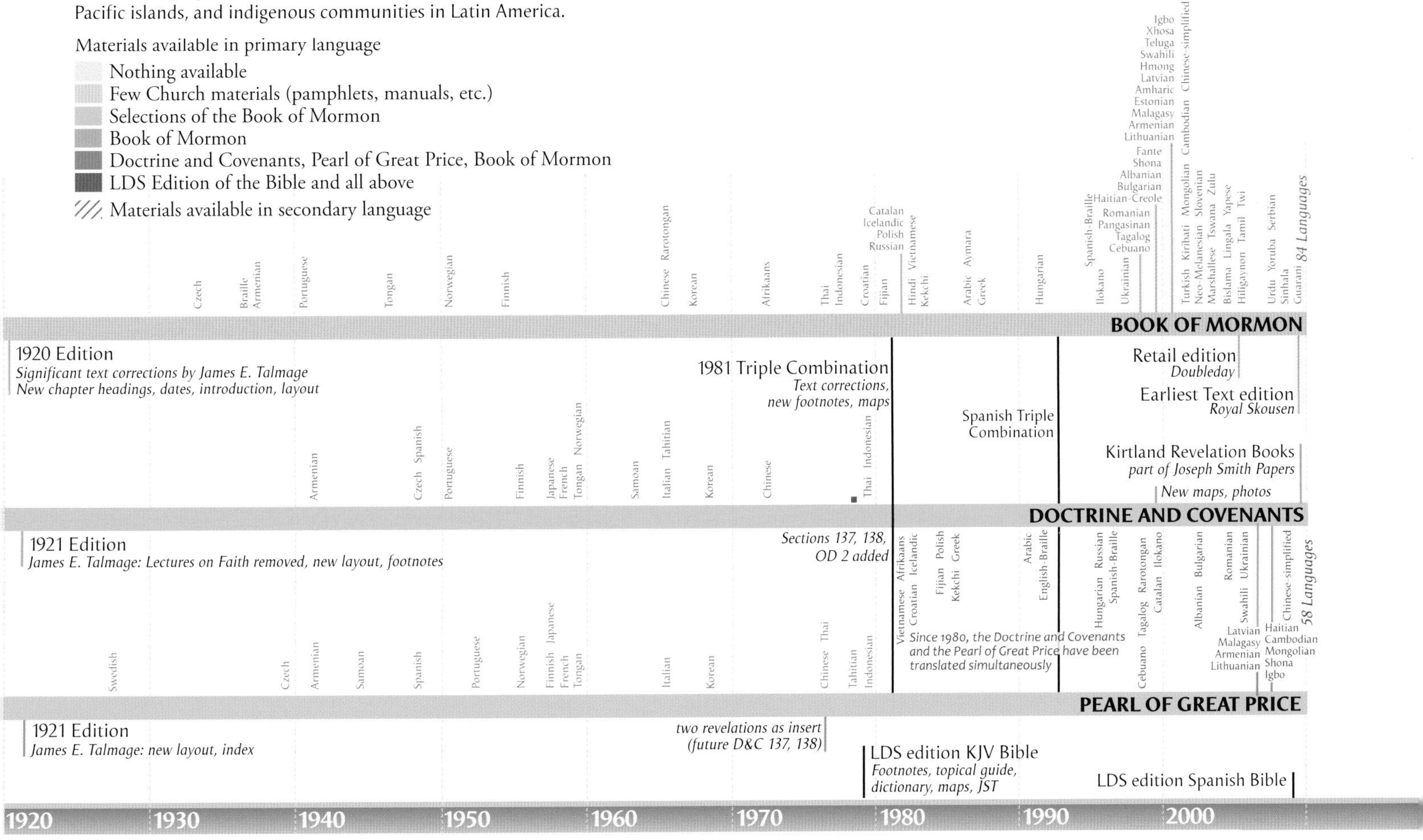

The First Year of the Church of Christ

April 1830–January 1831

EARLY BELIEVERS of the Book of Mormon gathered together in the small New York communities of Palmyra, Colesville, and Fayette. In Palmyra, believers met in the Joseph Smith Sr. farmhouse. In Colesville, other believers met in the Joseph Knight home, and in Fayette, the Peter Whitmer Sr. log cabin. About 50 believers met in obedience to revelation on Tuesday, April 6, 1830, at the Whitmer home, to organize the Church of Christ (later renamed The Church of Jesus Christ of Latter-day Saints). The meeting was opened with prayer, emblems of the Savior's sacrifice were blessed and passed, and "the Holy Ghost was poured out upon us to a very great degree—some prophesied, whilst we all praised the Lord, and rejoiced exceedingly," recalled Joseph Smith. He was acknowledged as "a seer, a translator, a prophet, an apostle of Jesus Christ, an elder of the Church through the will of God the Father, and the grace of your Lord Jesus Christ" (D&C 21:1).

After the organizational meeting, missionaries were called to share news of the restored gospel. The first missionary called was Samuel Smith, Joseph's brother. He ventured from Palmyra with copies of the Book of Mormon filling his knapsack. After traveling thirty miles the first day, he slept under an apple tree, having "been turned out of doors that day" for the fifth time. The next day, he journeyed eight miles to Bloomington, New York, where he met John P. Greene, a Methodist preacher, who consented to take a book on his next preaching tour. In the following fifteen months, Smith traveled over 4,000 miles, preaching from Maine to Missouri.

The most arduous early mission was served by Oliver Cowdery, Peter Whitmer Jr., Ziba Peterson, and Parley P. Pratt. In October 1830, they began their journey to share the Book of Mormon with Indian tribes, known among Mormons as Lamanites. Near Buffalo, New York, they preached to the Cattaraugus Indians. From Buffalo they traveled to Mentor, Ohio, where they converted Reverend Sidney Rigdon and many of his congregation (see p. 28). They then journeyed to Sandusky, Ohio, to preach to the Wyandot Indians. From Sandusky they traveled to Cincinnati and then 200 miles to St. Louis. For the last 300 miles, they trudged through trackless wastes of snow to Independence, Missouri, about 1,500 miles from where they had started. Parley P. Pratt claimed that they had "preached the gospel to tens of thousands of Gentiles and two nations of Indians; baptizing, confirming, and organizing many hundreds of people into churches."

As these missionaries were spreading the gospel of Jesus Christ, others did likewise. Jared Carter preached from Ohio to Benson, Vermont, and Ebenezer Page preached in Chenango, New York. While these and other missionaries shared the good news, Joseph extended an invitation to all early converts to attend three conferences of the Church at the Whitmer home in Fayette. On June 9, 1830, at the first conference, "much exhortation and instruction was given, and the Holy Ghost was poured out upon us in a miraculous manner." On September 26–28, 1830, at the second conference, Joseph was appointed to "receive commandments and revelations in this church" (D&C 28:2). On January 2, 1831, at the third conference, Joseph received a revelation commanding his followers to settle in Ohio: "Wherefore, for this cause I gave unto you the commandment that you should go to the Ohio; and there I will give unto you my law; and there you shall be endowed with power from on high" (D&C 38:32).

In obedience to the revelation, faithful Colesville Saints departed from Ithaca, New York, bound for Ohio. They were followed by the Fayette Saints with Lucy Mack Smith leading the first contingent and Thomas B. Marsh the second. Martin Harris led the next group from Palmyra in late May 1831. Editor E. B. Grandin noted their departure and printed in the *Wayne Sentinel*, "Several families, numbering about fifty souls, took up their line of march from this town last week for the promised land." The Harris group journeyed to Buffalo, New York, via the Erie Canal. They then went by boat on Lake Erie to reach the Fairport Harbor in Ohio. From Fairport, they journeyed overland to Kirtland, arriving in early June 1831.

Susan Easton Black

The First Year, 1830–31

- **6 April** First organizational meeting of the Church held at the Whitmer log home in Fayette, New York
- **June** "Visions of Moses" received by Joseph Smith as he begins the Bible translation
- **9 June** First conference of the Church held in the Whitmer home
- **26–28 September** Second conference of the Church held in the Whitmer home
- **October–November** Missionaries to the Lamanites convert some 130 residents in the Kirtland, Ohio, area
- **December** First revelation on gathering to Ohio received (D&C 37)
- **2 January** Third conference of the Church held in the Whitmer home
- **25 April** Colesville Saints depart from Ithaca bound for Ohio
- **May** Lucy Mack Smith leads first contingent of Fayette Saints; Thomas B. Marsh leads the second; Martin Harris leads a contingent of Palmyra Saints

Apr 1830 | May | Jun | Jul | Aug | Sept | Oct | Nov | Dec | Jan 1831 | Feb | Mar | Apr | May | Jun

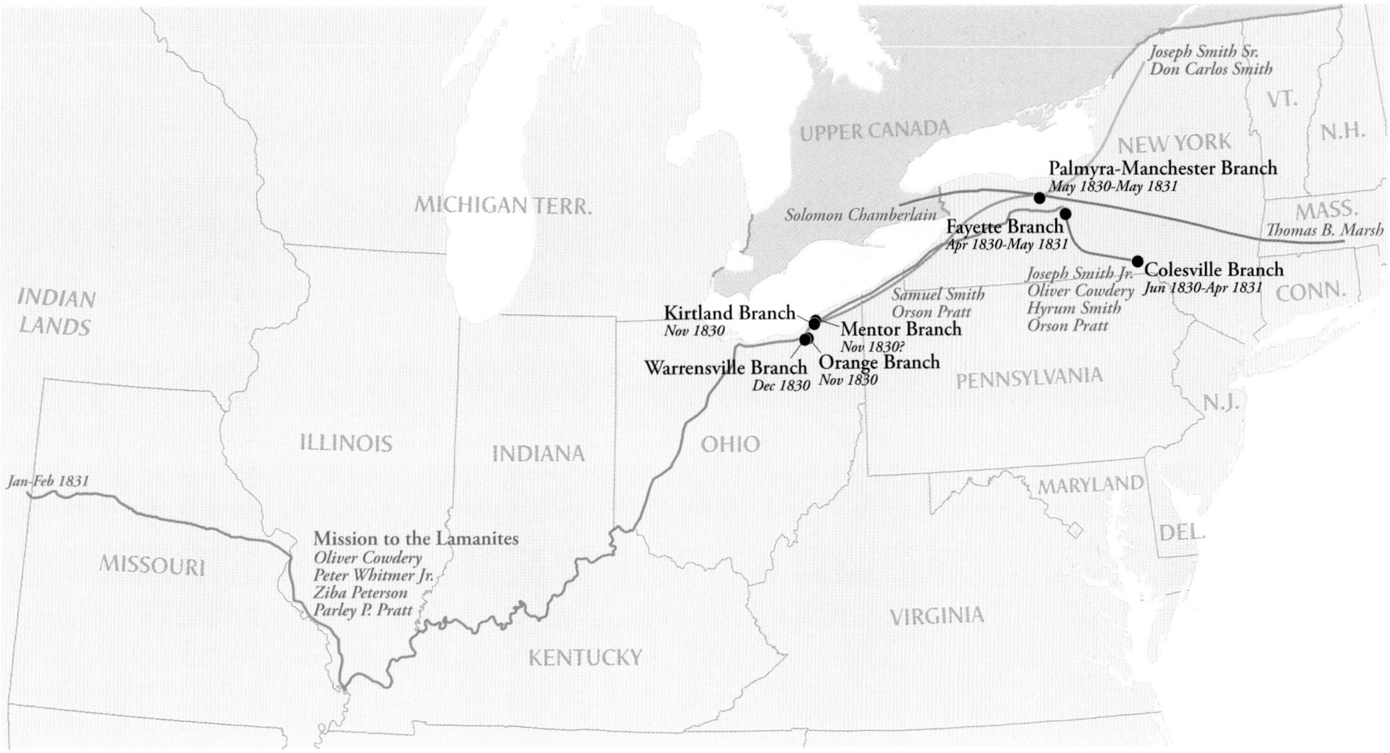

Early Missions

Before the Book of Mormon was fully printed and bound, early believers carried excerpts hundreds of miles to share with relatives and friends. Thomas B. Marsh carried 16 loose pages of the Book of Mormon to Charlestown, Massachusetts, to read to his family. Solomon Chamberlain took 64 pages to Canada. After traveling 800 miles through the Canadian wilderness, he stated, "I exhorted all people to prepare for the great work of God that was now about to come forth."

The missionaries to the Lamanites journeyed from New York to Missouri sharing the word of God with Native Americans and others. Joseph Smith Sr. and Don Carlos Smith traveled to St. Lawrence County, New York, to share the Book of Mormon with relatives. Hyrum Smith traveled to Colesville and Fayette, New York, to preach to early converts. Samuel Smith and Orson Pratt journeyed from New York to Kirtland, Ohio, to preach the word of God. The results of these missionary labors were the formation of major branches of the Church in New York and Ohio in 1830.

Gathering to Ohio

After the revelation was given to gather to Ohio (D&C 37), each of the three New York branches departed as soon as possible. The Colesville Branch gathered in Ithaca, New York, in April 1831, where they traveled by boat across Cayuga Lake. The Fayette Branch, about fifty in number, traveled in two companies under the direction of Lucy Mack Smith and Thomas B. Marsh. Both the Colesville and Fayette companies rode barges down the Cayuga and Seneca Canal (completed 1828) to the Erie Canal, riding it to Buffalo, there boarding a steamship across Lake Erie (still icy in May) to Fairport Harbor, Ohio, the nearest port to Kirtland.

About fifty of the Palmyra/Manchester Saints, under the leadership of Martin Harris, made a similar journey soon after, arriving in Kirtland in time to attend the June 1831 conference.

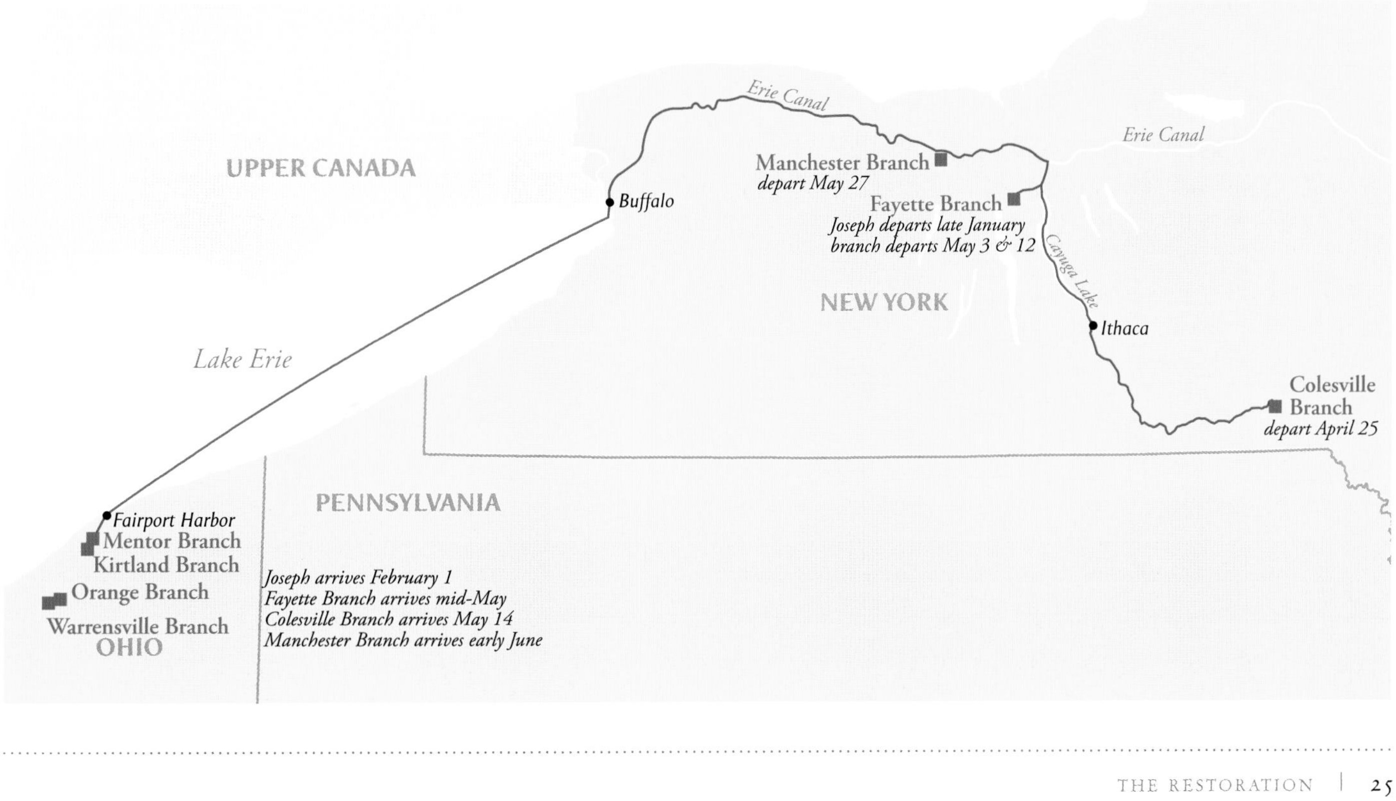

The Travels of Joseph Smith Jr.

1805–1844

Joseph Smith traveled far more extensively than many might assume. During his short life he traveled mostly in the eastern United States, but he also visited Canada at least twice. He and his family resided in six states and he traveled in sixteen states. His travels took him to large cities such as Boston, New York City, Philadelphia, and Washington, D.C. He also visited smaller cities such as Salem, Massachusetts; Providence, Rhode Island; Albany, New York; and Springfield and Quincy, Illinois. Along his way, he visited dozens of towns and villages across the eastern United States.

As he traveled, Joseph Smith employed several common modes of transportation. He walked, rode horseback, traveled by wagon and team, journeyed by stage coach, sailed on river boats and canal barges, and even traveled by rail.

The reasons the Mormon Prophet traveled are many and varied. While still in his youth, he traveled to Salem, Massachusetts, to recuperate from a serious leg operation (see p. 14). As a member of a large family, he often visited family members who lived in other locations. As he visited Church members, he gave counsel and pronounced blessings. Joseph Smith traveled for the purpose of preaching the gospel, both during short visits and longer, more formal stays, such as his missions to Canada. Many of his journeys involved legal matters. He was forced to travel when he was under arrest or being imprisoned. Often, he visited lawyers, judges, and government officials to seek legal advice. Sometimes he traveled to other places to attend court sessions or hearings. Once he even visited with President Martin Van Buren in the White House, seeking assistance for Mormon losses incurred in Missouri. Closely related to legal matters are his travels to take care of Church financial concerns, such as seeking funds from banks in New York and money in Salem. He also purchased supplies for the Church storehouse from eastern merchants. In military matters, he recruited for Zion's Camp and then led members of the camp from Ohio to Missouri in 1834. During an earlier visit to Missouri, he took part in the dedication of Missouri as a gathering place for the Saints. On numerous occasions, he traveled to distant communities to hold Church conferences and conduct Church business. Some of his trips included selecting sites for the establishment of possible settlements by Church members. He loved to travel with family and friends for recreational purposes, such as cruising on the Mississippi.

During his extensive travels, Joseph Smith had some interesting and unusual experiences. While traveling by stagecoach to Washington, D.C., he succeeded in bringing runaway horses under control, thus averting a serious accident. En route to Missouri with Zion's Camp, he prophesied concerning events related to the Book of Mormon. People listening to him preach in Ontario, Canada, told of the power of his testimony and countenance. During a visit to Montrose, Iowa, he prophesied that the Mormons would become a mighty people in the Rocky Mountains.

Donald Q. Cannon

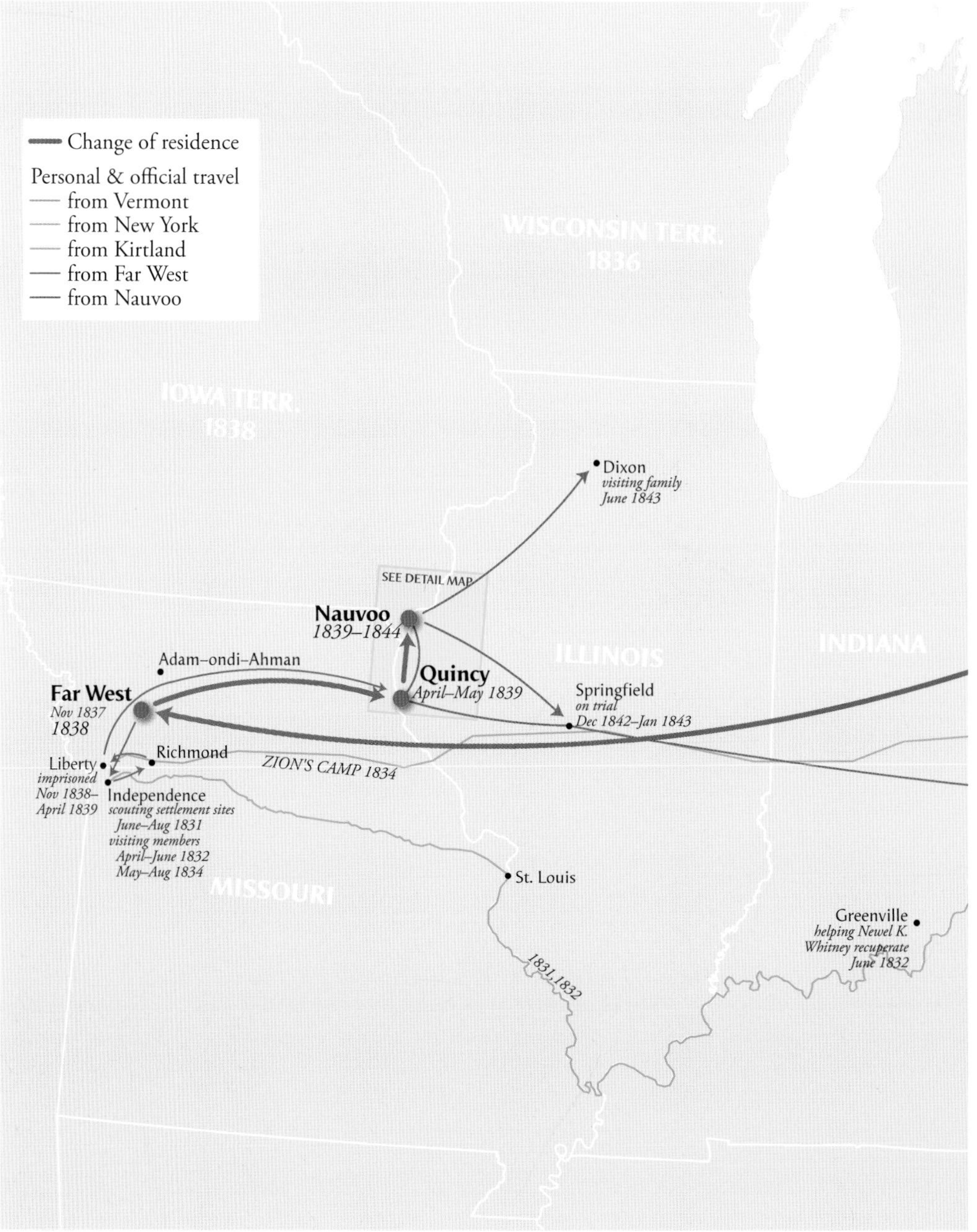

Kirtland Area

While living in northeastern Ohio, Joseph traveled extensively in the area surrounding Kirtland. He held Church conferences in Hiram, Orange, Amherst, Norton, and New Portage. Joseph visited family members in Chardon, Fairport, and Painesville. He preached the gospel as a missionary in Shalersville, Ravenna, and Huntsburg.

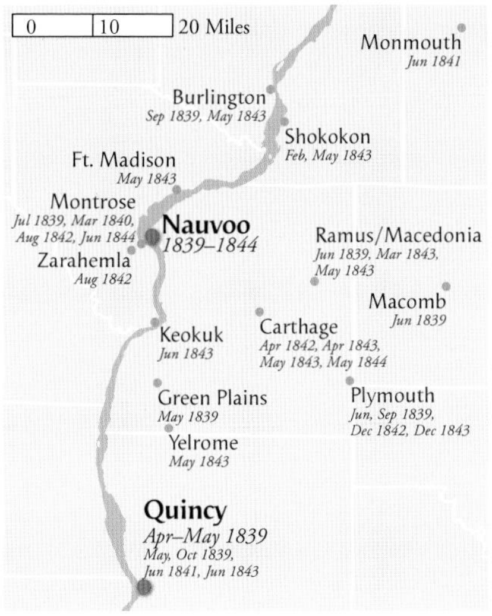

Nauvoo Area

Most of Joseph Smith's travels during the Nauvoo Era (1839–44) were in eastern Iowa and western Illinois, fairly close to Nauvoo. He visited family in Green Plains, Plymouth, and Macomb. Joseph held Church meetings in Quincy, Ramus, and Yelrome. He visited Quincy, Keokuk, Fort Madison, and Burlington while cruising on the *Maid of Iowa* on the Mississippi River.

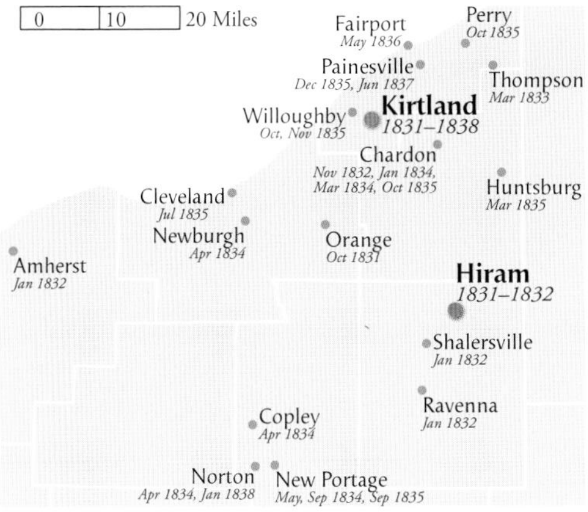

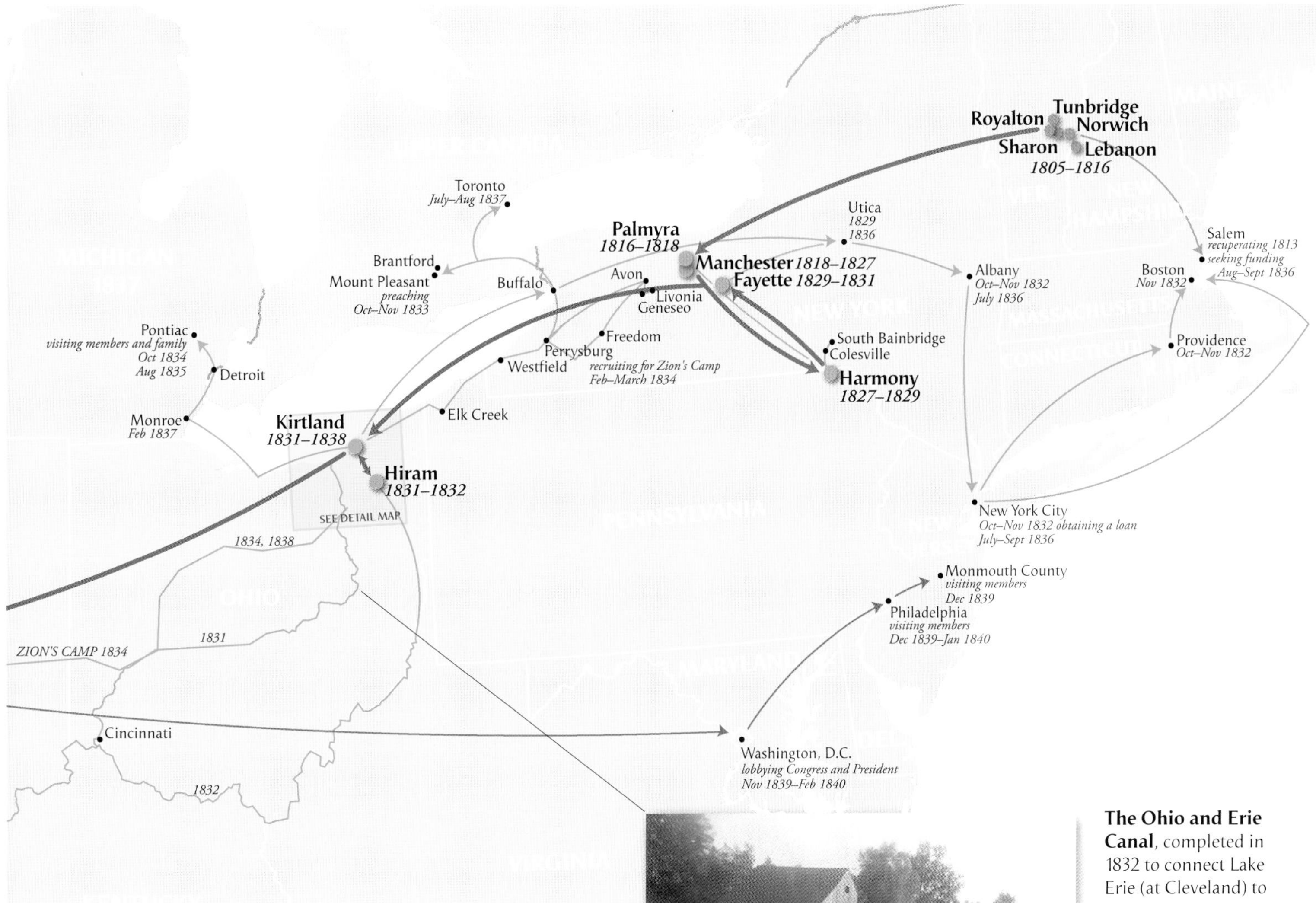

The Ohio and Erie Canal, completed in 1832 to connect Lake Erie (at Cleveland) to the Ohio River, was one of many routes used by Joseph Smith when he traveled between Kirtland and Missouri.

The Western Reserve

1826–1838

KNOWN TODAY SIMPLY AS THE WESTERN RESERVE, this 120-mile strip of land in northeastern Ohio was owned by the state of Connecticut. In 1795, Connecticut sold the land to a group of land developers who divided it and resold smaller land parcels, mostly to New England residents (leading to a predominantly New England culture and heritage in the area). The revelations commanding the Saints to move here identify the Western Reserve as "The Ohio" (D&C 37–39).

The center of the region for the Church was the city of Kirtland, where the first temple was built (see p. 30). Although the name Kirtland is usually understood as being the town or city of Kirtland, it was also used to refer to the wider area encompassing the Western Reserve. This is evidenced by nine references in the Doctrine and Covenants to the "land of Kirtland." Church growth in the Western Reserve resulted from missionary conversions in the area and from Saints gathering from other areas of the United States and Canada. Most of those who gathered sailed across Lake Erie, arriving at Fairport Harbor. They then walked 12 miles to Kirtland and settled either in or near Kirtland.

Conversions resulted from missionaries who traversed the Western Reserve beginning in 1830 with the missionaries to the Lamanites (see p. 24). Conversions in the Western Reserve were augmented significantly by Sidney Rigdon, a Reformed Baptist and Campbellite minister. Sidney had almost exclusively taught belief in the Bible and its pure doctrines. Early baptisms and leadership came primarily from his many Baptist and Campbellite congregations. Following his November 1830 conversion in Mentor, hundreds were then baptized from his wide circle of influence. Many of those baptized became Church leaders in the First Presidency, Quorum of the Twelve, Presiding Bishoprics, Seventies, stakes, and auxiliary organizations.

Karl Ricks Anderson

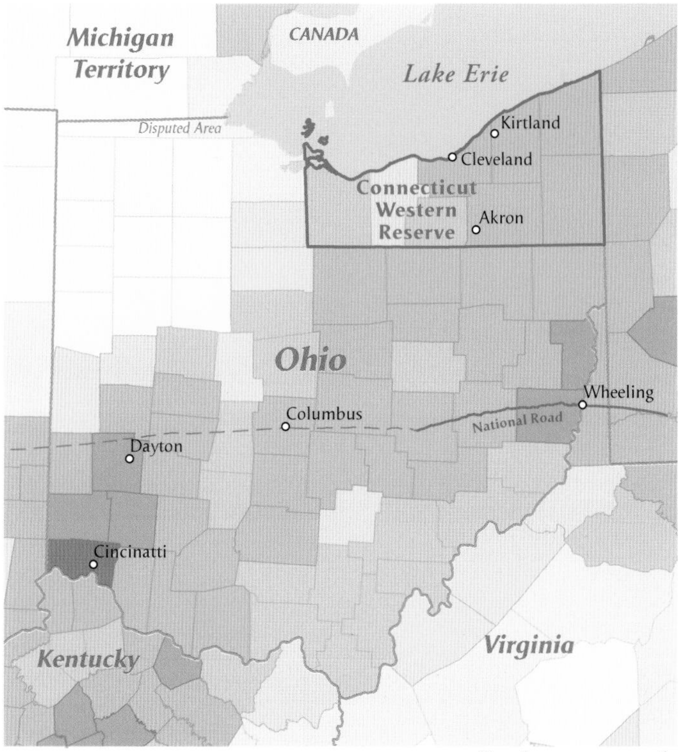

People per square mile
1830 census
- less than 3
- 3–5
- 6–10
- 11–20
- 21–50
- 51–100
- over 100

The Connecticut Western Reserve got its name when the states were relinquishing their western land claims to the new federal government in 1786; Connecticut retained this small part of its claim until 1800.

Although the Western Reserve was surveyed and available for settlement after the Connecticut Land Company purchased the land in 1795, growth was slow until the Erie Canal made the shoreline area more accessible. Meanwhile, the southern portion of the state was growing rapidly, aided by the Ohio River and the National Road.

In 1830, the area designated as the Connecticut Western Reserve was a lightly populated but rapidly growing frontier; early resident Eliza R. Snow described it as being "the jumping off place."

The Church in Ohio

1796 U.S. General Moses Cleaveland is sent by the Connecticut Land Company to survey the unsettled, Indian-occupied Western Reserve

1799 The family of Frederick G. Williams moves to the Western Reserve, the first of dozens of families who are converted when missionaries arrive in 1830

1825 Sidney Rigdon moves to the Western Reserve, begins preaching for the Reformed Baptist and Campbellite movements

1830 In November, the missionaries to the Lamanites arrive in the Western Reserve and baptize Sidney Rigdon and well over 100 of his followers

1831 D&C 64:21 declares that the Saints are to stay in Kirtland for five years

1831 Joseph Smith moves to Kirtland, followed by other Church members from New York and Pennsylvania

1831–32 Hiram, Ohio, becomes Church headquarters for one year when Joseph Smith moves there, causing many members to move to Hiram

1833–36 The Kirtland Temple is built, causing many members to move close to Kirtland

1834 The Kirtland Stake is created

1838 Most Ohio Church members move to Far West, Missouri; over 500 leave in July in a group called the "Kirtland Camp"

1841 Remaining members are asked to leave Ohio and move to Nauvoo; the Kirtland Stake is discontinued

1800 | 1810 | 1820 | 1830 | 1840

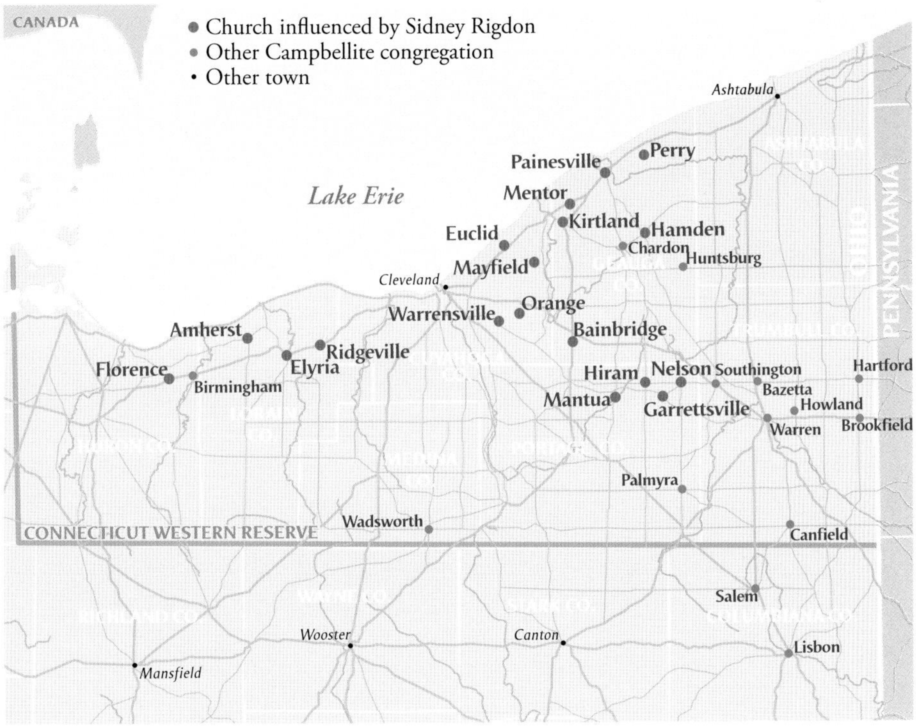

Sidney Rigdon, a well-trained and experienced Baptist minister from Pittsburgh, first preached in the Western Reserve from 1820 to 1822. Returning to Pittsburgh, he became a prominent Baptist minister, but soon joined the Disciples of Christ movement of Alexander Campbell, which broke from the Baptist Church to try to restore primitive Christianity as Campbell interpreted it. Rigdon, a dynamic and profound speaker, returned to the Western Reserve in 1825 at age 33, and soon established several Campbellite branches, and had a significant influence on many more.

Following his November 1830 conversion to Joseph Smith's Church of Christ, hundreds of his followers from these congregations were baptized. A revelation in December 1830 said that Sidney had been "sent . . . to prepare the way before me, and before Elijah . . . and thou knewest it not" (D&C 35:4).

Mormon Settlement in Ohio

Church growth in the Kirtland, Madison, and Amherst areas began with the Lamanite missionaries (see p. 24). Sidney Rigdon's influence led to widespread conversions in the areas in which he had preached. Growth in the Hiram area was accelerated when Joseph Smith moved there and he and Sidney were sent on their local preaching mission. All areas were impacted by seemingly constant missionary efforts. Although it is not entirely clear where branches of the Church existed in this area, especially near Kirtland, the places identified as branches were determined by researching Church periodicals, personal journals, and land records of early members.

After the widespread dissensions of 1837 and 1838, most of those loyal to Joseph left for Missouri, but enough remained to keep several branches operating, and the area actually saw a great deal of growth during the early days of Nauvoo.

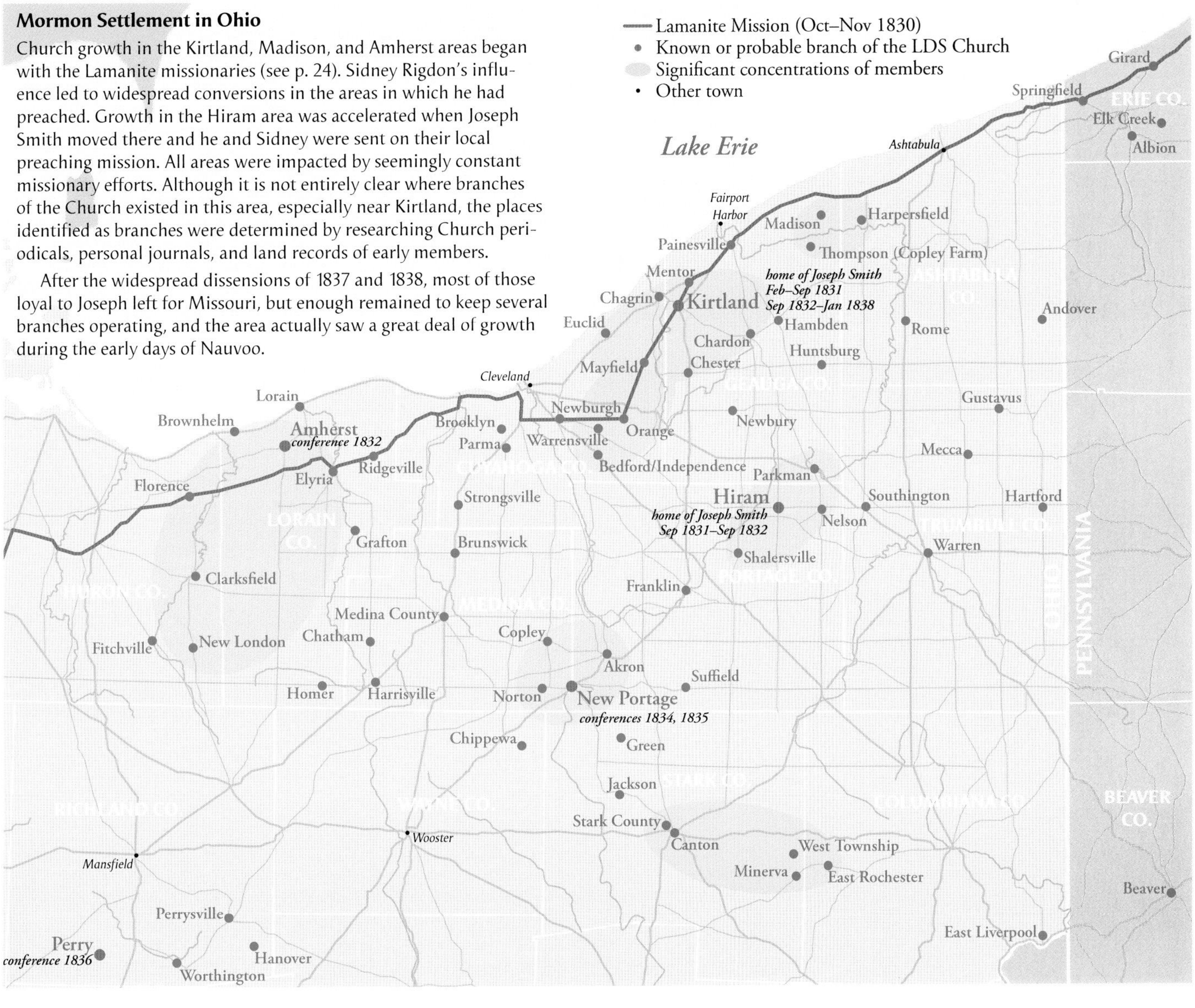

Kirtland, Ohio

1831–1838

KIRTLAND WAS ONE OF MANY TOWNS started by settlers who bought land from the Connecticut Land Company (see p. 28); in fact, it was named after Judge Turhand Kirtland, one of the company partners. When Parley P. Pratt and three other missionaries arrived from New York in 1830, they converted many local citizens to the new Church of Christ, including Newel K. Whitney, A. Sidney Gilbert, and Isaac Morley. Joseph Smith and his family arrived from New York in early February 1831, initially rooming with the Whitney family.

Soon, most of the members from New York arrived, and the village became the first gathering place for members of the Church (see p. 24). By 1837, there were more than 1,500 Saints in Kirtland Township, and many more in the surrounding area. The Mormons built hundreds of homes and several public buildings during this period. Some of the original buildings have survived, while others have been rebuilt, some as recently as 2002.

Kirtland was the headquarters for the Church from 1831 to 1837, its most formative period. Forty-six sections of the Doctrine and Covenants were received here (see p. 22), instituting most of the unique doctrines, practices, and organization of the LDS Church.

In Kirtland, the Church first attempted (and ultimately failed) to build a utopian "Zion" social and economic system. An ideal city plan was laid out (see p. 44), a temple was built, and the Kirtland Safety Society (a kind of bank) was instituted to help fund the building of this "stake of Zion." The United Firm (also known as the United Order) was an organization that managed the economic affairs of the Church, presided over by nine of the leading brethren. Four of these men were residents of Kirtland: Joseph Smith, Sidney Rigdon, Jesse Gause, and Newel K. Whitney. Five lived in Missouri: Oliver Cowdery, Edward Partridge, Sidney Gilbert, John Whitmer, and William W. Phelps (D&C 82:11–12). When Jesse Gause left the Church, Frederick G. Williams replaced him as a member of the Firm and became a member of the First Presidency of the Church (D&C 81; 92:1). Later, John Johnson (D&C 96:6–9) and Martin Harris were added to the Firm. These 12 men held properties in trust and cared for the poor by supervising the bishop's storehouse. They also purchased land and assisted in the construction of the Kirtland Temple.

At the dedication of the reconstructed Kirtland historic site in 2003, President Gordon B. Hinckley remarked, "There is something unique and wonderful about what happened here. . . . Nothing like it has occurred anywhere else in the history of the Church, either before or since." He concluded: "As I sat here my mind stretched across the earth. I saw this little infant Church—not born here, but nurtured here and blessed here and tested here, and tried here—grow and expand across the earth" (Church News, May 24, 2003).

Keith W. Perkins and Mark L. Staker

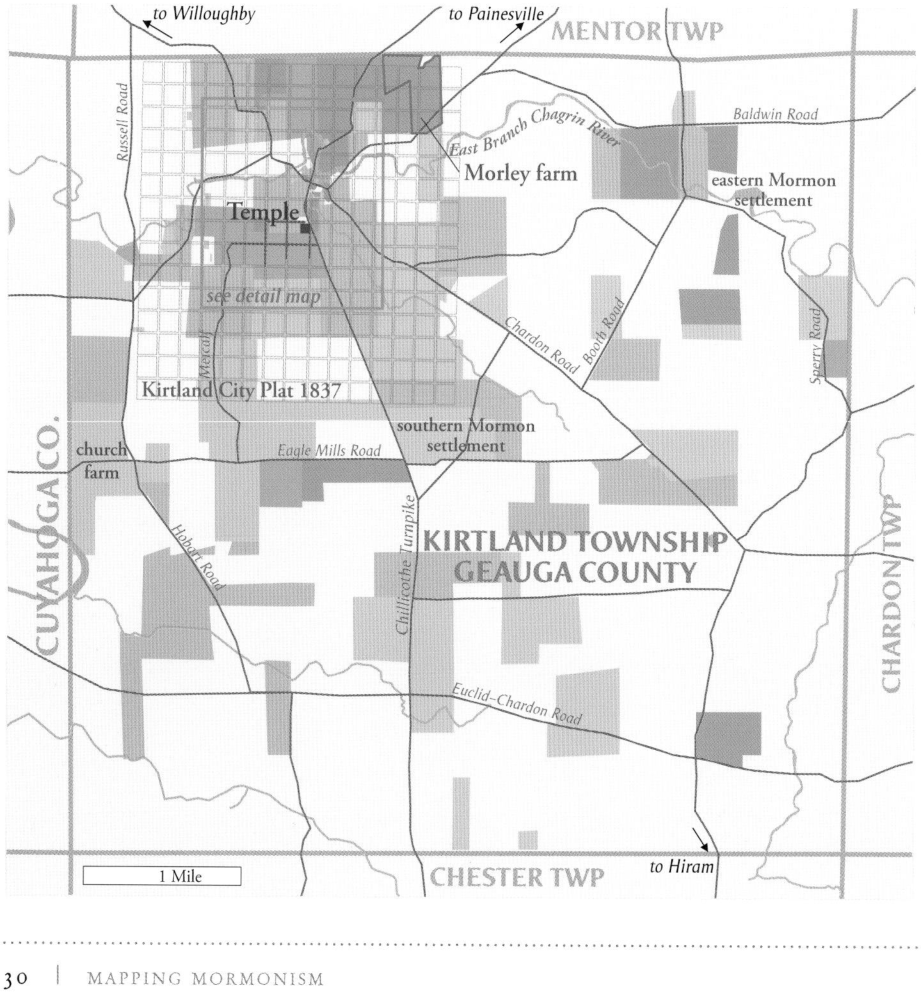

Mormon Land Owners in Kirtland

Among the Kirtland residents converted by Parley P. Pratt and his companions in 1830 were several significant landowners. For example, Isaac Morley owned a large farm. It was on his farm that many of the early Kirtland converts had been living, and it was there that the first high priests were ordained in 1831.

As the Saints gathered to Ohio, those with sufficient money purchased much of the land surrounding Kirtland village. In addition, much land was purchased in the name of the Church. In April 1833, Joseph Coe and Ezra Thayre arranged to purchase, for the Church, the Peter French farm of 103 acres for $5,000. It was on a small portion of this property that the Kirtland Temple was later built. On October 5, 1836, another large farm, consisting of 239 acres, was purchased by the Church for $11,777.50.

On this land the Church planned to enlarge the city according to the City of Zion plan (see p. 44), but only a few short streets were ever constructed before Joseph and most of his loyal followers were forced to leave in 1838.

Mormon-owned land
- already owned by 1830 converts
- purchased 1831–32
- purchased 1833–35
- purchased 1836–38

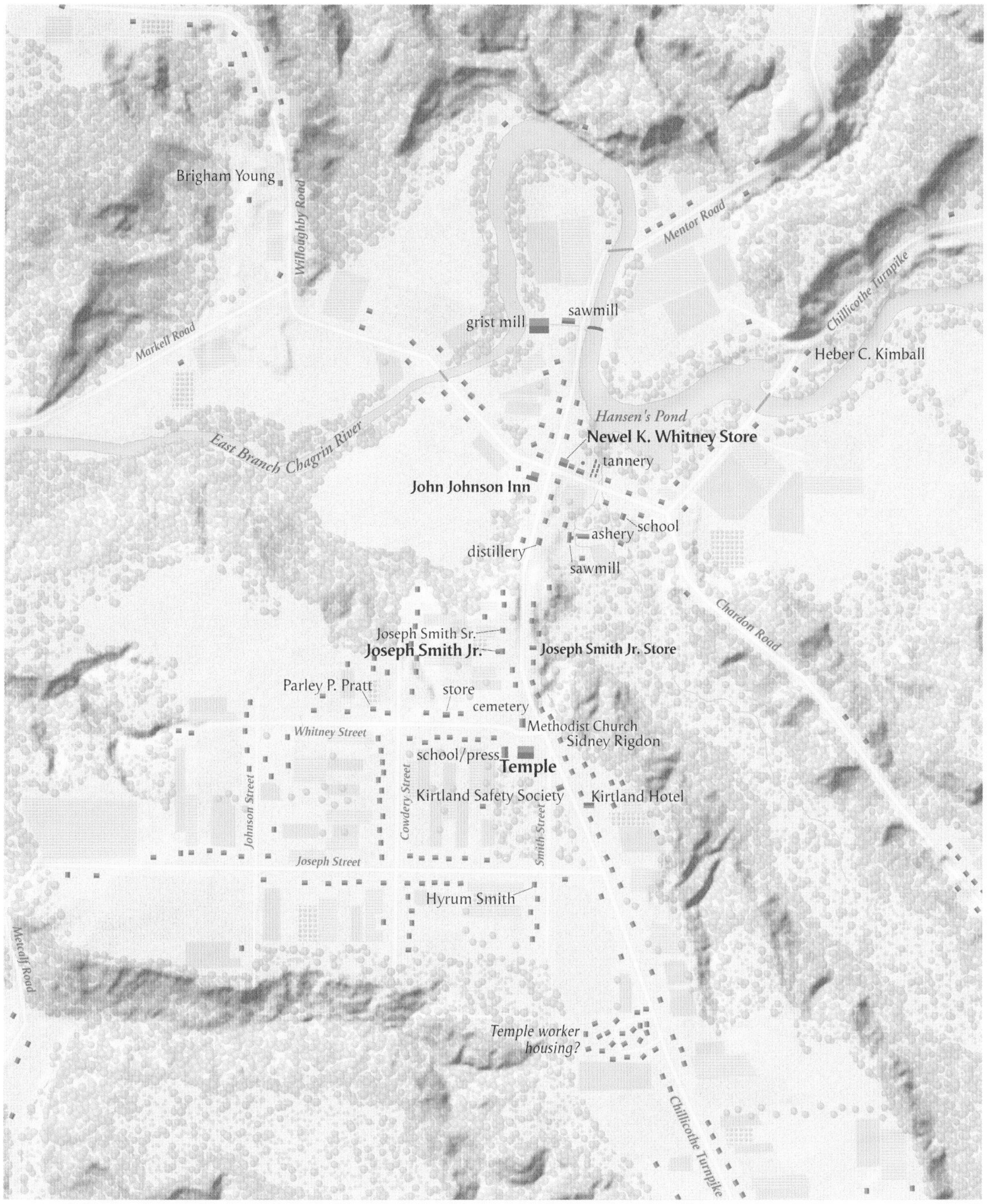

Kirtland in 1837

Initially, the focus of the village was in "the flats" south of the Chagrin River. At this time, the Newel K. Whitney store at the crossroads was essentially the headquarters of the Church: Joseph Smith had an office there, and the School of the Prophets—a training program for priesthood leaders and missionaries—was held upstairs.

By 1835, a new city was emerging on "the Bluffs" to the south, centered on the temple and following the planned grid pattern of the City of Zion (44). However, only a few of the 225 planned blocks (covering an area twice the size of this map) were developed before disaffected Church leaders drove Joseph out of Kirtland, along with most of the members of the Church loyal to him.

It should be noted that this reconstruction is not entirely certain. Some features have survived to the present (including the temple and the Whitney store); many locations are known from extensive historical and archaeological evidence, but some homes shown here are only conjectures based on general statements of the geography of Kirtland.

Kirtland Temple

The most prominent Kirtland structure (then and now) is the stately House of the Lord, the first Latter-day Saint temple. It overlooks the city from the top of the hill. The design, measurements, and functions of the Kirtland Temple were given by revelation. Its interior was to be 55 feet wide and 65 feet long and to have a lower and a higher court. The lower part of the inner court was to be dedicated "for your Sacrament offering, and for your preaching, and your fasting, and your praying, and the offering up of your most holy desires unto me, saith your Lord." The higher part of the inner court was to be "dedicated unto me for the school of mine apostles" (D&C 95:13–17).

The external design of the Kirtland Temple is typical of New England protestant meetinghouses, but the arrangement of the interior is unique. On each of the two main floors are two series of four-tiered pulpits, one on the west side, the other on the east. These are symbolic of the offices of the Melchizedek and Aaronic Priesthoods and accommodated their presidencies. The third floor contained offices and school facilities.

The Saints completed the temple in less than three years. The cornerstone was laid at the southeast corner on July 23, 1833, and it was dedicated on March 17, 1836. The temple became the center of life for the Saints, housing the School of the Prophets and Elders. There are three important revelations associated with the Kirtland Temple: D&C 109, 110, and 137. The last records the visit of the Father and the Son. "The heavens were opened upon us, and I beheld the celestial kingdom of God" and saw "the blazing throne of God, whereon was seated the Father and the Son" (D&C 137:1, 3). The temple is now owned and operated by Community of Christ (see p. 192).

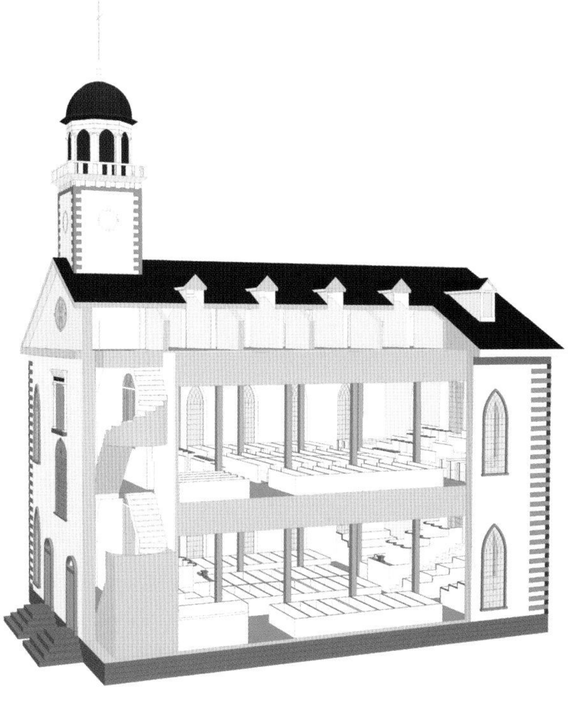

The Settlement of Zion

1831–1833

Oliver Cowdery and a vanguard of Mormon missionaries sent to the Lamanites (D&C 28:8–9; 30:5; 32:1–2) arrived in Jackson County, Missouri, on January 13, 1831. Lacking a government permit to continue teaching the American Indians west of the state, the missionaries returned to an unfriendly Jackson County (population 2,800). Cowdery said they found the county filled with "Universalists, Atheists, Deists, Presbyterians, Methodists, Baptists," and others who were scornful of them. In July, Joseph Smith arrived from Kirtland, Ohio, and proclaimed Jackson County "the land of promise, and the place for the city of Zion," with Independence as "the center place" (D&C 57:2–3). Independence, the county seat, contained a "courthouse built of brick, two or three merchant stores, and fifteen or twenty dwelling houses, built mostly of logs hewed on both sides." William W. Phelps, a New York newspaper editor with the Prophet, wrote that the old citizens had come principally from "Tennessee, Kentucky, Virginia, and the Carolinas" and possessed "customs, manners, modes of living, and a climate entirely different from the Northerner."

Upon dedicating Jackson County as the location of Zion in Kaw Township on August 2, and the next day locating the temple site "not far from the the courthouse" (D&C 57:3), Joseph Smith directed Bishop Edward Partridge to buy and distribute land to the Saints under an economic system of consecration and stewardship (D&C 42:30–33). After the Prophet returned to Ohio, Bishop Partridge finished purchasing 2,136 acres of land and established five settlements in the county. At Independence, Phelps and Cowdery established the *Evening and the Morning Star*, a Church newspaper, and printed the Prophet's revelations about Zion, and A. Sidney Gilbert operated a Church store.

By summer 1833, a robust Mormon immigration from the Northeast had settled in the county. Their growing numbers angered the citizens over economic, cultural, religious, and political differences, particularly over fear of losing political control. "It requires no gift of prophecy," stated a July 20 citizen's proclamation against the Mormons, "to tell that the day is not far distant when the civil government of the county will be in their hands; when the sheriff, the justices, and the county judges will be Mormons." At the courthouse square that day, a gathering of 500 citizens protested against the Mormons, their poverty, their unrestrained zeal for Zion, and against what they said was the "grossest superstition" in their belief in revelation and in spiritual gifts. The citizens assaulted the bishop, tore down the printing house, and attacked the Church store. A climax erupted that fall after the Mormons appealed to the courts for redress. On October 31, a mob destroyed the Whitmer settlement and damaged others. During the next two weeks, the most violent citizens whipped men, terrorized women and children, vandalized property, and drove 1,200 Mormons from the county.

continued on page 34

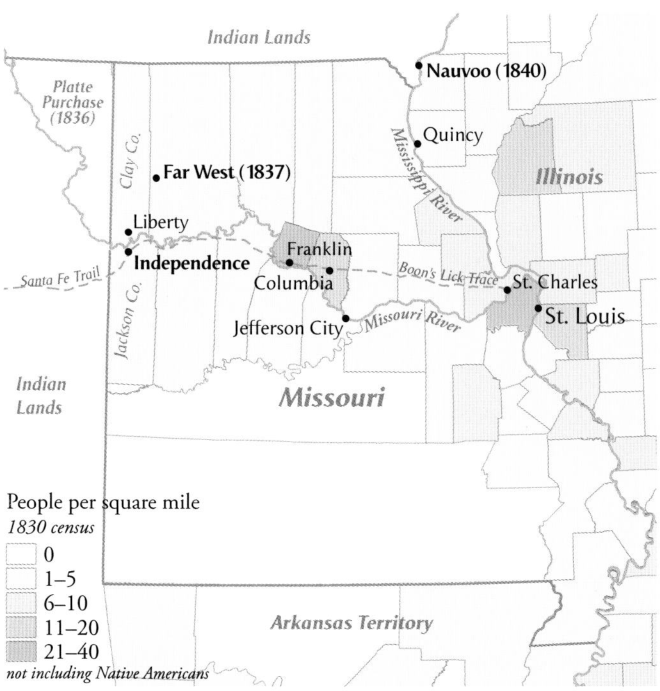

Missouri in 1830

When the Mormons arrived in western Missouri in 1831, it was the farthest American frontier, sparsely settled with towns scattered along the Mississippi and Missouri rivers. In 1821, the year Missouri became a state, Mexico was opened for American trade, and the Santa Fe Trail was born at Franklin, passing west through the Osage Indian lands of current Jackson County. Jackson County was organized in 1826, named for General (and future president) Andrew Jackson. It was originally 80 miles long, but the southern portion was organized into Van Buren County in 1833, with some functions still dependent on Jackson County until 1835. The 1830 Indian Removal Act authorized President Andrew Jackson to establish Indian lands west of the state, where he quickly moved the Osages and others, opening Jackson and Clay Counties to immigrants, predominantly from the South.

Major Events in Missouri

- **2 Aug 1831** Joseph Smith dedicates Zion
- **20 Jul 1833** Mob attacks Mormon leaders in Independence, destroying the press
- **11 Sep 1833** Saints in 5 settlements in Jackson County organized into 10 branches
- **Nov 1833** Mobs drive 1,200 Mormons from Jackson County
- **Nov–Dec 1833** Impoverished Mormon refugees camped along Missouri River bottoms
- **19 Jun 1834** Joseph Smith and Zion's Camp arrive in Clay County
- **Jun 1834** Thirteen members of Zion's Camp and two local Mormons die of cholera
- **7 Jul 1834** Joseph Smith organizes Clay County Stake
- **Jun 1836** Clay County citizens request that Mormons leave the county
- **Jul 1836** Stake leaders explore upper Ray County to find a new settlement area
- **29 Dec 1836** The Missouri Legislature creates Caldwell and Daviess Counties

1831 1832 1833 1834 1835 1836

Independence, Missouri, 1833

A view of Independence at the height of Mormon settlement, looking toward the southwest. The white outline shows the original plat of the town of Independence, while yellow outlines show LDS purchases in town and to the west. Independence was established in 1827, two years after the Osage Tribe ceded Missouri's western strip to the state. The old Osage Trace became the route to Santa Fe, passing west through the upper edge of the county and through Independence, where it branched. The western link, called the Westport Road, extended to the Native American lands to the west and also gave the Mormons access to their settlements in Kaw Township. Independence, which Washington Irving observed to be a "little straggling frontier village" in 1832, was primarily peopled by hearty frontier men from the southern states. These settlers cleared their timbered lots, planted corn fields, built rustic houses, and opened businesses. The two nearby river landings (Independence Landing two miles north and Blue Mills Landing six miles northeast) brought to the village adventurers, Indian traders, trappers, explorers, and those who had reason to break loose from the constraints of civilization.

1. **Temple Lot:** Joseph Smith ceremonially laid the cornerstone of the temple in Zion, August 3, 1831. The lot was part of a larger LDS purchase that had enough residents for its own branch by 1833.
2. **Partridge home and Church school:** Bishop Edward Partridge lived on the corner of the temple purchase. The Church built a two-story log schoolhouse next to his home.
3. **Jackson County stewardships:** Most Saints lived on Church-owned land west of Independence, in the Blue River valley and beyond at the edge of the prairie.
4. **First Boggs home and Whitmer tailor shop:** In June 1832, Peter Whitmer Jr. rented a room from Lilburn W. Boggs, the future governor, and operated a tailor shop. Mary Elizabeth Rollins, teenage niece of A. Sidney Gilbert, worked for Whitmer and stitched the facing of Lt. Gov. Boggs's inaugural suit.
5. **First bishop's storehouse:** In February 1832, A. Sidney Gilbert, the bishop's agent, purchased the vacated Jackson County log courthouse (1828–1831) for a residence and to use temporarily as the bishop's storehouse. During the twentieth century it was moved and renovated; Judge (and future U.S. president) Harry S Truman briefly held county court there, and it is now the oldest standing courthouse west of the Mississippi and the oldest building in Missouri once owned by Mormons.
6. **Brick courthouse:** The second courthouse, a two-story brick structure, was completed in 1831. This courthouse is referred to in D&C 57:3 to identify the location of the temple lot. On July 20, 1833, a citizens' mob demonstrated against the Mormons by tarring and feathering Bishop Edward Partridge and Charles Allen on the north part of the square. Later that day on the square, a citizens' committee and a Mormon committee signed an agreement for the Mormons to leave the county partly by the end of 1833 and completely by April 1834. On February 24, 1834, Mormon witnesses under guard by the state militia appeared before court here to prefer charges against members of the mob for the damage against the Saints in July 1833, but the mob spirit present in the town forced an end to the hearings.
7. **W. W. Phelps press:** William W. Phelps printed the *Evening and the Morning Star* in this two-story brick building and was printing the Book of Commandments on July 20, 1833, when a mob destroyed the building and scattered the type in the street.
8. **Gilbert and Whitney store:** This building functioned both as a business and as the bishop's storehouse. On November 1, 1833, it was broken into by the citizens and the goods were scattered into the street.
9. **Jackson County jail:** On November 1, 1833, several Mormon leaders were confined in the basement dungeon of this log jail, allegedly to protect them from the mob. In 1842, Orrin Porter Rockwell spent eight months in a second jail on this site awaiting trial (see site #12).
10. **Noland house:** After Joseph Smith and others were arrested at Far West on October 31, 1838, they were brought to Independence and temporarily held at this frontier log hotel. They were treated kindly and allowed to walk the streets freely without guard.
11. **Jones H. Flournoy house:** Flournoy resided here when he sold 63 acres of his farm to the west to Bishop Edward Partridge for the temple lot. In November 1838 the house was owned by General Moses Wilson of the state militia, who entertained Joseph Smith and other prisoners here. The house would later be moved and renovated as a museum by the RLDS Church (now Community of Christ, see p. 136).
12. **Second Boggs home:** After his term as governor, Lilburn W. Boggs moved to this house across from the public spring where emigrating wagons often camped. Here on May 6, 1842, an unknown gunman tried to assassinate Boggs at his home; Orrin Porter Rockwell was accused of the attempt (supposedly at Joseph Smith's behest) but was acquitted.

The Settlement of Zion

continued

Most of the Mormon refugees crossed the Missouri River into Clay County. Without sufficient food or clothing, the exiles spent the next several weeks barely surviving on the Missouri River bottoms. "The banks of the Missouri was now being lined with campfires of the little suffering multitude," wrote an observer. In December, William W. Phelps wrote to Joseph Smith, "Our clothes are worn out and we want the necessities of life" and asked for instructions. Meanwhile, friendly citizens hired the refugees to work the mills, slaughter hogs, make brick, cut cordwood, and perform other menial tasks. Lyman Wight said that his people eked out a subsistence "like men of servitude." A friendly landowner wrote, "The Mormons, in the main, were industrious, good workers, and gave general satisfaction to their employers, and could live on less than any people I ever knew."

By spring 1834, Joseph Smith answered the call to help. At Kirtland, Ohio, he organized Zion's Camp, a paramilitary relief party, to aid the state militia in escorting the exiles back to their lands in Jackson County (see p. 38). But once in Clay County and fearing an outbreak of civil war, Joseph instead chose to negotiate a settlement, which would never fully materialize. Meanwhile, he organized the exiled Saints into a stake at the Wight settlement, with David Whitmer, William W. Phelps, and John Whitmer as the presidency. Church members continued to gather to Missouri, believing that they would soon cross the Missouri River to redeem Zion (D&C 105:13, 31). Mormons individually purchased land until they owned 3,640 acres scattered across the southern part of Clay County. For two years, they appealed to the courts and to the government for redress in Jackson County but received no help (D&C 101:86–89).

The gathering into Clay County forced the hand of their formerly friendly neighbors by 1836. In June, local leaders in heated meetings at Liberty requested that the Mormons leave the county to prevent "the horrors and desolations of a civil war." Mobs soon harassed the Saints in the eastern county settlements and turned back caravans of emigrants. Consequently, in a "covenant of peace," the Church leaders in Clay County announced that they would find a new home. Phelps and Partridge bought land twenty-five miles northeast of Liberty, and in December, the Missouri legislature established Caldwell County around those lands as a place designated for Mormon settlement. There the Mormon leaders would try again to establish a place for their people.

Max H Parkin

Jackson and Clay Counties, 1831–1833

While most of the population of Jackson and Clay counties lived on scattered homesteads in the woodland fringe, Latter-day Saints established dense communities (five in Jackson County 1831–33, several more in Clay County 1834–36).

1. **Lamanite Mission:** On January 31, 1831, Oliver Cowdery and Parley P. Pratt preached to the Delaware Indians before they were forced to leave the Indian Lands.
2. **Whitmer Settlement:** On August 2, 1831, Joseph Smith had Sidney Rigdon dedicate the land for Zion at this site, which became the chief Mormon settlement in Kaw Township and the focus of fighting in 1833.
3. **Fishing River Camp:** Zion's Camp arrived in Clay County on June 19, 1834, camping between two branches of the Fishing River. That night a severe storm struck, flooding the rivers and the road west, preventing attacks by gathering mobs.
4. **Cooper's Farm:** On June 21, local government and militia officers met with Joseph Smith and other leaders of Zion's Camp at their new campsite and mutually signed an accord to resolve their difficulty through negotiation. This agreement replaced the Mormon plan to petition Missouri's governor Daniel Dunklin to use state militia to escort them at that time back to their homes in Jackson County. On June 22, Joseph Smith received a revelation (D&C 105) to disband Zion's Camp.
5. **Rush Creek Camp:** On June 24, Zion's Camp established its third camp in Clay County. Immediately, cholera attacked the camp, killing thirteen members and two local Latter-day Saints living nearby, including the Lord's storekeeper, Algernon Sidney Gilbert.
6. **Wight Settlement at Michael Arthur farm:** On July 3, Colonel Lyman Wight began to discharge members of Zion's Camp under Joseph Smith's direction. On July 7 at Wight's house, Joseph Smith organized a stake for the Saints in their Missouri exile, with David Whitmer as president, W. W. Phelps and John Whitmer as assistants, and a high council of twelve men.
7. **Liberty Jail and Courthouse:** After Joseph Smith and several others were arrested at Far West in October 1838 and were held in Independence for a few days, they had a preliminary hearing at the Fifth Judicial District in Richmond before Judge Austin A. King. After the court found "probable cause" to hold Joseph Smith and others for treason, etc., they were taken to the Liberty Jail for confinement because Caldwell County, the site of the alleged crimes, had no jail. They were incarcerated here for several months until April 1839. In January, Joseph Smith and Sidney Rigdon were taken to a hearing at the Clay County courthouse a few doors away. They were defended by their attorney Alexander Doniphan, who had recently saved Joseph Smith's life at Far West, Caldwell County, and his legal assistant Peter Burnett, later first governor of California.

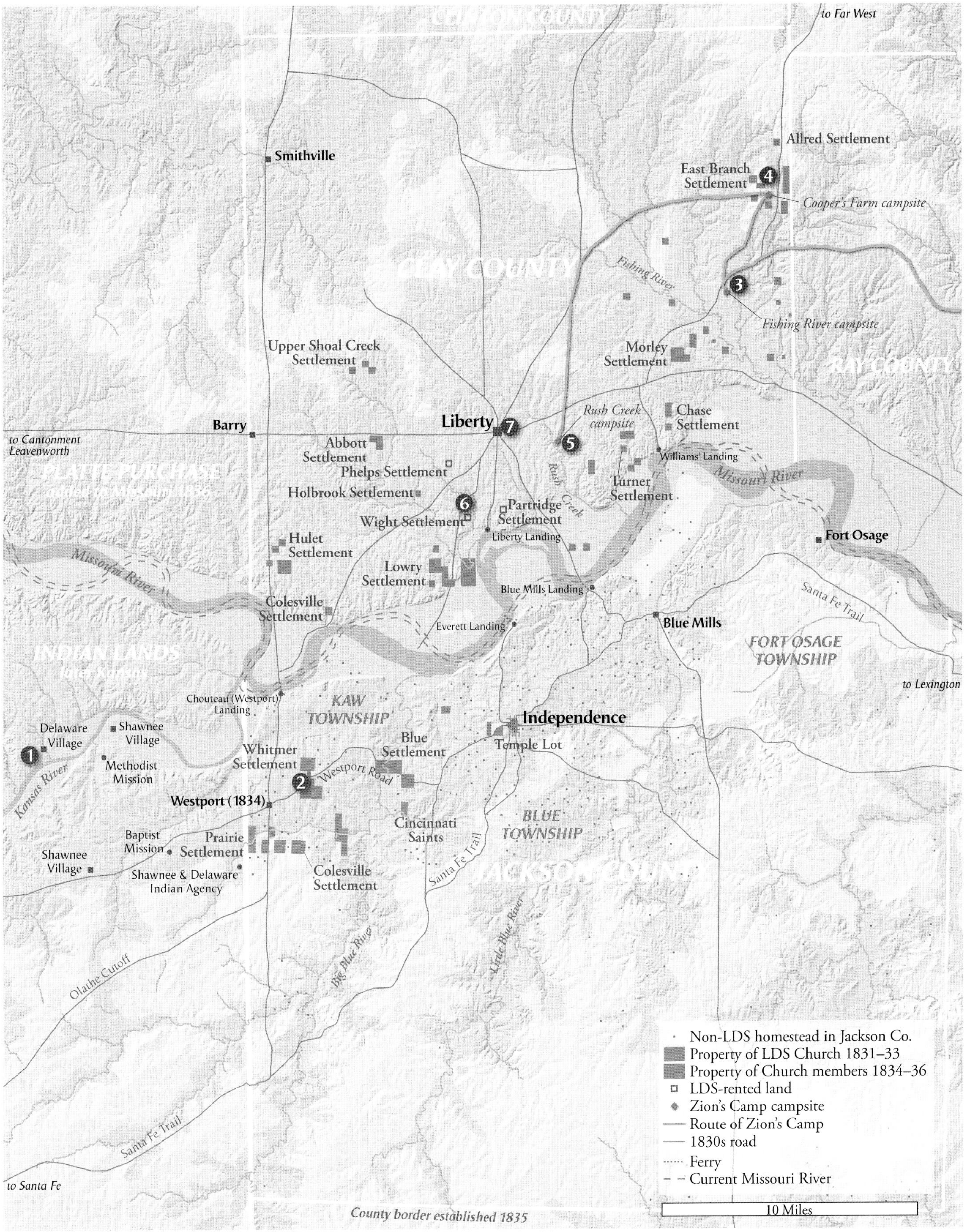

to Far West
CLINTON COUNTY
Smithville
Allred Settlement
East Branch Settlement
Cooper's Farm campsite
CLAY COUNTY
Fishing River
Fishing River campsite
Upper Shoal Creek Settlement
Morley Settlement
RAY COUNTY
Liberty
Barry
to Cantonment Leavenworth
Rush Creek campsite
Chase Settlement
Abbott Settlement
Phelps Settlement
Williams' Landing
PLATTE PURCHASE
Holbrook Settlement
Rush Creek
Missouri River
Turner Settlement
Partridge Settlement
Wight Settlement
Liberty Landing
Fort Osage
Hulet Settlement
Lowry Settlement
Blue Mills Landing
Santa Fe Trail
Colesville Settlement
Everett Landing
Blue Mills
FORT OSAGE TOWNSHIP
INDIAN LANDS
to Lexington
Chouteau (Westport) Landing
KAW TOWNSHIP
Independence
Delaware Village
Shawnee Village
Temple Lot
Blue Settlement
Whitmer Settlement
Methodist Mission
Kansas River
Westport Road
Westport (1834)
BLUE TOWNSHIP
Cincinnati Saints
Baptist Mission
Prairie Settlement
Shawnee Village
Shawnee & Delaware Indian Agency
Colesville Settlement
JACKSON COUNTY
Little Blue River
Big Blue River
Olathe Cutoff
Santa Fe Trail
to Santa Fe
County border established 1835
Non-LDS homestead in Jackson Co.
Property of LDS Church 1831–33
Property of Church members 1834–36
LDS-rented land
Zion's Camp campsite
Route of Zion's Camp
1830s road
Ferry
Current Missouri River
10 Miles

The Church in the Kirtland-Missouri Era

1831–1838

DURING THE 1830S, the Church of Christ was both expanding and concentrating. As missionaries traveled across the United States, Canada, and eventually England, they converted thousands and created at least 300 new branches. However, they also preached the Gathering, encouraging their new proselytes to pack up and join the Saints in Kirtland or Missouri. Thus, branches would often be organized with a few members, grow to several dozen, then disappear within a year or two. This trend would continue and further expand during the Nauvoo Era (see p. 60).

Having two centers of gathering some 800 miles apart presented many challenges to Joseph and other leaders, but they were able to build a strong presence in both areas. However, this presence came much to the chagrin of antagonistic neighbors, and by the end of 1838, most faithful Latter-day Saints had been forced out of both Missouri and Ohio.

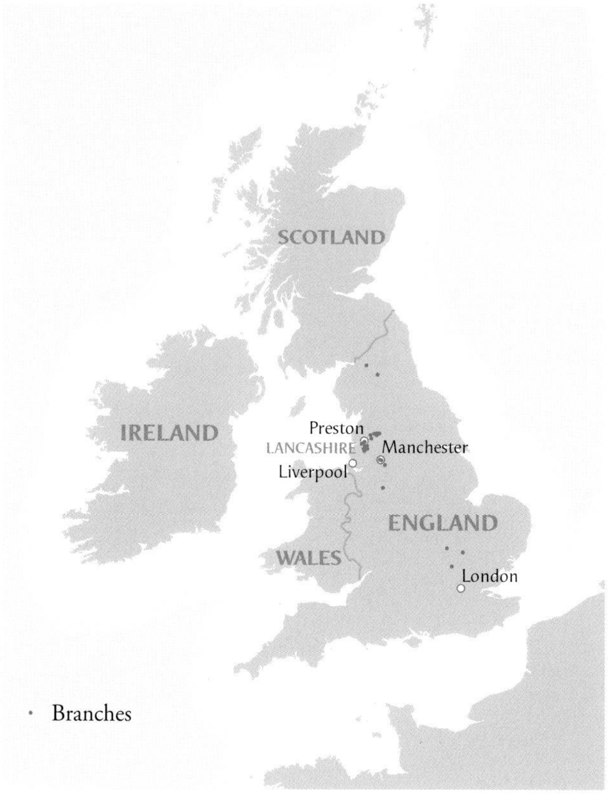

The first mission to Britain (1837) was centered in Lancashire, where missionaries found many converts in both the cities and the country. Of the 27 known branches organized by 1839 and shown here, 19 were within 20 miles of Preston.

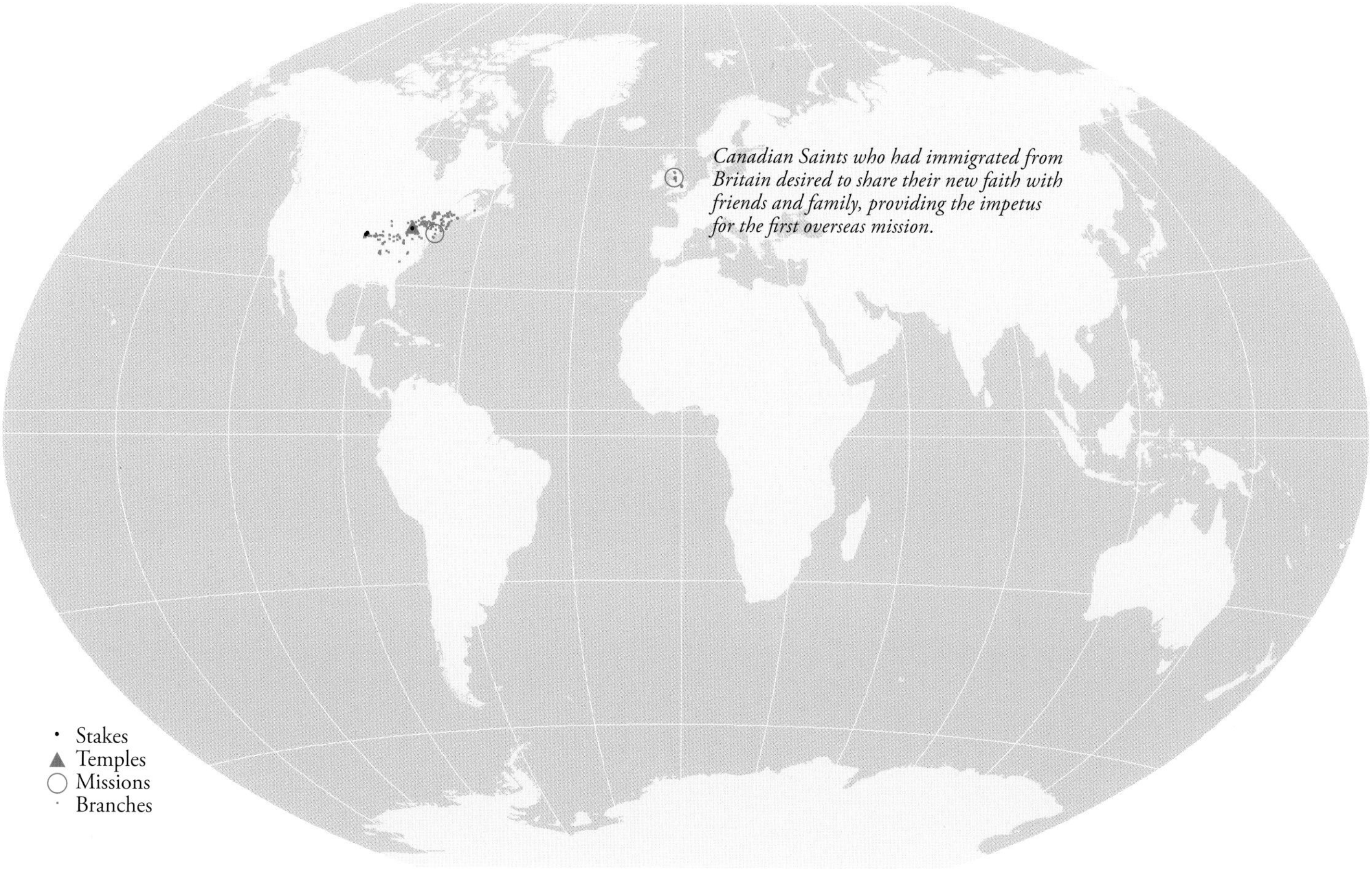

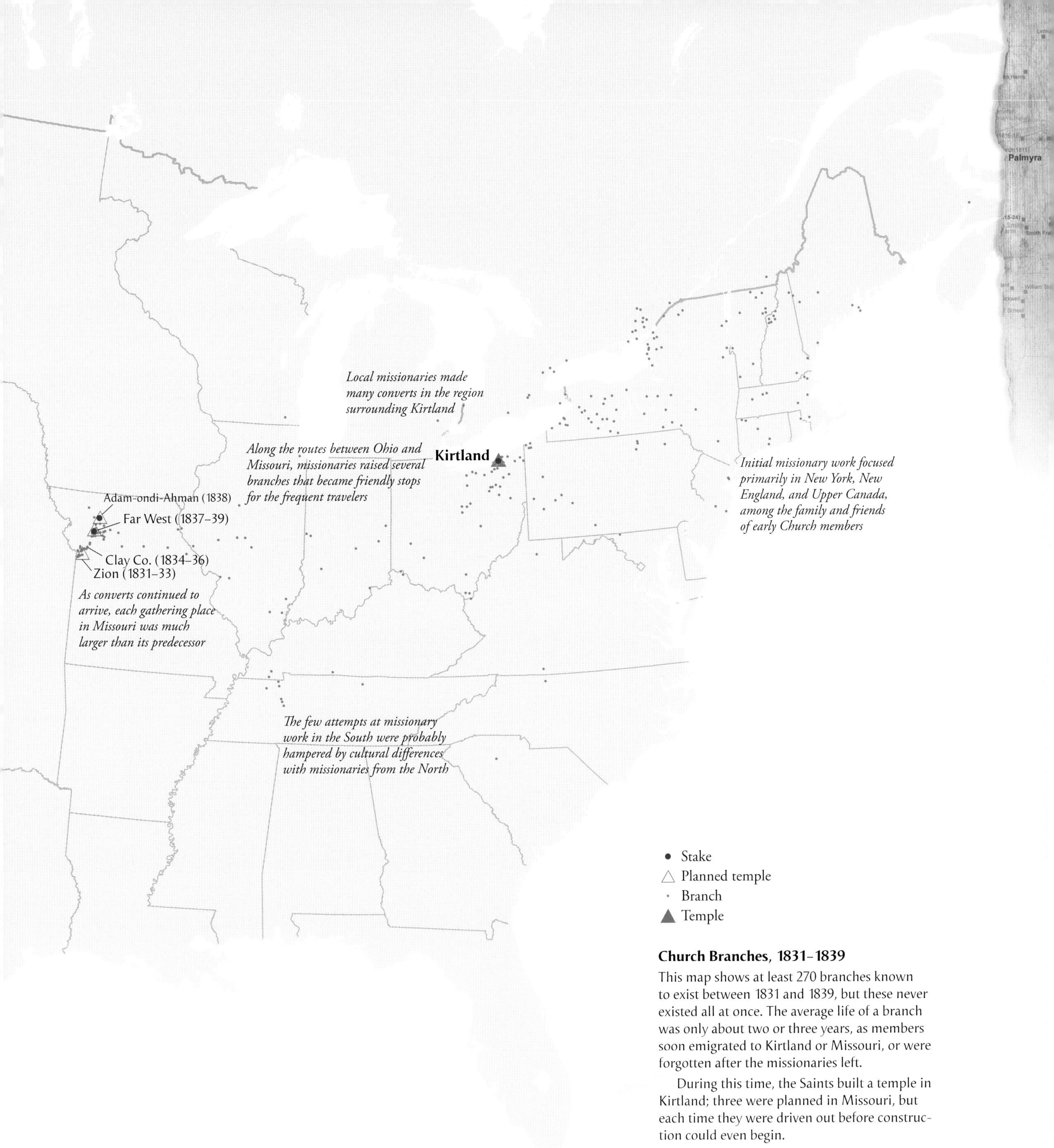

Local missionaries made many converts in the region surrounding Kirtland
Kirtland
Along the routes between Ohio and Missouri, missionaries raised several branches that became friendly stops for the frequent travelers
Adam-ondi-Ahman (1838)
Far West (1837–39)
Clay Co. (1834–36)
Zion (1831–33)
As converts continued to arrive, each gathering place in Missouri was much larger than its predecessor
Initial missionary work focused primarily in New York, New England, and Upper Canada, among the family and friends of early Church members
The few attempts at missionary work in the South were probably hampered by cultural differences with missionaries from the North
Palmyra
Stake
Planned temple
Branch
Temple

Church Branches, 1831–1839

This map shows at least 270 branches known to exist between 1831 and 1839, but these never existed all at once. The average life of a branch was only about two or three years, as members soon emigrated to Kirtland or Missouri, or were forgotten after the missionaries left.

During this time, the Saints built a temple in Kirtland; three were planned in Missouri, but each time they were driven out before construction could even begin.

Note: This map cannot show names and details about each branch, but detailed information can be found on the companion website, mappingmormonism.byu.edu.

Major Events in the Kirtland–Missouri Era

1831 New York Mormons settle in Kirtland and Jackson County

1833 Mormons are expelled from Jackson County, Missouri

Saints begin to settle in the Far West area of Missouri **1836**

British Mission opens **1837**

1838 Kirtland members loyal to Joseph Smith move to Far West

Mormons expelled from Missouri **1839**

1831 | 1832 | 1833 | 1834 | 1835 | 1836 | 1837 | 1838 | 1839

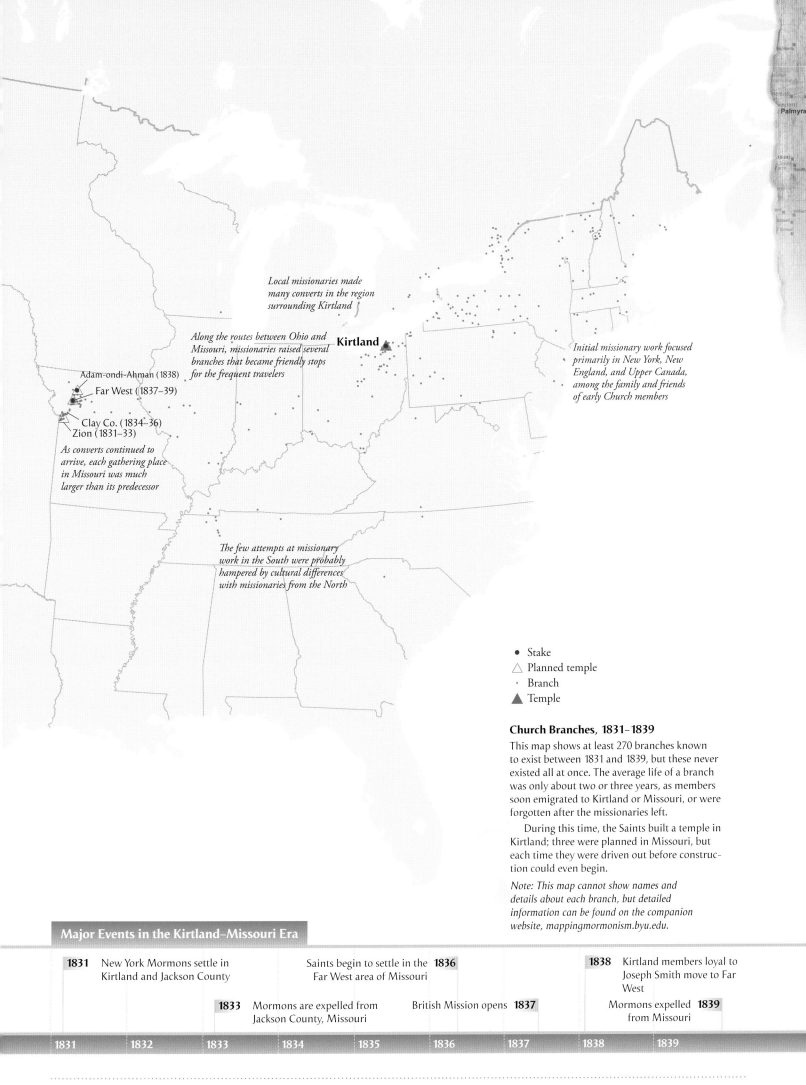

Travel Between Ohio and Missouri

1831–1838

The establishment of two major Mormon centers some 800 miles apart necessitated frequent travel between Ohio and Missouri, for which the Saints used various modes of transportation. Perhaps the most frequent and common mode of travel, especially among those who intended to permanently settle in Missouri, was by wagon. Although wagon travel was often slow and tedious, generally taking several weeks or months to complete the journey, it provided an effective means to transport the furnishings and equipment of an entire household. Travelers could often find lodging along the way in the homes of members who had been converted by earlier missionaries.

A faster but more expensive means of transportation was by commercial stage or private carriage. Church leaders would often employ this type of travel when engaged on a short-term mission, or to attend a special meeting or conference and then return home. Stage or carriage travel was also more comfortable, and the traveler enjoyed stops for food and overnight lodging at stage stations and taverns.

Mormons making the journey between Ohio and Missouri could travel a portion of the way along the National Road (sometimes called the Cumberland Road), which in the 1830s ran from Maryland through southwestern Pennsylvania, central Ohio, and Indiana, and terminated in Vandalia, Illinois (the original state capital). However, by 1834, Mormons traveling from Ohio generally left the National Road in Indiana, striking out on a direct westerly course toward northern Missouri.

The distance could also be negotiated by means of waterways, including canals and rivers. By 1832, it was possible to travel the entire way from northeastern Ohio to western Missouri by water via the Ohio and Erie Canal (see p. 26), and the Ohio, Mississippi, and Missouri rivers. Travel aboard canal boats and steam paddle wheelers afforded the most wealthy travelers the luxury of almost carefree travel, complete with meals and onboard room accommodations.

Weather often played havoc on the overland Mormon migrant. Seasonal rain, snow, humidity, and extreme temperatures caused not only discomfort but also delays and even cancellations in travel plans. Accidents and sickness could also make the journey more difficult.

Throughout the 1830s, several thousand Latter-day Saints made their way to and from Ohio and Missouri, literally making the route a two-way Mormon thoroughfare. However, in spite of the time and distance separating the Saints living in each region, the Church succeeded in maintaining communication and interaction between the two Mormon centers.

Alexander L. Baugh

Trips to Missouri, 1830–1838

Only a few examples of the dozens of trips taken by Church members between Ohio and Missouri are shown here, demonstrating the various means of travel and transportation employed. The preferred and most comfortable mode of travel was by riverboat, but it was costly. Most of the Saints, however, regardless of whether they were traveling in groups, as a family, or individually, journeyed by wagon, carriage, or on foot, although some employed multiple means. For example, the missionaries to the Lamanites, who journeyed to western Missouri in 1830–31, traveled about half the route by foot and half by steamer (see p. 24). When Joseph Smith made his first trip from Ohio to Missouri and back during the summer of 1831, he went by wagon, canal boat, stage, steamer, and on foot. The Colesville Branch, consisting of about seventy Mormons, made their way to Missouri that same summer almost entirely by boat. In most instances, travel time between Ohio and Missouri took three to four weeks, although for those who primarily walked (e.g., Hyrum Smith and John Murdock's 1831 mission) or who were transporting entire households by wagon (e.g., Kirtland Camp), the trip could take six to eight weeks or even longer.

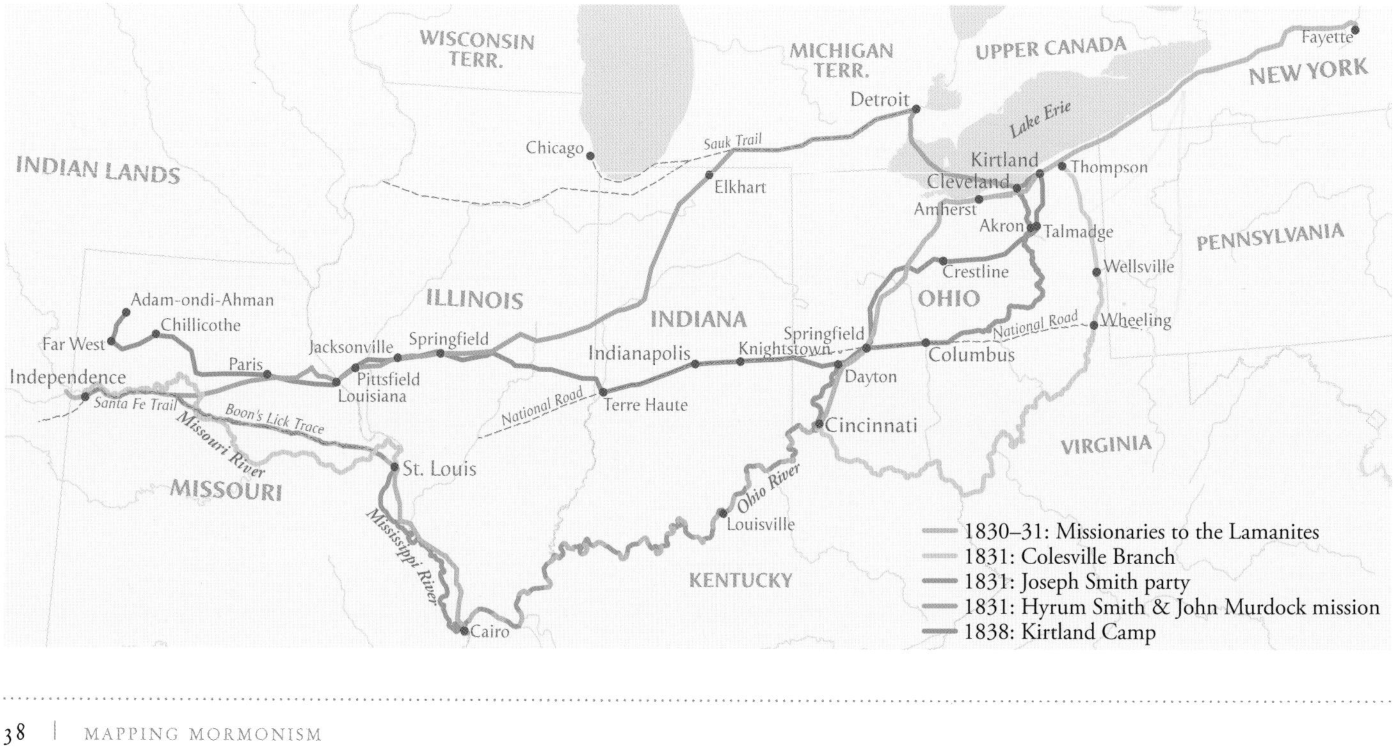

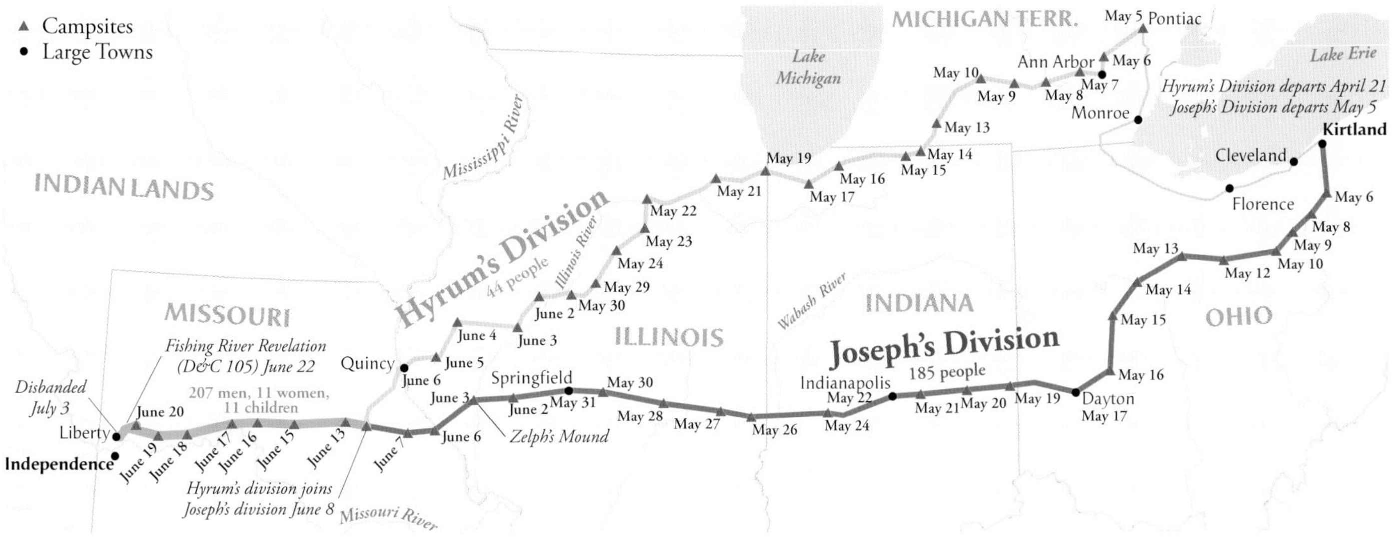

Zion's Camp, 1834

Zion's Camp was a Mormon military expedition company that marched to Missouri in 1834, intending to help the Saints reclaim the lands in Jackson County from which they had been expelled in November 1833 (see page 34).

On May 1, 1834, a group of 20 men left Kirtland. Five days later, the main company of 85 men under the leadership of Joseph Smith departed. The same day, Hyrum Smith and Lyman Wight led a smaller group of seventeen persons from Pontiac, Michigan, intending to join with the main body en route. As the company proceeded west, additional men and volunteers fell in with the main company, increasing their ranks and numbers. On June 8, following a month of travel through Ohio, Indiana, and Illinois, picking up recruits along the way, the two groups met at the Salt River Branch in Monroe County, Missouri. Now Zion's Camp consisted of a force of just over 200 men. In the meantime, the Mormons learned that Missouri Governor Daniel Dunklin would not lend state military assistance as promised and advised the Saints to seek redress through the courts. Dunklin's position meant that the main objective of Zion's Camp—to help the Saints repossess their Jackson County property—could not be achieved.

In late June, after arriving in Clay County where the main body of Missouri Saints had located, Joseph Smith received revelatory instructions informing the members of Zion's Camp that they should disband and return to their homes in the East. On July 3, the men were officially discharged. Members did not return to Ohio in one large body but made their way home in smaller groups. Before beginning the return trip, Joseph Smith spent a few days in Clay County instructing the leaders and organizing a stake in Missouri (see p. 34). He left around July 12, arriving back in Kirtland around August 1, after nearly a three-month absence.

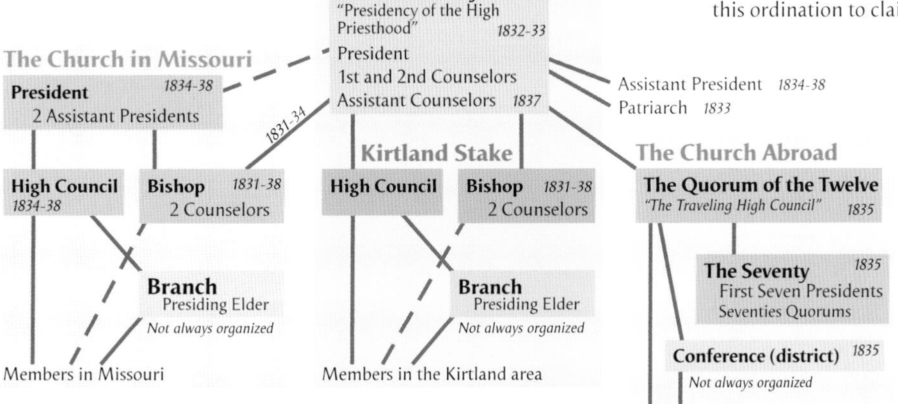

During this time, the branch president presided at meetings, while the bishop managed the Law of Consecration, church-owned lands, and other temporal affairs; they also acted as judges in disputes and disciplinary matters, until the High Council assumed that responsibility in 1834.
** February-October 1838, Kirtland Stake had a separate presidency after Joseph Smith left*
** June-November 1838, a second stake was formed in Adam-ondi-Ahman, Missouri*

Church Organization, 1832–1838

During the 1830s, ecclesiastical quorums, councils, and offices were established to administer the spiritual and temporal affairs of the Church. At the organization of the Church in 1830, leadership was simple: Joseph Smith and Oliver Cowdery presided over the Church as first and second elders. Over the next several years, the numerical and geographical growth of the Church necessitated a more complex leadership structure.

Each congregation, called a branch, was led by a presiding elder (also known as a branch president). The priesthood (elders, priests, teachers, and deacons) had responsibility for carrying out the work of the Church in each branch. Branches varied in size but generally consisted of only a few families holding worship services in members' homes.

The first addition was the bishop (February 1831), established to oversee the temporal aspects of the Church, including the law of consecration. However, a bishop was not the leader of a congregation until the 1850s.

In March 1832, the "presidency of the high priesthood" (initially, the presidency of the quorum of high priests) was organized with a president (Smith) and two counselors and functioned until the official organization of the First Presidency in March 1833. Ten months later, in December 1833, Joseph Smith established the office of patriarch, ordaining his father, Joseph Smith Sr.

As membership increased, the 800-mile separation between gathering places in Ohio and Missouri made close supervision impossible, and more local authority was needed. On February 17, 1834, the Kirtland Stake of Zion was created with a three-man presidency (Joseph and his counselors) and a twelve-man high council. On July 3, Joseph installed a similar organization in Clay County, Missouri, with David Whitmer as "President of the Church in Missouri." This division occasionally caused some confusion, as it was not clear whether the Missouri presidency was completely subordinate to the Kirtland presidency (i.e., Joseph Smith), and Whitmer would later use this ordination to claim succession to Church leadership.

On December 5, 1834, Oliver Cowdery was ordained to the office of "assistant president," coinciding with his previous calling as second elder. This essentially elevated Cowdery to be second only to Joseph Smith (and the presumptive heir). Hyrum would later hold this position until he was killed.

On February 14, 1835, the Quorum of the Twelve Apostles was constituted. Initially, the Twelve's authority was that of a "traveling high council," with jurisdiction only outside the jurisdiction of stake high councils (see p. 46). Two weeks later, the First Quorum of Seventy was established as a quorum of dedicated missionaries under the direction of the Twelve.

The organization of the Church continued to evolve in response to geographic growth, in Nauvoo (see p. 58), Utah (p. 128), and globally (p. 164).

Early Missions

1831–1844

Missionary work has been a central concern of The Church of Jesus Christ of Latter-day Saints since its earliest days. The revelations given to Joseph Smith proclaimed the opening of a new and final dispensation of the gospel of Jesus Christ, which was to be taught in all the nations of the world. Initially, missionary work was informal, with new converts taking the message of the Restoration to their own families and neighbors. An early revelation declared, "If ye have a desire to serve God ye are called to the work" (D&C 4:3–4). Thus, many of the earliest elders like Frederick G. Williams, Levi Hancock, Jared Carter, Zera Pulsipher, and even Brigham Young served missions without a formal call to do so (see p. 24). Each was led by the Spirit, and the harvest of their work created the first congregations of baptized believers. The first missionary tract was the scriptures, and the preaching of the missionaries described therein, such as Paul, served as models for these first missionaries.

The mission to the Lamanites (American Indians) proceeded from a specific call (D&C 28:8; 30:5; 32:1–3, see p. 24). Although the four elders had little success in their intended goal of preaching to the American Indians, they were instrumental in preparing the future gathering places in Kirtland (see p. 28) and Independence (see p. 32). In February 1831, Joseph Smith moved the headquarters of the Church to the area of Kirtland, Ohio, and it remained the center of missionary work for a decade. Kirtland was an ideal location, being close to water routes and well-traveled roads going in all directions. Here more formal calls were given and more formal structures began to emerge. Missionaries were to travel two by two and were to travel in all the directions of the compass (D&C 42:6, 63). And here the converted members were reminded that they accepted a lifetime missionary assignment with their membership (D&C 88:81). While there still remained some of the informality of the earliest years, gradually Joseph Smith had to give the missionary work more formal structure due to the growth of the Church. Church conferences, missionary training (schools of the prophets and of the elders), the publishing of Church newspapers for internal communication and supervision, and membership record keeping emerged during the Kirtland era.

Occasionally, specific individuals were called by revelations to full-time preaching (e.g., D&C 44:1,3; 45:64; 52:7–10, 22–32; 60:1–9; 66:1, 5–8; 75:6–18; 75:30–36; 79:1; 80:1–3; 99:1; 112:1–4), with instructions and counsel regarding the qualities they should exhibit (e.g., D&C 4). The earliest missionaries were elders, but ordained seventies became the norm after they were first called in 1835: about 90 percent of Mormon missionaries in the nineteenth century were seventies. Church growth in the 1830s eventually required that better records be kept of baptized members, that missionaries carry official licenses for preaching (by the end of 1836, 285 licenses had been issued), and that more specific mission assignments be given. In time mission areas were designated as conferences and so reported in the Church periodicals. The calling of Apostles and Seventies in 1835

continued on page 42

Timeline

- **1830** First missionary work in Canada; by 1835, there are many branches
- **10 Aug 1832** First known regional conference of elders in Benson, Vermont: a gathering of missionaries, not local leaders
- Calling of Apostles and Seventies provides priesthood structure for scattered branches **1835**
- Opening of British Mission **1837**
- John P. Greene called as first regional president in the United States, over the "Eastern States" **6 May 1839**
- British soldier William Donaldson called to be a missionary while serving in India; uncertain whether he served **1839**
- British seventeen-year-old William James Barratt called to preach the gospel while living in Australia **Jul 1840**
- James Howard serves briefly in Hamburg, Prussia **Sep 1840**
- Orson Hyde travels to Britain, Germany, and the Holy Land without his companion John E. Page **1840–41**
- Joseph Smith calls Harrison Sagers to Jamaica, Joseph Ball to South America, but neither serve **1841**
- Addison Pratt and companions begin mission in French Polynesia **1843**
- Orson Hyde and George J. Adams called to Russia, but never serve **1843**
- Johann Greenig (a German converted in England) preaches briefly in Germany **1844**
- **6 Apr 1844** Hundreds of missionaries called, with regional presidents and scheduled regional conferences; all of Western Hemisphere proclaimed as Zion, lessening the importance of gathering
- Almost all missionaries return to Nauvoo as they learn of Joseph's death **Jul 1844**
- **16 Oct 1844** High priests called to preside over conferences and develop them into stakes rather than gather to Nauvoo
- Due to persecution in Hancock County and the need to finish the temple immediately, most missionaries and conference presidents recalled **1845**

1830 1831 1832 1833 1834 1835 1836 1837 1838 1839 1840 1841 1842 1843 1844

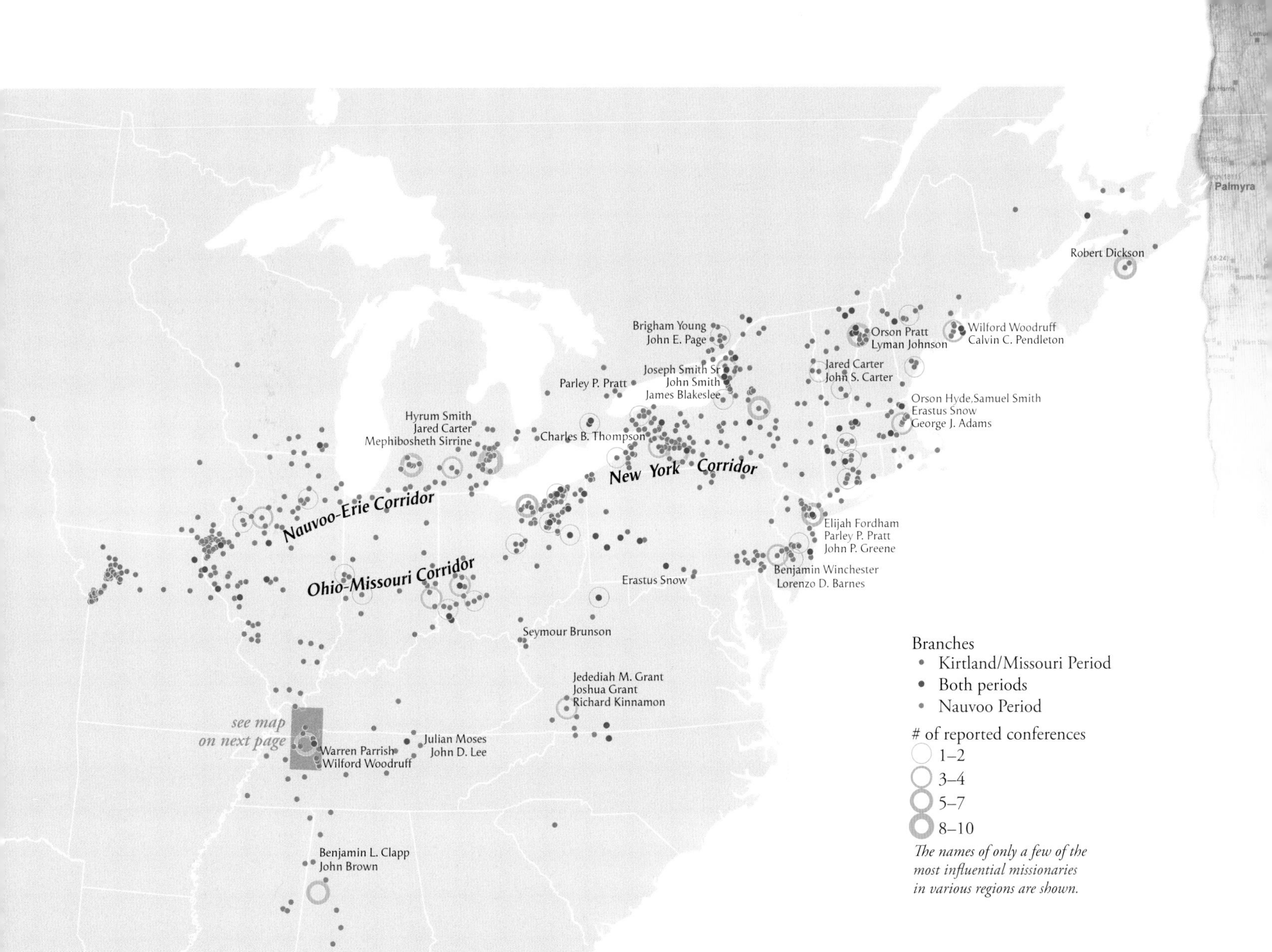

Note: This map cannot show names and details about each branch, but detailed information can be found on the companion website, mappingmormonism.byu.edu.

Missionary Work in the U.S. and Canada

During the lifetime of Joseph Smith, missionaries spread throughout the United States and British Canada. As they found converts, they organized them into branches—small congregations (often as small as 6–7 members) with a presiding priesthood holder, preferably an elder, but often an adult teacher or priest. The distribution of branches found during this period reflects several different types of missionary labor:

- "Friends and family" missionaries returned to their hometowns to share their new faith with those they knew, and established many of the early branches in New England and New York.
- "Wandering" missionaries preached as they traveled through the countryside, eventually forming corridors of rural branches along major travel routes, such as between Kirtland and Missouri.
- "Circuit Rider" missionaries traveled within a region, repeatedly preaching at friendly locations until a cluster of branches was created, over which they would voluntarily preside.
- Urban missionaries, taking their cue from experiences in England, used rented halls and advertising to establish a presence in major cities, leading to very large branches.

Fewer missionaries served in the South, probably due to cultural differences as well as distance, so branches there were limited to isolated pockets built up by dedicated long-term missionaries such as Jedediah M. Grant and Wilford Woodruff.

According to the 1830 organizational revelation of the Church (D&C 20), the priesthood holders in each region (missionaries and local members) were to hold quarterly conferences to strengthen each other and conduct business. These were not held regularly until 1834, but after they were promoted and implemented by the newly called Apostles in 1835 (see p. 46), regular conferences were reported in many regions, especially in western New York and Michigan. These conferences also served as regional administrative units (the same way the term was used in the Methodist Church), eventually being renamed districts as used in missions today.

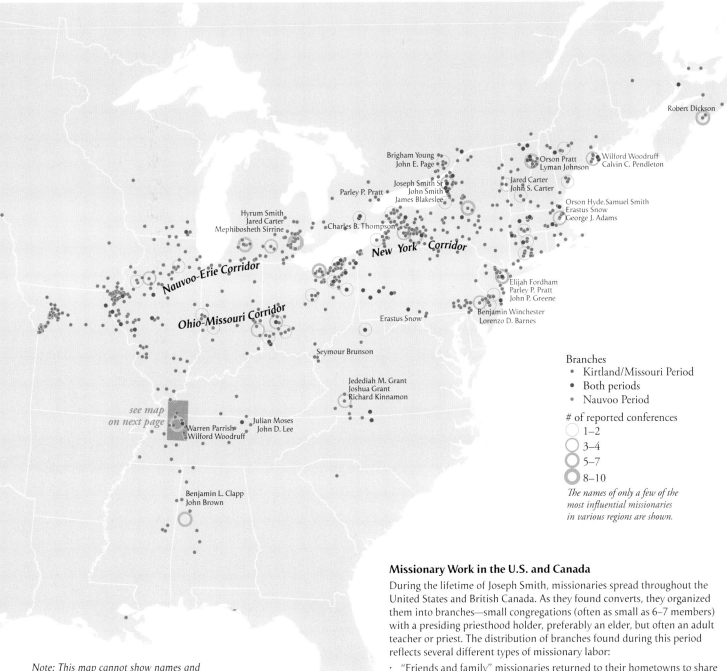

Early Missions

continued

brought more formal organization to the missionary work, even though their specific responsibilities were only gradually spelled out (D&C 107). By 1837, Mormon missionaries were moving into the larger towns and cities, and for the first time a missionary literature began to appear that could both reach the larger audience of the towns and could reply to the growing criticism of the Mormons and their message. In 1837 the first missionaries were called to travel to England to introduce the gospel there (see p. 46).

David J. Whittaker

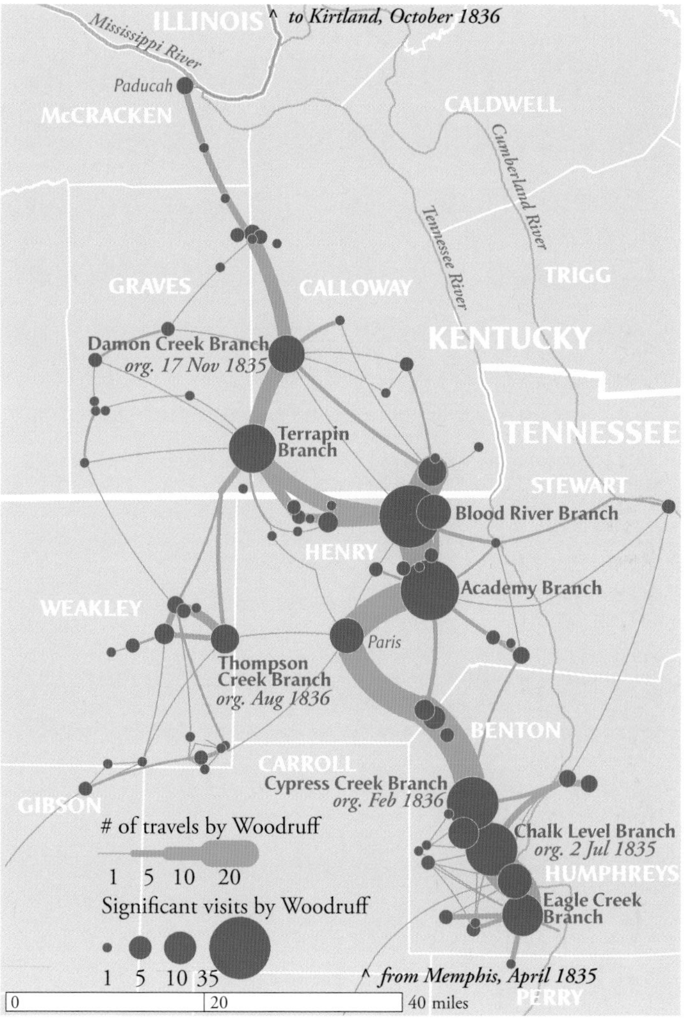

The first mission of Wilford Woodruff (1835–36) began with little success as he wandered through southern Missouri and Arkansas, but he soon became one of the greatest missionaries of the Church. The 28-year-old priest, a convert of little over a year, happened upon Warren Parrish in Tennessee in April 1835, where he and David Patten had baptized a few people and set up three branches before Patten had returned to Kirtland (soon to become an Apostle).

Under Parrish's tutelage, Willford (as he then spelled his name) became a dynamic preacher and adopted the "circuit rider" style of missionary work. Parrish ordained him an elder just before leaving in July, and for the next several months, Woodruff was the only holder of the Melchizedek Priesthood in the region. He traveled back and forth between the branches, preaching, baptizing, organizing, marrying, burying the dead, strengthening, and disciplining the more than 100 new members in "his" mission. Among these converts were protégés he trained to become leaders in the Church, such as Abraham O. Smoot (from Blood River Branch) and Benjamin Clapp (from Terrapin Branch). By the time he completed his 18-month sojourn in Tennessee and Kentucky, he had baptized at least 70 people, organized four branches, and traveled 5,000–7,000 miles within this small region.

Foreign Missions in Joseph Smith's Day

Missionaries first gained converts in Upper Canada (the future Ontario) in 1832, and their success among recent British immigrants led to the opening of Britain (see p. 46), which would be the most successful mission in the Church for decades. Following divine injunctions, Joseph Smith wanted missionaries to visit all the nations and islands of the sea to teach the gospel, and although most of the earliest foreign missions were short-lived, they reveal a serious commitment to take the gospel message to all nations. Some calls were opportunistic: English members who were traveling to Germany, India, and Australia for various reasons were called to preach the gospel while they were there. Other missionaries were called to places well beyond what was easy to accomplish; most were not fulfilled.

One of the most successful missions was to the Society Islands (Tahiti). In the spring of 1843, Addison Pratt, Benjamin F. Grouard, Noah Rogers, and Knowlton F. Hanks (who died at sea) were called by Joseph Smith to travel to the South Pacific to teach the gospel. Originally intending to go to the Sandwich Islands (Hawaii), they instead stayed in French Polynesia, serving the first foreign-language mission in the Church. They arrived on April 30, 1844, on Tubuai Island, where Pratt stayed. Rogers and Grouard sailed to Tahiti, arriving on May 14, 1844. Rogers returned to America in 1845, but Pratt and Grouard remained for several years longer, baptizing about 2,000 Polynesians. By the time Pratt had returned to the United States, he had circumnavigated the globe, probably the first Mormon to do so.

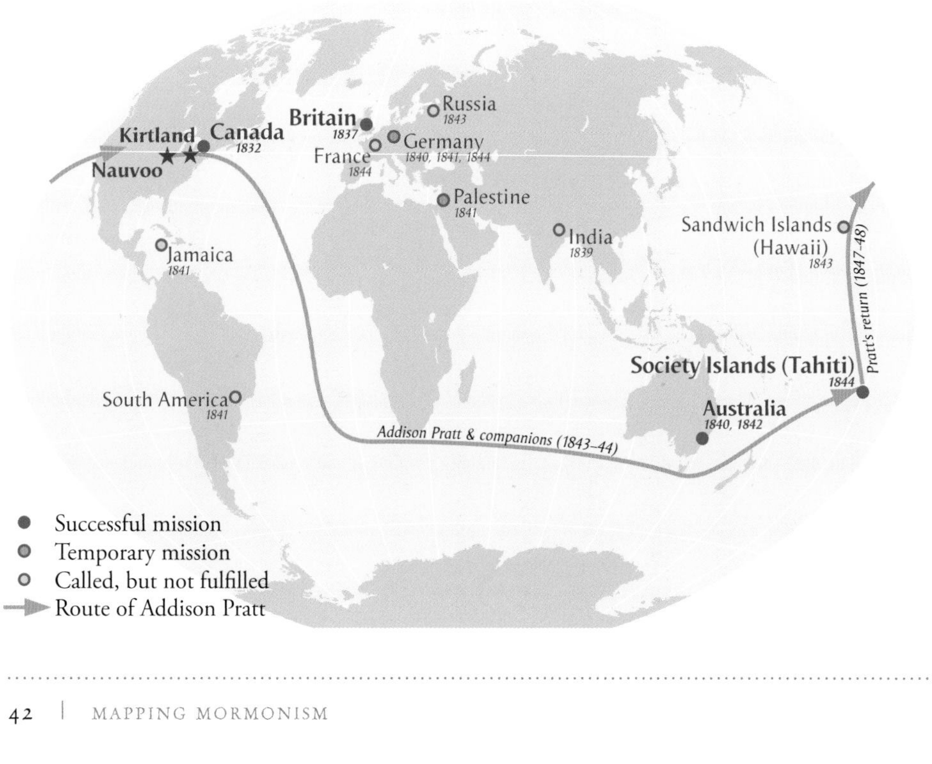

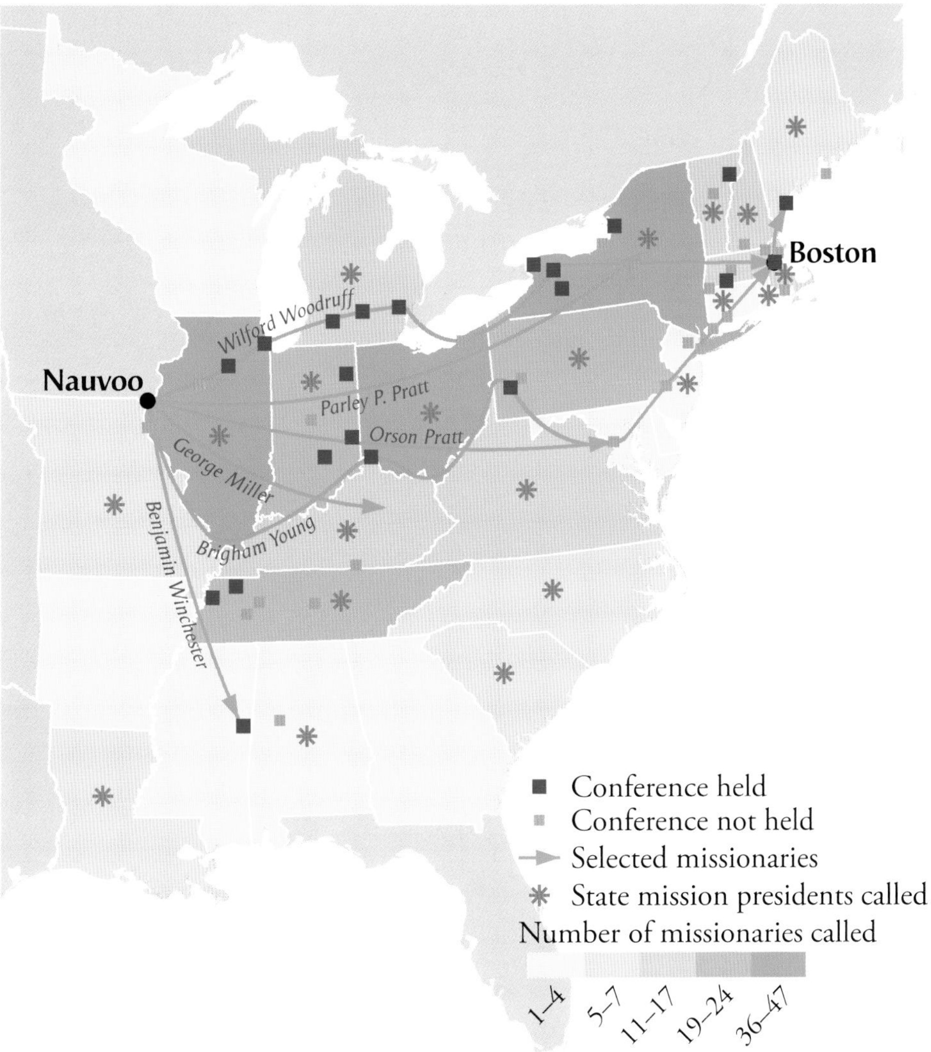

Joseph Smith's Presidential Campaign

After a trip to Washington, D.C., in 1840 and a letter-writing campaign in 1843, Joseph recognized that the U.S. government, including the likely 1844 presidential candidates, were unwilling to help the Mormons. He therefore declared his own candidacy for president of the United States. He published a pamphlet entitled *General Joseph Smith's Views of the Powers and Policy of the Government of the United States,* espousing generally moderate stances on the issues of the day. The campaign was launched at general conference in April 1844, combined with a greatly expanded and reorganized missionary effort (including the first regional mission presidents). Regional priesthood conferences doubled as campaign rallies. His campaign was cut short by his murder in June 1844, even as several of the Twelve were campaigning in Boston.

State Mission Presidents Called April 1844

Maine	Josiah Butterfield
New Hampshire	Willard Snow & Howard Egan
Massachusetts	Daniel Spencer*
Rhode Island	William Seabury
Connecticut	E. H. Davis
Vermont	Erastus Snow*
New York	Charles W. Wandell* & Marcellus Bates
New Jersey	Ezra T. Benson*
Pennsylvania	D. D. Yearsley & Edson Whipple
Virginia	Benjamin Winchester & S. C. Shelton
North Carolina	Alexander McRae & Aaron Razer
South Carolina	Alonzo LeBaron
Kentucky	John D. Lee
Tennessee	Abraham O. Smoot* & Alphonzo Young
Alabama	Benjamin L. Clapp*
Louisiana	J. B. Bosworth
Ohio	Lorenzo Snow*
Indiana	Amasa Lyman* & George P. Dykes*
Michigan	Charles C. Rich* & Harvey Green*
Illinois	E. H. Groves & Morris Phelps
Missouri	A. H. Perkins & John Lowry

** known to have served in the state by July 1844*

Eastern States Mission, 1844–45

At the April 1844 conference, Joseph Smith began to downplay the gathering in the United States, declaring the entire continent as Zion and envisioning a standardized mission structure of presidents and conferences that would develop strength in local branches, building them into future stakes. In October, Brigham Young reinforced this message, calling high priests to move their families to various conferences to preside over the stakes-in-embryo.

During 1844 and 1845, this was implemented better in some regions than others but was certainly best carried out in the Eastern States Mission. Under an Apostle who personally presided over the New York City area were a dozen or so conferences, each with a presiding high priest who called quarterly meetings to gather reports, train priesthood holders, and conduct priesthood business.

One reason for the relative success of this mission was a newspaper published in New York City, *The Prophet* (renamed *The Messenger* in 1845), which reported on mission activities, forwarded news from Nauvoo, and published inspiring messages. As with the *Millennial Star* in Britain, this periodical strengthened the cohesiveness of members (and the line of authority) in the eastern States.

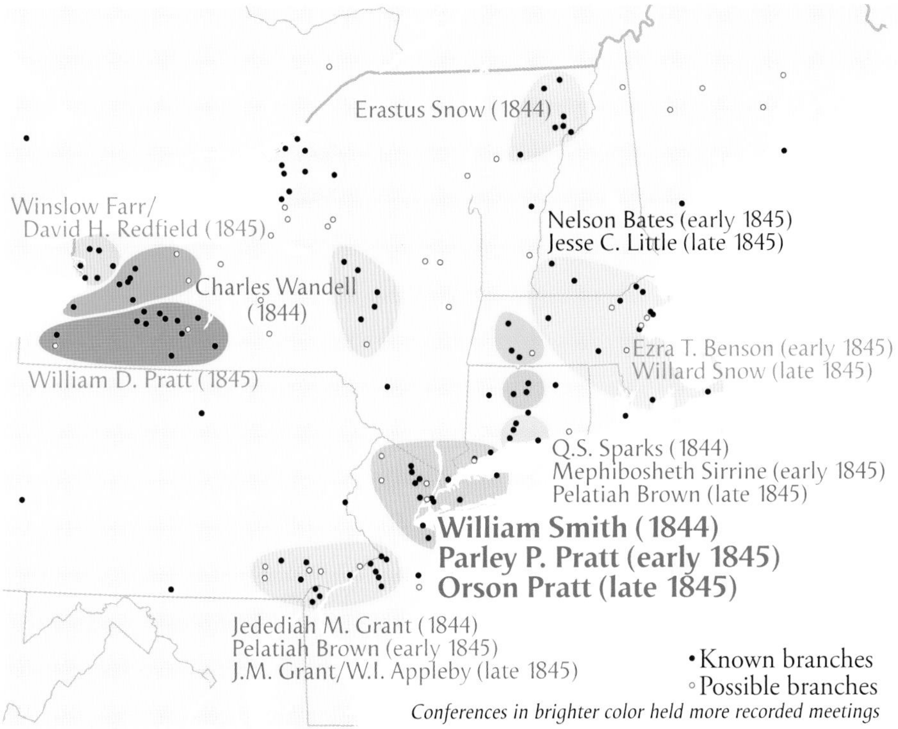

The City of Zion Plat

1833–1900

On June 25, 1833, Joseph Smith sent a proposed town plat to Church leaders in Missouri. This plan, which became known as the City of Zion Plat, was never followed to the letter but quickly became a model repeated in Mormon towns in the Midwest and in the West.

One of the central aspects of the teachings of the Prophet Joseph Smith was the vision of a utopian "Zion" society. In addition to the crucial spiritual, social, and economic elements of Zion was a vision of an ideal settlement. At a time when frontier towns across the Midwest were primarily established to serve the dispersed farmsteads that characterized settlement in the region, Smith taught that Church members should live in organized towns where "the farmer and his family . . . will enjoy all the advantages of schools, public lectures, and other meetings. His home will no longer be isolated, and his family denied the benefits of society."

Smith's ideal City of Zion had lots for about 15,000 residents, with very wide streets, relatively small lots, and most importantly, a central plaza of religious (rather than civic) buildings. The City of Zion Plat was never canonized as a revelation from the Prophet and was never implemented exactly as drawn (the Saints were evicted from Jackson County before they could even make an attempt). When it was implemented in Kirtland, Ohio (see p. 30), and Far West, Missouri (see p. 48), several revisions were made to the plan to make it more practical, setting aside more commercial and civic spaces with narrower streets but retaining a central focus on the temple. The next planned Mormon city, Nauvoo, was significantly different, with much narrower streets, much smaller blocks, much larger lots, and a temple outside the original plat (at the most prominent site in the area, rather than at the geometric center).

After the Mormons removed to the Great Basin, they established hundreds of communities that incorporated some aspects of the City of Zion Plat. Salt Lake City was the first, and became the model for many other communities. All streets were to be 132 feet wide plus an additional twenty feet for sidewalks and a twenty-foot setback for each home. Blocks in Salt Lake City were ten acres in size, as in Smith's plat, but with eight large lots of one and one-half acres per block (except the central temple square). The large lots allowed each settler to provide basic foodstuffs from their city lot, with more substantial farmland south of the city (see p. 84). Salt Lake City's street-naming system was centered on the temple, with the central streets adjacent to the temple lot named North Temple, South Temple, West Temple, and East Temple (now Main Street), while other streets in the original plat of the city were simply numbered consecutively based on their location and distance from the first four streets (First North, First East, etc.). Contrary to popular belief, the street numbering system that is ubiquitous in Utah today (100 South, 200 South, etc.) was not part of the original plan but was adopted in the 1940s (see p. 128).

The urban bias of Joseph Smith and Brigham Young is still evident in the Mormon West landscape, with its nucleated villages and in the establishment of the "benefits of society" that Joseph saw in urban life as the Mormon settlers established schools, universities, theatrical societies, musical groups, and other social activities beyond Church meetings. Thus, while the City of Zion Plat may not have ever been fully implemented, the underlying ideas it represented are found across the Mormon West.

Richard H. Jackson

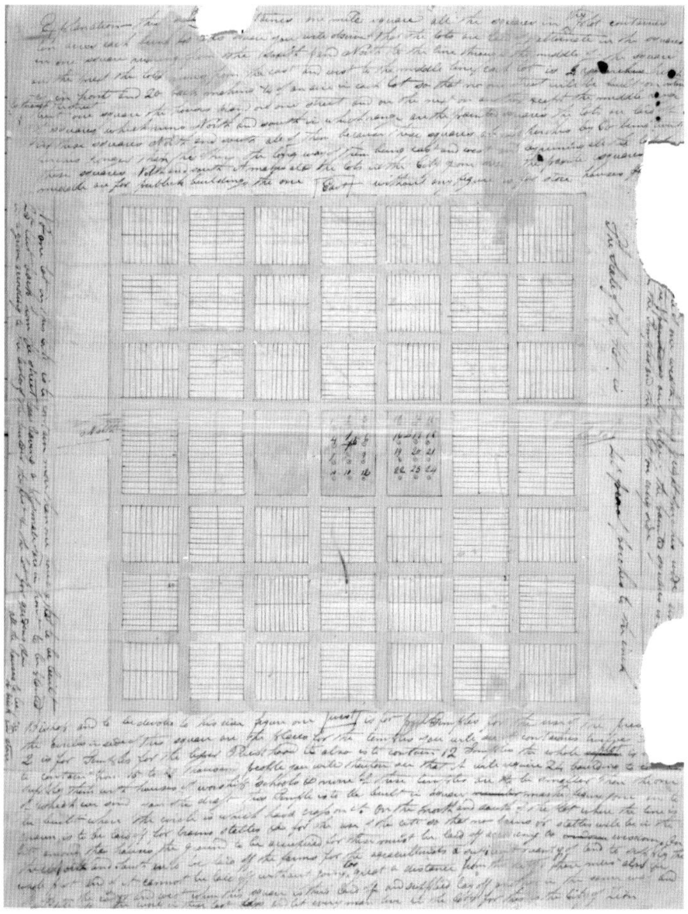

The Original Plat of the City of Zion appears, at first glance, typical of midwestern towns, but it had several unique characteristics, including extremely wide streets (132 feet) and two sizes of blocks. The central tier of large rectangular blocks was made up of 32 lots, each one-half acre in size, while the rest of the blocks were square but with only 20 one-half acre lots. Two of the larger blocks were reserved for "temples" (24 in total, mostly Church administration offices), while a third was for public buildings, businesses, and open space. Lots were rectangular with lots on each block alternating their orientation so that houses did not face other houses across the street. The house lots were intended to be large enough for the residents to have the gardens, trees, and animals common to frontier subsistence community life. Farmland to support more extensive crops such as corn and wheat was to be allocated outside of the town. According to the marginal notes included with the plat, the Prophet anticipated that each community would grow only to a population of 15,000 to 20,000, whereupon another would be created farther away to allow adequate farmland for both.

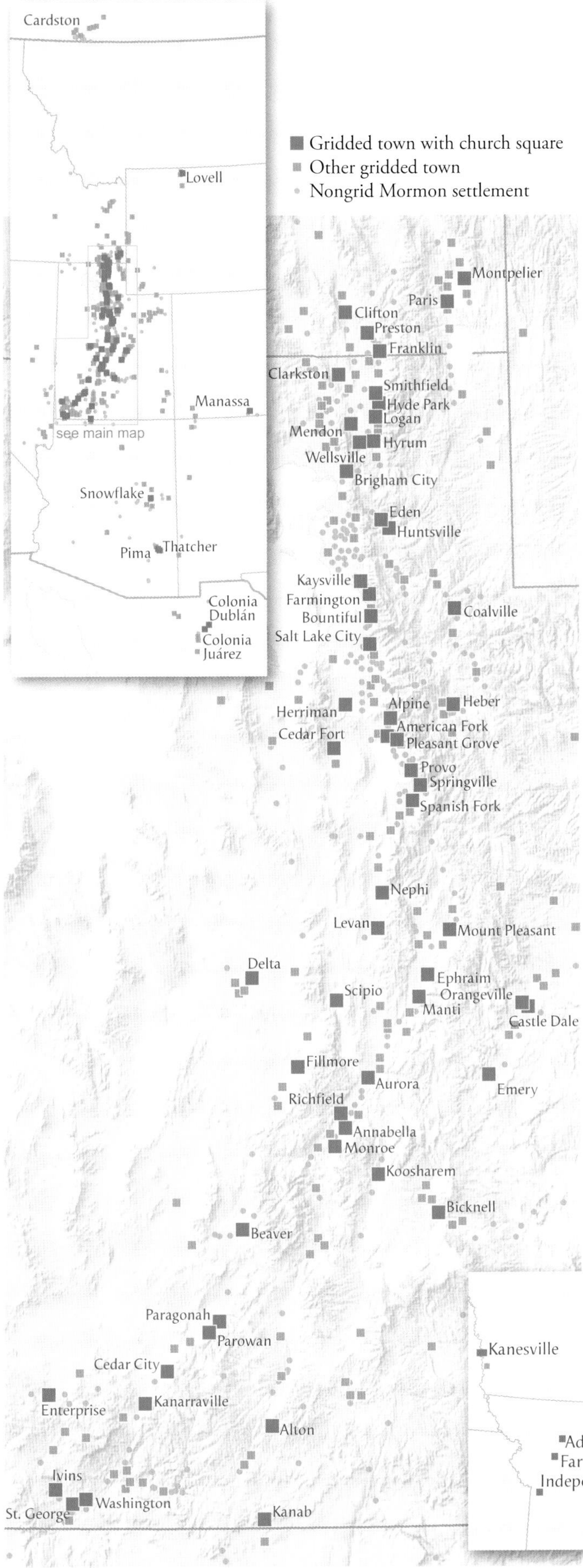

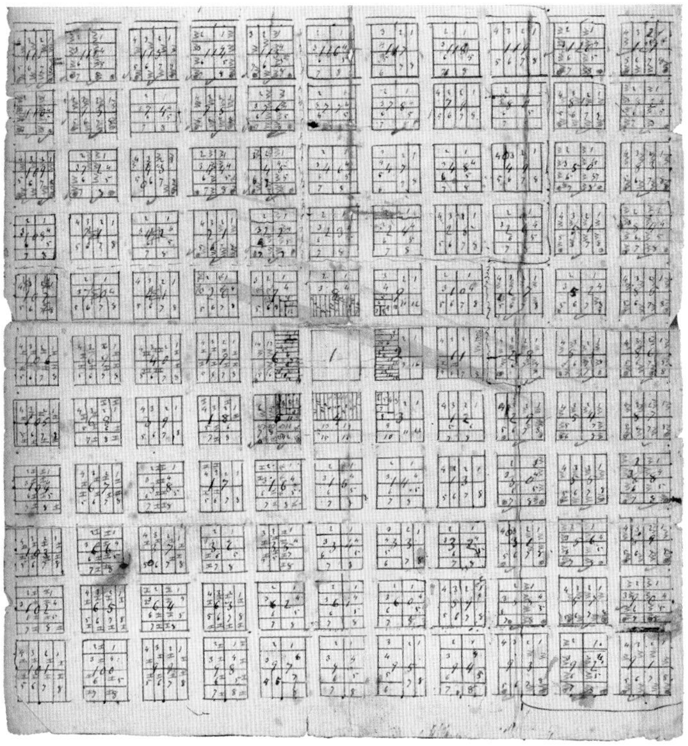

Far West, Missouri, surveyed in 1836, was one of the first true implementations of the City of Zion Plat, with some significant changes. It had four 132-foot-wide streets bordering a central square, but other streets were only 82.5 feet wide, and all blocks were square with only eight lots per block. The central square was encircled by very small lots for commercial uses. This arrangement was very similar to the typical midwestern county seat (for example, Independence and Liberty, Missouri), but with a Church meetinghouse replacing the central courthouse. A later revision and expansion (see p. 48) included public squares (to be used for parks, schools, and churches) every half mile.

Towns inspired by City of Zion principles are concentrated in the Mormon Corridor of Utah and southern Idaho but are also found in Mormon settlements in Canada, Arizona, and Mexico. Although there is some variety in the precise details, several principles of Joseph's City of Zion Plat distinguish the platted Mormon communities, such as extremely wide streets (often 132 feet wide, even in communities of only a few hundred people); very large lots with barns, farm animals, gardens, etc. in town; and a religious, rather than civic, central square. These settlements followed the model of Salt Lake City for three basic reasons. First, many communities were founded by groups "called" by Brigham Young, often including many familiar with the Salt Lake model. Second, the rectangular grid was simple to plat and survey; and third (perhaps most importantly), many of the communities were surveyed by one or two individuals sent out from Salt Lake City by Brigham Young.

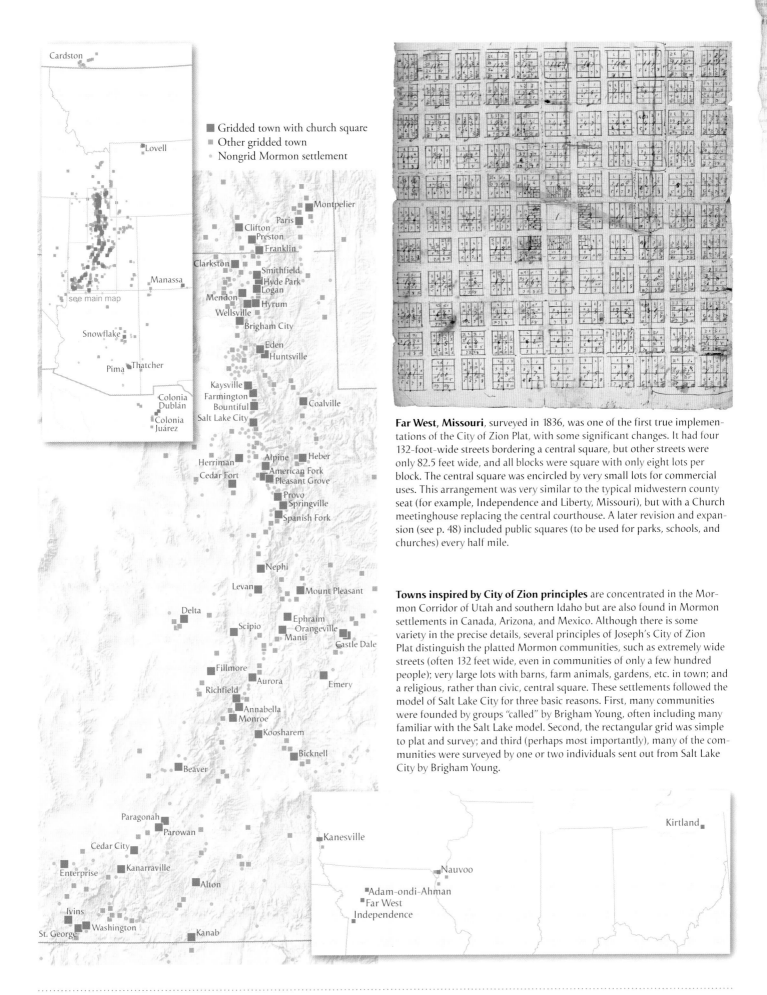

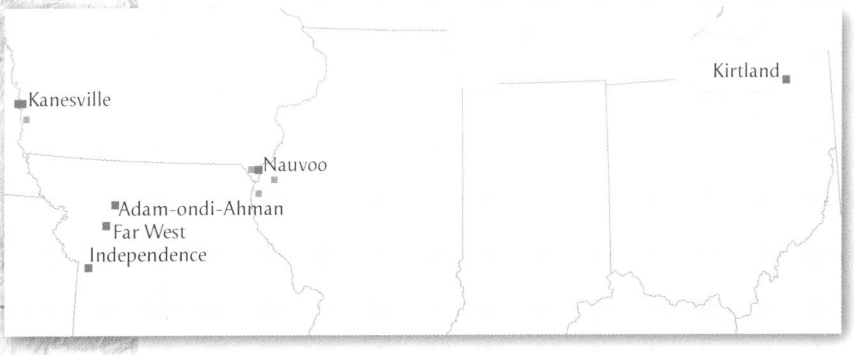

The Twelve Apostles

1835–1846

Between February 1835 and August 1841 the duties and responsibilities of the Quorum of the Twelve Apostles expanded dramatically. When first organized on February 15, 1835, they formed a "traveling presiding high council," with a commission to carry the gospel into the world and minister to members in the scattered branches, but with no authority where stakes of the Church were already organized (D&C 18:26–37; 107:35–39). A few months later, Quorum members undertook their first mission as a group, spending five months traveling from Kirtland, Ohio, to Farmington, Maine, preaching and conducting Church business as they traveled. They organized the first geographic conferences and worked to better organize the branches in the mission field. However, in the chaotic events of 1837 and 1838 in Ohio and Missouri, a number of the original Quorum left the Church, and several new members were called to replace them (D&C 118).

Between 1837 and 1841 there were two apostolic missions to the British Isles. In addition to converting almost 6,000 people, it was during these missions that the Twelve (at least the nine that went) brought their Quorum into its full flowering. In a relatively short time, they laid the organizational foundation for the most successful missionary program of the Church in the nineteenth century, organized an extensive emigration program, and established a major publishing program. Their shared experiences welded them together as a quorum while far from Church headquarters and Joseph Smith's immediate presence.

These nine Apostles had proven their mettle, and Joseph Smith gradually gave them increased authority, with direct responsibility over Church finances, emigration, publishing, Nauvoo city government, and organized stakes of the Church in addition to the missionary responsibilities they had already enjoyed. The Twelve composed the "inner circle" of Joseph's most trusted friends (even more so than the counselors in the First Presidency), being the first to receive the temple endowment, plural marriage, and membership in the Council of Fifty. When Joseph Smith was murdered in June 1844, the Quorum of the Twelve (the nine, at least) were most prepared to carry on where Joseph left off.

David J. Whittaker

1835 Mission of the Quorum of the Twelve Apostles

During the summer of 1835, the Quorum of the Twelve undertook their first mission as a group (and their only mission with all twelve). They traveled east from Kirtland, Ohio, under the leadership of President Thomas B. Marsh. The Apostles traveled together and separately, as they found opportunities to preach; the two Apostles shown in the map kept a diary of their travels, showing the similarities and differences of their routes.

Along the way, they called together conferences in which various items of Church business could be conducted. During this mission, "conference" took on a second meaning: in addition to being meetings where Church members conducted business and received instruction, they were permanent geographical regions consisting of a dozen or more branches (the term continued until "district" gradually replaced it in the early twentieth century). The conferences also helped the missionaries in the area organize their proselytizing efforts, helping the Church transition from its earlier freelance missionary work (see p. 42) into a more systematically organized effort.

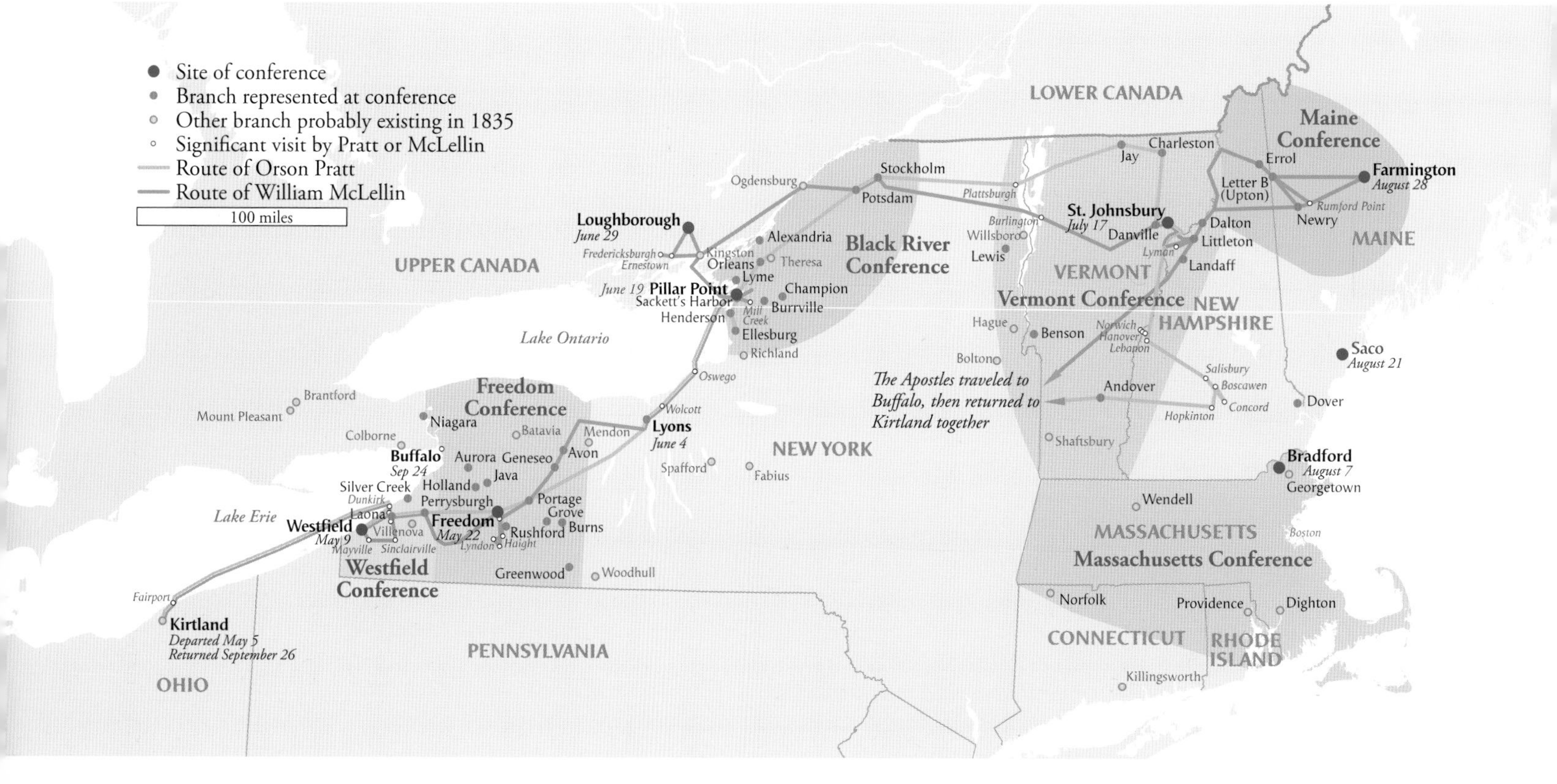

Missions of the Apostles to the British Isles

During the life of Joseph Smith, the Quorum of the Twelve Apostles led two missions to the British Isles. Heber C. Kimball and Orson Hyde established the first mission (1837–38), concentrating their efforts in the area of Preston and the River Ribble Valley of Lancashire, finding about 1,500 converts. From 1839 to 1841, the second mission, nine Apostles under the leadership of Brigham Young consolidated the success of the first mission, then expanded south into the Staffordshire potteries, Birmingham, Herefordshire, and eventually London. Orson Pratt went north to Scotland, while John Taylor opened the Isle of Man and northern Ireland. Meanwhile, Parley P. Pratt took charge of the *Millennial Star* newspaper, laying the foundation for a British publishing program that would become very important to the Church.

The success of these two missions had a great impact on the Church, establishing one of the most important missionary programs in the nineteenth century and an organized emigration program that would continue to provide convert-settlers for the extensive colonization and settlement of the American West. Their work prepared them for the leadership roles they would take on after the death of Joseph Smith in 1844, as well as providing a cadre of converts who were loyal to the Twelve over all other claimants to Church leadership (see p. 66).

Orson Hyde to the Holy Land

Reports of the successes of missionaries were a regular feature in early Mormon periodicals, highlighting the spread of the work and the increase of faith. One of the most interesting was the April 1842 printing in England of Orson Hyde's booklet "A Voice from Jerusalem." It contained a number of Hyde's letters, detailing his journey to and from Jerusalem, and the wording of the prayer he offered on the Mount of Olives on October 24, 1841, blessing the land for the return of the Jews.

Called with fellow Apostle John E. Page at the conference of April 1840, he left Nauvoo for the East the next week. Page stayed behind in Ohio, but Hyde went on to Europe. After spending some time with his brethren of the Twelve on their mission in England, Hyde traveled through Europe and the Middle East, returning to Nauvoo in December 1842. Although his attempts at preaching in Germany were not successful, the intended goal in Jerusalem was accomplished. Along the way, his reports were regularly published in the *Millennial Star* and the *Times and Seasons*. Hyde's account would serve as a model for later foreign mission accounts: Lorenzo Snow's "The Italian Mission" (1851), Orson Spencer's "The Prussian Mission" (1853), and Erastus Snow's "One Year in Scandinavia: Results of the Gospel in Denmark and Sweden" (1851).

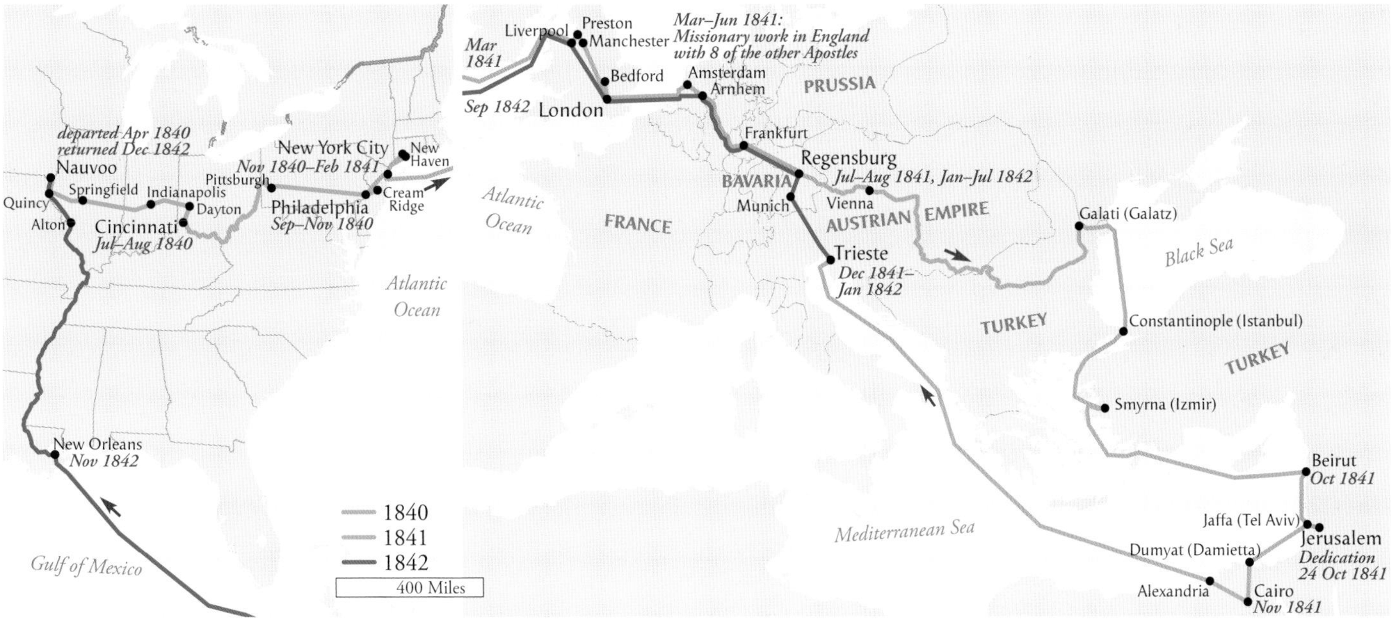

Timeline

June 1829 Joseph Smith and Oliver Cowdery ordained as Apostles when given the Melchizedek Priesthood

June 1829 Three Witnesses promised to find and call the Twelve Apostles (D&C 18)

Quorum of the Twelve Apostles organized **15 Feb 1835**

First group mission to the eastern States **Summer 1835**

First mission to Britain led by two Apostles **1837**

Entire Quorum called to go to Europe **8 Jul 1838**

1840–41 Nine Apostles serve mission in Britain, including Orson Hyde, who goes on to Germany and Palestine

Several members of the **1841** Twelve are first instructed by Joseph Smith on polygamy

Apostles given increased **16 Aug 1841** authority

4 May 1842 First full endowments given: 3 of 8 are Apostles

Council of Fifty organized **11 Mar 1844** with the Twelve at the core

Aug 1844 Twelve confirmed by Nauvoo members as caretakers for the Church

Brigham Young ordained as **Dec 1847** President of the Church

1828 | 1830 | 1832 | 1834 | 1836 | 1838 | 1840 | 1842 | 1844 | 1846

Settling Northern Missouri

1836–1838

FOLLOWING THE EXPULSION of the Mormons from Jackson County, Missouri, in November 1833, the majority of Church members relocated in Clay County (see p. 34). Although Clay's residents were much more fair-minded than Jackson's old-time settlers, by 1836 continued Mormon immigration caused local residents to feel the Mormon stay in Clay County had been long enough. Rather than resorting to physical violence, Clay's citizenry opted to allow the Mormons to relocate peacefully and even offered assistance.

In the spring of 1836, Missouri Church leaders began searching out possible sites for permanent settlement in the region of Missouri north of Ray County (then not organized within any county). After conducting explorations of the region, Mormon officials began making a number of land purchases in what would become Caldwell County. The most significant of these purchases took place on August 8, 1836, when W. W. Phelps and John Whitmer of the Missouri presidency purchased a square mile (640 acres), near Shoal Creek from the local government land office as the main place of Mormon settlement in the region. The site was subsequently named Far West.

During the fall 1836 Missouri legislative session, Alexander W. Doniphan, Clay County's representative to the state legislature and the Mormons' hired attorney, introduced legislation proposing the creation of a county for the Mormons north of what was considered "incorporated" Ray County. Doniphan initially proposed the county be 24x24 square miles. However, a number of non-Mormons living between the 53rd and 54th township lines protested being included in the Mormon county, so this region (called the Buncombe Strip—6x24 square miles) was attached to Ray County, leaving the proposed Mormon County at 18x24 square miles. As discussions progressed, Doniphan began to fear that the bill to organize one county exclusively for the Mormons might not pass, so he proposed that a second county also be created, to be called Daviess, directly north of the proposed Mormon county. The bill passed the legislature, and on December 29, Governor Lilburn W. Boggs signed it into law. Mormons purchased most of the lands owned by earlier settlers and began to move to Caldwell County in earnest. Soon, Daviess County also attracted many Mormons, especially after Adam-ondi-Ahman was identified as a place of great spiritual significance.

Alexander L. Baugh

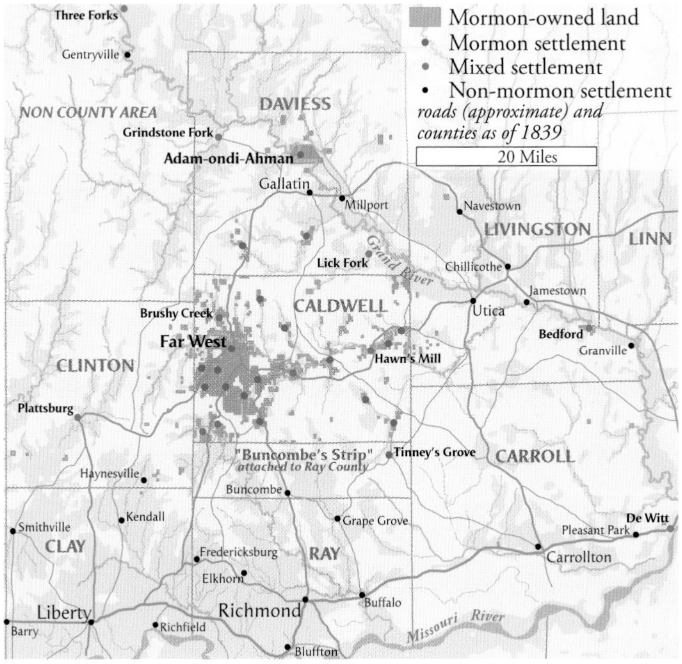

Mormon Settlement in Northern Missouri, 1839

Population figures for the number of Mormons living in northern Missouri just prior to their expulsion from the state in 1839 are difficult to determine because no census data exists. Although some Mormon narratives mention as many as 10,000–15,000 Latter-day Saints living in the region, these figures are probably too high. More careful estimates place the number of Mormons living in Caldwell County at approximately 5,000–5,500, with another 1,000–1,250 residing in Daviess County. Additionally, perhaps another 200–250 Mormons were scattered throughout other surrounding counties (Clay, Clinton, Ray, Carroll, and Livingston) or were living in nearby unincorporated regions. Therefore, at its height, the Mormon population of northern Missouri was likely around 6,000–7,000.

Missouri, 1836–1839

May 1836 Missouri Church leaders search out possible sites in "unincorporated" Ray County and begin making land purchases for a possible Mormon settlement

8 August 1836
W. W. Phelps and John Whitmer purchase 960 acres of land in behalf of the Church, including one square mile (640 acres) that became Far West

29 December 1836
Missouri Governor Lilburn W. Boggs signs the bill creating Caldwell and Daviess Counties, the former specifically for Mormon settlement

3 July 1837
The foundation for the Far West Temple is excavated

14 March 1838
Joseph Smith arrives in Far West and takes up permanent residence

4 July 1838
LDS leaders formally dedicate the Far West Temple site

6 August 1838
Mormons living in Daviess County attempt to vote in the state-wide elections and a skirmish breaks out in Gallatin, marking the beginning of the Mormon–Missouri War

31 October 1838
Joseph Smith and several other Church leaders are taken into custody by Missouri militia officials

1 December 1838 Joseph Smith, Sidney Rigdon, Hyrum Smith, Lyman Wight, Alexander McRae, and Caleb Baldwin are put in Liberty Jail

February 1839
The Mormons begin evacuating Caldwell County and temporarily relocate in Adams County, Illinois

16–22 April 1839
En route to Columbia, Missouri, Joseph Smith and his prison companions are released by their guards and make their way to Quincy, Illinois

26 April 1839
Brigham Young and the Twelve return from Quincy, Illinois, to Far West to rededicate the Far West Temple site and officially begin their mission to Great Britain

1836 1837 1838 1839

Caldwell and Daviess Counties, 1839

From 1836 until early 1839, Caldwell County became the main settlement location for Mormons gathering to northern Missouri. Land parcels could be purchased from the government land office at nearby Lexington, generally for $1.25 per acre. Although Far West became the main place of Mormon gathering, smaller settlements were established on or near the creeks, typically bearing the name of the original inhabitants. These outlying settlements were generally scattered clusters of farms, not platted villages.

A few Mormons began settling Daviess County in 1837, but most came in 1838. Land transactions in Daviess were different than in Caldwell; because it was not yet open to government sale, settlers filed a preemptive claim for up to 160 acres. The tenant could then live on the property and make improvements with the expectation that when the federal government officially offered the land for sale, he would have the first rights to buy the land. Adam-ondi-Ahman (Diahman for short) soon became the largest settlement in the county (platted as a city much like Far West), but other Mormon settlements also arose, soon coming into conflict with the non-Mormon settlers, who were building towns such as Gallatin and Millport. Unlike Kirtland and Nauvoo, when the Mormons abandoned their settlements in 1839 (see p. 50), they were not reinhabited by other settlers but became ghost towns, eventually reverting to farmland.

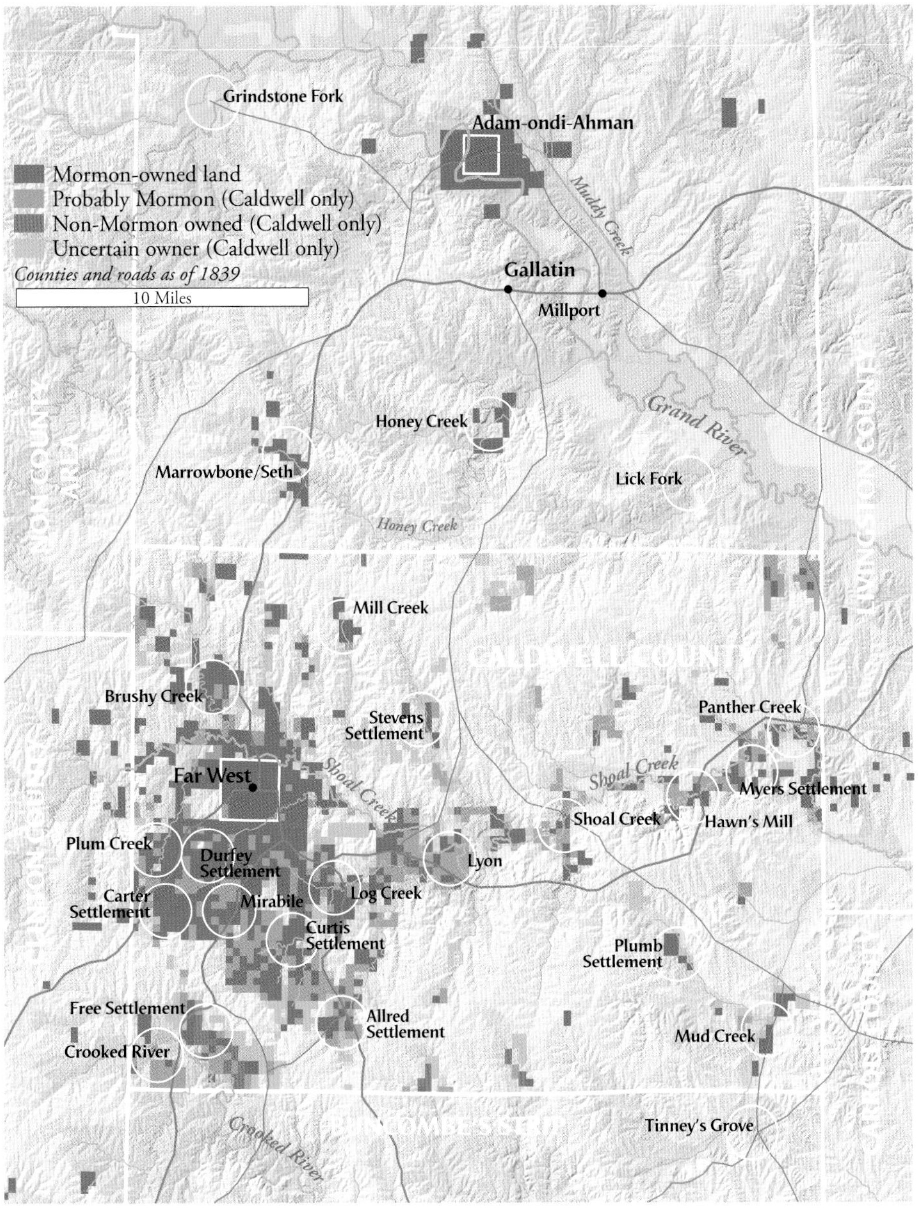

Far West, Missouri

Located in Mirabile Township in Caldwell County, Far West was the largest Mormon settlement in northern Missouri. Although its existence was relatively short-lived (1836–39), it became the center of the religious, political, and social activities of the Latter-day Saints living in the region. Originally, Far West was to have been one square mile according to the City of Zion plan (see p. 44) but was soon expanded to two miles square (four times its original size). Joseph Smith took up permanent residence in the community on March 14, 1838, making it the new headquarters of the Church. On July 4, during a festive celebration, a site was dedicated for a temple on the town's public square.

By the early summer of 1838, Far West was a thriving community consisting of 150 homes, several stores, blacksmith shops, a printing establishment, a school, and two hotels. Throughout the summer and early fall, the community continued to increase in number and size as companies of Mormon immigrants arrived from the East. As hostilities increased in the fall, large numbers of Mormons from outlying areas, particularly Daviess County, took up temporary residence in or near Far West before leaving the state beginning in early 1839.

Far West disappeared almost as quickly as it had appeared. Dissident John Whitmer, who had originally purchased most of the town site, turned the former town into a farm. On this aerial photograph, it is clear that the former town is now cropland; nothing more than a few foundations have been found.

The Mormon-Missouri War

1838–1839

When they arrived in Missouri, the Latter-day Saints found themselves to be very different from the other settlers. In the first place, Missourians came largely from the frontier mold—independent, suspicious of outsiders, and relatively irreligious. The large population of Mormons that inundated northwestern Missouri in 1838 was communal, devout, and partly foreign-born. Secondly, the Mormons presented a political threat to the unorganized Missourians, since they tended to vote as a bloc. Finally, and perhaps most significantly, Mormons soon outnumbered Missourians in Caldwell and Daviess counties, thus gaining significant political and economic clout (see p. 48).

While moderates dominated both groups, prejudice and bigotry among radicals on both sides inevitably led to tensions. The pattern of events that led to the earlier expulsion of the Saints from Jackson County repeated itself in northwestern Missouri: the Saints arrived, the locals felt threatened by the continual influx of Mormons and saw their peculiar neighbors as a threat to their own society. They responded by attacking the Mormons and seeking their departure from their communities. While both sides were active in the fighting, rumors of a full-scale Mormon "rebellion" led Governor Lilburn W. Boggs to issue an order in the autumn of 1838 to the state militia to drive the Mormon populace from the state.

The Mormon surrender in Far West came with four conditions: surrender of key Mormon leaders, including Joseph Smith; disarmament of citizens in Far West; repayment of war damages by the Mormons; and their departure from the state by February of 1839. With Joseph Smith in jail, the responsibility of protecting Mormon interests in Missouri fell to Brigham Young, Heber C. Kimball, and Edward Partridge. After consolidating in Far West, Church members began to leave Missouri in November. Mormons made tremendous sacrifices of land and personal property as they evacuated Daviess and Caldwell counties. Some families made the entire trek barefoot, while others attempted to wrap their feet in rags to protect them from the frozen earth. By mid-February, a steady stream of Saints was traveling along the rugged roads to Palmyra, Missouri, and across the Mississippi to Quincy, Illinois. Soon, only the poorest remained in Missouri. With help from Saints already relocated, by mid-April the last Mormons had left Far West.

Upon reaching Quincy, the Saints were met with kindness and generosity by the residents of Adams County. The governors of Illinois and Iowa responded with similar humanity. Some Saints purchased new farmland in the surrounding area (see p. 58), while other searched for a new gathering place.

The exodus from Missouri constituted the first organized move of the Church from one central location to another. It prepared the Saints for an exodus on a much larger scale eight years later.

Sean Cannon

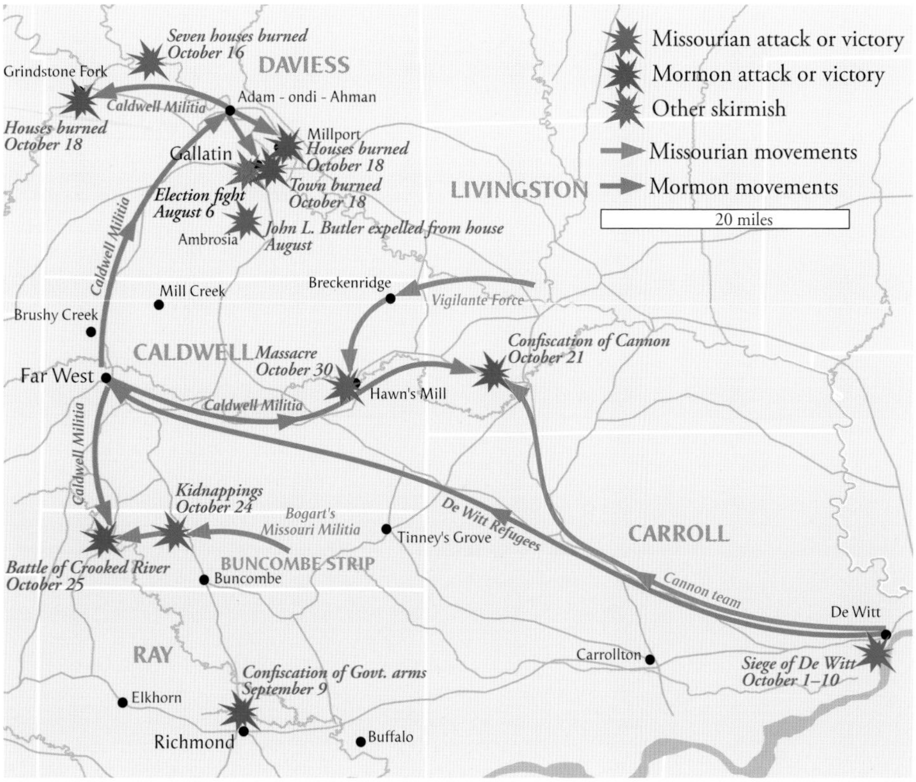

The Mormon–Missouri War was precipitated by Missourian fears that the rapidly immigrating Mormons would dominate not only Caldwell County, which had been set aside for Mormon settlement (see p. 48), but also Daviess County, which was supposed to be a non-Mormon County, then continue to expand into surrounding counties. The Missourians were especially anxious about political control, leading to a skirmish on election day in August at the polls in Gallatin.

Both sides felt slighted by the fight, and heated rhetoric soon gave way to raids on homes. This in turn led to more violent retaliatory strikes by both sides, culminating in the Battle of Crooked River and the Hawn's Mill Massacre. Biased reports of the fighting painted a picture of Mormons in open rebellion against the Missouri government.

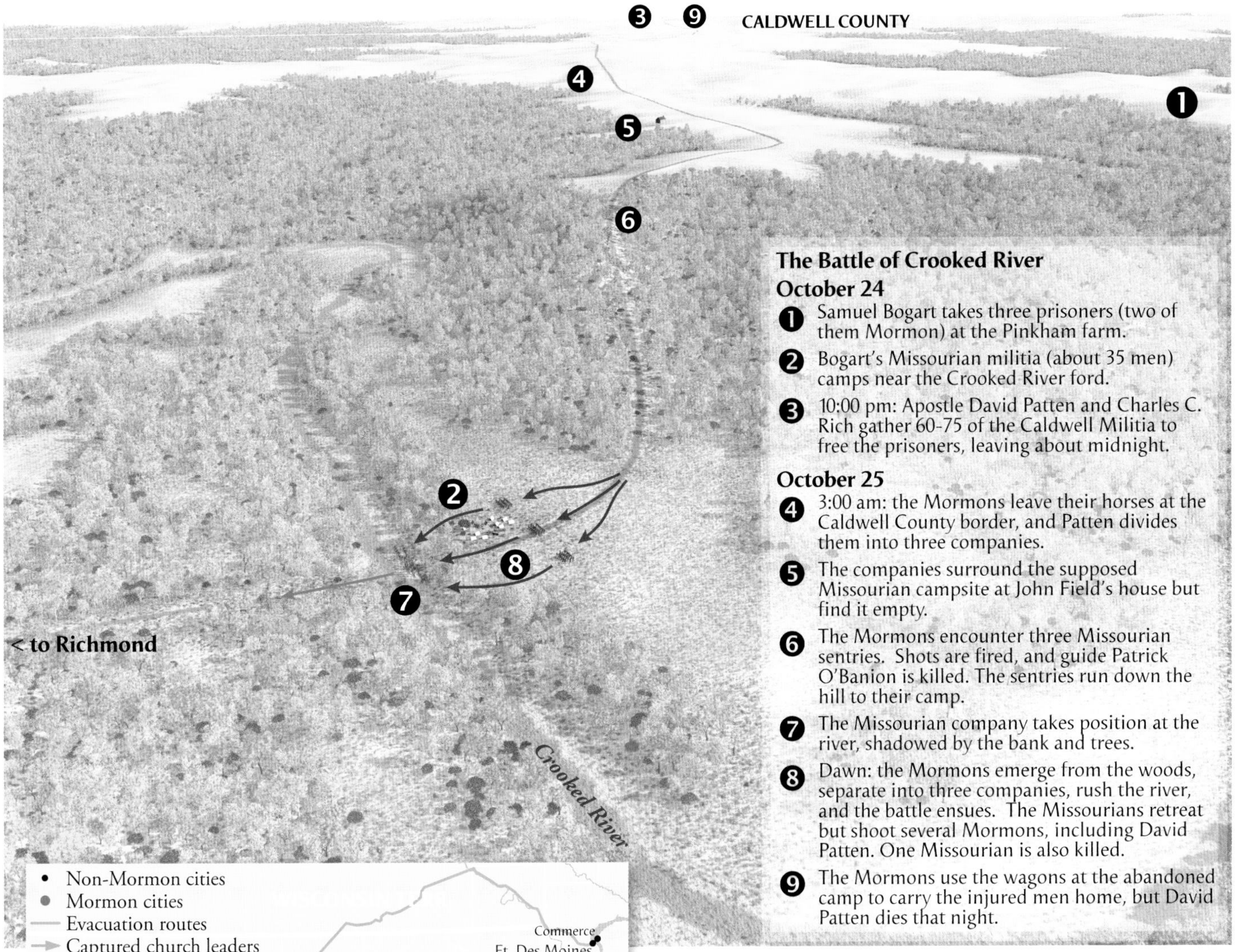

CALDWELL COUNTY
< to Richmond
Crooked River
The Battle of Crooked River
October 24
1 Samuel Bogart takes three prisoners (two of them Mormon) at the Pinkham farm.
2 Bogart's Missourian militia (about 35 men) camps near the Crooked River ford.
3 10:00 pm: Apostle David Patten and Charles C. Rich gather 60-75 of the Caldwell Militia to free the prisoners, leaving about midnight.
October 25
4 3:00 am: the Mormons leave their horses at the Caldwell County border, and Patten divides them into three companies.
5 The companies surround the supposed Missourian campsite at John Field's house but find it empty.
6 The Mormons encounter three Missourian sentries. Shots are fired, and guide Patrick O'Banion is killed. The sentries run down the hill to their camp.
7 The Missourian company takes position at the river, shadowed by the bank and trees.
8 Dawn: the Mormons emerge from the woods, separate into three companies, rush the river, and the battle ensues. The Missourians retreat but shoot several Mormons, including David Patten. One Missourian is also killed.
9 The Mormons use the wagons at the abandoned camp to carry the injured men home, but David Patten dies that night.

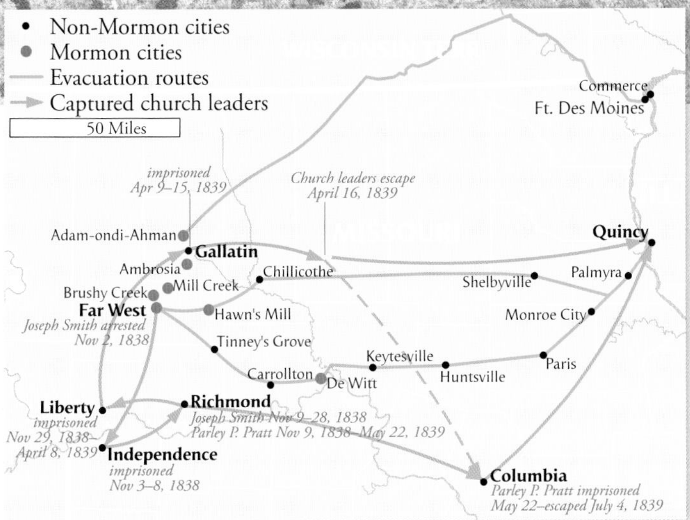

Non-Mormon cities
Mormon cities
Evacuation routes
Captured church leaders
50 Miles
Commerce
Ft. Des Moines
imprisoned Apr 9–15, 1839
Church leaders escape April 16, 1839
Adam-ondi-Ahman
Gallatin
Quincy
Ambrosia
Chillicothe
Palmyra
Brushy Creek
Mill Creek
Shelbyville
Far West
Joseph Smith arrested Nov 2, 1838
Hawn's Mill
Monroe City
Tinney's Grove
Keytesville
Paris
Carrollton
De Witt
Huntsville
Liberty
imprisoned Nov 29, 1838–April 8, 1839
Richmond
Joseph Smith Nov 9–28, 1838
Parley P. Pratt Nov 9, 1838–May 22, 1839
Independence
imprisoned Nov 3–8, 1838
Columbia
Parley P. Pratt imprisoned May 22–escaped July 4, 1839

Exodus from Missouri, 1838–1839

After the extermination order was issued, the Saints were forced to leave Missouri whichever direction they could. Fear of Indian attacks in the West probably kept the move directed eastward. Some families strayed into Iowa, but most made the 200-mile journey northeast toward Quincy, Illinois, the closest major town across the state line, tending to follow established roads. From personal accounts of the trek, a northern route extending eastward from Far West through Chillicothe and Shelbyville to Quincy, and a southern route connecting Far West with Tinney's Grove, Keytesville, Huntsville, and Quincy, appear to have been the prevalent routes.

Leaving Missouri, 1838–39

6–7 Aug "Election Day Fight" erupts at Gallatin when Saints are forbidden to vote; Joseph Smith leads 150 men to protect Adam-ondi-Ahman; they surround Justice Adam Black's home, insisting he sign a statement vowing to administer justice fairly; he files a complaint of intimidation

13 Aug–24 Sep Saints ordered to leave Carroll County; Joseph Smith and Lyman Wight arrested and freed on bail pending a grand jury trial; state militia musters several times

1–11 Oct De Witt Mormons besieged by 400 vigilantes from Carroll and five other counties; soon surrender and flee to Far West

14–24 Oct Joseph Smith and Sidney Rigdon lead 400 men to Daviess County to protect the Saints, burning Gallatin and Millport and expelling almost all non-Mormons from the county

25–27 Oct Three Mormons and one Missourian are killed in the Battle of Crooked River as a company of Mormons tries to free prisoners held by the militia

30 Oct 200 militia from Livingston County massacre 18 Saints at the small settlement of Hawn's Mill

31 Oct Militia surrounds Far West; Joseph Smith and about 80 leaders surrender as hostages

Nov 1838 The Mormons surrender, military occupies Far West

Winter 1838–39 Mormon exodus from Missouri

August | September | October | November | December

Commerce, Illinois

1824–1839

North of the point where the Des Moines River empties into the Mississippi (at Keokuk), the Great River passes through 12 miles of rapids between 100-foot bluffs that separate the river from the flat prairies on either side. At the head of these rapids is a wide horseshoe bend that forms a peninsular floodplain on the east side. The area is heavily wooded with a wide variety of hardwood trees, and grass grows abundantly; springs at the base of the bluffs have made the lowlands boggy. Such is the physical character of the place where Commerce was established in the early nineteenth century.

The area had been inhabited by Native Americans for hundreds of years. Most recently, the Sac and Fox under Chief Quashquema lived in a village at the head of the rapids, but by 1820 they had moved west, and settlers began arriving.

By 1830, the scattered settlement, called Venus, was large enough to have a post office, and in 1833 a town was platted on the river. However, it attracted only a few residents, even when replatted under the name Commerce. The area attracted many speculators, some of whom platted the adjacent Commerce City and Montrose across the river. However, the Panic of 1837 killed the real estate boom, and by the time the Latter-day Saints arrived in 1839, the area was still sparsely settled.

Donald Q. Cannon & Brandon S. Plewe

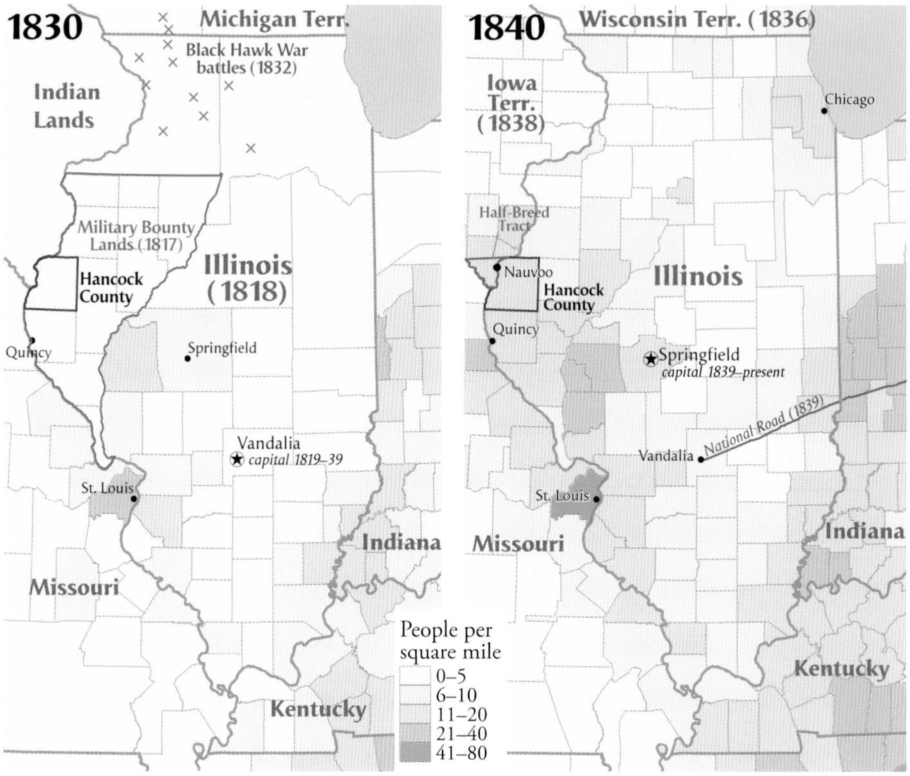

The Illinois Frontier

After statehood in 1818, Illinois's population was concentrated in the south and near St. Louis. Much of the land west of the Illinois River was granted to veterans of the War of 1812, but few settled there due to the remaining American Indians.

After the Black Hawk War (1832), lands in western Illinois and eastern Iowa (including the Half-Breed Tract across from Nauvoo) were available for white settlement, and the frontier rapidly expanded northward (and west from Indiana).

Land speculation by easterners (e.g., the Hotchkiss and Kimball groups) and locals (e.g., Isaac Galland) was rampant in this frontier environment, leading to many "paper towns" like Commerce City, and land title that was often dubious.

Commerce town plat, recorded May 20, 1834, by Alexander White and Joseph Teas. Their earlier plat of Venus, which covered the same area with different lot numbering, has not survived. Very few lots were sold, and in 1837, White's widow sold the remainder of the north half to Horace Hotchkiss, who later sold it to the LDS Church; Teas sold the south half to Charles Munson, who retained it in absentia throughout the Mormon period. ▶

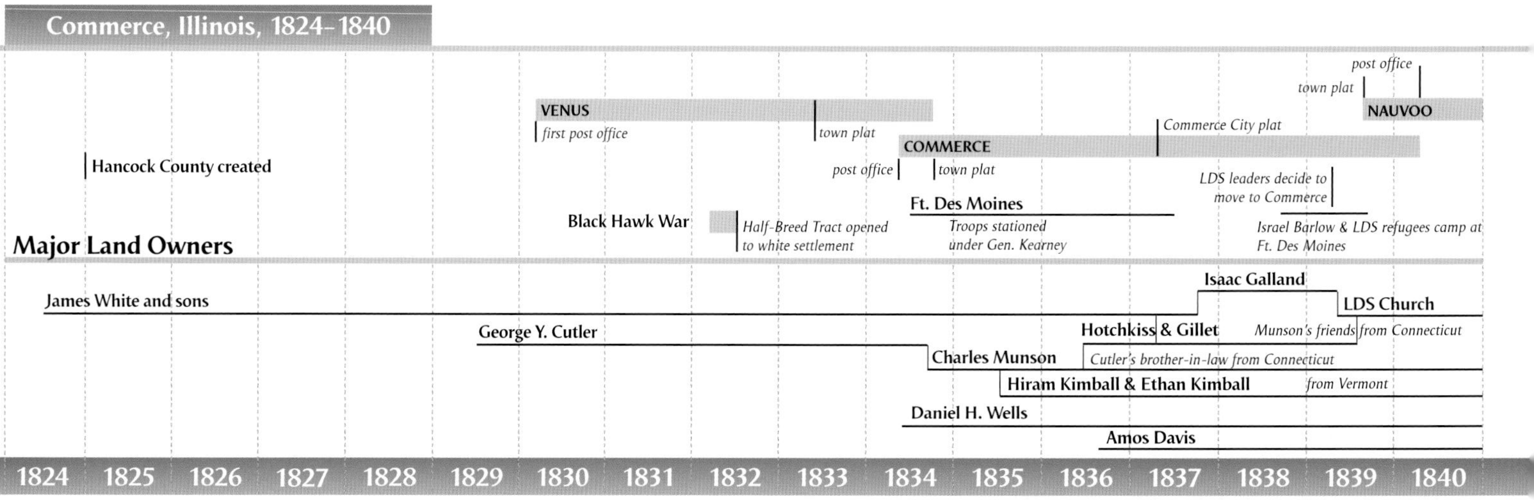

Commerce in Spring 1839, as Joseph Smith might have first seen it. Although the residents and speculators had great plans for Commerce and Commerce City, it was only a hamlet of a few houses (to the left) surrounded by boggy woodlands. The stone house built in 1829 by James White, then inhabited by Isaac Galland, can be seen at right. Just behind it is the Hugh White home, which would soon become the nucleus of Nauvoo. Homesteads were scattered on the bluffs along the road to Carthage.

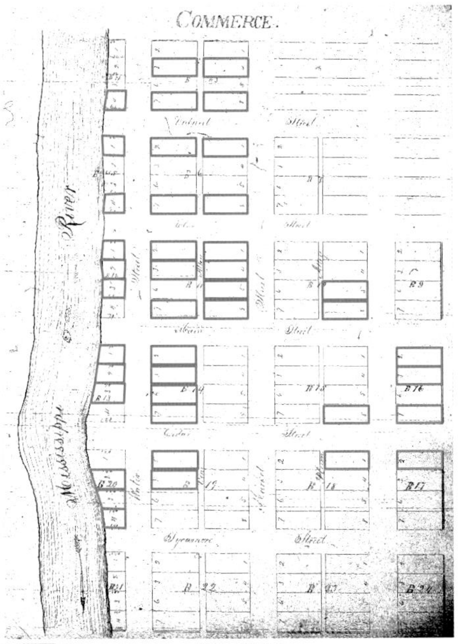

Lots purchased by 1839

Commerce lands in 1839

James White, the first permanent settler, purchased the southern peninsula in 1824 and built a two-story stone house from which he and his sons guided boats through the rapids. Led by the Whites, the settlement of "Venus" included perhaps twenty scattered homesteads by 1833 when the first town plat was surveyed.

Land speculators soon followed the settlers, buying up homesteads and military grants that were never occupied. Connecticut native George Cutler, the first postmaster, had a house in Venus but bought more than a hundred acres of prairie on the bluffs. After his death, brother-in-law Charles Munson and friends Horace Hotchkiss and John Gillet (who all stayed in Connecticut) began buying acreage. Hotchkiss and Gillet created a plat for a second town called Commerce City in 1837, but when the Panic of 1837 hit, they did not sell any lots.

In places, the Mississippi River was half its current width and contained many islands before the construction of the Keokuk Dam in 1819.

Commerce City (1837)
no lots sold

Venus (1833)
replatted as Commerce (1834)

James White stone house (1829)

During the early 1800s, Quashquema's band of Sac and Fox lived at the head of the rapids. At times, they also lived in Cut Nose Village across the river.

Ft. Des Moines

The Hugh White homestead was built in 1805 by Indian agent William Ewing, and became Joseph Smith's first home in 1839. It and the Hibard homestead to the East still stand.

Louis Tesson was the first white settler in the area, but his 1799 homestead and orchard were abandoned by 1810.

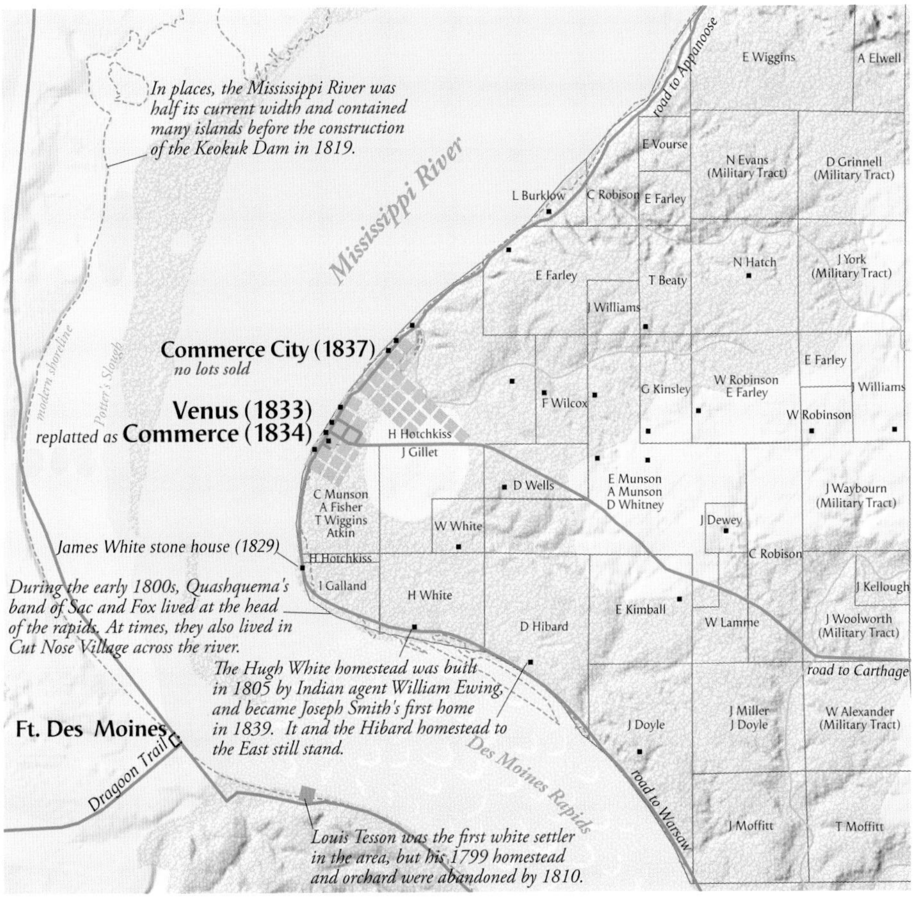

Fort Des Moines was a U.S. Dragoon (cavalry) post established by Stephen W. Kearny from 1834 to 1837 to protect settlers in the Half-Breed Tract. A Sac and Fox settlement called Cut Nose Village had been here. After it was abandoned, settlers attempted to found a town called "Montrose" but were hampered by questionable land titles until 1850. Mormon refugees from Missouri, led by Israel Barlow, spent the winter of 1838–39 in the barracks.

Buying Nauvoo

1839–1843

Forcibly driven from Missouri in 1839, most of the Mormons took up refuge in the vicinity of Quincy, Illinois (see p. 50), while they considered whether to settle in one place again or disperse themselves among non-Mormons. Meanwhile, Mormon exiles living in abandoned Fort Des Moines at Montrose, Iowa, met Isaac Galland, who held claims to large swaths of land in Iowa in addition to his farm in Commerce, Illinois (see p. 52), that he was willing to sell to the Saints. After his escape from Missouri, Joseph Smith visited the nascent village on May 1, 1839, and saw an opportunity for a new gathering place for the Saints.

The Church, through Joseph and his bishops, immediately began to purchase land in the area from both residents and eastern speculators on terms that seemed reasonable at the time. Soon they owned almost all of the "flats" along the river. Here Joseph Smith envisioned a city on a grand scale, giving it the name Nauvoo (a Hebrew word meaning "beautiful"). The horseshoe bend in the Mississippi and the panorama created by the heavily wooded hills certainly made Nauvoo a beautiful place, although much of it was swampy and needed to be drained.

Church surveyors platted Nauvoo in September 1839 with a square grid system, similar to the earlier City of Zion plat (see p. 44), but with some significant differences. There was no central religious or civic square set aside and no downtown of small commercial lots. Rather than the plan to have small lots inside the city and farms beyond, city lots (just over 500 of them) were four acres each. In fact, Nauvoo was more similar to other American cities than to earlier Mormon cities.

As Mormons poured into the new city, neighboring landowners (mostly non-Mormons) recognized an opportunity and began to subdivide their land, tripling the amount of urban property available. Also, many residents were willing to sell parts of their large city lots, further subdividing Nauvoo. This led to competition and conflicting goals for Church leaders: they knew that most of the incoming Saints were poor and needed land as cheaply as possible, but they also needed to make a significant profit from sales of the original Nauvoo plat to repay the mortgage.

By its height in 1845, Nauvoo consisted of over 1,500 acres of city lots (about half of the land within the city limits), housing over 12,000 people. When the Saints largely abandoned the city in 1846, the Church assigned three men to act as trustees to sell the Saints' land on their behalf. Speculators such as Phineas Kimball were able to buy up large amounts of the city for a fraction of its value, later selling the city to the French Icarians (a utopian community), then to German immigrants. However, the city has never regained the population it had in 1845.

Brandon S. Plewe & Donald Q. Cannon

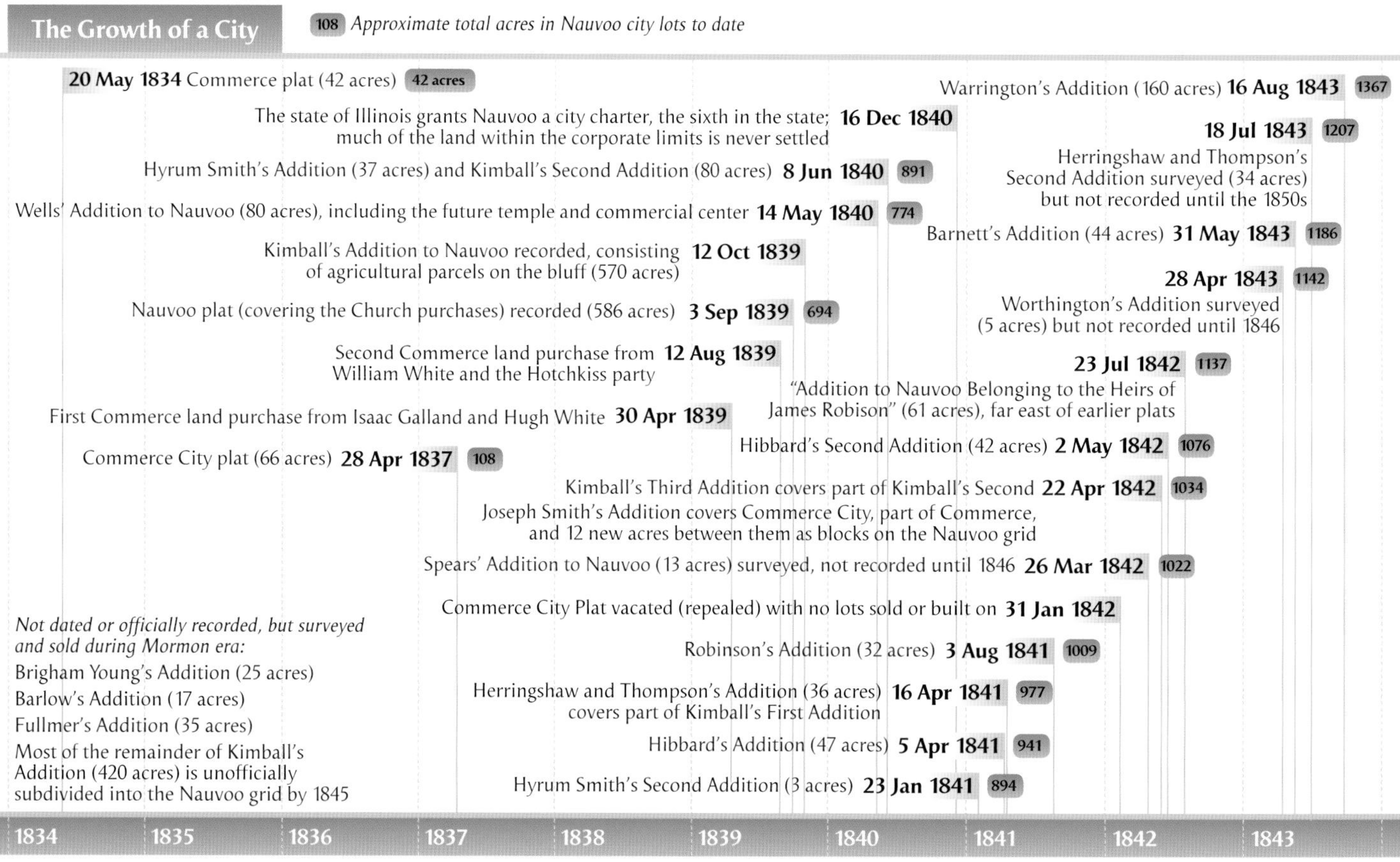

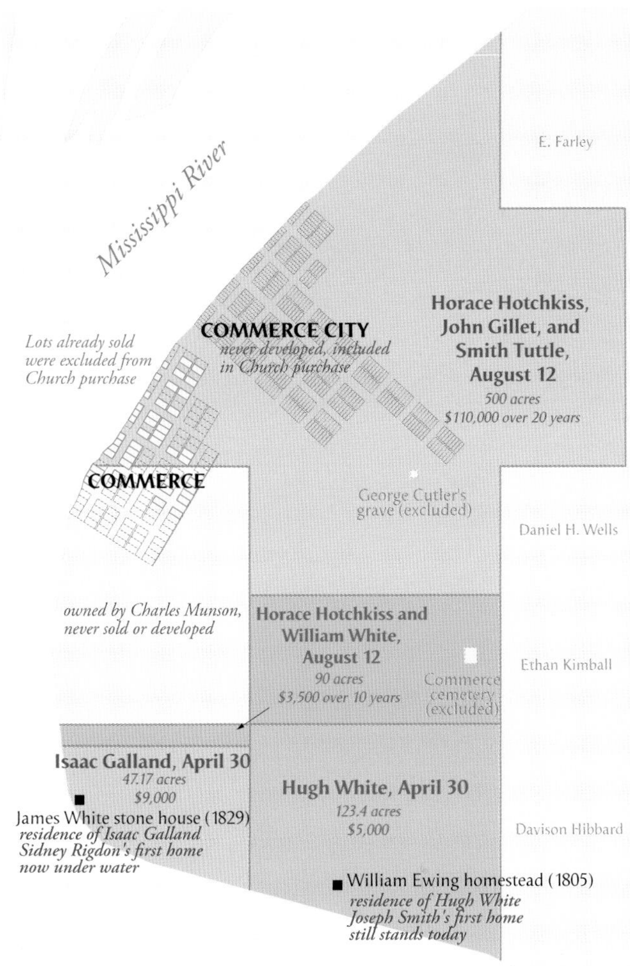

The Church purchased more than 750 acres in the Commerce area in 1839, including the farms of local residents and the property of speculators who lived in Connecticut. The latter included Commerce City, a town that had been platted but had failed to sell any lots due to the Panic of 1837. The massive mortgage that Joseph Smith signed for this property was to be paid for through the sale of lots, but soon became a major personal burden for him (among the factors that led to his declaring bankruptcy in 1842). It was difficult to balance the need to charge profitable prices for lots against his desire to house the thousands of poor immigrants who were arriving and against the interests of friends and family who were competing with the Church to sell their own lots in other parts of Nauvoo. One scheme was for gathering Saints to trade the title to the property they were leaving in the east to Hotchkiss for credit against the mortgage, for which they received property in Nauvoo. However, the debts were not paid until lands owned by Smith and the Church were sold off in 1853.

The survey of Nauvoo departed significantly from the City of Zion Plat proposed seven years earlier (see p. 44). It was laid out in a grid, as were most midwestern cities of that time. However, it lacked the small lots that had been meant to build a tight-knit community, although further subdivision of lots soon increased density in the core areas of the city. It also lacked the blocks set aside for public uses and the temple. Instead, the temple block was purchased on a prominent site at the crest of the bluff, completely outside of the original Church survey. Without an official public square, outdoor civic and church meetings were typically held on an unsold block below the temple called "the Grove" or at the foot of Main Street in front of Joseph Smith's home.

Soon after Nauvoo was surveyed, adjacent landowners quickly recognized the growth potential of the city as the gathering place for the Saints and began subdividing their property to sell to immigrants. These developers included old Commerce settlers like Daniel H. Wells and Davison Hibbard, Church members, and distant speculators. The first addition, created by Ethan Kimball, was laid out as small farms, but subsequent plats followed the Nauvoo Grid, and by 1845 almost all of Kimball's addition had been gridded (the surveys for most of which were never officially recorded with the county).

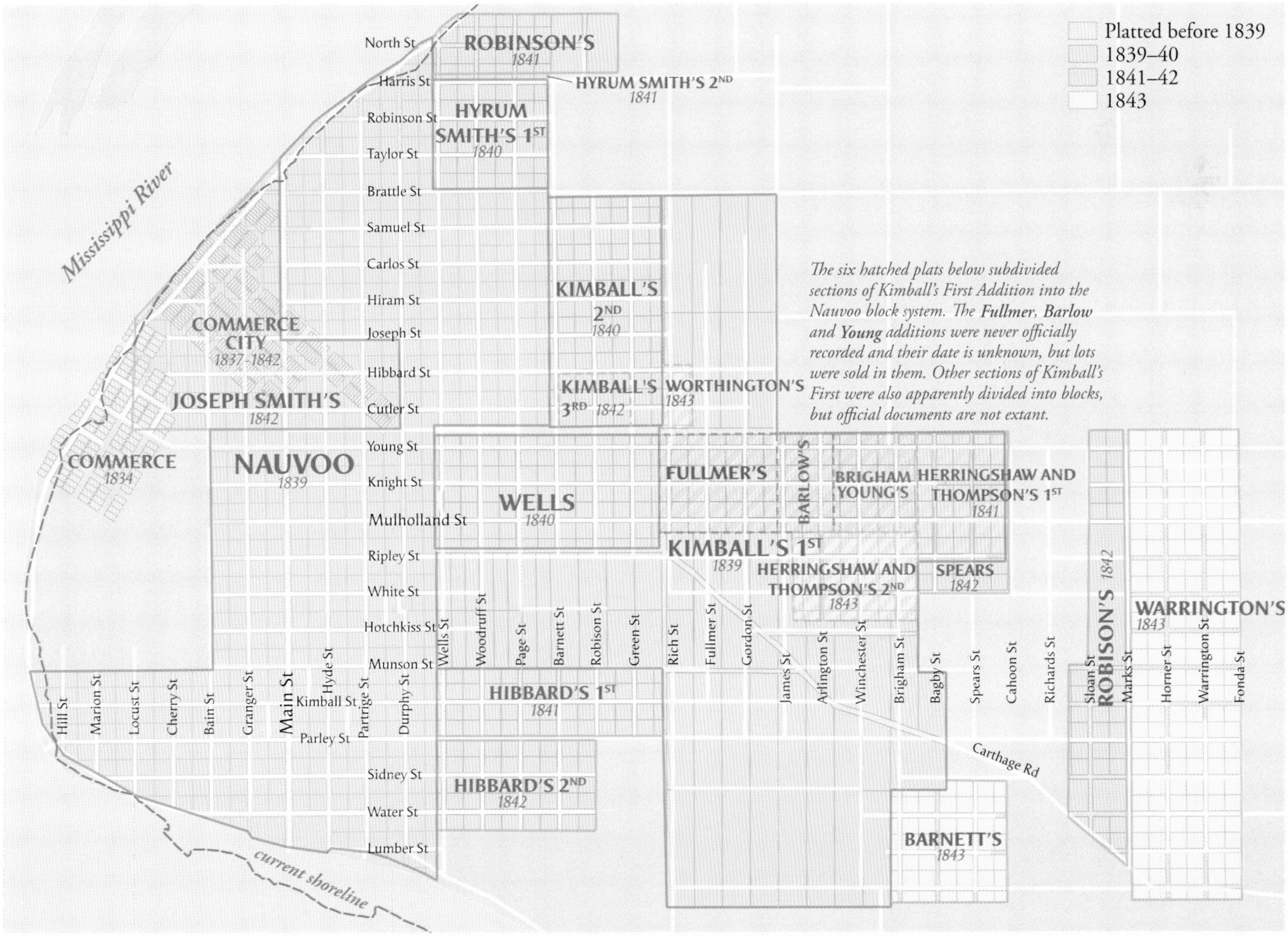

Building Nauvoo

1839–1846

Joseph Smith envisioned building a city on a monumental scale—one that was systematic, orderly, and carefully planned. It was to be a home for the Saints, a beacon to the world. The city he planned would contain 150 blocks, each with 4 one-acre lots. Streets would run north–south and east–west.

Before public buildings could be erected, homes had to be built. At first these homes were crude and uncomfortable, including sod huts and rude cabins. As time went on, better cabins and eventually frame and brick homes dotted the landscape. Lumber for these homes came from trees in the vicinity, such as cottonwood, walnut, and hickory. Later, a mission was sent to the Wisconsin Pineries, some 500 miles north of Nauvoo, to obtain lumber and float it down the Mississippi River. Some of the Saints managed to build substantial brick homes. One of the largest was the Heber C. Kimball home, built on one corner of his one-acre lot.

As the city grew and modest prosperity developed, public buildings were erected. One of the most important public buildings was Joseph Smith's Red Brick Store. This building was much more than a store. It also served as a public meeting place where both temporal and spiritual business was conducted. Other public buildings included the Masonic Hall, Seventies Hall, Music Hall, and the Times and Seasons Complex.

The crowning building achievement was, of course, the Nauvoo Temple. This magnificent structure was built by the sacrifice of the people of Nauvoo on the edge of the bluffs, overlooking the Mississippi River and the Iowa side of the river. It was the most prominent building in the city.

Donald Q. Cannon & Brandon S. Plewe

Nauvoo Temple

In January 1841, Joseph Smith received a revelation (D&C 124) commanding the Saints to build a temple in Nauvoo. The temple, a magnificent edifice for its day, was erected by a people who had very few financial resources. In place of monetary donations, members tithed their time to work on the building. Like the Kirtland Temple (see p. 30), most of the space was dedicated to public Church meetings; endowment and sealing ceremonies were reserved for the attic story. After Joseph's martyrdom (see p. 62), finishing the temple was the primary goal of the Church. It was dedicated even as the Saints were leaving for the West.

The LDS Church has recently reconstructed the original Nauvoo Temple on the original temple site. The new building has the same exterior but an interior in keeping with modern temple designs. The new temple is as much a tourist attraction as a functional building (see p. 136), helping visitors visualize the city of Nauvoo as it once was.

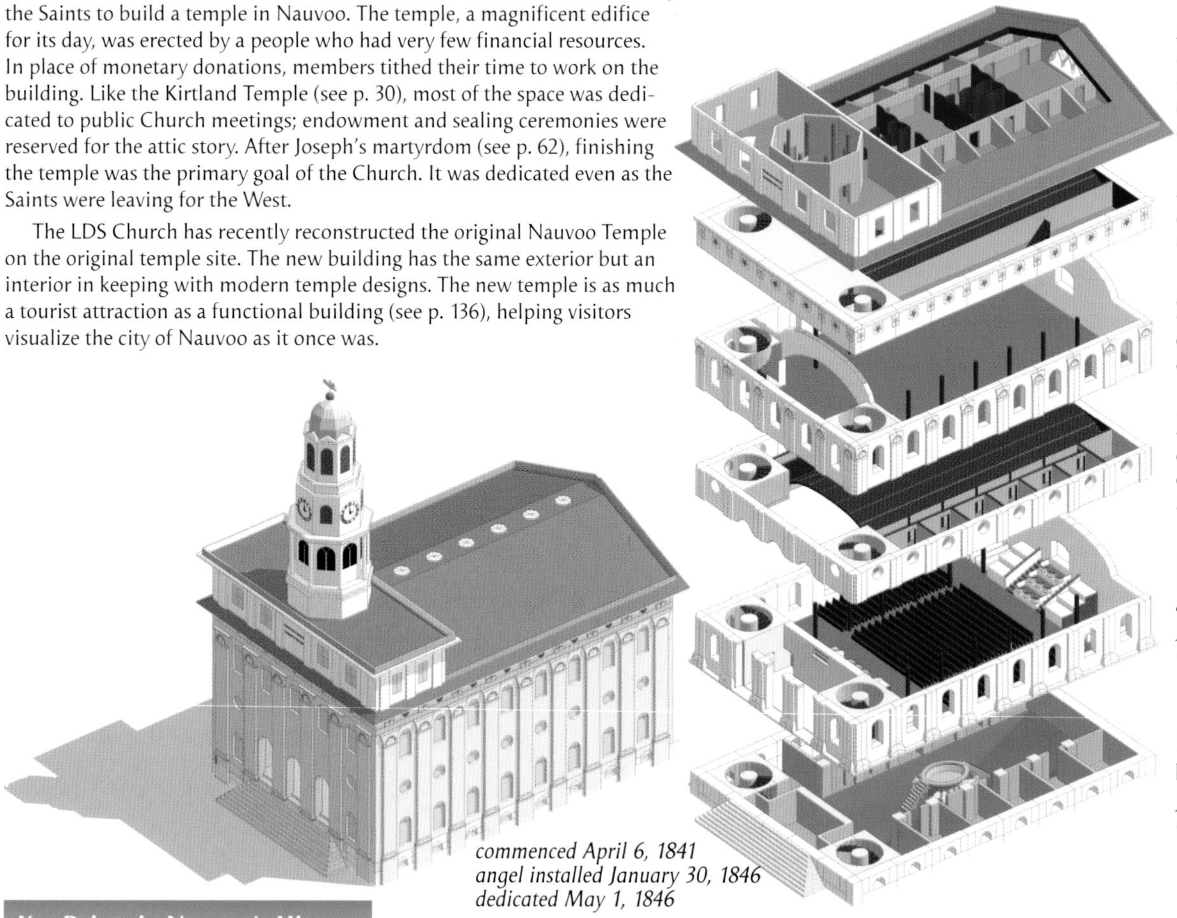

Key Points in Nauvoo's History

- **3 Sep 1839** Nauvoo City Plat
- **Fall 1840** Temple groundbreaking
- **16 Dec 1840** Charter of City of Nauvoo granted by Illinois Legislature
- **18 Nov 1841** Baptisms begun in font in temple basement
- Nauvoo City Charter revoked **24 Jan 1845**
- Nauvoo Temple dedicated **1 May 1846**
- Battle of Nauvoo **10–12 Sep 1846**

1839 | 1840 | 1841 | 1842 | 1843 | 1844 | 1845 | 1846

Nauvoo in 1845

This diorama was constructed for the Nauvoo Visitors' Center (see p. 138) based on extensive research into the settlement of the city. It shows that by the spring of 1845, settlement had spread over almost all of the area that had been platted (see p. 54). Grid streets and homes were even expanding into the rugged (and thus less valuable) terrain in the northern part of the city (to the left in this photograph). The almost-completed temple occupied the most prominent location on the bluff overlooking the Mississippi River. Despite the pressure of thousands of incoming Mormons, the Church never purchased or developed the land of Charles Munson (pictured in the center foreground), although a few families built small cabins along its edges, living as squatters.

Nauvoo Homes

By 1845, Nauvoo may have had as many as 15,000 residents, living in homes ranging from tiny cabins to multistory brick houses. The most valuable land lay around the two commercial centers on lower Main Street and on the bluff behind the temple, and between these two centers. Here lived Nauvoo's prominent residents, including Joseph Smith's inner circle of confidants. These included the Twelve Apostles; the Council of Fifty, a group charged with preparing for the Kingdom of God and the Saints' move west; those who had received the endowment; and those who had entered into plural marriages. Joseph's most trusted aides, his brother Hyrum and nine of the Twelve Apostles, were members of all of these groups.

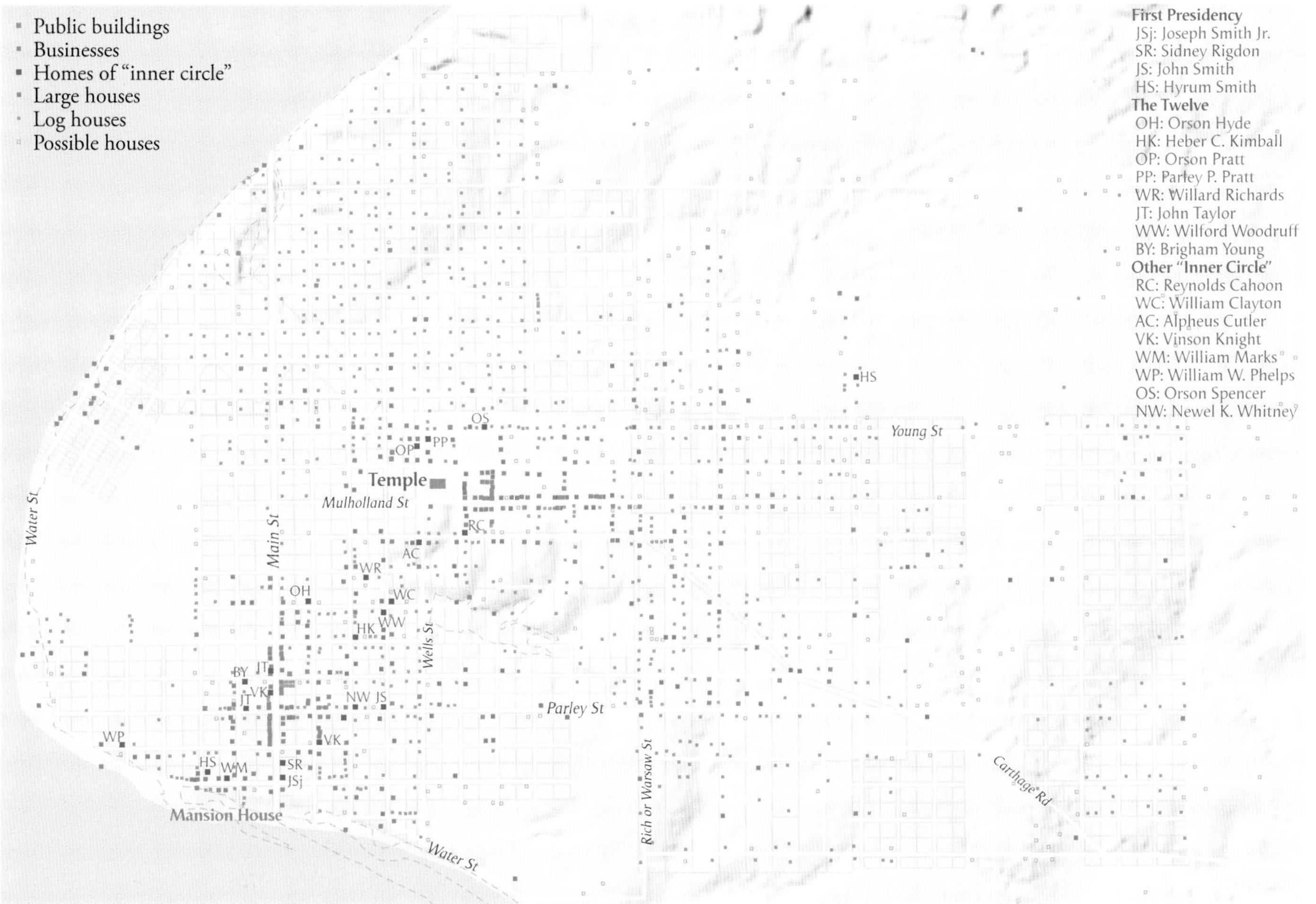

Greater Nauvoo Region

1839–1846

Although Nauvoo was the main settlement of the Mormons in Illinois, it was certainly not the only community founded by the Saints in the Prairie State. In fact, Joseph Smith and his followers established as many as 17 communities in Hancock County besides Nauvoo. Settlements also sprang up across the Mississippi River in Lee County, Iowa.

Joseph Smith referred to these settlements in a meeting in March 1841: "There is a wheel; Nauvoo is the hub; we shall drive the first spoke in Ramus, second in La Harpe, third in Shokoquon, fourth in Lima; the other half of the wheel is over the river." Ramus (also known as Macedonia and renamed Webster after the Mormons left) was the second largest Mormon settlement in Hancock County. It was built on the lands of the Perkins family (who had converted there years before Nauvoo was settled); the family of Joel Johnson also played an important role there. Ramus was large enough to have a stake and a meetinghouse, an unusual practice in the early Church because most meetings were held in homes or outdoors.

The settlements in Lee County composed the Iowa Stake, the most prominent of these being Montrose, built on the site of old Fort Des Moines, where the Mormon refugees from Missouri had gathered in 1839. In the western part of Montrose, Mormons surveyed a new city called Zarahemla, although it is uncertain how much was built before it was abandoned in 1846.

Beyond Lee and Hancock Counties, the Mormons lived in many other settlements in both Iowa and Illinois. Most of them surrounded Quincy, where the 1839 refugees from Missouri had been welcomed and from which the Saints had spread in search of new homes. Some established new settlements such as Lima, but in most cases they moved into existing towns, such as Columbus, Geneva, Pleasant Vale, and Bentonsport. Some of these areas, distant from Nauvoo, became substantial enough for additional stakes to be created.

This entire settlement pattern was very fluid. It grew and contracted and, in most cases, did not constitute a permanent presence of Latter-day Saints. As anti-Mormon persecution and violence increased, Church leaders encouraged members to gather into Nauvoo. As early as 1842, most of these outlying Mormon communities had been abandoned or at least severely depleted.

Donald Q. Cannon & Brandon S. Plewe

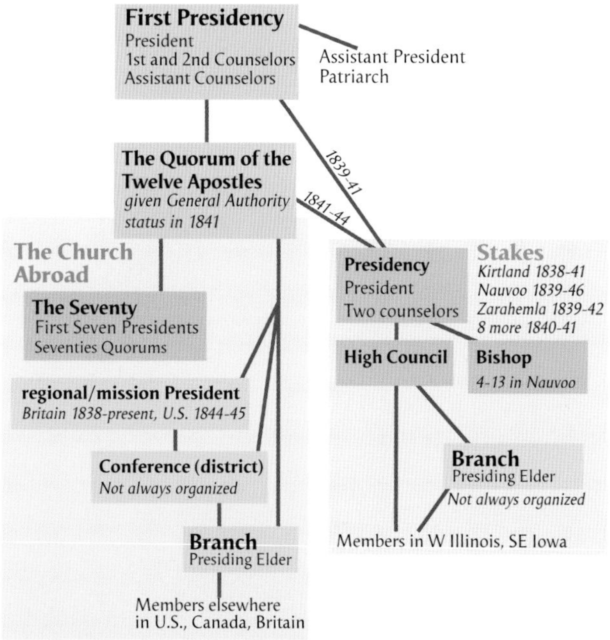

Church Organization in the 1840s

During the Nauvoo era, Joseph Smith made many significant changes to the organization of the Church (compare to the chart on p. 38). Some of these changes resulted from apostasies in Ohio and Missouri. In the First Presidency, Hyrum Smith was added as Assistant President (and presumptive heir) and Patriarch in 1841. Also, in Nauvoo the Quorum of the Twelve played a much greater role in governing the Church than it had previously, due to their success in England (see p. 46) and in orchestrating the exodus from Missouri (see p. 50). Seventies quorums proliferated, with dozens by 1844.

Several stakes were organized, Nauvoo being by far the most important, with a presidency, high council, and, by 1843, 13 bishops (who were still not ecclesiastical leaders over separate congregations but administrators of temporal affairs). Most of the new stakes in this period were not regional groups of congregations as they are today but were merely large branches (200–300 or more members) that had additional leadership in addition to the traditional presiding elder, such as a high council and a bishop. It is even unclear how much jurisdiction the Nauvoo Stake had over surrounding settlements. Only the Iowa Stake (also known as the Zarahemla Stake) has a clear record of jurisdiction over multiple branches. This vague structure evolved gradually until the modern hierarchy of stakes, wards, and branches was standardized in 1877 (see p. 128).

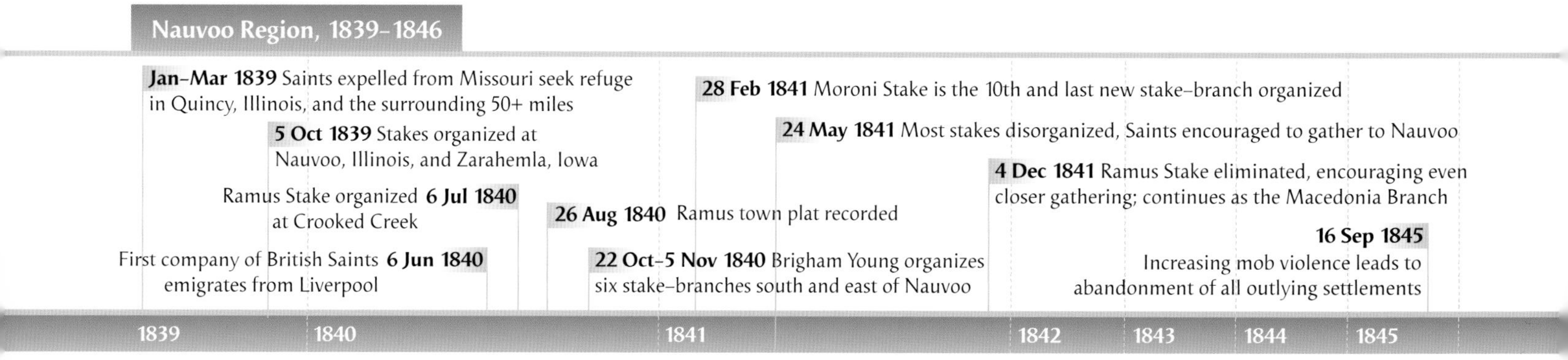

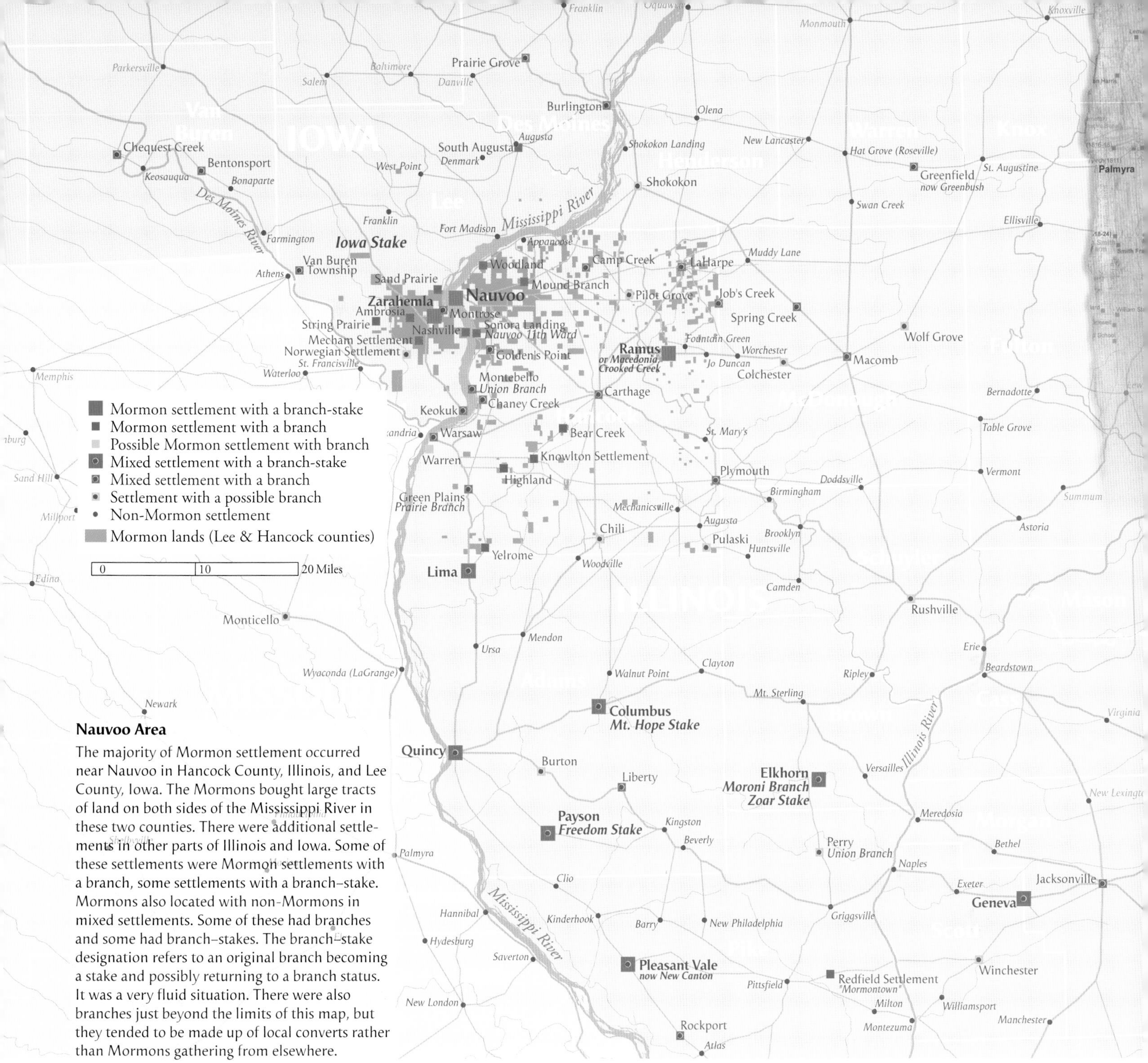

Nauvoo Area

The majority of Mormon settlement occurred near Nauvoo in Hancock County, Illinois, and Lee County, Iowa. The Mormons bought large tracts of land on both sides of the Mississippi River in these two counties. There were additional settlements in other parts of Illinois and Iowa. Some of these settlements were Mormon settlements with a branch, some settlements with a branch–stake. Mormons also located with non-Mormons in mixed settlements. Some of these had branches and some had branch–stakes. The branch–stake designation refers to an original branch becoming a stake and possibly returning to a branch status. It was a very fluid situation. There were also branches just beyond the limits of this map, but they tended to be made up of local converts rather than Mormons gathering from elsewhere.

Lee County Purchases

The southern half of Lee County, Iowa, was called the Half-Breed Tract, because it had been set aside in 1824 for people of mixed white and Native American parentage who were often rejected by both communities. Starting in 1834, the government allowed these people to personally own and sell land, and the area was swamped with speculators, including Isaac Galland. In 1839, the Church (through Bishop Vinson Knight) purchased over 20,000 acres from Galland on generous terms.

Although many Mormons moved to Iowa, including Brigham Young and John Smith, Nauvoo soon surpassed Montrose in size. A persistent issue with developing the Iowa land was dubious title, because Galland and other speculators had often purchased the same land from different natives who did not have clear title themselves. The issue eventually reached the U.S. Supreme Court in 1850; although the Church was not directly involved in the case, the court's decision invalidated all of the Church's claims to ownership.

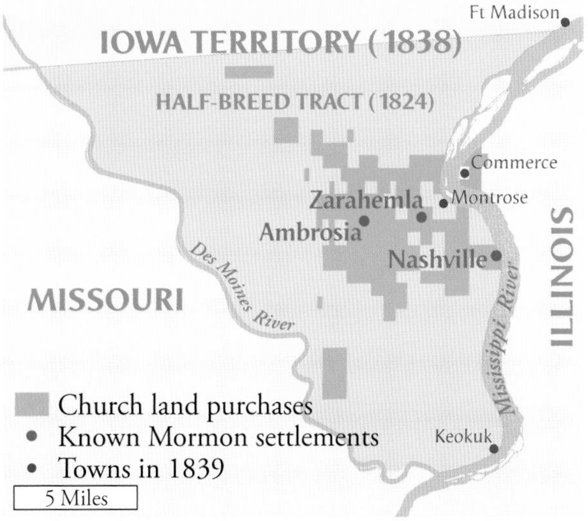

The Church in the Nauvoo Era

1839–1846

Nauvoo, Illinois, faced its share of challenges but was more successful than most frontier boomtowns. The stability and security it provided enabled the Apostles and the Seventy to make frequent missions to the eastern and southern United States, Canada, Britain, and beyond, increasing Church membership rapidly. Almost 750 branches existed sometime between 1839 and 1846.

As converts gathered to Nauvoo (see p. 104) and the surrounding area, its population swelled. Neighbors again became wary of Mormon political and economic power, as well as increasingly unique doctrines such as the rumors of polygamy, leading to the assassination of Joseph and Hyrum Smith and the expulsion most of the Saints. Many of those who remained followed leaders other than Brigham Young and formed alternative Church organizations (see p. 64).

SCOTLAND
IRELAND
ENGLAND
WALES
The greatest concentration of converts was in the boom cities of the Industrial Revolution in the West Midlands, where wealth and poverty both abounded.
In rural Herefordshire, Wilford Woodruff converted dozens of entire congregations of the United Brethren.

During the single year of the Second Apostolic Mission to Britain (1840–41), membership quadrupled to almost 6,000, not including 800 emigrants to America. The 315 British branches that existed during this period were much more concentrated than in the United States, primarily in dense urban areas.

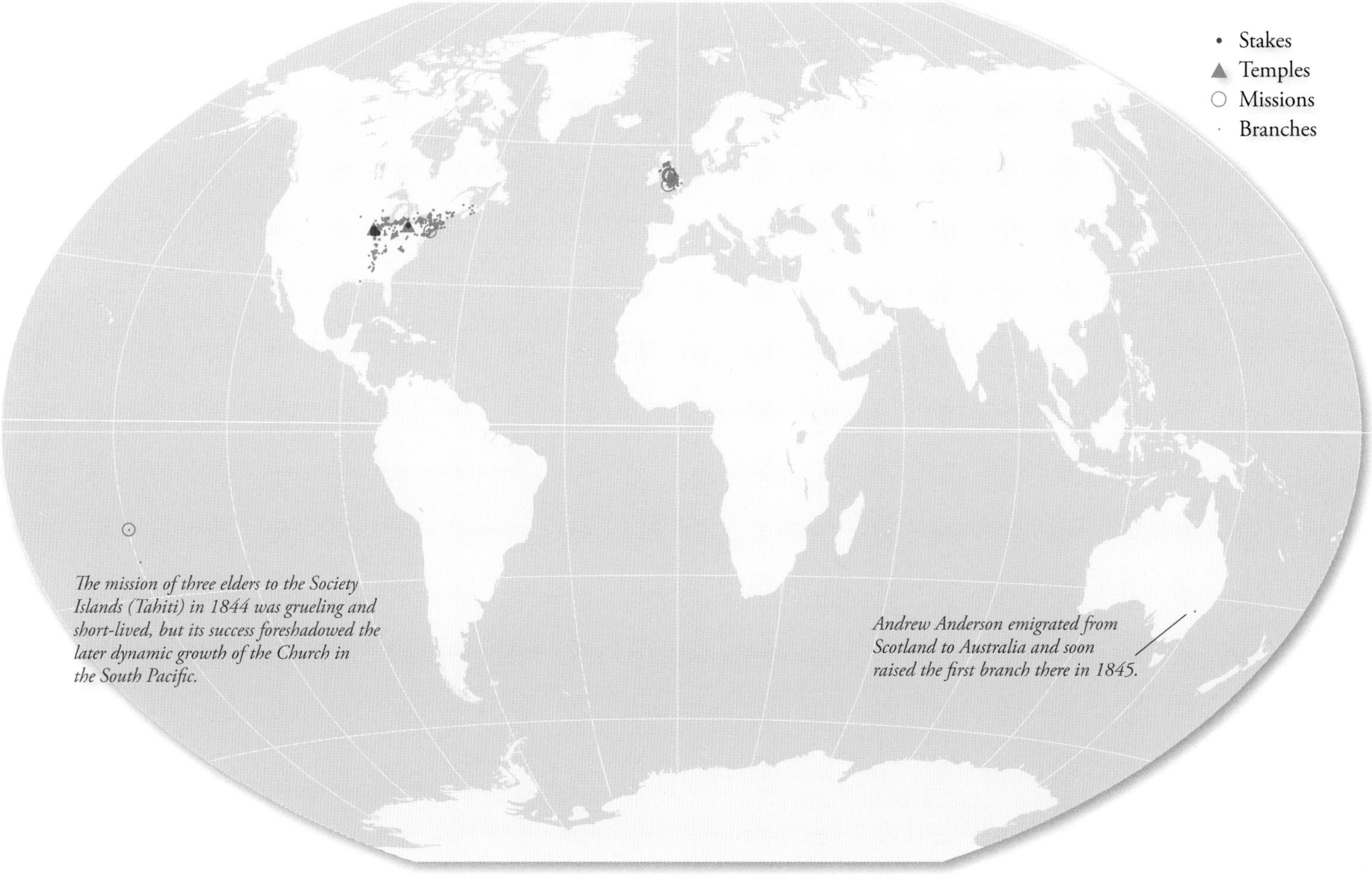
• Stakes
▲ Temples
○ Missions
· Branches
The mission of three elders to the Society Islands (Tahiti) in 1844 was grueling and short-lived, but its success foreshadowed the later dynamic growth of the Church in the South Pacific.
Andrew Anderson emigrated from Scotland to Australia and soon raised the first branch there in 1845.

The scattered branches of the Midwest were largely unaware of the major doctrinal, organizational, and ritual developments in Nauvoo and would later form the nucleus of new churches opposed to the Twelve.
Kirtland
Nauvoo
The 1840s saw a new focus on the large cities of the East Coast. Boston, New York, and Philadelphia each had branches of several hundred members.
Hundreds of loyal members remained in the Kirtland area and even continued to meet in the temple. Easterners gathering to Nauvoo often stayed there.
For a few months in 1840–41, several "stakes" (large branches with a high council) were created beyond Nauvoo, until they were disbanded in a renewed call for gathering.
The Church spread to several clusters in the South, but was still much smaller than in the North.
Stakes
Branches
Temples
Conferences

An increasing missionary force led to widespread conversions; there were probably more than 400 branches across the United States at the time of the Martyrdom. However, most of these were small (10–50 members) and short-lived, quickly depleted by the gathering to Nauvoo.

Note: This map cannot show names and details about each branch, but detailed information can be found on the companion website, mappingmormonism.byu.edu.

Major Events in the Nauvoo Era

Apr 30 Joseph Smith purchases land in Commerce, Illinois

5 Oct Nauvoo Stake organized

1840–41 Apostolic mission to Britain

August First British immigrants arrive in Nauvoo

April Nauvoo Temple construction begins

27 Jun Joseph and Hyrum Smith murdered in Carthage, Illinois

Battle of Nauvoo **10–15 Sep**

Mormons begin to leave Nauvoo **Feb 1846**

1839 | 1840 | 1841 | 1842 | 1843 | 1844 | 1845 | 1846

Conflict in Hancock County

1842–1846

As the number of Latter-day Saints in Hancock County dramatically increased, especially in Nauvoo, other citizens became concerned, believing that Joseph Smith and his followers would soon dominate the region politically, economically, religiously, and socially. Community leaders, including Thomas Sharp, Thomas Gregg, and William Roosevelt, organized the Anti-Mormon Party in 1841 as a political bloc, but in time they turned to violence to drive Joseph Smith and the Mormons from the state.

A number of events exacerbated the sour relations between the Illinois Mormons and their neighbors, including Missouri's repeated attempts to extradite Joseph Smith, rumors of plural marriage, and Smith's declaration of candidacy for president of the United States. However, the destruction of the *Nauvoo Expositor* press was the final straw. Despite personal efforts by the governor to impose justice on both sides, a local mob killed Joseph and Hyrum Smith in the Carthage Jail on June 27, 1844.

Following the Martyrdom, as this seminal event became known, an uneasy truce lasted for over a year, but in the autumn of 1845, the anti-Mormons stepped up their use of intimidation and violence against the Latter-day Saints. They burned Mormon homes and outbuildings, as well as crops in areas outside of Nauvoo, all in an effort to cause the evacuation of all Latter-day Saints from Illinois. In the end they were successful, and on October 1, 1845, Brigham Young announced that he and his people would leave Nauvoo in the spring of 1846 and resettle in the West. Government officials won assurances that the Anti-Mormon Party would restrain and withhold further violence and permit the Mormons to depart in peace.

There was comparative peace as thousands of Saints crossed the Mississippi River into Iowa during the late winter and spring of 1846 while finishing and dedicating the temple (see p. 72). However, the pace was not enough for the Anti-Mormons, and in the fall of 1846 the few Mormons remaining in Nauvoo, most of whom were poor, old, or sick, were driven from the city in what is called the Battle of Nauvoo. With the departure of these last Latter-day Saint refugees, the Anti-Mormon Party met on January 9, 1847, and discussed building a monument that would immortalize non-Mormon deeds and be a fitting tribute to the "six brave men who had lost their lives" in what historian Annette P. Hampshire called "The Triumph of Mobocracy." The monument never became a reality. Perhaps the fact that, as a *Burlington Hawk Eye* reporter wrote of Nauvoo, "No fair hand was there and no breath was heard save the rustling zephirs of heaven," was monument enough.

Kenneth W. Godfrey

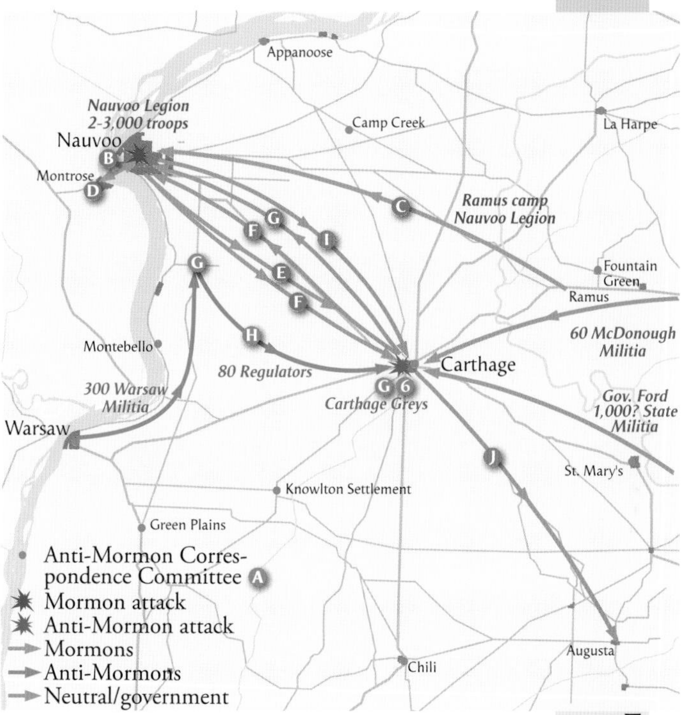

Appanoose
Nauvoo Legion 2-3,000 troops
Nauvoo
Montrose
Camp Creek
La Harpe
Ramus camp Nauvoo Legion
Fountain Green
Ramus
60 McDonough Militia
Montebello
80 Regulators
Carthage
300 Warsaw Militia
Carthage Greys
Gov. Ford 1,000? State Militia
Warsaw
St. Mary's
Knowlton Settlement
Green Plains
Augusta
Chili
Anti-Mormon Correspondence Committee
Mormon attack
Anti-Mormon attack
Mormons
Anti-Mormons
Neutral/government

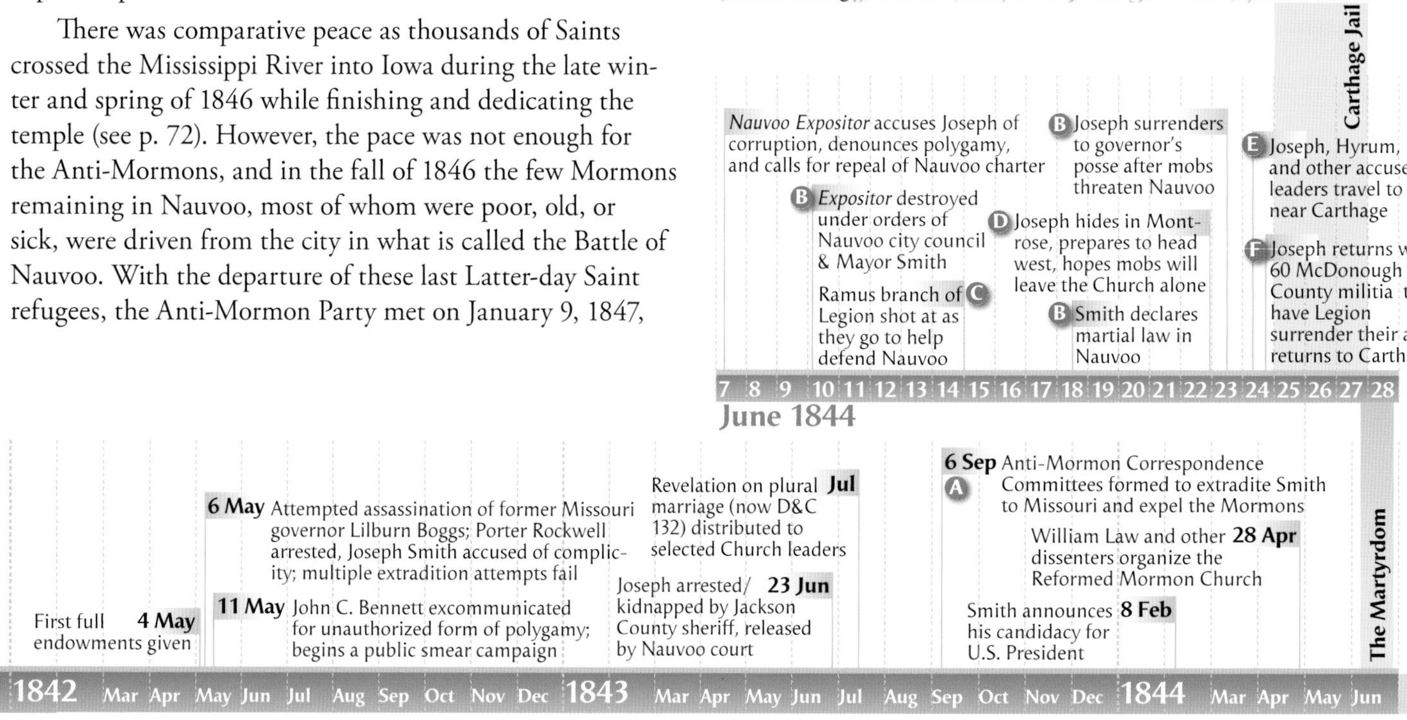

Carthage Jail
Nauvoo Expositor accuses Joseph of corruption, denounces polygamy, and calls for repeal of Nauvoo charter
B Joseph surrenders to governor's posse after mobs threaten Nauvoo
E Joseph, Hyrum, and other accused leaders travel to near Carthage
B *Expositor* destroyed under orders of Nauvoo city council & Mayor Smith
D Joseph hides in Montrose, prepares to head west, hopes mobs will leave the Church alone
F Joseph returns with 60 McDonough County militia to have Legion surrender their arms; returns to Carthage
Ramus branch of Legion shot at as they go to help defend Nauvoo C
B Smith declares martial law in Nauvoo
7 8 9 10 11 12 13 14 15 16 17 18 19 20 21 22 23 24 25 26 27 28
June 1844
6 Sep Anti-Mormon Correspondence Committees formed to extradite Smith to Missouri and expel the Mormons A
Revelation on plural marriage (now D&C 132) distributed to selected Church leaders Jul
6 May Attempted assassination of former Missouri governor Lilburn Boggs; Porter Rockwell arrested, Joseph Smith accused of complicity; multiple extradition attempts fail
William Law and other dissenters organize the Reformed Mormon Church 28 Apr
Joseph arrested/ kidnapped by Jackson County sheriff, released by Nauvoo court 23 Jun
11 May John C. Bennett excommunicated for unauthorized form of polygamy; begins a public smear campaign
First full endowments given 4 May
Smith announces his candidacy for U.S. President 8 Feb
The Martyrdom
1842 Mar Apr May Jun Jul Aug Sep Oct Nov Dec 1843 Mar Apr May Jun Jul Aug Sep Oct Nov Dec 1844 Mar Apr May Jun

5:12 Men charge past jail guards and climb the stairs; finding the dungeon
4 empty, attack the bedroom; others remain outside, shooting at the windows

5:13 Hyrum killed by a shot to the face

5:14 While Joseph and Richards hold the door, John Taylor goes to the window,
5 is shot four times, rolls under the bed

5:15 While Richards knocks down gun barrels through the door with his cane,
6 Joseph runs to the window; shot several times from behind and below; falls through the window, dying within moments

7 Mob rushes outside to see Joseph

8 Richards, uninjured, hides with John Taylor in the dungeon room

9 Mob returns, but someone yells "the Mormons are coming!" and disperses before finding survivors

Mob gathers at edge of town **4:30 pm**

4 pm treason hearing adjourned to next day

Mormon company stays with Governor Ford in hotel

2 Return to dungeon room for protection

10 am Governor parades Joseph and Hyrum before militia

3 Move to jailor's bedroom for comfort

4 pm Hearing on riot charge; defendants released on bail until the 29th

Joseph & Hyrum arrested for treason due to Nauvoo martial law

1 Stay in debtor's cell of jail

5 am Three of Joseph's companions depart, leaving Joseph, Hyrum, John Taylor, and Willard Richards

G Ford disbands militias, including Thomas Sharp's militia; leads company of dragoons to defend and pacify Nauvoo

H Sharp leads "disbanded" Warsaw regulators to Carthage

6:30 Ford returns to Carthage
I

12:00 Fearing Mormon attack,
J Ford and most Carthage residents flee to south

Tues June 25 | Wed June 26 | Thu June 27

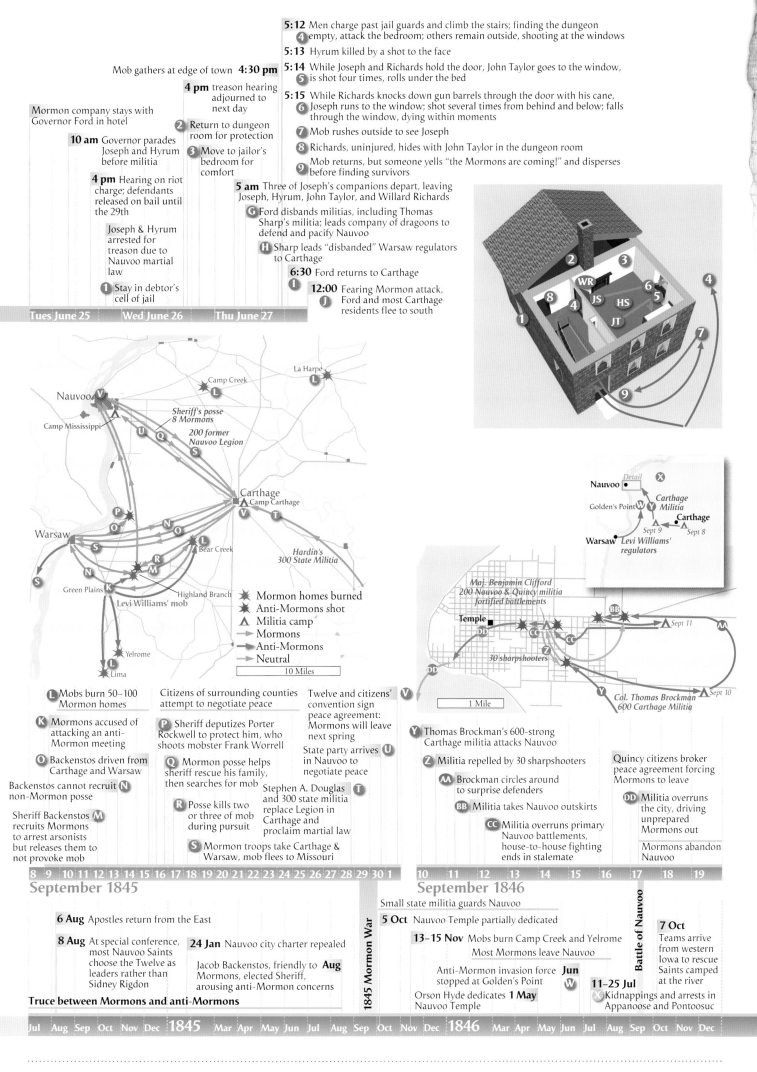

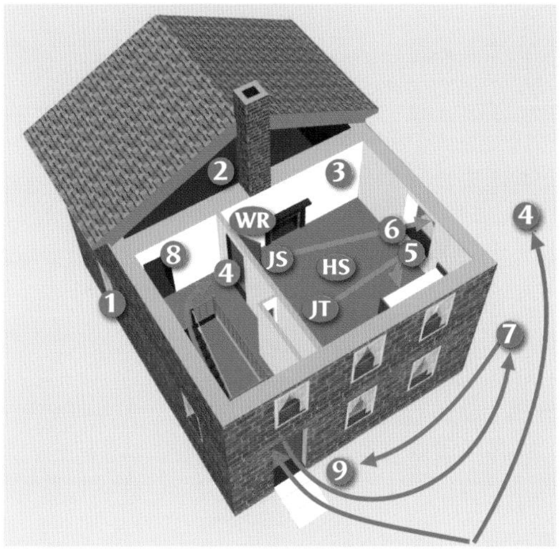

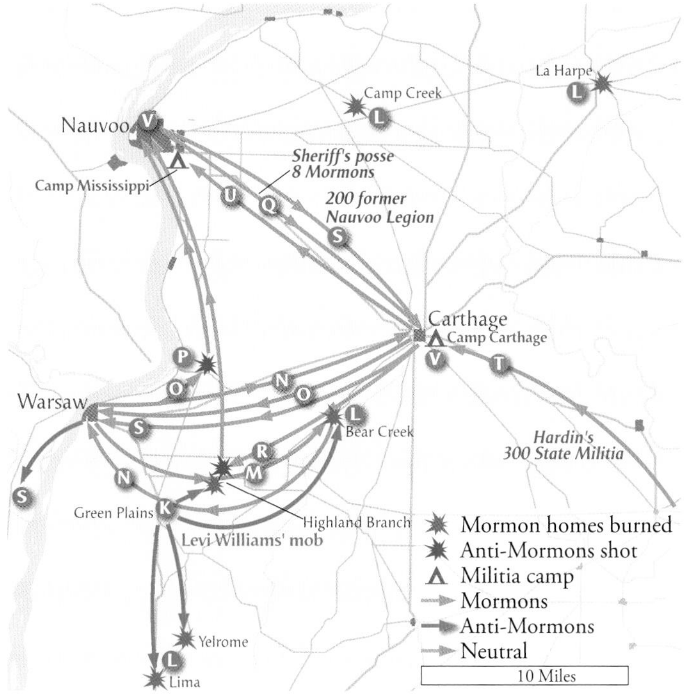

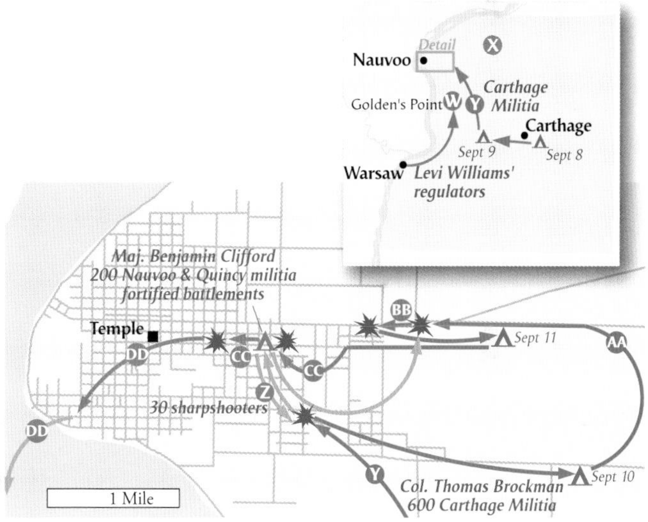

L Mobs burn 50–100 Mormon homes

K Mormons accused of attacking an anti-Mormon meeting

O Backenstos driven from Carthage and Warsaw

Backenstos cannot recruit N non-Mormon posse

Sheriff Backenstos M recruits Mormons to arrest arsonists but releases them to not provoke mob

Citizens of surrounding counties attempt to negotiate peace

P Sheriff deputizes Porter Rockwell to protect him, who shoots mobster Frank Worrell

Q Mormon posse helps sheriff rescue his family, then searches for mob

R Posse kills two or three of mob during pursuit

S Mormon troops take Carthage & Warsaw, mob flees to Missouri

Twelve and citizens' V convention sign peace agreement: Mormons will leave next spring

State party arrives U in Nauvoo to negotiate peace

Stephen A. Douglas T and 300 state militia replace Legion in Carthage and proclaim martial law

Y Thomas Brockman's 600-strong Carthage militia attacks Nauvoo

Z Militia repelled by 30 sharpshooters

AA Brockman circles around to surprise defenders

BB Militia takes Nauvoo outskirts

CC Militia overruns primary Nauvoo battlements, house-to-house fighting ends in stalemate

Quincy citizens broker peace agreement forcing Mormons to leave

DD Militia overruns the city, driving unprepared Mormons out

Mormons abandon Nauvoo

8 9 10 11 12 13 14 15 16 17 18 19 20 21 22 23 24 25 26 27 28 29 30 1 | 10 11 12 13 14 15 16 17 18 19

September 1845 | September 1846

6 Aug Apostles return from the East

8 Aug At special conference, most Nauvoo Saints choose the Twelve as leaders rather than Sidney Rigdon

24 Jan Nauvoo city charter repealed

Jacob Backenstos, friendly to **Aug** Mormons, elected Sheriff, arousing anti-Mormon concerns

Truce between Mormons and anti-Mormons

1845 Mormon War

Small state militia guards Nauvoo

5 Oct Nauvoo Temple partially dedicated

13–15 Nov Mobs burn Camp Creek and Yelrome

Most Mormons leave Nauvoo

Anti-Mormon invasion force **Jun** stopped at Golden's Point W

Orson Hyde dedicates **1 May** Nauvoo Temple

Battle of Nauvoo

7 Oct Teams arrive from western Iowa to rescue Saints camped at the river

11–25 Jul
X Kidnappings and arrests in Appanoose and Pontoosuc

Jul Aug Sep Oct Nov Dec **1845** Mar Apr May Jun Jul Aug Sep Oct Nov Dec **1846** Mar Apr May Jun Jul Aug Sep Oct Nov Dec

The Succession Crisis

1844–1865

Joseph Smith's supporters during his lifetime vastly outnumbered any of the detractors who tried to challenge his leadership and prophetic role. There were challenges to Smith's authority during his lifetime, but most quickly evaporated, and those that survived his death pale in comparison to what happened in the summer of 1844. After he died, his supporters became fragmented over the dual issues of administrative and prophetic succession. Some who supported Smith in life now wrestled for control over the Church he founded and contended against each other for prominence.

At an emergency August 1844 conference at Nauvoo, Brigham Young urged the Church to sustain the Twelve Apostles as an interim "second presidency" with Sidney Rigdon as a counselor to that presidency. Rigdon argued that as the remaining member of the First Presidency he should succeed as President or act as a "guardian" for the Church. Both of the arguments had merit, but those present voted for Young's plan. Rigdon rejected this action and began to gather his own adherents, especially after he left Nauvoo and traveled among the branches.

The third major early faction was led by James Strang, who emerged about the same time but was not part of the special conference. His claim of angelic visitation and new scripture, his personal charisma, and his dynamic missionary force attracted many members who saw a similarity to Joseph. At one time, he may have drawn half of the members in the United States, but his church gradually dissipated as he made doctrinal changes, declared himself king, and was eventually murdered; one or two hundred members remain loyal to this day.

Other groups followed leaders who either claimed spiritual manifestations, membership in Joseph's inner circle (e.g., the Council of Fifty), or the backing of a major leader, such as Apostles John E. Page or William Smith. As the years passed, many of the emergent denominations dissipated as members (including Page and Smith) became disappointed with the new prophets and looked elsewhere for leadership. Many of these disillusioned Saints eventually coalesced around the idea of "young Joseph," Joseph Smith's eldest son, being a literal heir to his father's mantle. The leaders of their New Organization were successful in uniting many of the branches in the Midwest, especially when young Joseph himself joined late in 1859. This formed the basis for the

continued on page 66

Minor Succession Churches

In addition to the major movements shown at right, a variety of fragments of the original Church emerged in various parts of the United States in the years following Joseph Smith's death. Some churches tried to preserve the memory of Joseph and the complete doctrine he revealed (as they interpreted it), such as Alpheus Cutler. Some proclaimed Joseph a fallen prophet and aimed to return the Church to its pre-Nauvoo "purity," such as those following David Whitmer, Granville Hedrick, Sidney Rigdon, and William McLellin. Others gradually became less and less "Mormon," as new doctrines were proclaimed by the candidate prophet, such as Charles B. Thompson, Francis Gladden Bishop, and James Colin Brewster.

Some of these movements were able to attract hundreds of followers for short periods of time, but none had the lasting power of the major successor churches.

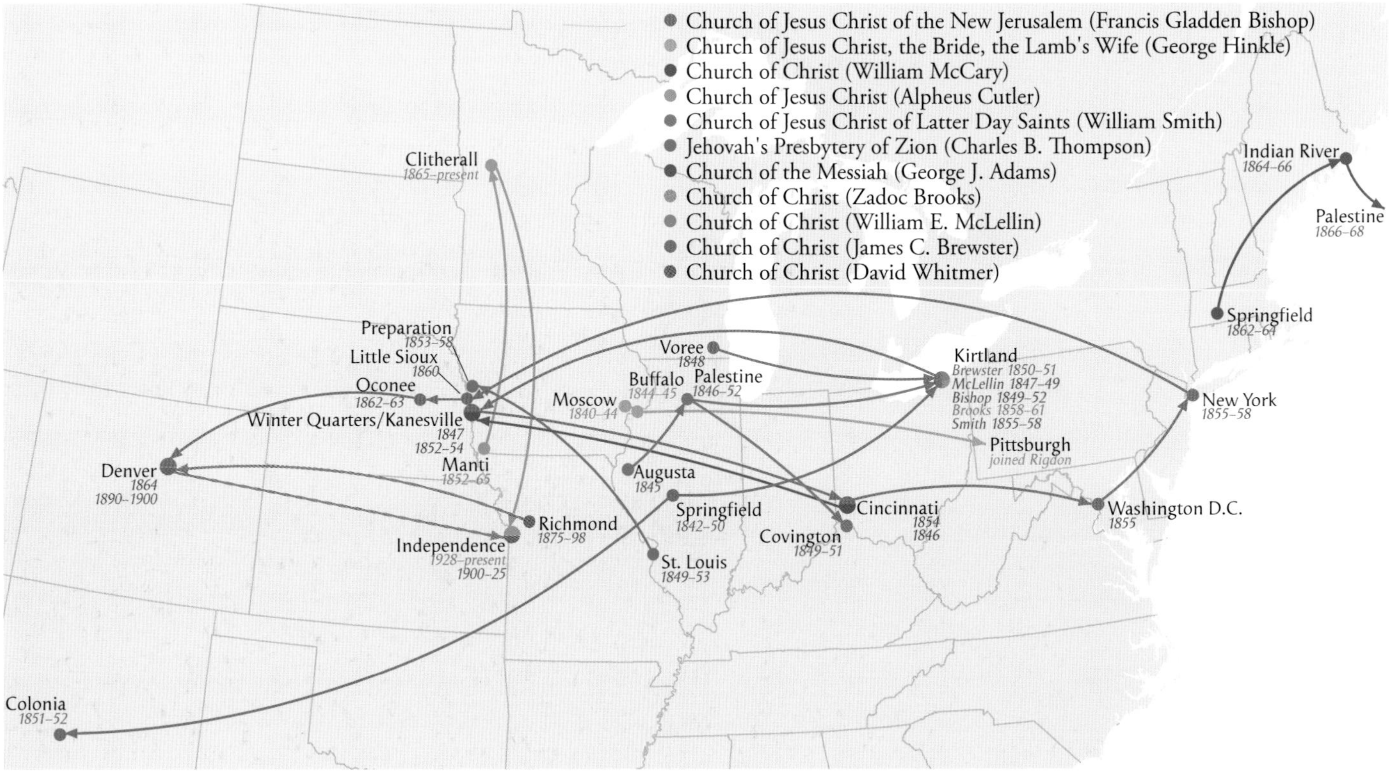

The Church of Jesus Christ of Latter-day Saints

Brigham Young, 8 Apostles

Membership:
1850: 20,000?
2010: 14,000,000

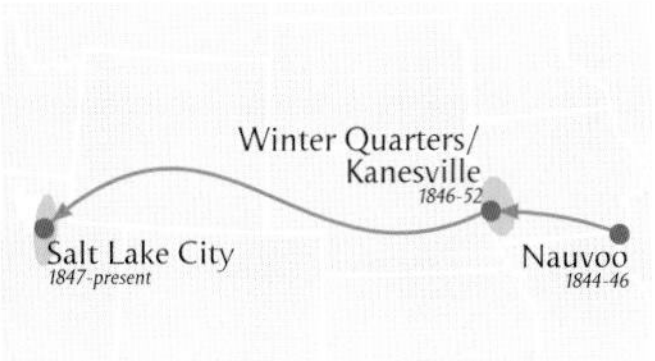

colored areas were major concentrations in 1850

At the emergency August 1844 conference at Nauvoo, Brigham Young convinced most Nauvoo residents that the Twelve Apostles should lead the Church rather than have a new prophet immediately. In 1847, Young reorganized the First Presidency, with himself as president. His followers included most of the residents of Nauvoo, about half of the members in the rest of the United States, and virtually all of the British church. This was the only major successor church that accepted the new doctrines and practices introduced by Joseph Smith before he was killed (and the only one that claims that he did introduce them), including temple ceremonies, baptism for the dead, and polygamy, and was the only church to adopt the British spelling of "Latter-day" instead of "Latter Day."

Community of Christ (formerly Reorganized Church of Jesus Christ of Latter Day Saints)

Jason Briggs, Zenas Gurley, Joseph Smith III

Membership:
1861: 400?
2010: 250,000

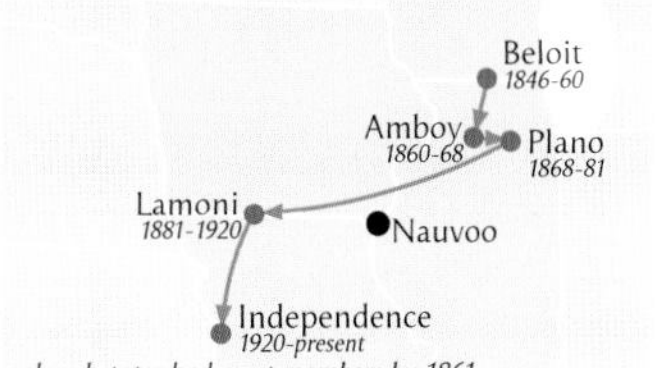

colored states had most members by 1861

Jason Briggs led a nucleus of branches in southern Wisconsin at the time of the Martyrdom, which were soon joined by Zenas Gurley, another local leader. After breaking with Strang in 1850, and believing that Joseph had ordained his son to be heir, they formed the "New Organization" and began to encourage "Young Joseph" to continue his father's work. Joseph III was ordained in 1860 as president of the Church of Jesus Christ of Latter Day Saints ("Reorganized" was added in the 1870s for clarification). Soon, they had gathered most of the midwestern Saints opposed to Brigham Young and polygamy. In 2001 the denomination adopted the name Community of Christ (see p. 192).

Church of Jesus Christ of Latter Day Saints

James J. Strang

Membership:
1850: 4,000–6,000?
2010: 100–300?

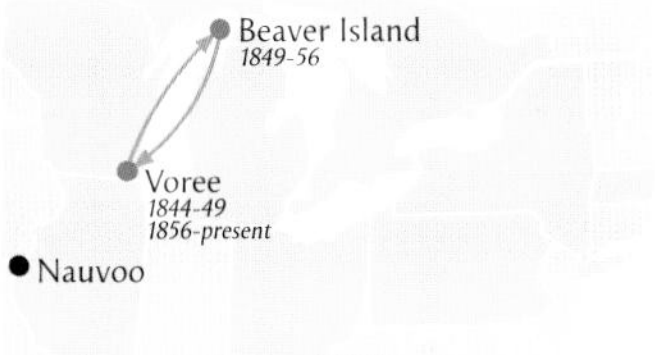

colored states had at least 100 followers

Almost immediately after the Martyrdom, Strang, a recent convert, was proclaiming an appointment by Joseph Smith as heir, an angelic ordination, and new scripture. Many members who wondered whom to follow saw similarities to Joseph, bolstered by Strang's personal charisma and a dynamic missionary force. At one time, he may have drawn half of the U.S. members, but his Church gradually dissipated as he made doctrinal changes (such as practicing polygamy after initially rejecting it), declared himself king, and was eventually murdered. One or two hundred members remain loyal to this day, divided between an incorporated Church and independent adherents.

Church of Christ

Granville Hedrick, John E. Page

Membership:
1867: 100?
2010: 9,000

No known picture

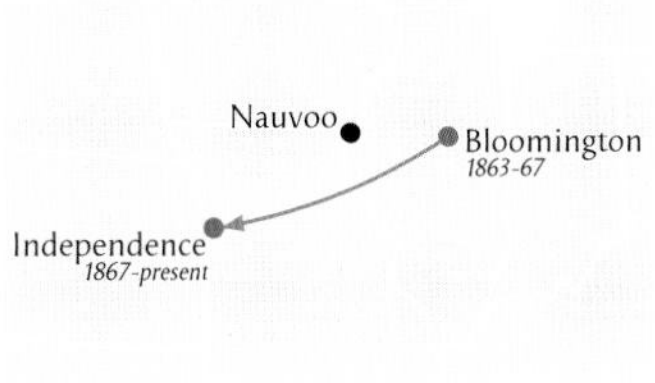

Hedrick was an elder who led several branches in central Illinois following the death of Joseph Smith. They considered affiliation with various leaders but rejected them all. After attracting Apostle John E. Page, the Church of Christ was formally reorganized in 1863 with Hedrick as "President of the High Priesthood." The Church moved to Independence in 1867 (the first to return to Missouri), purchasing the original site of the temple (leading to their nickname "the Temple Lot Church").

Church of Christ (1844–47)
Church of Jesus Christ of the Children of Zion (1863–1884)

Sidney Rigdon

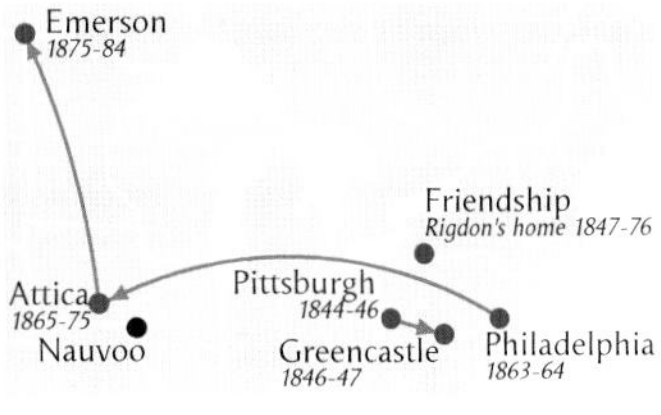

At the August 1844 conference, Sidney Rigdon, as the only remaining member of the First Presidency, argued that he should be a caretaker for the Church until a new prophet emerged. Rigdon organized his followers in 1844, headquartered at Pittsburgh, Pennsylvania, adopting the original name, Church of Christ. After a failed attempt to create a utopian community in 1847, the Church fell apart but was revived in the early 1860s by the encouragement of some of his loyal followers. After gathering to a new community in Canada (without Rigdon), by 1884 most of the remaining members had joined with the Community of Christ.

Church of Jesus Christ

William Bickerton

Membership:
1867: 300?
2010: 12,500

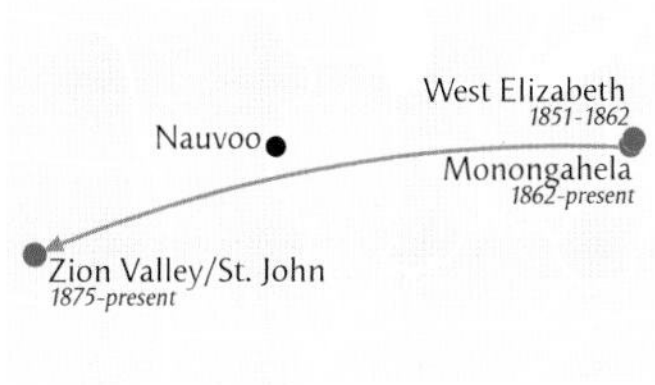

Bickerton, an immigrant, was baptized in Sidney Rigdon's church in 1845. After its demise, he briefly joined Brigham Young's church, but left when plural marriage was publicly announced in 1852. After a visionary experience, Bickerton was ordained as president and prophet of the Church of Jesus Christ in 1861 in Pennsylvania. Eventually rejecting most of the later teachings of Joseph Smith but believing strongly in the call to preach to the Lamanites, he eventually founded a new community in Kansas to be a base for missions to the Native Americans. The Church of Jesus Christ has a presence in the United States and in dozens of nations around the world.

Church of Jesus Christ of Latter Day Saints

Lyman Wight

Membership:
1858: about 100

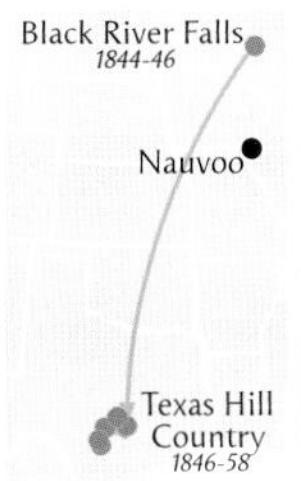

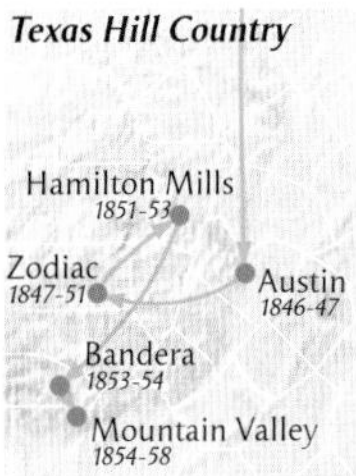

Wight was ordained an Apostle in 1841 and was leading the timber harvesting mission in Wisconsin at the time of the Martyrdom. The rest of the Twelve hesitantly permitted him to lead the Wisconsin colony to Texas (see p. 68), but he never reconciled with Brigham Young's leadership and was dropped from the Twelve in 1848. Although never considering himself a prophet, he eventually organized a separate church that accepted the temple ceremonies, including plural marriage, and built their own temple in 1850. Although briefly aligned with William Smith, a complete union of their churches was never realized. He died unexpectedly in 1858 while on a mission to Native Americans in southern Texas. Most of his followers joined the Reorganized Church after his death.

The Succession Crisis

continued

Reorganized Church of Jesus Christ of Latter Day Saints, now the Community of Christ.

Initially numbering more than a dozen, by the time the fragmentation period came to a conclusion in the early 1860s, there were two primary denominations and a few small ones, whose styles of organization and basic tenets represented different aspects of the original Church. Why did this division occur, and why were some factions more successful than others?

One reason for the schism is that Joseph Smith Jr. had demonstrated that one could be a disciple of Jesus Christ and run a growing church without a highly educated clergy. Anyone, regardless of age or circumstance, could access the heavens and hear the voice of God. These ideas contributed to the schismatic tendencies within the religious movement Smith founded by giving many of his followers the confidence that they could lead in his stead.

Smith himself appears to have suggested at least eight succession possibilities during his lifetime, such as Oliver Cowdery and Hyrum Smith (Assistant Presidents), David Whitmer (ordained a president of the Church in Missouri in 1834), the Twelve Apostles (his closest advisors in 1844), and his young son Joseph.

Another reason was that there were, in effect, three different churches: the Nauvoo Stake, the scattered branches throughout the United States and Canada, and the British Mission; each consisted of roughly a third of the 30,000 members in 1844. Nauvoo had the largest concentration of members, including the leadership. There Joseph introduced new doctrines, temple ceremonies, the Council of Fifty, and plural marriage, often to only a select few who he felt were prepared for the innovations (including the Apostles). The branches were largely unaware of these new developments, except what little was published in the *Times and Seasons* and frequent rumors that gave them a negative slant. They were thus largely living in the Church of the Kirtland–Missouri period. The result was that most at Nauvoo supported Brigham Young's continuance of these practices, while the majority of the members in the outlying branches supported other alternatives, often attributing the changes to Young himself. They were joined by several from Nauvoo (including a few leaders) who were well aware of, but opposed to, the new doctrines. Britain was in a similar state to the branches, except that they were very loyal to the Twelve, who had personally converted most of them.

The groups that were able to survive and thrive were those that could mobilize resources and build a strong administrative structure. Brigham Young and the eight members of the Twelve loyal to him had control of the Church newspaper, the temple, and other assets. Strang was able to very quickly build a force of missionaries to garner support in the branches, and he coalesced a group of leaders personally opposed to Young. Only when these leaders left Strang did his movement decline. In turn, Jason Briggs and Zenas Gurley were able to effectively build a grassroots movement in the midwestern branches that would lead to the New Organization.

Rivalry and animosity between the surviving churches over the matter of succession lasted throughout the nineteenth and twentieth centuries, although recently there has been a civil dialogue between them. Those who gathered in Nauvoo during the summer of 1844 were all believers but not uniform in their thinking. They remained faithful, to the best of their understanding, to the work of Joseph Smith Jr. but did so in a vast array of expressions and experiences.

Steven L. Shields

Voree, now on the western outskirts of Burlington, Wisconsin, was established in 1844 by James J. Strang as a gathering place for his followers. Strang said that the name meant "garden of peace." Between 1844 and 1850, hundreds or even thousands lived here, building homes and businesses with stone from their own quarry, including the house shown here in which the church newspaper, the *Voree Herald*, was printed. A temple was even begun, but when dissension and poverty threatened the settlement in 1850, Strang created a new gathering place on Beaver Island in Lake Michigan. After being shot by dissidents in June 1856, he returned to Voree, dying weeks later in this house. After most of his followers left, the town was largely abandoned, and very few buildings have survived to the present.

Joseph Smith's leadership was challenged a few times during his life, but when he died, the Church fragmented, with many members seeking the legitimate successor to their beloved Prophet. Many candidates vied for followers, some from the existing leadership, some from the rank and file. Most churches soon evaporated or merged into a few major groups.

Most of the leaders of the Church in 1844 followed Brigham Young, while others searched for years for a spiritual home. In addition, many leaders who had left the Church years earlier saw an opportunity to renew their Mormon beliefs, especially in "primitive" movements that returned to the doctrine and practices of the Kirtland or even New York eras.

Divergent Paths of the Restoration

- – – Unorganized following
- —— Organized church
- ● Date of church organization
- ······ Schism to/from another church
- —— Claim as authorized successor

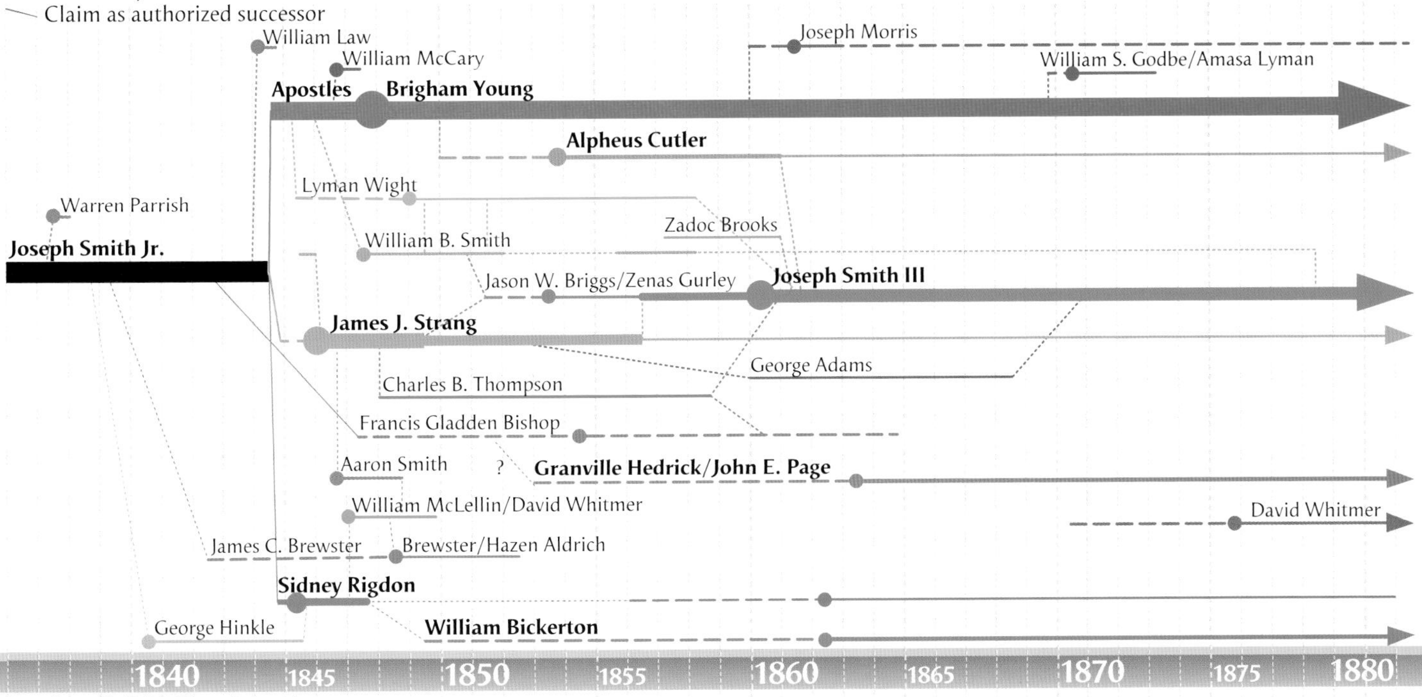

Destiny of 1844 Church Leaders

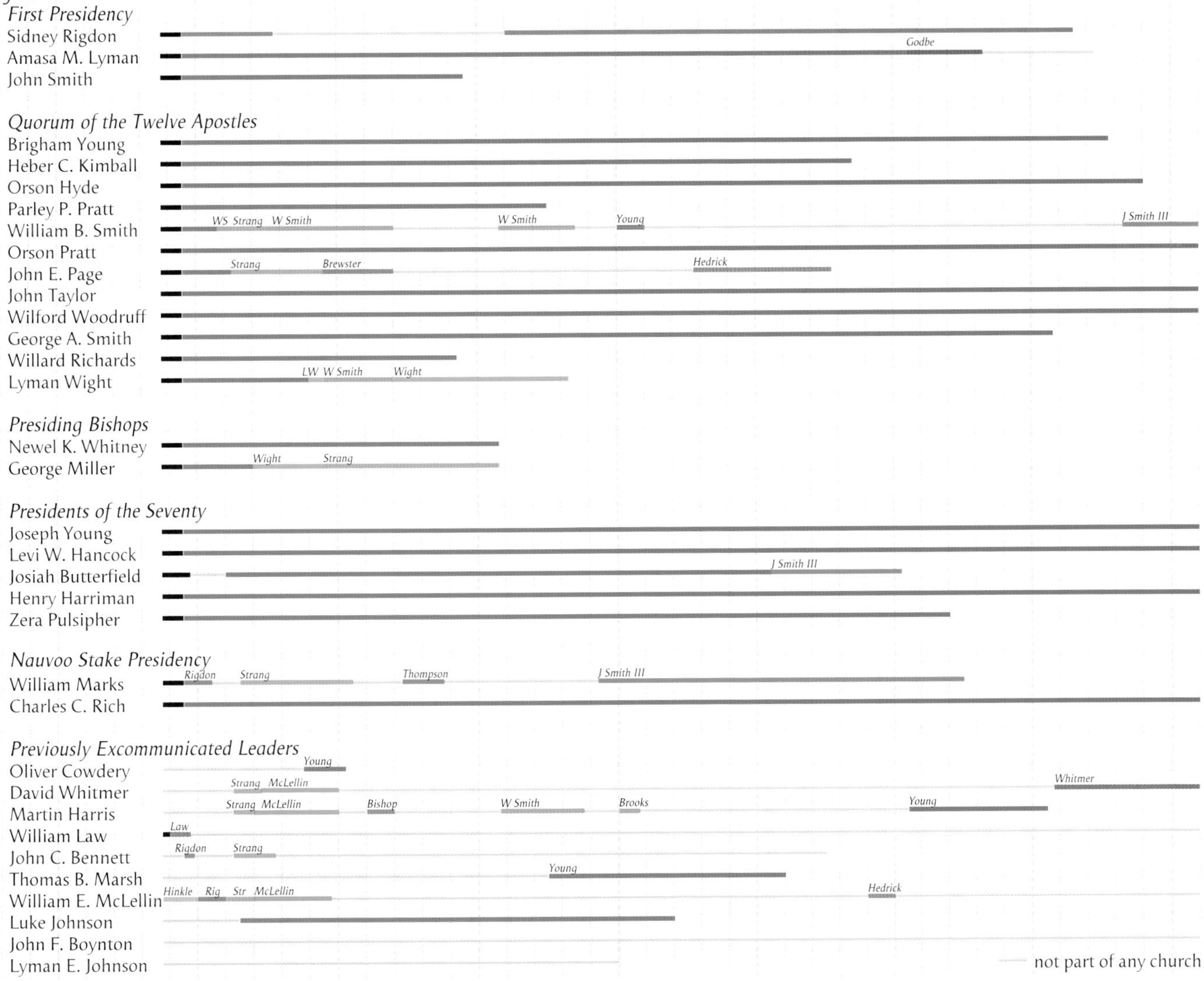

Planning the Exodus

1842–1846

CHURCH MEMBERS SOMETIMES ASSUME that the Saints crossed the plains in 1847 with only a vague idea of where they were going. However, they were completing a journey that had been thoroughly planned for many years.

By the early 1840s, the American West attracted Joseph Smith as a permanent place of refuge for his people and for proselytizing among Native Americans. News buzzed about Upper California, Oregon, New Mexico, and the new Republic of Texas, areas the United States wanted to acquire. In early 1842, Church leaders discussed finding a Rocky Mountain refuge, and Joseph Smith proposed the "Great Western Measure" to investigate unoccupied western locations for a homeland. He created a Council of Fifty to lead the secular affairs of the Saints, including oversight of the planning of possible migrations. In early 1844 he declared the whole western hemisphere was Zion, and he invited friends to form companies to find suitable settlement sites.

After Joseph's death that June, the Twelve set their priorities to first finish the temple, then find a new gathering place in the West. James Emmett and Lyman Wight, zealous council members, led companies to resettle in Dakota and Texas, respectively. Both claimed prior authority from Joseph, and rejected the Twelve's request to be patient. Emmett's company eventually rejoined the main body of the Saints at Council Bluffs, but Wight's followers eventually left the Church altogether, with only a few returning later.

During meetings in March and April 1845, the Twelve and the Council of Fifty discussed ways to explore the West, particularly Upper California. In April, Elder John Taylor wrote a song: "Upper California! O! That's the land for me." That spring, Oneida Nation convert Lewis Dana and others met with tribes in the middle Missouri River region, gaining approvals for Mormon settlements among them. The Council studied all of the maps, guides, and reports they could find. In one plan they called for 300 men and families to go on a western expedition in spring 1846, then changed the number to perhaps 1,500 men without families, including the Twelve, then favored total evacuation from Nauvoo and vicinity. In October 1845, Brigham Young told Illinois Governor Thomas Ford the Saints probably would resettle at Vancouver Island in British North America (Canada), likely a ruse to obscure the intended Upper California destination (which included today's Utah).

Alternative settlement locations were still being considered as Brigham Young crossed Iowa in 1846, but by the summer of 1846, Church leaders were clearly in agreement that the new home of the Church would be the valleys at the base of the Wasatch Mountains.

William G. Hartley

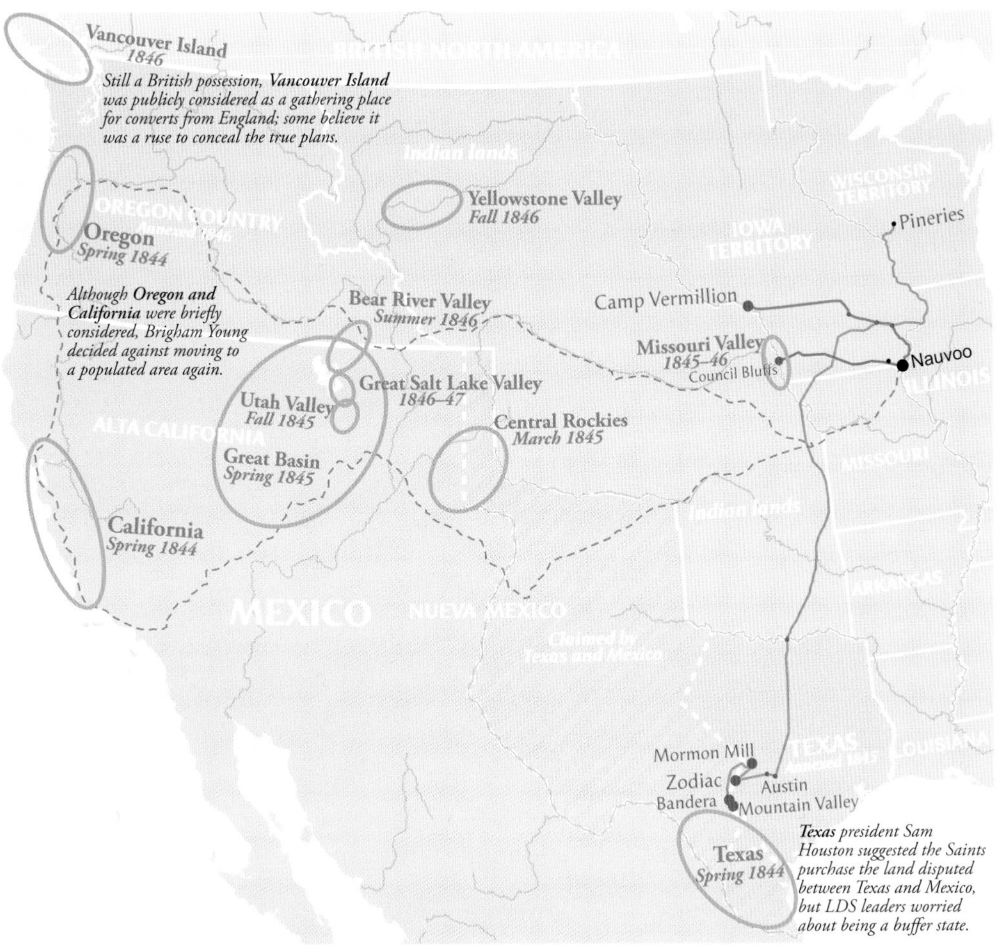

The Great Western Measure

Sites considered for resettlement

Oregon & California Expedition (1844)
On February 20, Joseph Smith and the Twelve began recruiting a company to explore New Mexico, California, and Oregon. By March 11, James Emmett and 19 others had volunteered, but Joseph's martyrdom put the expedition on hold.

James Emmett Company (1844–46)
After Joseph's death, Emmett renewed the expedition as a mission settlement among the Sioux. Despite the Twelve's wishes, he led 150–200 Saints from Nauvoo in September 1844. After wintering in central Iowa, they established Camp Vermillion in the spring, which lasted a year.

Lyman Wight (1845–1858)
In March 1844, Apostle Lyman Wight proposed settling in the Texas Republic, which Joseph considered before his death. Against the advice of the Twelve, Wight and 150 Wisconsin Saints left in 1845, settling in 6 new towns before Wight died in 1858. Most of the group eventually joined the RLDS Church.

Lewis Dana (1845)
On April 24, Lewis Dana (a converted Oneida) and four others were sent by the Twelve to explore the West for resettlement locations. They were able to secure permission from the Pottawattomi Indians to settle (temporarily) in western Iowa.

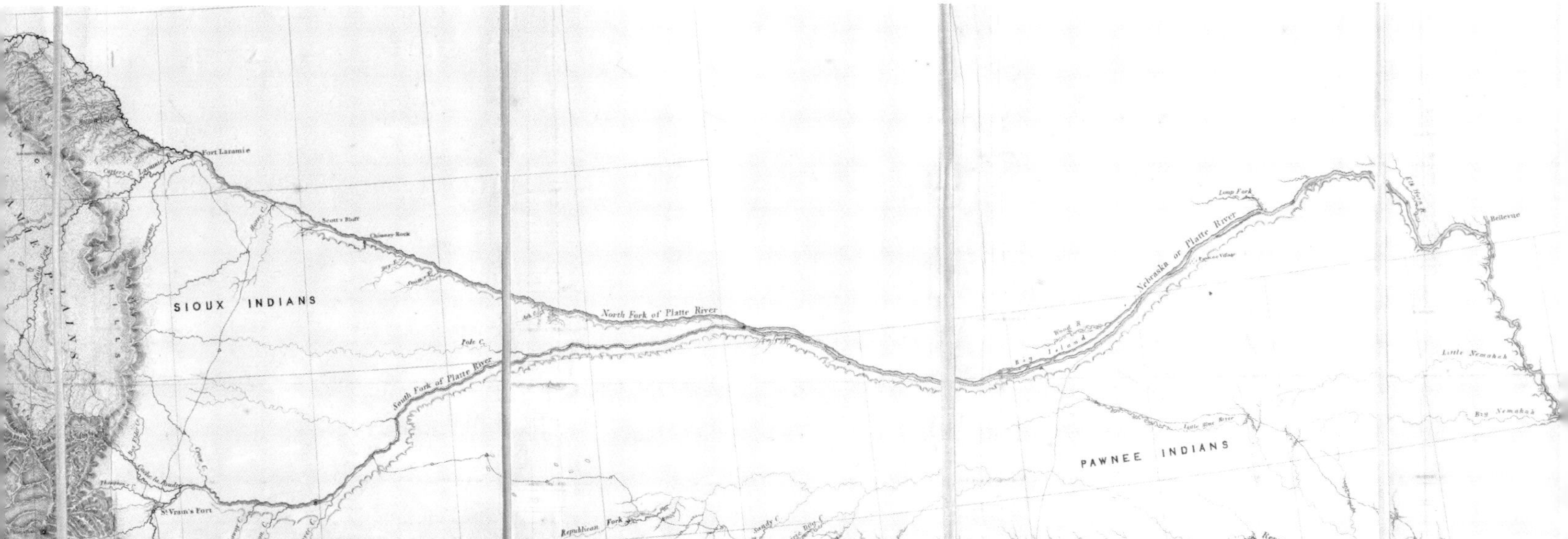

1845 John C. Frémont Map

As the Council of Fifty considered the various options for moving the Saints, it obtained every map and report on the West it could. Although they were incomplete and in many cases inaccurate by today's standards, they were nevertheless an invaluable resource; the Exodus could not have been successful without the knowledge provided.

Among the resources was a copy of the March 1845 report to Congress of John C. Frémont's expeditions of 1842 and 1843–44 (courtesy of Senator Stephen A. Douglas). His reports included this map by Frémont's cartographer, Charles Preuss. On the first exploration, Frémont surveyed the Platte River "up to the head of the Sweetwater" at South Pass. During the second he made a circuit that included boating on the Great Salt Lake during the outbound trip and examining Utah Lake on the return.

The Twelve paid particular attention to information about the Great Salt Lake Valley and regions nearby. In December 1845, several of the Twelve met in the Nauvoo Temple and read from Frémont's reports: on the 20th, Apostle Franklin D. Richards read part to Brigham Young and others of the Twelve, and on the 29th, Apostle Parley P. Pratt read from the journal to Brigham Young and Heber C. Kimball.

Three days before the 1847 pioneers left Winter Quarters on April 7th, Thomas Bullock made for their company a sketch of Fremont's topographical map of the "road to Oregon." During the pioneer journey to the Great Salt Lake, they generally followed Fremont's maps as well as S. Augustus Mitchell's new 1846 map of the West.

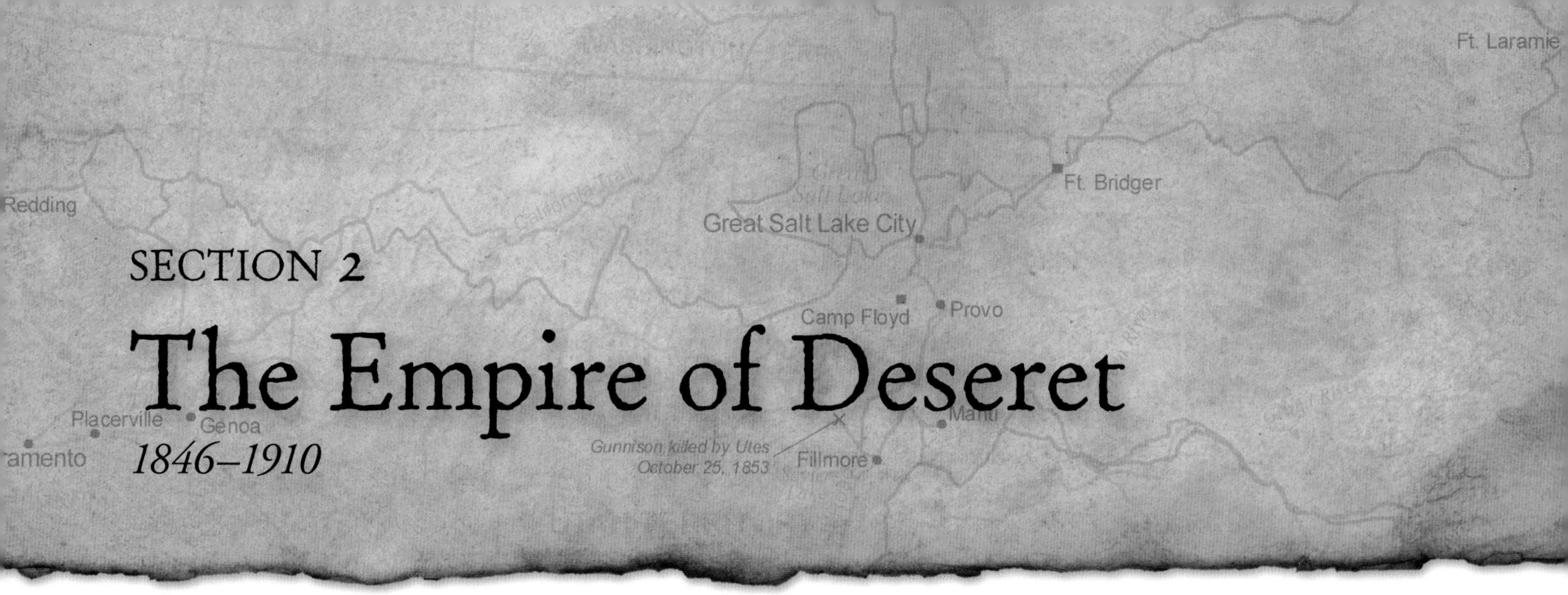

SECTION 2

The Empire of Deseret

1846–1910

CONFLICT IN THE AMERICAN MIDWEST drove the LDS people to seek refuge in the Indian lands of western North America. In the arid Great Basin in 1847, they again began building a community. They were guided by Brigham Young's vision of a vast empire called Deseret. Under his direction the migration of most of the population of Nauvoo and surrounding LDS communities was accomplished, as well as that of thousands of members from other parts of the United States and Europe, comprising the largest organized migration in U.S. history. It demonstrated the organizational and cooperative ability of Church leaders and members, even in trials such as the handcart disaster of 1856. That ability shaped the geography of the West as Young's vision took root as far as Canada and Mexico.

The uniqueness of Mormon settlement gave rise to distinct political, social, and economic practices, including attempts to develop cooperative businesses, women's suffrage, plural marriage, and the women's Relief Society. As the settlements grew, Young's vision of Deseret was overwhelmed by national pressures, resulting in a much smaller Territory and State of Utah. The process was not without conflict as the Saints came in contact with Native Americans and as "gentiles" immigrated to the Intermountain Region, drawn by economic opportunities. Ultimately, the Mormons abandoned their most unique practices, such as plural marriage and a theocratic political economy. Despite the "Americanization" of the Church, the dream of the Empire of Deseret has been ingrained in the cultural landscape of the Intermountain West.

1840 1850 1860 1870

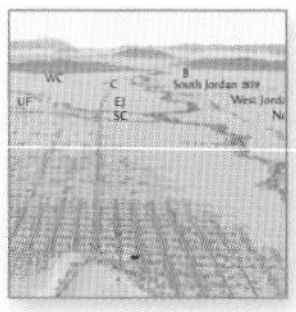

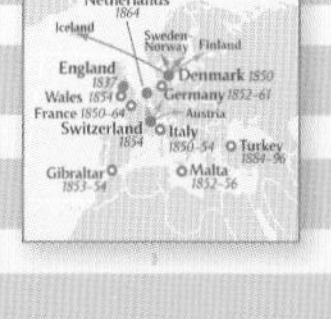

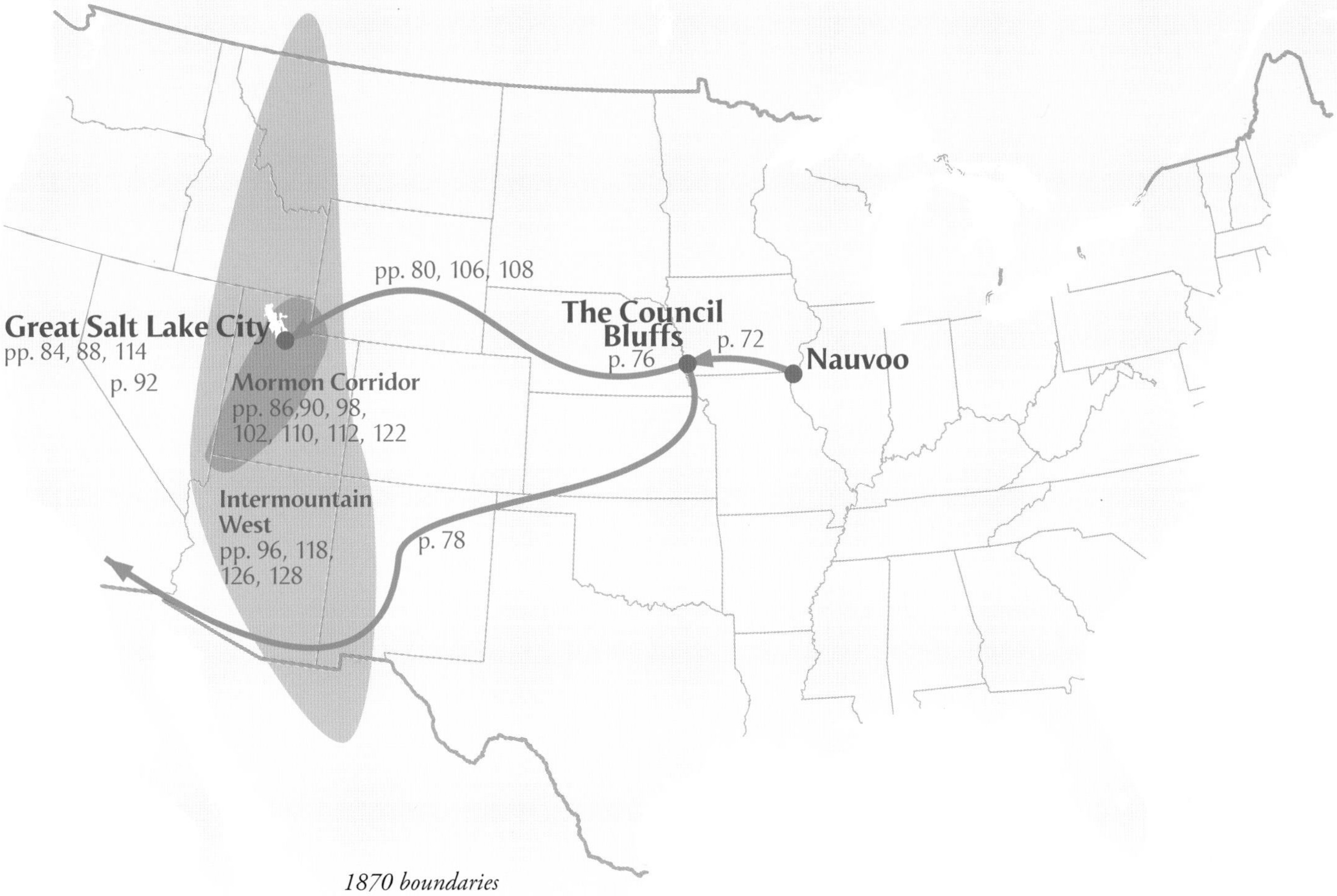

1870 boundaries

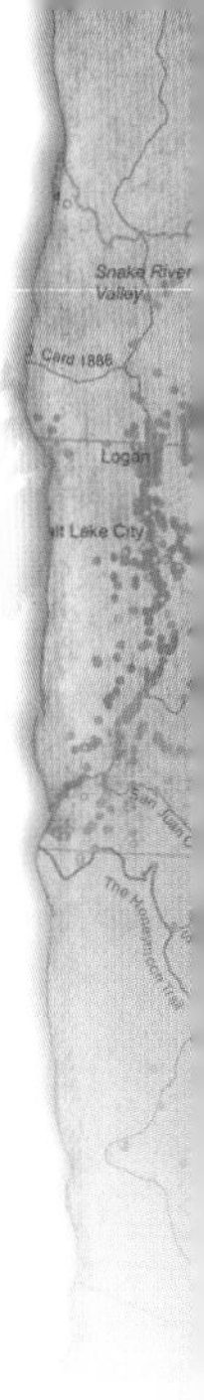

1880 | 1890 | 1900 | 1910

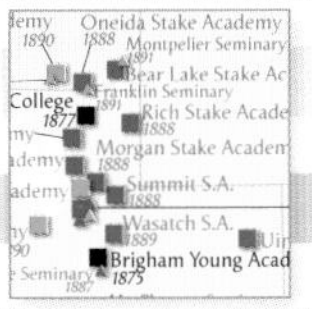

Plural Marriage p. 122

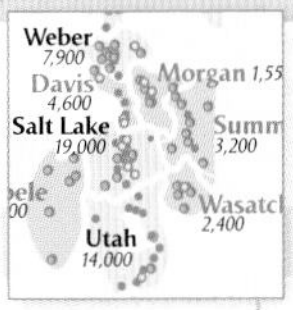

Church Academies p. 126

The Emergence of Modern Stakes and Wards p. 128

The Pioneer Presidents p. 130

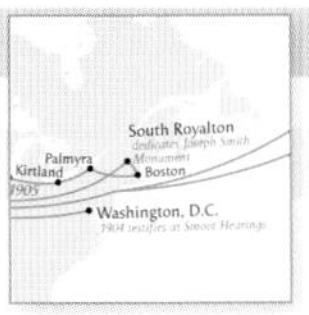

The Church in 1910 p. 132

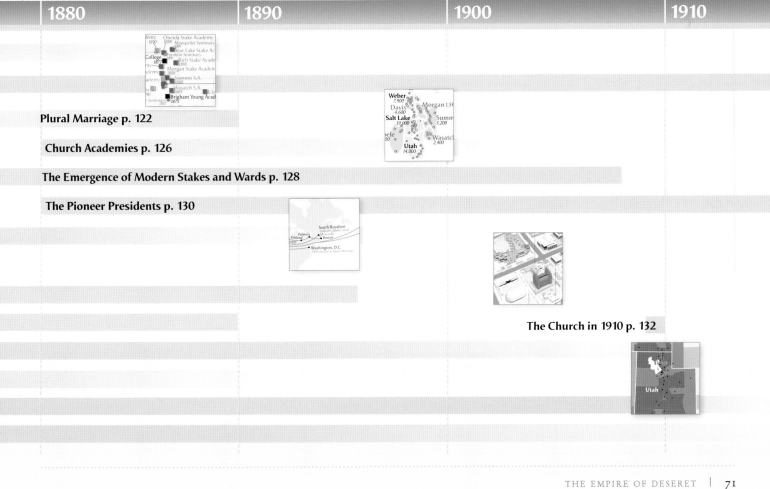

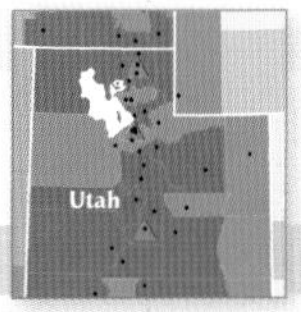

The Exodus Begins

1846

By late summer 1845, Church leaders, facing anti-Mormon pressures, decided that the more than 17,000 Saints living in and around Nauvoo should leave the next spring for a new home in the West. Plans called for 100 companies and 2,500 wagons. By December, 3,285 families were thus organized. Then, in the nearly finished temple, more than 5,000 Saints received temple endowments that winter to prepare them for the trek west.

By January's end, threats to stop the exodus and prosecute LDS leaders forced the Twelve to leave early with an advance company of 2,500 people. This "Camp of Israel" traveled through the mud and snow of early spring, staying close to the Missouri border so they could trade with Missouri settlements for feed and food. At Locust Creek Camp, where William Clayton wrote "Come, Come, Ye Saints," leaders decided to cross the Missouri River not at Banks Ferry in Missouri but at "the Council Bluffs" (as the region had been called since the visit of Lewis and Clark), so they led the company northwesterly across uncharted prairies. After establishing way stations at Garden Grove and Mount Pisgah, the company reached the Missouri River on June 13, finishing their 300-mile Iowa crossing in three and a half months.

Meanwhile, in mid-April, the main exodus from Nauvoo began. Because the earlier departures had fragmented the original company organizations, people now left on their own in small groups. After two Apostles dedicated the temple on April 30 and May 1, people turned west. Some 12,000 Saints comprised this spring exodus. Hundreds stayed in the small towns of eastern Iowa to work, but the majority caught up with the Camp of Israel in just four weeks by following better roads.

continued on page 74

NORTH AMERICA
see inset
New York City
departed 4 February 1846
Yerba Buena (San Francisco)
31 July
Sandwich (Hawaiian) Islands
20–30 June
near Cape Verde Islands
25 February
SOUTH AMERICA
CALIFORNIA
Sutter's Fort
(Sacramento)
Stockton (1849)
Yerba Buena
(San Francisco)
New Hope
Monterey
Juan Fernandez Island
4–9 May
Cape Horn
10 April

Voyage of the *Brooklyn*

Apostle (and Eastern States Mission president) Orson Pratt appointed Samuel Brannan to lead an LDS company from New York by sea to California. Brannan chartered the *Brooklyn*, a Yankee trader sailing ship, and recruited 239 passengers. Also on board were Brannan's printing press, paper and type, three flour mills, irons for a saw mill, saddles, ploughs, carts, grindstones, school books, muskets, lead and powder, and seeds. The captain and crew numbered 17.

On February 4, 1846, the *Brooklyn* left New York City for a 24,000-mile voyage. After encountering a severe Atlantic storm, it rounded Cape Horn and made a weather-induced stop at the Juan Fernandez Islands. After a stop in the Sandwich Islands (Hawaii), it reached the village of Yerba Buena (soon renamed San Francisco) on July 31 after 177 days at sea. Twelve had died and three were born.

Brooklyn passengers settled in Yerba Buena, the first city in the American West settled by Latter-day Saints, then set up New Hope, a colony in the San Joaquin Valley that fizzled when Utah, not California, became the Church's gathering place. Brannan eventually left the Church to seek his fortune, becoming California's first millionaire but dying destitute in 1889.

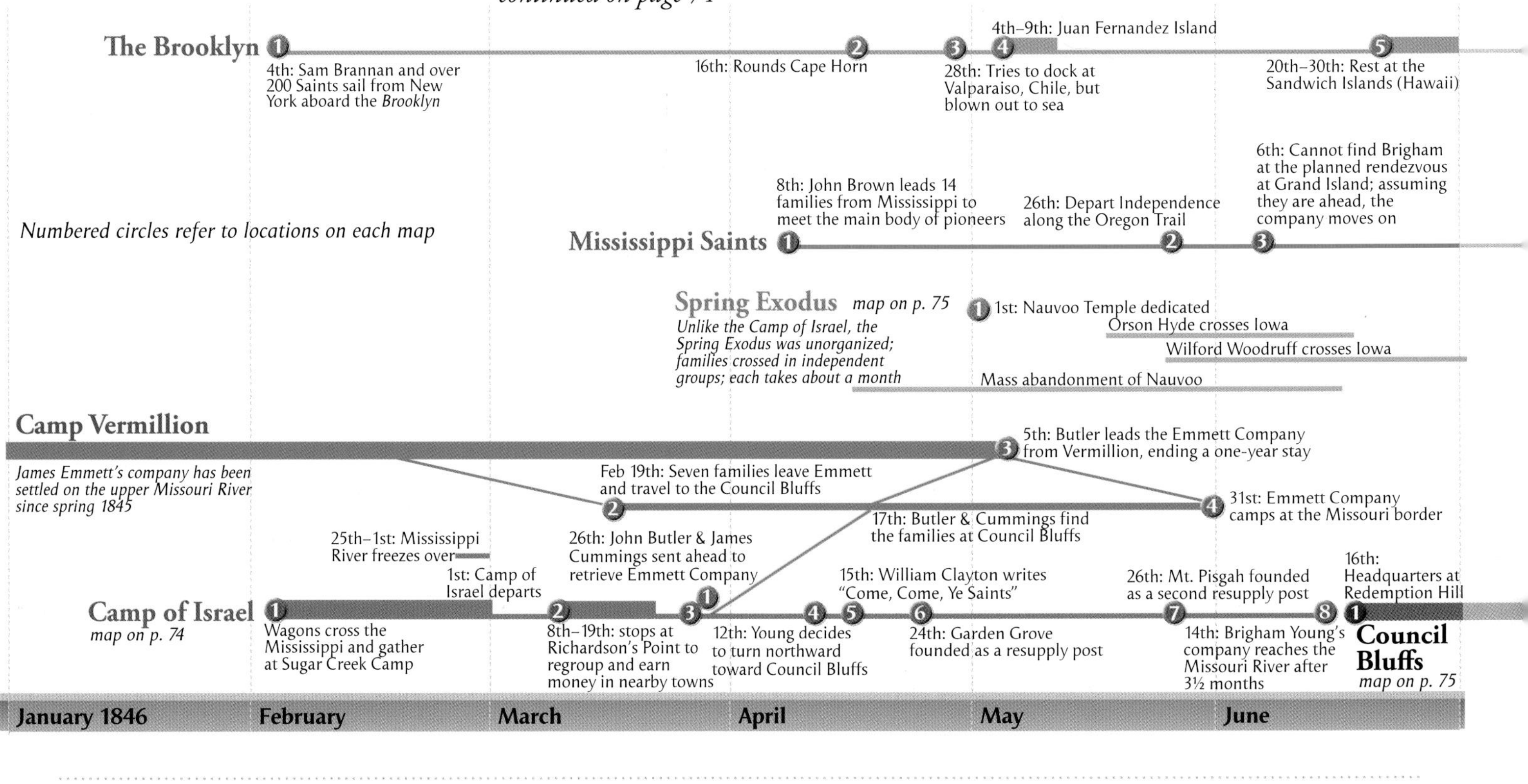

The Brooklyn
4th: Sam Brannan and over 200 Saints sail from New York aboard the Brooklyn
16th: Rounds Cape Horn
28th: Tries to dock at Valparaiso, Chile, but blown out to sea
4th–9th: Juan Fernandez Island
20th–30th: Rest at the Sandwich Islands (Hawaii)
Numbered circles refer to locations on each map
Mississippi Saints
8th: John Brown leads 14 families from Mississippi to meet the main body of pioneers
26th: Depart Independence along the Oregon Trail
6th: Cannot find Brigham at the planned rendezvous at Grand Island; assuming they are ahead, the company moves on
Spring Exodus map on p. 75
Unlike the Camp of Israel, the Spring Exodus was unorganized; families crossed in independent groups; each takes about a month
1st: Nauvoo Temple dedicated
Orson Hyde crosses Iowa
Wilford Woodruff crosses Iowa
Mass abandonment of Nauvoo
Camp Vermillion
James Emmett's company has been settled on the upper Missouri River since spring 1845
Feb 19th: Seven families leave Emmett and travel to the Council Bluffs
5th: Butler leads the Emmett Company from Vermillion, ending a one-year stay
17th: Butler & Cummings find the families at Council Bluffs
31st: Emmett Company camps at the Missouri border
Camp of Israel
map on p. 74
25th–1st: Mississippi River freezes over
1st: Camp of Israel departs
26th: John Butler & James Cummings sent ahead to retrieve Emmett Company
15th: William Clayton writes "Come, Come, Ye Saints"
26th: Mt. Pisgah founded as a second resupply post
16th: Headquarters at Redemption Hill
Wagons cross the Mississippi and gather at Sugar Creek Camp
8th–19th: stops at Richardson's Point to regroup and earn money in nearby towns
12th: Young decides to turn northward toward Council Bluffs
24th: Garden Grove founded as a resupply post
14th: Brigham Young's company reaches the Missouri River after 3½ months
Council Bluffs
map on p. 75
January 1846
February
March
April
May
June

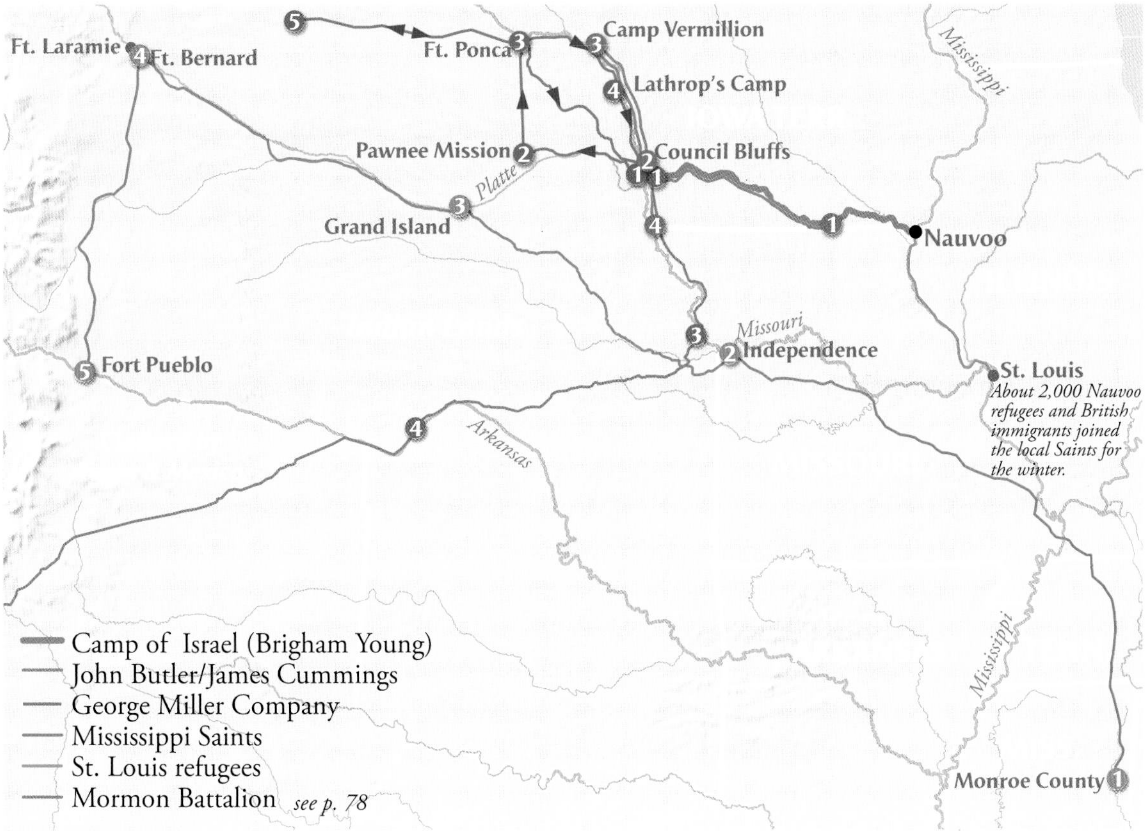

1846 Expeditions

During 1846, several Mormon expeditions were moving westward. James Emmett had led a company across Iowa to establish Camp Vermillion in the southeastern tip of today's South Dakota. Brigham Young sent John Butler (one of Emmett's company who had been visiting Nauvoo) and James Cummings ahead to Camp Vermillion, from which they brought the camp down to Council Bluffs to meet the main body of Saints.

After reaching the Missouri River, President Young sent George Miller's company, including some of Emmett's company, and two other companies toward the Rocky Mountains. After salvaging the remains of a mission abandoned when Indian wars made the area unsafe, they accepted the Ponca Indians' offer to winter with them to the north. There, about 500 Saints built Fort Ponca. Finding no feasible route west, in spring they moved down to Winter Quarters. Both Miller and Emmett eventually became disaffected, but almost all Ponca sojourners rejoined the Mormon trek west.

During the Nauvoo exoduses, about 1,500 Saints went to St. Louis to live until they were prepared to emigrate to the Rockies. Meanwhile, John Brown led a company of Mississippi converts to Fort Laramie to join the Mormon emigration. When the main body didn't come, the proprietor of a small fort in Pueblo invited them to spend the winter there. Soon they were joined by three detachments of sick soldiers and women from the Mormon Battalion; the merged group left the next spring, arriving in the Salt Lake Valley a few days after Brigham Young (see p. 80).

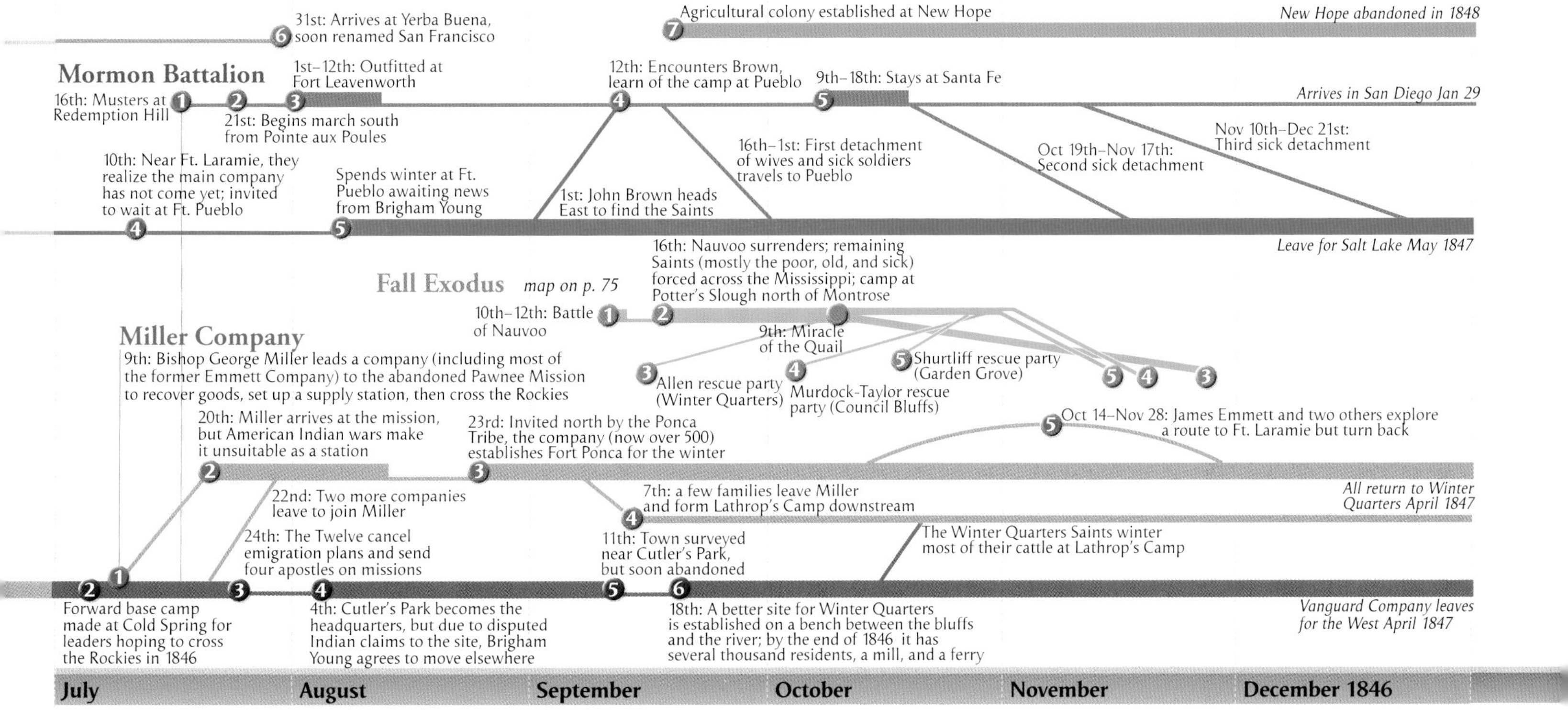

The Exodus Begins

continued

In July, U.S. Army officers enlisted nearly 500 men from camps scattered across Iowa (see p. 78); although they left their families to make their own way to the West, their pay proved to be a godsend to the homeless Saints. During July and August 1846, several thousand Saints at the Bluffs crossed the Missouri River. Brigham Young originally intended to send as many as possible across the Rocky Mountains and was able to send Bishop George Miller ahead with three companies, but everyone soon realized that it was too late in the season and established semipermanent camps, the largest at Winter Quarters (see p. 76).

After the "Battle of Nauvoo" (see p. 62), mobs drove out some 700 Saints still in the city. Forced across the Mississippi, those too poor or sick to go west set up riverside camps, where three rescue companies soon arrived to help them relocate to the West.

Parallel to the gradual abandonment of Nauvoo were expeditions of Saints from elsewhere to the West, including the more than 200 eastern Mormons who sailed on the *Brooklyn* to Yerba Buena (San Francisco) and a company of Saints from Mississippi who found themselves hundreds of miles ahead of Brigham Young and who sought refuge for the winter in a small fort at Pueblo (and would in turn provide refuge for the many wives and sick soldiers detached from the Mormon Battalion).

When 1846 ended, Nauvoo was mostly vacant, its homes and gardens and orchards deteriorating, and the temple desecrated. Exiles were scattered throughout the West. Those at Winter Quarters, Ponca, Mount Pisgah, Garden Grove, and Pueblo suffered through the winter. Hundreds in Iowa towns and 1,500 in St. Louis lived under better circumstances. Battalion soldiers then were crossing deserts now part of Arizona and California, and the *Brooklyn* Saints worked and lived in California. To bring these groups together as a Church community again required that a new homeland be found in the Intermountain West.

William G. Hartley

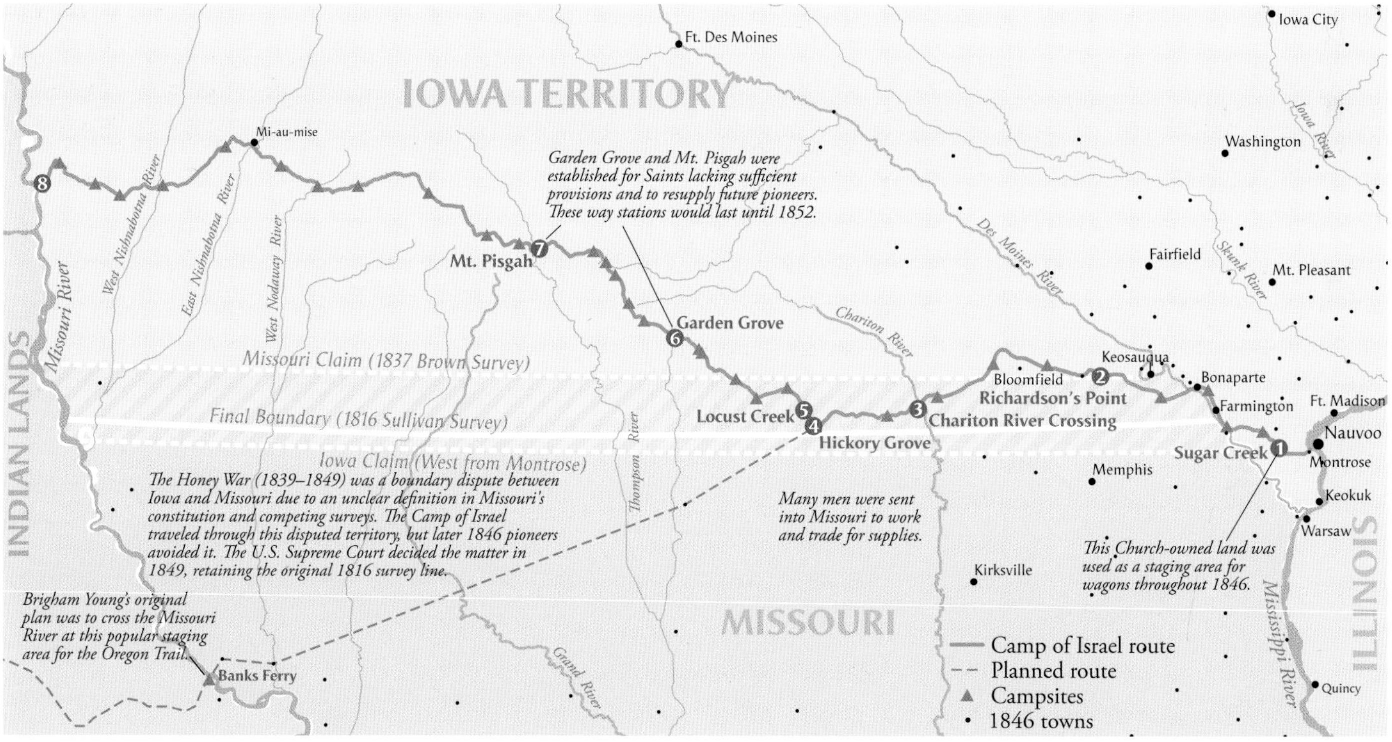

Camp of Israel, February–June 1846

In October 1845, the Twelve announced plans to evacuate Nauvoo the next spring and seek a homeland in the West. About 17,000 Saints in the Nauvoo region had six months to get ready. Saints struggled to sell properties and construct or purchase wagons, teams, and provisions for the trek west. Plans called for at least 2,500 wagons.

By January 1846, rumors that the Twelve might be arrested or prevented from leaving caused them to leave early as a vanguard company with anyone ready to go. During February some 2,500 Saints gathered at the Sugar Creek encampment in Iowa, whom Young organized as a "Camp of Israel." Spring rain and mud slowed the way, forcing the Camp to take 3.5 months to cover the 300 miles to the Missouri River.

Initially they passed along existing roads. During extended stops, men worked for locals; for example, the brass band performed for pay in Keosauqua. The company hugged the Missouri border so they could trade with settlers to the south for livestock feed. Deciding not to cross Northern Missouri (in which Mormons were still in danger) as originally planned, they turned northwest toward the Council Bluffs area, blazing a new trail. At this turning point, William Clayton wrote the hymn "Come, Come, Ye Saints." Moving on, they created Garden Grove and Mount Pisgah as temporary settlements for those without means to continue, eventually reaching the Missouri River in mid-June.

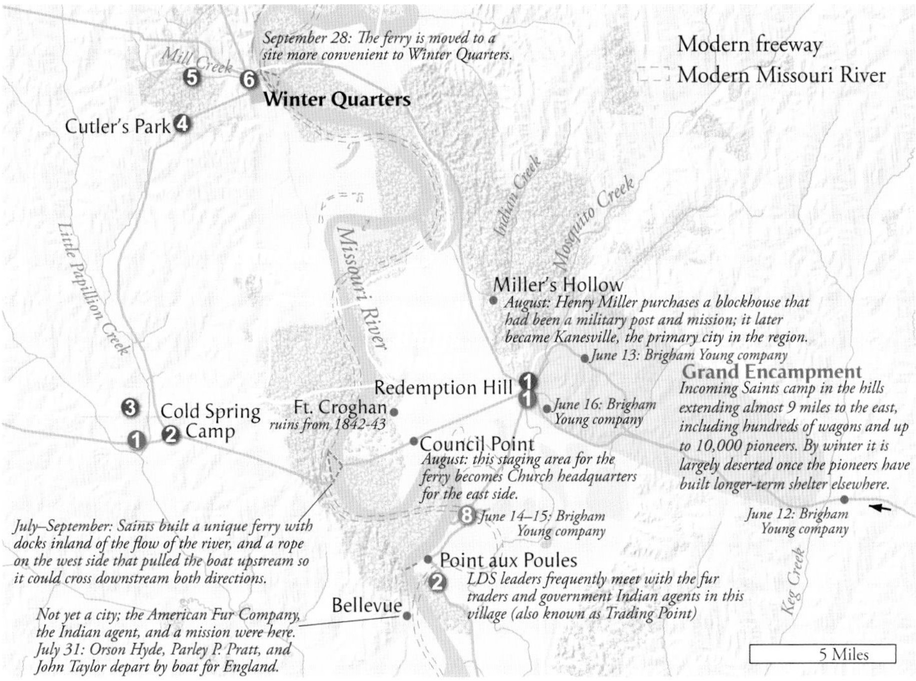
September 28: The ferry is moved to a site more convenient to Winter Quarters.
Modern freeway
Modern Missouri River
Mill Creek
5
6
Winter Quarters
Cutler's Park 4
Little Papillion Creek
Missouri River
Indian Creek
Mosquito Creek
Miller's Hollow
August: Henry Miller purchases a blockhouse that had been a military post and mission; it later became Kanesville, the primary city in the region.
June 13: Brigham Young company
Grand Encampment
Incoming Saints camp in the hills extending almost 9 miles to the east, including hundreds of wagons and up to 10,000 pioneers. By winter it is largely deserted once the pioneers have built longer-term shelter elsewhere.
Redemption Hill
June 16: Brigham Young company
3
Cold Spring Camp
Ft. Croghan
ruins from 1842-43
Council Point
August: this staging area for the ferry becomes Church headquarters for the east side.
June 12: Brigham Young company
July–September: Saints built a unique ferry with docks inland of the flow of the river, and a rope on the west side that pulled the boat upstream so it could cross downstream both directions.
June 14–15: Brigham Young company
Point aux Poules
LDS leaders frequently meet with the fur traders and government Indian agents in this village (also known as Trading Point)
Keg Creek
Bellevue
Not yet a city; the American Fur Company, the Indian agent, and a mission were here. July 31: Orson Hyde, Parley P. Pratt, and John Taylor depart by boat for England.
5 Miles

Saints Enter Council Bluffs

When Brigham Young's company reached the Missouri River in mid-June, they camped on the bluffs while they planned their next move. The next month Captain James Allen mustered about 500 men to serve in the Mexican War. Then Church leaders built a unique ferry that was guided diagonally downstream both ways by hemp cables, which were then used to haul it back upstream.

Five successive camps were made west of the Missouri River in 1846 as the plan to send at least a few pioneers to the Rocky Mountains that summer was shelved. A winter campsite at Cutler's Park was established by an agreement with the Otoe-Missouria and Omaha tribes. However, when the two nations began to quarrel over which had right to the land (and therefore the Saints' rent), LDS scouts found a better site on unclaimed land and soon laid out the city of Winter Quarters (see p. 76).

Meanwhile, on the east side of the river, thousands of weary Saints continued to arrive. By late summer they had formed a nine-mile-long "Grand Encampment" in the hills southeast of today's Council Bluffs, Iowa, where they waited for further instructions. They soon ran out of nearby wood, while their extensive herds of livestock quickly cropped off most of the lush grass. When the creeks and springs dried in the heat of summer, they were forced to find more permanent places to settle, either in Winter Quarters or scattered across southwestern Iowa (see p. 76).

Spring and Fall Exodus, May–November

Perhaps 12,000 Saints left for the West during the second wave of migration in April, May, and June 1846, once the Nauvoo Temple was dedicated and grass began growing on Iowa's prairies. Unlike the Camp of Israel, they traveled not in one large company but separately as families or small groups as soon as they were ready. White-topped wagons dotted the green prairies. Most traveled on better, more direct routes than the first company, requiring only a month or less to cross Iowa. In fact, the routes were so much better that spring emigrants began catching up to the Camp of Israel at Mt. Pisgah. By July 1st, Brigham Young, who had started with 500 wagons, counted 1,800 wagons between Pisgah and Council Bluffs, with more coming.

That September, mobs forced Nauvoo's last 700 or so Mormons across the Mississippi River (see p. 62). Half of them lacked means to go west, so they lingered in "Poor Camps" in the swamps along the Iowa shore of the river. Exposed and hungry, they experienced a "miracle" when weary quail flopped into their camp one day. Rescue wagon companies from Council Bluffs and Garden Grove soon arrived to bring them west. By October, Nauvoo was bereft of Mormons and became a partial ghost town filled with vacant houses and untended gardens, orchards, and farms.

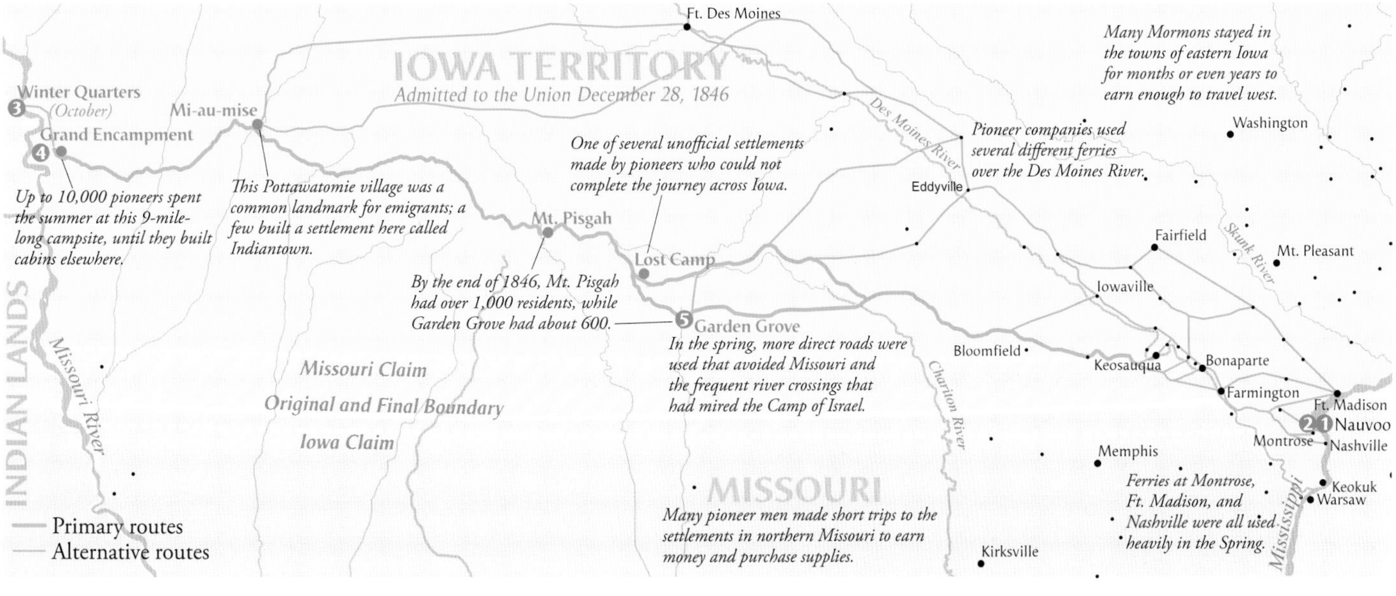
Ft. Des Moines
IOWA TERRITORY
Admitted to the Union December 28, 1846
Many Mormons stayed in the towns of eastern Iowa for months or even years to earn enough to travel west.
Winter Quarters
3 (October)
Mi-au-mise
Grand Encampment
4
Des Moines River
Pioneer companies used several different ferries over the Des Moines River.
Washington
One of several unofficial settlements made by pioneers who could not complete the journey across Iowa.
Eddyville
Up to 10,000 pioneers spent the summer at this 9-mile-long campsite, until they built cabins elsewhere.
This Pottawatomie village was a common landmark for emigrants; a few built a settlement here called Indiantown.
Mt. Pisgah
Lost Camp
Fairfield
Skunk River
Mt. Pleasant
INDIAN LANDS
By the end of 1846, Mt. Pisgah had over 1,000 residents, while Garden Grove had about 600.
Iowaville
5 Garden Grove
In the spring, more direct roads were used that avoided Missouri and the frequent river crossings that had mired the Camp of Israel.
Bloomfield
Keosauqua
Bonaparte
Missouri River
Missouri Claim
Original and Final Boundary
Iowa Claim
Chariton River
Farmington
Ft. Madison
2 1 Nauvoo
Montrose
Nashville
Memphis
MISSOURI
Ferries at Montrose, Ft. Madison, and Nashville were all used heavily in the Spring.
Keokuk
Warsaw
Mississippi
Primary routes
Alternative routes
Many pioneer men made short trips to the settlements in northern Missouri to earn money and purchase supplies.
Kirksville

The Middle Missouri Valley

1846–1853

About 15,000 Latter-day Saints fleeing Illinois in 1846 made an unexpected stop on their way to the Rocky Mountains. After the four-month struggle across Iowa to the Missouri River, the beginning of "Indian Country" (see p. 72), large numbers of men, women, and children were too sick, exhausted, and destitute to cross the plains that summer.

Instead, they established a temporary settlement at Winter Quarters, which became the headquarters of the Church that winter. For two years, it was the primary outfitting post for thousands preparing to cross the plains for Utah, until they were forced to abandon the settlement, which was on lands reserved for native tribes.

Meanwhile, Iowa was much more promising as a stopping point for LDS pioneers. Just before the Saints arrived at the Missouri River, the 2,250 Pottawatomi, Ottawa, and Chippewa indians had agreed to sell their lands in southwestern Iowa for new lands in Kansas, moving there in 1847. The Mormons took advantage of this newly available land, quickly spreading over 40 miles to the north, south, and east of their original camp (in modern Council Bluffs), looking for adequate locations of wood, water, and grass. Their grain, corn, potatoes, and vegetables flourished in the loess soil (ancient wind-blown dust) of Nebraska and western Iowa. Because the land would not be officially available for sale until 1854, the Mormons were squatters, claiming "preemption rights" to the land (i.e., when the land became available, those already living there had the first right to purchase it).

They built roads, bridges, and ferries to connect the expanding settlements to Kanesville (now Council Bluffs), which was the central trading city, regional Church headquarters, and seat of their nascent government. Mormons continued to join the exodus along the trail through Iowa and up the Missouri River by steamboat. Decades later, assistant Church historian Andrew Jenson estimated that almost 32,000 members migrated through the Middle Missouri Valley between 1846 and 1853. Starting in 1849, 10,000 California Gold Rushers bought all kinds of supplies in Kanesville, allowing Mormon farmers to sell virtually all of their supplies of grains and vegetables and enabling them to buy needed supplies to move west to the Salt Lake Valley. Usually, entire communities reorganized as pioneer companies and emigrated together. In 1852, Brigham Young issued an ultimatum for all loyal Saints to come to Great Salt Lake City, and by 1853 most (but not all) of the Mormon population was gone from Iowa and Nebraska, replaced by a new influx of farmers and traders who built the modern Omaha/Council Bluffs area.

Gail Geo. Holmes

Winter Quarters, Church Headquarters 1846–48, Looking South

When Cutler's Park, the first site chosen to spend the winter of 1846–47, led to tensions between the Indian nations who claimed the land (see p. 72), a new site was found on a tableland 40 or 60 feet above and west of the Missouri River. About 2,500 Saints, including Church leaders, established Winter Quarters in September. The city was carefully platted, and log and dugout dwellings were quickly constructed, as shown in this diorama at the Winter Quarters Visitors' Center. Ultimately, 22 wards were organized with bishops to look after the poor and the families of Mormon Battalion volunteers marching to California. The ferry was moved up river to Winter Quarters, where it could be used by arriving pioneers and for communicating with the expanding settlements on the east side of the river.

The residents suffered through the bitter winter of 1846–47; by spring, more than 300 men, women, and children were buried in the cemetery atop the bluff overlooking the city. The Apostles and bishops worked tirelessly for the safety, supply, and spiritual welfare of the community. It was here that Brigham Young received a revelation (D&C 136), with guidance for organizing pioneer companies. The vanguard company left Winter Quarters in early April (see p. 80), followed by about 2,000 total that year.

Thousands of Mormons moved in and out of the city until June 1848, when the U.S. Indian agent at Bellevue insisted they leave Indian lands. Winter Quarters was abandoned, and the remaining Saints either headed west or settled in Iowa, which had a much larger Mormon population by then. Later resettled as Florence, it became one of the primary outfitting posts for Mormons and non-Mormons headed west (see p. 80).

Settlements, 1846–53

Jun 1846 First LDS pioneers arrive at Council Bluffs

Jul 1846 Pottawattamie High Council created; first headquarters at Council Point

Sep 1846 Winter Quarters founded

Dec 1846 First Iowa branch organized at the Blockhouse (Kanesville)

Dec 1847 Brigham Young first sustained as Church President in Kanesville

1848 Iowa legislature creates Pottawattamie County

Jun 1848 Winter Quarters abandoned, almost 40 new branches created by Saints resettled in Iowa

1852 Brigham Young calls scattered Saints to gather to Salt Lake

May 1853 The last known settlers loyal to Brigham Young emigrate

1860 Missionaries representing the New Organization (RLDS) reconvert many scattered Saints

1846 | 1847 | 1848 | 1849 | 1850 | 1851 | 1852 | 1853 | 1854 | 1855 | 1856 | 1857 | 1858 | 1859 | 1860

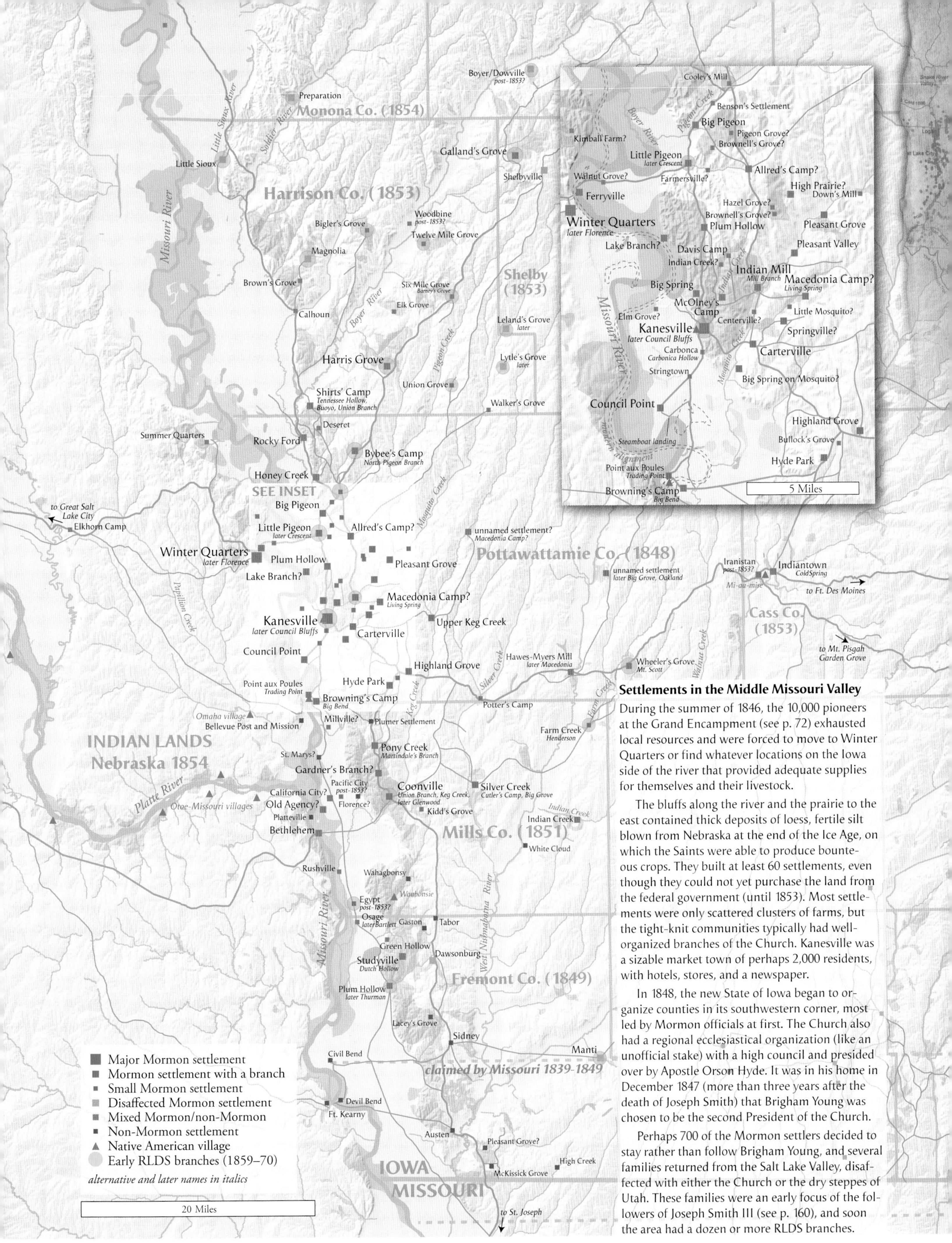

Settlements in the Middle Missouri Valley

During the summer of 1846, the 10,000 pioneers at the Grand Encampment (see p. 72) exhausted local resources and were forced to move to Winter Quarters or find whatever locations on the Iowa side of the river that provided adequate supplies for themselves and their livestock.

The bluffs along the river and the prairie to the east contained thick deposits of loess, fertile silt blown from Nebraska at the end of the Ice Age, on which the Saints were able to produce bounteous crops. They built at least 60 settlements, even though they could not yet purchase the land from the federal government (until 1853). Most settlements were only scattered clusters of farms, but the tight-knit communities typically had well-organized branches of the Church. Kanesville was a sizable market town of perhaps 2,000 residents, with hotels, stores, and a newspaper.

In 1848, the new State of Iowa began to organize counties in its southwestern corner, most led by Mormon officials at first. The Church also had a regional ecclesiastical organization (like an unofficial stake) with a high council and presided over by Apostle Orson Hyde. It was in his home in December 1847 (more than three years after the death of Joseph Smith) that Brigham Young was chosen to be the second President of the Church.

Perhaps 700 of the Mormon settlers decided to stay rather than follow Brigham Young, and several families returned from the Salt Lake Valley, disaffected with either the Church or the dry steppes of Utah. These families were an early focus of the followers of Joseph Smith III (see p. 160), and soon the area had a dozen or more RLDS branches.

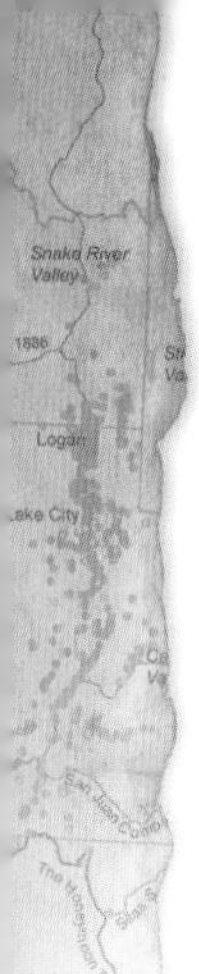

The Mormon Battalion

1846–1847

In January 1846, Brigham Young authorized Jesse Little to meet with national leaders in Washington, D.C., and seek government aid for migrating Latter-day Saints. Arriving in the capital eight days after Congress declared war on Mexico, Little met with President James K. Polk, who offered to pay them to raise a battalion of 500 men. Little committed a Mormon battalion to join Colonel Stephen Watts Kearny, commander of the Army of the West, to fight for the United States in the Mexican War.

Kearny appointed Captain James Allen to enlist soldiers from the Mormons encamped in Iowa Territory. At first, Allen was met with suspicion, until Brigham Young vigorously endorsed the endeavor, enthusiastically exclaiming, "Let the Mormons be the first to set their feet on the soil of California. . . . Hundreds would eternally regret that they did not go, when they had the chance." Young also recognized the importance of showing the Saints' loyalty to the United States government and promised that the Church would care for the families of the soldiers.

An estimated 543 men volunteered, accompanied by 33 women and 51 children. At Fort Leavenworth, they received weapons, accoutrements, and a clothing allowance of $42. After Captain Allen's sudden death, Lt. Colonel A. J. Smith marched them to Santa Fe, where they were heralded by a 100-gun salute. In Santa Fe, Smith was replaced by Lt. Colonel Philip St. George Cooke. The remaining soldiers journeyed down the Rio Grande del Norte and crossed the Continental Divide. While moving up the San Pedro River, they were attacked by a herd of wild cattle. They continued their march toward Tucson, where they anticipated a fight with the garrisoned Mexican soldiers. The conflict did not ensue. They then camped near the Gila River. After two weeks of camping, the battalion crossed the Colorado River and entered California. Their military march from Council Bluffs to California was over. "History may be searched in vain for an equal march of infantry," penned Colonel Cooke. "Half of it has been through a wilderness where nothing but savages and wild beasts are found, or deserts where, for lack of water, there is no living creature."

By the time they reached California, the war was already over. To complete their enlistment, some soldiers were assigned to garrison duty at San Diego, San Luis Rey, and Ciudad de los Angeles, while others were designated to accompany General Kearny back to Fort Leavenworth. The battalion soldiers were mustered out of the military at Ciudad de los Angeles, one year from the date of their enlistment. Eighty-one soldiers chose to reenlist and serve eight additional months in Company A of the Mormon Volunteers.

The sacrifice and patriotism of the Mormon Battalion is honored by Mormons and other westerners, due to its many contributions to the West (California in particular), at sites such as the Mormon Battalion Visitors' Center in San Diego, the Fort Moore Pioneer Memorial in Los Angeles, the Kanesville Tabernacle in Iowa, and the Mormon Battalion Monument.

Susan Easton Black

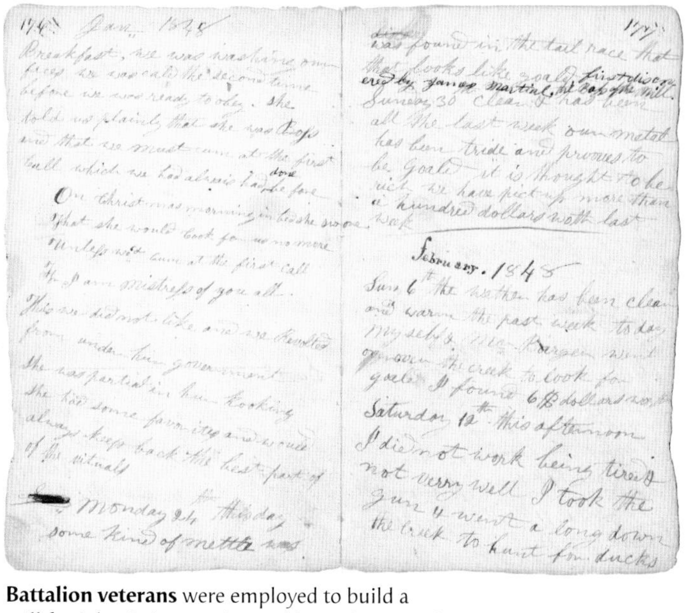

Battalion veterans were employed to build a mill for John A. Sutter when gold was discovered on January 24, 1848. Henry W. Bigler documented the discovery in his diary.

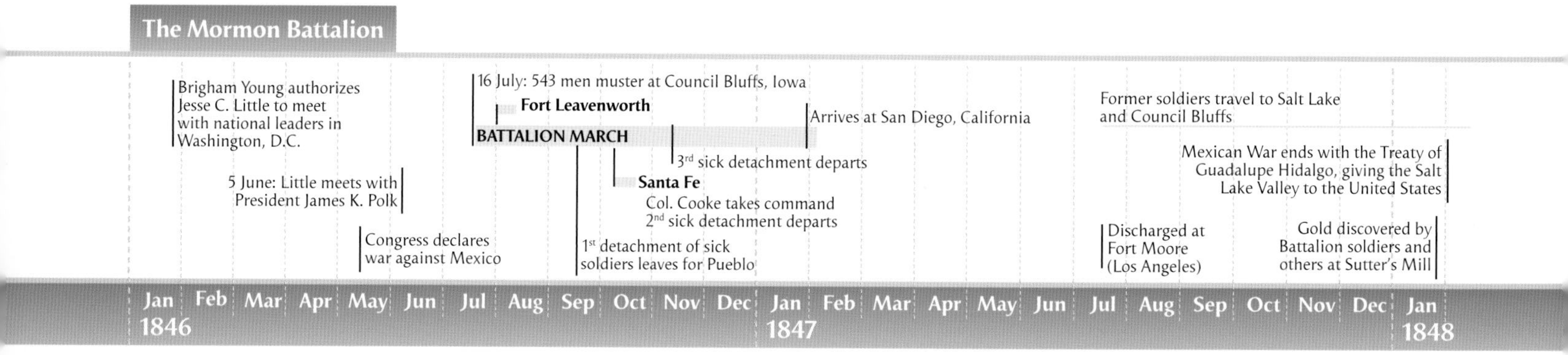

The Mormon Battalion
Brigham Young authorizes Jesse C. Little to meet with national leaders in Washington, D.C.
5 June: Little meets with President James K. Polk
Congress declares war against Mexico
16 July: 543 men muster at Council Bluffs, Iowa
Fort Leavenworth
BATTALION MARCH
1st detachment of sick soldiers leaves for Pueblo
3rd sick detachment departs
Santa Fe
Col. Cooke takes command
2nd sick detachment departs
Arrives at San Diego, California
Former soldiers travel to Salt Lake and Council Bluffs
Discharged at Fort Moore (Los Angeles)
Mexican War ends with the Treaty of Guadalupe Hidalgo, giving the Salt Lake Valley to the United States
Gold discovered by Battalion soldiers and others at Sutter's Mill
Jan Feb Mar Apr May Jun Jul Aug Sep Oct Nov Dec
1846
Jan Feb Mar Apr May Jun Jul Aug Sep Oct Nov Dec
1847
Jan
1848

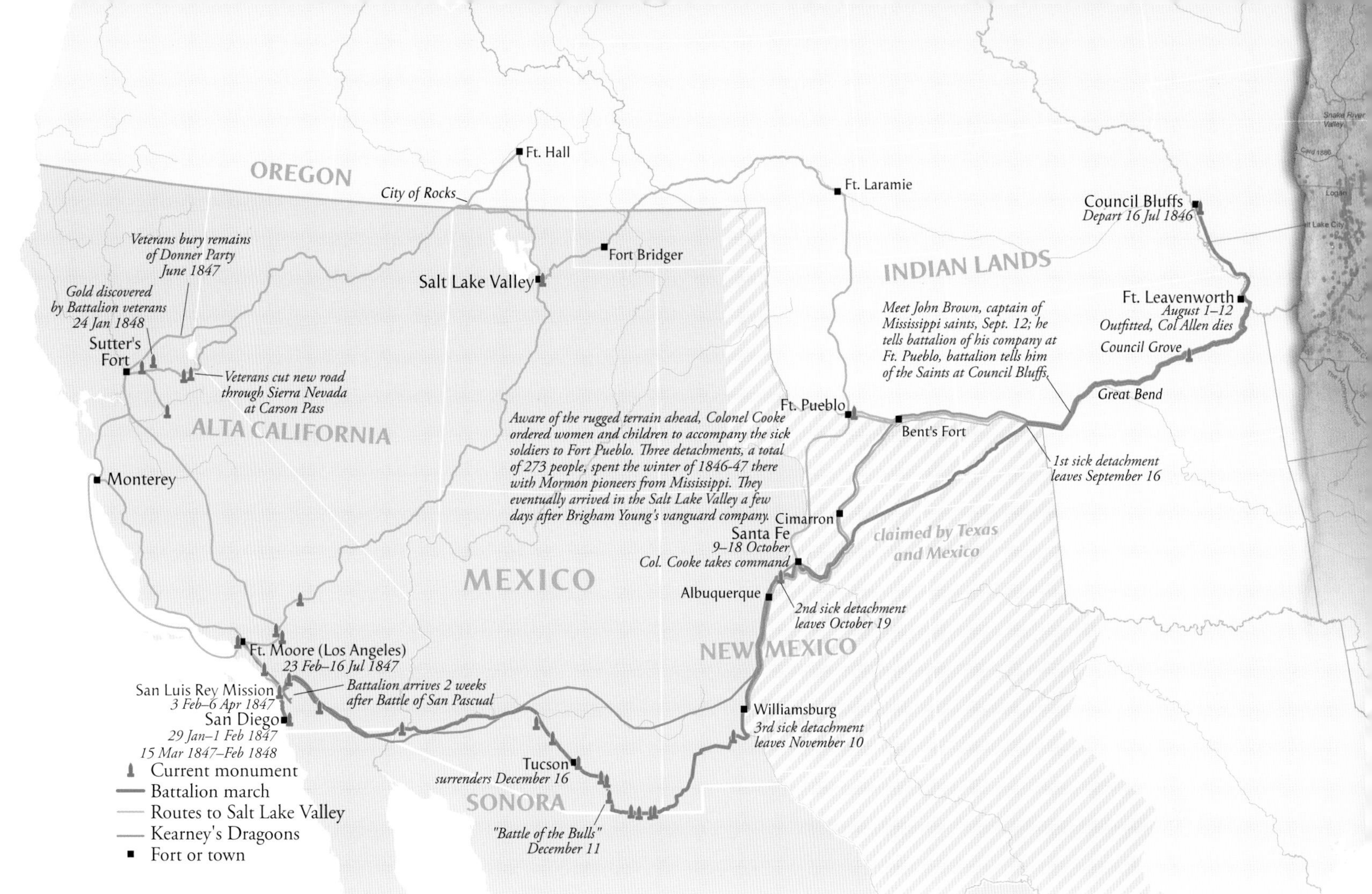
OREGON
Ft. Hall
City of Rocks
Ft. Laramie
Council Bluffs
Depart 16 Jul 1846
Fort Bridger
Salt Lake Valley
INDIAN LANDS
Veterans bury remains of Donner Party June 1847
Gold discovered by Battalion veterans 24 Jan 1848
Sutter's Fort
Veterans cut new road through Sierra Nevada at Carson Pass
ALTA CALIFORNIA
Meet John Brown, captain of Mississippi saints, Sept. 12; he tells battalion of his company at Ft. Pueblo, battalion tells him of the Saints at Council Bluffs
Ft. Leavenworth
August 1–12
Outfitted, Col Allen dies
Council Grove
Great Bend
Ft. Pueblo
Bent's Fort
Aware of the rugged terrain ahead, Colonel Cooke ordered women and children to accompany the sick soldiers to Fort Pueblo. Three detachments, a total of 273 people, spent the winter of 1846-47 there with Mormon pioneers from Mississippi. They eventually arrived in the Salt Lake Valley a few days after Brigham Young's vanguard company.
1st sick detachment leaves September 16
Monterey
Cimarron
Santa Fe
9–18 October
Col. Cooke takes command
claimed by Texas and Mexico
MEXICO
Albuquerque
2nd sick detachment leaves October 19
NEW MEXICO
Ft. Moore (Los Angeles)
23 Feb–16 Jul 1847
San Luis Rey Mission
3 Feb–6 Apr 1847
Battalion arrives 2 weeks after Battle of San Pascual
San Diego
29 Jan–1 Feb 1847
15 Mar 1847–Feb 1848
Williamsburg
3rd sick detachment leaves November 10
Tucson
surrenders December 16
SONORA
"Battle of the Bulls"
December 11
Current monument
Battalion march
Routes to Salt Lake Valley
Kearney's Dragoons
Fort or town

The march of the Mormon Battalion was one of the longest military marches in United States history. They followed a few weeks behind Stephen Watts Kearney's Army of the West, so each city they reached was already in American hands (except Tucson, which surrendered without a fight). Among their major contributions were the wagon roads they pioneered across the mountains and deserts. Due to the length of the march and the Battalion's many contributions to the West, monuments and trail markers have been placed along the battalion route in New Mexico, Arizona, and Colorado, including the Mormon Battalion Memorial Visitors' Center in San Diego.

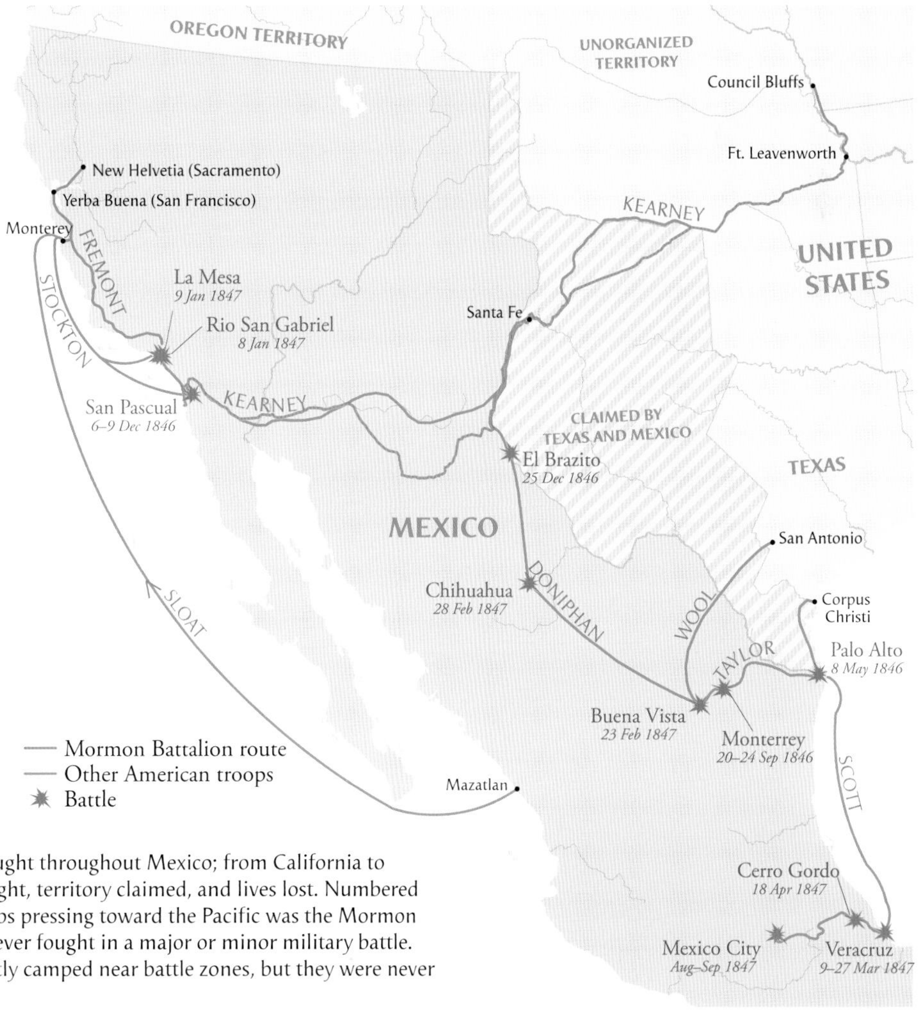
OREGON TERRITORY
UNORGANIZED TERRITORY
Council Bluffs
Ft. Leavenworth
New Helvetia (Sacramento)
Yerba Buena (San Francisco)
Monterey
FREMONT
KEARNEY
UNITED STATES
STOCKTON
La Mesa
9 Jan 1847
Rio San Gabriel
8 Jan 1847
Santa Fe
San Pascual
6–9 Dec 1846
KEARNEY
CLAIMED BY TEXAS AND MEXICO
El Brazito
25 Dec 1846
TEXAS
MEXICO
San Antonio
Chihuahua
28 Feb 1847
DONIPHAN
WOOL
SLOAT
Corpus Christi
TAYLOR
Palo Alto
8 May 1846
Buena Vista
23 Feb 1847
Monterrey
20–24 Sep 1846
SCOTT
Mormon Battalion route
Other American troops
Battle
Mazatlan
Cerro Gordo
18 Apr 1847
Mexico City
Aug–Sep 1847
Veracruz
9–27 Mar 1847

The Mexican War was fought throughout Mexico; from California to Veracruz, battles were fought, territory claimed, and lives lost. Numbered among the American troops pressing toward the Pacific was the Mormon Battalion. The battalion never fought in a major or minor military battle. Mormon soldiers frequently camped near battle zones, but they were never called upon to fight.

Pioneer Trails

1847–1869

THE MOST ORGANIZED and long-lasting movement of pioneers to the western United States was the Mormon exodus from the Mississippi and Missouri rivers to the valleys of the Great Basin. It began in 1846 with the Mormon migration to the Council Bluff area (see p. 72) after their expulsion from Nauvoo, Illinois, on the east bank of the Mississippi River. Here they prepared to launch their thousand-mile journey to the Salt Lake Valley.

In 1847 the first company started westward under the leadership of Brigham Young, blazing a new road to Fort Laramie in modern Wyoming; from here, they followed the Oregon Trail and the Hastings Cutoff to the Salt Lake Valley. Along the way, they took careful notes of locations, mileage, and landmarks; these notes helped them produce a detailed guide book to aid future Mormon migrants.

They were soon joined by ten other companies that same year. This was just the beginning of multiple wagon trains that brought thousands of Mormons west over the next 22 years. They were usually organized into companies under a captain elected by the group or appointed by Church leaders. Companies varied in size from just a few families to large companies of 500 or more. The largest company, under Brigham Young in 1848, included 1,220 persons and over 300 wagons. Wagon trains with large numbers traveled more slowly because it took them longer to ford the rivers or cross with ferries. The wagons were generally pulled by two or four oxen, depending on the size of the wagon and the weight of the load. Oxen were stronger than horses and mules and better able to forage on native prairie vegetation, requiring less feed to be carried as part of the load.

Companies had to leave in the early spring when spring runoff made the rivers difficult to cross and the roads were muddy. Heavy rains could hold up a wagon train for several days or even weeks. Other than weather, the greatest danger was cholera, sometimes hitting the camps before they ever started their journey. Some wagon trains had problems with Native Americans, but on the whole they were able to keep hostilities to a minimum by sharing some of their meager supplies.

The actual number of Mormons who came across the plains is unknown. Official Church reports tallying each company included team drivers that were counted as part

continued on page 82

The 1847 Vanguard Company

On April 7, 1847, the day after a general conference at Council Bluffs, Brigham Young began organizing a wagon train to head for the Salt Lake Basin. This vanguard company consisted of 143 men, 3 women, and 2 children and included a number of Apostles and other Church leaders; it was intended to be a scouting group to prepare for the families to follow. The train was held up for a week at the Elkhorn River to await the arrival of John Taylor, who was coming from England with some scientific instruments, including sextants, barometers, and a telescope, which allowed Orson Pratt to determine the latitude, longitude, and elevation of important landmarks along the way. The company also took a cannon with them to help guard against any Indian attacks. They were able to design and construct an odometer, which was attached to a wagon wheel to measure the distance they traveled each day. They noted the flora and fauna, soils, and rock formations along the way.

They stayed on the north side of the Platte and North Platte rivers until they reached Fort Laramie to avoid interaction with Oregon-bound travelers on the south side. Because they were the first wagon train to take this route, crews were sent ahead with tools to build the road through difficult terrain, knowing that many wagon trains would be following them. The rivers were running high with spring runoff, so they stopped to build ferry rafts and left crews behind to assist the companies that would follow that summer.

At Fort Laramie, they crossed to the south side of the river and followed the Oregon Trail across most of Wyoming. At Fort Bridger they followed the Hastings Cutoff to the southwest, used by the ill-fated Donner-Reed Party the year before. The first scouts entered the Salt Lake Valley on July 22 and were already plowing fields when Brigham Young arrived two days later, uttering the iconic words, "This is the right place; drive on." Many of the men did not stay long, hurrying back east to prepare to bring their families.

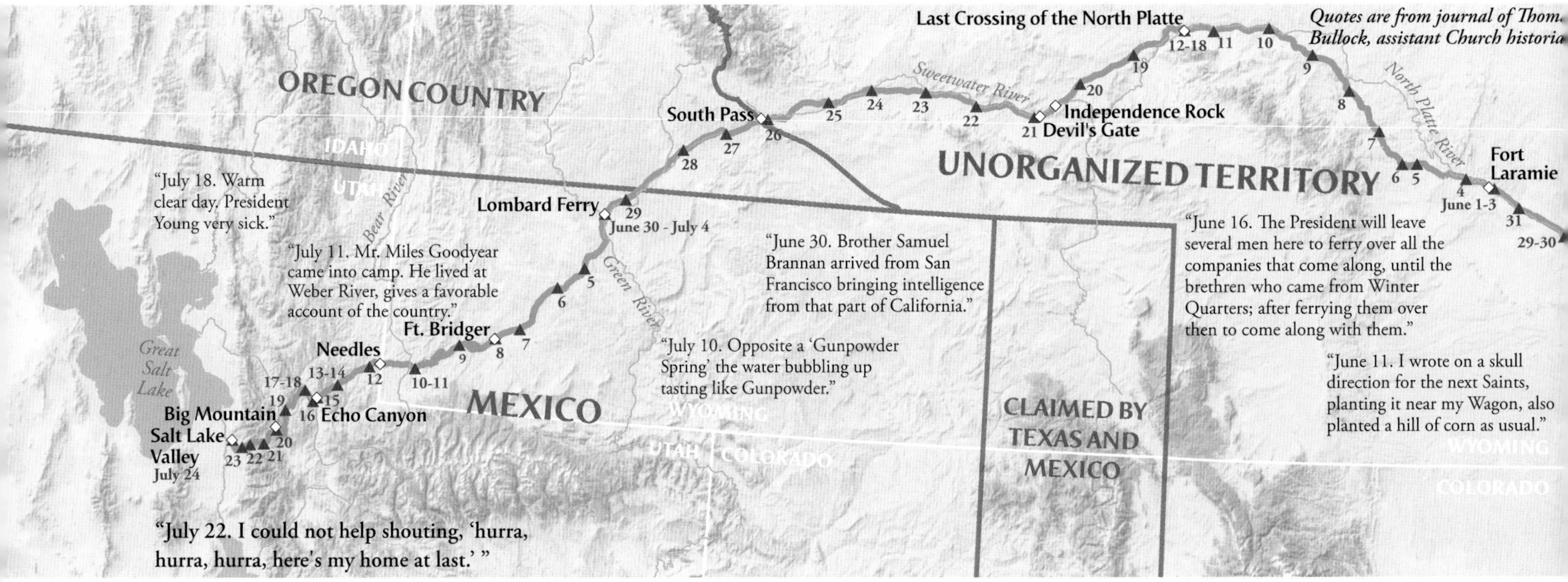

Last Crossing of the North Platte
Quotes are from journal of Thom[as] Bullock, assistant Church historia[n]
OREGON COUNTRY
South Pass
Sweetwater River
Independence Rock
Devil's Gate
North Platte River
Fort Laramie
June 1-3
UNORGANIZED TERRITORY
IDAHO
UTAH
Bear River
"July 18. Warm clear day. President Young very sick."
Lombard Ferry
June 30 - July 4
"June 30. Brother Samuel Brannan arrived from San Francisco bringing intelligence from that part of California."
"June 16. The President will leave several men here to ferry over all the companies that come along, until the brethren who came from Winter Quarters; after ferrying them over then to come along with them."
"July 11. Mr. Miles Goodyear came into camp. He lived at Weber River, gives a favorable account of the country."
Green River
Ft. Bridger
Great Salt Lake
Needles
"July 10. Opposite a 'Gunpowder Spring' the water bubbling up tasting like Gunpowder."
"June 11. I wrote on a skull direction for the next Saints, planting it near my Wagon, also planted a hill of corn as usual."
Big Mountain
Echo Canyon
MEXICO
Salt Lake Valley
July 24
CLAIMED BY TEXAS AND MEXICO
WYOMING
UTAH
COLORADO
"July 22. I could not help shouting, 'hurra, hurra, hurra, here's my home at last.' "

1
2
3
4
5
6
7
8
9
10
S

Looking south over Meridian Peak across the Salt Lake Valley as it probably looked when the Mormon pioneers arrived in 1847. The valley was predominantly covered in tall prairie grass, with groves of willows, cottonwoods and box elder trees in the streambeds. The northwest part of the valley was less hospitable, with poor soil, alkaline deposits, salt marshes, and brackish ponds (such as Decker Lake, visible to the right). It was dotted with campsites utilized intermittently by Utes and Shoshones.

Arriving in the Salt Lake Valley, July 1847

July 22

1 George A. Smith and Orson Pratt climb Donner Hill and get the first view of the valley

2 Smith and Pratt lead the advance party down to a creek (now 1700 S 500 E) to camp

23

3 Men explore northward as far as the Hot Springs

24

4 The camp moves to a better creek (City Creek, near 300 S State), where they begin digging irrigation ditches and planting potatoes

5 Brigham Young and the sick party enter the valley and come to the new camp

25 Sunday

The pioneers rest and worship

26

6 Young and eight others climb Ensign Peak to survey the valley and plan the city

27

7 Young and others explore westward to the edge of Tooele Valley and swim in the Great Salt Lake

First of combined Battalion detachment and Mississippi Company arrive from Pueblo

28

A semipermanent fort is built (now Pioneer Park) 10

Orson Pratt calculates the coordinates and elevation of the temple site then begins to survey the city lots

8 Orson Pratt leads a group up Traverse Mountain to see Utah Valley

9 Young identifies the site of the future temple

August

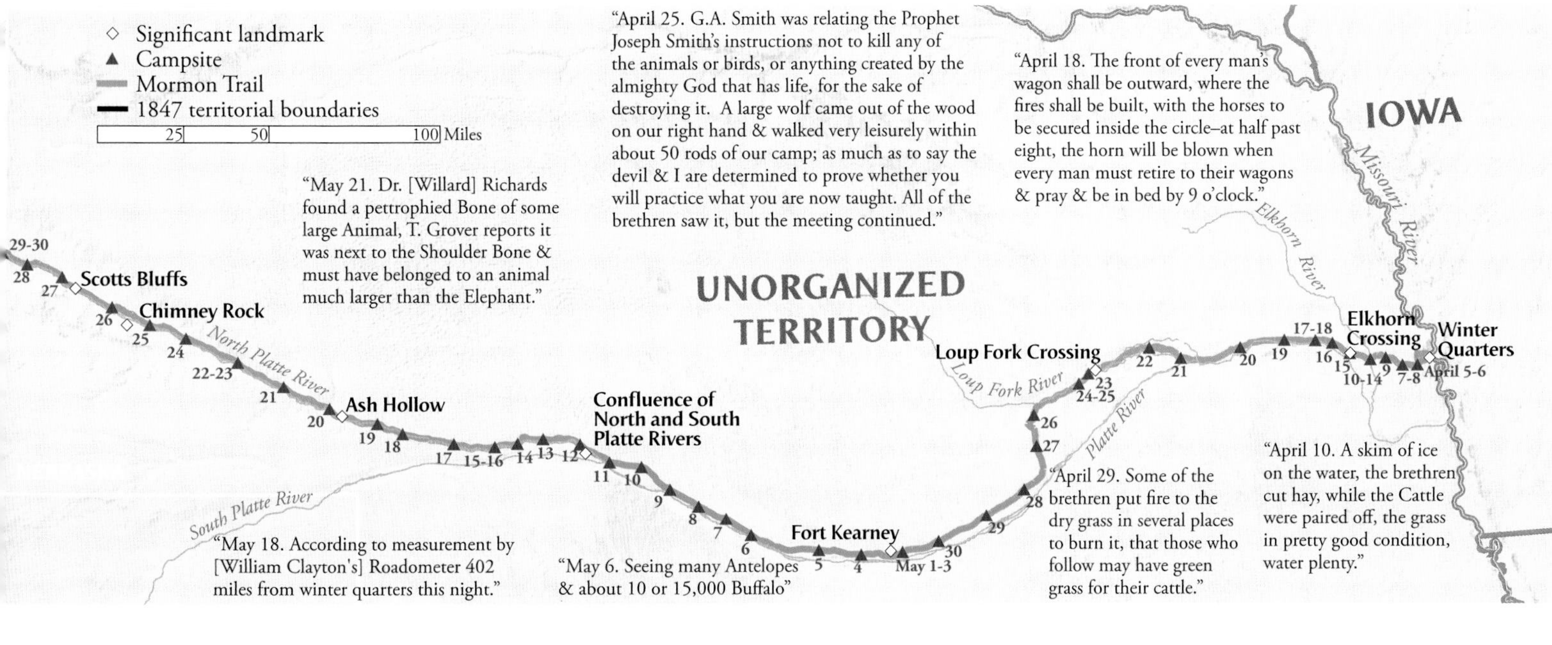

◇ Significant landmark
▲ Campsite
Mormon Trail
1847 territorial boundaries
25 50 100 Miles
"April 25. G.A. Smith was relating the Prophet Joseph Smith's instructions not to kill any of the animals or birds, or anything created by the almighty God that has life, for the sake of destroying it. A large wolf came out of the wood on our right hand & walked very leisurely within about 50 rods of our camp; as much as to say the devil & I are determined to prove whether you will practice what you are now taught. All of the brethren saw it, but the meeting continued."
"April 18. The front of every man's wagon shall be outward, where the fires shall be built, with the horses to be secured inside the circle–at half past eight, the horn will be blown when every man must retire to their wagons & pray & be in bed by 9 o'clock."
IOWA
Missouri River
Elkhorn River
"May 21. Dr. [Willard] Richards found a pettrophied Bone of some large Animal, T. Grover reports it was next to the Shoulder Bone & must have belonged to an animal much larger than the Elephant."
UNORGANIZED TERRITORY
Scotts Bluffs
Chimney Rock
North Platte River
Ash Hollow
Confluence of North and South Platte Rivers
Loup Fork Crossing
Loup Fork River
Platte River
Elkhorn Crossing
Winter Quarters
April 5-6
Fort Kearney
May 1-3
South Platte River
"May 18. According to measurement by [William Clayton's] Roadometer 402 miles from winter quarters this night."
"May 6. Seeing many Antelopes & about 10 or 15,000 Buffalo"
"April 29. Some of the brethren put fire to the dry grass in several places to burn it, that those who follow may have green grass for their cattle."
"April 10. A skim of ice on the water, the brethren cut hay, while the Cattle were paired off, the grass in pretty good condition, water plenty."

Pioneer Trails

continued

of multiple companies. It is also likely that several thousand came with California- or Oregon-bound trains, joined with professional freight trains, or came on their own and were not reported. The total number of Mormon pioneers was likely about 60,000. Non-Mormons came as well, including territorial appointees, soldiers (see p. 110), merchants, miners (see p. 112), and tourists.

In 1869, the Union Pacific Railroad was completed to Utah, making the journey considerably easier but bringing to a close an era in which the physical and spiritual strength of the Saints was forged on the Great Plains.

Wayne Wahlquist

Variant Pioneer Trails

Between 1847 and 1869, a wide variety of outfitting posts were used for organizing and equipping the pioneer companies. Some years, small companies started their trek from very different starting points, including several from California and four that began in southern Texas. The latter were composed of Texas converts to Mormonism and European converts who had migrated from New Orleans seeking employment. The locations changed for various reasons, but economics was the primary factor. The cost of purchasing and collecting the wagons and oxen was substantial, and when the organizers felt that the local merchants were charging unreasonable rates, they found a new location where expenses could be reduced. Some posts were used exclusively by Mormon agents, while others were shared with emigrants to California and Oregon.

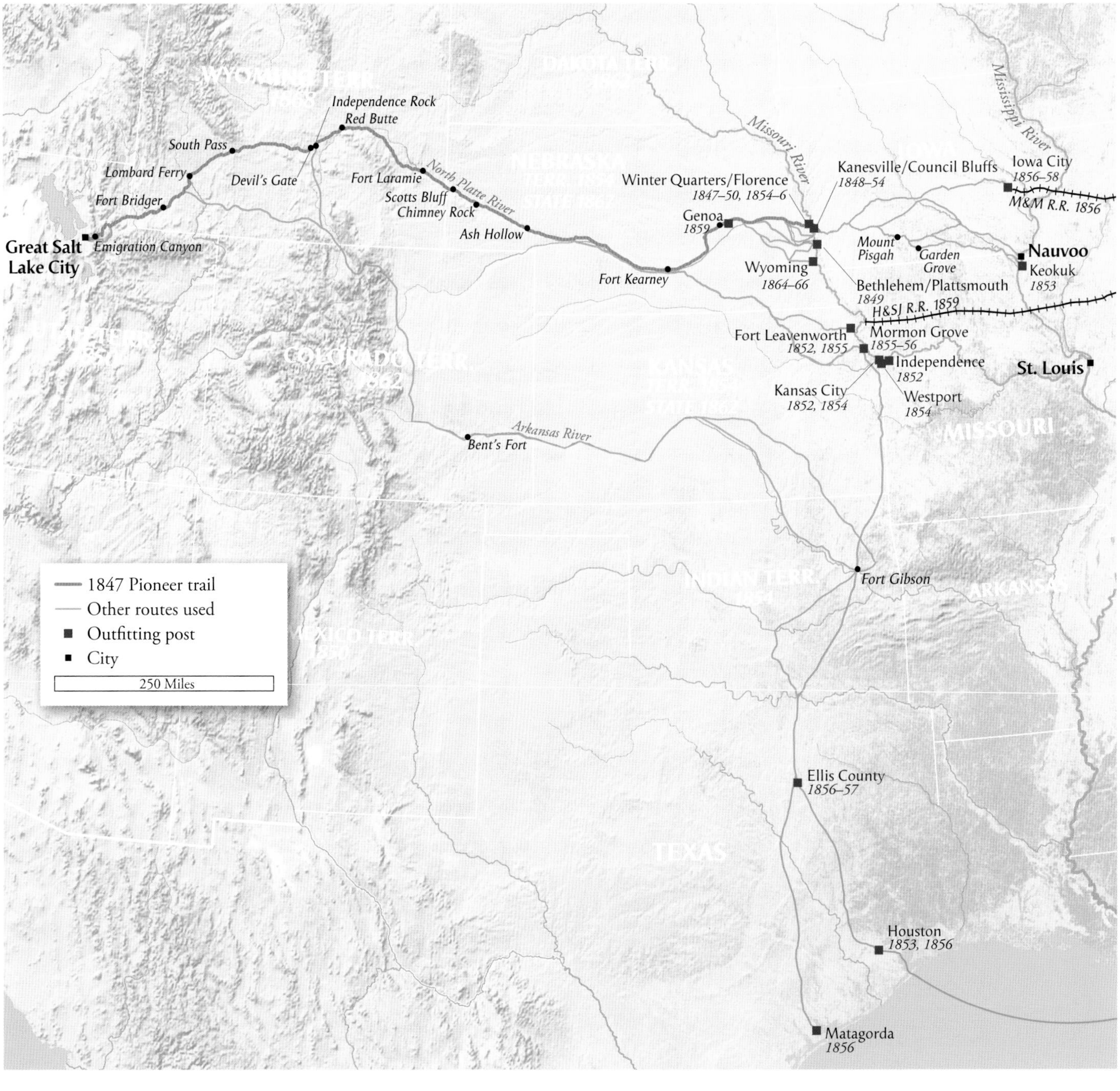

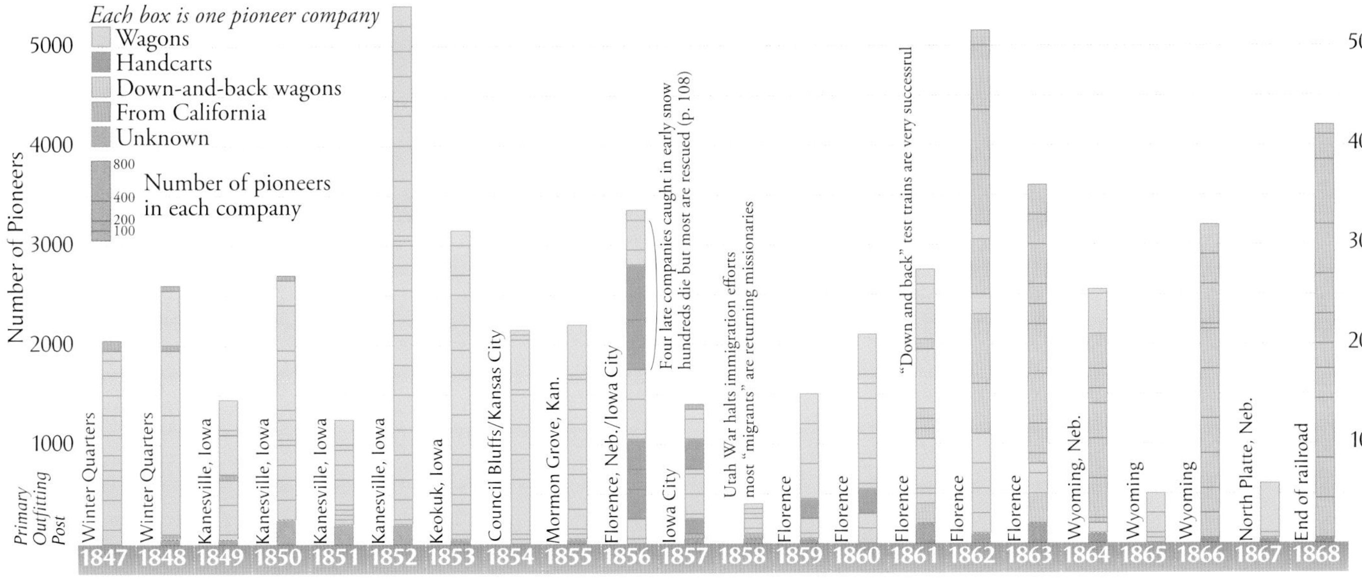

Modes of Transportation on the Trail

During the early part of the Exodus, most of the European Mormons entered the United States through the port of New Orleans and then made their way up the Mississippi and the Missouri rivers by riverboats to the outfitting posts. However, cholera and malaria took a heavy toll among these European converts, and a wagon team was often prohibitively expensive for the poor immigrants. In 1856, Brigham Young introduced a new innovative solution, handcarts (see p. 106). Five companies made the journey that first year, followed by two in 1857, one in 1859, and two in 1860, the last two leaving from Florence, Nebraska, rather than Iowa City, because by that time the rail line had reached Omaha.

The second major innovation began in 1861 after a private wagon freight train was able to make the 1,000-mile trip both directions in one season. This approach reduced costs, improved safety (since experienced drivers drove the wagons), and reduced the large surplus of wagons and oxen accumulating in Salt Lake City. The Church called on bishops and stake presidents to recruit experienced men with teams and wagons to go to the Missouri River and bring the European converts to Zion. From then until the coming of the railroad, almost all pioneers traveled by these down-and-back companies. In 1865 and 1867, a combination of the Black Hawk War (see p. 98) and social and economic stresses in Utah made it too difficult to send any two-way wagon trains to pick up new immigrants, and immigration was reduced to a trickle.

The Coming of the Railroad

In 1867, a new outfitting post was established at North Platte, the end of the continental railroad. In 1868, it moved first to Laramie then to Benton just east of present Rawlins, and finally to Green River, Wyoming. The last wagon train traveled from Salt Lake City to Green River, Wyoming, and back. The continental railroad was completed in 1869, ending the overland wagon trains. From then on, Mormon immigrants could take the train all the way to Salt Lake City at a fraction of the cost and time.

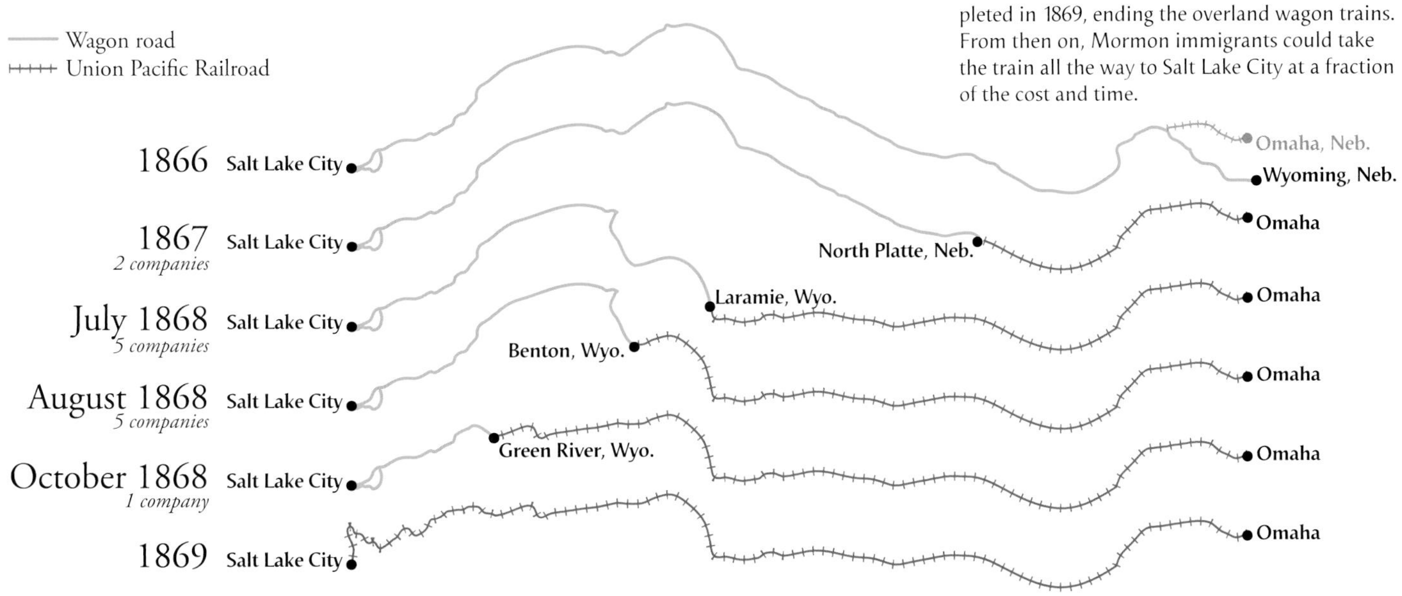

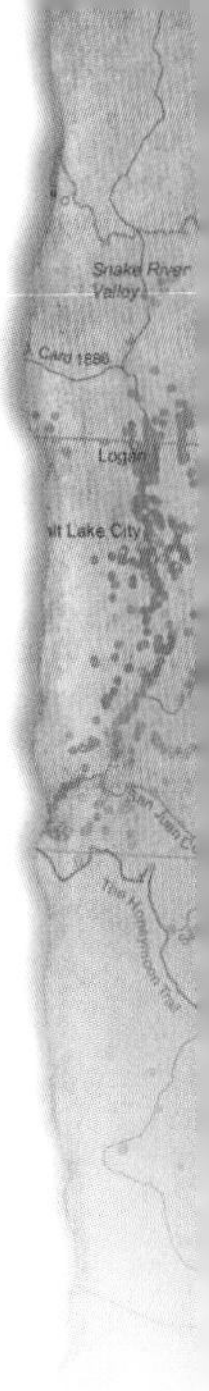

Settling the Salt Lake Valley

1847–1870

Arriving on the edge of the Salt Lake Valley in July 1847, the Mormon pioneers gazed upon a pleasing vista. Dramatic mountain peaks, some of them still capped with snow, ringed the valley. "We gazed with wonder and admiration upon the most fertile valley spread out before us for about twenty-five miles in length and sixteen miles in width, clothed with a heavy garment of vegetation," recorded Wilford Woodruff. The Saints admired the glistening waters of the Great Salt Lake and the thick, 6-foot-high grass that carpeted much of the valley. In the river bottoms, Parley P. Pratt reported, the grass was green and "very luxuriant," but elsewhere the tall grass was "nearly dried up for want of moisture." The soil in the eastern half of the valley was "fertile friable loam." West of the Jordan River, sagebrush predominated in the drier, poorer soil. Timber in the valleys was generally scarce, although clusters of cottonwood, box elder, and scrub oak dotted the courses of creeks and streams.

The land appeared to be unoccupied by American Indians, but the Mormons received many visits from the nearby residents during their first month in the valley. They learned that bands of Shoshones (from Weber Valley) and Utes (from Utah Valley) frequented the hot springs on the northern edge of the valley and hunted and gathered in the Salt Lake Valley (see p. 98). When representatives of these bands tried to sell land to the Mormons for weapons, Brigham Young declined, stating that the land belonged to God and that there was ample acreage for all.

Although they began to plant crops in the valley and decided to winter there, the pioneers continued to investigate other possible sites for a final encampment. On July 27, they met and determined to plant a city along City Creek. Subsequently, Orson Pratt and Henry Sherwood surveyed the city's original plat.

As the population grew in subsequent years, the city's boundaries expanded to include additional plats. Arriving in the valley in 1849, a correspondent for the *New York Tribune* discovered a thriving community. He described "an extensive and cultivated valley" with fields of wheat, corn, potatoes, oats, flax, and green vegetables. On the east benches he passed "extensive herds" of livestock. In the city itself, single-story wood and adobe homes flanked by gardens, orchards, and fledgling shade trees lined the streets.

Soon, pioneers located along other creeks in the valley, establishing farm villages and mills, followed in the 1860s by mines in the mountains and eventually smelters. By 1870, twenty-three years after the first settlers arrived, Salt Lake County's population had grown to more than 18,000. Of that number, nearly 13,000 resided in Salt Lake City proper, while 700 lived in mining camps and over 4,000 inhabited farming districts in the valley.

Notwithstanding the productivity of the valley's farms and ranches, the march of civilization was a two-edged sword: the semi-arid grasslands soon deteriorated under excessive grazing. In 1865, Orson Hyde lamented that where stands of luxuriant grasses once predominated "there is now nothing but the desert weed, the sage, the rabbit-bush and such like plants that make very poor feed for stock."

Brian Q. Cannon

Settling the Salt Lake Valley

1847 Plat A, consisting of 135 blocks, is surveyed by Orson Pratt and Henry Sherwood

1848 Lots in Plat A are formally allocated to residents by Brigham Young and Heber C. Kimball using a lottery system

1848 Plat B, consisting of 63 blocks east of the original city, is surveyed

1848 Groups of farmers settle Sugarhouse, East Millcreek, Spring Creek (Holladay), and South Cottonwood (Murray), North Jordan (Taylorsville) and West Jordan

1849 Plat C, consisting of 84 blocks west of the original city, is surveyed

1849 5- and 10-acre agricultural plots south of the city are allocated to city dwellers based on need and ability to farm them productively

1849 Groups of farmers settle Brighton (now Poplar Grove/Glendale), English Fort (Granger), Union Fort, Butterfield (Herriman) and Willow Creek (Draper)

1851 East Jordan (Midvale) is settled

1859 South Jordan is settled

1847 | 1848 | 1849 | 1850 | 1851 | 1852 | 1853 | 1854 | 1855 | 1856 | 1857 | 1858 | 1859 | 1860 | 1861

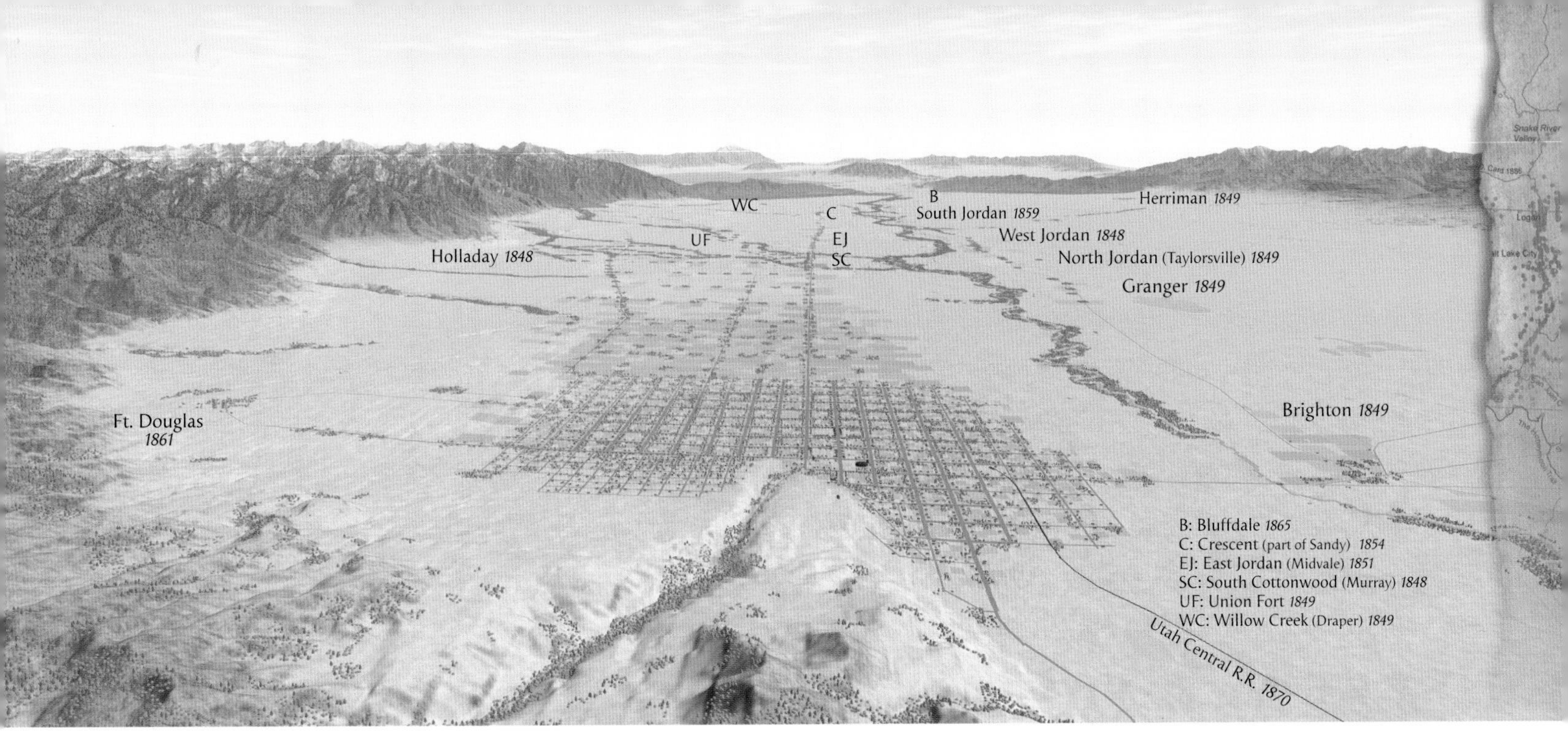

Looking south across the Salt Lake Valley, one can see the outlines of Salt Lake City as it would have appeared about 1870 (compare to 1847 view on p. 80). Note the newly completed Salt Lake Tabernacle on the temple block. The central business district was concentrated between West Temple and 2nd East and between South Temple and 3rd South, especially along East Temple (now Main Street). To the east, Fort Douglas had been established in 1862 by soldiers from California under the command of Col. Patrick Edward Connor. Smaller blocks comprising 2.5 acres with four lots were platted in what became the Avenues neighborhood of Salt Lake. Just beyond the city was the intensively cultivated "Big Field." Distinct settlements had appeared beyond this along the courses of Mill Creek and Big and Little Cottonwood Creeks, and along the Territorial Road (now State Street) and the main road west of the Jordan River (now Redwood Road). The Utah Central Railroad, completed in 1870, carried passengers from its terminus on Salt Lake's west side northward to the transcontinental line in Ogden.

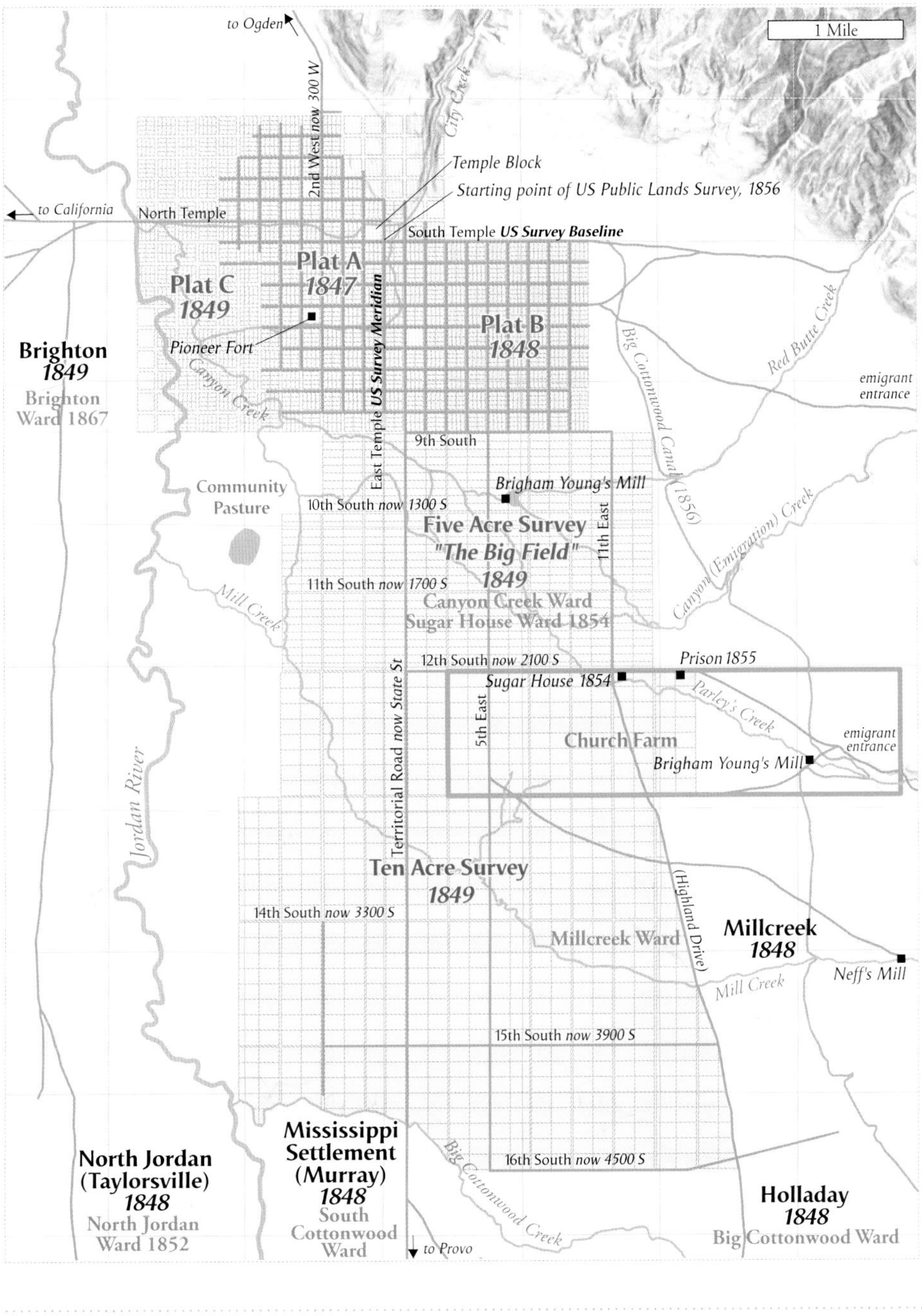

Great Salt Lake City and its agricultural districts were surveyed in the first few years of settlement. City blocks of ten acres were divided into eight lots, each large enough for vegetable gardens, fruit trees, and outbuildings. The survey of Plat A also included three public squares and a temple block. City dwellers could farm larger fields in the Big Field, which was subdivided into five-acre lots. In the ten-acre lots to the south, families typically lived on their farms. Although planners originally contemplated gridded plots of 20, 40, and 80 acres in the southern half of the valley, these were never implemented, as southern settlers surveyed irregular fields according to the terrain, roads, or creeks. In 1856, federal surveyors began a regular public lands survey (commonly known as "township and range") of the valley, shown in pink, which did not match the existing land use. Contrary to settlers' fears, the government allowed these existing surveys and ownership to stand. The pattern shown here has influenced the urban development of the northeast valley to this day, but the federal one-mile square sections dominated the later development of the west side of the Salt Lake Valley.

Exploring Utah

1847–1861

DURING THE TWO DECADES following the Saints' initial migration to the Salt Lake Valley in 1847, at least 60,000 converts followed. The Church sponsored explorations of present-day Utah to accommodate the influx by finding sites for new settlements and to stake claim to the surrounding territory. The Church also emphasized preaching to the American Indians (see p. 98), and several missions were sponsored to begin the process. These expeditions and missions played key roles in the Mormon settlement of the West. Surveying parties ascertained possible locations for settlements, noting climate, terrain, timber, and mineral resources. Many sites described in these reports became Mormon settlements (see p. 96).

The motives for the federal government to explore the region included surveying and fortifying the overland trails and identifying feasible routes for the construction of a transcontinental railroad. In Washington, D.C., a political battle was waged to determine which city would become the eastern terminus. Proposed northern, central, and southern routes brought the Army Corps of Engineers west. Many of the routes they surveyed soon became roads used by stage coaches, express riders, emigrants, and the telegraph.

Jay H. Buckley

Government Explorers

In 1849, Captain Howard Stansbury of the Army Corps of Engineers traveled west on the Oregon Trail. His orders were to survey locations for military posts to assist immigrants on the trail, locate a route for a supply artery between the trail and Salt Lake City, survey the Great Salt Lake Valley, make observations of Mormon and Indian communities, and discover available natural resources. He surveyed the region of the Great Salt Lake and Utah Lake. Stansbury's return route was south of the existing trail on a more direct course, which remains one of the expedition's most significant contributions. His trail became the preferred route for stage coaches, Pony Express riders, and the Union Pacific Railroad.

Lieutenant John W. Gunnison, who had earlier assisted Captain Stansbury, was selected to explore the possibility of a railroad route between the 38th and 39th parallels. In October 1853, Gunnison and seven others were massacred by Pahvant Utes near Sevier Lake. The Gunnison massacre had lasting effects: false accusations of Mormon involvement greatly strained the Church's relationship with the federal government and contributed to the tensions that led to the Utah War of 1857 (see p. 110). Edward G. Beckwith was granted permission to continue Gunnison's survey to the Pacific. Railroads eventually followed portions of his route.

Although initially sent to California, Lt. Col. Edward J. Steptoe also agreed to investigate the Gunnison massacre. He built a road through west-central Utah (along the route earlier found by John Reese, shown at right) and nearly became the new governor of the territory. His military presence further strained Mormon-Federal relations. James H. Simpson was General Albert Sidney Johnston's chief topographical engineer. He led two expeditions east from Camp Floyd through the Wasatch and Uinta mountain ranges to Fort Bridger. More important were his surveys west, which improved on Steptoe's routes through the Great Basin to California. These roads were used by Pony Express riders, the overland stage, and pioneers.

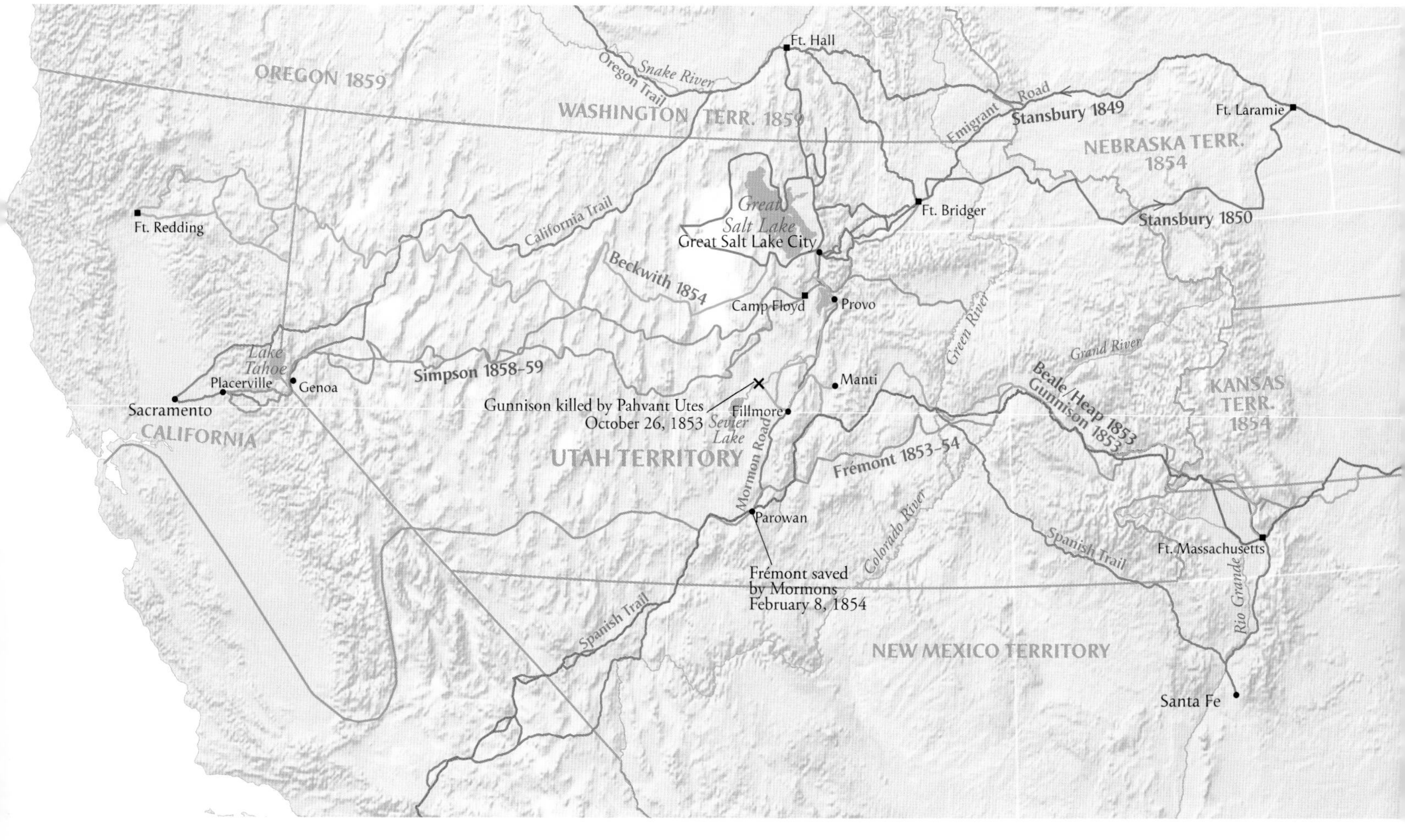

Pioneer Explorers

The first exploring expedition undertaken by the Mormon pioneers was led by Parley P. Pratt in 1847, traveling on horseback through the Utah, Rush, and Tooele valleys. Jesse C. Little led another group north along the Great Salt Lake's eastern shore to Miles Goodyear's fort near the Weber River and then to Cache Valley, finding both sites favorable for farming and grazing.

To answer Salt Lake Valley's need for supplies, Mormon Battalion veteran Jefferson Hunt led a group south along what became the "Mormon Corridor" connecting southern Utah and Los Angeles, returning with seed and cattle. Brigham Young envisioned multiple settlements along this corridor and asked Parley P. Pratt to survey the route. During the winter of 1849–50, Pratt and 50 men explored southern Utah as far as the Virgin River. They reported on 26 sites suitable for settlements, most of which were settled within a few years. In 1852, Young sent Albert Carrington to explore the area west of present-day Fillmore to locate lead deposits. Carrington followed the Sevier and Beaver rivers, finding both mineral deposits and settlement sites. Later expeditions extended further west, finding little to encourage colonization there.

John C. L. Smith explored the upper Sevier and Virgin rivers and found favorable locations for future towns such as Panguitch. William Gardner led an expedition up the Weber and down the Provo River in 1853. He reported potential sites for timber, grazing, settlement, and roads. Exploration of the Uinta Basin occurred in 1861, as Young sent territorial surveyor Jesse W. Fox and a separate party from Provo to locate settlement sites. Their unfavorable report discouraged Mormons from settling the region for many years.

In addition to exploratory expeditions, the Church sent many missionaries to settle among the American Indians and preach to them (see p. 98). These included Alfred Billings and the Elk Mountain Mission near present-day Moab; Thomas S. Smith's establishment of Fort Lemhi among the Bannocks in Idaho; Orson Hyde and the Green River Mission; and Jacob Hamblin's expedition to the Hopis. These missions achieved limited success and eventually dissolved. Their more lasting impact was the number of promising locations they found for future colonization (see p. 96).

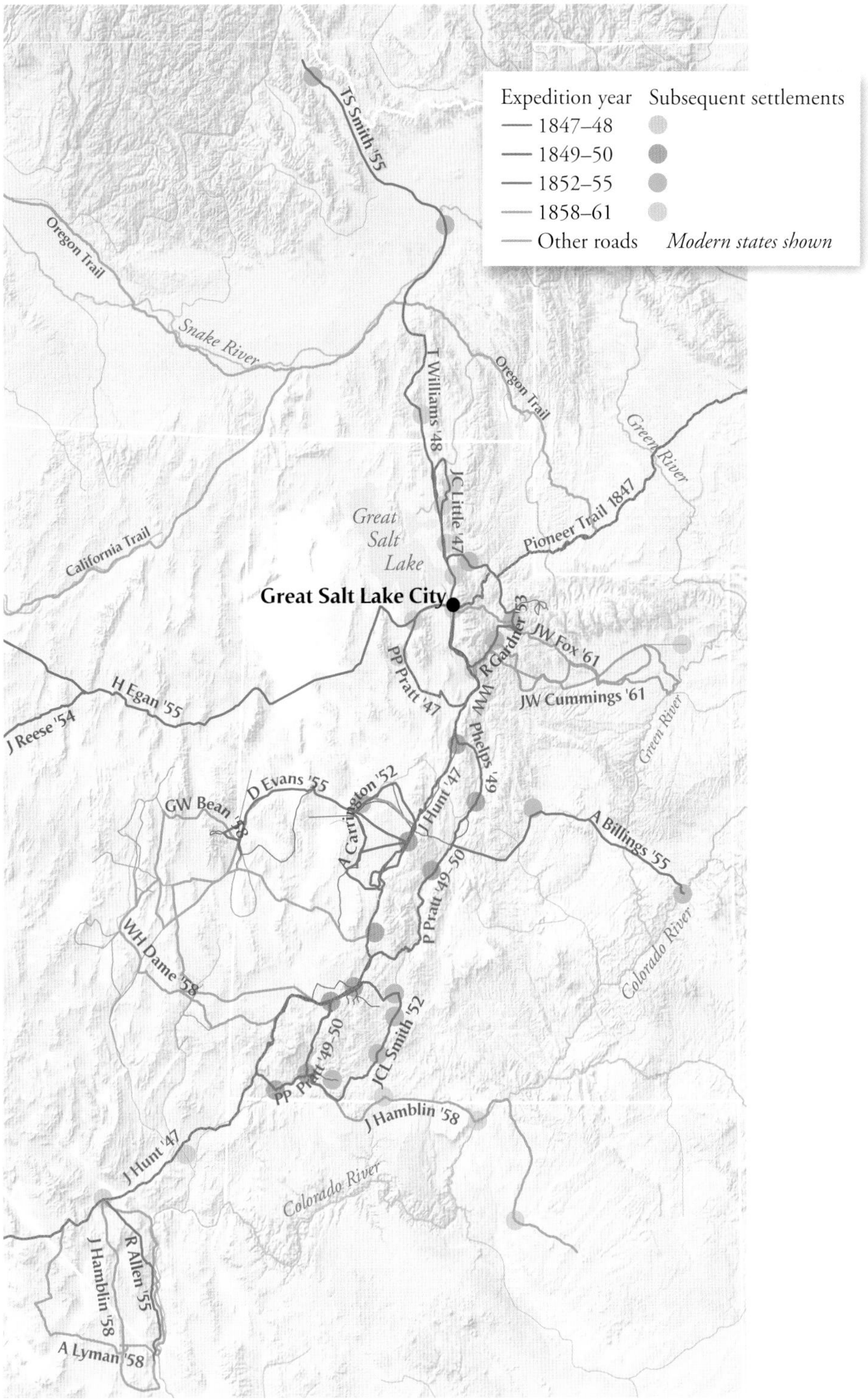

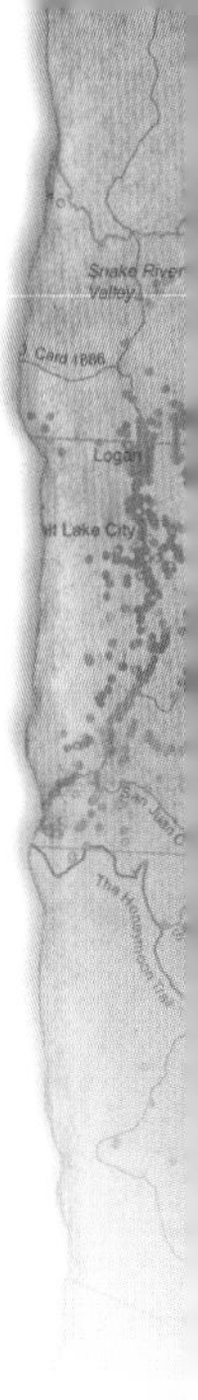

Exploring Utah

Cities in parentheses were settled directly based on report of expedition

- **Aug 1847** Jesse C. Little to Weber and Cache valleys *(Ogden)*
- **Nov–Dec 1847** Mormon Battalion veteran Jefferson Hunt pioneers route from Los Angeles to Salt Lake
- **Dec 1847** Parley P. Pratt to Utah and Tooele valleys *(Provo, Tooele)*
- **Feb 1848** T. Williams to Ft. Hall
- **Nov 1849–Feb 1850** Parley P. Pratt to southern Utah *(Nephi, Parowan, Fillmore)*
- **Aug 1849** W. W. Phelps to Sanpete Valley, climbs Mt. Nebo *(Manti)*
- **Sep 1852** William & Robert Gardner to upper Weber and Provo rivers *(Kamas, Heber)*
- Albert Carrington **1852** to Sevier Lake
- **Jun 1852** John C.L. Smith to upper Sevier and Virgin valleys *(Orderville, Panguitch)*
- Bannock Indian **May 1855** Mission *(Ft. Lemhi)*
- **25 Oct** Gunnison killed by Pahvants
- **1853** John W. Gunnison Expedition to explore central rail route
- **1854** E.G. Beckwith completes expedition
- **1853** Edward F. Beale & Gwin H. Heap explore central rail route
- **1853–1854** John C. Frémont's 5th expedition
- **8 Feb** rescued by Parowan Mormons
- **1854** John Reese pioneers direct route from Salt Lake City to Carson Valley
- **May 1855** Elk Mountain Mission *(Moab, Castle Dale)*
- **May–Jul 1855** David Evans to Snake Valley, Wheeler Peak
- **Jun 1855** Rufus Allen down the Colorado River
- **Sep 1855** Howard Egan pioneers shortcut to Sacramento in 10 days
- James W. Cummings & **Aug 1861** Jesse W. Fox to Uinta Basin *(Vernal)*
- **Mar–Apr 1858** Jacob Hamblin, Amasa Lyman down the Colorado River
- **Apr–Jun 1858** George W. Bean and William H. Dame into the West Desert *(Panaca)*
- **Oct–Dec 1858** Jacob Hamblin across the Colorado to Hopi villages
- **May–Jun 1859** James H. Simpson expedition guided by John Reese across Great Basin

1847 | 1848 | 1849 | 1850 | 1851 | 1852 | 1853 | 1854 | 1855 | 1856 | 1857 | 1858 | 1859 | 1860 | 1861

Settling the Wasatch Front

1847–1890

Historians and other commentators on Utah's past have tended to view the nineteenth-century Beehive Territory as an agrarian commonwealth; the state is still often viewed as relatively rural. However, according to the federal census, Utah has generally been about as urban as the rest of the United States, and well above average in recent years. Utah's most urban region lies along the Wasatch Front, a series of valleys bordered by the Wasatch Mountains on the east and the Great Salt Lake and the Oquirrh Mountains on the west, anchored by Salt Lake City, Ogden, and Provo.

As pioneer companies entered the Salt Lake Valley throughout 1847, it became clear that Great Salt Lake City would not be able to accommodate everyone, and many settlers began to look for their own lands. Settlement quickly proceeded to the north and south. Prior to 1860, almost all new settlements were along the Wasatch Front, with some notable exceptions such as San Bernardino, Carson Valley, Sanpete County, and Iron County (see p. 96). This region contained the most fertile agricultural land, milder winters than the valleys in the mountains, and the most extensive and easily diverted streams for irrigation, including the Weber, Ogden, Jordan, American Fork, Provo, and Spanish Fork rivers, and several creeks in the Salt Lake Valley.

Although many of the outlying Wasatch Front settlements began as scattered farms, almost all were soon laid out as urban villages with the familiar Utah grid pattern (see page 44). The reasons for Utah's rapid urbanization are not hard to find. When settlers began to arrive in Utah during the late 1840s and early 1850s (many from British cities), they promoted a mercantilist rather than agrarian economy. While the latter encourages self-sufficiency of the individual, the former encourages self-sufficiency of the community (especially important for the isolated Church to survive). Community leaders preached this, and the towns became centers of economic and population growth. Homegrown businesses produced and sold commodities as diverse as shoes, overalls, wagons, and plows. The Church formed Zion's Cooperative Mercantile Institution (ZCMI) and factories to develop a local economy (see p. 118).

Just as important, Utah's principal mineral lodes bordered the Wasatch Front on the east and west, in the Wasatch and Oquirrh Mountains. The cities in the valley drew in the wealth of these mining districts, processed the minerals, and sent them on to national and worldwide markets. At the same time, these cities served as distribution points for locally grown and imported agricultural commodities and other essential goods and services, encouraging further urban growth. Lastly, foreign immigrants (primarily European LDS converts) tended to settle in the cities first, where they were able to form tight-knit communities.

Thomas Alexander

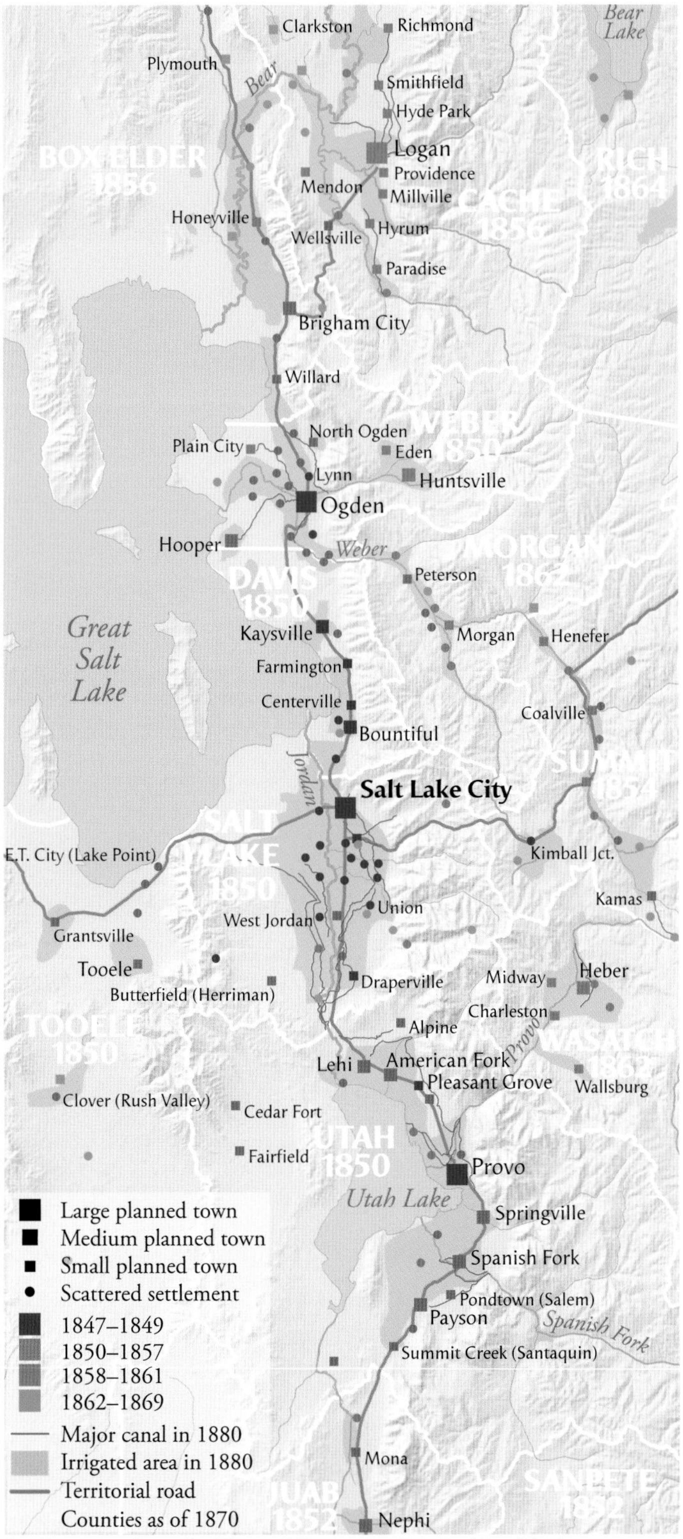

Settlements along the Wasatch Front closely coincide with the most productive agricultural regions of nineteenth-century Utah. In 1847, pioneers were already moving to the north and south of Salt Lake City to claim prime land. The earliest settlements would become the major towns of each valley. Some were planned settlements, to which settlers were called by Church leaders, but most pioneers settled where they chose because of relatives or friends, a desire to build "the kingdom," or economic opportunities; this scattered pattern was predominant in most of the Salt Lake Valley. In each community, settlers organized to construct canals to divert water for irrigation, to herd cattle and sheep, and to make and trade goods and services. Businesses included blacksmiths, haberdasheries, dressmakers, shoemakers, coopers, and the other necessities of life in the nineteenth century.

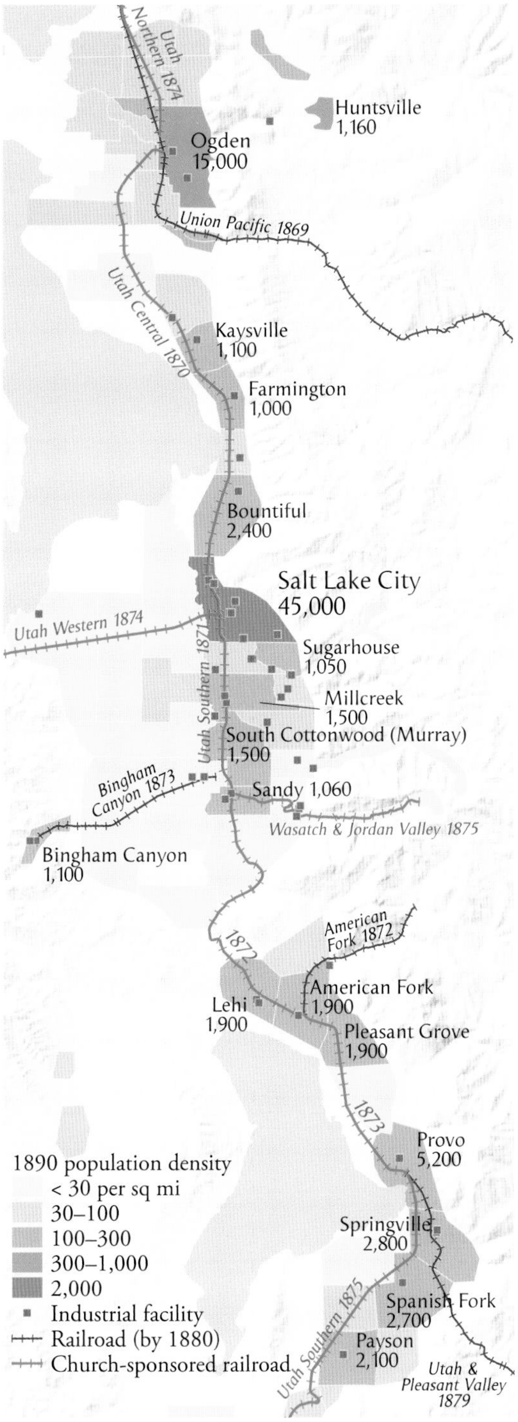

The Wasatch Front Becomes Urban

Historically, urban development in the United States has resulted from four factors: commerce, manufacturing, mining, and ideology. All four of these factors promoted the development of Utah's Wasatch Front. Established because of religious ideology, Salt Lake City, Ogden, and Provo all served as commercial centers, especially as railroads connected them to each other (an effort initially begun by the Church itself) and to the outside world.

Commodity extraction soon began. In 1849 parties engaged in lumbering and in extracting salt from the Great Salt Lake. Entrepreneurs organized the West Mountain Mining District in 1863, and commercial mining exploded after the shipment of the first load of copper in 1868. Mining led to the founding of towns such as Eureka (1869), Alta (1871), and Murray (1872) for mining, milling, and smelting and the influx of thousands of non-Mormon miners and merchants to the cities (see p. 112).

Manufacturing began with early entrepreneurs (especially millers) or with the cooperative efforts of Mormon settlements (see p. 118). These operations usually began small, but many soon expanded to provide goods for the entire region. In Salt Lake City, the Utah Manufacturing Company (1868) produced wagons, carriages, and agricultural machinery. Entrepreneurs in Provo established the Provo Woolen Mills. At Brigham City the cooperative organized a large number of manufacturing enterprises. As an adjunct of commerce, each of these businesses marketed their products in Utah communities and elsewhere.

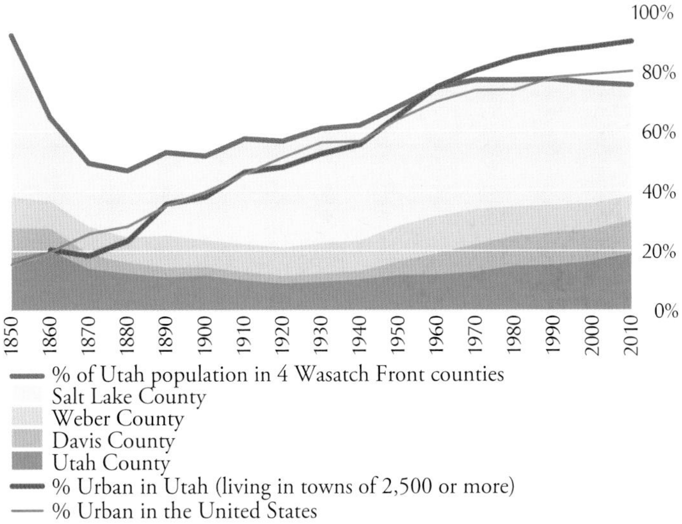

Urbanization in Utah

Utah has generally been considered a rural state, but in terms of the percentage of people living in urban areas (defined by the U.S. Census as places of 2,500 or more residents), Utah urbanized at essentially the same rate as the remainder of the United States. Although the Wasatch Front was the heart of the Mormon colony, it lost its population dominance during the 1860s and 1870s as settlement rapidly expanded (see p. 96). It gradually regained its importance during the twentieth century due to its concentration of non-farm jobs. In fact, since World War II, Utah has been more urban than the U.S. average. By 2010, Utah was the eighth most urbanized state in the nation, surpassing such reputedly urban states as Pennsylvania, New York, and Illinois. Even "rural" Utahns tend to live in villages rather than on scattered farms, as encouraged by the City of Zion ideals (see p. 44).

Settling the Wasatch Front

- **1847** Salt Lake City, Bountiful, and Farmington settled
- **1847** First diversion of water from City Creek to irrigate crops
- **1848** Ogden, Centerville, Holladay, West Jordan
- **1849** Provo and Kaysville; Perpetual Emigrating Fund organized
- **1850** First diversion of water from the Jordan River
- **1851** Brigham City
- **1852** Legislature authorizes county courts to allocate water supplies
- **1853** Provo Canal and Irrigation Company authorized to divert ½ of Provo River for irrigation
- **1855** Cottonwood Canal Company incorporated; Springville settlers authorized to divert ½ of Spanish Fork River
- **1859** First dam constructed on Jordan River
- **1863** West Mountain Mining District organized
- **1868** First shipment of copper ore from Utah; Zion's Cooperative Mercantile Institution (ZCMI); Provo Woolen Mills
- **1869** Transcontinental Railroad completed; first shipment of fruit on railroad from Ogden
- **1870** Utah Central Railroad from Ogden to Salt Lake City
- **1872** Salt Lake County's dam at Jordan River outlet of Utah Lake
- **1873** Bingham and Camp Floyd R.R. to Bingham Canyon, Utah Southern R.R. completed to Provo, Utah Northern R.R. completed to Logan
- **1874** Ogden stockyards
- **1875** South Jordan Canal
- **1882** Jordan and Salt Lake City Canal
- **1887** Chambers of Commerce in Salt Lake City and Ogden
- Utah Sugar Company **1889**

1845 | 1850 | 1855 | 1860 | 1865 | 1870 | 1875 | 1880 | 1885

President Brigham Young

1847–1877

DURING **J**OSEPH **S**MITH'S LIFETIME, Brigham Young had been a man on the move. On foot, by wagon, stage, or canal boat, in a few cases by train, steamer, or sail, he traveled thousands of miles several times from Ohio to Missouri and from Illinois to New York, and once across the Atlantic (see p. 46). After three trips across the Great Plains in 1847 and 1848, he established his residence in Salt Lake City and turned his back on the East forever. Even the ease and speed of travel on the transcontinental railroad after 1869 failed to entice him from his mountain retreat.

But the traveling did not stop. From 1847 to 1877, Brigham Young spent more time on the road than ever before; by horse and carriage, then by rail, he traveled approximately 40,000 miles. He explored new territory to personally assess resources and judge the settlement potential of valleys, mountains, and deserts. Many trips involved important meetings with Indian leaders (see p. 98).

Most journeys were primarily pastoral in nature, visiting and encouraging the Saints in their widespread villages and homes. Such visits enhanced community, unity, and loyalty; they helped people to persevere in difficult circumstances; and they demonstrated that each community was considered important. Whether Latter-day Saints lived 45 miles, 80 miles, or 300 miles from Salt Lake City, most could count on at least one yearly visit from President Young.

These trips were grueling, as he spent weeks on the rough roads, delivering dozens of sermons. Tired horses could be exchanged along the way, but Young and his party had to endure happily for the good of the settlers. In fact, some of Young's greatest sermons and programs were inspired on these trips, including the United Order (in St. George in 1874, see p. 118) and the reorganization of the priesthood (also in St. George in 1877, see p. 128).

The personal attention "Brother Brigham" gave to the Saints was one key to the success of his leadership and was crucial to the successful colonization of the Great Basin when it was extremely difficult to make a living.

Ronald K. Esplin

Travels of President Young

During his tenure, President Brigham Young undertook hundreds of trips for various purposes. Nearby towns along the Wasatch Front were most often visited (Young traveled to or through Provo and Davis County at least 100 times each), especially when the railroad made day trips convenient in the 1870s. The President made nearly two dozen trips to southern Utah, even before he purchased a winter home in St. George in 1870; side trips to Manti and Sanpete Valley were common on these journeys. Extended trips northward were just as common, through Ogden to Logan and the Bear Lake Valley. Beyond these primary corridors, Young also tried to visit some of the new, small, struggling settlements at the outer reaches of Mormon civilization, such as Fort Lemhi, Idaho (1855), the Muddy River Valley, Nevada (1870), and Pahreah (1870).

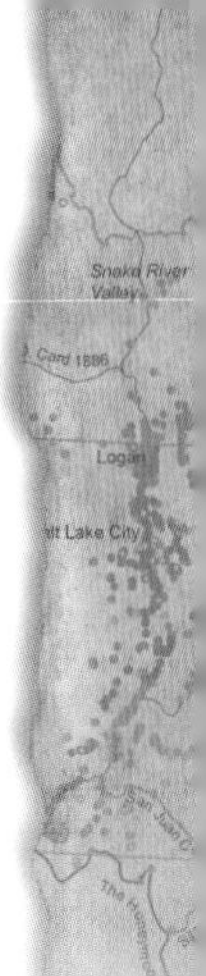

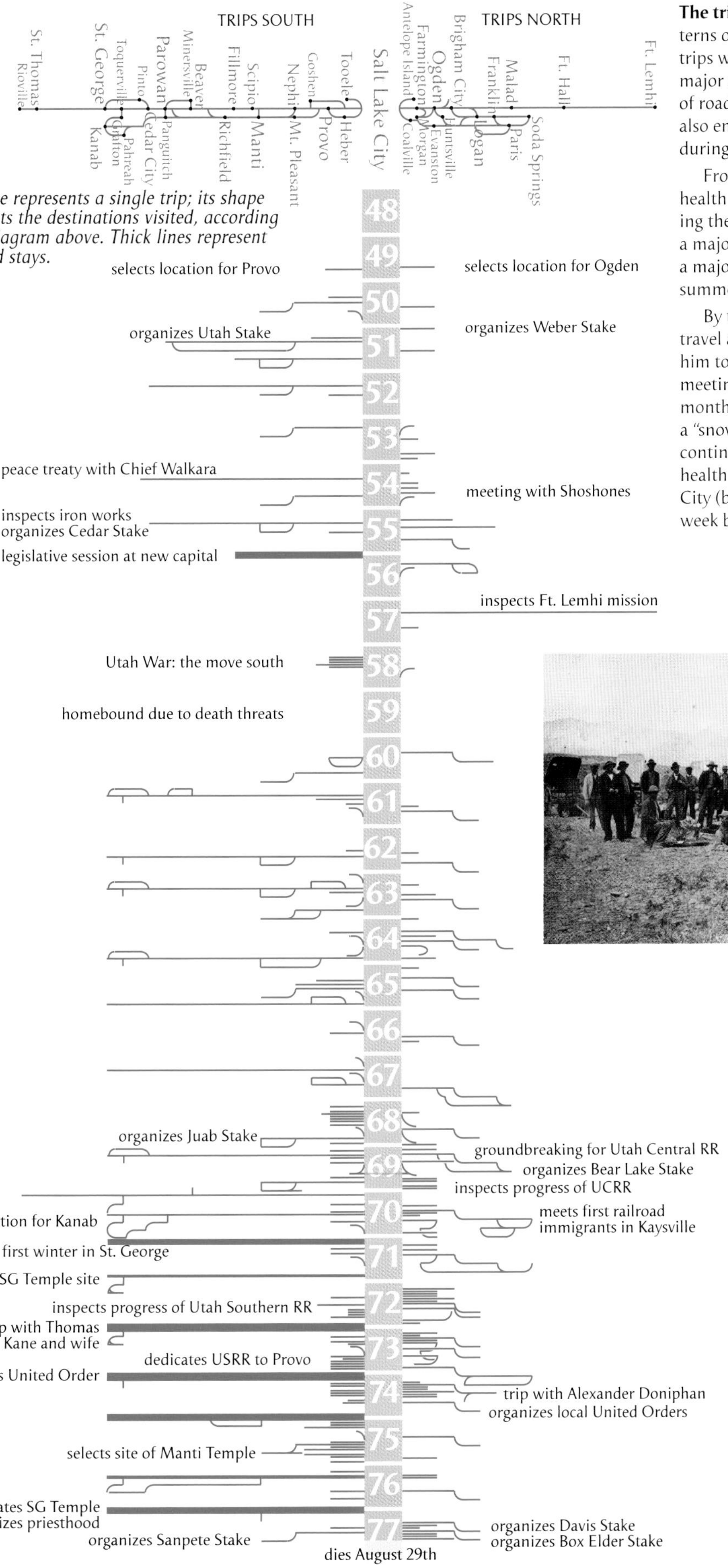

Each line represents a single trip; its shape represents the destinations visited, according to the diagram above. Thick lines represent extended stays.

The trips taken by Brigham Young show distinct patterns over time, as shown in this timeline. His earliest trips were more exploratory, directing the locations of major settlements but were not frequent due to the lack of roads. Most trips were along the Wasatch Front. He also enjoyed boating out to Antelope Island with friends during these years.

From 1856 to 1859, he traveled very little, due to ill health and occasional house arrest by hostile judges. During the 1860s, he established an annual pattern of taking a major trip south (usually to St. George) each winter and a major trip north (to Logan or Bear Lake Valley) each summer.

By the 1870s, the expanding railroad network made travel along the Wasatch Front almost trivial, allowing him to regularly attend stake conferences and business meetings. In his 70s, he stayed in St. George for several months each winter (shown as thick lines), beginning a "snowbird" trend that retired northern Utahns have continued in "Utah's Dixie" to this day. Old age and poor health did not stop Brigham: his final tour was Brigham City (by train) to organize the Box Elder Stake just one week before he passed away.

Brigham Young (seated near the center with a top hat) and his entourage at the Colorado River in 1870, near the mouth of the Virgin River. This was the farthest he traveled from Salt Lake City after 1847.

Each visit was a scene of pageantry and celebration, as well as gospel teaching. Young typically traveled with a large entourage of church leaders, family, friends, and invited guests, as well as supplies. In each town, they were often escorted through town by local leaders in a grand procession; bands played while settlers cheered from the sides of the street. Public banquets and parties commonly followed.

Deseret and Utah Territory

1849–1896

THE QUEST FOR SELF-GOVERNMENT AS A STATE was a major priority for the LDS Church during the nineteenth century. From 1849 to 1896, the goal gradually evolved from a theocracy, the Kingdom of God on earth, into an attempt to become fully reintegrated as Americans. The frontier of Mexico offered a perfect opportunity to build an independent, isolated community, avoiding the competition that had led to their eviction from every previous gathering place (the option of not gathering at all was not seriously considered).

However, when the Mexican War ended, the Saints found themselves back in the United States, so the vision was altered slightly to conform to American standards: the Kingdom of God would become a state. Given the rapid growth of the Church and the relatively low capacity of the Intermountain West for agriculture, Church leaders knew they would need a very large amount of land, far beyond what they then occupied. They also knew that economic independence would require access to the ocean. When leaders convened to create a constitution for their proposed State of Deseret, they claimed almost 440,000 square miles (almost all of the current states of Nevada, Utah, Arizona, and parts of all surrounding states), even though the Mormons had only settled less than a tenth of that.

From 1850 to 1868, the U.S. Congress gradually whittled Utah Territory (a name they preferred) down to a fifth of the size of Deseret. During this period, the Mormons were generally at odds with Congress, largely due to the practice of polygamy (see page 122). The shrinking boundaries of Utah Territory have often been portrayed as one more way in which the federal government persecuted the Saints. However, anti-Mormon sentiment, while ever-present, actually had little impact on boundaries. Although several radical proposals were made to punish the Mormons by drastically shrinking or even eliminating Utah, the bills that were enacted were generally rational attempts (given the limited knowledge Congress had of western geography) to provide self-government for each emerging cluster of settlements, including the Mormons. The pre-war politics of slavery had far more influence on Utah's boundaries than religious intolerance.

Despite six official petitions for statehood from the territorial assembly, and although Utah Territory met the de facto standard for statehood by the 1870s (i.e., a population equal to the allocation for a member of Congress), it would have to wait until 1896 for statehood, after the Church abandoned polygamy. By this time, Mormons comprised about 67% of the population of the state (the proportion has remained relatively constant ever since), and Utah contained over 80% of the Mormons in the Intermountain West. To this day, most Americans still tend to equate the state of Utah with the Church. Although it is as democratic as any other state and the Church itself is politically neutral, the predominance of voting Mormons has had a lasting impact on the government of the state (see page 188).

Brandon S. Plewe

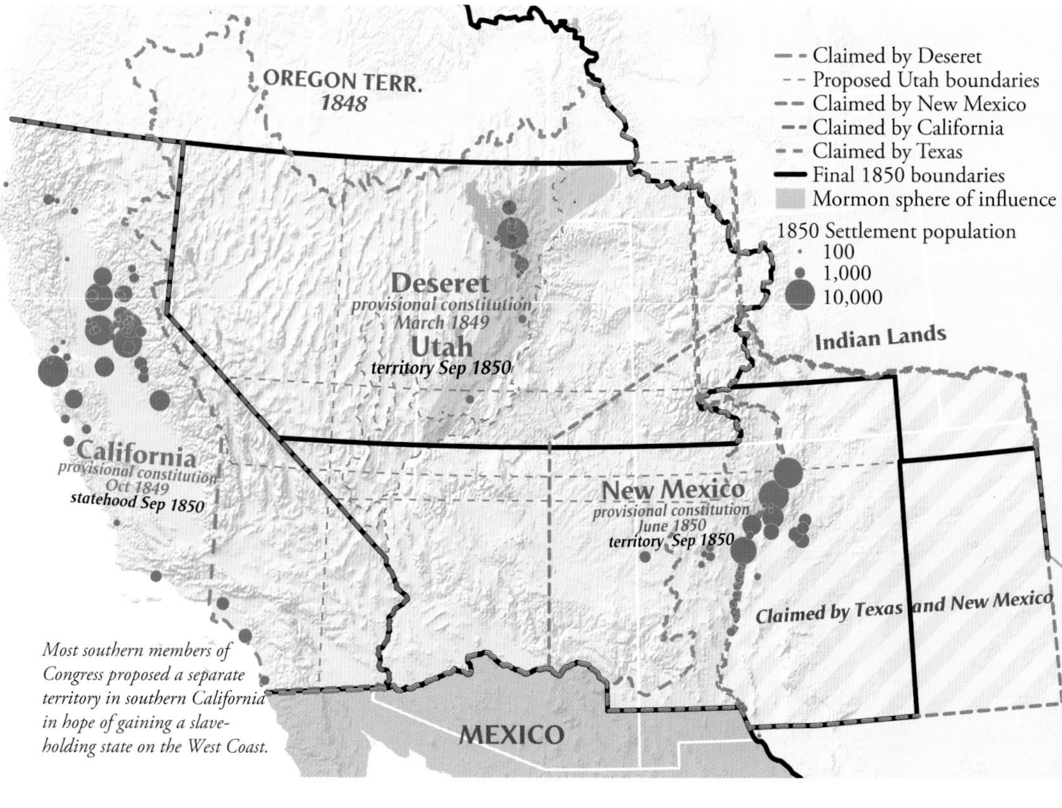

1849–1850

In 1848, the 500,000 square miles that Mexico sold to the United States to end their war (see p. 78) included the Spanish settlements in New Mexico and California and the Mormons in the Salt Lake Valley. When Congress failed to organize territories for them, each region formed its own provisional government. The State of Deseret claimed an immense area, far beyond what was settled or even explored by Mormons. The Deseret government operated for over a year, with a legislature, courts, and county governments. In the 1850 session, Congress had four overlapping claims to deal with, as well as the issue of whether or not slavery would be allowed in the new territories. It had previously been outlawed by the Mexican government, but Deseret's constitution was silent on the issue (a few southern converts had brought slaves to the West). With little anti-Mormon sentiment, the general consensus was to grant all the Mormon-settled area to Utah. The numerous proposed boundaries, included dividing California, granting everything but California to Utah, and granting it all to New Mexico. In the end, the Great Compromise of 1850 gave California what it requested and divided the remaining territory evenly between Utah and New Mexico, with a boundary that paid little attention to the landscape but that has survived to this day.

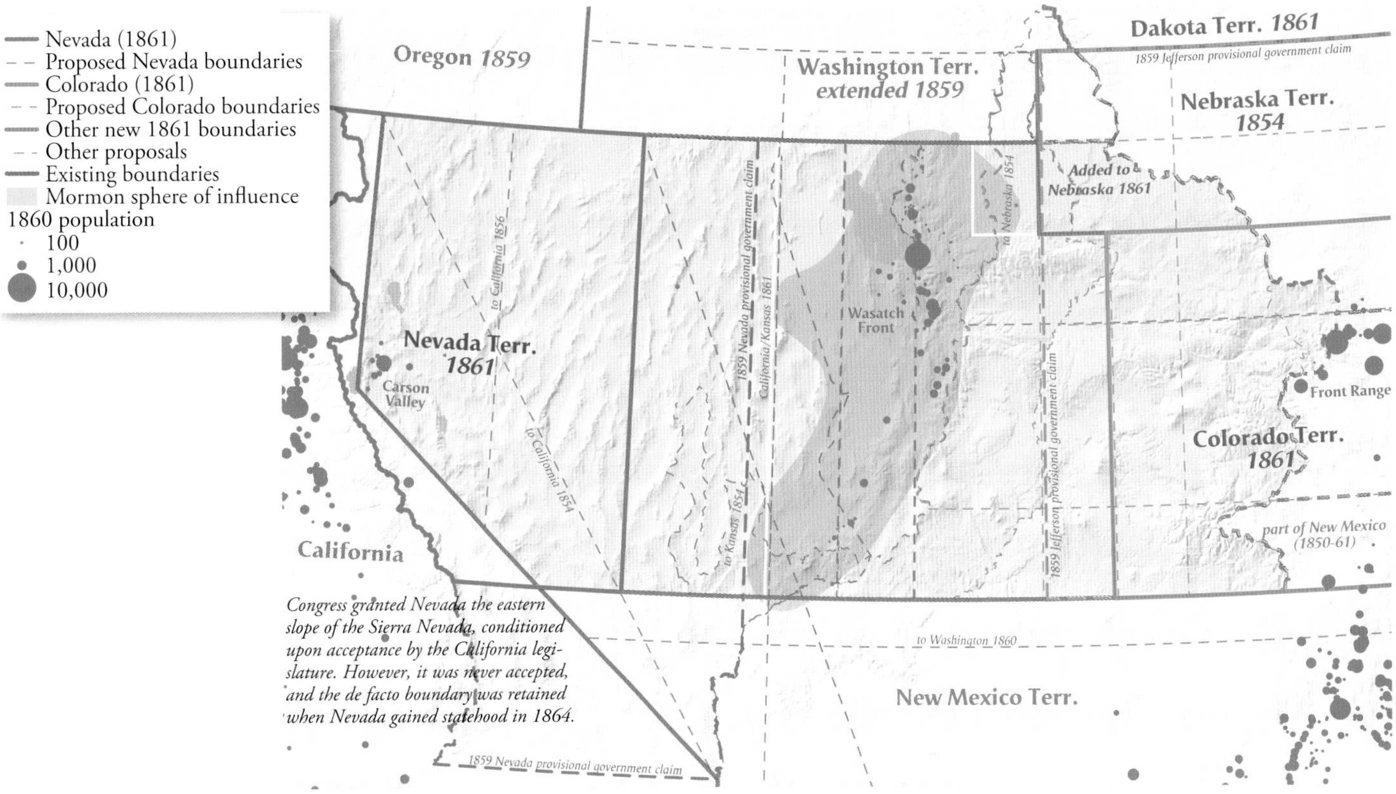

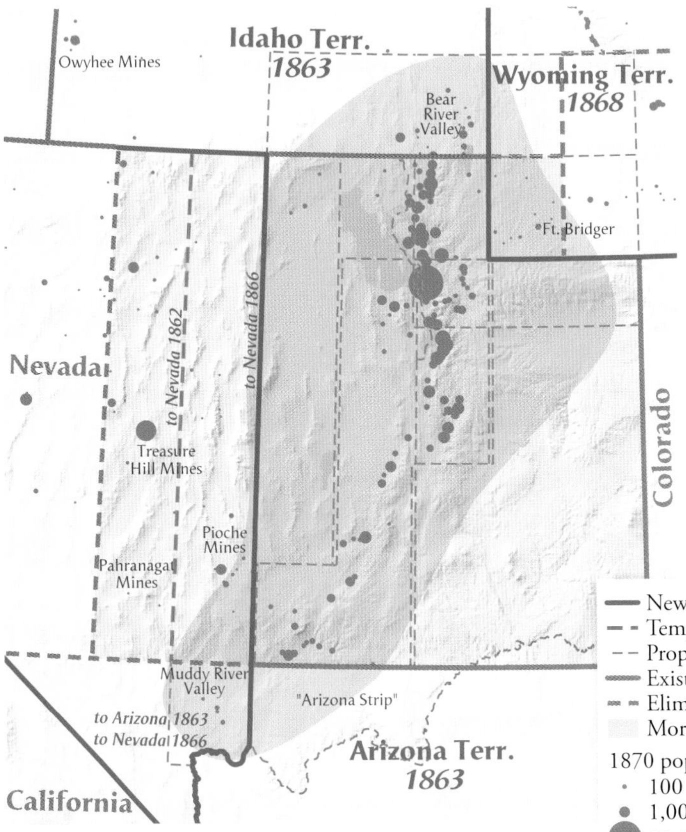

1854–1861

By 1856, new settlements, largely focused on mining, had been established along the eastern side of the Sierra Nevada and the Front Range of the Rockies. These areas were impractically distant from their territorial governments (Utah and Kansas, respectively), and, following earlier tradition, they created their own provisional governments and requested validation by Congress; the future Coloradans requested the name "Jefferson Territory." However, slavery politics was at an all-time high in Congress, and every proposal regarding the territories engendered extensive debate between northern and southern extremists. Anti-Mormon feelings were also present, especially among the Republicans who had declared polygamy as barbaric as slavery. Fortunately for the Saints, the most extreme proposals to eliminate Utah between Nevada and Colorado failed. However, a resolution did not occur until the election of Lincoln and the subsequent secession of several southern states left the North firmly in control, who soon divided Utah between the three settlement cores with relatively logical boundaries.

1862–1872

The Republican hegemony during and after the Civil War eliminated the issue of slavery from debate concerning the western territories but raised the prominence of anti-polygamy (and anti-Mormon) influences on policy (see p. 122). In addition to various laws aimed to outlaw polygamy and punish the Church for practicing it, boundaries were attempted as a form of pressure. Proposals to severely reduce or even eliminate Utah Territory failed, as did proposals to grant Utah statehood and additional territory in exchange for abandoning polygamy. In the end, Utah's boundaries were only reduced when outlying areas were settled by non-Mormons who preferred to have their own governments.

Timeline

- **1846–1848** Mexican-American War
- **Jul 1847** Mormon Pioneers arrive in Alta California in Mexico
- **2 Feb 1848** Treaty of Guadelupe Hidalgo
- **May 1849** Provisional State of Deseret organized
- **Jun 1850** Provisional State of New Mexico organized
- **Sep 1850** Compromise of 1850 creates California, Utah, and New Mexico
- **Sep 1859** Constitution of provisional Nevada
- **Oct 1859** Constitution of provisional Jefferson (Colorado)
- **28 Feb 1861** Nevada & Colorado territories created from Utah Territory
- **Oct 1864** Nevada granted statehood
- **1862–1866** Nevada expanded, removing mining camps from Utah Territory
- **1868** Wyoming Territory created, including northeast corner of Utah Territory
- **1868–1872** Failed proposals to reduce, eliminate, or enlarge Utah
- Utah granted statehood **1896**

1845 1850 1855 1860 1865 1870 1875 1880 1885 1890 1895

Missions of the 19th Century

1849–1890

Missionary work was a major part of Brigham Young's life after he joined the Church in 1832. By the time he became the acting leader of the Church in 1844, he had served ten missions. Although as President he was unable to serve in the field, he continued to emphasize missionary work. During his 30-year tenure, Church membership grew from 30,000 to 115,065, and there were about 2,530 missionaries called to serve full-time missions. On average, about 80 missionaries were called each year. Excluding member missionary work (which has always been important), the formal missionary work during Brigham Young's administration was modest and must be seen as a part of the larger patterns of emigration to and colonization in the American West. Church calls could just as easily be extended for individuals and families to settle a new community or to establish new crops or industries in the Great Basin as to serve proselytizing missions. Missionaries tended to be called at an older age than is now the practice, and in many cases the length of missionary service was longer. The missionaries came from the Seventies Quorums of the Church, and many of those called left families at home while they served. All of these missions were under the direction and supervision of Brigham Young and the Quorum of the Twelve Apostles.

President Young built on the earlier calls issued by Joseph Smith and then expanded the work into continental Europe and to other countries around the world. Although many of the missions in countries that were opened during the 1849–52 initiative did not survive, it suggests how seriously Brigham Young took the command to carry the gospel to all the world.

While the missionary force was reduced during the Utah War (see p. 110) and during the several years of isolation following, President Young began to reopen missions near the end of his life, starting with the eastern United States. This renewed effort continued to expand for the rest of the century.

Throughout his presidency, Brigham Young taught the importance of missionary work: "When I came into this Church, I started right out as a missionary, and took a text, and began to travel on a circuit. Truth is my text, the Gospel of salvation my subject, and the world my circuit" (*Journal of Discourses 9:137*).

David J. Whittaker

19th Century Missions

During Joseph Smith's lifetime, most missionaries served in the eastern United States and Canada, with a few going to the new mission in Great Britain. The worldwide expansion from 1850 to 1854 resulted in long-term success in Australia, Switzerland, and Scandinavia, but most of the missions closed when missionaries were recalled during the Utah War. Work was very limited during the darkest days of polygamy-related persecution, but missions and missionaries started to re-expand during the 1870s. After the Manifesto (1890) publicly ended polygamy, improved relations with the rest of the world, and a crop of young second-generation members led to a rapid increase in missionary work in the 1890s.

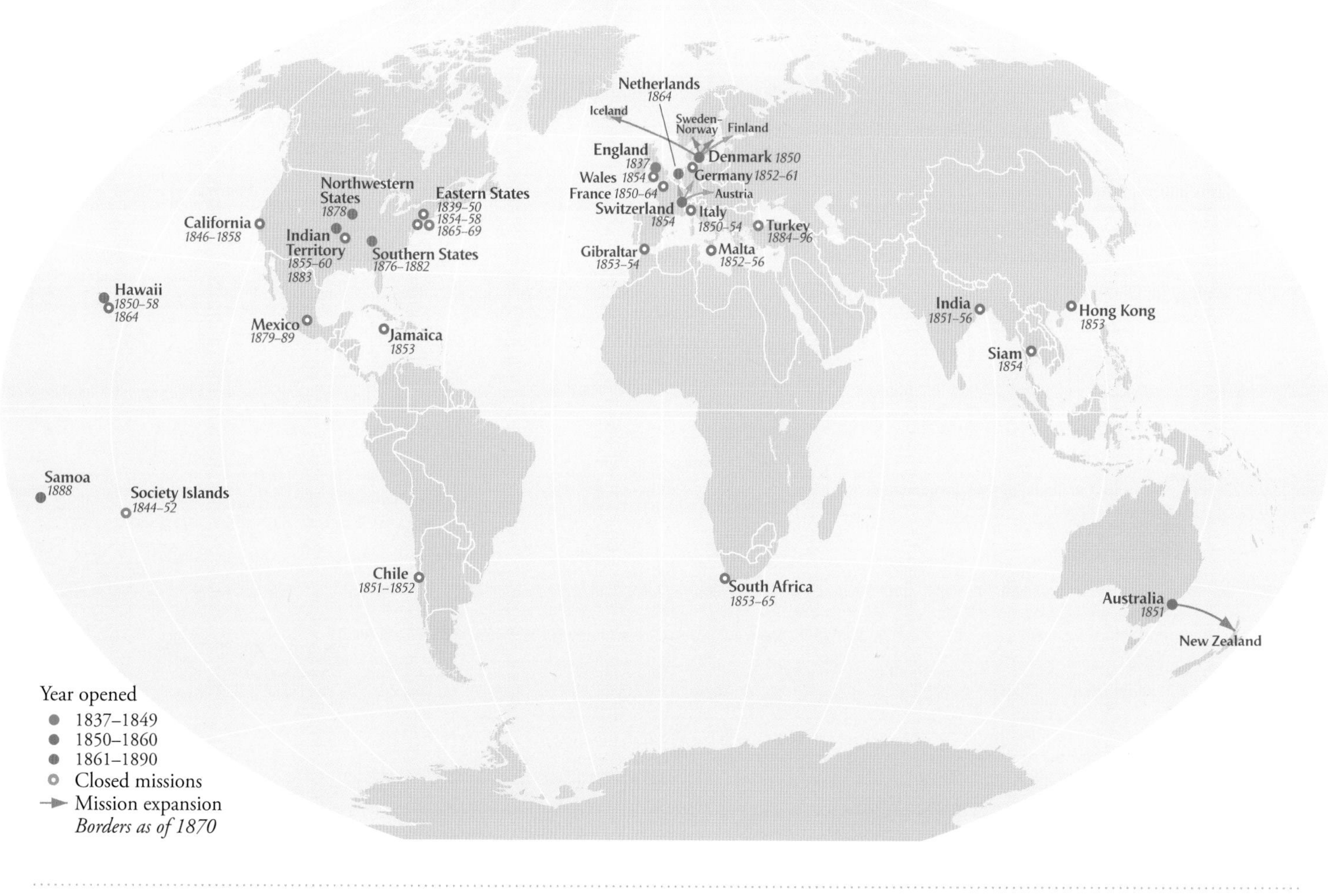

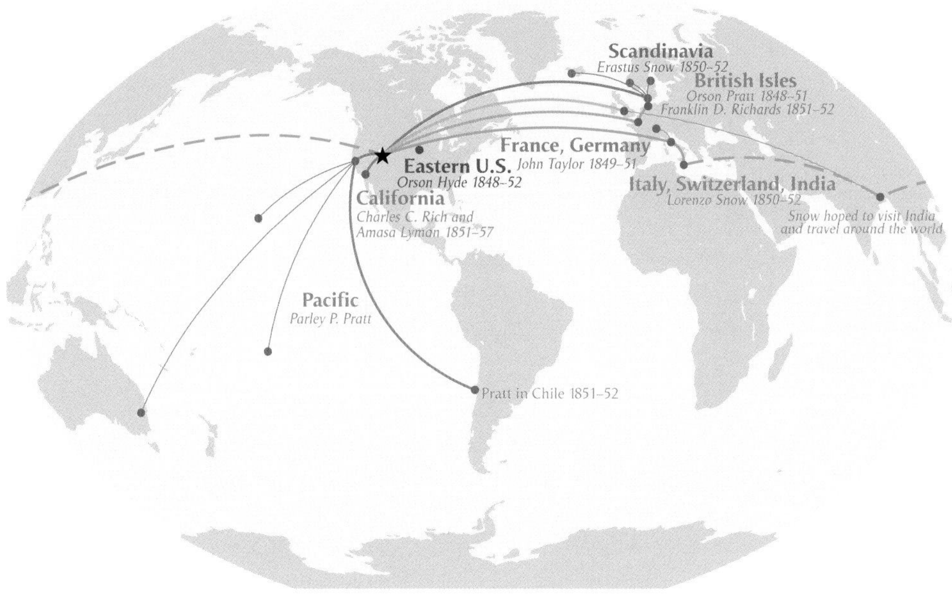

The 1849 Mission Plan

In 1849, Brigham Young announced a grand plan for expanding global missionary work, assigning each Apostle to a section of the world (foreshadowing the area system of the latter twentieth century; see p. 164) and sending them out with many other missionaries to open new countries. The focus on Europe may have been inspired by the wave of revolutionary movements there in 1848. In 1849 the Italian, French, and Scandinavian missions were opened; in 1850 missionaries were in Switzerland and Hawaii. Apostle Parley P. Pratt, assigned to the presidency of the Pacific Region, visited Chile in 1851, published the first Spanish language tract in 1852, and sent missionaries again to Australia in 1853. In 1852 additional missionaries were called to Gibraltar, South Africa, India, Ceylon, Siam (Thailand), and Hong Kong. While most of these initial attempts met with limited success, major long-term centers were opened in Europe (especially Scandinavia and Switzerland) and the Pacific (especially Australia).

The demographics of missionaries in the nineteenth century were quite different than today's young elders. They were typically married men, called from the quorums of Elders and Seventies. Each served for as long as he could, typically one to three years. Statistics have shown that younger men tended to serve longer missions to more remote countries (at the extreme, missionaries to the Pacific Islands averaged 30 years old and served an average of 35 months), while older men tended to serve shorter missions within the United States (where the average missionary was 40 years old, serving for 10 months). From 1860 though the 1880s, most missionaries were called to Europe until work in the United States was reopened in earnest by President Wilford Woodruff.

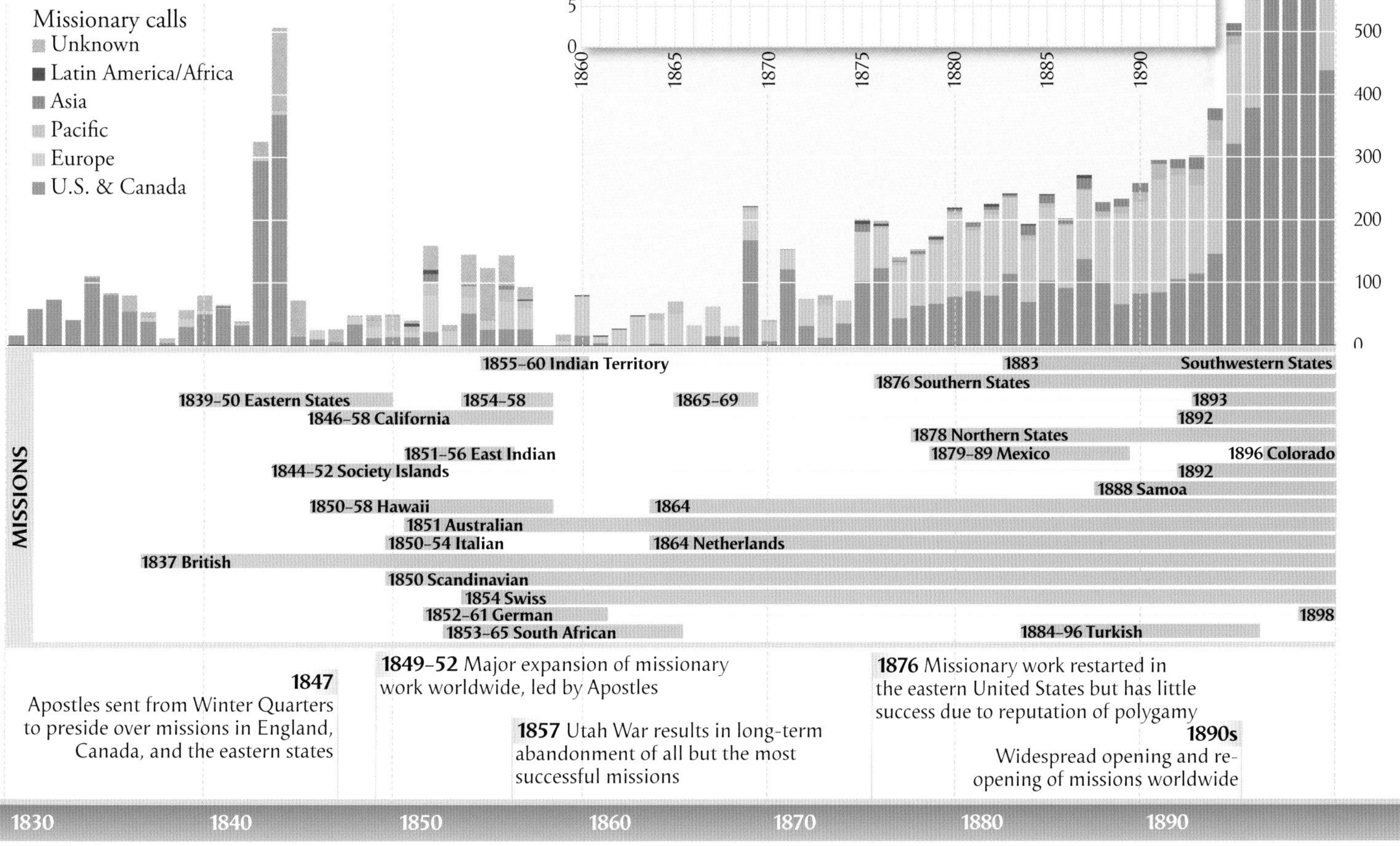

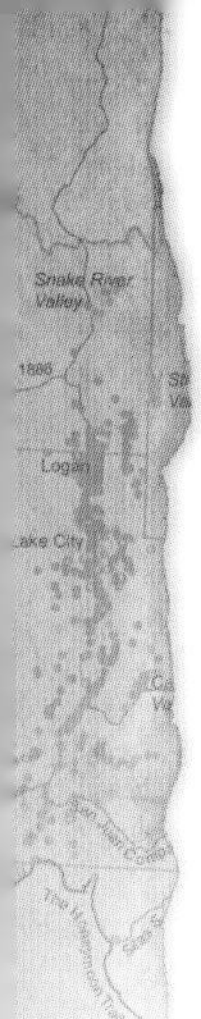

Intermountain Colonization

1847–1899

Mormon colonization resulted in the establishment of approximately 100 settlements within the first ten years of the Saints' arrival in the Salt Lake Valley in July 1847. By the end of the nineteenth century an estimated 500 communities had been settled throughout the Intermountain West.

Two broad geographical divisions of these settlements can be recognized: those in the Mormon Corridor stretching from southern Idaho to southeastern Nevada along the eastern edge of the Great Basin, and those beyond the Mormon Corridor. Many of these colonization efforts were organized by Church leaders, who called a group of settlers to occupy a specified site based on reports of surveying parties (see page 86). These first colonizers typically included individuals possessing the variety of skills needed for successful colonization.

By 1849, initial settlements were planted in each of the valleys of the Wasatch Front. Then came the colonization of several outlying valleys along the Mormon Corridor. Early settlement efforts were largely to the south of Salt Lake City, reflecting Brigham Young's belief that it was too cold for successful agriculture in the Cache Valley and also reflecting his desire to extend colonization toward the Pacific Ocean. Some of these outposts were attempts to make the Mormon colony economically self-sufficient, such as the iron mission to Parowan and the cotton mission to St. George. Others, such as the Cache Valley colony to the north, occurred as settlers independently moved onto new lands as population pressure increased in the earlier settlements.

While the central Mormon Corridor was being established, settlements were also begun in far flung locations reflecting Young's vision of a vast State of Deseret, such as San Bernardino, California, the Carson Valley of today's Nevada, Fort Supply and Fort Bridger in what is now Wyoming, Fort Lemhi in Oregon Territory (near today's Salmon, Idaho), and Las Vegas. Of these, San Bernardino was most successful, reaching a population of 1,400 by 1855, but all of these outlying settlements were abandoned in 1857 as Brigham recalled the settlers during the Utah War (see page 110).

Later expansion beyond the Mormon Corridor was primarily the result of individuals or groups moving to a new location to capitalize on economic opportunities, although the Church sometimes gave capital and encouragement to organize joint stock companies to develop economic activities. The settlers in these outlying areas usually came from existing fringe settlements, such as St. George or Logan.

Completion of the transcontinental railroad in 1869 and subsequent railroads (many initially funded by the Church) opened new lands to settlement as the railroad companies sold their land grants from the federal government. Mormons, always feeling the pressure in existing settlements from the constant influx of immigrant converts, took advantage of these opportunities. This was especially true in eastern Idaho and along the Oregon Short Line (owned by the Union Pacific) and routes toward Montana and Oregon. By 1883, settlements in the Snake River Valley were so promising that the Church was formally encouraging Mormons to migrate to the area.

Other Mormon settlements in the West were established in scattered pockets wherever member-explorers found sufficient land and water, including southwestern and north central Wyoming, eastern Nevada, eastern Arizona, southern Colorado, northwestern New Mexico, and outside the United States in southern Alberta and northern Mexico. The latter two became especially important as a refuge where Mormons could escape prosecution for polygamy. Charles Ora Card of Logan was directed in 1886 by Church President John Taylor to find a settlement site in Canada. Cardston was established as the central community, but other settlements were soon established nearby (see p. 208). Mormon settlers also fled to the south to escape prosecution for polygamy, founding several communities in northern Mexico within 200 miles of the U.S. border in Chihuahua and Sonora beginning in 1885 (see p. 218).

Richard H. Jackson

Intermountain Colonization

- **1847** Salt Lake City established
- **1848** Weber Valley (Ogden)
- **1849** Utah Valley (Provo), Tooele Valley, Sanpete Valley
- **1851** Box Elder, Pahvant, Parowan, and Juab valleys; San Bernadino, California; Carson Valley, Nevada
- **1853** Fort Supply, Wyoming
- **1855** Las Vegas, Nevada and Fort Limhi, Idaho
- **1856** Cache Valley; Beaver; Cotton Mission
- **1857–58** Abandonment of outlying settlements
- **1859** Logan
- **1864** Bear Lake Valley
- **1864** Sevier Valley
- **1865** Southern Nevada
- **1876** Northeastern Arizona
- **1877** Castle Valley and Vernal, Utah; Mesa, Arizona
- **1878** Pocatello and Blackfoot, Idaho; San Luis Valley, Colorado
- **1879** Bluff, Utah; Rexburg, Idaho; Star Valley, Wyoming
- **1885** Northern Mexico
- **1887** Southern Alberta
- Big Horn Basin, Wyoming **1893**
- White Pine Valley, Nevada **1897**

1845 · 1850 · 1855 · 1860 · 1865 · 1870 · 1875 · 1880 · 1885 · 1890 · 1895

Settling the Intermountain West

Brigham Young's plan to establish a transportation corridor from the Pacific Coast through Mormon settlements stretching to Salt Lake City ended when San Bernadino was abandoned by the Mormon colonists, but the Mormon Corridor between southeastern Idaho and southeastern Nevada has continued to be the core of the Mormon culture area. Beyond the Corridor, settlement expanded into eastern Utah and surrounding states, then into Mexico and Canada. Most of these later settlements were not centrally planned, but were typically settled by groups of pioneers from an existing settlement that had reached its population capacity. For example, the settlers of eastern Arizona were primarily from St. George and southern Utah.

Stake Tabernacles

Tabernacles were constructed by Mormons as places where large numbers of Church members from a regional stake (see p. 128) could gather for counsel and teaching. In many respects, the temples at Kirtland and Nauvoo had more in common with these tabernacles than later temples. Shortly after establishing Salt Lake City and selecting the Temple Block, a temporary tabernacle, or bowery, was constructed of poles with a brush cover. It and subsequent buildings were eventually replaced by the magnificent current structure (see p. 114).

Tabernacles represented the success of a town as it became a stake, and were constructed of the best materials and handiwork that local residents could afford. They housed quarterly stake conferences that gathered members from the wards and branches in all the surrounding settlements. Construction of tabernacles ended in the mid-twentieth century as multipurpose stake centers replaced them (see p. 160). A few are still used for Church events, but most have since been destroyed or transformed into museums or civic buildings.

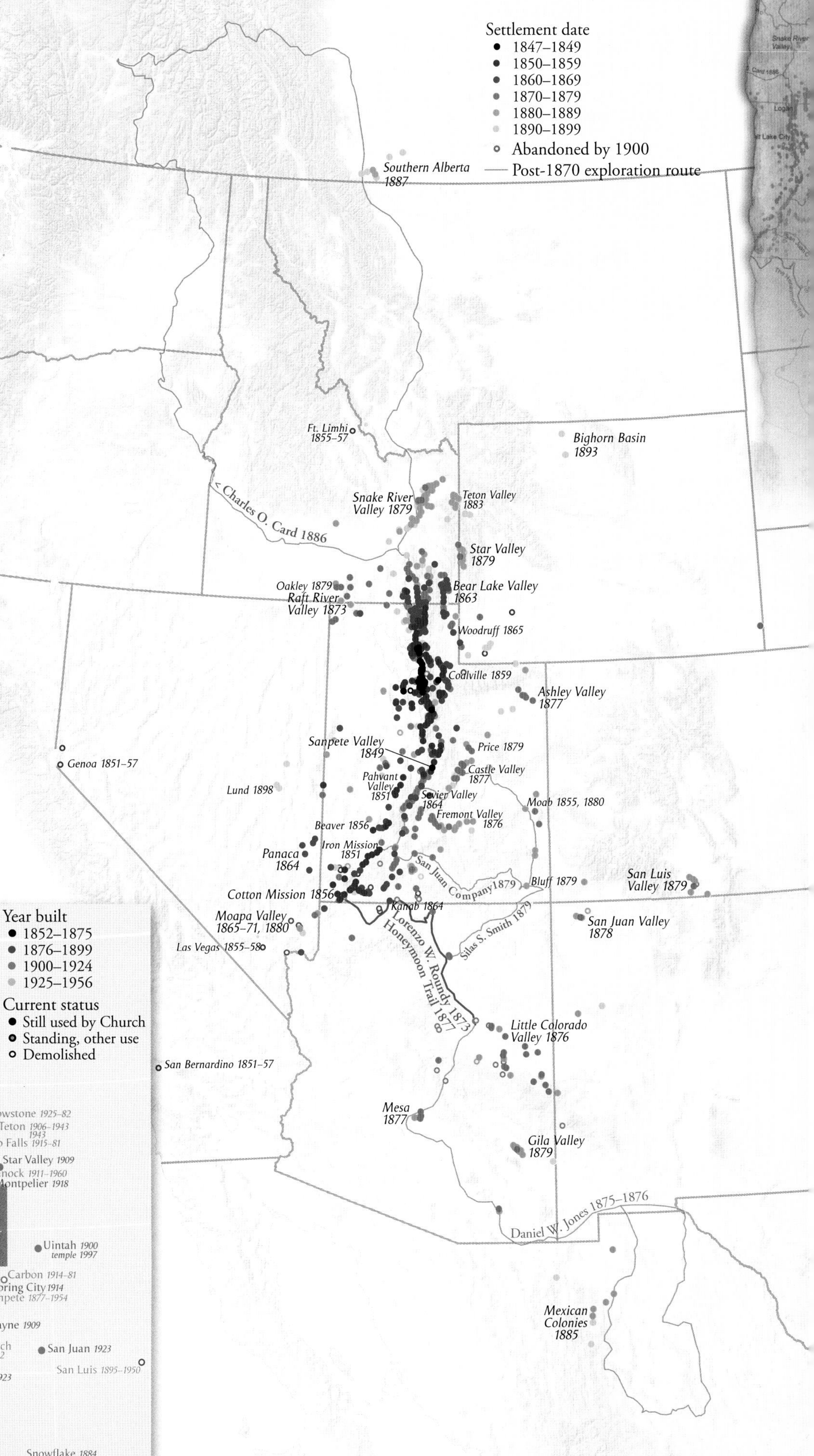

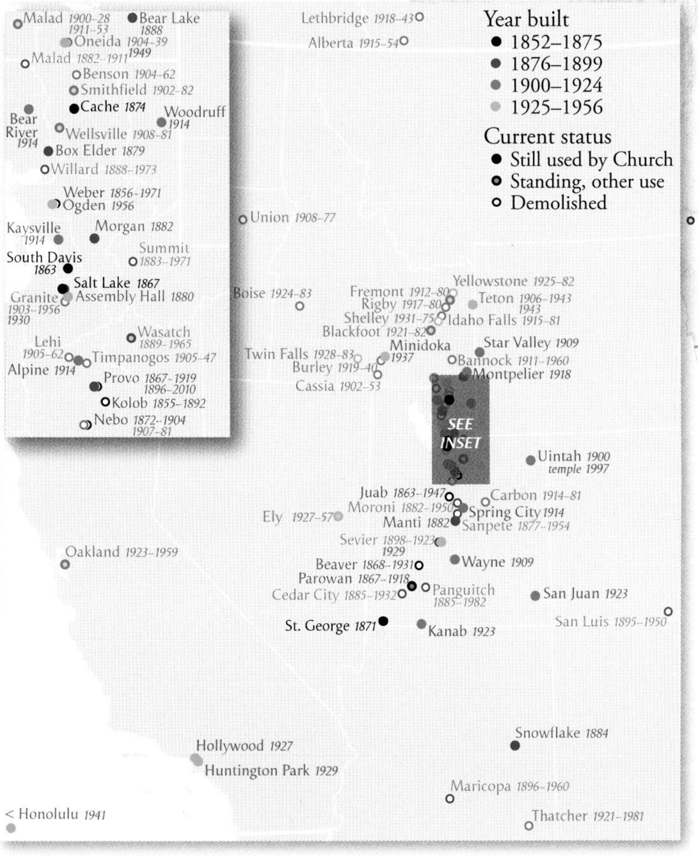

Mormon-Indian Relations

1847–1890

RELATIONS BETWEEN Latter-day Saints and American Indians opened on a hopeful note owing to a perceived special relationship based on the Book of Mormon. Indeed, its title page stated that the book was "an abridgment of the record of the people of Nephi, and also of the Lamanites—written to the Lamanites, who are a remnant of the house of Israel." Therein, the prophet Mormon had stated that if the Lamanites would believe in Christ and be baptized, it would "be well with [them] in the day of judgment" (Mormon 7:10). Based on the then-universal belief that all indigenous tribes were descendants of the Lamanites, early members felt that they had a natural kinship with the natives and that their destiny was to convert the American Indians en masse to the religion of their forefathers as part of the promised gathering of Israel.

Lamanite missionary efforts started within months of the organization of the Church and have continued ever since. These efforts have been sporadic but concerted, typically focusing a great effort on selected nations for a few months or years. While there have been converts, branches, and wards organized, and even leaders produced, large-scale conversions have been rare.

As the pioneers began to settle in Utah, relations were complicated as both peoples sought to accommodate each other in the very limited oases of the Wasatch Range. But the vast influx of settlers after 1848 turned out to be overwhelming as the natural flora and fauna of the oases, which had sustained the natives for centuries, were replaced by the Saints with wheat and cattle.

Initially, the leaders of both groups wanted to have a peaceful, even complementary, relationship. In 1849, Chief Walkara of the Sanpitch band of Utes invited the Saints to come to his valley and teach his people to farm; he was even baptized (likely more as a token of friendship than a true conversion). Mission farms would be set up in several locales where the two peoples dwelt side-by-side, but these efforts met with limited success. Although this policy of "civilizing the savages" is seen as imperialistic and egotistical by the standards of today's pluralistic society, the views of Brigham Young and other Church leaders toward native relations were much more positive (and pragmatic) than most Americans of his day. In recalling the militia from a potential conflict, General Daniel H. Wells explained, "If we pursue the same course that people generally do against the Indians we may expect to expend more time and money in running after

continued on page 100

Indian Nations and Bands in 1847

When the pioneers arrived in the Great Basin, the area that would become Utah was home to five major American Indian nations. Although they were already in contact with Europeans (especially through the New Mexico slave trade), they still had a primarily semi-nomadic, hunter-gatherer culture with minimal agriculture. The Salt Lake Valley turned out to be an advantageous location for the Mormons to settle, as it was a "no-man's land" shared between the several groups. However, settlement soon expanded into areas heavily used by the original inhabitants, especially in Utah and Sanpete valleys, leading to competition for resources and conflict.

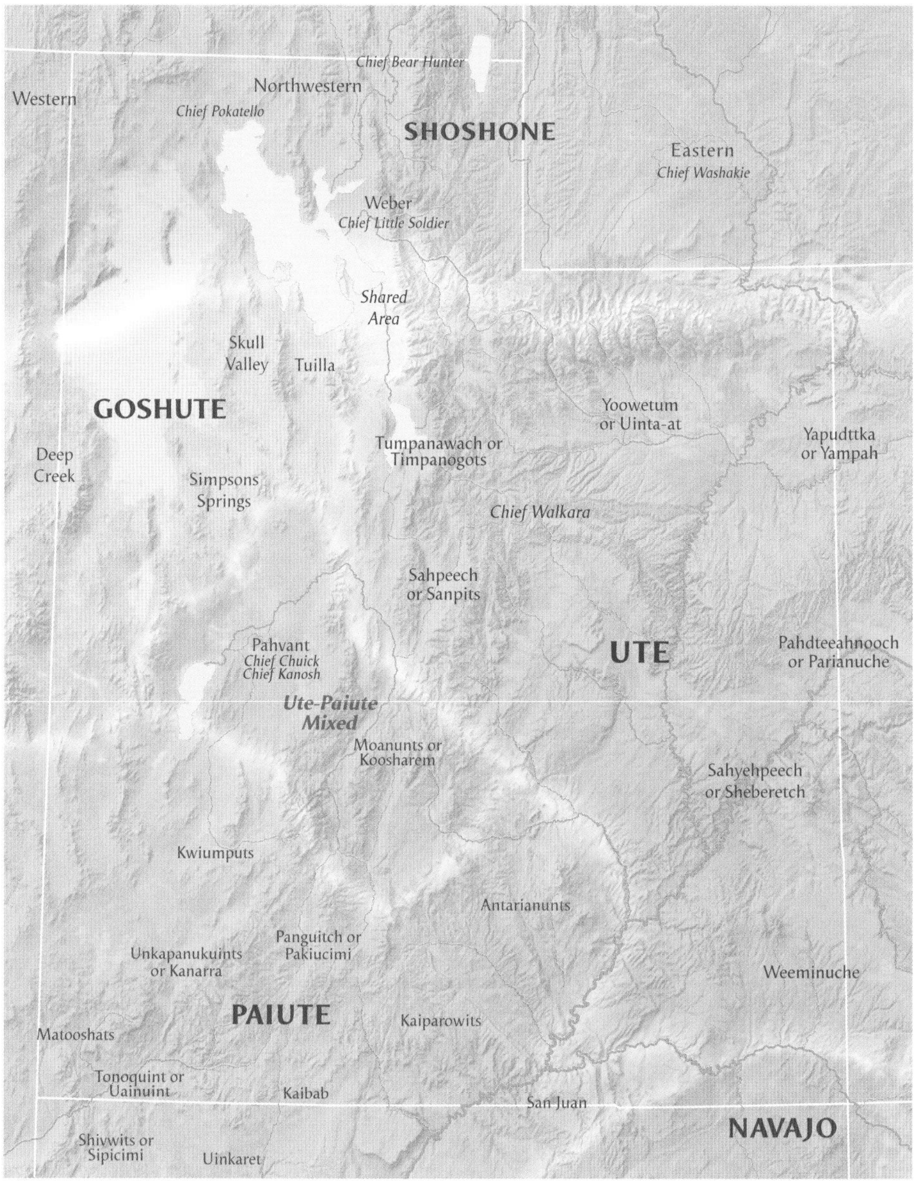

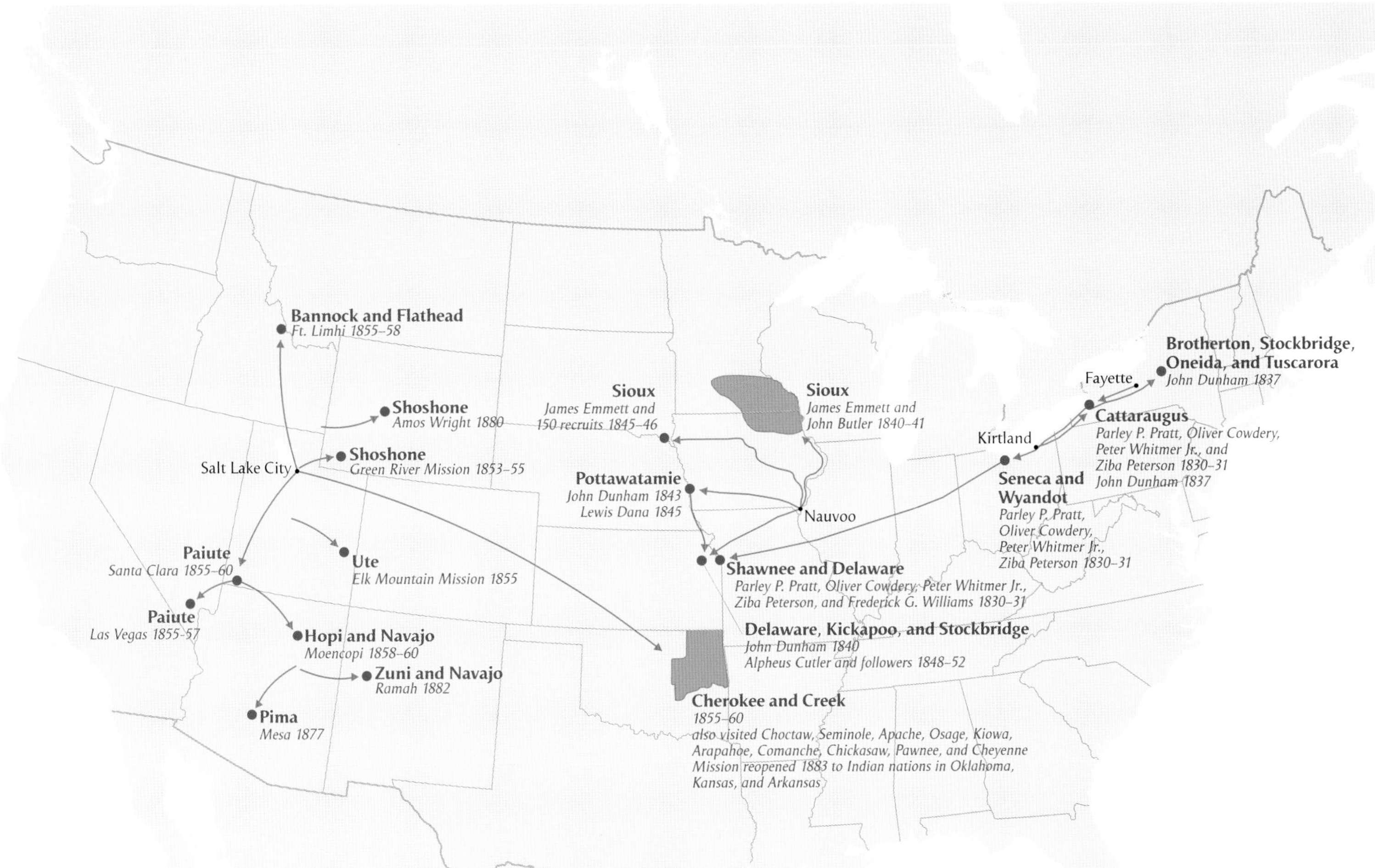

Missions to the Lamanites

The first LDS mission to American Indians commenced soon after the Church was established in 1830. Called by revelation, several elders traveled north in October, where they spent one day with the Cattaraugus tribe near Buffalo, New York, then on to Ohio, where they visited "for several days" with Wyandots near Sandusky. They next traveled to Missouri, "crossed the frontier" (into Kansas Territory) for a very brief visit with the Shawnees, then on "across the Kansas River," where they spent several very successful days with the Delaware chief and his people until "ordered out of Indian country" by government authorities. Further missionary work with American Indians was curtailed thereafter owing primarily to the serious difficulties experienced by the Saints in Ohio and Missouri commencing in 1831.

Minimal contact with Native Americans recommenced when the Saints removed west after being forced out of Illinois in 1846. The next attempt at missionary work among Indians was in the mid-1850s, when missions, or mission farms, were established among the Shoshone near Ft. Bridger; Bannocks at Fort Limhi on the Salmon River; Paiutes at Las Vegas Springs, Nevada; and Utes near Moab, Utah. All these were abandoned under hostile pressure by 1858. Mission and farm efforts to make accommodation with surrounding Indian tribes (including Goshutes, Navajos, Hopis, Zunis, Sioux, and Assiniboins) continued sporadically throughout the nineteenth century and into the first half of the twentieth century, again with minimal results.

Timeline

Mar 1849 First Mormon–Ute conflict at Battle Creek (Pleasant Grove)

Summer 1849 Brigham Young meets Chief Walkara, who invites the Mormons to settle in Sanpete Valley

1851 Early Indian farms

Jul 1853–May 1854 Walker War

1853–55 First missions from Salt Lake City to American Indians

Several Indian reserves created **1856**

Ute Reservation created in Uinta Basin **1861**

Bear River Massacre; U.S. military attacks Shoshones **29 Jan 1863**

1860–63 Battles between military and Goshutes

10 Apr 1865–67 Black Hawk War

Jan 1866 Navajo raids on southern Utah settlements

1872 All Utes in Utah forced to relocate to Uinta Reservation

An entire band of Shoshones is **1880** converted, establishes farming settlement near Idaho border

Navajo Reservation **1884** expands into Utah

1845 | 1850 | 1855 | 1860 | 1865 | 1870 | 1875 | 1880

Mormon-Indian Relations

continued

Indians than all the loss sustained by them." Such reasoning can be considered the preamble to Brigham Young's July 1851 pronouncement "that it is cheaper by far . . . to pay such losses than to raise an expedition . . . to fight Indians."

Unfortunately, no matter how often, or how strongly, conciliatory efforts were attempted by the Church leadership, as often as not those efforts were defied by residents in the outlying settlements, who faced the strains between the two peoples on a daily basis and much closer at hand. Conflict over issues such as: who would control the limited usable land, the awesome cultural gap, assumptions that American Indians could or would accommodate to drastic changes in their way of life, the lack of compassion on both sides, and the lack of viable policies, inevitably led to tragedy, especially for the American Indians. There was a typical downward spiral of competition and conflict: pioneer agriculture and grazing pushed out traditional Indians food resources; hungry Indians stole cattle; pioneers raided Indian camps to retrieve the cattle, often killing a few Indians in the process; and Indians raided pioneer settlements in retaliation. This often led to pitched battles and even massacres and other atrocities on both sides. As a result, two wars were fought with the Utes, and battles with other tribes were common.

As a result, efforts to achieve mutual accommodation were insufficient to achieve a better end, and the bitterness generated has to a considerable degree continued into the present.

Howard A. Christy

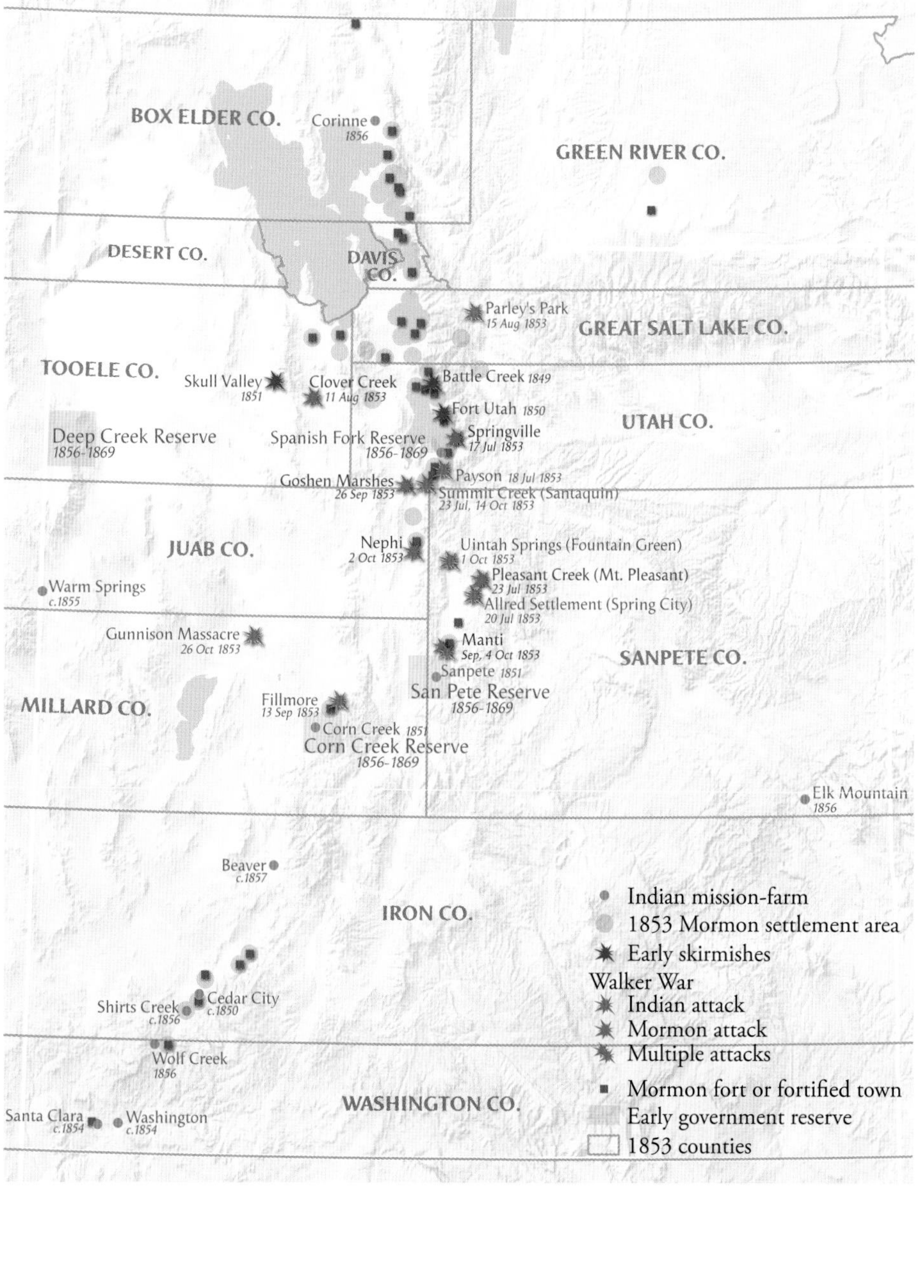

Early Indian Farms and the Walker War

Bloodshed commenced in 1849 at Battle Creek, east of today's Pleasant Grove, owing to reports of theft. Militia men were dispatched from Great Salt Lake City with orders "to take such measures as would put a final end to depredations in future," a policy that had repercussions over the next two years. Open warfare commenced in January 1850 on the Provo River near Fort Utah. Troops again sent from Great Salt Lake City viciously quelled the disturbance a month later on the lake shore south of the Provo settlement. In June 1851, militia responded again to reported stock losses, this time in Tooele Valley.

In 1853, open warfare commenced, again in Utah Valley, when an argument over a simple trade of fish for flour lit the match on what has been called the Walker War. Brigham Young immediately dispatched orders that "no retaliation be made and no offense offered but for all to act entirely on the defense until further orders"—to no avail. Discipline cracked and a spate of brutal killings occurred as each side retaliated against the other. Apparently exasperated by such indiscipline and carnage, in October Brigham Young pleaded: "Brethren we must have peace. We must cease our hostilities and seek by every possible means to reach the Indians with a peaceful message." In the spring of 1854, after offering full amnesty, Governor Young met with Chief Walkara in the chief's tent, blessed a sick child, purchased a slave as a further gesture, and the war was over.

Although small efforts at farming assistance by Mormons (doubling as proselytizing missions) began as early as 1850, federally supported Indian farms—Corn Creek in Millard County, Twelve Mile Creek in Sanpete County, and Spanish Fork in Utah County—were initiated in cooperation with territorial officials in 1855–56, and a few other, smaller efforts were initiated in later years. These enterprises were only minimally and briefly successful, and all failed for any number of reasons, including insufficient funding and lack of commitment or interest either from governmental officials, surrounding settlers, or the Indians intended as beneficiaries.

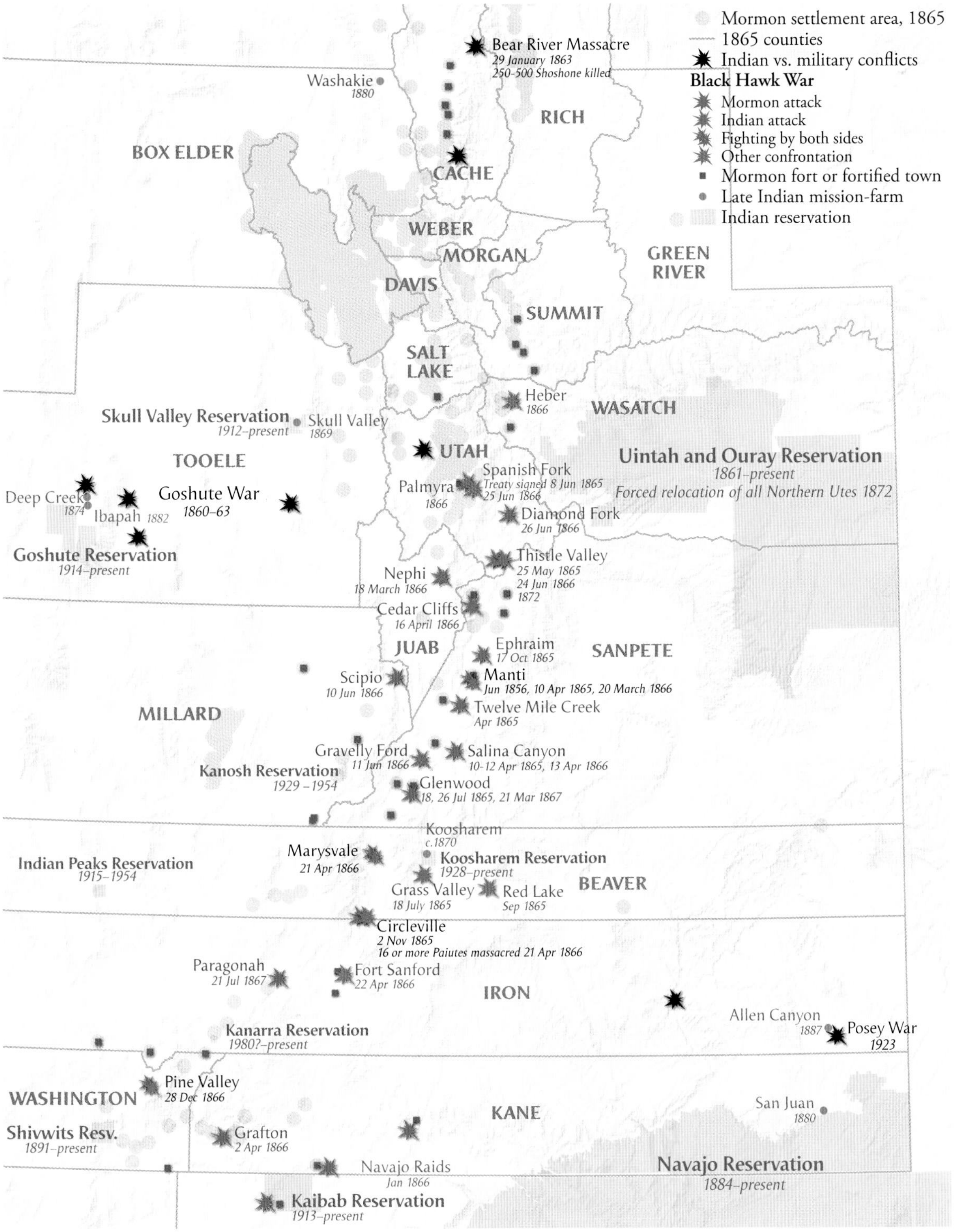

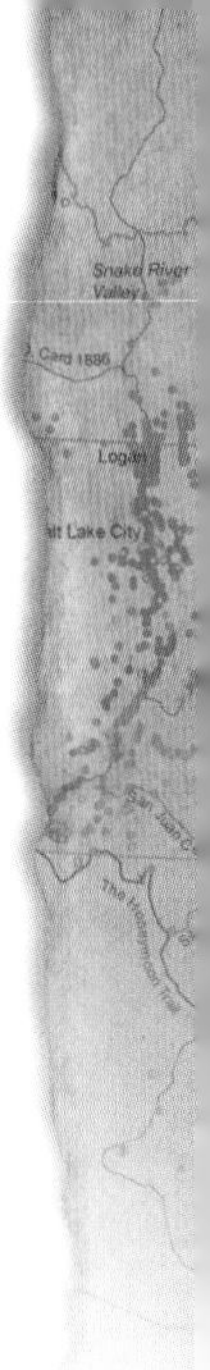

The Black Hawk War and Indian Reservations

Tentative peace prevailed for about ten years—until 1865 when the Walker War was largely repeated by the Black Hawk War, which occurred generally for the same reasons, in the same locales, and with similar losses of both life and property on both sides. At this point, territorial and Church leaders decided that separation was the only option for peace, which meant (as in the rest of the United States) forced relocation of the natives to lands the white settlers did not want. Hostile encounters, generally with the U.S. military rather than Mormon settlers, continued sporadically until as late as 1923.

The Relief Society

1854–1881

The Relief Society of The Church of Jesus Christ of Latter-day Saints organizes women for charitable service, spiritual nurture, and sisterly connection. Established in 1842, it has functioned as a counterpart and complement to adult men's priesthood quorums. Interruptions in its early operations were rectified by the late 1860s, and since that time it has been a permanent part of the local and general Church structure.

On March 17, 1842, twenty women met with Joseph Smith and other priesthood leaders above his store in Nauvoo to create a new organization headed by Emma Hale Smith. The institution, named the Female Relief Society of Nauvoo, paralleled other women's benevolent societies, but the women differentiated their group from "the popular institutions of the day" because it was organized "according to the law of Heaven—according to a revelation." Membership rapidly expanded from the original twenty members to over 1,300 members, who left an impressive record of humanitarian work in two years. The last recorded meeting of the Female Relief Society of Nauvoo took place on March 16, 1844.

Nearly seven years after the arrival of Latter-day Saints in the Great Basin, in 1854 the Female Relief Society was reestablished by women working with ward bishops. They sewed clothing for American Indians, ministered to poor and immigrant Saints, wove carpet for meetinghouses, and helped clothe the militia staving off U.S. troops in 1857 (see p. 110). Most of these societies did not last long, but Brigham Young called for their reestablishment in 1867–68. At that time, he appointed his plural wife Eliza R. Snow, who had been the Society's secretary in Nauvoo, to assist bishops in organizing ward societies. They multiplied rapidly and labored to minister to the poor and also to establish cooperative stores and granaries and help fund immigration and temple construction. Central leadership from Snow and other leading women helped standardize organizational structure and process, connected women across wards in such shared endeavors as medical services (including supporting selected women in receiving advanced medical training in the East), and published the semi-monthly *Woman's Exponent.*

Snow and other women also helped create organizations for young women and children, organizing the first "Young Ladies' Department of the Cooperative Retrenchment Association" in 1870 and the first "Primary Association" in 1878 in Farmington. At first, Snow was unofficially esteemed as "President of the Latter-day Saint Women's Organizations," until the three organizations—Relief Society, Primary, and the Young Ladies National Mutual Improvement Association (now Young Women)—were clearly distinguished under separate presidencies in 1880. Each of these has been led and managed by women ever since.

Over the years, Relief Society has adapted to meet the needs of successive generations of women, opening new possibilities for education, self-expression, and service. It has contributed significantly to welfare, social services, and literacy within and beyond the Church and advocated for women, children, and families in local, national, and international forums. The Church-wide correlation program of coordinating administration under the priesthood starting in the 1960s ended Relief Society's self-directed finances, magazine, and lessons and moved its weekday meetings to Sunday—changes that both challenged its longtime members and enabled it to become an essential component of branches, wards, and stakes as the Church expanded throughout the world.

Jill Mulvay Derr

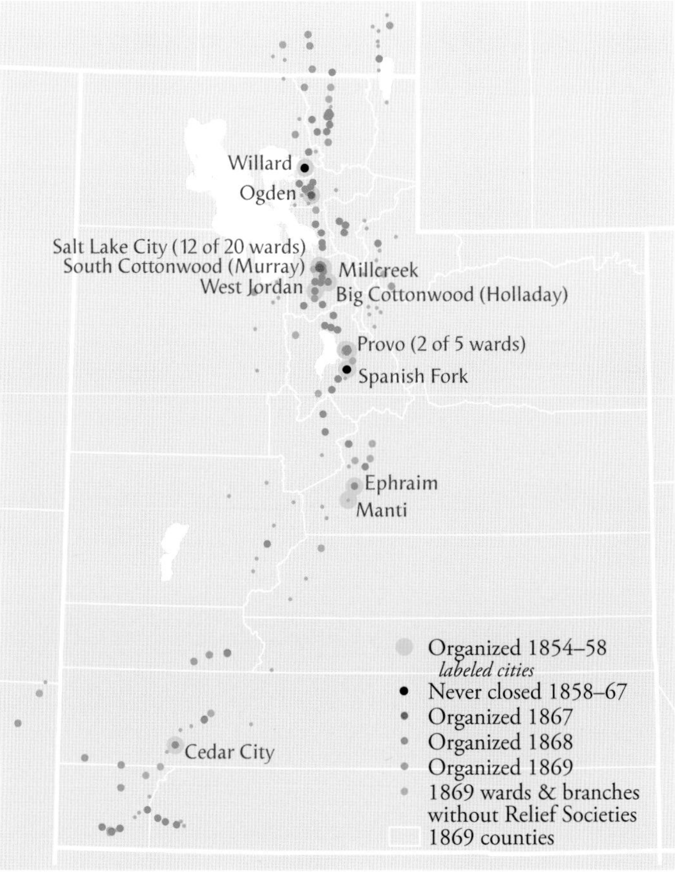

Early Relief Societies

Local branches of the Latter-day Saint women's Relief Society were organized in two distinct periods. In 1854, women formed Relief Societies (sometimes known as Indian Relief Societies) in at least 24 wards as a response to Church leaders' call to minister to neighboring Indians. They sewed clothing for Indian women and children and assisted the poor. Most of these early societies waned around 1858, due to the disruption of the move south during the Utah War (see p. 110). At the close of 1867, Brigham Young called for the reorganization of Relief Societies in every ward, as he anticipated both a major influx of poor immigrant Saints and the need for women's support in upholding a self-sufficient Mormon economy (see p. 118). Young appointed Eliza R. Snow to work with bishops and leading women to establish the Relief Society more widely than previously and, significantly, on a permanent basis. There were at least 102 Relief Societies in operation by 1869, although about two dozen could not be verified well enough to be shown here.

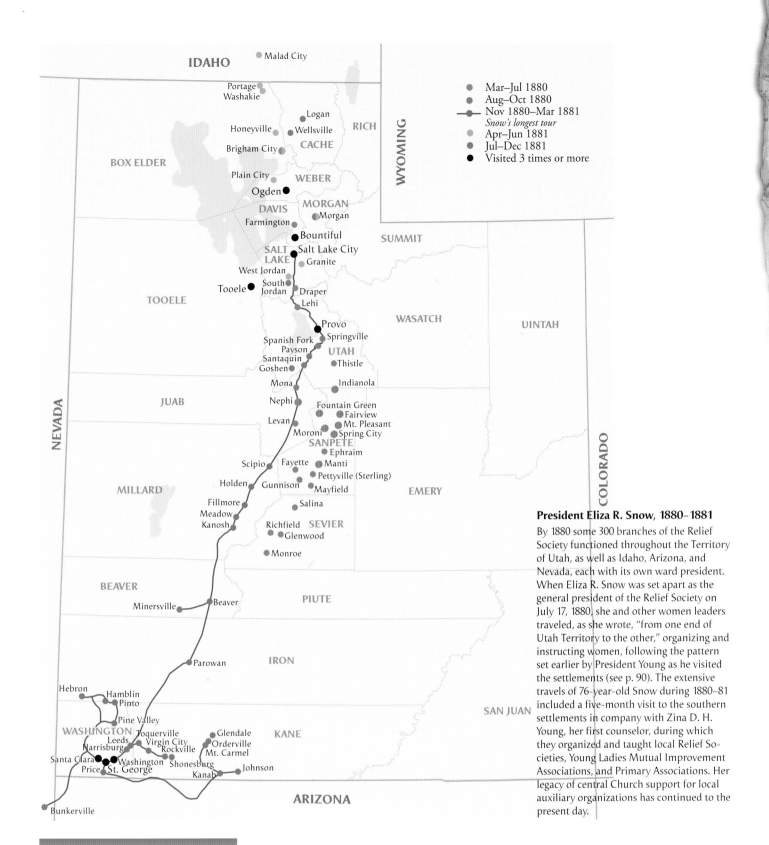

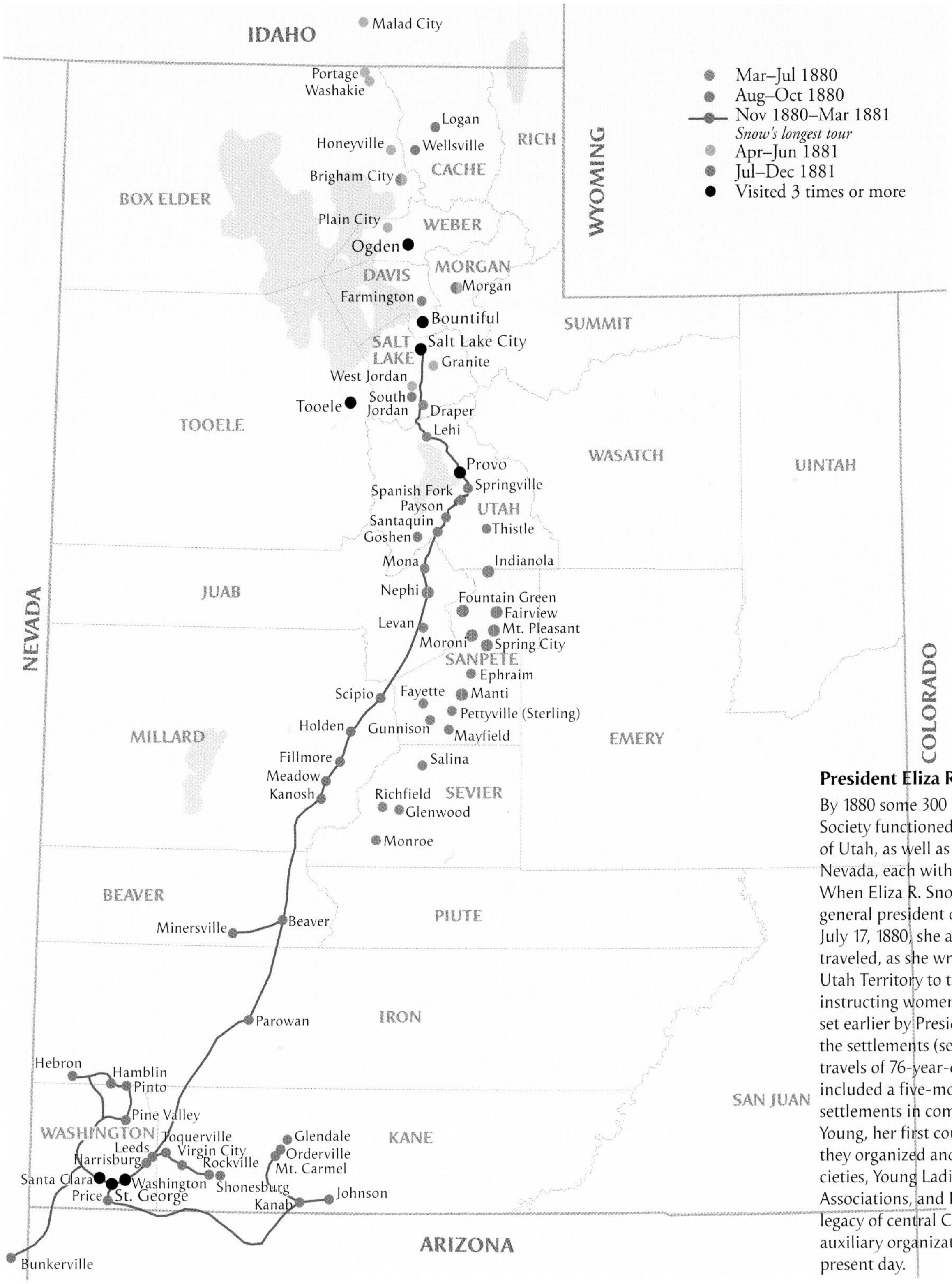

President Eliza R. Snow, 1880–1881

By 1880 some 300 branches of the Relief Society functioned throughout the Territory of Utah, as well as Idaho, Arizona, and Nevada, each with its own ward president. When Eliza R. Snow was set apart as the general president of the Relief Society on July 17, 1880, she and other women leaders traveled, as she wrote, "from one end of Utah Territory to the other," organizing and instructing women, following the pattern set earlier by President Young as he visited the settlements (see p. 90). The extensive travels of 76-year-old Snow during 1880–81 included a five-month visit to the southern settlements in company with Zina D. H. Young, her first counselor, during which they organized and taught local Relief Societies, Young Ladies Mutual Improvement Associations, and Primary Associations. Her legacy of central Church support for local auxiliary organizations has continued to the present day.

The Development of Relief Society

17 Mar 1842 "Female Relief Society" organized by Joseph Smith at Nauvoo, with his wife Emma as president

16 Mar 1844 Last known meeting in Nauvoo

Women organize first "Indian Relief Society" in Great Salt Lake City **Feb 1854**

Brigham Young calls for ward societies; many are soon formed **Jun 1854**

Most ward Relief Societies cease meeting **1858**

Dec 1867
Brigham Young calls for reorganizing Relief Societies in every ward

Apr 1868
Eliza R. Snow writes article in *Deseret News* on purpose of Relief Society

27 May 1870
First "Young Ladies' Department of the Cooperative Senior and Junior Retrenchment Association" (now Young Women) formally organized

1872–1914 *Woman's Exponent* journal

19 Jul 1877
First stake Relief Society presidency organized in Ogden

Aug 1878 Aurelia S. Rogers organizes first Primary Association for children in Farmington

19 Jun 1880
John Taylor calls Snow as general president of the Relief Society and calls general presidents of the Primary and YLMIA

1840 | 1850 | 1860 | 1870 | 1880

Gathering to Zion

1840–1890

THE UNIVERSAL CALL TO GATHER was received by the Prophet Joseph Smith during the second conference of the Restored Church, less than six months after its organization in 1830 (D&C 29:7–8). From then on, missionaries encouraged their converts to join the main body of the Saints, first in Kirtland (1831–37, p. 30), Missouri (1831–38, pp. 32, 48), then Nauvoo (1839–46, p. 56).

At first the Saints were gathered from only the United States and Canada, until the British Mission was opened in 1837 (see page 46). The Apostles baptized thousands during their second mission to Britain (1840–41), encouraging the new Saints to gather. Soon after the Apostles arrived, the first company of British Saints boarded a ship for America, followed by thousands more. These British immigrants gathered first to Nauvoo (1840–1846) and later to Utah after the Saints selected a new gathering place in the valleys of Utah in 1847. Most entered the United States at New Orleans, since the cheapest way to reach Nauvoo was by steamboat. Church agents were stationed in Liverpool and New Orleans to charter transportation and help the Saints on their way.

By 1850, missionary work was expanded in Europe (see page 94), and by 1852 Scandinavian converts began to gather along with the British, joined by converts from Germany, Switzerland, Italy, and France. With the increasing volume of immigration and Salt Lake City a thousand miles further away than Nauvoo, agents were dispatched to find the cheapest route to Utah, even if it were not the fastest. This was usually (but not always) through New York City, then on a train to the Midwest, then by wagon, handcart (see p. 106), or eventually rail across the plains and mountains.

By the end of the nineteenth century, about 90,000 converts had gathered to America, including approximately 55,000 British and 25,000 Scandinavians. In addition, missionaries were also finding success in Australia and New Zealand, and hundreds of those converts gathered to America via the Pacific Ocean.

By 1890, Church leaders began to encourage foreign converts to remain in their homelands. However, converts continued to gather by their own means, even after a stronger call to stay in 1911 from President Joseph F. Smith. The gathering in this form officially ended in the early 1950s, when President David O. McKay issued a call for Saints to "gather" together in their own homelands (see page 158) and backed it up through the creation of stakes, meetinghouses, and temples worldwide (see pages 162, 182, 184).

Fred E. Woods

Immigration to Nauvoo began with a company of 40 British converts aboard the new ship *RMS Britannia* on June 6, 1840, led by English convert John Moon. After entering the United States at New York on July 20, the group divided. Some traveled via the Erie Canal and Great Lakes, reaching Nauvoo in early fall (the same route taken by the second British company a few months later); the others traveled through Philadelphia, Pittsburgh (where they were forced to spend the winter), and St. Louis, before arriving in Nauvoo on April 16, 1841. A third 1840 company sailed to New Orleans then took a riverboat to Nauvoo.

This third route turned out to be the fastest and cheapest, and almost all Nauvoo-era emigrants used it, traveling as large companies organized by Church agents in Liverpool and New Orleans. Occasionally, small groups traveled by their own means and by their own routes, such as three groups in 1841 that sailed from Bristol to Quebec. In total, nearly five thousand British Saints sailed to Nauvoo between 1840 and 1846 on 34 Mormon company voyages and 13 additional LDS voyages not chartered by the Church.

After arriving in Nauvoo in the first company, Francis Moon wrote back to his native homeland in England (published in the *Millennial Star*) to describe the favorable temporal and spiritual conditions that now surrounded him at Nauvoo. He referred to Nauvoo as a refuge in the troubled last days, further noting that a purpose of gathering the people of God in any age was to "build a sanctuary to the name of the Most High." Moon's glad tidings to his British homeland, other letters from early LDS immigrants, and counsel from general Church leaders encouraged the British Saints to gather.

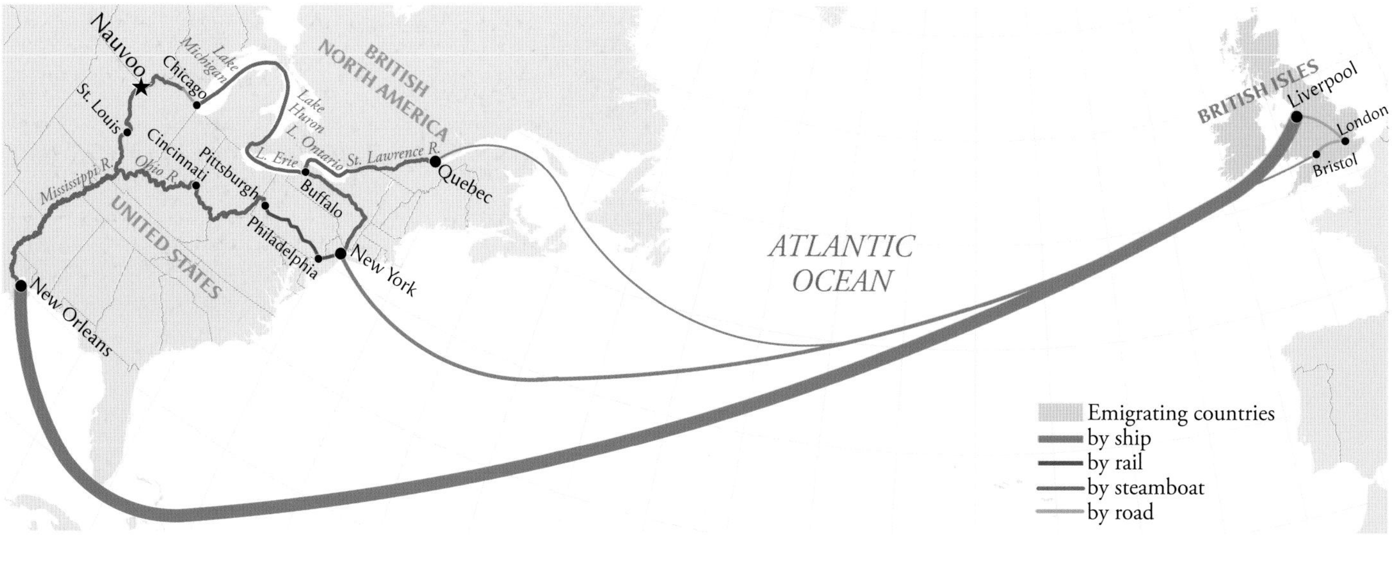

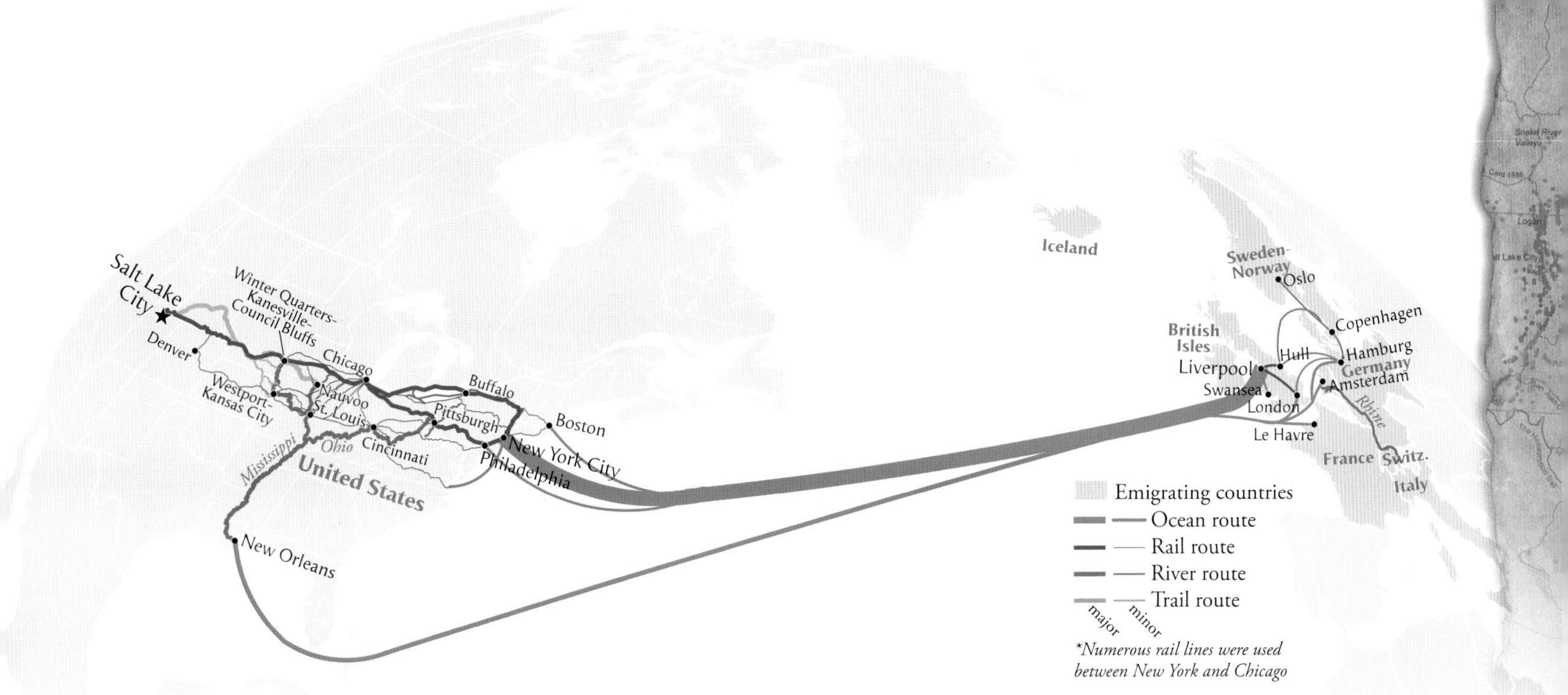

Gathering to Utah was influenced by an "emigration revelation" received by Brigham Young near the banks of the Missouri River at Winter Quarters on January 14, 1847 (D&C 136:1). This instruction not only provided a much-needed administrative map to guide the Mormon pioneers across the plains to the Salt Lake Valley but also provided a divine pattern of principles and promises for all segments of the journey, whether it be by sail, rail, or trail.

Experienced leaders, such as returning missionaries, guided the Saints across the ocean, the eastern United States, and the Great Plains. LDS agents at Liverpool, New Orleans (1840–1855), New York (1855–1889), and frontier outfitting posts chartered transportation and offered provisions and trail supplies. Church leaders published updated travel guidelines in LDS periodicals such as the *Latter-day Saints' Millennial Star*, *The Mormon* (New York), the *St. Louis Luminary*, and *The Frontier Guardian* (Kanesville).

The rise of steam power greatly aided the Mormon gathering. After 1867, Latter-day Saints traveled by steamships, which were much faster than sailing vessels. Railroads were taken as far west as they went; when the transcontinental railroad was completed in 1869, Latter-day Saint converts were able to cross the ocean and the eastern United States and reach Utah in about three weeks. This was in stark contrast to the earlier sailing voyage of a month (to New York) or two (to New Orleans) and several months to cross the United States by boat, wagon, and foot.

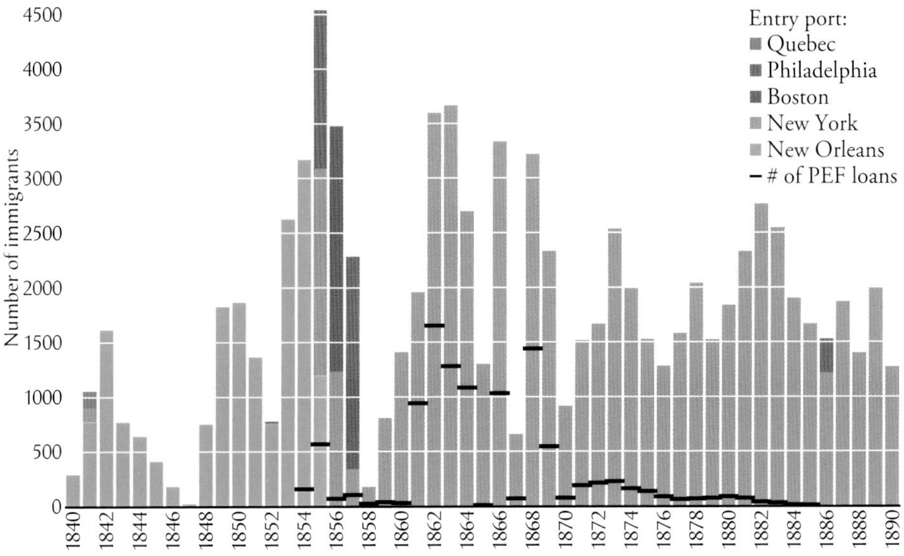

Immigration over the Years

In 1840–41 three LDS voyages entered North America at Quebec and three at New York before proceeding on to Nauvoo. All other voyages launched from Liverpool bound for Nauvoo (1840–46) disembarked at New Orleans. Vessels continued to use this same port, plying up the Mississippi and Missouri rivers to frontier outfitting posts until the route was changed to eastern ports in the spring of 1855. The reason for this alteration can be traced to a letter sent by President Brigham Young in 1854 to Elder Franklin D. Richards at Liverpool: "You are aware of the sickness liable to assail our unacclimated brethren on the Mississippi river, hence I wish you to ship no more to New Orleans, but ship to Philadelphia, Boston, and New York, giving preference in the order named." However, the vast bulk of immigration passed through New York because Castle Garden, the first U.S. immigration depot, had been erected there in 1855.

In 1849, the Church launched a revolving loan (1849) known as the Perpetual Emigrating Fund (PEF) to assist those who could not afford the high costs of traveling for months by land and sea to reach Zion. Once they were settled, they were expected to repay the loan to fund later immigrants; not everyone was able to repay, but enough did to keep the program running. In all, over 10,000 loans totaling over $1.2 million were made before the U.S. government shut it down in 1887 as part of their anti-polygamy laws.

Gathering to Zion

1830 Saints first commanded to gather

1836 Keys of gathering restored by Moses to Joseph Smith and Oliver Cowdery

1837 First overseas mission (Great Britain) to gather Israel led by Elder Heber C. Kimball

1840 First group of British converts leave England to gather to Nauvoo, Illinois

1847 Saints commence gathering to the Salt Lake Valley

1849 Perpetual Emigrating Fund is launched to bring converts to Zion

1852 Emigration of Scandinavian converts is launched

1855 Eastern ports favored over New Orleans due to river sickness and NY immigration depot

1856 Handcarts introduced to lessen costs of gathering to Utah

1861 Church wagon trains sent from Utah to aid immigrants coming to the Salt Lake Valley

1869 Transcontinental railroad completed; Church begins using steamships

1890 Immigration from abroad begins to decline as the Saints are told to build Zion locally

European immigration **1932** records no longer kept for Saints gathering to America

London England Temple **1958** is dedicated, which aids in Saints building Zion at home

1830 1835 1840 1845 1850 1855 1860 1865 1870 1875 1880 1885 1890

Handcart Pioneers

1856–1860

The Mormon handcart plan grew out of a deep commitment to the principle of the gathering (see p. 104) and the economic realities of transporting thousands of impoverished Saints to Utah. The Perpetual Emigrating Fund (PEF) gave travel assistance to the faithful needy through a system of donations and loans, but by the autumn of 1855, there was simply not enough money in the fund to buy wagons and oxen for the journey across the plains as thousands had done (see p. 80). Church President Brigham Young saw the use of handcarts as the solution to this problem. Two-wheeled carts cost a fraction of what covered wagons did, and having people pushing and pulling the handcarts would almost eliminate the considerable expenditure for purchasing oxen. Only a few draft animals would be required to pull a small number of provision wagons, in which the sick could ride if necessary.

Although this method of traveling demanded that the immigrants make substantial sacrifices and involved arduous daily labor, the "Lord's poor" eagerly embraced the plan during its first year of operation, 1856. During that year, the missionaries enthusiastically promoted the system, and loans were readily available to the poor who wished to try the handcarts, despite the fact that this policy plummeted the PEF deeply into debt. In subsequent years, the handcart plan was far less popular.

In spite of the hardships of handcart travel, the foremost consideration was the cost of the journey. Expenses were kept at a bare minimum. The labor was exhausting, the provisions were scant, and hunger was common; but the Saints paid the personal price and gathered to Zion the hard way. The plan indicated that supply wagons from Utah would meet them in Wyoming. In 1857, supply outposts were established, but they only lasted that year. When and where relief supplies would reach the companies was always uncertain; the longer the wait for relief, the greater the hardship. In September 1859, the Rowley Company suffered near-starvation near the Green River.

The handcart era lasted only four years, from 1856 through 1860, excluding 1858. Of the more than 60,000 Mormon immigrants between 1847 and 1868 (see p. 82), only slightly more than 3,000 used handcarts, about four percent of the total. Two-thirds (2,000) of the handcart pioneers came in 1856 in five companies. Another five companies totaling one thousand persons traveled by handcart in the remaining years: two groups in 1857, one in 1859, and two in 1860. Despite the hardships the immigrants endured, the handcart method proved feasible for continuing the gathering of the poor with less expense to the Perpetual Emigrating Fund. Each year the Church made improvements in the plan. However, after 1860 handcart travel became obsolete when another plan, the Church "down-and-back" teams (see p. 80), demonstrated greater success with even less monetary expense.

Ideally, the handcart trains would leave Florence, Nebraska Territory, in June or July and arrive in the Salt Lake Valley during September or early October before winter storms. Eight companies followed that schedule, reaching the valley without major incident. However, the Willie and the Martin companies of 1856 met with disaster. They set out from Florence several weeks too late to cross the mountains safely, but Church agents still sent the immigrants forward, trusting that faith would protect them. The companies still had hundreds of miles to travel when winter struck in mid-October. Snowbound and starving, the handcart pioneers desperately needed help. Although assistance eventually came from Utah (see p. 108), more than 200 immigrants lost their lives. The enormous tragedy of 1856, caused by the mistake of starting too late, was the largest disaster of the American westward migration. Considering the bitterness of the weather, coupled with the shortage of food and lack of shelter, it is astonishing that more did not perish. The Church's rescue effort saved the belated immigrants from utter destruction.

Lyndia McDowell Carter

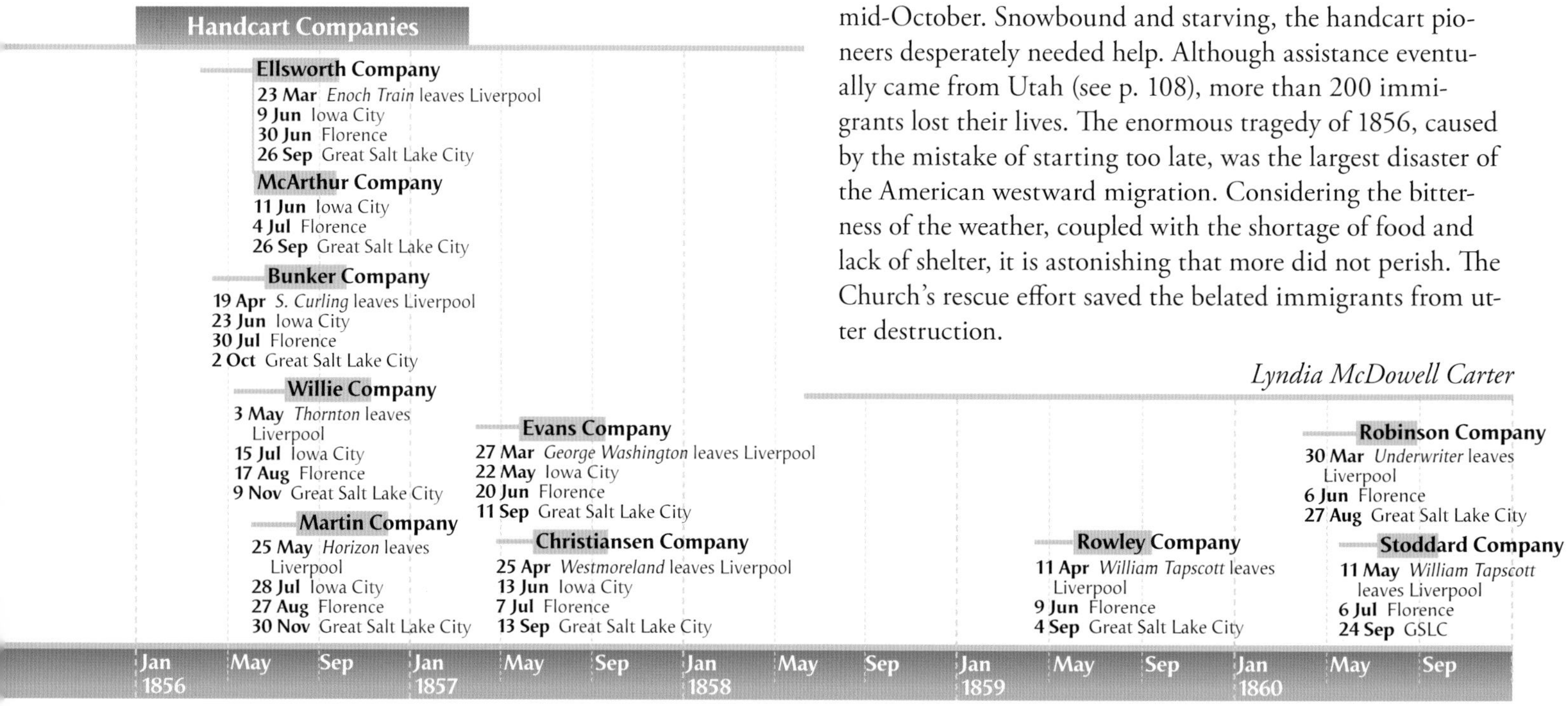

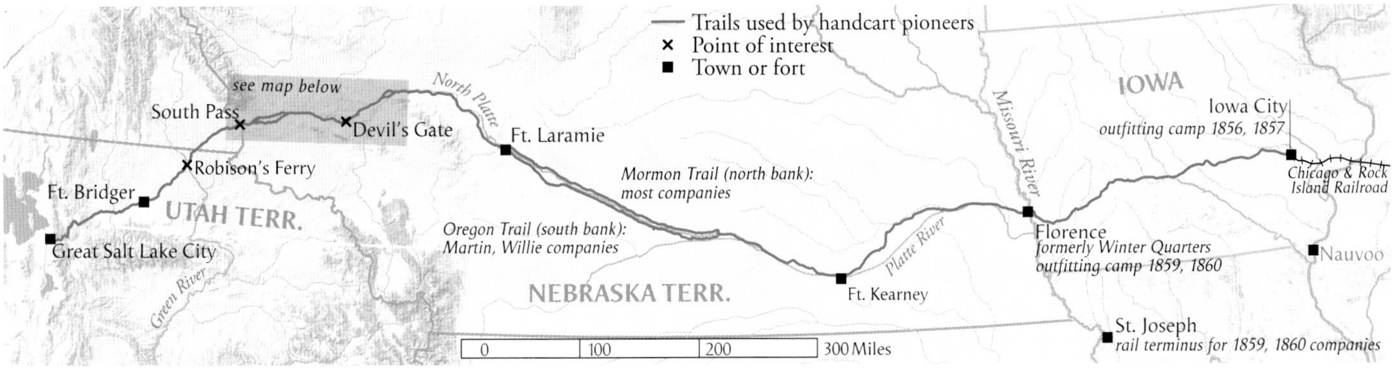

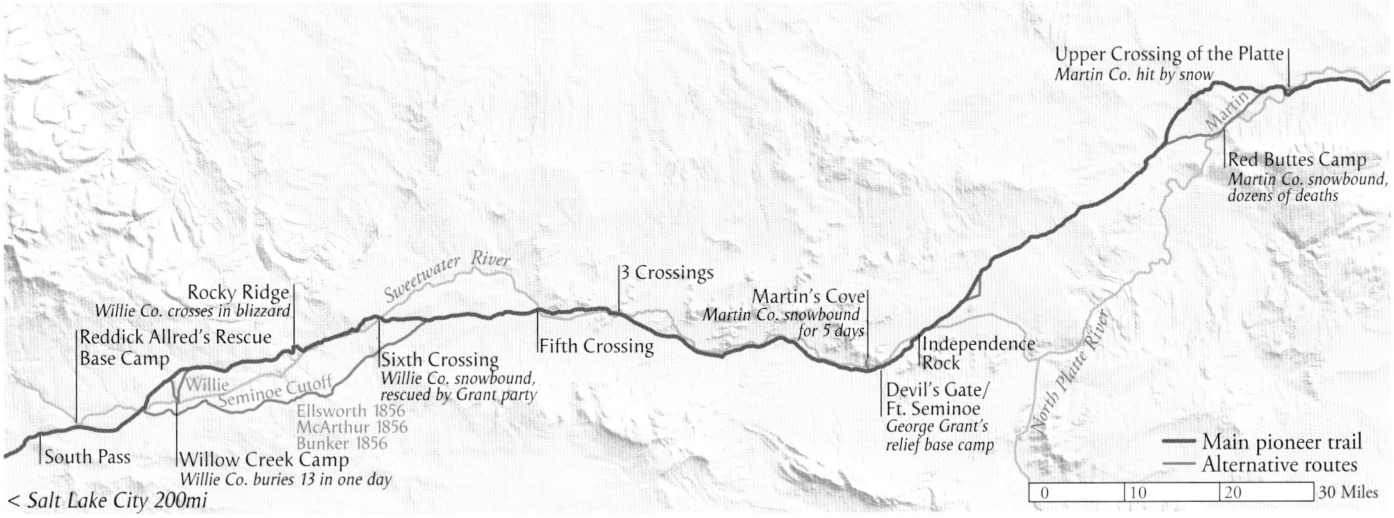

The handcart trail essentially began in Liverpool, England. Church members from Great Britain, Scandinavia, and parts of Europe met there and sailed to the United States together in Church-chartered ships (see p. 104). The emigrants traveled steerage to minimize expenses. The voyage took four to seven weeks or longer.

Landing at New York, Boston, or Philadelphia, the immigrants piled into railroad cars, often little better than cattle cars, and traveled immigrant class about eight days to the Mormon outfitting camps. Occasionally steamboats provided part of the transportation.

In 1856 and 1857, the outfitting campground was outside of Iowa City, Iowa, the terminus of the railroad. The travelers then tugged their carts across Iowa and re-supplied at Florence, Nebraska. In 1859 and 1860, they got all the way to Florence by train and steamboats, which saved them nearly 300 miles of walking with their carts in Iowa's intense summer heat and humidity. At the outfitting post, all companies experienced a wait of one to six weeks as carts were built and preparations made.

The handcart route from Florence ran on the north side of the Platte River, then followed the north side of the North Platte River to Fort Laramie, where it crossed to the south side. (The Willie and Martin companies of 1856 crossed to the south side of the North Platte just west of the confluence of the two forks of the Platte River.) In eastern Wyoming, the handcart pioneers followed the trail along the river, crossing it twice, then forded it one last time to the north side at today's city of Casper. Then the immigrants cut across country to the Sweetwater River, along which they traveled, crossing it nine times before reaching South Pass. In 1856, some of the companies traveled the Seminoe Cutoff on the south side of the Sweetwater. From South Pass, the trail followed the Big Sandy River to the Green River, then to Fort Bridger, down Echo Canyon, and over the Wasatch Mountains. Most companies entered the Salt Lake Valley through Emigration Canyon, except the 1860 companies, which went down Parley's Canyon to the City of the Saints.

The 1856 Handcart Tragedy

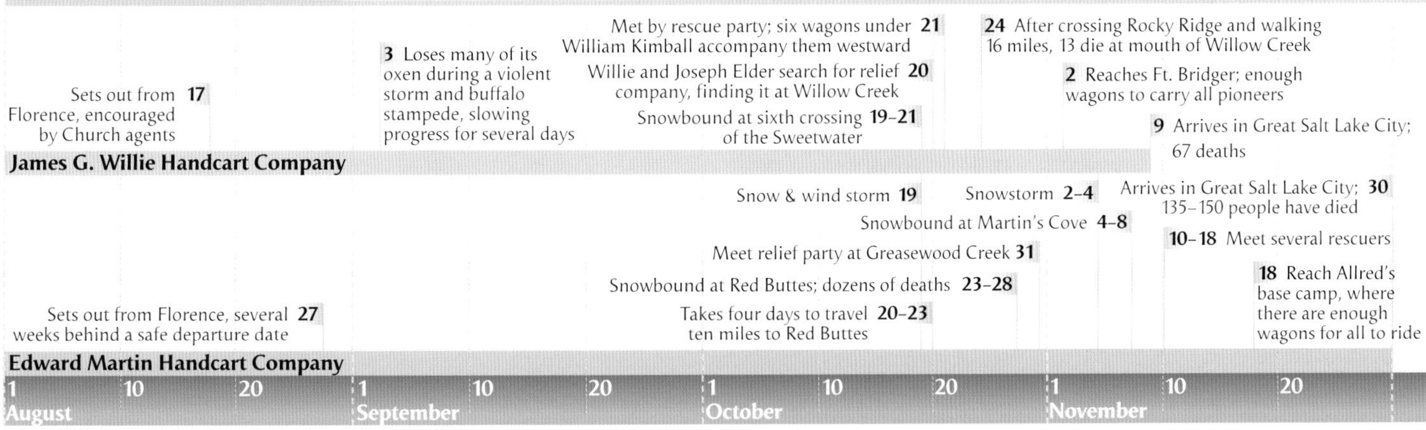

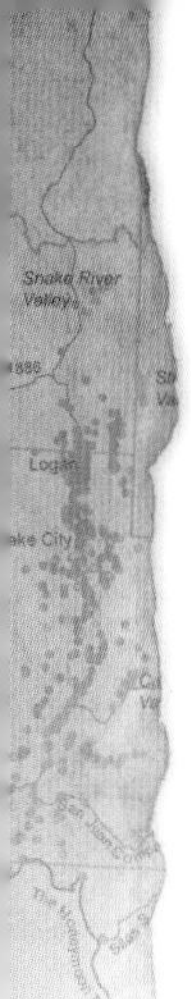

Rescuing the Martin and Willie Companies

1856

More than 1,400 immigrants, in two handcart companies led by James G. Willie and Edward Martin, and two wagon companies led by John A. Hunt and William Hodgetts, left Florence too late to ensure a safe journey to the Salt Lake Valley. Apostle Franklin D. Richards, who had met them along the way as he was returning from Europe by carriage, reached the valley on October 4 and notified Brigham Young of the belated companies. Expecting that the immigrants would be caught by winter storms, Brigham Young devoted general conference to call for donations and volunteers to go to their relief.

Church members generously donated anything they could spare. Wagons with teams of horses or mules were loaned for the relief effort, then filled with clothing, bedding, provisions, flour, and feed for the animals. Serving as teamsters and other relief workers, men answered the call to help, including several recently returned missionaries (such as William Kimball), who felt deep concern for the immigrants they had sent out too late from the frontier. This initial wave of relief left Salt Lake Valley on October 7; some of them did not return until November 30 with the Martin Company.

In mid-October winter struck with all its fury and would not cease. The rescuers and especially the handcart immigrants suffered in the snow, icy wind, and frigid temperatures. The first relief company met the Willie Company at the sixth crossing of the Sweetwater. The starving, freezing, weary immigrants needed much more aid than the few wagons and limited provisions could provide, but the men from Utah abundantly gave of their strength, energy, and compassion, as well as renewing hope.

William Kimball and six wagons helped the Willie Company continue west, while eight wagons and the rest of the men went on to find the Martin Company and the two wagon trains. On the last day of October, they met the emaciated and freezing Martin Company. The relief company had been on the road so long that they had to ration their few remaining provisions and spent the next month helping the pioneers get to the Salt Lake Valley.

A second call for volunteers came late in October, after nothing had been heard from the first relief company. Volunteers, wagons, teams, and provisions came from many communities. The first wagons of this second wave of relief met the Willie Company near Green River, with many more at Fort Bridger, carrying them into Great Salt Lake City on November 9.

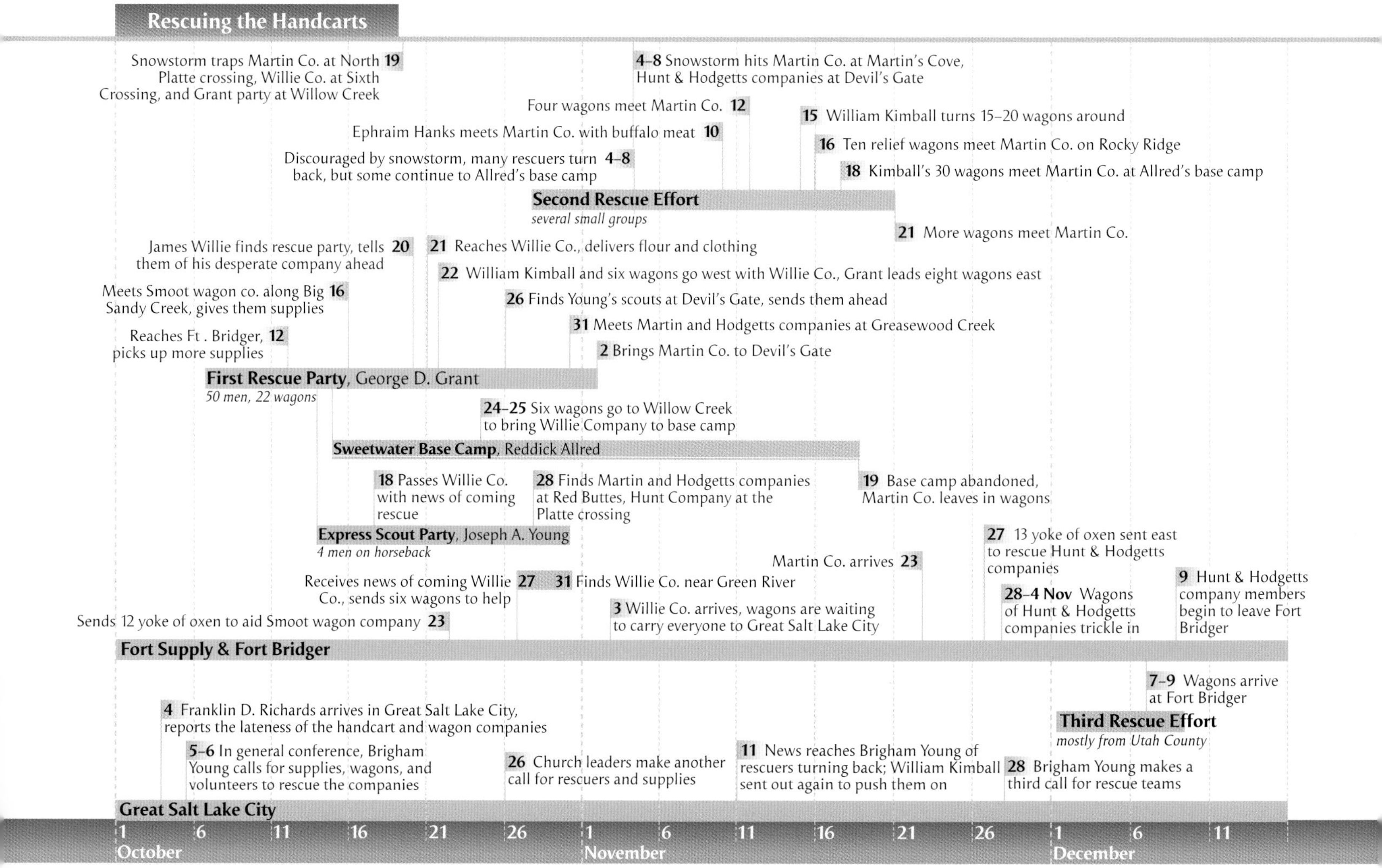

Rescuing the Handcarts
Snowstorm traps Martin Co. at North Platte crossing, Willie Co. at Sixth Crossing, and Grant party at Willow Creek 19
4–8 Snowstorm hits Martin Co. at Martin's Cove, Hunt & Hodgetts companies at Devil's Gate
Four wagons meet Martin Co. 12
Ephraim Hanks meets Martin Co. with buffalo meat 10
Discouraged by snowstorm, many rescuers turn back, but some continue to Allred's base camp 4–8
15 William Kimball turns 15–20 wagons around
16 Ten relief wagons meet Martin Co. on Rocky Ridge
18 Kimball's 30 wagons meet Martin Co. at Allred's base camp
Second Rescue Effort
several small groups
21 More wagons meet Martin Co.
James Willie finds rescue party, tells them of his desperate company ahead 20
21 Reaches Willie Co., delivers flour and clothing
22 William Kimball and six wagons go west with Willie Co., Grant leads eight wagons east
Meets Smoot wagon co. along Big Sandy Creek, gives them supplies 16
26 Finds Young's scouts at Devil's Gate, sends them ahead
Reaches Ft. Bridger, picks up more supplies 12
31 Meets Martin and Hodgetts companies at Greasewood Creek
2 Brings Martin Co. to Devil's Gate
First Rescue Party, George D. Grant
50 men, 22 wagons
24–25 Six wagons go to Willow Creek to bring Willie Company to base camp
Sweetwater Base Camp, Reddick Allred
18 Passes Willie Co. with news of coming rescue
28 Finds Martin and Hodgetts companies at Red Buttes, Hunt Company at the Platte crossing
19 Base camp abandoned, Martin Co. leaves in wagons
Express Scout Party, Joseph A. Young
4 men on horseback
27 13 yoke of oxen sent east to rescue Hunt & Hodgetts companies
Martin Co. arrives 23
Receives news of coming Willie Co., sends six wagons to help 27
31 Finds Willie Co. near Green River
9 Hunt & Hodgetts company members begin to leave Fort Bridger
28–4 Nov Wagons of Hunt & Hodgetts companies trickle in
3 Willie Co. arrives, wagons are waiting to carry everyone to Great Salt Lake City
Sends 12 yoke of oxen to aid Smoot wagon company 23
Fort Supply & Fort Bridger
7–9 Wagons arrive at Fort Bridger
4 Franklin D. Richards arrives in Great Salt Lake City, reports the lateness of the handcart and wagon companies
Third Rescue Effort
mostly from Utah County
5–6 In general conference, Brigham Young calls for supplies, wagons, and volunteers to rescue the companies
26 Church leaders make another call for rescuers and supplies
11 News reaches Brigham Young of rescuers turning back; William Kimball sent out again to push them on
28 Brigham Young makes a third call for rescue teams
Great Salt Lake City
1 6 11 16 21 26 1 6 11 16 21 26 1 6 11
October
November
December

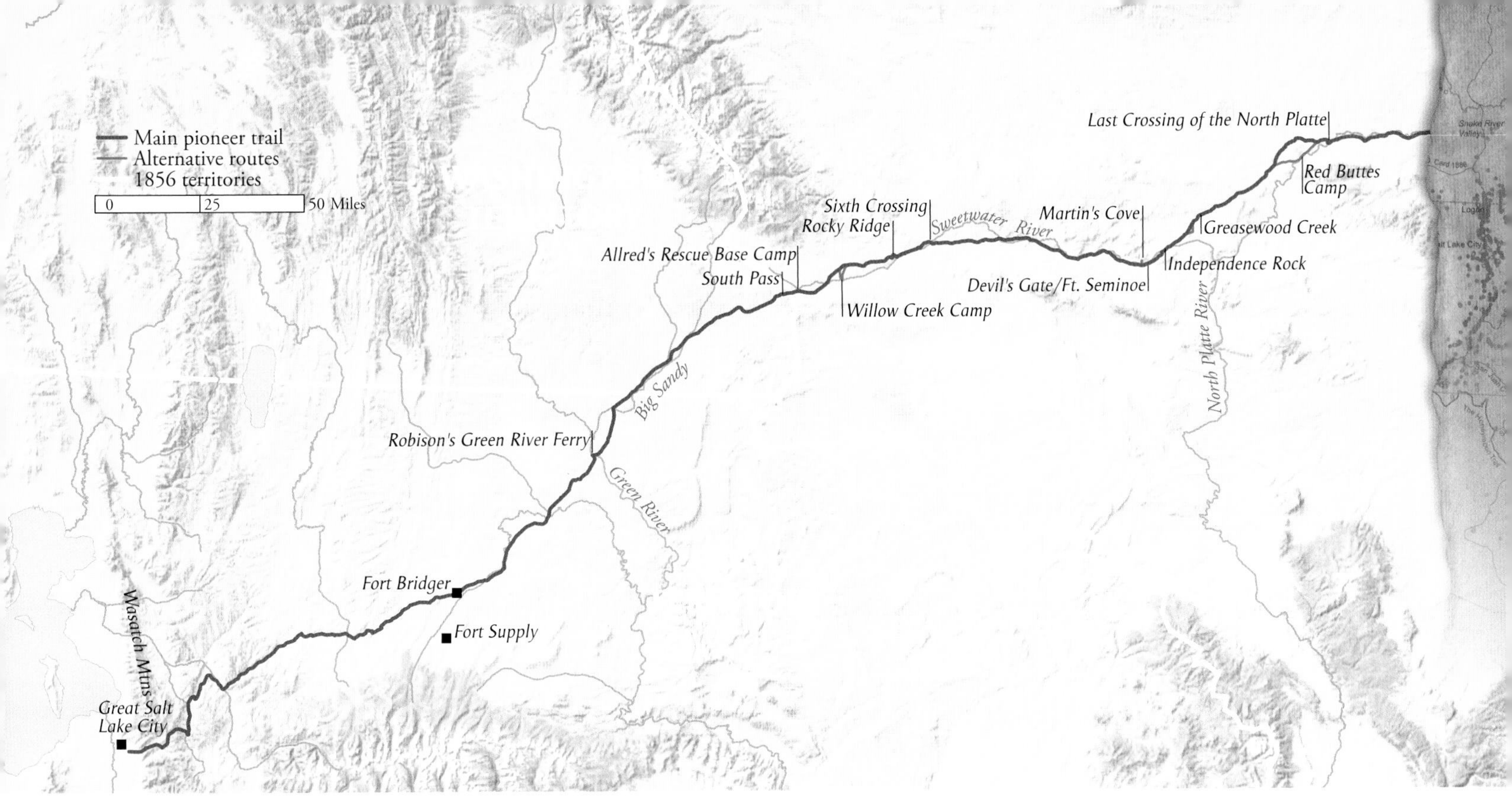

Many other wagons from the second relief drove on to meet the Martin Company still far to the east. Unfortunately, as the days passed, the weather worsened, and when there was still no news from the initial relief party and the Martin Company, these teams became discouraged and retreated to the Fort Bridger area. When Brigham Young heard of this reversal, he sent messengers to turn them back to their duty. These messengers got the wagons going in the right direction, along with teams from Fort Supply. The wagons arrived at the relief base camp east of South Pass in time to meet the Martin Company as it staggered in. The next day, teamsters found places in the wagons for all the Martin Company, and the rescue teams then rushed toward Salt Lake City. One hundred and four wagons bearing the survivors of the Martin Company drove into the city the last day of November.

Having only a little support left to them, the Hunt and Hodgetts wagon companies, also suffering from hunger, wind, cold, and the loss of many oxen and some wagons, slowly struggled on to Green River. There additional teams from Fort Supply helped them to Fort Bridger. A third wave of relief from Utah came to them there and brought them the remainder of the way, arriving in mid-December.

The men who went to the rescue of the late immigrants were heroes, but many others contributed to the relief effort. As the snow deepened, work groups went into the mountains to keep the road open, particularly over Big Mountain, so the wagons and immigrants could come through. The relief effort did not end upon the immigrants' arrival. Destitute, starving, emotionally and physically traumatized, many severely ill from exposure and disabled with frozen limbs, the immigrants required homes, food, clothing, nursing care, and emotional support. With very limited resources, the citizens of Utah took the survivors into their homes and provided for their needs, sometimes for months, while they recovered.

Lyndia McDowell Carter

Going to the Rescue

Following the Mormon emigrant trail, the initial relief company headed east over the Wasatch Mountains. Flour and animal feed were cached at Fort Bridger and Green River. At the Big Sandy, the relief group met and assisted the Smoot wagon train. Just east of South Pass, they set up a base camp led by Reddick Allred. Moving on, the relief teams were hit by the October 19 storm and were forced to shelter near the mouth of Willow Creek, where Captain Willie found them. The next day, they found the Willie Handcart Company snowbound at the sixth crossing of the Sweetwater. There the relief company split: six teams helped the Willie Company continue west; eight teams went east to find the Martin Handcart Company. These eight wagons under Captain Grant encountered the scouts waiting near Devil's Gate, unable to locate the Martin Company. While Grant established a base camp at Fort Simcoe, a small abandoned post there, he sent three scouts forward, who found the Martin and Hodgetts companies snowbound at Red Buttes; the Hunt wagon company was ten miles east at the last crossing of the North Platte. The scouts got the companies moving, then rushed to Devil's Gate with the news. Hurrying forward, the relief teams intercepted the Martin Company at Greasewood Creek (today's Horse Creek). Helping the Martin, Hunt, and Hodgetts companies to Devil's Gate, they all waited there for the wagon companies. The handcart company moved into a cove in the mountains two miles west (later called Martin's Cove) to wait out another ferocious winter storm.

Meanwhile, the Willie Company climbed Rocky Ridge and pushed sixteen miles to the Sweetwater River below the mouth of Willow Creek. There they buried fifteen people. Six wagons from the base camp came to them there and assisted them westward. Wagons from Fort Supply and Utah met them between Green River and Ham's Fork. At Fort Bridger, there were enough relief wagons to take all of the Willie Company into Salt Lake City.

On that same day, November 9, Grant got the Martin Company and the wagon companies moving again from Devil's Gate and Martin's Cove. During the next several days, they met the lone Ephraim Hanks and a few small relief groups. Finally, the Martin Company struggled into Allred's base camp. There, many more relief workers packed all the survivors into waiting wagons that rushed them to Salt Lake City, where they arrived November 30. The Hodgetts and Hunt wagon companies moved slowly on under their own power with assistance from fresh ox teams, mostly from Fort Supply. Eventually they reached Green River and with additional help from Fort Supply, they made it to Fort Bridger. A third wave of relief teams brought them on to the Salt Lake Valley in mid-December.

Utah War

1857–1858

In 1857 tensions between Utah Territory and the federal government reached a breaking point. Members of Utah's legislature sent memorials to Congress asking that men of their own liking be appointed to territorial offices. Unsuitable federal appointees, they said, would be sent away.

Within days of receiving the memorials, the federal government also received letters from three earlier appointees charging that Utah was in a state of rebellion. The letters and memorials led U.S. President James Buchanan to send a substantial portion of the U.S. Army to accompany new appointees to Utah. The army could quell any rebellion and assure the seating of Buchanan's new appointees. Buchanan did not inform then territorial governor Brigham Young of his purposes.

Having been driven out of Missouri and Illinois by the territorial militias of those states, the Saints viewed the approach of soldiers with suspicion. When Young became aware that the newly dispatched army was to be headed by General William Harney, he concluded the army had hostile intentions, since Harney had a reputation for brutality. Young and territorial militia general Daniel H. Wells put Utah's militia, called the Nauvoo Legion, on alert. They also asked citizens to conserve grain and prepare arms and clothing for a potentially long siege.

In September 1857, during this period of unrest, 50–60 militiamen in southern Utah, aided by Indians, killed some 120 California-bound emigrants in an atrocity that became known as the Mountain Meadows Massacre.

Later that month, Young issued a martial law proclamation that formally put Utah on a war footing. Under the direction of Wells, territorial forces harassed approaching federal troops, who were finally stopped in their approach by snowstorms. The U.S. forces and territorial appointees established their winter quarters near Fort Bridger.

Meanwhile, in March-April 1858, Young organized a mass exodus from Salt Lake City and other northern settlements, in case hostilities broke out; most refugees camped in Utah Valley for the next three months. At the same time, explorations were made in southern and western Utah to find potential permanent resettlement sites; none were found to be suitable. They did find a military exploring party steaming up the Colorado River.

Thomas L. Kane of Pennsylvania, a longtime friend of the Saints, negotiated a settlement between Young and Utah's newly appointed governor, Alfred Cumming. Two commissioners sent by Buchanan helped formalize a peace accord, and on June 26, 1858, the army marched through a nearly deserted Salt Lake City. From there the troops eventually moved southwest and established a military encampment called Camp Floyd.

Richard E. Turley Jr. and John Eldredge

Actions of the Utah War

U.S. troops began leaving Fort Leavenworth, Kansas, for Utah in June 1857. From Devil's Gate forward, Mormon militiamen watched the army's movements. They sought to slow the troops' advance by stampeding their stock, burning grass, and setting supply trains on fire. The first hostilities occurred near South Pass, and continued harassment forced the troops to winter in present-day Wyoming, finally marching through Salt Lake City in June 1858 and establishing Camp Floyd southwest of there.

Meanwhile, Church leaders sent exploring parties to verify rumors of military expeditions coming up the Colorado River and to search for possible resettlement sites.

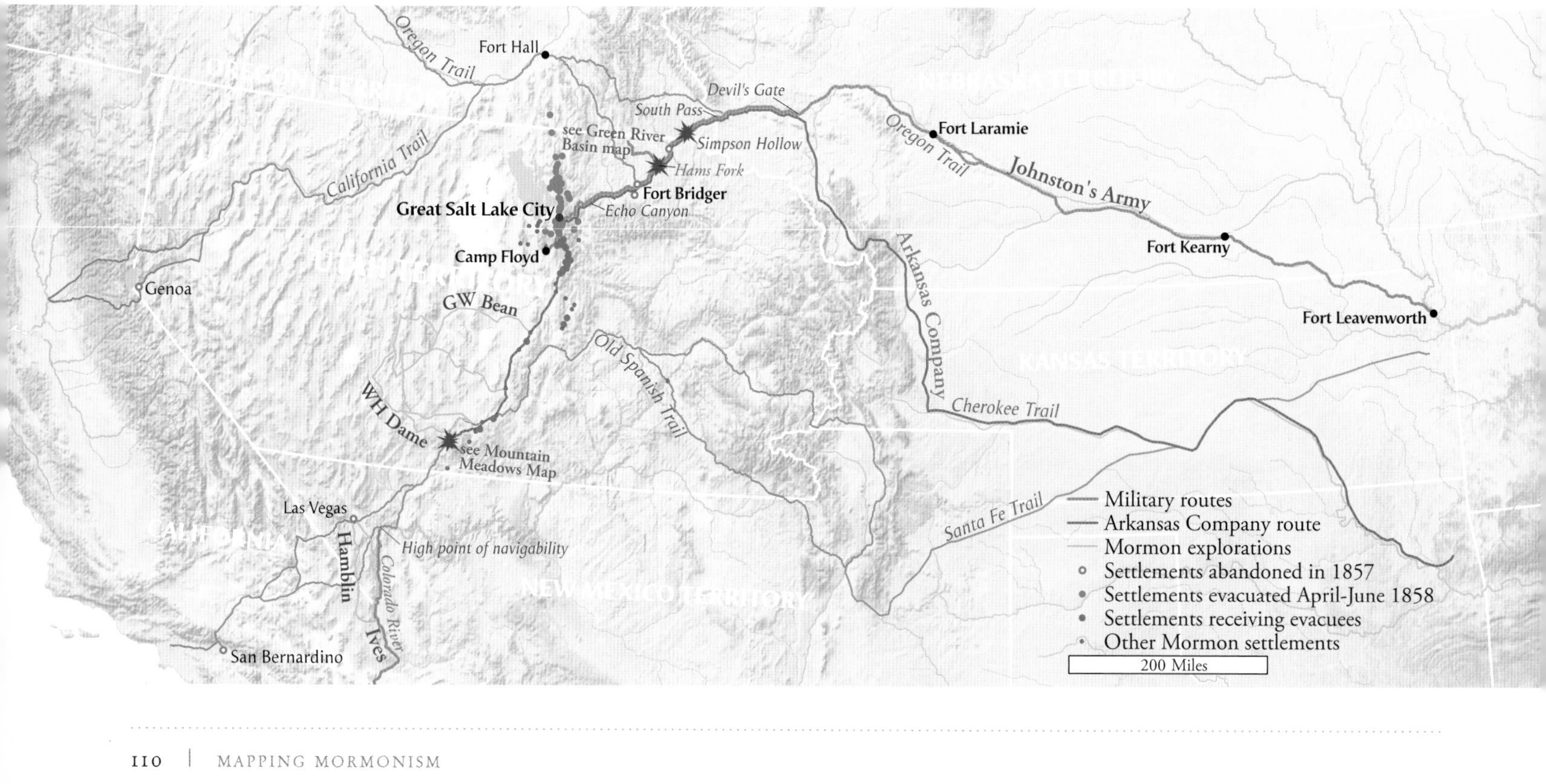

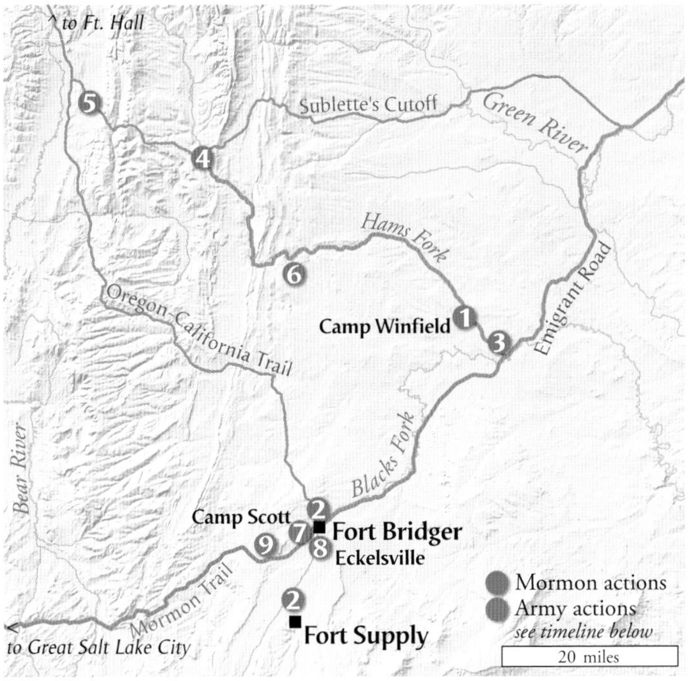

The Green River Theater

The vanguard of the U.S. Army, led by Colonel Edmund B. Alexander, arrived at Hams Fork in late September and established Camp Winfield. During the army's stay there, the two sides came as close to pitched battles as at any time during the Utah War. Rumors of large Mormon forces to the north caused Alexander to abandon his march to Fort Hall. After a severe November storm killed most of their draft animals, U.S. troops were forced to establish winter quarters on Camp Scott on Blacks Fork. The camp incorporated the ruins of Fort Bridger, which had been burned by Mormons. They stayed here from late November 1857 through early June 1858, while negotiations took place that led to a peaceful resolution.

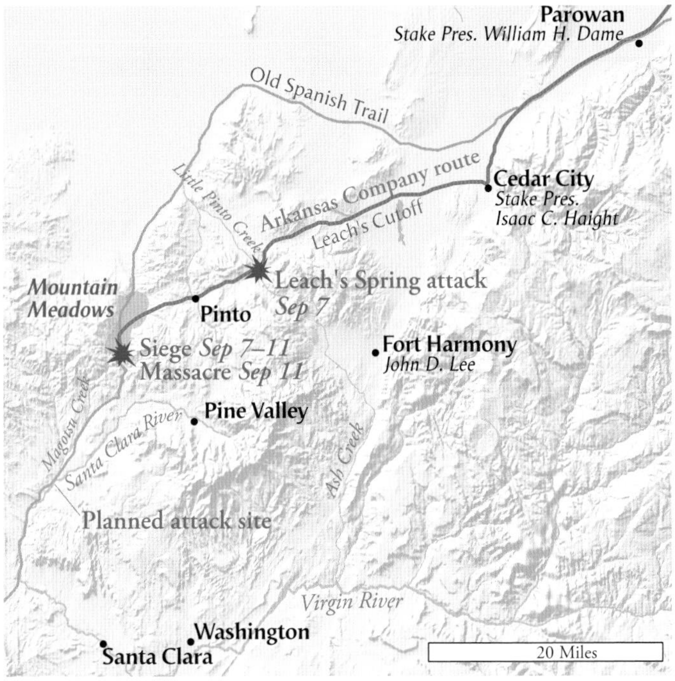

The Mountain Meadows Massacre

On September 11, 1857, some 120 California-bound emigrants, led by Alexander Fancher, were killed by local Mormon men aided by Indians. Only 17 small children survived. Historians have debated possible reasons why a generally peaceful people would commit such an atrocity. As members of the Arkansas company traveled south from Salt Lake City, they had minor run-ins with local residents, but their journey was mostly peaceful until they reached Cedar City, the last major settlement in Southern Utah. There they were denied much-needed supplies. After tensions between the emigrants and Cedar City residents, local leaders called on John D. Lee to orchestrate an attack on the emigrants, which he did at Mountain Meadows. After three largely unsuccessful assaults, Cedar City leaders sent additional militiamen to the Meadows, and the combined Mormon and Indian force killed almost the entire emigrant company. Although several of the conspirators were eventually indicted for the massacre, only John D. Lee was tried, convicted, and executed for his role in the crime.

Utah War, 1857–58

28 May Gen. Winfield Scott issues orders for army to Utah

Army begins to leave **18 Jul** Ft. Leavenworth

Rumors of the army **23 Jul** coming to Utah are confirmed

First Nauvoo Legion troops **13 Aug** called to active service

Missionaries in U.S. and **mid-Aug** outlying settlements called home

Col. Albert Sydney Johnston assigned **Aug 28** command of the Utah Expedition

MOUNTAIN MEADOWS

First attack at Mountain Meadows; **7 Sep** Mormons fire on two emigrants at Leach's Spring

Arkansas company besieged

At "Tan Bark Council" in Parowan, William **10 Sep** H. Dame approves killing the emigrants

Arkansas company massacred **11 Sep** by local militia and Indians

8 Sep Capt. Stewart Van Vliet's advance party notifies Brigham Young of the coming army

15 Sep Young declares martial law throughout Utah Territory

18 Sep Saints begin to abandon Genoa

Nauvoo Legion scouts see U.S. **22 Sep** Army at Devil's Gate

Late Sep Legion fortifies Echo Canyon

GREEN RIVER BASIN
see numbers on map above

Late Sep ❶ Col. Alexander establishes temporary Camp Winfield, where news of martial law in Utah arrives

3–4 Oct ❷ Saints abandon and burn Ft. Bridger and Ft. Supply

5 Oct Legion Maj. Lot Smith sets fire to supply train at Simpson Hollow

❸ 11 Oct Nauvoo Legion runs off 700 head of army cattle

11 Oct Alexander leads army northward to circumvent Mormon defenses

❹ 16 Oct Capt. Randolph Marcy's men fire forty shots at Nauvoo Legion group led by Maj. Lot Smith; two horses are hit and one man's hat is shot off, but they escape

❺ 16 Oct Army captures Legion Maj. Joseph Taylor and William Stowell as prisoners of war

❹ 18 Oct harassed by Mormons and weather, Alexander turns his troops back

❻ 26 Oct Army fires on Legion scouts, who escape unharmed

3 Nov Col. Albert Sydney Johnson takes command of the troops at Blacks Fork

❼ Mid-November Army sets up winter quarters at Camp Scott near ruins of Fort Bridger

❽ 19 Nov New Gov. Alfred Cumming arrives with cavalry, establishes camp of Eckelsville as seat of territorial government

21 Nov Cumming officially orders Mormons not to rebel

❾ Winter Legion troops watch U.S. troops from Bridger Butte

Nov–Feb San Bernardino abandoned

Feb 1858 Indians attack Ft. Lemhi, which is soon abandoned

Thomas L. Kane arrives **25 Feb** in Great Salt Lake City to negotiate peace

Mar–Apr Kane negotiates with Cumming

21 Mar Young advises northern Saints to temporarily move south

Mar–Jul The Move South

Mar–Apr Jacob Hamblin finds soldiers steaming up the Colorado River

Apr–Jul White Mountain expedition cannot find suitable settlement sites in the western desert

12 Apr Cumming arrives in Great Salt Lake City

7 Jun Peace commission arrives in GSLC

13 Jun Peace treaty signed

26 Jun Army passes through Great Salt Lake City

May 1858 | June | July | August | Sept | Oct | Nov | Dec | January 1858 | February | March | April | May | June | July

The Gentiles

1862–1910

While most people think of Utah as the capital of Mormondom—and rightly so—the Saints were preceded by American Indians (see p. 98), Spanish explorers, missionaries, and fur trappers. Although the Mormons chose Utah as a remote location outside the boundaries of the United States where they could pursue their unique way of life unmolested by "Gentiles,"* they were never fully able to do so, for the United States tended to follow them. The Treaty of Guadalupe-Hidalgo, which ended the Mexican War in 1848, brought Utah within the boundaries of the United States. The Gold Rush of the following year brought streams of travelers through Utah, and the Utah War of 1857–58 (see p. 110) brought soldiers from across the United States.

The real end of Mormon isolation, though, began with the completion of the transcontinental railroad in northern Utah on May 10, 1869. Very soon local spur lines were constructed, which brought larger and larger parts of the territory into connection with the transcontinental line. Although the railroad provided easy access to eastern manufactured goods and markets for Utah agricultural products, it inaugurated a process of change that ultimately doomed Utah's unique theocratic political system, its polygamous society, and its agricultural economy.

Another important agent of change was the development of mining. The agricultural village was a fundamental element of Mormon culture, so even after Utah's rich subterranean resources were discovered, primarily silver and coal, Mormons were discouraged from exploiting them because it would necessitate living and working outside the village and would produce inequalities in wealth that would erode the social fabric. Conversely, the soldiers stationed in Utah were encouraged to explore by their commander, Colonel Patrick Connor, who correctly foresaw that a mining boom would attract diverse multitudes to dilute the Mormon hegemony of Utah. Irish and Italian Catholics, Greeks, and others flocked to the mining communities in the Wasatch and Oquirrh mountains and Carbon County.

Salt Lake City—Utah's political, financial, and cultural capital—became a microcosm of the increasing diversification of Utah life at the turn of the twentieth century. The City–County Building's monumental architecture symbolized an emerging secular political maturity. The city's emerging capitalist economy was centered on Exchange Place, and religious diversity was evidenced in churches like the Roman Catholic Cathedral of the Madeleine, St. Mark's Episcopal Cathedral, and the First Presbyterian Church.

Some of the non-Mormons who came to Utah were motivated not by a quest for wealth, but by hostility to Mormonism, and the late nineteenth century was a time of religious antagonism. Protestant groups, particularly the Presbyterians, Congregationalists, and Methodists, failed to defeat Mormonism in outright debate and then sought to undermine it by mission schools. Basic education had been largely the responsibility of LDS wards, which varied widely in quality, as qualified teachers and books were often in short supply. The Protestant schools were of uniformly high quality, with well-trained teachers and abundant educational materials provided by donations from eastern congregations. The strategy behind them was that Mormon parents, seeking the best available education for their children, would be tempted to send them to the Protestant schools, where the teachers would not only educate them but convert them as well. The strategy yielded very few conversions, but it did expose the inadequacies of the ward schools and led to the establishment of the LDS Academy system (see p. 126) and an effective public school system in the 1890s.

Gary Topping

**Note: The Mormon use of the term "Gentile" had its origin during the lifetime of Joseph Smith, who taught that the Saints were adopted into the House of Israel upon baptism, joining the Jews and the Lamanites (Native Americans); thus the Jewish term "gentile" applied to all others. It was used extensively by Utah Mormons during Brigham Young's administration but gradually fell out of favor by the end of the nineteenth century as the Church endeavored to improve its public image by reducing the use of divisive language. Ironically, it was increasingly used by non-Mormons in Utah to identify and unify themselves as a minority "other." By the early twentieth century, neither group used the term very often.*

Timeline

- **1862** Ft. Douglas established
- **1866** First Catholic church in Utah
- **1869** Completion of the transcontinental railroad
- **1869** First Godbeite protest against Brigham Young
- **1874** Consecration of St. Mark's Episcopal Cathedral
- **1875** Opening of Wasatch Academy, a Presbyterian school in Mt. Pleasant
- **1875** Opening of Salt Lake Collegiate Institute, a Presbyterian college in Salt Lake City, now Westminster College
- **1894** Completion of City-County Building
- **1905** Dedication of First Presbyterian and First United Methodist Churches
- **1907** Samuel Newhouse begins construction of Exchange Place
- **1909** Dedication of the Cathedral of the Madeleine
- **1915** Completion of Utah State Capitol

1860 | 1870 | 1880 | 1890 | 1900 | 1910

Non-Mormons in Utah Territory

The Spanish empire fell apart during the eighteenth and early nineteenth centuries largely through neglect growing from the perception that there was no more gold and silver in the New World. This map shows how egregiously wrong that perception was for Utah, and similar maps for California, Nevada, and Colorado would show the same thing. The red lines not only depict the expanding railroad network linking more and more of those mining and agricultural communities; they also represent the gradual infusion of the new blood of capitalism and commerce that caused such fundamental changes in Utah life.

Although Fort Douglas would remain an active military post until very recent times, the other military installations were the wave of the past, not the future. As settlers pressed out into remote parts of the territory, the sad story of the defeat of the American Indians was played out in Utah as elsewhere in the nation, and military protection became unnecessary.

When Father Lawrence Scanlan (later the first Catholic bishop of the Diocese of Salt Lake) complained in 1888 that the Protestants "have schools in every small settlement in the Territory of Utah," he was scarcely exaggerating, as this map shows. By the turn of the century only a few would remain, as funding for public schools increased dramatically.

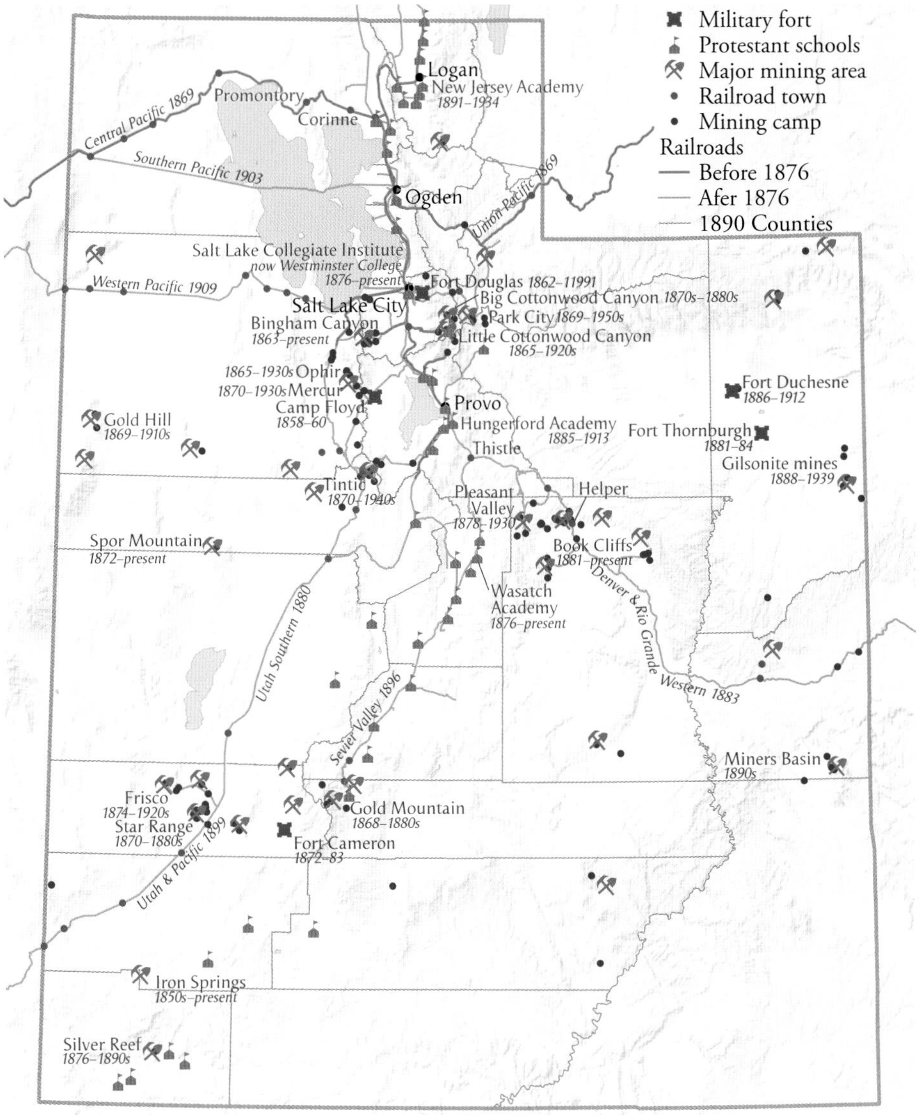

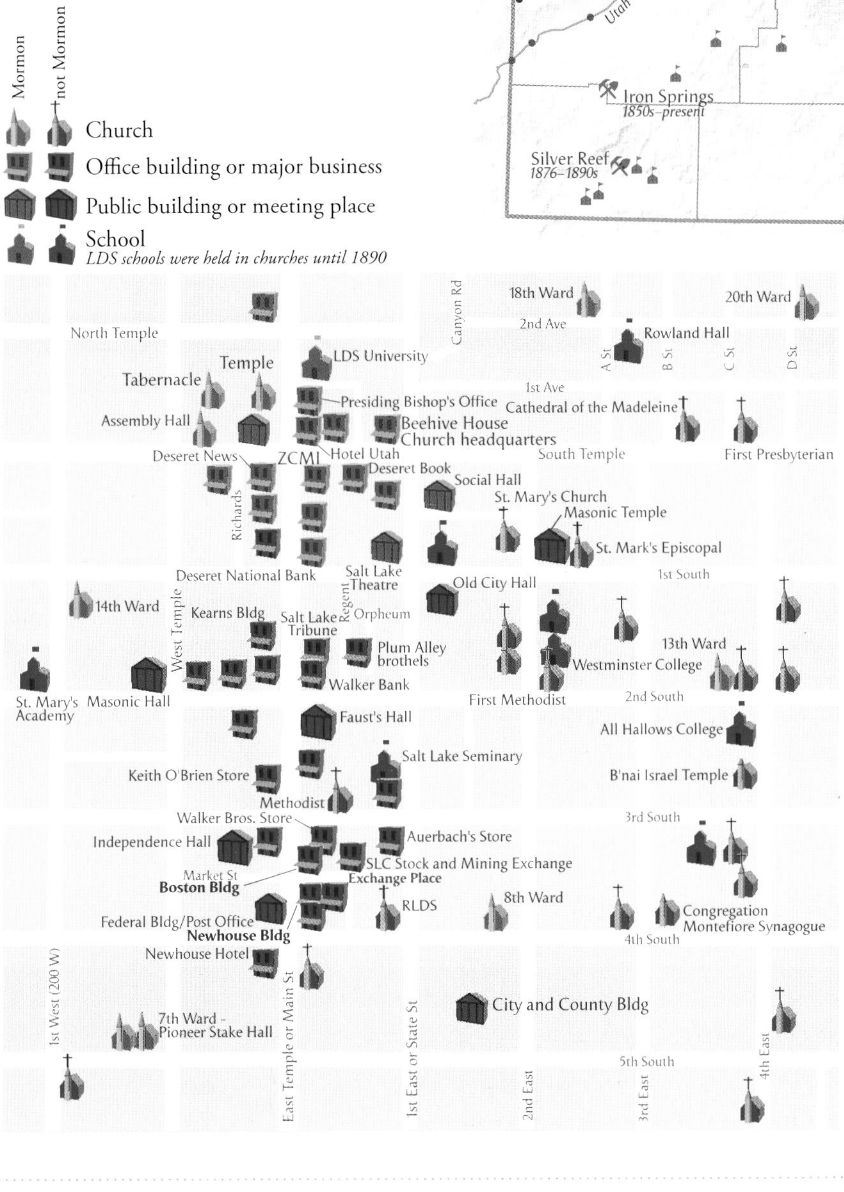

Salt Lake City's Two Downtowns, Early 1900s

The non-Mormon population in Utah was most conspicuous in mining communities like Bingham Canyon, Park City, and Carbon County. Salt Lake City, the capital of the territory and state and headquarters of The Church of Jesus Christ of Latter-day Saints, offered natural attractions to non-Mormons as well. The city offer political and commercial opportunities, and non-Mormon religions established their Utah headquarters in Salt Lake City as well. By the turn of the twentieth century, the capital had become two cities. With few exceptions, the Mormon part of the city was in the north surrounding the temple, while the non-Mormons clustered along the southern part of Main Street from Second to Fourth South. Exchange Place, anchored by the twin Boston and Newhouse Buildings (above) was its heart. This division has survived (subtly) to the present.

Church Headquarters

1847–present

Beginning in 1830, the fledgling Church of Christ was composed of small regional congregations, subject to removal and relocation, without a discernable core. Not until Joseph Smith's identification of Kirtland, Ohio and Independence, Missouri, as gathering sites in 1831 did a concept of a Church center or headquarters form. The early center of Church administration was typically the residence of its prophet, Joseph Smith Jr.

Starting in 1831, revelations and administrative strategies included the provision for physical structures to accomplish the Lord's purposes for his people. Temples became the centerpiece around which Church administration and the Saints' lives revolved. First in Independence, then in Kirtland, Far West, and Nauvoo, the "City of Zion" (see p. 44) plan was centered on a central public square containing temples and buildings to accomodate priesthood needs in governing Church operations. A Kirtland revelation given in May 1833 (D&C 94) indicated that besides plans to build the Lord's "house" there, the Saints should also build a "house for the presidency" (an administration building) and a printing press adjacent to the temple. The subsequent plan for Zion (Independence) included 24 "temples": in addition to the "House of the Lord," the rest were a variety of administrative and public buildings. In each case, the headquarters served two functions: worship, including typical Sunday meetings, general and stake conferences, and temple ceremonies; and administration offices for those who devoted their time to carrying forth the work of the Church.

These functions continued in the Salt Lake Valley. Among the first matters attended to was the identification of the temple site around which the city would be built. The forty acres initially planned for Church operations in Great Salt Lake City were soon pared to the ten acres that presently constitute Temple Square, the symbolic heart of the Church to the present day. A number of worship-related structures have been housed within the walls of Temple Square, including the early boweries (rudimentary outdoor pavilions for public worship) and Endowment House (a temporary building for conducting temple ceremonies), as well as the iconic domed tabernacle and the temple that took forty years to construct.

The block to the east, initially owned by Brigham Young and other leaders, quickly gained a variety of administrative offices and functions, especially the tithing yard, which gathered in-kind donations. It has been the administrative headquarters of the Church ever since, now anchored by the granite, Classical Revival Church Administration Building (still housing the offices of the President) and the 28-story modernist Church Office Building. In addition, since 1900, a third function has emerged: tourism, welcoming the members and non-members who visit Salt Lake City. Tourism has necessitated museums, visitors' centers, and the Hotel Utah,

continued on page 116

The headquarters of the Church started in 1848 with Brigham Young's small adobe home, but other administrative functions soon occupied the block, especially the substantial shops and yards in which members' tithing-in-kind (primarily agricultural products) was collected and redistributed to the poor. Meanwhile, the first ecclesiastical buildings were built on the Temple Block during the 1850s to house Sunday meetings (attended by everyone in the city; ward sacrament meetings originated later) and temple ceremonies; construction on the temple itself was halted (and the foundation hidden) during the Utah War. Surrounding the Temple Block were the homes of the First Presidency, Apostles, and other prominent leaders.

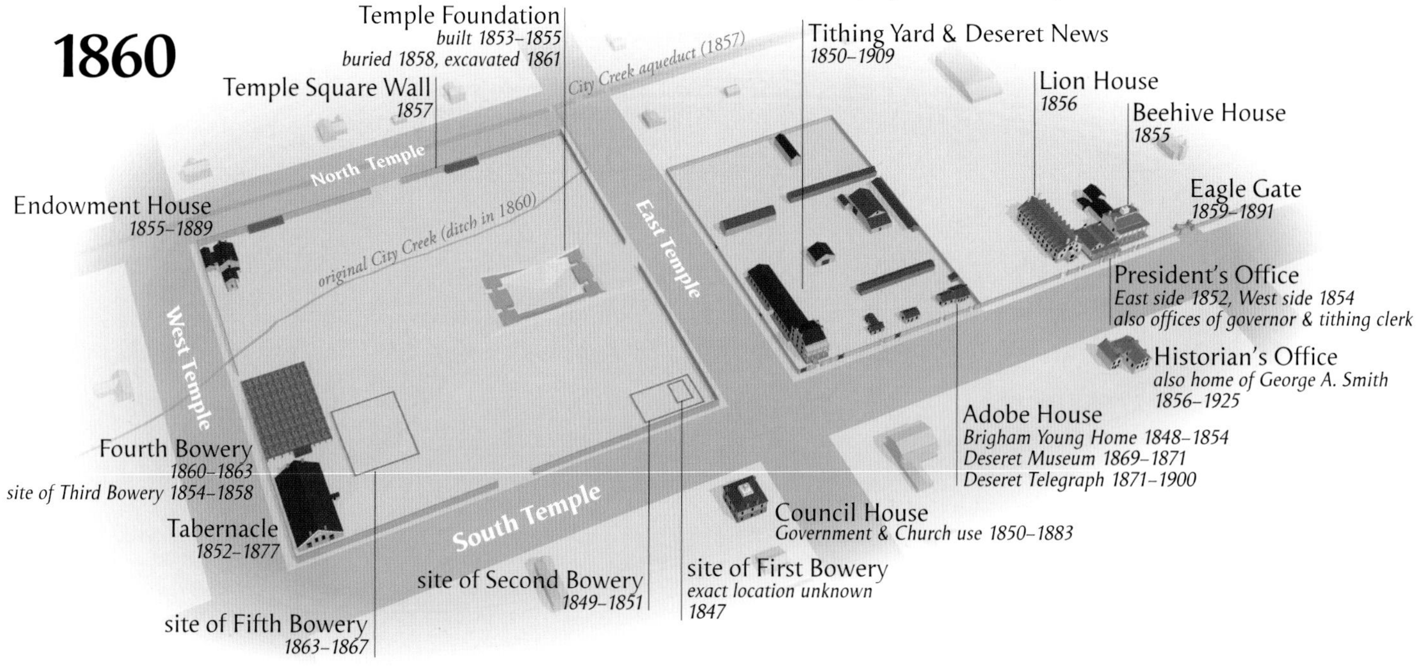

1900

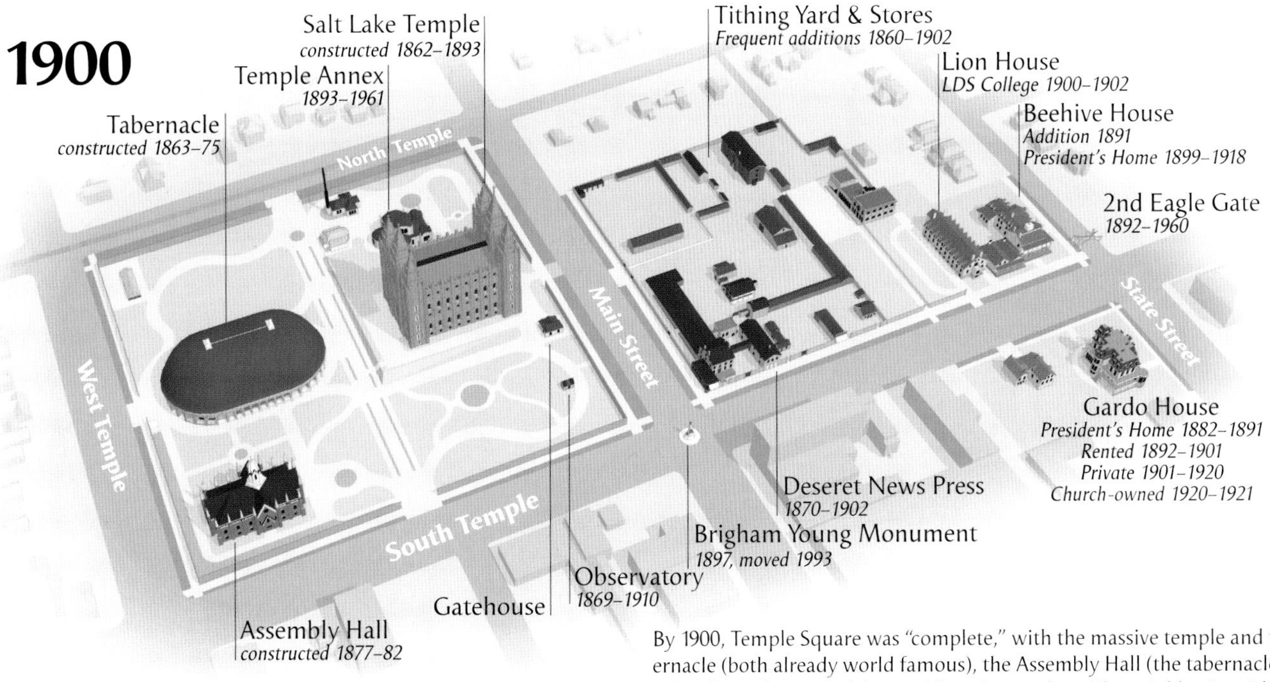

By 1900, Temple Square was "complete," with the massive temple and tabernacle (both already world famous), the Assembly Hall (the tabernacle for Salt Lake Stake), and elaborate Victorian gardens. The neighboring tithing yard had been augmented with the offices and press of the *Deseret News*, food processing facilities for tithing products, and even temporary housing for destitute immigrants. Across the street was the Gardo House, often called "Amelia's Palace" after the wife of Brigham Young for whom it was built. Probably the best example of a Victorian mansion on Salt Lake City, it was at times the presidential home of John Taylor and Wilford Woodruff before being rented, sold, then razed in the 1920s. Presidents Lorenzo Snow and Joseph F. Smith lived in the Beehive House.

Church Buildings in Downtown Salt Lake City

1847 Temple Square surveyed as the center of Great Salt Lake City

1847–51 Temporary boweries (open-air pavilions) used for church meetings

1848 Brigham Young's first home built; later used as the President's office, museum, and telegraph office

1850–88 Council House, built as governmental headquarters but also used for Church meetings

1850–1909 Tithing Yard used for gathering and distributing in-kind donations

1852–77 First Tabernacle

1852 President's Office constructed as part of Brigham Young's home

1853–55 Initial construction of Salt Lake Temple foundation

1854–67 New boweries constructed as membership outgrows the tabernacle

1855 Beehive House, Brigham Young's primary home

1855–89 Endowment House serves as a temporary temple

1856 Lion House, home to additional wives of Brigham Young; later used for administrative, educational, and tourist uses

1856 Historian's Office

1857 Temple Square Wall

1861–93 Salt Lake Temple constructed

1863–75 Construction of the tabernacle

1870–1902 *Deseret News* occupies part of the tithing complex

1877–82 Construction of Assembly Hall (Salt Lake Stake tabernacle)

Gardo House built for one **1882** of Brigham's wives; later the home of Church Presidents and wealthy families

1897 Monument constructed to honor Brigham Young to commemorate the 50-year anniversary of the pioneers

1901–31 LDS University constructed on administrative block

1904–76 Bureau of Information built to serve tourists; gradually expanded into a full museum

1910–62 Bishop's Building

1910–62 Deseret Gymnasium built by the Church to encourage wholesome recreation

1911 Hotel Utah

1917 Church Administration Building, primary offices of General Authorities to the present

1925–62 Missionary Home

1925–52 Primary Children's Hospital, eventually moved to the Avenues

1931 LDS University reduced to LDS Business College; most buildings converted to Church administration

1953–73 Expanding bureaucracy requires the Church to purchase or rent several office buildings in surrounding downtown

Relief Society Building **1956**

North Visitors' Center **1963**

1965–97 Second Deseret Gym north of Temple Square

Salt Lake Temple remodeled, **1966** with addition and new annex buildings

Church Office Building **1972**

South Visitors' Center replaces the museum **1978**

1984–85 Museum of Church History and Art, and Family History Library expand the campus to the west

1993 Hotel Utah renovated for Church use and renamed the Joseph Smith Memorial Building

Conference Center and **2000** Main Street Plaza

Church History Library **2009**

1845 | 1865 | 1885 | 1905 | 1925 | 1945 | 1965 | 1985 | 2005

Church Headquarters
continued

one of the most elegant buildings in the city when it was built in 1911. Although it was converted from a hotel into administrative offices in 1993, it still features a considerable amount of space devoted to serving visitors.

As the Church has grown, it has repeatedly outgrown older worship, administration, and tourism facilities, and older buildings have periodically been replaced by new, larger, buildings. This has tended to occur in spurts, especially in the 1850s, 1901–17, and 1963–78.

As one walks through the plaza connecting the Church Administration and Church Office buildings, one can easily forget that the headquarters campus (now about 40 acres, as originally envisioned by Brigham Young) required generations of labor and commitment. What appears commonplace to modern observers seemed imaginary to adventurer Richard F. Burton, who in 1860 upon learning plans for the Salt Lake Temple observed that it "will probably never be completed." Through foresight and many modifications over the years, Church headquarters has served an expanding domestic and international membership.

Ronald O. Barney and W. Randall Dixon

Once the Church retired its debt in the early twentieth century, and ended the practice of tithing-in-kind, it was able to build several buildings to meet the growing needs of the Church. The Church Administration Building on South Temple Street anchored a new downtown campus, including the headquarters of the Presiding Bishop's departments, the Hotel Utah (one of the Church's many non-ecclesiastical endeavors to improve the economic health of downtown Salt Lake City), and the Deseret Gymnasium (intended to provide a "wholesome" recreational facility for members). The four-building campus of LDS University was built between 1901 and 1919; when most church schools were closed in 1931 (see p. 126), all but the business and music departments were closed, and administrative departments took over the other buildings, including the rapidly expanding collection of the Genealogical Society of Utah (see p. 152). The Missionary Home, a gathering place for newly called missionaries to receive their temple endowments and short-term training, initially occupied a series of houses originally built by the Young family; it outgrew these facilities in the missionary surge of the 1960s (see p. 178), moving first to a hotel, then to an abandoned school until the Missionary Training Center was built in Provo.

Other proposed buildings, including a larger replacement for the tabernacle and an archives building, were never built (although buildings for similar purposes were built recently). On the temple block, facilities were built to host the growing numbers of tourists coming to see the world-famous temple and tabernacle, and several monuments were erected to honor the pioneer forefathers of the second and third generation Utahns.

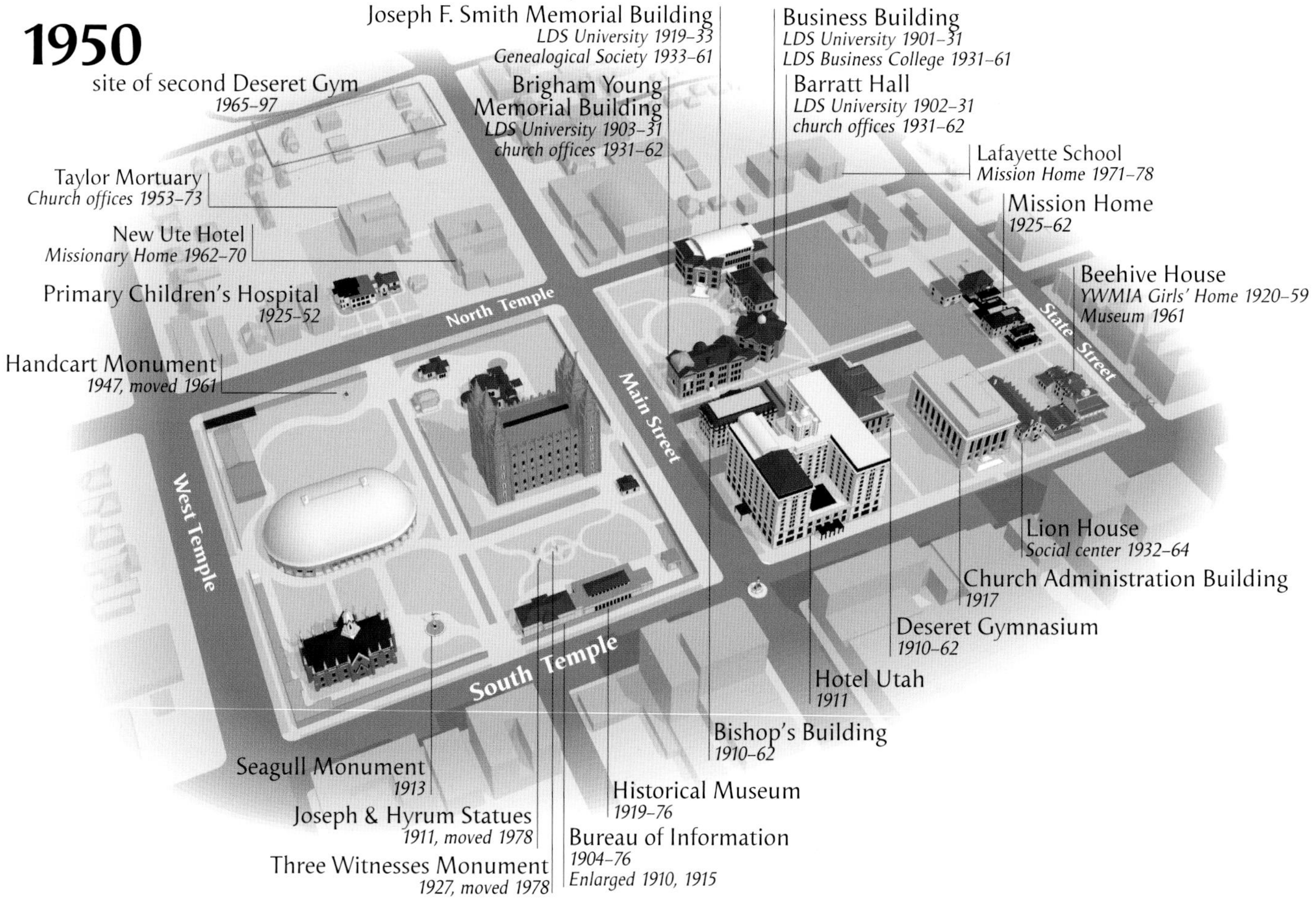

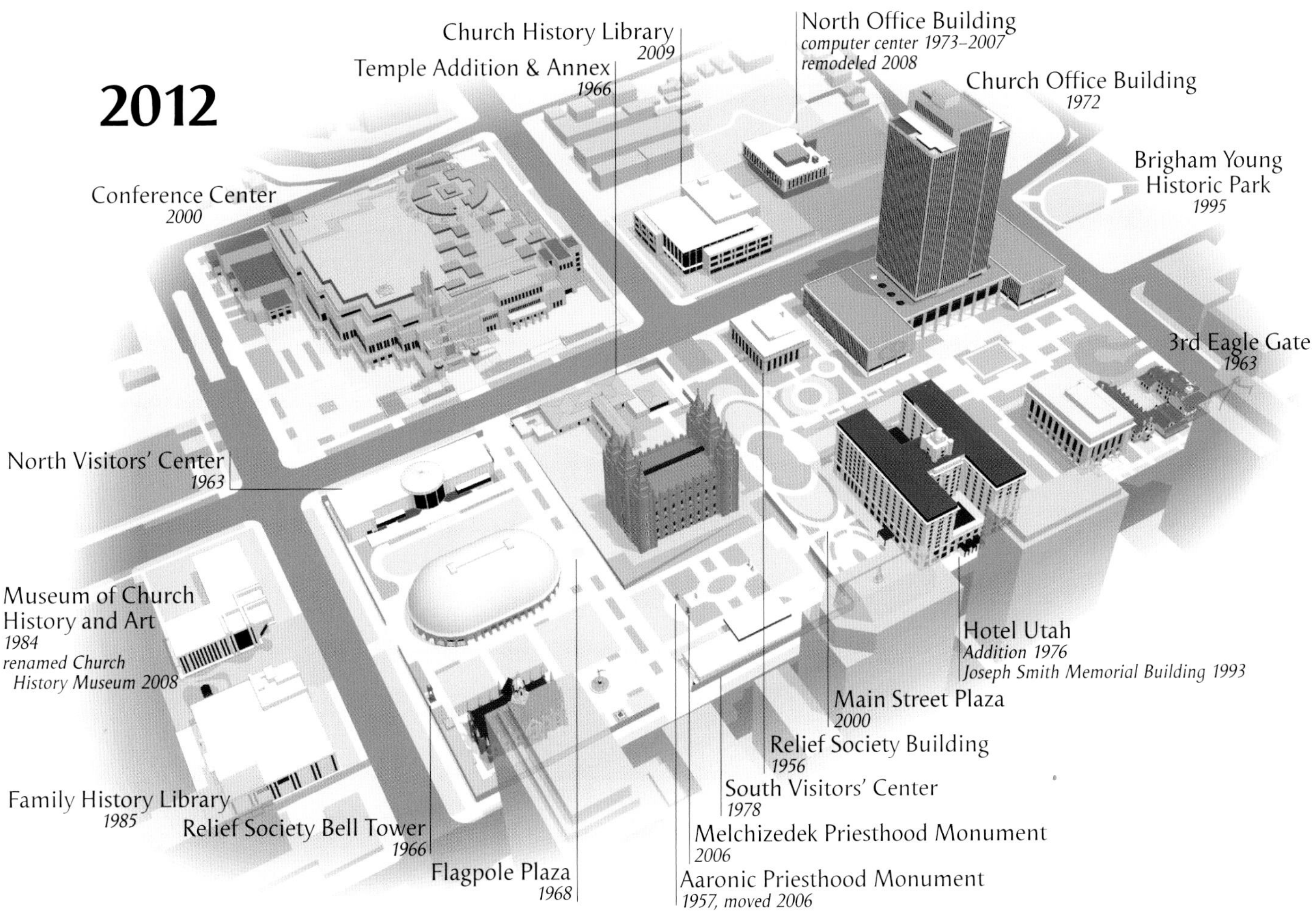

By the late 1950s, the growing Church had again outgrown its home. Church departments and agencies were housed in thirteen separate buildings around the city. The Relief Society Building, built to house the auxiliary organizations in 1956, helped, but the real solution (in the height of modernism) was to build a skyscraper. Most of the older administrative buildings were replaced by an underground parking garage, a large plaza, and the 24-story Church Office Building, occupied in 1972 and dedicated in 1975. Meanwhile, Temple Square was enhanced by the construction of new visitors' centers, the enlargement of the temple complex, and remodeled gardens.

Church growth continued to require additional space. Three buildings devoted to preserving and sharing historical records and artifacts have been built: the Family History Library, Church History Museum, and Church History Library. In April 1996, President Gordon B. Hinckley announced the construction of a vast new auditorium just north of Temple Square (the location of the second Deseret Gym) for general conferences to replace the aging, outgrown, 6,000-seat Tabernacle (restored and repaired 2005–2007). The Conference Center was, at the time of its dedication in April 2000, the largest fan-shaped auditorium of its kind in the world: over 21,000 people can be comfortably seated for the Church's general conferences each April and October. Built from the same quarry that furnished stone for the Salt Lake Temple and Administration Building, the 1.4 million-square-foot building is topped by a six-acre landscaped roof garden requiring 25,000 cubic yards of soil.

Church-owned Property in Downtown Salt Lake City in 2012

The LDS Church has owned much of the property surrounding the Temple for decades, gradually acquiring even more. Most of the surrounding land has been developed for commercial and residential purposes, including the headquarters of former and current Church-owned businesses such as Zions Bank, ZCMI, the Deseret News, Deseret Book, and KSL Broadcasting. By retaining the land and developing it, the Church has been able to ensure a very high level of aesthetic and economic quality for its home, most recently in the development of City Creek Center (see p. 118). It is also able to "bank" the land for the gradual expansion of the headquarters campus, such as the recent conversion of a parking lot into the Church History Library. All of the non-religious land is held in the name of Property Reserve, Inc., the for-profit real estate subsidiary of the Church, which isolates its taxable business interests from its ecclesiastical functions supported by tithing funds, which are housed on lands owned by the Presiding Bishopric.

Economic Development

1868–1920

As converts streamed into Utah in the nineteenth century, the Church faced the challenge of promoting sufficient economic growth to sustain a rapidly growing population. The economic condition of most Church members would have been improved by staying in the East, but they would not have been able to sustain Church communities in the face of aggressive opposition. Although settlers were drawn to other parts of the West by economic factors (especially mining), Utah and much of the Great Basin were settled by people modtived by religious conviction. Utah had less mineral wealth, less timber, and less agricultural potential than most of the surrounding western states. Consequently, Utah households were poorer than those in surrounding states. Both Church leaders and individual households had to find ways to sustain the Church and its members economically while retaining the strength of the predominantly Mormon settlement and communities in the Great Basin.

There were several key strategies. First, Church leaders pushed exploration and subsequent settlement of any land suitable for agricultural production, although water quickly became a key constraint. Over time, incoming settlers had to settle in valleys further away from Salt Lake City and onto more economically marginal land, as migration put pressure on the available economic resources. Second, the Church used its religious authority to initiate cooperative ventures to increase capital formation, expand economic diversity, and encourage economic independence from the outside world. This cooperation was important for the construction of the infrastructure—railroads and highways—as well as for irrigation projects. It was also instrumental in the creation of new industries such as sugar production. Third, the Church invested in education to create a more productive labor force, and prepare members for the economy of the twentieth century (see p. 126).

By the end of the nineteenth century, migration out of Utah was relieving some of the economic pressures on the limited resources. Some of the out-migration was Church-organized, but most migrants simply moved to surrounding states for better economic opportunities. Utah was not destined to be a state with a large agricultural sector nor a state with advantages in natural resources, but the strategies noted above promoted sufficient economic growth to sustain the Church and members' households during the gathering phase.

Clayne L. Pope

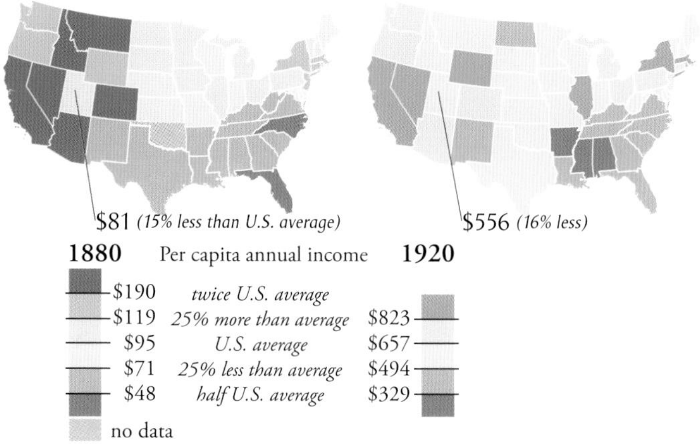

Utah's economic status was unique among western states. As a whole, the West was the richest region in the nineteenth century (in large part due to its mining-dominated economy and small population). By 1920, mountain states had converged toward the national average. Utah remained consistently below the national average through both the nineteenth and twentieth centuries. Today, the lower personal income per capita is due to the higher birth rate in Utah. This was less important in 1880 and 1920, when the general population had larger families.

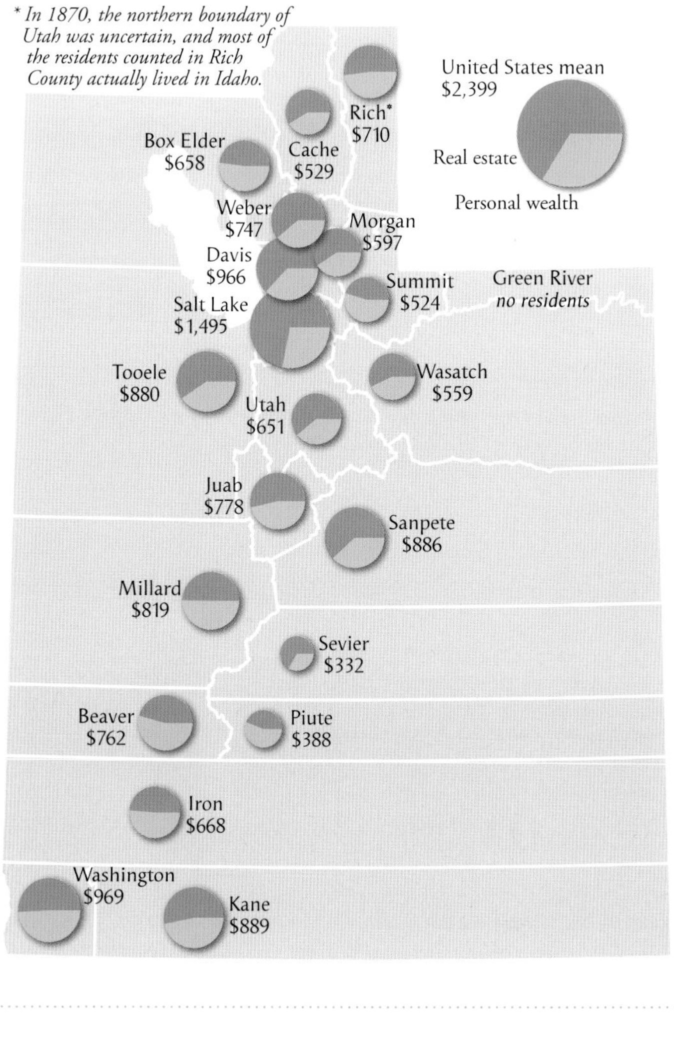

On balance, Utah households owned less than 40 percent of the wealth of the average U.S. household. Migration from settled counties to new settlements reduced household wealth. Households in Salt Lake County were, on average, substantially richer than households in outlying counties. One important element not illustrated by the map is the advantage in wealth from early arrival in Utah. Households residing in Utah since 1850 owned over 300% of the average wealth of 1870 households in Utah.

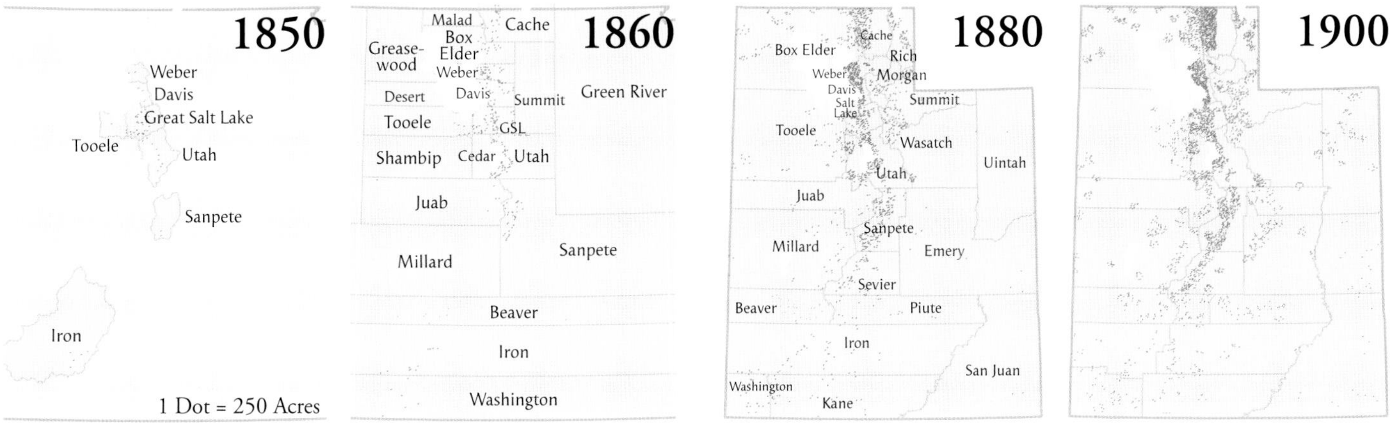

Agricultural land expanded significantly for many years, but it is probably more important to realize how much of Utah could never be improved for agricultural production. In 2008, Utah had agricultural output of $1.5 billion compared to $3.5 billion in Arizona, $6.4 billion in Idaho, and $6.5 billion in Colorado. There is simply less agricultural potential in Utah because of the rugged topography, poor soils, and limited available water. Nevertheless, early pioneers exploited the agricultural land to the maximum extent possible.

Church-Related Economic Activities

The Church concentrated its economic efforts on provision of infrastructure and marketing opportunities to move the economy away from subsistence agriculture, often "filling in the gaps" where a traditional market economy could not see profit. In addition, the Church sought to address the growing economic inequality in Mormon communities during the nineteenth century. In 1850, Utah households were poor, but there was relative equality. As settlement and development proceeded, the level of income of some members rose more than others; the United Order movement was specifically designed to address this challenge, but with little long-term success. Over time, as the intermountain economy became more integrated with the rest of America, most Church-owned corporations were closed or privatized, with only a few exceptions where an ecclesiastical purpose remained (such as broadcast and print media).

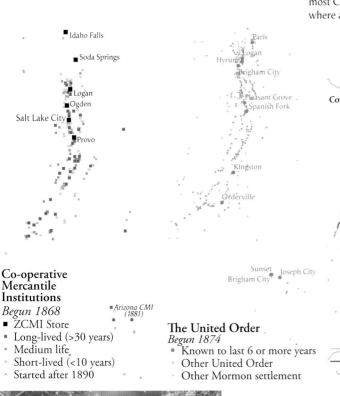

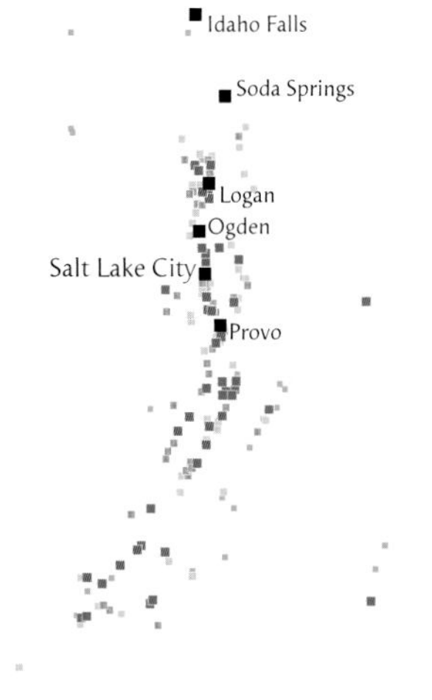

Co-operative Mercantile Institutions

Begun 1868

- ZCMI Store
- Long-lived (>30 years)
- Medium life
- Short-lived (<10 years)
- Started after 1890

The United Order

Begun 1874

- Known to last 6 or more years
- Other United Order
- Other Mormon settlement

Railroads in 1890
Church-sponsored
Settlements, 1890

Beet-growing lands

Church-owned sugar factories
open beyond 1941
- Amalgamated Sugar Co.
- Utah–Idaho Sugar Co.

closed by 1941
- Amalgamated Sugar Co.
- Utah–Idaho Sugar Co.
- Consolidated Wagon & Machine Co. agents

City Creek Center, built 2006–12, continues the Church's long tradition of supporting the economic well-being of its home. Built on 2½ blocks (23 acres) of Church-owned land adjacent to Temple Square, this $3 billion project, a partnership of the Church (funded by its corporate interests, not tithing) and other developers, combines residential, retail, and office space in a project that promises to improve the image and vitality of the LDS Headquarters neighborhood. More visitors downtown translates to more visitors to Church sites, which is a benefit to the Church far beyond any profits realized.

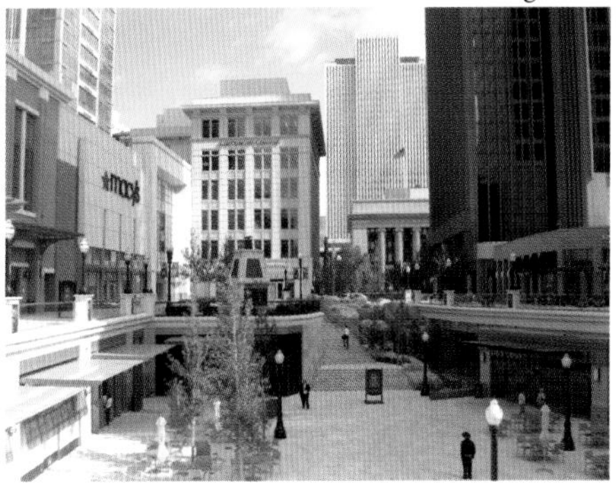

The Church in 1870

IN THE FACE OF REPEATED PERSECUTION, President Brigham Young felt that the only way to strengthen the Church was through isolation. The trials of the pioneer trek and settling the Utah wilderness strengthened the members of the Church, bolstered by expanding missionary success in Europe. Under Brigham Young's vision, a "Mormon Corridor" was established with settlements stretching from Idaho to California (see p. 96), although many outlying settlements were abandoned during the Utah War (see p. 110). The negative reputation of polygamy (see p. 122) and the Mountain Meadows Massacre forced the closure of nearly all missionary work in the United States. In 1870, missionaries actively preached only in a few European and Pacific countries (see p. 94). However, the intermountain core was rapidly growing in both population and geographic area, accelerated by the transcontinental railroad making immigration easier.

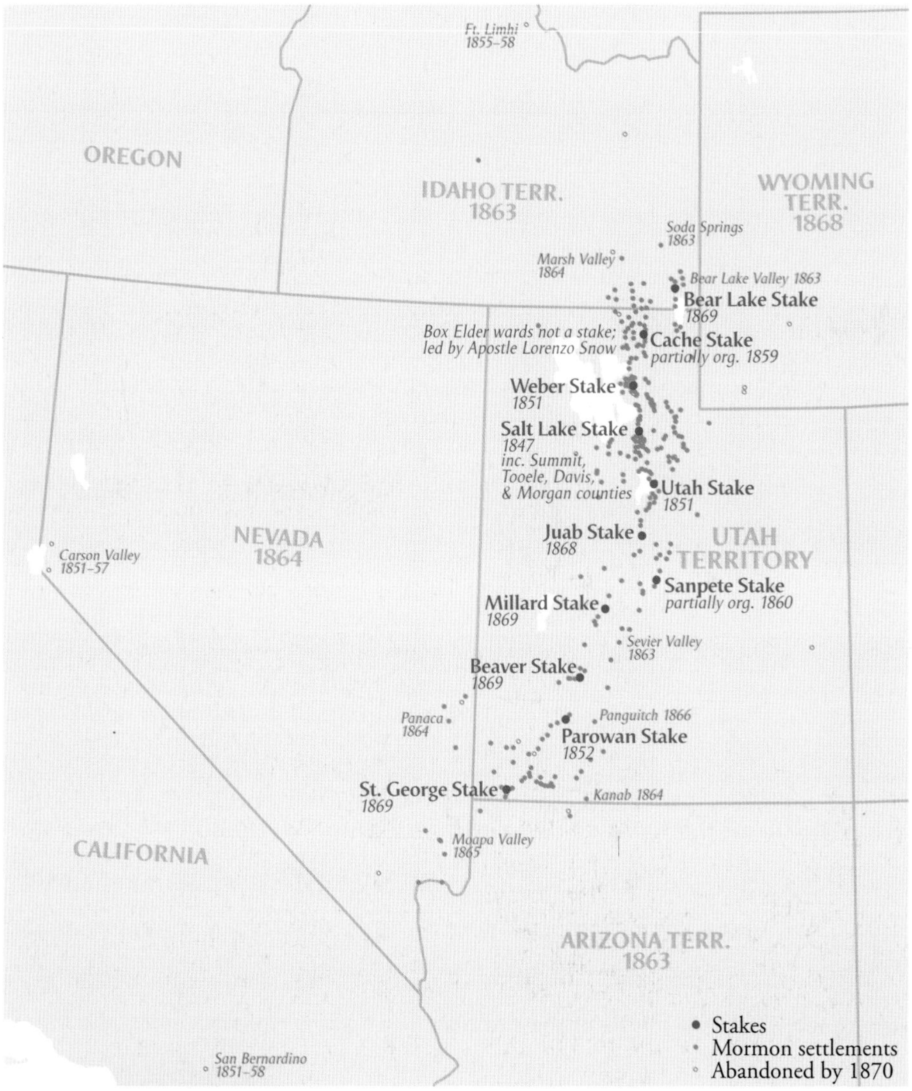

By 1869, the "Mormon Corridor" was established as a string of settlements from southern Idaho, through Utah, into southern Nevada. Although the greater Mormon empire of Deseret had been retracted when colonies in western Nevada and California were abandoned during the Utah War, the Corridor would soon expand into central and eastern Utah (aided by the resolution of the Black Hawk War and the forced relocation of the Utes; see p. 98), Arizona, Idaho, Wyoming, Mexico, and Canada (see p. 96).

Timeline

- **1846** Kanesville–Winter Quarters region settled
- **1847** The first pioneer companies arrive in the Salt Lake Valley
- **1850** Utah Territory created
- **1850–52** Expeditionary missions begun worldwide, half survive
- **1851** Membership in Britain peaks at 33,000, more than in Utah
- **1852** Settlements in western Iowa abandoned
- **1856–60** Handcarts used to cross the plains
- **1857** The Utah War
- **1862** "Down-and-back" wagons dominate emigration to Utah; the Morrill Act passed, the first federal anti-polygamy law
- **1867** The Relief Society is reorganized
- **1869** First immigrants arrive by the Union Pacific Railroad; ZCMI begun

1845 | 1850 | 1855 | 1860 | 1865

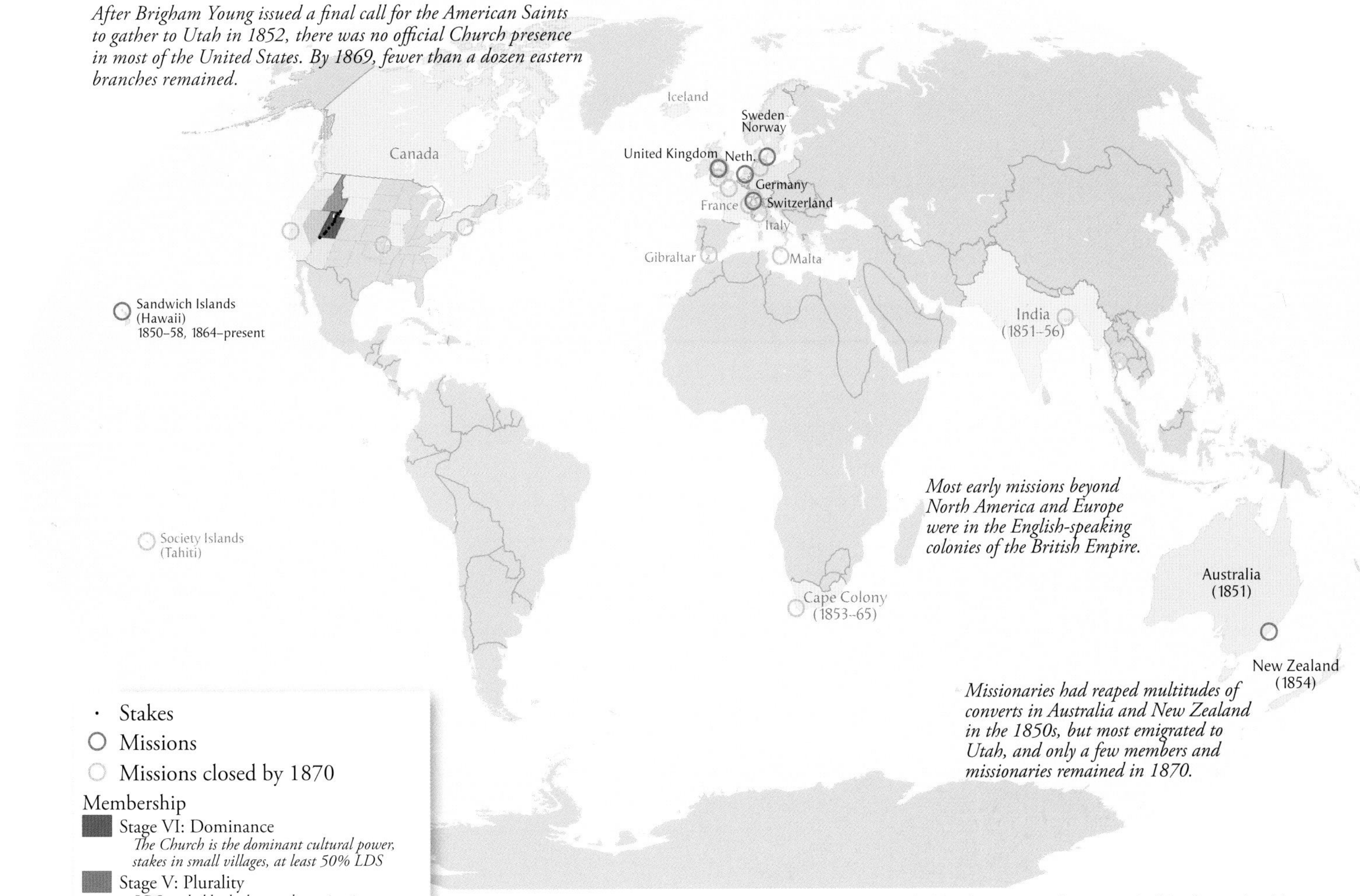
After Brigham Young issued a final call for the American Saints to gather to Utah in 1852, there was no official Church presence in most of the United States. By 1869, fewer than a dozen eastern branches remained.
Iceland
Sweden-Norway
Canada
United Kingdom
Neth.
Germany
France
Switzerland
Italy
Gibraltar
Malta
Sandwich Islands (Hawaii) 1850–58, 1864–present
India (1851–56)
Society Islands (Tahiti)
Cape Colony (1853–65)
Most early missions beyond North America and Europe were in the English-speaking colonies of the British Empire.
Australia (1851)
New Zealand (1854)
Missionaries had reaped multitudes of converts in Australia and New Zealand in the 1850s, but most emigrated to Utah, and only a few members and missionaries remained in 1870.
Stakes
Missions
Missions closed by 1870
Membership
Stage VI: Dominance
The Church is the dominant cultural power, stakes in small villages, at least 50% LDS
Stage V: Plurality
LDS probably the largest denomination, a major influence, at least 1 LDS in 10
Stage IV: Pervasive
Most people personally know a Mormon, stakes cover the country, at least 1 LDS in 50
Stage III: Widespread
Wards and stakes in most cities, most people have heard of Mormons, at least 1 LDS in 500
Stage II: Established
Significant, permanent presence; has a stake in the largest cities, at least 1 LDS in 5,000
Stage I: Pioneering
Few members, branches, districts legally open to missionaries
Stage 0: Restricted
Very few members, mostly expatriates no proselytizing, usually restricted by law
no Church presence

The late 1860s were probably the most reclusive period in the entire history of the Church. Most of the expeditionary missions of the early 1850s (see p. 94) had failed, and, with the onset of the Utah War, most missionaries throughout the world (including the eastern United States) were recalled. By 1869, northern Europe was the only significant area of missionary work.

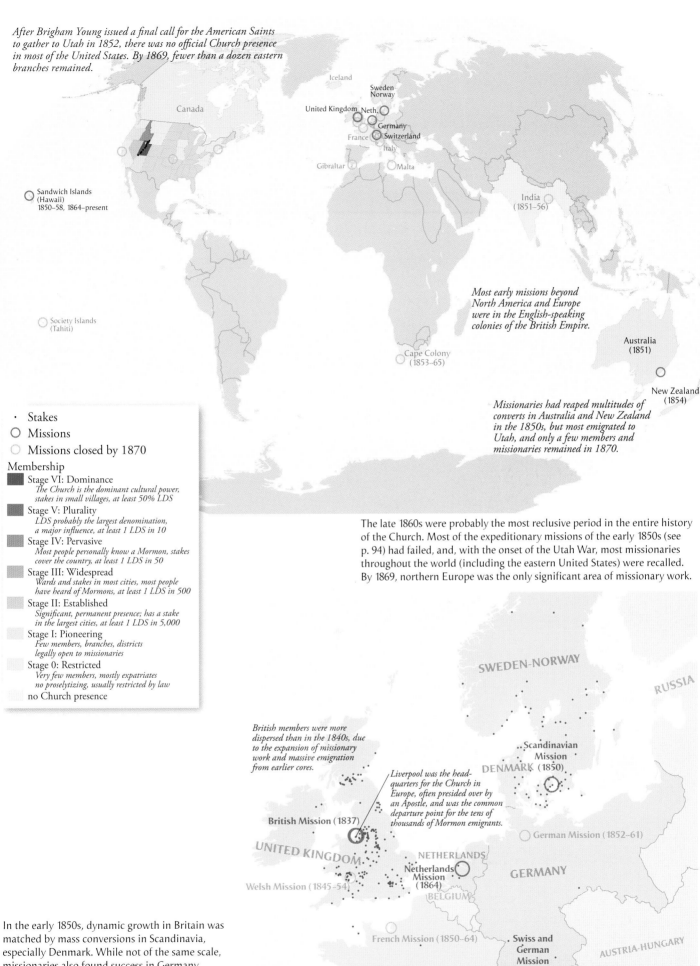

SWEDEN-NORWAY
RUSSIA
British members were more dispersed than in the 1840s, due to the expansion of missionary work and massive emigration from earlier cores.
Scandinavian Mission (1850)
DENMARK
Liverpool was the headquarters for the Church in Europe, often presided over by an Apostle, and was the common departure point for the tens of thousands of Mormon emigrants.
British Mission (1837)
German Mission (1852–61)
UNITED KINGDOM
NETHERLANDS
Netherlands Mission (1864)
GERMANY
Welsh Mission (1845–54)
BELGIUM
French Mission (1850–64)
Swiss and German Mission (1850)
AUSTRIA-HUNGARY
FRANCE
SWITZERLAND
Italian Mission (1850–54)

In the early 1850s, dynamic growth in Britain was matched by mass conversions in Scandinavia, especially Denmark. While not of the same scale, missionaries also found success in Germany, Switzerland, and the Netherlands. During the 1860s, emigration outpaced conversion, decreasing the numbers of remaining members, but branches were still widespread.

Plural Marriage

1841–1904

HOW DOES ONE UNDERSTAND A PHENOMENON as complex and perplexing as nineteenth-century Mormon polygamy (or polygyny, the proper term)? Non-Mormons have long struggled to come to terms with this unique practice, joined by modern Mormons, asking questions such as that asked by a 1866 hearing on "The Condition of Utah" before the Congressional Committee for the Territories: "what proportion of the Mormon people are practical [practicing] polygamists?" Answers ranged from one-sixth to one-half. Twenty years later (April 4, 1885) an epistle of the First Presidency stated that "the male members of our Church who practice plural marriage are estimated as not exceeding but little, if any, two per cent, of the entire membership." In the U.S. Senate's Smoot Hearings (1904–07), President Joseph F. Smith, after asking stake presidents to count the number of "polygamous families" within their precincts, claimed "only about 3 or 4 percent of the entire male population of the Church have entered into that principle." Facing intense national prosecution after 1885, Church leaders understandably tried to minimize the importance of "The Principle," as the practice itself waned. Consequently, the impression persists, even among Mormons, that relatively few members, mainly the elite, ever practiced polygamy.

The incidence of plural marriage among Mormons actually varied considerably over time, probably peaking during the "Mormon Reformation" of the late 1850s, when many brethren "requested [and received] the Privilege" of adding another spouse. The estimates above also exclude the wives and children, who accounted for much more of the plural population than married men. In examining the LDS marriage system's evolution in Manti, Utah, Kathryn Daynes calculated the percent of men, women, and children living in plural families from nineteenth century censuses as 25% (1850), 43% (1860), 36% (1870), 25% (1880), and 7% (1900). A study of Brigham City's plural households in 1870, adding a few servants to family members, produced similar figures. In both towns, polygamists' properties occupied a prominent position. Furthermore, the polygamous population of a settlement changed with births, deaths, divorces, and migration. Most of little Virgin City's polygamists in 1870 had moved elsewhere by 1880, causing a sharp decline (40% to 5%) in its plural marriage population.

The geography of plurality also reflected the tendency of dozens of polygamists to keep families in two or more towns; in 1870, for instance, Joseph S. Murdoch had three wives in Heber while living with two others in the Muddy River Mission of Nevada. With numerous wives, even "Brother Brigham" found it desirable to relocate many of them.

continued on page 124

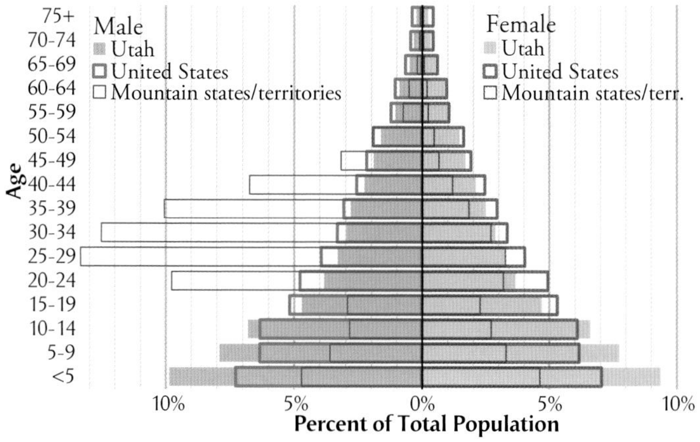

The 1870 population pyramid of Utah reveals an unusually fertile population, with 58 percent under 20 years old and, surprisingly, slightly more men than women in each age group 20–54. The male surplus resulted from the presence of a sizable and mostly male "Gentile" population tied to the railroad, military and mining camps, and Salt Lake businesses, although it was not nearly as skewed as the surrounding frontier states and territories (the hollow boxes). Also, polygamous husbands with wives in different towns were sometimes counted twice.

Timeline

5 Apr 1841 Joseph Smith's first authenticated plural marriage (to Louisa Beaman)

12 Jul 1843 First written record of Joseph Smith's revelation on plural marriage (D&C 132)

29 Aug 1852 LDS Church's first public acknowledgement of its practice of polygamy

1856 Republican Party denounces polygamy and slavery as "twin relics of barbarism"

1862 Morrill Anti-Bigamy Act passed by U.S. Congress aimed at Mormon polygamy

House passage of Cullom Bill sparks series of "Great Indignation Meetings" by LDS women **Jan 1870**

1874 Elizabeth W. Kane publishes *Twelve Mormon Homes* to express her sympathy for plural wives

1878 Ladies Anti-Polygamy Society of Utah founded; publishes the *Anti-Polygamy Standard* in 1880

1882 Enactment of Edmunds Act by Congress to prosecute Mormons for unlawful cohabitation

1887 Passage of Edmunds-Tucker Act to dissolve the Church as a corporation

1890 President Wilford Woodruff issues Manifesto prohibiting new plural marriages in the United States

President Joseph F. Smith issues "Second" Manifesto **1904** forbidding new plural marriages anywhere

1840 1845 1850 1855 1860 1865 1870 1875 1880 1885 1890 1895 1900 1905 1910

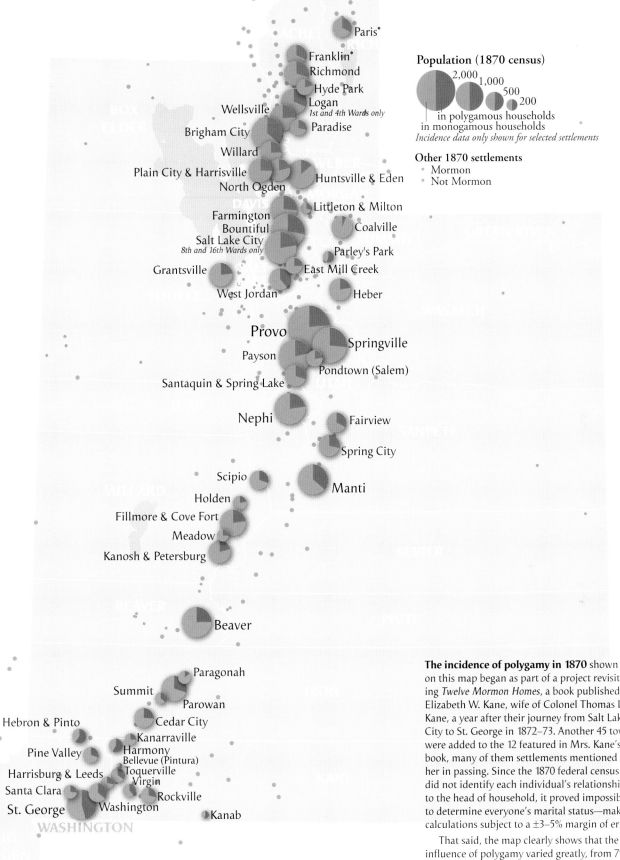

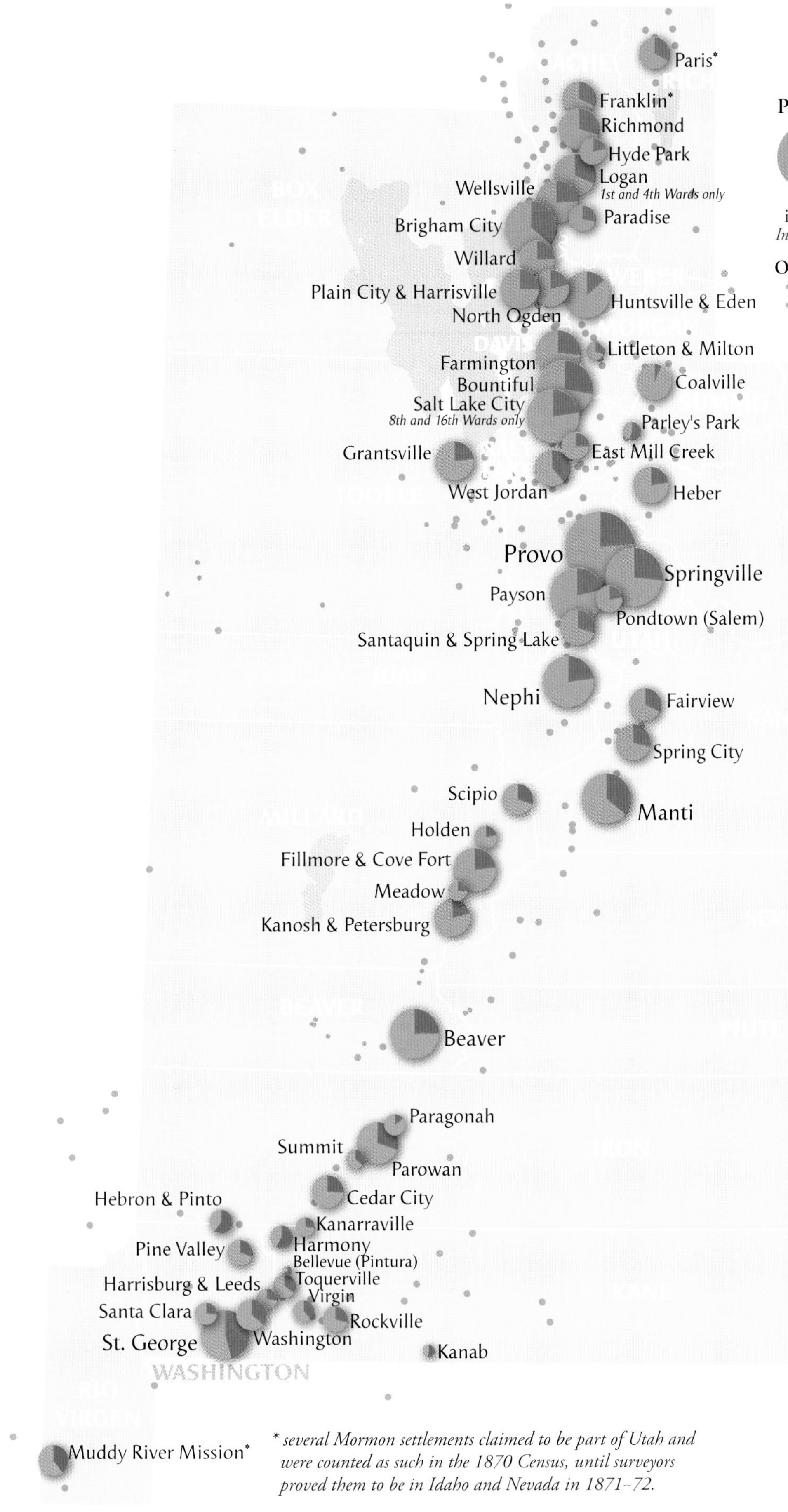

** several Mormon settlements claimed to be part of Utah and were counted as such in the 1870 Census, until surveyors proved them to be in Idaho and Nevada in 1871–72.*

The incidence of polygamy in 1870 shown on this map began as part of a project revisiting *Twelve Mormon Homes*, a book published by Elizabeth W. Kane, wife of Colonel Thomas L. Kane, a year after their journey from Salt Lake City to St. George in 1872–73. Another 45 towns were added to the 12 featured in Mrs. Kane's book, many of them settlements mentioned by her in passing. Since the 1870 federal census did not identify each individual's relationship to the head of household, it proved impossible to determine everyone's marital status—making calculations subject to a ±3–5% margin of error.

That said, the map clearly shows that the influence of polygamy varied greatly, from 7% in Coalville to 68% in Bellevue (now Pintura). In tiny towns like the latter, one plural family could skew the figure significantly. Also, since most polygamists did not take a second wife for the first 5 to 15 years of their married life, towns with a high proportion of younger couples usually had fewer plural families. That may explain Hyde Park's lower percentage, compared to Logan's and Wellsville's in 1870, even though Stake President Charles O. Card labeled it Cache Valley's most polygamous place for its size in 1887.

Plural Marriage

continued

Larger towns with high levels of plurality—most notably St. George—had long-term resident Apostles (see p. 128). From its founding in 1861, St. George's Apostle, Erastus Snow, encouraged "Celestial Marriage" as much as his distant cousin Lorenzo did in Brigham City. Salt Lake County's West Jordan Ward was nearly 40% polygamous, thanks perhaps to the example set by Bishop Archibald Gardner's well-known "family village" of 30 souls. Even in wards with monogamous bishoprics, such as Heber City and East Mill Creek, plural rates were sometimes surprisingly high (20–25%).

Those who discount polygamy's importance may think the 25–30 percent average figure proves that a majority of nineteenth-century Mormons never practiced it. But demographers insist a stable population cannot sustain a polygamous population higher than that. Given the balanced male-female ratio of Utah's 1870 population, how many husbands could marry a second wife, especially when competing with the small but significant number who claimed three or more? Only by courting females much younger than they, often teenagers, could men approach the limits of polygamy imposed by demography. Some added wives with seeming ease. Other men, like St. George's Charles L. Walker, tried for more than a decade before finally finding a second spouse.

Another important factor was that many monogamous wives privately opposed the practice. Plural marriages ending in divorce must have deterred some from entering polygamy again and discouraged their children from ever practicing it. Extreme poverty or occasional apostasy kept others outside the "plural circle." Notations in the 1880 Utah census margins often labeled inhabitants as "Gentile," "Apostate," or "Josephite [RLDS] Mormon."

Even under optimal circumstances, only a minority could have practiced the Principle. Those who did often occupied central parts of town and exercised disproportionate influence in their communities. By adding polygamists' closest monogamous relatives—parents, siblings, married children, and in-laws—one could argue that by 1880 close to a majority of the Mormon population was directly or indirectly affected by a practice much more prevalent than generally acknowledged. "Polly Gamy" (coined by one plural wife) clearly played a powerful role in expanding Brother Brigham's "Great Basin Kingdom" well beyond Utah's borders and in integrating the diverse people who gathered to Zion (see p. 104).

Lowell C. Bennion

Perregrine Sessions, called an "Exemplary Elder" by his leaders, served several missions and married nine women, six of them compatible enough to live initially in the same house and to pose with him in front of it. In 1858, when a reporter from Olympia, Washington, asked him why he had two wives, he expressed his belief that the larger his posterity, the greater his blessings in the next life. According to a possibly apocryphal family story, at a later date "the most recent bride said to the others, 'Why does he want to marry again? It seems like we three are enough.' One of the two responded, while looking knowingly at the other, 'That's what we said when he wanted to marry you.'" Ten of Bountiful's 35 polygamists in 1870 had three or more wives.

Brigham City, 1880

Less than 20% of the husbands claimed multiple wives in 1870, but by 1880 they owned almost 30% of the developed lots, many close to the court house or tabernacle. No other town north of Salt Lake City quite matched Brigham City's level of plurality, perhaps because of the long-term presence and influence of Apostle Lorenzo Snow, who also managed Mormondom's most successful co-operative (see p. 118). In 1870, he and his two counselors in the Box Elder Stake presidency and the ten city councilors accounted for about 6% of the city's husbands, but their mostly plural households held almost 16% of the population. Some polygamous families were even larger than those of the leaders.

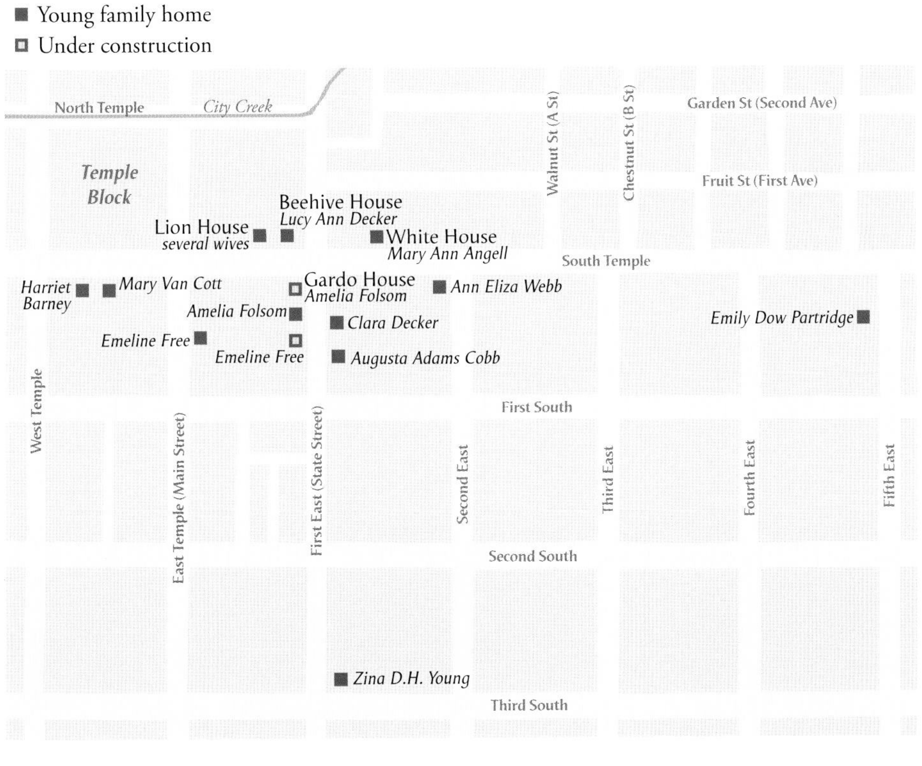

Brigham Young's wives in about 1873 did not all live in the crowded Lion House; about half lived elsewhere to accommodate their families' needs for more space and privacy. Most of the additional dozen homes were located within a block of the Beehive and Lion Houses. In addition, he placed Eliza Burgess in Provo, where the Kanes stayed in 1872–73, and Lucy Bigelow in St. George. The latter's house proved too small to accommodate visitors, prompting the President to acquire a bigger house (and office) for his winter sojourns in Dixie (see p. 90).

Church Academies

1875–1933

EDUCATION, BOTH SECULAR AND RELIGIOUS, has always been a high priority of The Church of Jesus Christ of Latter-day Saints. "Seek ye out of the best books words of wisdom," the Doctrine and Covenants proclaims (D&C 88:118). Consistent with this revelation, the Church became involved in numerous educational endeavors in Ohio, Missouri, and Illinois. However, these ventures were relatively small when compared with the magnitude of the Church's efforts in the West.

During the last quarter of the nineteenth century and the first decade of the twentieth century, the Church established as many as 56 schools in five western states, Canada, and Mexico. Most of these institutions served as elementary or secondary schools but some eventually became colleges and even universities.

When the Church began establishing academies in Utah during the 1870s, there were no public secondary schools in the territory. In addition, in the 1860s and 1870s the Protestants and Catholics had founded numerous excellent mission schools in the Utah Territory (see p. 112). A large percentage of their students were Latter-day Saints, so Church leaders felt a need to provide education for their own youth rather than entrusting them to others.

The first academy founded by the LDS Church was Brigham Young Academy, established in Provo, Utah, in 1875. It later became Brigham Young University. Two years later, Brigham Young organized the Church's second academy in Logan, Utah, calling it Brigham Young College. Like its sister institution in Provo, this academy served as a teacher training school and even a four-year liberal arts college for a time. The Church sponsored only these two academies until 1886 when it authorized the Beaver Stake Academy and the Salt Lake Stake Academy (now LDS Business College).

Emery Stake Academy, 1906. This school in Castle Dale operated from 1889 to 1922, and was typical of those built in the small towns across the Mormon settlement area.

In 1888, the Church organized a General Board of Education with Karl G. Maeser as Superintendent and directed that all stakes establish an academy within their boundaries. As a result, during the next three years 26 academies were organized in the Intermountain West, including Sanpete Stake Academy (now Snow College), Bannock Stake Academy (later Ricks College and now Brigham Young University–Idaho), St. George Stake Academy (now Dixie State College), Weber Stake Academy (now Weber State University), and St. Joseph Stake Academy (now Eastern Arizona College).

Encouraged by the emphasis placed on education, smaller communities throughout the region soon began requesting schools of their own. Supporting the endeavor, Church leaders authorized approximately 20 additional schools, generally in stakes already sponsoring an academy. In an effort to avoid confusion with their sister institutions, these schools were called "seminaries," although they were more like small academies than the modern seminary model begun in 1912 (see p. 142). Meanwhile, from 1891 to 1910, the Church founded six more academies, including two international schools: the Juarez Stake Academy in Mexico, which is still in operation, and the Alberta Stake Academy in Canada.

By the 1920s, public high schools and colleges, supported by the Church's newly formed modern seminary and institute programs, created duplication with the more expensive academies. Financial burdens caused the Church to close or transfer to the state all but four of its remaining academies: Brigham Young University, LDS Business College, Ricks College, and Juarez Academy (see p. 142). Even though most of the schools are no longer in existence, for more than a half-century they played an important role in the history of education in the Intermountain West. They were the learning and cultural centers for dozens of communities.

Scott C. Esplin and Arnold K. Garr

Timeline

1875 Brigham Young Academy founded

1877 Brigham Young College established

1888 General Board of Education formed; all stakes instructed to create academies

1890–92 Most early seminaries founded

1893–95 Financial crisis causes several academies to close

Modern seminary system begun **1912**

1921–33 Church closes or transfers to the states most remaining academies

Institute program established **1926**

Church retains Brigham Young University, LDS Business College, Ricks College (now BYU–Idaho), and Juarez Academy **1933**

1875 1880 1885 1890 1895 1900 1905 1910 1915 1920 1925 1930

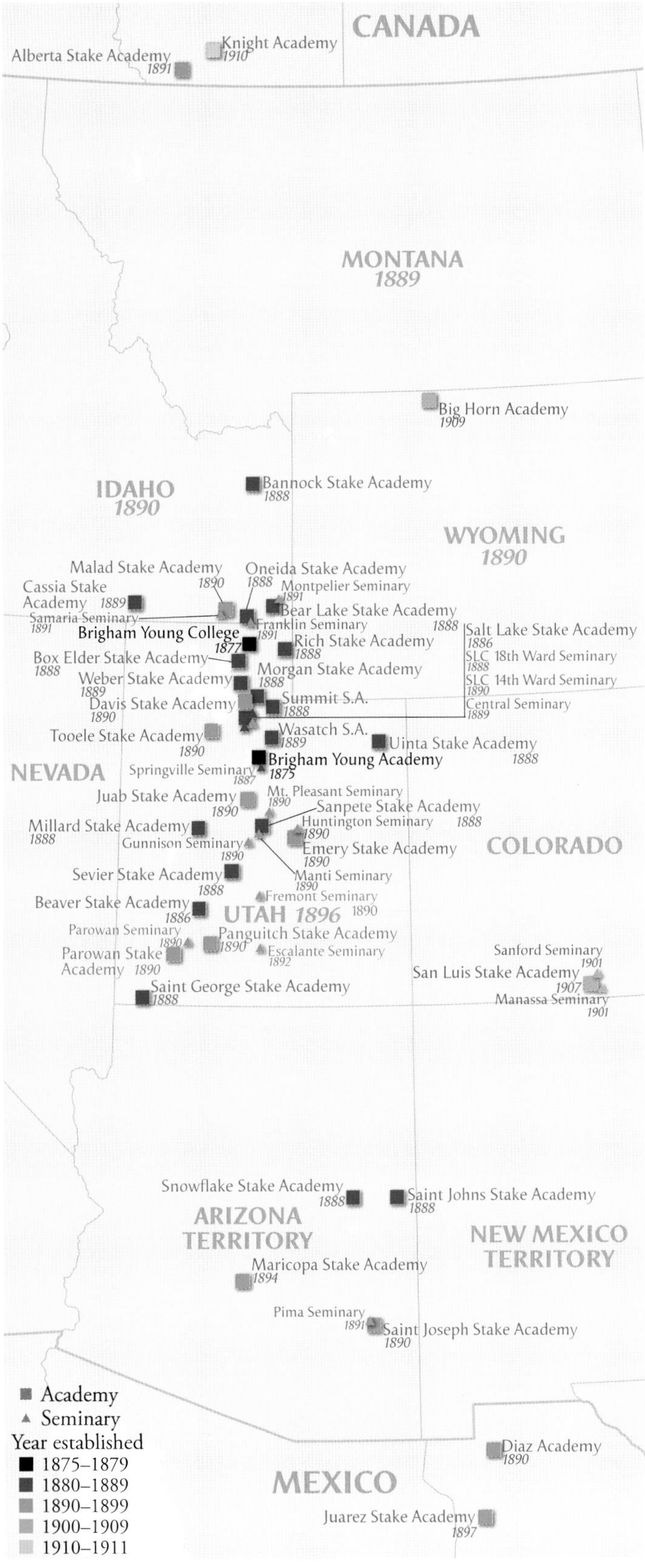

The Growth of Academies, 1875-1911

Thirty-six academies and as many as 20 seminaries marked Church influence in education during the late nineteenth and early twentieth centuries. From the Knight Academy in Canada to the Juarez Stake Academy in Mexico, the system served the educational needs of thousands of Latter-day Saint youth throughout the Intermountain West. Patterned after the original Brigham Young Academy in Provo, Utah, and Brigham Young College in Logan, Utah, the bulk of the schools originated when President Wilford Woodruff instructed in 1888 that each stake implement a private secondary school. Some were successful for decades while others soon closed. A second wave of Church schools began during the early twentieth century as Church leadership responded to the educational needs of its members in more remote locations. Most of these later schools introduced secondary education to isolated pockets of Church membership.

The Decline of Academies, 1894-1933

Through the years, the educational environment of the Intermountain West changed, causing the Church to modify its educational programs and eventually discontinue the academy system. In 1890 the Utah Territory established a non-sectarian public school system which duplicated the secular courses taught by the academies. These public schools were free, whereas the academies charged tuition. In 1912 the Church founded the modern seminary program, followed by the institute program in 1926 (see p. 140), which competed with the religion courses taught by the academies. Finally, the Great Depression put a tremendous financial burden on the Church Educational System in the 1930s. Therefore, by 1933 the Church had either closed or transferred to the states all but four of its academies, three of which had become full colleges.

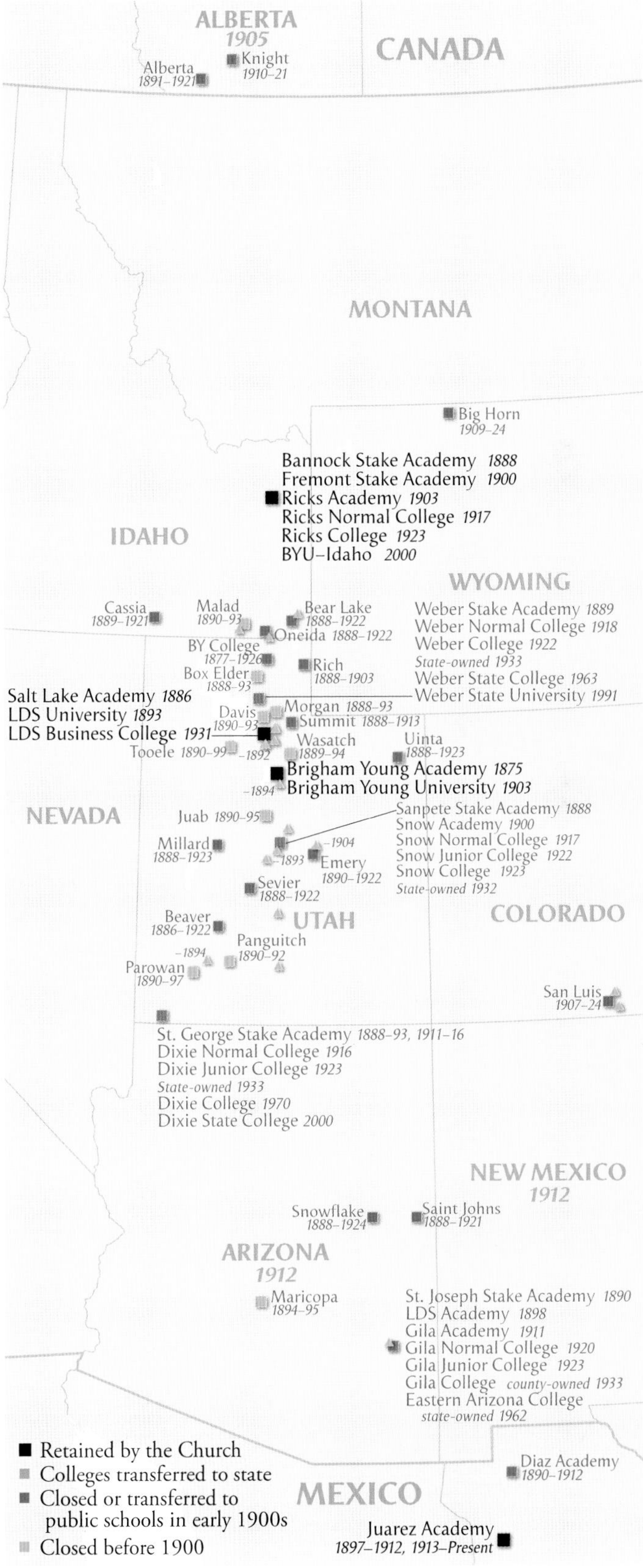

The Emergence of Modern Stakes and Wards

1834–1909

Today's Latter-day Saints would probably not recognize the congregations of Joseph Smith's lifetime (see pages 38, 58). When introduced, branches (1830), stakes (1834), and wards (1840) functioned differently than today, and changed frequently. In Winter Quarters and the early days of Salt Lake City, this pattern continued: the entire settlement (the stake) met together on Sunday, while bishops' wards were not congregations, just districts for caring for the poor. During the 1850s and 1860s, increasing population and scattered settlement necessitated more manageable congregations, and modern notions gradually took hold with a ward as a single congregation with its own meetinghouse and a stake as a regional collection of wards and branches. However, there was still a great deal of ad hoc variety in local ecclesiastical governance.

At the dedication of the St. George Temple in 1877, Brigham Young announced that the organizational structure of the Church would be standardized. Priesthood roles and lines of authority (i.e., who reported to whom) were more clearly defined, and the nomenclature and structure for congregations were made consistent, as is familiar today: branches are small congregations led by a presidency, wards are large congregations led by a bishopric, and stakes are regional collections of wards and branches led by a presidency and high council. This new policy required a massive reorganization of wards and stakes across the settlements, which was not completed until a few months after President Young's death.

During the nineteenth century, the geographical creation and subdivision of wards and stakes were determined by travel distance, not by membership totals. A ward or branch covered a settlement, and a stake covered a valley or settlement region, no matter how many members it contained. Along the Wasatch Front, wards with several thousand members were common. This did not matter very much when most members were spectators in meetings and attendance rates were fairly low. However, President Lorenzo Snow started several initiatives to strengthen the activity of members (continued under President Joseph F. Smith), including making wards and stakes smaller to increase the sense of community and the opportunities of members to serve in "callings." This new optimal size for wards (about 150–200 active members) and stakes (about 10–12 wards) necessitated another sweeping reorganization of wards and stakes in the core area of the Church (the Wasatch Front) between 1900 and 1909.

Since then, stakes and wards have been regularly created and divided whenever increasing membership warrants (see p. 184), so that 100 years later, the Salt Lake Valley contains 169 stakes. These turn-of-the-century divisions have survived in a tangential fashion, though: when the State of Utah first developed its public school system during these years, it found the Wasatch Front stakes to be a convenient basis for its school districts (both names and boundaries, such as Granite, Jordan, Alpine, and Nebo), which have survived largely intact to this day.

Brandon S. Plewe

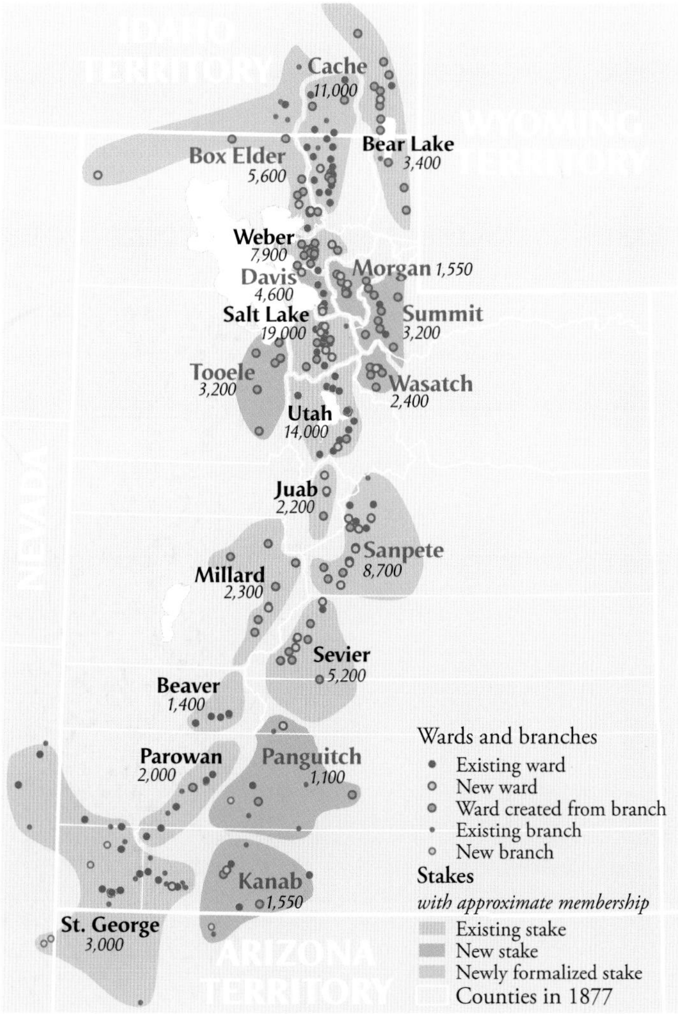

Before 1877: 10–13 stakes, 114 wards, 120 branches
After 1877: 20 stakes, 237 wards, 37 branches

The 1877 Priesthood Reorganization

By the 1870s, local congregations in the Mormon settlements were a mélange of administration, including branches with presidents; congregational wards with both bishops and presidents; non-congregational wards, precincts, and districts (with non-presiding bishops); regional bishops; and fully organized regional stakes. In addition, Cache, Sanpete, and Box Elder Counties functioned like stakes but were very rarely called such and were presided over by a resident Apostle (Ezra T. Benson, Orson Hyde, and Lorenzo Snow, respectively) rather than a presidency and high council. Most stakes had high councils and presidencies, but some only had one or the other. In his last initiative as President, Brigham Young standardized the local administrative structure of the Church and spent most of 1877 traveling across Utah with his Apostles, creating and reorganizing units according to the new pattern. The number of fully organized stakes was doubled, as was the number of wards, by far the most sweeping overhaul of the Church geography in its history, before or since.

Intermountain Stakes

From 1878 to 1899, as settlement expanded across the Intermountain West (see p. 96), new stakes and wards were quickly created when the new areas were too remote to be adequately served by the existing stakes, many times with very few members. In 1899, the San Juan Stake (covering the Four Corners region) had only 4 wards and 940 members. Meanwhile, ward and stake organization changed very little in the core settlement area for 23 years, despite continued population growth; for example, the Salt Lake Stake had 38,000 members in 48 wards in 1899.

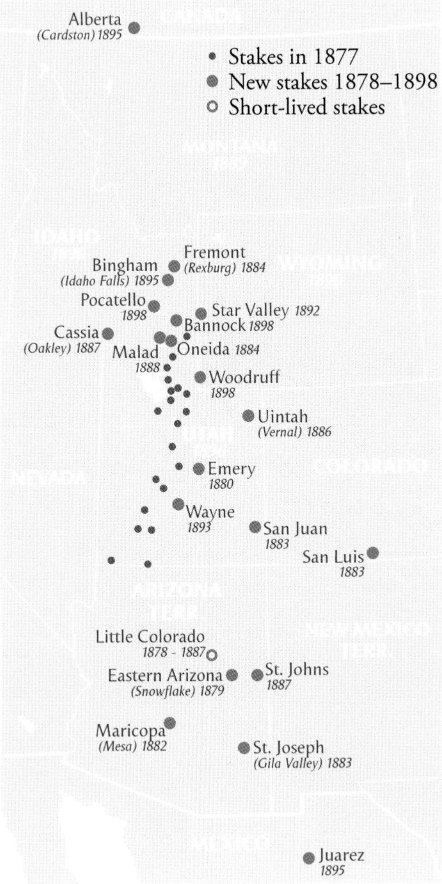

Subdivisions of Salt Lake Stake

In 1900, the new Church policy of creating smaller stakes and wards led to massive subdivision across Utah, but the greatest change was in the Salt Lake Valley, in which almost 40,000 members were part of a single stake. In 1900, the rural areas were split off into two new stakes, and in 1904, Salt Lake City was further divided into 4 stakes, while the number of wards in the valley increased from 48 to 71. This was especially pronounced in the rapidly suburbanizing farmland immediately south of Salt Lake City around Sugar House, which would see the creation of dozens of new wards in the next 20 years. At this time, large stakes were also divided in Sanpete (to 2 in 1900), Utah (3 in 1901), Cache (3 in 1901), Weber (3 in 1908) and Box Elder (2 in 1908) counties.

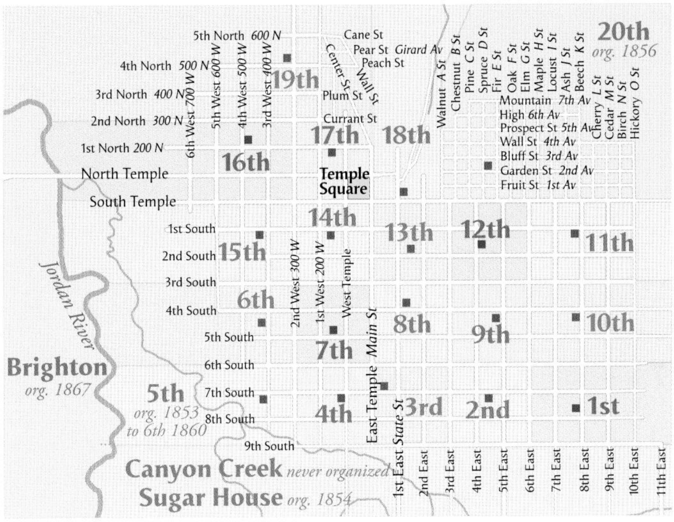

▪ Ward school/meeting house

Salt Lake City was divided into 19 wards in February 1849. Originally, these were not separate congregations as we think of them today; members of the entire city met together in the boweries on Temple Square (see p. 114); the bishops of each ward were initially responsible only for tithing, temporal affairs, and the Aaronic Priesthood holders but gradually adopted greater ecclesiastical authority. Ward schoolhouses built in the early 1850s were soon also used for other meetings, including Sunday services.

As shown here, the original street naming system was also quite different from that of today (shown in italics). "Main Street" and "State Street" came into use during the 1890s, and the grid coordinate system (e.g., 600 West) so closely associated to Utah was not fully implemented in Salt Lake City until 1972.

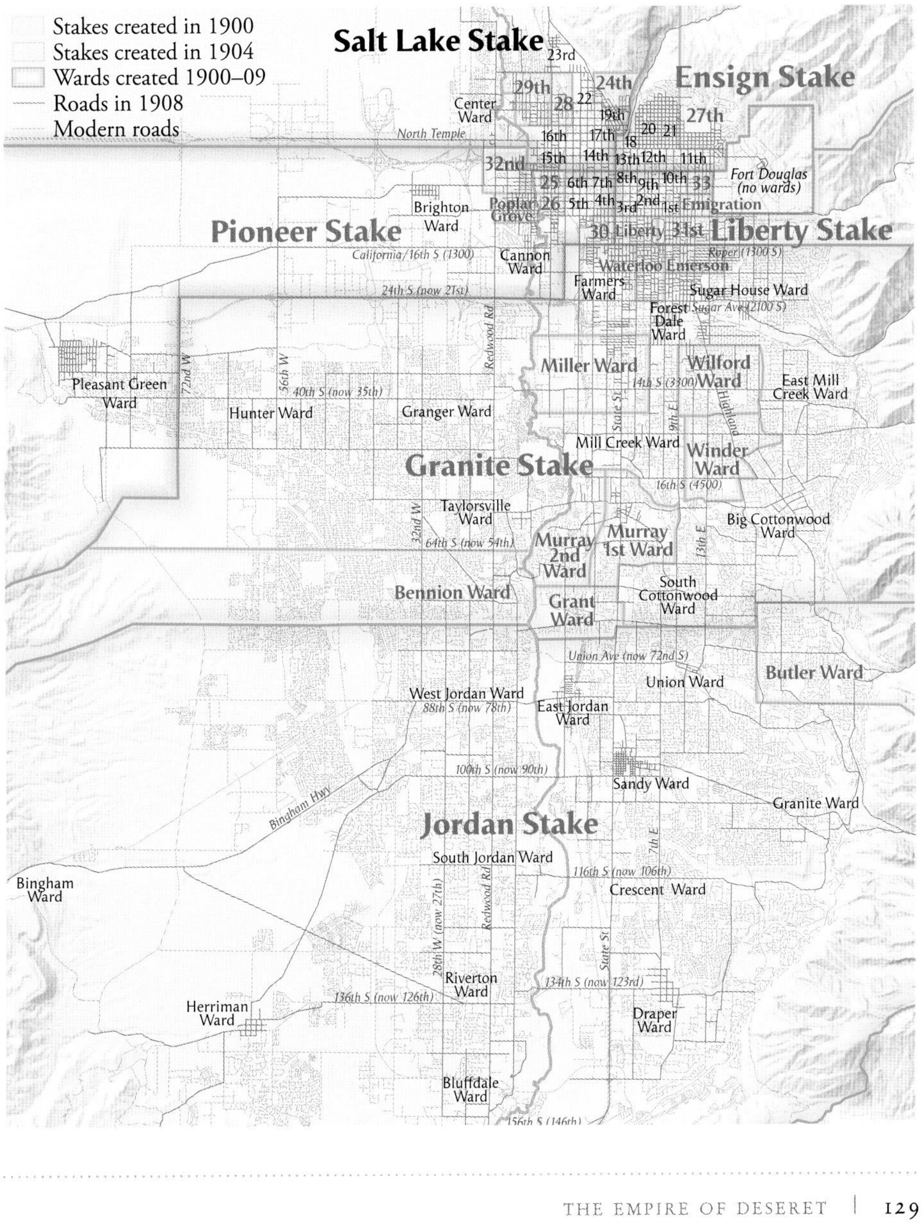

The Pioneer Presidents

1880–1918

THE TRAVELS OF THE SEVERAL PRESIDENTS after Brigham Young (see p. 90) varied greatly, depending on their health, advancing transportation technology, and other external forces. Their travels also provide insights into the personality and preferences of each prophet and the needs of the Church in his day.

President John Taylor (1880–87) traveled very little as President. His only significant trip was in January 1885 to Arizona and Mexico. Immediately upon his return, he was forced into hiding to avoid arrest for plural marriage (see p. 122); his exact whereabouts are mostly unknown, but he appears to have spent most of the last two years of his life relatively close to home.

President Wilford Woodruff (1889–1898) traveled extensively during his administration as Church President, using the widespread rail network of his day. On these trips, he would visit and counsel the local members, perform administrative business, and enjoy some sightseeing. The greatest Mormon diarist of the nineteenth century, Woodruff's journals have provided valuable insight into how much he enjoyed travel.

Probably due to age and ill health, President Lorenzo Snow (1898–1901) did not travel much during his brief tenure, other than one trip east immediately after he was sustained as President. However, he began several trends that would significantly affect the geography of the Church, such as expanding missionary work (including Japan) and subdividing the largest stakes in Utah (see p. 128).

President Joseph F. Smith (1901–1918) traveled the greatest distance of any President during this period, being the first LDS President to visit Europe. He also took several trips to Hawaii, which he had adopted as a home away from home since his first mission there as a young man. Of course, the methods of travel he used were far superior to those used by his predecessors.

Smith's successors, Heber J. Grant (1918–1945) and George Albert Smith (1945–1951) traveled far less often. Grant's only major international travel during his very long tenure was a tour of Europe in 1937, while Smith traveled very little other than an important trip to Mexico in 1946 (see p. 218). Although travel destinations and distances traveled varied, each President was eager to get out among the members and to preach the gospel.

Donald Q. Cannon

Wilford Woodruff (in front) and his entourage are shown here at the famed Hotel Coronado in San Diego where they stayed in 1896. George Q. Cannon, his counselor, is seated to Woodruff's left. The first Church President to travel extensively for pleasure, Wilford Woodruff was especially attracted to the West Coast. He once described Monterey, California, as a place whose beauty exceeded description. On a pleasure cruise to Alaska in 1893, he described in his journal the thrill of seeing glaciers, Eskimos, and whales.

Pioneer Presidents

JOHN TAYLOR

Oct 1880–Jul 1887 3rd President

Jan 1885 Tour of Arizona settlements

Feb 1885–Jul 1887 Taylor and other authorities in hiding

WILFORD WOODRUFF

Apr 1889–Sep 1898 4th President

Apr 1889 1st trip to San Francisco

Nov 1889 Canada

Aug 1890 Colorado, New Mexico, conferences with members and leaders

Sep 1890 Manifesto ends new plural marriages in the United States

3rd trip to San Francisco **Jun 1891**

1893 Chicago World's Fair

Vacation to Sitka, Alaska **Summer 1893**

4th trip to San Francisco, San Diego **Aug 1896**

Sep 1897 Portland and San Francisco

6th trip to San Francisco; died in the mansion of Isaac Trumbo **Aug 1898**

LORENZO SNOW: Sep 1898–Oct 1901 6th President

Oct 1898 Trans-Mississippi Exposition, Omaha

8 May 1899 "Windows of Heaven" sermon in St. George renews emphasis on tithing

JOSEPH F. SMITH: Oct 1901–Nov 1918 7th president

1904 Washington, DC, Smoot Hearings

Dec 1905 Joseph Smith Memorial dedicated in South Royalton, Vermont, as part of trip to Church history sites

Tour of Europe, **1906** first Church President to do so

1909 First presidential trip to Hawaii

Dedicates temple site in Alberta **Jul 27 1913**

1916 Hawaii

1917 Hawaii

1917 Tour of Utah

Dedicates site of Hawaii Temple **1 Jun 1915**

Hawaiian Temple dedicated by President Heber J. Grant **27 Nov 1919**

1880 | 1885 | 1890 | 1895 | 1900 | 1905 | 1910 | 1915

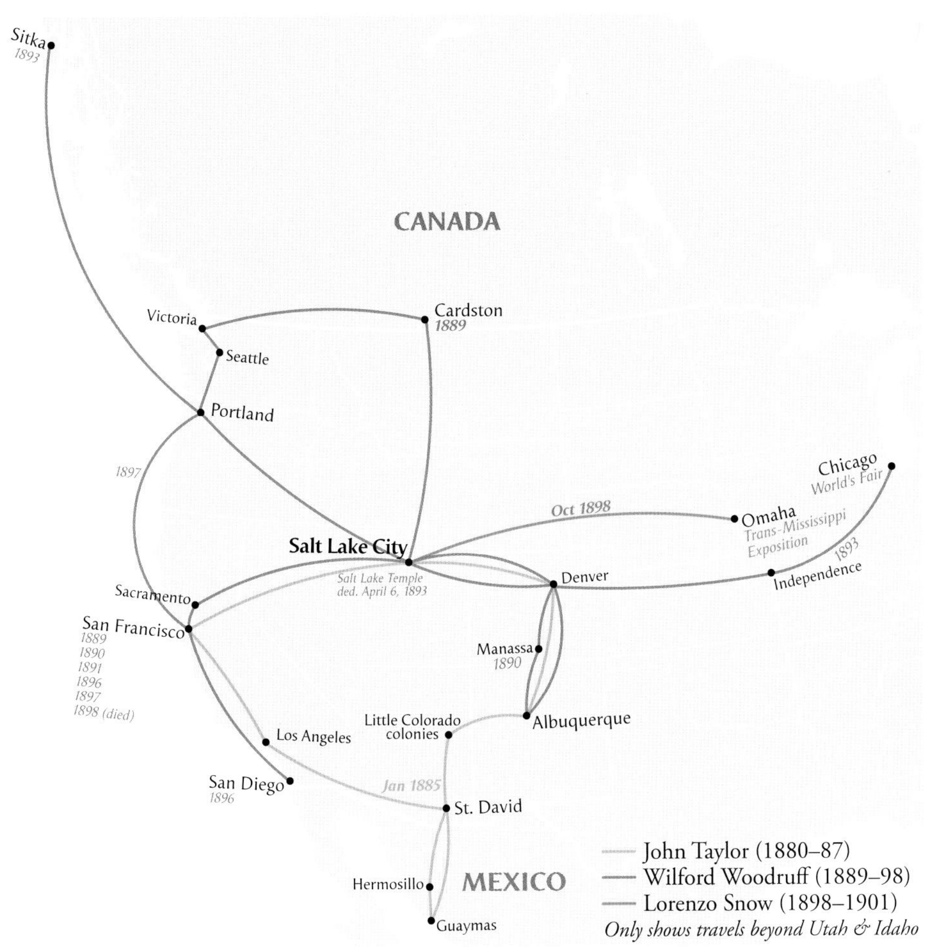

Presidents Taylor, Woodruff, and Snow

On his 1885 trip to the Southwest, John Taylor covered 5,000 miles in 24 days, thanks to the availability of railroads. He visited the young Arizona colonies, then rode the train into Hermosillo, Mexico (the first President to enter what is now Mexico), to investigate the possibility of purchasing land in Mexico for colonization (which was accomplished very soon after he left). There had been an idea to make the port of Guaymas the primary ocean access for immigrating converts and exporting Mormon goods, but this never came to fruition.

During his nine years as President of the Church, Wilford Woodruff traveled to several places outside of Utah. He frequently traveled to meet with members, most notably to the new Canadian colonies (1889) and to Colorado and New Mexico (1890). Some tours served multiple purposes; on a trip to Chicago in 1893, he visited the Chicago World's Fair (in which the Tabernacle Choir took second place in a competition) and saw the Buffalo Bill Wild West show, but he was also able to secure a loan for $250,000 to save Utah banks. His trip to Alaska was primarily a pleasure cruise.

His favorite destination was San Francisco, California. There he met with influential men such as Colonel Isaac Trumbo, Alexander Badlam Jr. (a nephew of lapsed Mormon leader Sam Brannan), and Judge Morris M. Estee to convince them to use their influence to obtain loans to keep the Church afloat, and with politicians such as Senator Leland Stanford who helped to seek statehood for Utah, or at helped lessen government persecution (see p. 92). These trips also led to the re-opening of missionary work in California in 1893 (see p. 206). President Woodruff passed away on his sixth California trip.

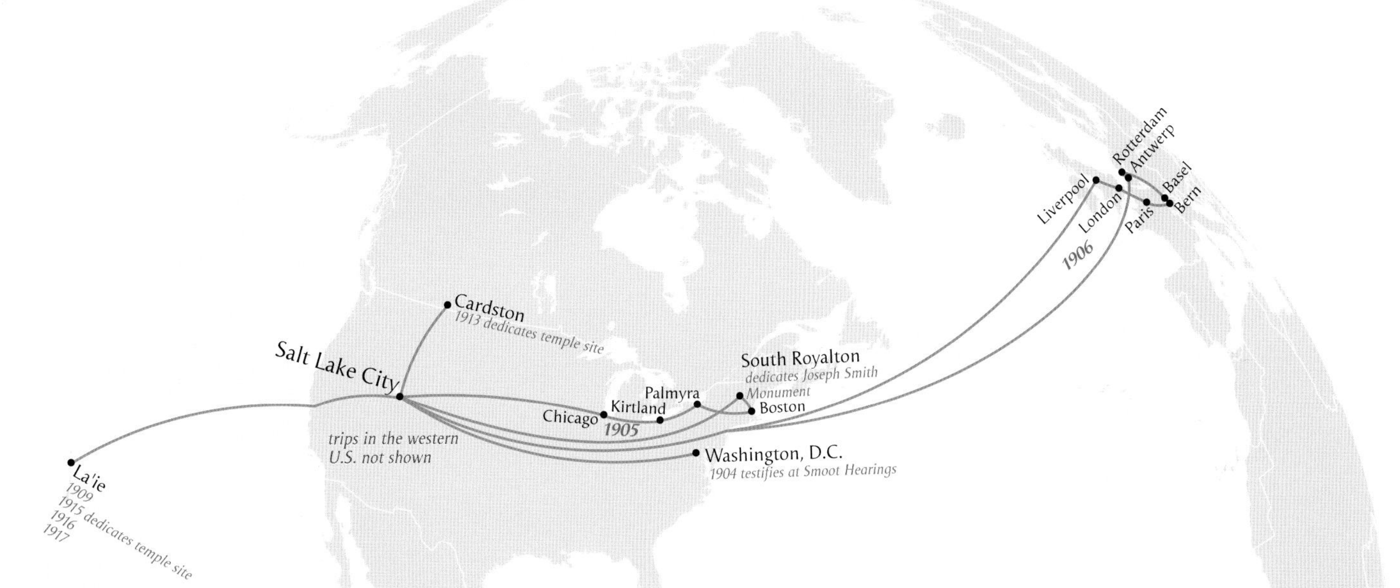

Travels of Joseph F. Smith

During his 17 years as President of the Church (1901–1918), Joseph F. Smith traveled extensively within the United States and beyond. Some trips were to conduct Church business, such as the congressional hearings on whether Reed Smoot was entitled to serve in the U.S. Senate (he eventually was allowed; see p. 188). This trip and another to the eastern states to dedicate the first Church-owned monument at a Church history site (and to visit other sites) were important to the goal of President Smith (the first second-generation member to become prophet) to improve the image and standing of the Church in America.

In 1906, Joseph F. Smith became the first Church President to travel to Europe while serving as President; he strove to meet local members and missionaries, as have other Presidents. While in Bern, Switzerland, Joseph F. Smith prophesied that "the time will come when this land [Europe] will be dotted with temples," which would be fulfilled almost 50 years later. This prophecy was important to President Smith's goal of slowing the Gathering and strengthening the Church beyond Utah.

President Smith made four trips to his beloved Hawaii (where he had served several missions) for various purposes, including dedicating a site for a temple that he would not live to see completed.

The Church in 1910

IN THE LATE NINETEENTH CENTURY, missionary work was rejuvenated in many parts of the world (see page 94). Tens of thousands of converts immigrated to the new Zion, primarily from Europe, aided by a well-organized transatlantic emigration program and transcontinental rails (see page 104). The core in Utah and Idaho was strengthened by institutions such as academies (see page 126), ZCMI (see page 118), and four new temples, while colonization spread to a wide area of the Intermountain West from Canada to Mexico (see page 96). The most distant colony, in Laie, Hawaii, even warranted a temple by 1919 (see p. 238). The remaining 15% of Church members were scattered in small branches throughout the rest of the world, especially Europe (where the Church had survived heavy persecution around the turn of the century), the East and West coasts of the United States, and the South Pacific. However, the Church had begun to discourage the gathering to Utah (aided by the increasingly restrictive immigration policies of the U.S. Government), leading to permanent growth in these areas throughout the twentieth century.

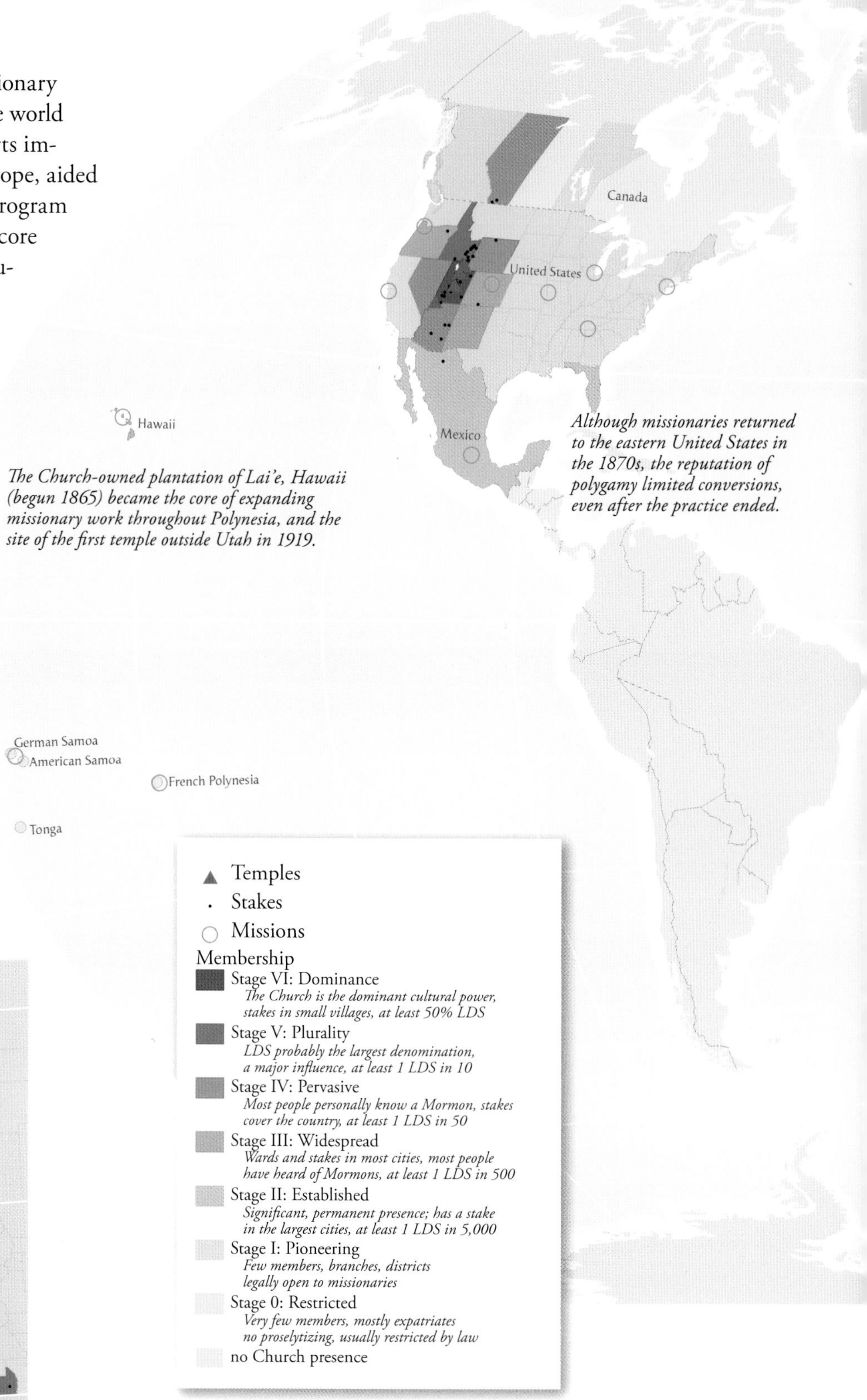

The Church-owned plantation of Lai'e, Hawaii (begun 1865) became the core of expanding missionary work throughout Polynesia, and the site of the first temple outside Utah in 1919.

Although missionaries returned to the eastern United States in the 1870s, the reputation of polygamy limited conversions, even after the practice ended.

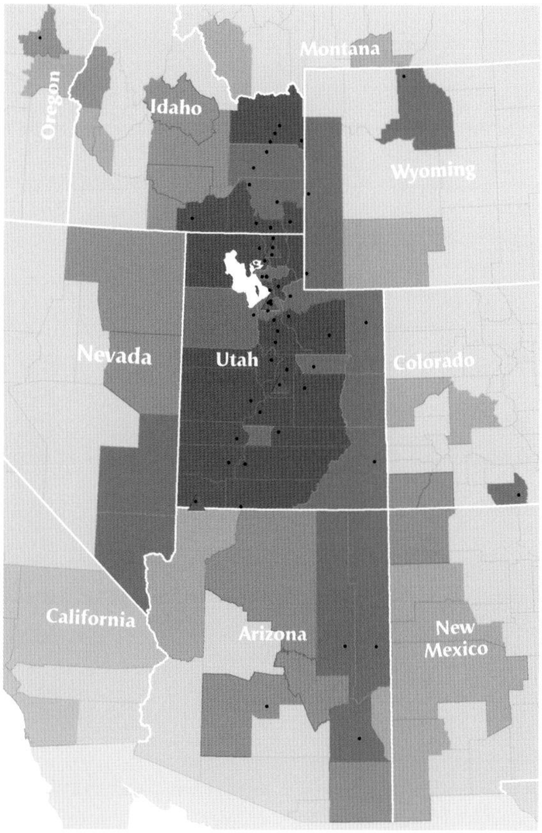

By the turn of the twentieth century, LDS settlers had expanded well beyond the corridor envisioned by Brigham Young in Utah and Idaho to create agricultural colonies in the surrounding states of Oregon, Nevada, Arizona, New Mexico, Colorado, and Wyoming, where they lived alongside non-Mormon communities. This spread was fueled by increasing numbers of immigrating converts, avoidance of persecution related to plural marriage, the availability of free land from the federal government, and the advent of federally funded large-scale irrigation projects that made agriculturally marginal lands prosper.

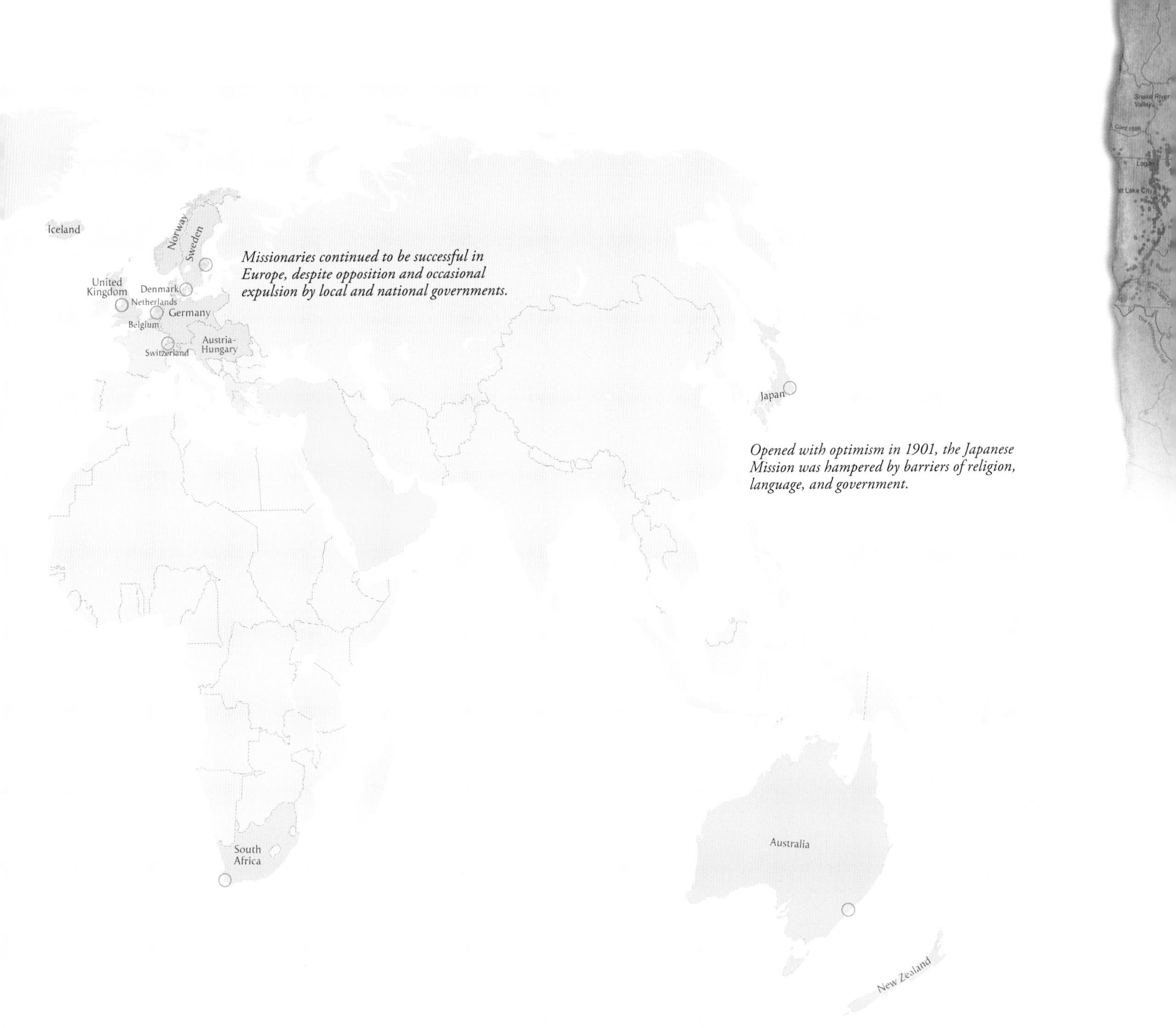
Iceland
Norway
Sweden
United Kingdom
Denmark
Netherlands
Germany
Belgium
Switzerland
Austria-Hungary
Missionaries continued to be successful in Europe, despite opposition and occasional expulsion by local and national governments.
Japan
Opened with optimism in 1901, the Japanese Mission was hampered by barriers of religion, language, and government.
South Africa
Australia
New Zealand

By the end of the nineteenth century, missionary work had expanded from its nadir in the 1870s (see p. 120) to include the entire United States, most of Europe, Australia and the Pacific, and South Africa. Although missions were intermittently opened and closed in places like France and the Ottoman Empire (Turkey), depending on changing government policies, the Church was beginning to establish a permanent presence around the world, which would become much more prominent by the 1950s (see p. 156).

The Church, 1870–1920

- **1875** Brigham Young Academy begun
- **1876** First colonies in Arizona established
- St. George Temple dedicated; Brigham Young dies **1877**
- John Taylor sustained as 3rd President **1880**
- **1884** Logan Temple dedicated
- **1885** Manti Temple dedicated
- **1887** Edmunds–Tucker Act against polygamy
- Wilford Woodruff sustained as 4th President **1889**
- **1890** Manifesto ends plural marriages
- **1893** Salt Lake Temple dedicated
- **1896** Utah becomes a state
- **1898** Lorenzo Snow sustained as 5th President
- **1900** Salt Lake Stake (55 wards) divided
- Joseph F. Smith sustained as 6th President **1901**
- Reed Smoot hearings and 2nd Manifesto **1904**
- **1905** Joseph Smith birthplace monument
- **1906** President Smith tours Europe
- **1907** First call to end the gathering to Utah
- **1914** European missions closed for World War I
- Heber J. Grant, 7th president **1918**
- Mass outmigration begins, especially to California **1918**

1870 · 1880 · 1890 · 1900 · 1910

SECTION 3

The Expanding Church

1912–present

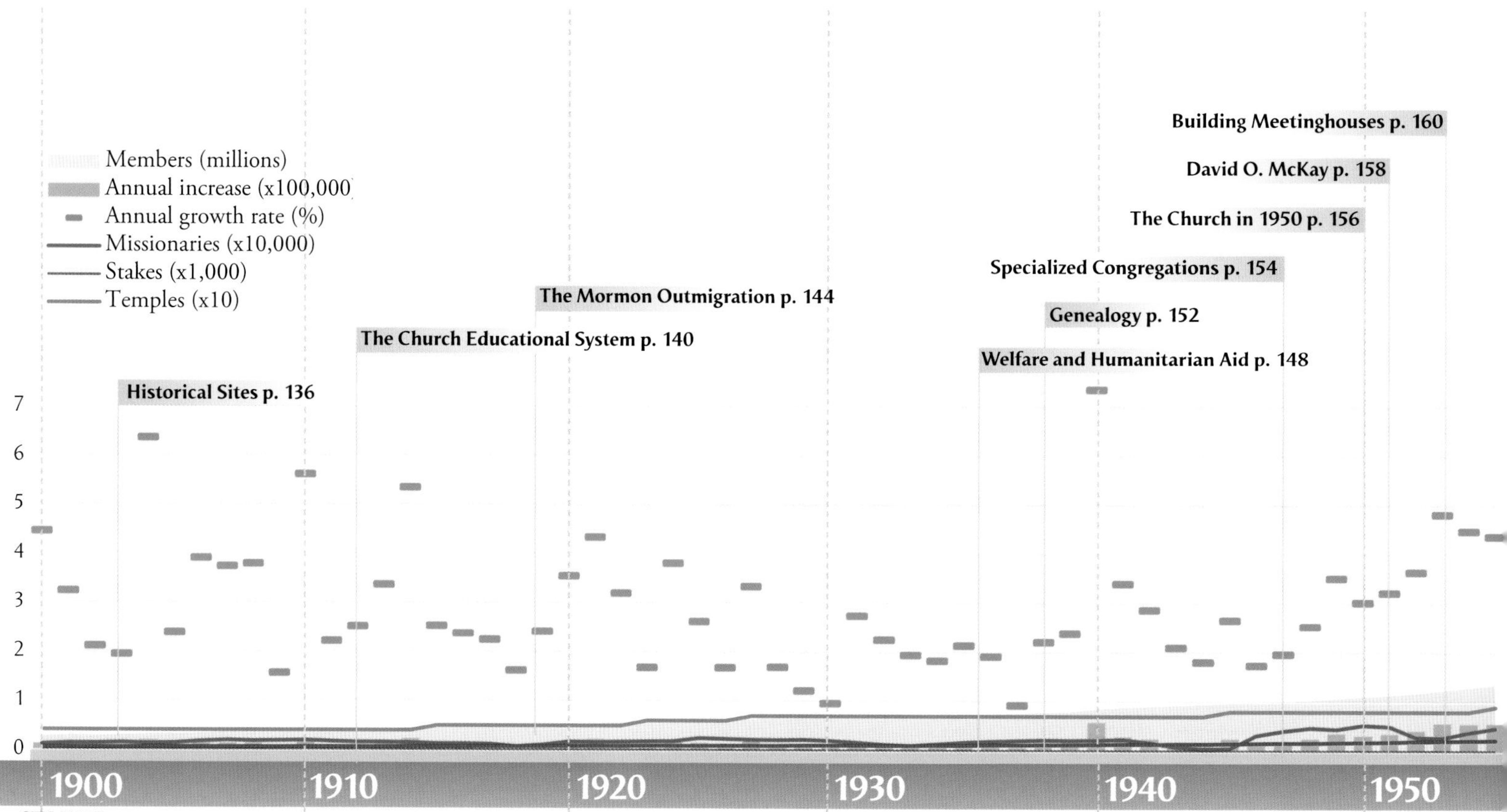

STAKES

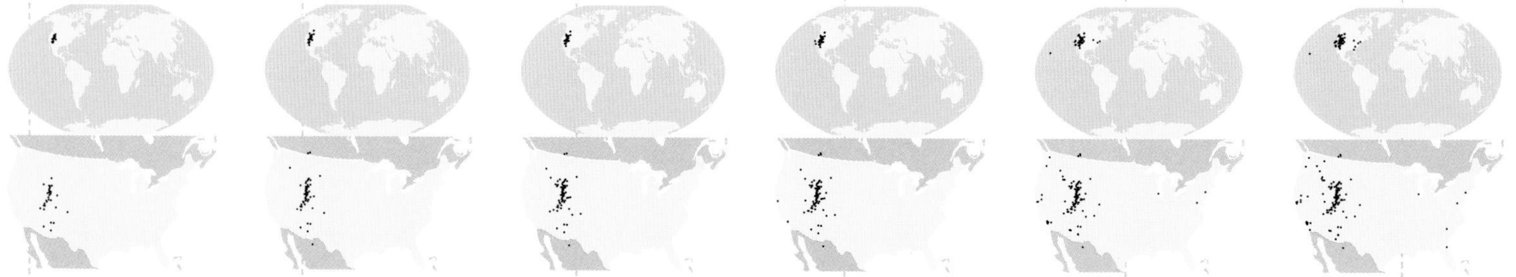

TEMPLES

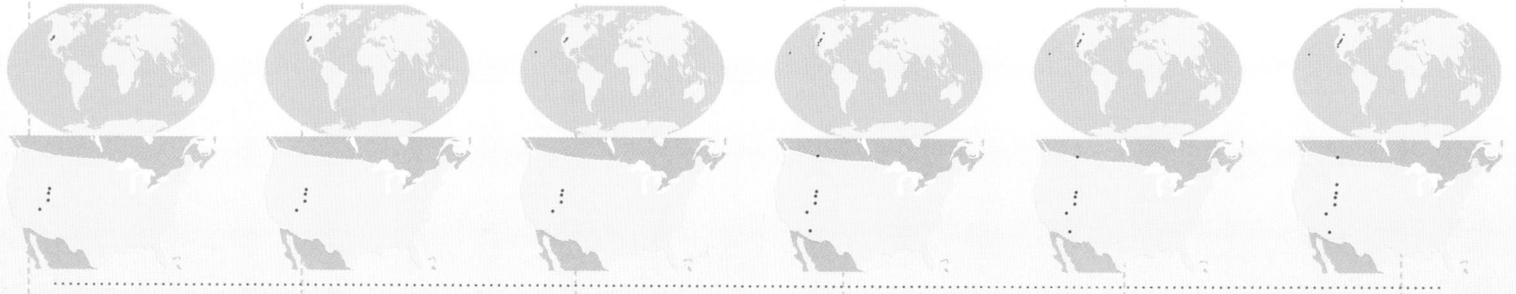

IN THE EARLY TWENTIETH CENTURY, there were fewer than 300,000 members of The Church of Jesus Christ of Latter-day Saints, but it reached 14 million members in 2010. The expansion of the Church from the Intermountain West to more than 150 countries of the world reflects a century of demographic, economic, political, social and technological changes.

Expansion due to the mass migration of members seeking education and jobs across the United States in the early part of the century gave way to international growth in later decades as the gathering of the nineteenth century ended. Over the past century, political changes have opened more and more countries to missionaries, while technology has allowed Church leaders in Salt Lake City to communicate and visit with far-flung congregations.

The growth of Church programs such as welfare and humanitarian aid mirrored this expansion. The Church Educational System grew from early high schools in Utah to elementary and secondary schools in Latin America and Polynesia, three universities in the United States, and the worldwide seminary and institute program providing both secular and sacred education to young members. As LDS membership has grown, so too has the influence of the Church in political, cultural, and social spheres.

Membership Distribution p. 174
Church Leadership p. 176
Missionary Work p. 178
Temples p. 182
Stakes p. 184
Cultural Ambassadors p. 186
Political Affiliation p. 188
Book of Mormon Geographies p. 190
Community of Christ p. 192
The Restored Church(es) p. 196
Three American Churches p. 198
The Future of the Church p. 202
The Church in 2012 p. 172

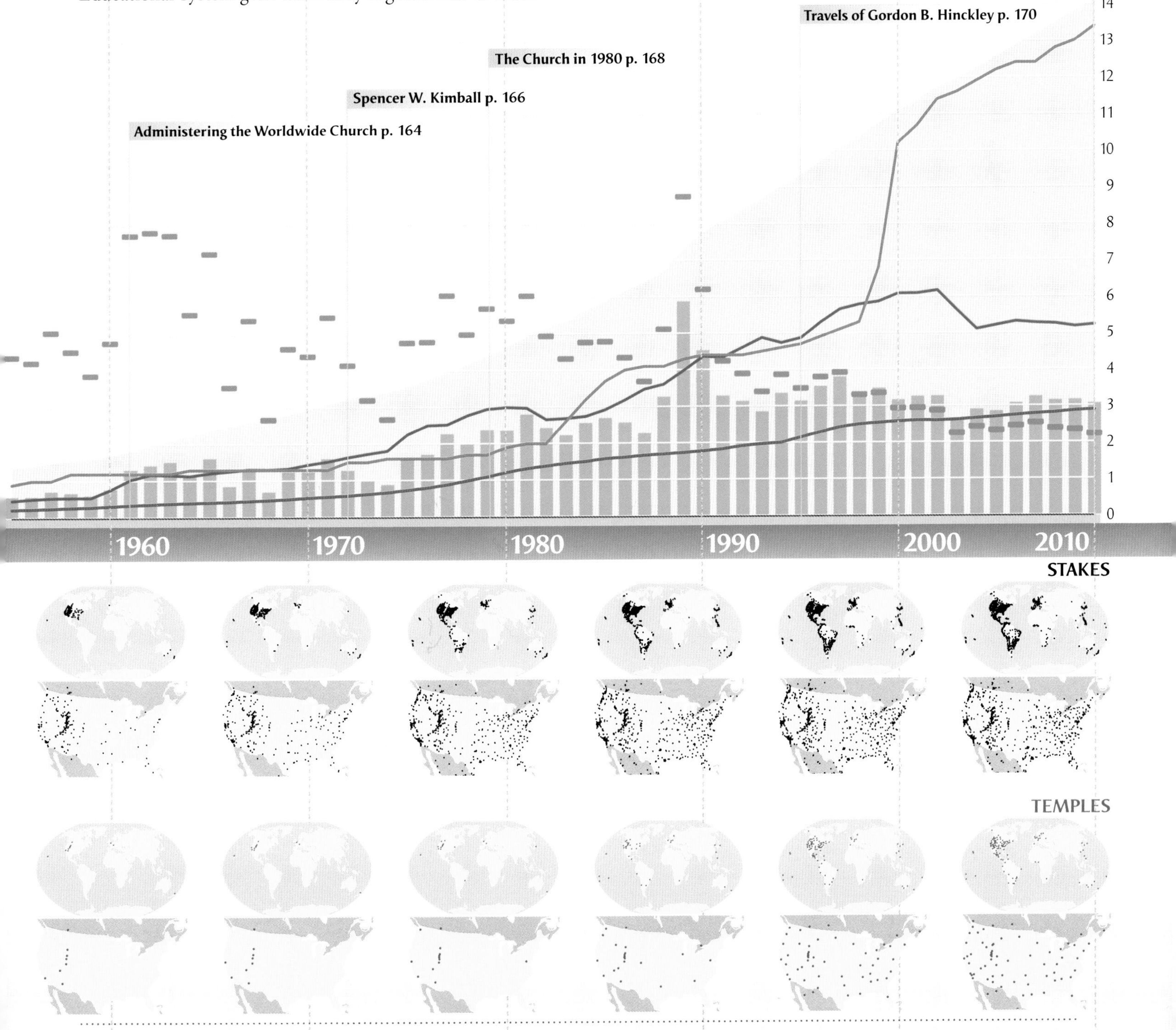

Historical Sites

1903–present

The Church of Jesus Christ of Latter-day Saints has been involved in preserving and commemorating important historical places for many years. Most memorialize the Church's origins, sacred events and places, and pioneer heritage. While Mormon heritage sites are scattered across the United States, Canada, and western Europe, the most important and famous attractions are in New York, Ohio, Missouri, Illinois, and Utah.

Initially, the Church showed little interest in the places of Mormon history due to financial constraints, other priorities, and a lack of desire to return to the scenes of persecution. However, President Joseph F. Smith, the first prophet who was not part of the early restoration, recognized the importance of preserving and promoting Church history and, as the Church retired its debt, he saw an opportunity. The acquisitions of Carthage Jail (1903) and the Solomon Mack farm in Vermont (1905), the sites of Joseph Smith's birth and death, mark the beginning of the Church's interest in obtaining sites important to its history and development.

Private individuals also played a major role in the early acquisition of property and helped to stimulate interest in a variety of projects. Church member Wilford C. Wood personally purchased a number of important sites in the mid-1900s, including the Nauvoo Temple lot, Adam-ondi-Ahman, the Liberty Jail site, and important properties in Ohio. Most of these were eventually sold or donated to the Church. In Nauvoo, the decision of a descendant of Heber C. Kimball to purchase and restore his ancestor's home became the catalyst for the preservation process and ultimately led to the creation of Nauvoo Restoration in 1962 as an independent organization (recently subsumed into the Church historical sites program). Its mandate was to restore and operate all of the facilities in Nauvoo and Carthage that depict the history of the Latter-day Saints.

Pioneer heritage is an important component of Mormon identity. Monuments, memorials, historical buildings, museums, and visitors' centers are physical reminders of the group's roots and history. Church members are encouraged to remember the hardships Mormon pioneers endured from the Church's beginnings in New York to the eventual migration and settlement of Utah and surrounding regions. Stories of their sacrifices, obedience, hard work, faithfulness, and willingness to overcome all types of adversity are used as examples that people in contemporary times should emulate in their own lives. Members are encouraged to visit these places to learn more about their history and enhance their faith. Annually, thousands of Latter-day Saints travel to the more famous Mormon locations in Palmyra, Nauvoo, Kirtland, and Winter Quarters. These trips have a similar lifetime impact and spiritual significance as pilgrimages in many other religions. Visiting the heritage locations helps make history become a reality and reinforces the lessons they have been taught and values they possess.

continued on page 138

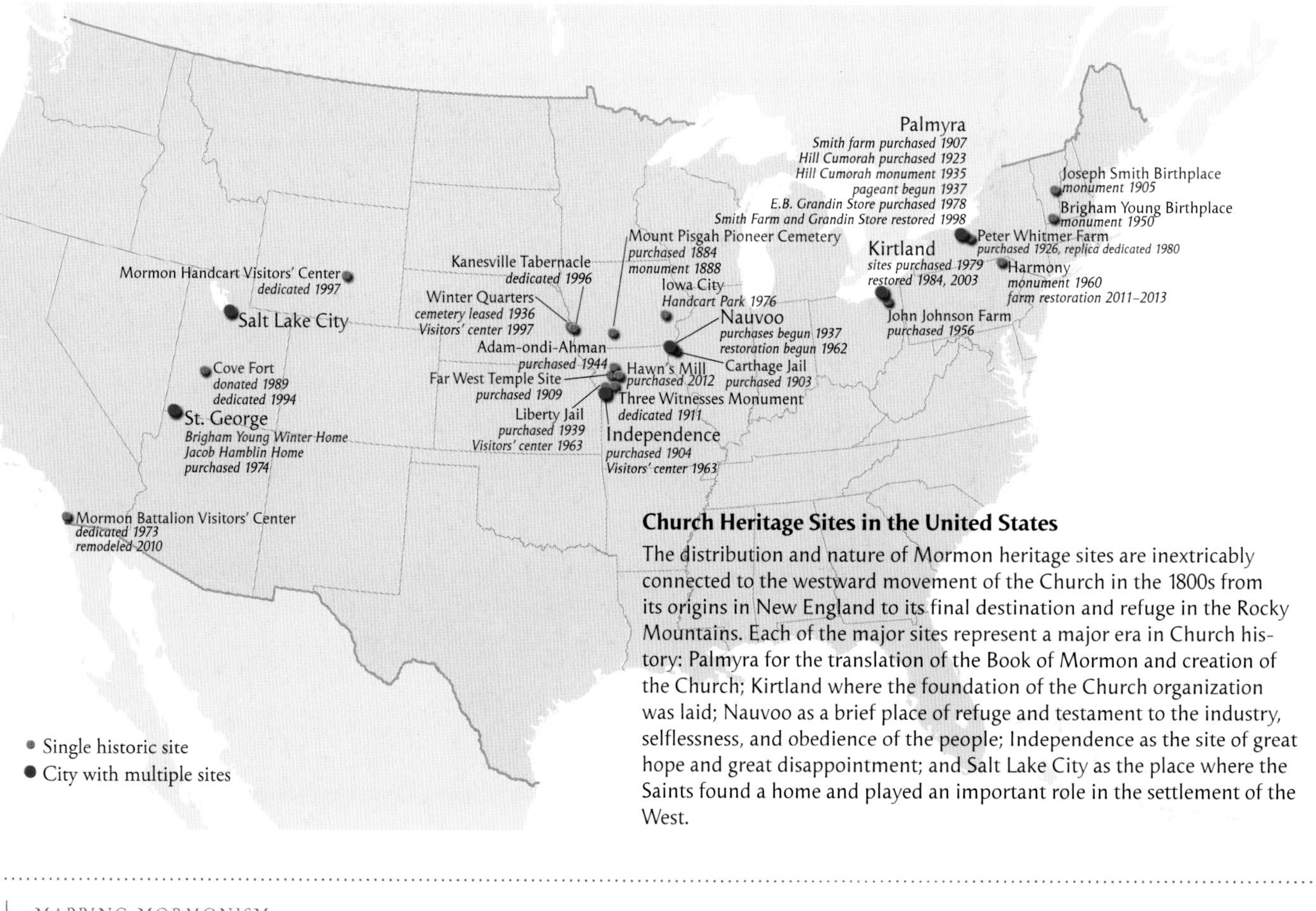

Church Heritage Sites in the United States

The distribution and nature of Mormon heritage sites are inextricably connected to the westward movement of the Church in the 1800s from its origins in New England to its final destination and refuge in the Rocky Mountains. Each of the major sites represent a major era in Church history: Palmyra for the translation of the Book of Mormon and creation of the Church; Kirtland where the foundation of the Church organization was laid; Nauvoo as a brief place of refuge and testament to the industry, selflessness, and obedience of the people; Independence as the site of great hope and great disappointment; and Salt Lake City as the place where the Saints found a home and played an important role in the settlement of the West.

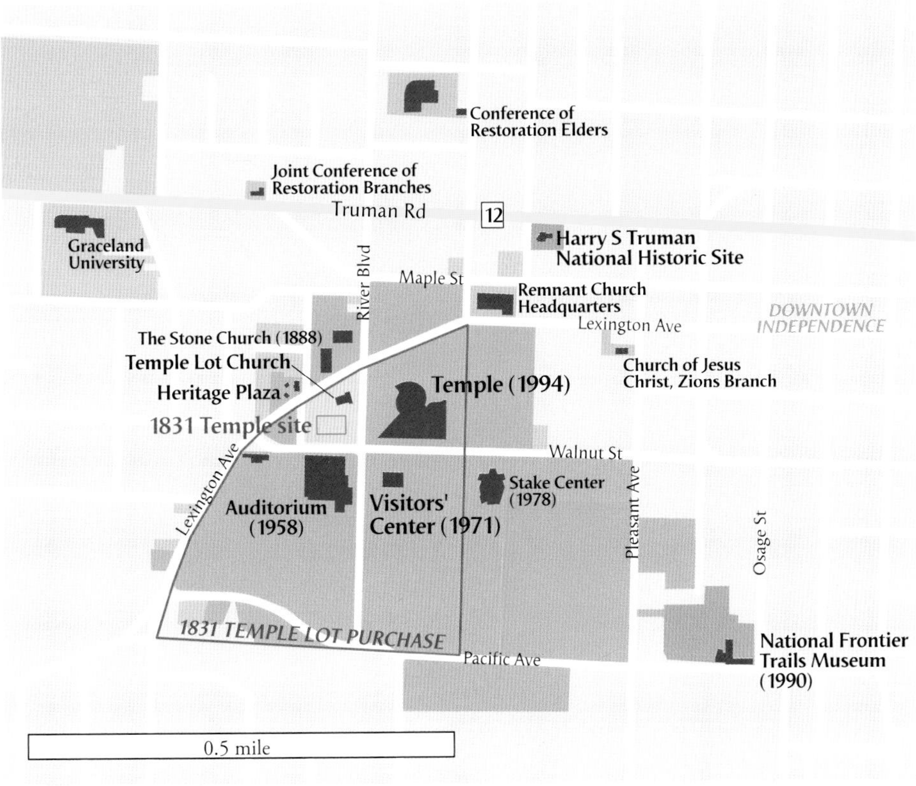

■ Building

Land and facility owner

- The Church of Jesus Christ of Latter-day Saints
- Community of Christ
- Central Development Association (Community of Christ)
- Other RLDS Groups
- Church of Christ (Temple Lot)
- Government

Heritage Sites in Independence, Missouri

The property purchased by the Church in 1831 for a temple (see p. 32) is one of the most significant, and certainly the most contested, sites relevant to Church history. Although the Saints were driven out before the temple could be built, the revealed call to build it was never rescinded, so the site is still considered sacred ground.

The followers of Granville Hedrick (see p. 64) were the first to return to Independence in 1867, purchasing a parcel that included the actual temple site (later finding the buried cornerstones); his Church has been nicknamed "the Temple Lot Church" ever since. After a lengthy lawsuit over the property with the Reorganized Church of Jesus Christ of Latter Day Saints (now Community of Christ) in the early twentieth century, the two sister churches have been relatively good neighbors. The real estate subsidiary of the Community of Christ also owns several surrounding residential and commercial properties to ensure the quality of the neighborhood. The "Utah Church" entered the picture in 1904, eventually building a large visitors' center. In recent years, groups breaking off from the Community of Christ (see p. 192) have established headquarters in the area.

The Mormon Battalion Vistors' Center, first built in 1973, was remodeled in 2010 with a greater focus on the history of the Battalion rather than the spiritual emphasis on the Church it had earlier had.

Heritage Sites Timeline

1903 Carthage Jail purchased

1904 The Church buys a 25-acre portion of the original temple purchase in Independence, Missouri

1905 Joseph Smith Birthplace purchased in Sharon, Vermont; Pres. Joseph F. Smith dedicates the birthplace monument

1909 80 acres of Far West purchased, including the temple site. By 1996 the Church owned 593 acres including the John Whitmer home

1911 Monument to the Three Witnesses dedicated in the Pioneer Cemetery in Richmond, Missouri.

1923–28 The Church purchases property near Palmyra, New York, including the sites of the Smith Family Farm, the Sacred Grove, and the primary portion of the Hill Cumorah

1926 Church purchases the 100-acre Peter Whitmer Farm in Seneca County, New York

1936 Winter Quarters Pioneer Cemetery leased from Omaha City

1937–51 Nauvoo Temple parcels purchased by Wilford Wood

1939 The Church purchases the house built on the foundation of the Liberty Jail; visitors'center dedicated in 1963

1944 Wilford Wood purchases 38 acres of Adam-ondi-Ahman for the Church (several hundred acres have been purchased since)

1950 Brigham Young Birthplace monument, Whittingham, Vermont

1956 John Johnson Farm, Hiram, Ohio, home of Joseph Smith for a year and site of many revelations

1959 Aaronic Priesthood Restoration Monument, Harmony, Pennsylvania

1962 Nauvoo Restoration, Inc., organized to coordinate private restoration efforts in Nauvoo

1972 Mormon Battalion Visitors' Center, San Diego

1976 Mormon Handcart Park and Nature Preserve, Coralville, Iowa, developed with Church funds on property owned by the University of Iowa

1980 To celebrate the sesquicentennial of the Church, Spencer W. Kimball broadcasts general conference from the newly reconstructed Peter Whitmer Home

1984 Newel K. Whitney Store restored

1989 Cove Fort donated to the Church by the Hinckley family

1996 Kanesville Historic Park, with a replica of the log tabernacle in which Brigham Young was sustained as Church President

1997 Sesquicentennial of first Mormon pioneers commemorated by dedication of Mormon Trail Center in Winter Quarters and Martin's Cove Visitors' Center in Wyoming

1998 Joseph Smith Sr. Farm in Palmyra restored to 1820s appearance

2003 Kirtland historical site restored, including several replica buildings

2010 Mormon Battalion Visitors' Center in San Diego reconstructed as a historically-focused tour site

2011 Restoration of sites at Harmony, Pennsylvania, begun

1900 | 1910 | 1920 | 1930 | 1940 | 1950 | 1960 | 1970 | 1980 | 1990 | 2000 | 2010 | 2020

Historical Sites

continued

Historical sites are also missionary tools, even though non-LDS visitors are typically a minority. An important function of many attractions, such as Temple Square, is to teach people about the Church. The fundamental message is that all people should come to Christ. At all of the locations people are reminded of the central role Jesus Christ plays in the LDS religion.

The balance between these historical and proselytizing roles has shifted over the years. Many sites were originally restored as museums displaying artifacts. During the 1980s and 1990s, most sites were significantly changed, focusing on Christ and doctrine; historical information could often be difficult to find. Since 1996, major remodeling projects in Palmyra, Kirtland, Winter Quarters, and San Diego have focused on telling a historical story in a spiritual context.

James A. Davis

The Newel K. Whitney Store in Kirtland was the site of several important revelations and other events between 1831 and 1838, and has been the heart of the LDS presence in Kirtland since it was purchased from Wilford C. Wood in 1979.

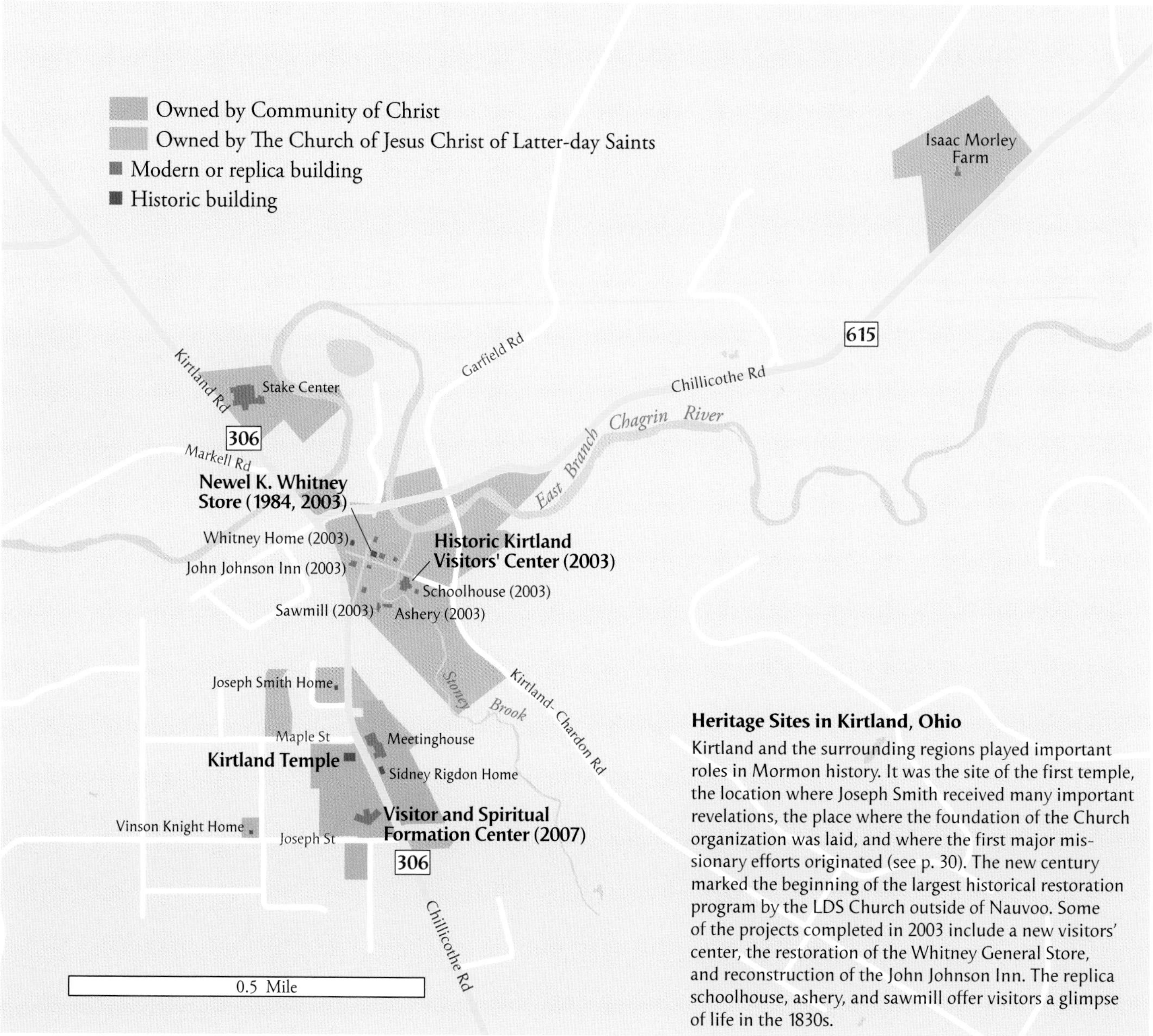

Heritage Sites in Kirtland, Ohio

Kirtland and the surrounding regions played important roles in Mormon history. It was the site of the first temple, the location where Joseph Smith received many important revelations, the place where the foundation of the Church organization was laid, and where the first major missionary efforts originated (see p. 30). The new century marked the beginning of the largest historical restoration program by the LDS Church outside of Nauvoo. Some of the projects completed in 2003 include a new visitors' center, the restoration of the Whitney General Store, and reconstruction of the John Johnson Inn. The replica schoolhouse, ashery, and sawmill offer visitors a glimpse of life in the 1830s.

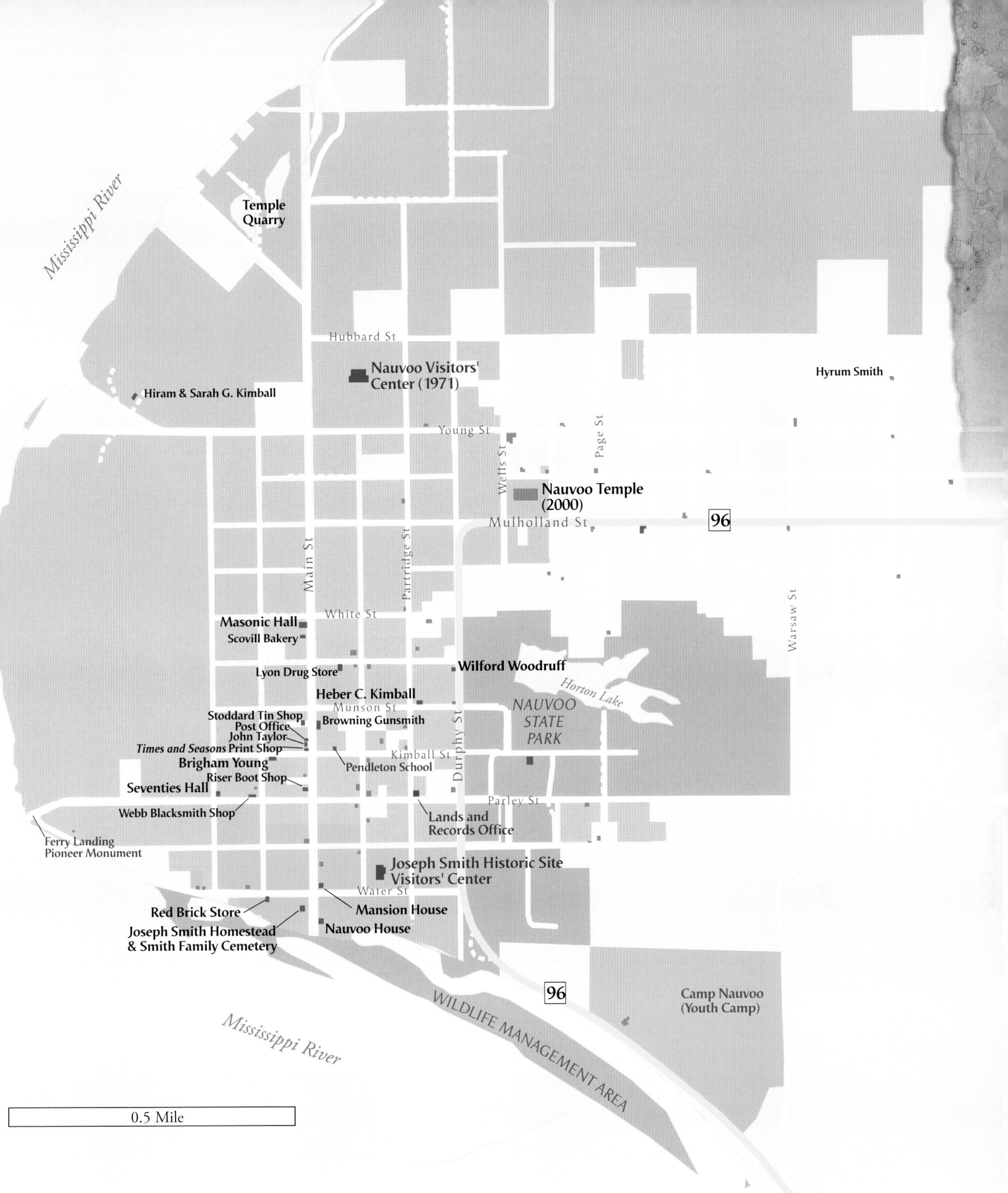

Heritage Sites in Nauvoo, Illinois

Nauvoo was by far the largest settlement of the Saints prior to the move to Salt Lake City (see p. 56). Historic Nauvoo is an example of how the actions and examples of one family led to the preservation and reconstruction of this historic Mormon town. Dr. James L. Kimball sparked interest in the restoration of Nauvoo after purchasing and restoring his grandfather Heber C. Kimball's home in the 1950s. He organized Nauvoo Restoration, Inc. (NRI) in 1962; it acquired and restored dozens of historic sites and homes in Nauvoo, eventually turning it into one of the largest historic reconstructions in the United States. NRI was eventually acquired by The Church of Jesus Christ of Latter-day Saints, and the facilities are now part of the Church's Historic Sites program.

Today there are several dozen sites, including restored homes and shops, visitors' centers, memorials, exhibits, and the beautiful, reconstructed Nauvoo Temple. Period-dressed missionaries at each site explain about the people and practices of Mormon Nauvoo.

The Church Educational System

1912–present

THE LATTER-DAY SAINTS have always valued education, for a variety of spiritual and temporal reasons (D&C 88:78–80). As have many other churches, the LDS Church has faced the questions of the balance between religious and secular education, and whether to encourage public schools or provide schools itself (at great expense). Throughout its history, the Church has taken one or more of three different approaches to these questions:

- Church-owned schools, whether local or boarding schools, provided both secular and religious instruction.
- Church meetings, such as Sunday School, Primary, and the Mutual Improvement Association (MIA) for teens, provided once-weekly religious instruction.
- Supplemental education, providing daily religious education to students attending public schools.

During the late nineteenth century, the Church schools approach was most common (see p. 126). This was a natural reaction to a particular educational environment with concentrated clusters of Church members, few or no public schools, and Catholic or Protestant schools eager to convert Mormons (see p. 112). The academies were moderately

continued on page 142

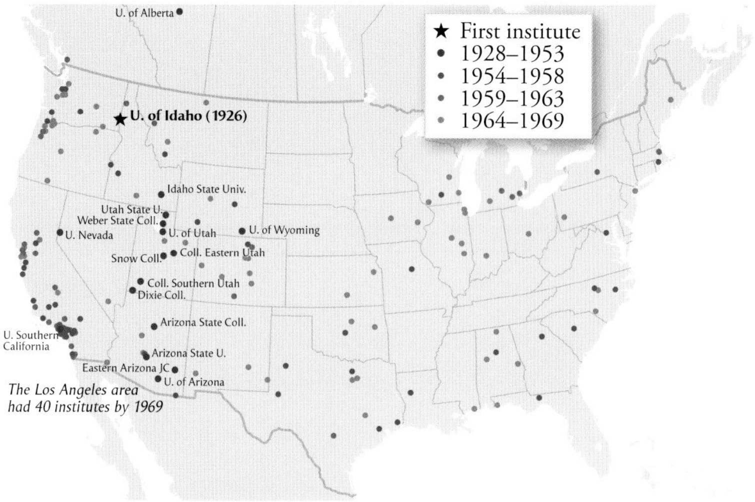

The First Institutes of Religion

As members moved beyond the traditional Mormon culture area, and as Church academies disappeared, LDS youth attended non-LDS colleges in increasing numbers. The success of the seminary program inspired Church leaders to encourage a similar extracurricular program at the college level. From the first "collegiate seminaries" at the University of Idaho and College of Southern Utah, the program (soon renamed Institutes of Religion) quickly spread throughout the West. By the 1950s, the Church had a policy to create a full institute (with a building and a full-time instructor) whenever a university had more than 100 active member students, but they also began establishing smaller institutes elsewhere, with classes taught by local members or missionary couples.

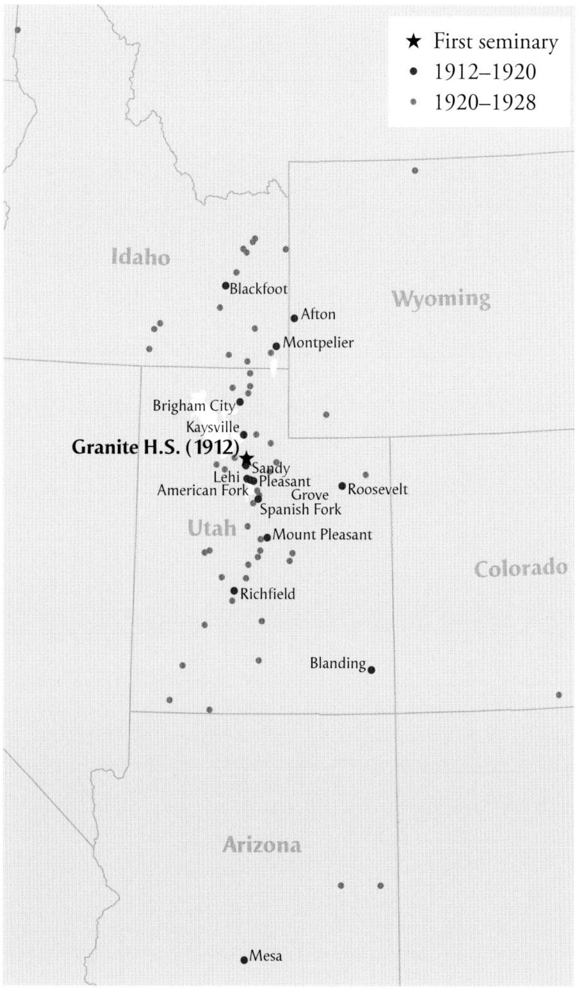

The Beginnings of Seminary

With the rise of public education in the Intermountain West, and the subsequent decline of the Church academies, many parents and leaders worried about the spiritual education of students. Joseph F. Merrill, a counselor in the Granite Stake presidency and a future Apostle, arranged with the local school district to release students to leave the school for one hour to attend seminary at a neighboring meetinghouse, taught by full-time instructors. By 1915, the Church Board of Education adopted the program and "release-time seminaries" were created as quickly as school boards and state governments would grant permission, primarily in communities with a major Church presence. Beyond this area, "daily seminaries" were eventually organized with courses taught by local members outside school hours, often in the early morning.

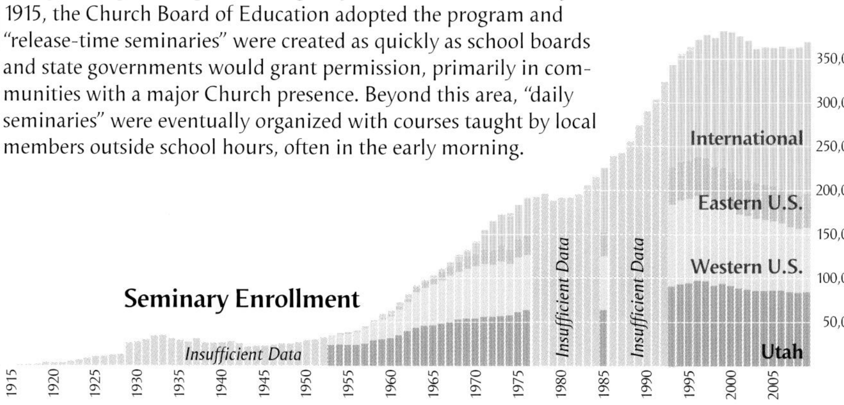

Enrollment in Seminary and Institute has generally grown due to the increase in Church membership and the introduction of programs tailored to youth outside the Intermountain West, such as early-morning and home-study seminary. Some programs have not survived, such as seminary in elementary schools (leading to the decline in the 1930s) and the Indian boarding seminaries (causing the decline in the 1970s). The recent decline is likely due to long-term demographic decline in the size of Mormon families.

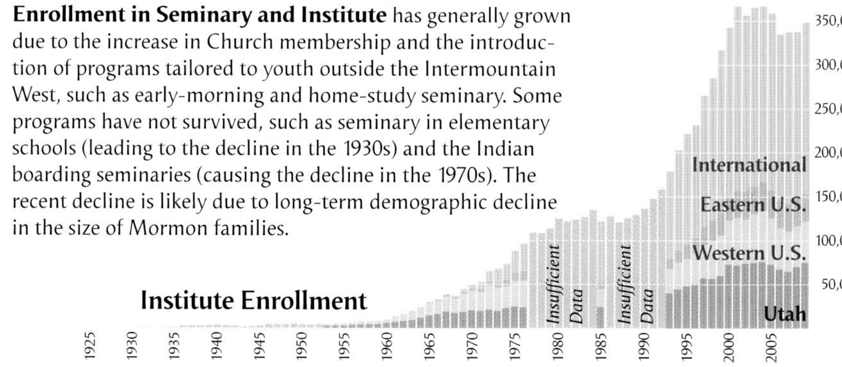

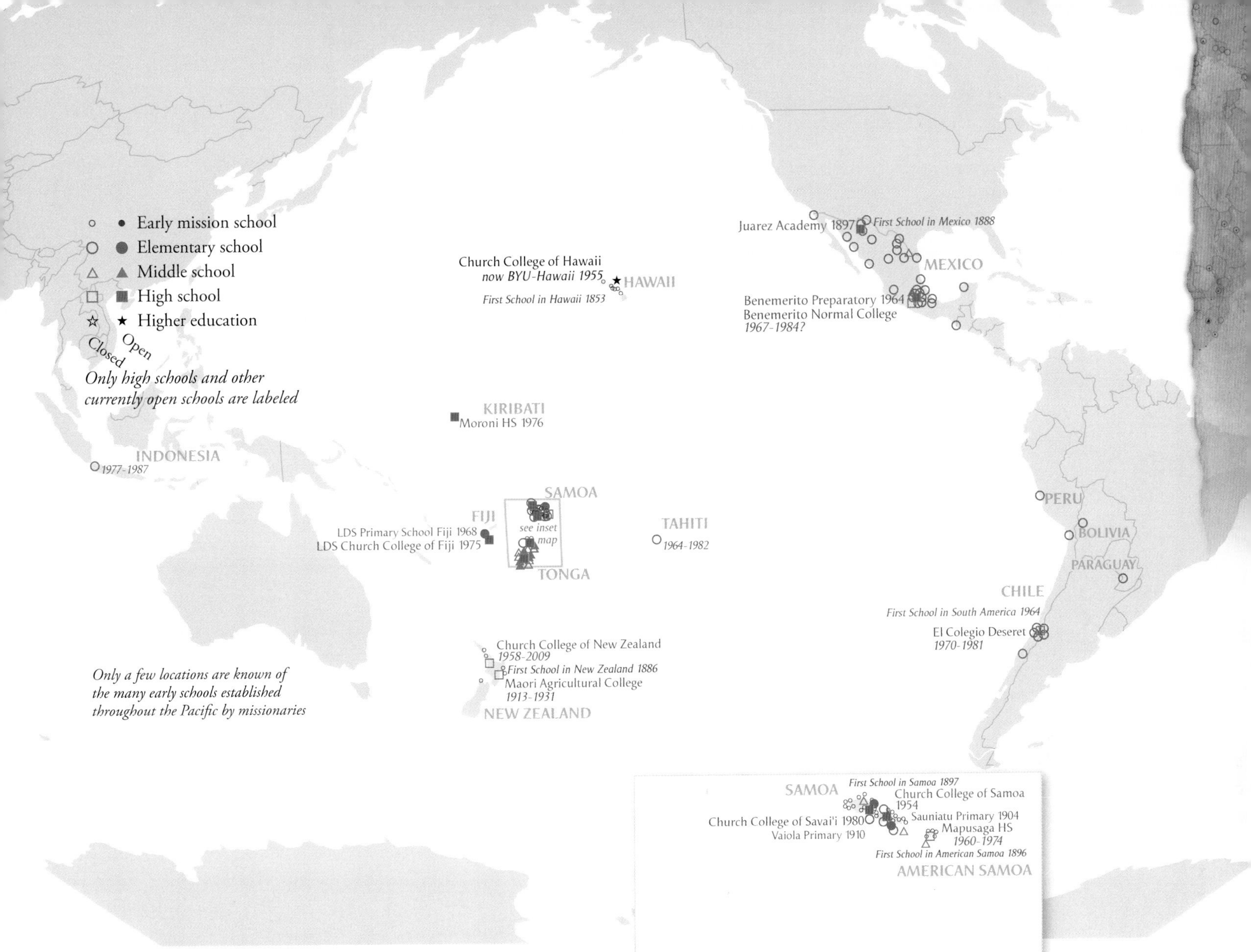

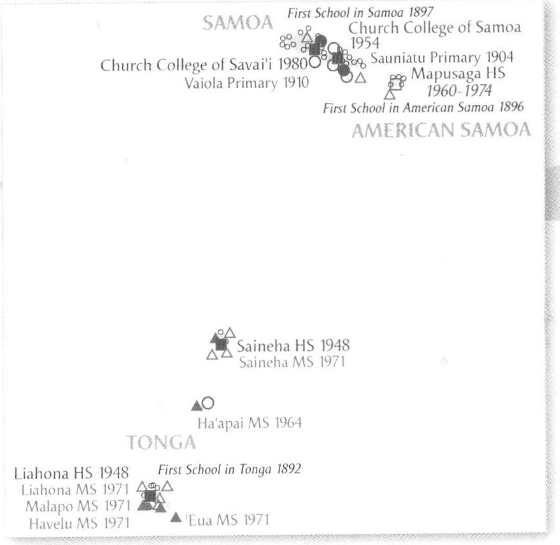

Church Schools in the Developing World

In the late 1800s, missionaries in the Pacific Islands started schools in many villages, largely for proselytizing, which were rather successful, despite the limited quality of the education (since the missionaries were not trained teachers). However, because the same conditions existed here as in Utah Territory earlier, they gradually received more resources and better teachers (often alumni of the schools themselves). The system expanded into secondary schools where large concentrations of members lived, culminating in the construction of the Church College of Hawaii (now BYU-Hawaii). Similar school systems were soon created in Mexico and South America, and by the mid-1970s, 75 elementary, middle, and high schools were operating. However, as public educational systems have improved, and as Church resources have been needed for ecclesiastical purposes, most of the schools have closed, and the future of those that remain open is uncertain.

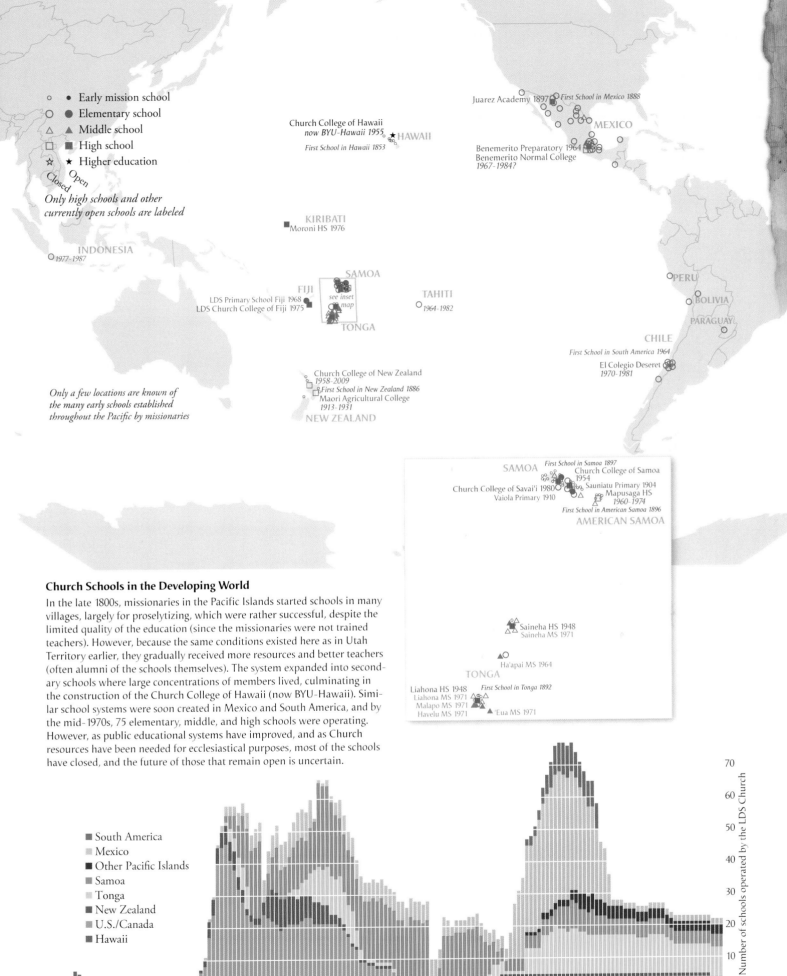

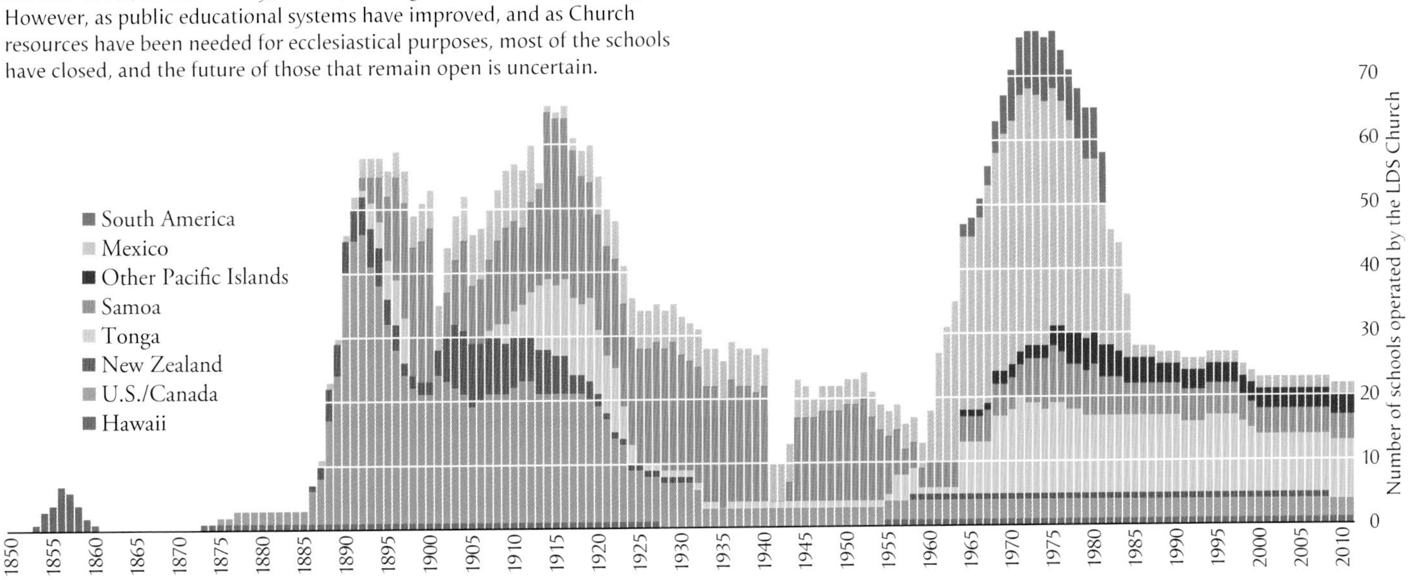

The Church Educational System

continued

successful at providing an education that integrated the sacred and the secular, but with the rise of free public education in Utah and surrounding states, the academies were neither needed nor sustainable, and almost all were eventually closed. In outlying areas such as Latin America and the South Pacific, members again encountered this environment, and again created Church-owned schools (with the additional purpose of conducting missionary work, as the Protestants had done in Utah).

With the decline of the academies, the need for religious education still existed, leading to the creation of seminaries for high school students and institutes of religion for college students, thus implementing a supplemental education approach. In this model, students typically receive an hour of instruction each day, either during, before, or after regular school hours (depending on school rules) at a site separate from the school itself (usually a meetinghouse or a nearby dedicated building). These were so successful (and so efficient financially) that they quickly spread across the Church, eventually including alternative approaches for teaching young members in numbers too small to justify full-time facilities and staff. Not only did seminaries and institutes replace Church schools in Utah; they have more recently replaced most Church schools in Latin America and the Pacific, as local public education systems have become sufficient. A supplemental program for elementary students has not existed since weekday Primary meetings were merged with Junior Sunday School in 1980.

The Church has retained four colleges and universities: Brigham Young University in Provo, Utah; BYU–Hawaii (formerly the Church College of Hawaii) in Laie; BYU–Idaho (formerly Ricks College) in Rexburg; and LDS Business College in Salt Lake City. At times, the future of even these have been in doubt, but since the 1950s they have grown and thrived, although they are not large enough to enroll all the LDS youth who wish to attend. Their success has thus led many to suggest building more, including a major effort during the 1950s that met with initial support of the Board of Education (the First Presidency and Quorum of the Twelve). However, this and other proposals have been rejected in favor of seminaries and institutes (and moderate expansion of the existing colleges and universities) for two reasons: 1) cost and 2) the value (despite risks) of young members interacting with the rest of the world.

This long-standing policy has not kept members from creating religious schools on their own. There are several successful independent private K–12 schools in Utah that publicly espouse LDS values while several members in the eastern United States purchased a failing college in 1996 and transformed it into Southern Virginia University, an LDS-themed liberal arts college with an enrollment of about 750 in 2010.

Brandon S. Plewe

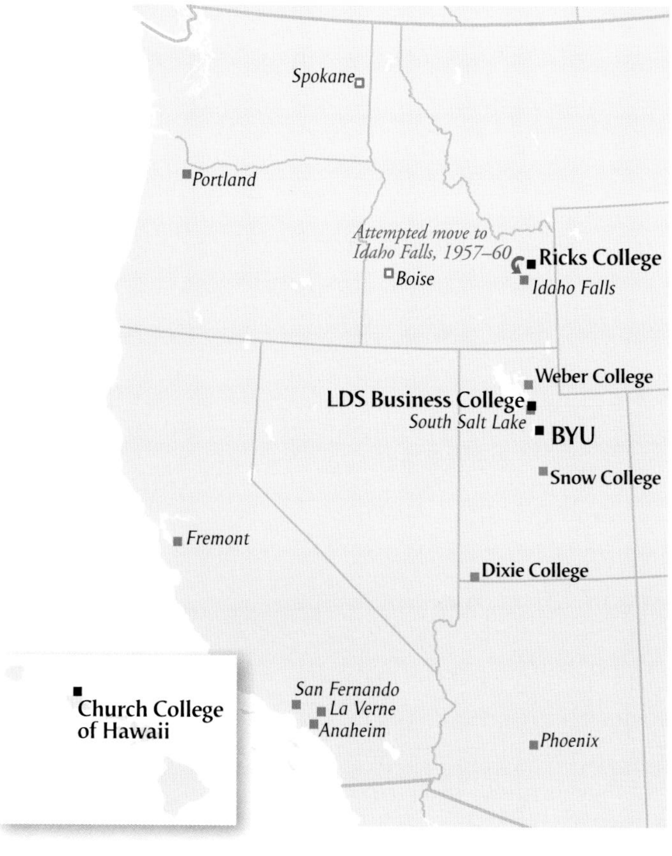

The Planned Higher Education System

From 1951 to 1964, Ernest L. Wilkinson served as both president of BYU and Church commissioner of education. Across the U.S., the GI Bill was bringing unprecedented numbers of students to college, including young Mormons. Wilkinson developed a grand vision for a Church system of higher education, similar to many state systems, consisting of several "feeder" junior colleges, with the best of their students going to the large flagship university in Provo. The first phase, repurchasing the schools that had been sold to the state 20 years earlier (Dixie, Weber, and Snow), was rejected in a statewide referendum.

Land was purchased in several western cities for new campuses, but none were built. Wilkinson's proposal to move Ricks College from Rexburg to Idaho Falls failed after two years of debate, the global meetinghouse construction program (see p. 160) was straining the finances of the Church, and the First Presidency realized that they could never build colleges fast enough to keep up with global membership growth.

The institute program was seen as a much more efficient way to aid the religious education of college students, and when Wilkinson handed all of the Church school system other than BYU to Harvey L. Taylor in 1964, the four original colleges were still the only ones, and have remained so to this day. Most of the land was sold, but 30 years later the Portland Temple was built on land purchased by Wilkinson.

- Existing campus
- Former Church schools almost reacquired 1954
- Property obtained 1957–58
- Proposed but not purchased

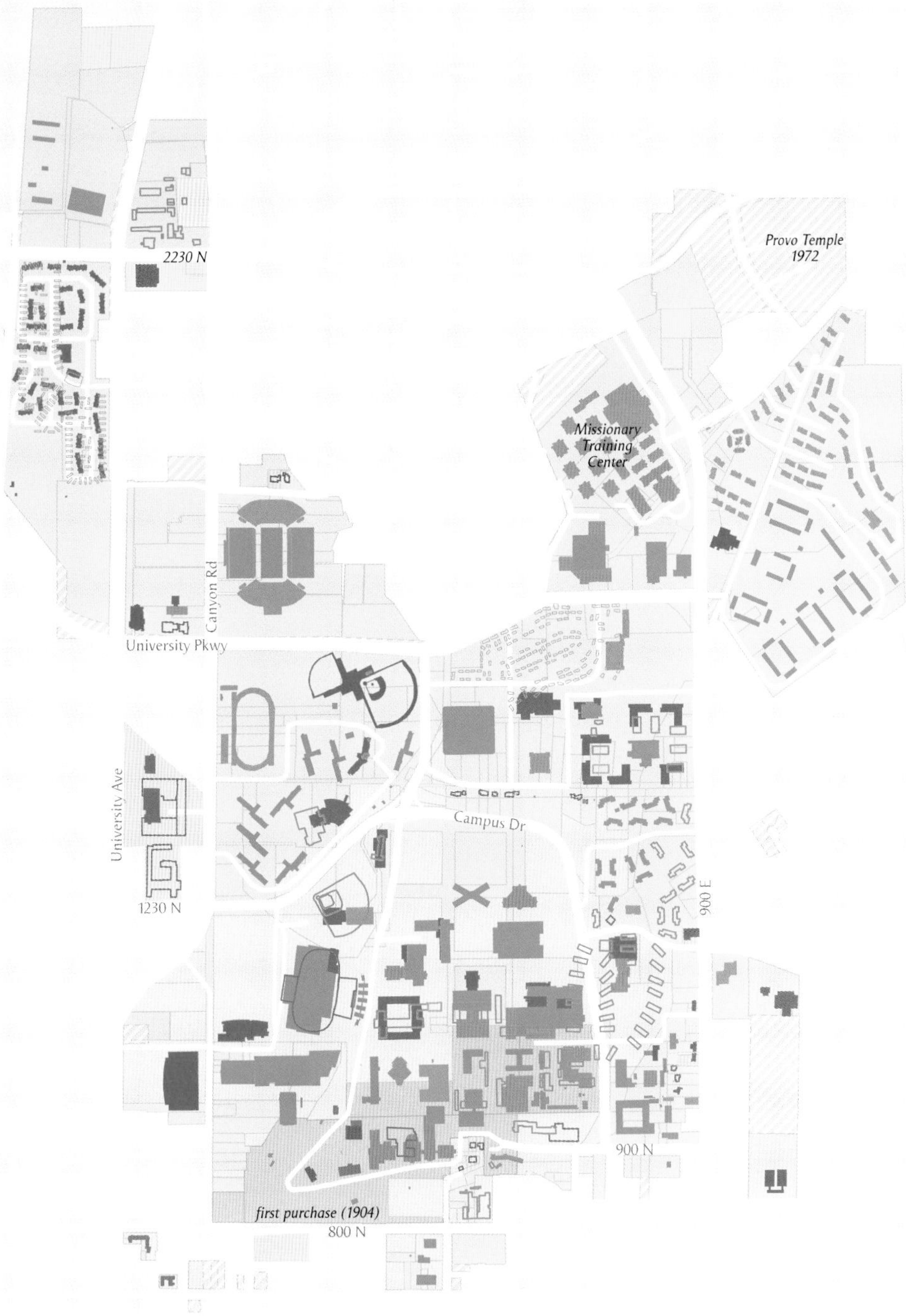

Expansion of the Brigham Young University Campus

Early in its history, the Brigham Young Academy was housed in several locations in downtown Provo, until it completed the large Academy Building in 1892. However, the newly renamed Brigham Young University quickly outgrew this and surrounding buildings.

In 1904, President Brimhall purchased the southwest corner of "Temple Hill" overlooking the city (so named because most residents thought a temple would someday be built there) from the city of Provo.

At that time, the bench beyond the purchased land was a scattering of orchards. Although finances were tight, land was acquired and buildings were constructed on the new "upper campus" as the university slowly grew. After World War II, the GI Bill led to rapid growth at universities across the United States, and BYU was no exception. In response, President Ernest L. Wilkinson spent the 1950s buying up as much land as possible (including entire residential neighborhoods) and spent the 1960s filling that land with new residential, academic, and administrative buildings. During his 20-year term, enrollment increased from 4,000 to 25,000, the campus from 230 to 660 acres, and academic building space from 800,000 to 5,000,000 square feet.

Enrollment was capped at 25,000 in 1972 (later extended to 30,000), so subsequent construction has generally slowed to updating or replacing older buildings, except where private donor funds have been available for expansion in targeted areas.

- 1903–21 Brimhall
- 1922–45 Harris
- 1946–50 McDonald, Jensen
- 1951–71 Wilkinson
- 1972–80 Oaks
- 1981–89 Holland
- 1990–95 Lee
- 1996–03 Bateman
- 2004– Samuelson
- Acquired existing building
- Building no longer standing
- No longer BYU property

Church Education

1903 Brigham Young Academy becomes Brigham Young University, with a primarily collegiate mission

Sep 1912 First modern seminary: Granite High School, South Salt Lake, Utah

1913–1931 Maori Agricultural College (New Zealand), the first Pacific secondary school

1915 Ricks Academy (secondary) becomes Ricks College

First institute of religion **1926** started at University of Idaho

Junior seminary, **1929–1958** an after-school program for children, thrives then gradually dissipates

Four colleges given to the states of Utah **1933** and Arizona, ending the academies era

Pacific Board of Education **Jul 1957** formed to coordinate schools in the Pacific

1931 LDS University disbanded, LDS Business College and McKune School of Music survive as separate institutions

Church College of Hawaii **1 Sep 1974** becomes BYU-Hawaii

1949 Ricks College a 4-year school

1950 First early-morning seminaries held in Southern California

1950s–1970s Indian seminaries, comprehensive boarding schools on reservations

9 Jul 1953 Unified School System organized, led by Ernest Wilkinson, who was also president of BYU

26 Sep 1955 Church College of Hawaii opens

Mar 1964 First schools in South America opened in Chile

1967 Home-study seminary piloted in the midwestern U.S.

Sep 1970 Educational programs consolidated into new Church Educational System (CES), with Neal A. Maxwell as commissioner. BYU enrollment cap

Perpetual Education **7 Aug 2001** Fund instituted to benefit young adults in developing nations

10 Aug 2001 Ricks College becomes BYU-Idaho, a 4-year college

1900 | 1910 | 1920 | 1930 | 1940 | 1950 | 1960 | 1970 | 1980 | 1990 | 2000

The Mormon Outmigration

1919–1970

SINCE THE CHURCH WAS FOUNDED, migration has played a crucial role in understanding the distribution of the Latter-day Saints in the United States. During the latter part of the nineteenth century, the strength of the Church rested on "the gathering" (see p. 104), migration from the Midwest and Europe to Utah, but the next century was characterized by "outmigration" from Utah (and Idaho) to other states. In 1900, over 70% of American Latter-day Saints lived in Utah (another 20% lived in the colonies elsewhere in the Intermountain West), whereas by 2000, Utah claimed less than one third of the nearly six million American Mormons. The other four million now lived in the other 49 states. From where did all of the non-Utah Church members appear? There was only a moderate increase due to births or conversions in these states; historical evidence suggests that the main reason for the expansion of wards and stakes nationwide was this "Great Outmigration."

Unlike the previous century, this movement was based on decisions by individuals and families; while the Church favored the idea of members moving to seek new jobs or higher education, there was never a general call for the Saints to leave. Latter-day Saint families, especially young adults, realized that there were few jobs and educational opportunities in Utah. In the early days, five cities, rich in educational and professional opportunities, were magnets for young Saints: Washington, D.C., New York City, Chicago, Los Angeles, and San Francisco.

The two World Wars accelerated the outmigration as many Saints moved to places such as Seattle, Detroit, and Washington, D.C., for employment in wartime industries. This continued after the war when veterans sought higher degrees on the GI Bill in universities from coast to coast, such as UCLA, Chicago, Indiana, Cornell, and Harvard. As these new Mormon enclaves increased in population, new branches of the Church were established. Most student-emigrants did not return to Utah but stayed in their new homes. In Utah, Brigham Young University and state universities expanded rapidly as well (see p. 140), increasing the pool of graduates searching for professional opportunities abroad.

As opposed to local members, often not numerous, the emigrants brought organizational skills honed by priesthood, auxiliary, and missionary experience. Their leadership encouraged a flood of migrants to follow seeking new opportunities, aided by affordable housing thanks to the postwar building boom. The list of destinations expanded to cities such as Phoenix, Las Vegas, Portland, and St. Louis. The southern states, largely ignored by migrants before the war, now became new targets of opportunity (see p. 210). In their new homes, Latter-day Saints were a minority, mingling with their non-Mormon neighbors and assimilating into American society. By the time the outmigration tide ebbed in 1970, the face of Mormonism in America had changed from a two-state entity to a national force, from a rural culture to the suburban mainstream, from an isolated "other" to yet another group of Americans.

continued on page 146

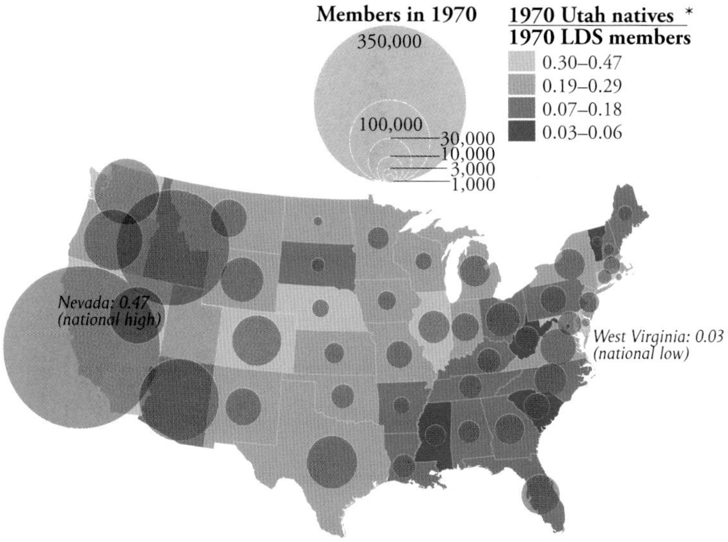

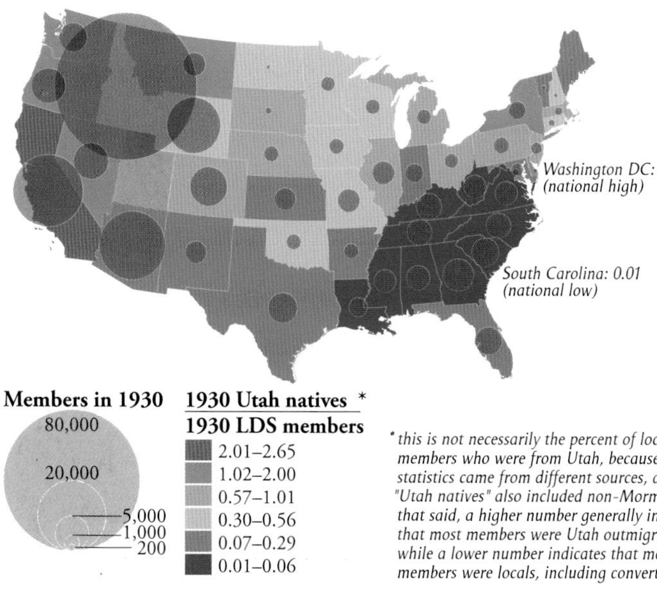

** this is not necessarily the percent of local members who were from Utah, because the statistics came from different sources, and "Utah natives" also included non-Mormons; that said, a higher number generally indicates that most members were Utah outmigrants, while a lower number indicates that most members were locals, including converts.*

Regional Dominance of LDS Outmigrants

These maps show the ratio between the number of residents of each state who were born in Utah (mostly, but not entirely, Mormon) and the number of LDS members in that state. In the midst of the outmigration in 1930, outmigrants from Utah made up the majority of members along the West Coast and in the major cities of the mid-Atlantic states and the Midwest. Conversely, in the South, the vast majority of Mormons were local converts and their descendants. Another sign of the relative success of missionary work in the South was that its total membership far outnumbered that of the North, even with the influx of Utahns adding to the latter. By 1970, the outmigration had reached the South, especially in the booming cities in Texas, Georgia, and Florida, but they were still the minority (see p. 210). Across the United States, the proportion of outmigrant Mormons had dropped drastically; as the outmigration trend slowed, former migrants had children who were native to their adopted states, and local missionary work saw more success.

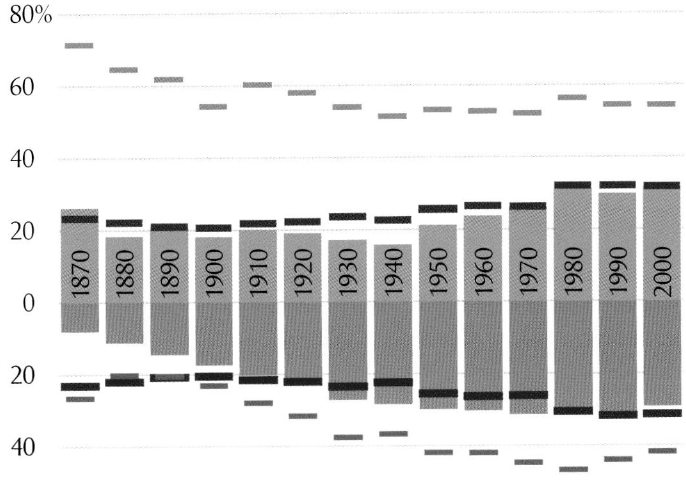

Interstate Migration

In the late nineteenth century, Utah was a net importer of Americans, but by 1910, the percentage of native Utahns who had left the state (in red) was rapidly increasing, becoming higher than the percentage of Utah residents who were from other states (in green). This pattern of "net emigration" continued through 1970, significantly exceeding the national average during the Great Depression and the postwar economic boom. In recent years, those who have come and those who have left have been relatively balanced. Throughout this period, however, Utah's population was far less mobile than in surrounding mountain states, in which mass migrations came and went in earlier years based largely on mining booms and busts.

- % of Utah residents born in other states
- % of residents of any state born in another state
- % of mountain states residents born in other states

- % of Utah natives living in another state
- % of natives of any state living in another state
- % of mountain states natives living in another state

foreign-born not included

Utahns Abroad

During the early twentieth century, natives of Utah (mostly but not exclusively Mormons) migrated to a number of locations. California was the primary destination, where for many years, the flow from Utah was significantly larger than from neighboring states, even though California was consistently the national leader in immigration from the rest of the country. Throughout the century, Utahns moved to neighboring states in significant numbers. Destinations in the Northwest, East Coast, and the Midwest were also important, but Utahns were often outnumbered by migrants from other Mountain states (possibly due to reverse migration from declining mining areas). One notable exception was the Washington, D.C., area, which appears to have attracted a disproportionate number of Utahns (presumably led by Mormon federal employees).

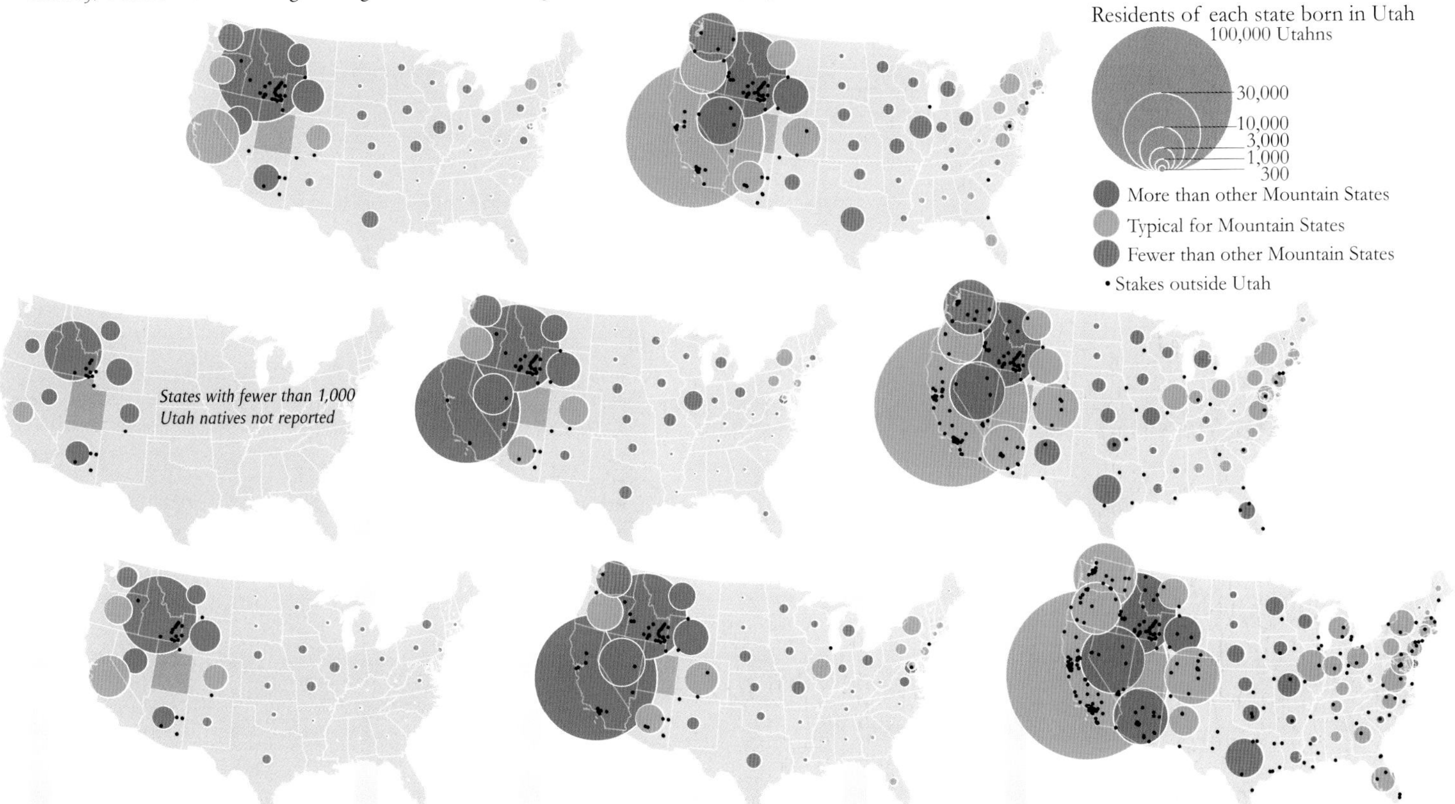

1900–1920 Federal water reclamation projects throughout western U.S. open new lands to agricultural development, drawing Mormon farmers beyond the traditional core

1901 Bighorn (Lovell, Wyoming) and Union (La Grande, Oregon) Stakes, first beyond the Mormon core

1903 Apostle Reed Smoot elected Senator, beginning a flow of Mormons to work in Washington, D.C., that continues to this day

1917–1918 Military industries during World War I attract large numbers of young Mormons to Los Angeles and Oakland

21 Jan 1923 Los Angeles Stake, first in California; by 1935 there were 7 stakes

9 Dec 1934 New York Stake formed with mostly outmigrant leadership

30 Jun 1940 Washington, D.C., Stake formed with Ezra Taft Benson as president

1945 The GI Bill leads to thousands of Mormon veterans attending college throughout the United States

Oct 1953 New stakes in Dallas and Houston come on the heels of increased migration to the South

1970 Mormon migration to California slows dramatically, likely due to slowing economic opportunity

1900 1910 1920 1930 1940 1950 1960 1970 1980

The Mormon Outmigration

continued

Among the variety of migrants from traditional Mormon cores were many young professionals who would become major leaders in their local LDS Churches as well as secular corporations, institutions, industry, and government. The outmigrants shown here were well-known pioneers in moving to various locations across the nation, both for employment and advanced degrees, but their paths are typical of thousands of lesser-known Mormons.

G. Wesley and Marian Ashby Johnson

J. Reuben Clark Jr. 1871–1961

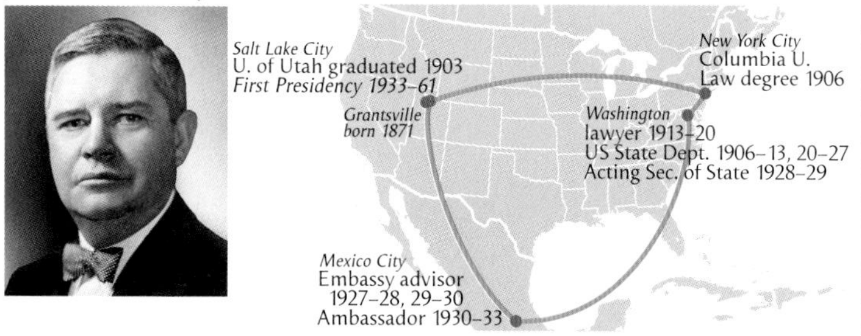

Lawyer and diplomat. Undersecretary of State; as ambassador to Mexico, helped the Church improve its status there (see p. 218). When called to the First Presidency, he was not an Apostle and had never even been a bishop.

Edgar B. Brossard 1889–1980

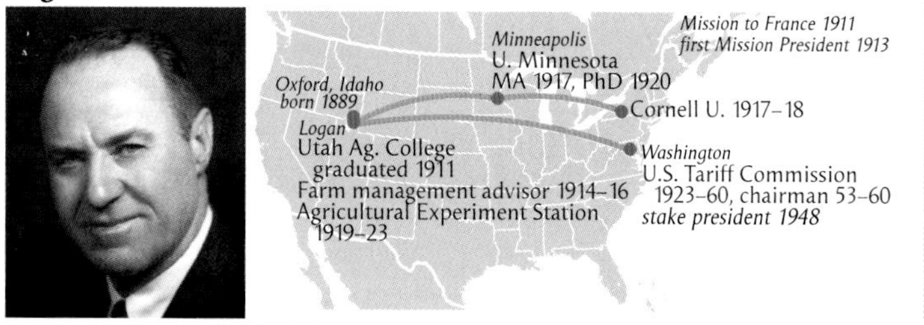

Businessman. Established the LDS French Mission, eventually head of the U.S. Tariff Commission. Longtime president of LDS Washington D.C. Branch, helped to build monumental chapel (see p. 160).

Ezra Taft Benson 1899–1994

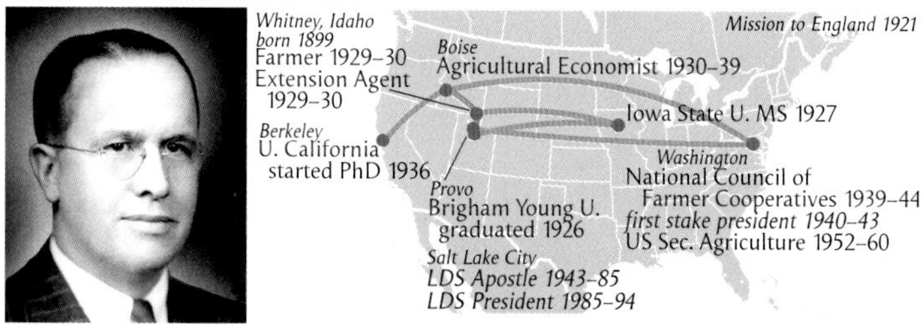

Helped foster the formation of farmers' cooperatives. While head of an association of these cooperatives in Washington, he was the first president of the stake. As an Apostle, he was Dwight D. Eisenhower's Secretary of Agriculture (the first LDS member of the cabinet). Eventually became the President of the Church.

G. Stanley McAllister 1900–1970

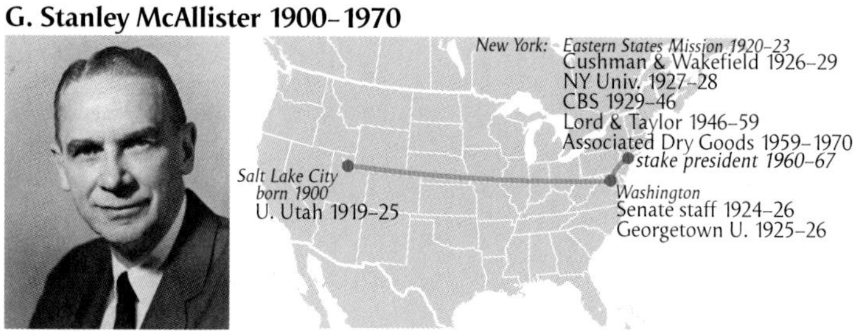

Businessman. Held technical and executive positions in broadcasting (CBS) and retailing (Lord & Taylor). As New York stake president, he directed the successful LDS pavilion at the 1964 World's Fair (see p. 212).

Reed Smoot 1862–1941

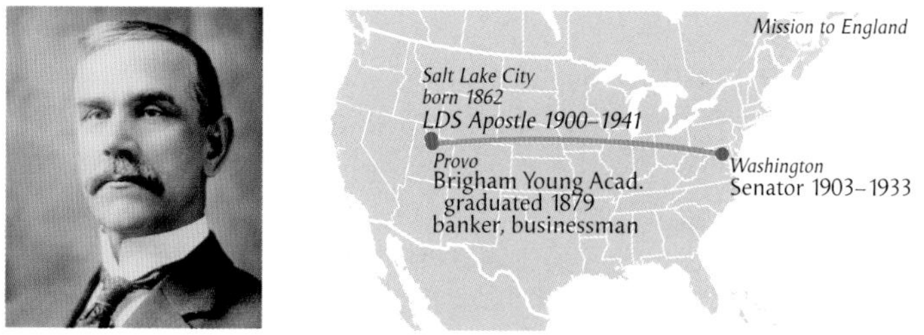

Served in the U.S. Senate while an Apostle. Helped create the National Park Service and chaired the Senate Finance Comittee, secured passage of the Smoot-Hawley Tariff in 1930.

Harvey Fletcher 1884–1981

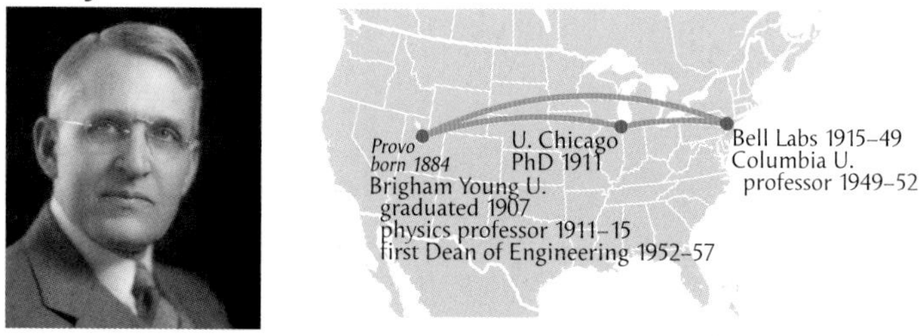

Physicist. As a student helped Robert Millikan with experiments that would win the Nobel Prize. As director of Bell Labs, made several discoveries and inventions, including the hearing aid.

Marriner S. Eccles 1890–1977

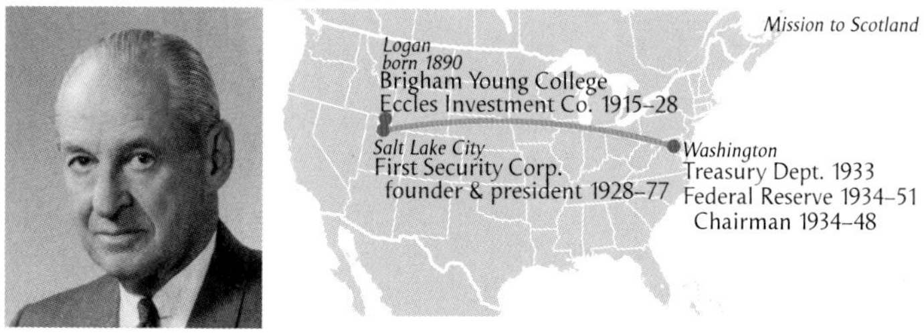

Banker and businessman, heir of timber magnate David Eccles. His success in forming First Security Corporation led to service as chairman of the Federal Reserve; he later helped create the World Bank.

Ernest L. Wilkinson 1899–1978

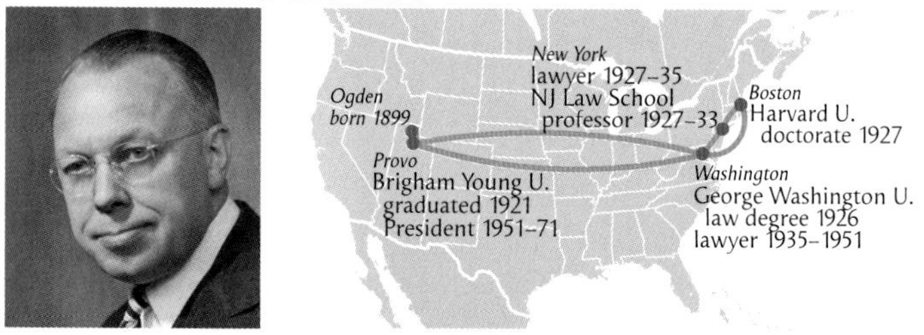

Lawyer. Represented Native Americans in landmark claims suit, president of Brigham Young University and commissioner of LDS Education (see p. 142), unsuccessfully ran for Senate.

J. Willard Marriott 1900–1985

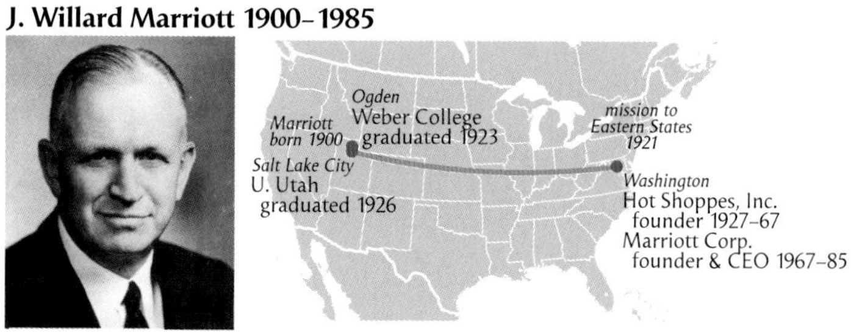

Entrepreneur. Turned Hot Shoppes restaurant chain into a major hospitality empire, including Marriott Hotels. A major donor to Brigham Young University and the University of Utah.

John K. Edmunds 1900–1989

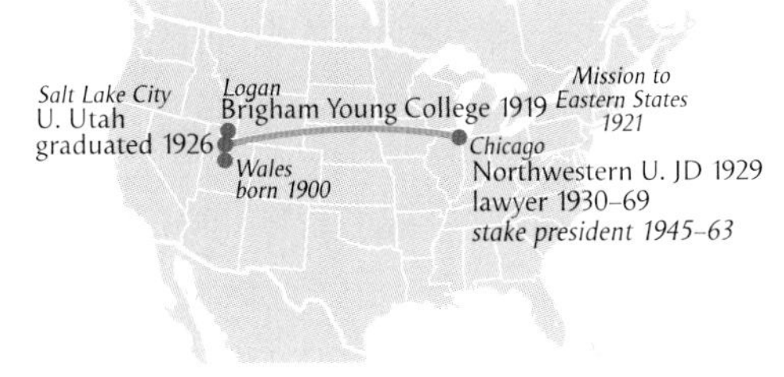

Lawyer. Primary leader of the Church in Chicago for many years. Edmunds, McAllister, and Marriott served missions together. In his retirement, served as president of the Southern California Mission and the Salt Lake Temple.

Henry Eyring 1901–1981

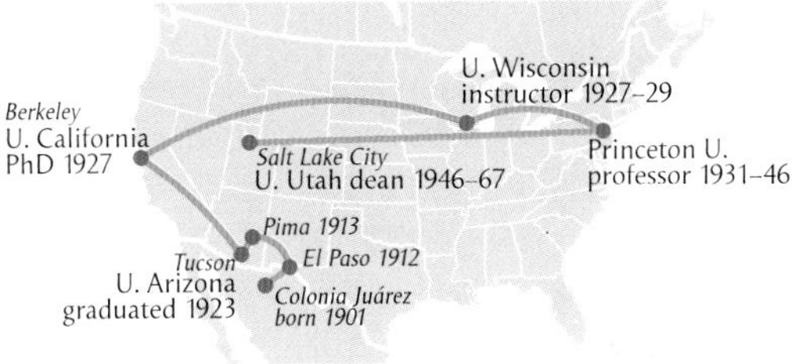

Theoretical chemist. Made several award-winning discoveries and published more than 600 papers. A brother-in-law of Spencer W. Kimball, his son Henry B. Eyring became a Counselor in the LDS First Presidency.

Howard Stoddard 1901–1971

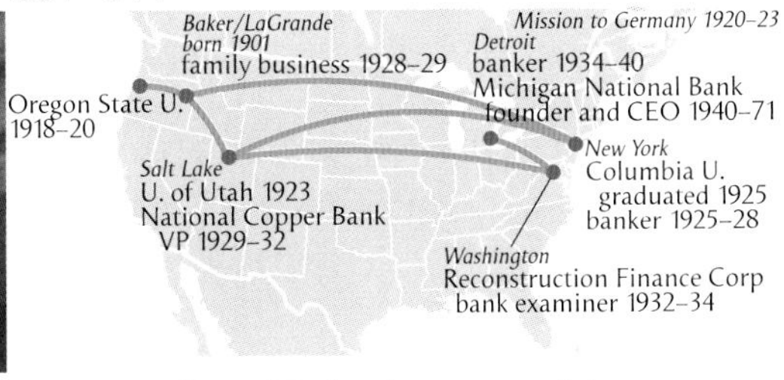

Banker, his father was a partner of David Eccles. As an agent of the government Reconstruction Finance Corporation, he helped Detroit banks survive the Depression, then merged several to form the Michigan National Bank.

H. Taylor Peery 1901–1964

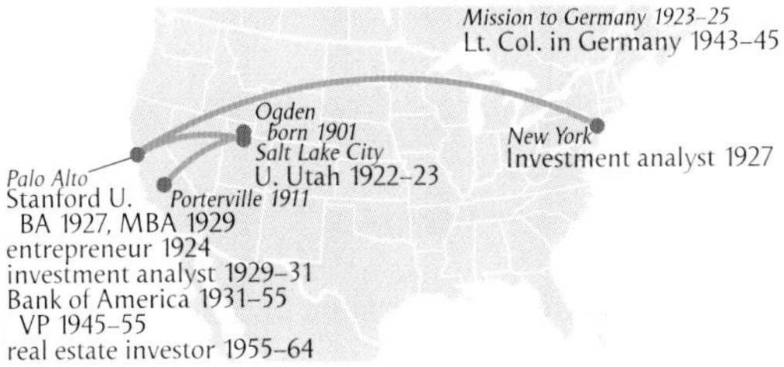

Businessman and financier. Eventually becoming vice president of Bank of America. He left to start a real estate investment company, which has become one of the largest in the Bay Area.

Harold F. Silver 1901–1984

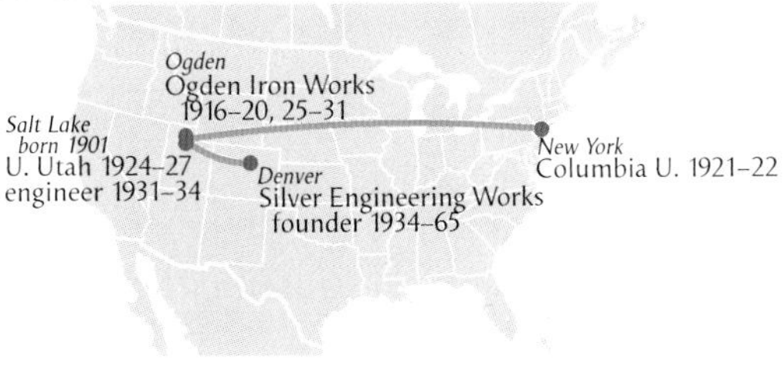

Engineer. Invented several machines for the sugar industry and mining. Founded a machinery and metals distribution company. Civic and Church leader in Denver.

David M. Kennedy 1905–1996

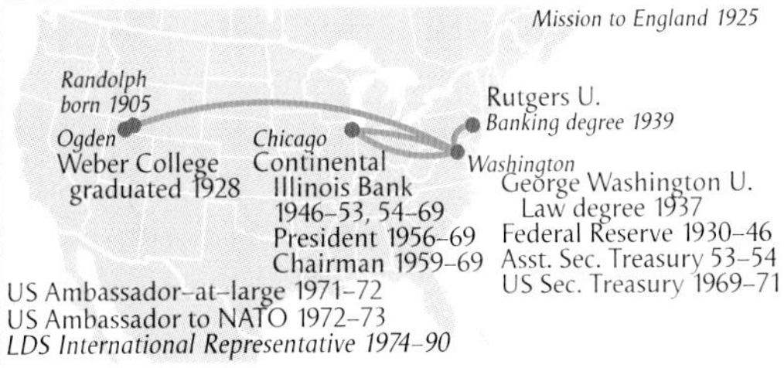

Bank executive and Lawyer. Served as Richard Nixon's Secretary of the Treasury, until asked by President Spencer W. Kimball to serve as a special international ambassador for the Church (see p. 166).

George Albert Smith Jr. 1905–1969

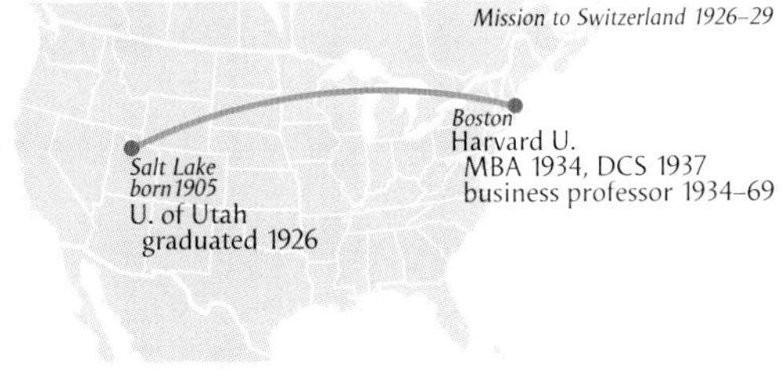

Business professor, son of the prophet. First LDS professor at Harvard, major contributor to management practice, pioneering the field of business ethics. Leader of the Church in the Boston area.

Esther Peterson 1906–1997

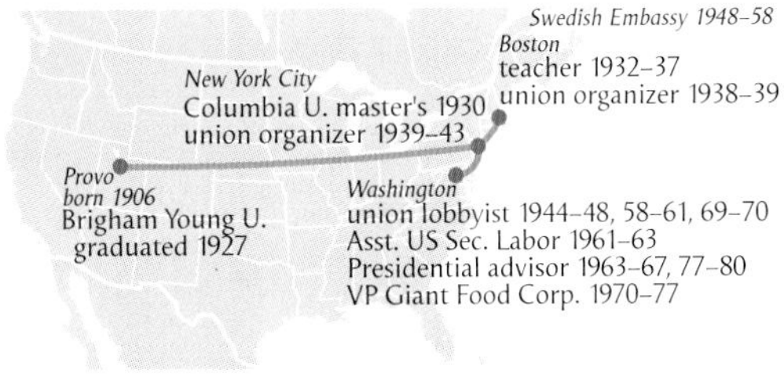

Starting as a teacher, she became a major advocate of women and a leader in the union movement. Served as Jimmy Carter's main consumer advocate, receiving the Presidential Medal of Freedom.

George W. Romney 1907–1995

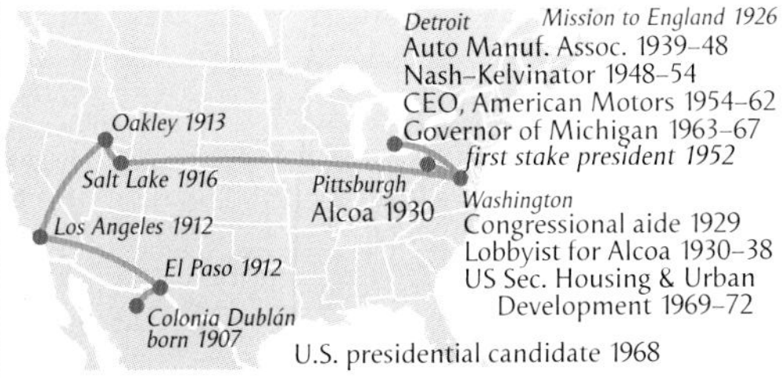

Businessman. Worked in several jobs in manufacturing until becoming CEO of American Motors in 1954. Governor of Michigan, Richard Nixon's Secretary of Housing & Urban Development, and ran for U.S. president in 1968.

Roy Oscarson 1909–1996

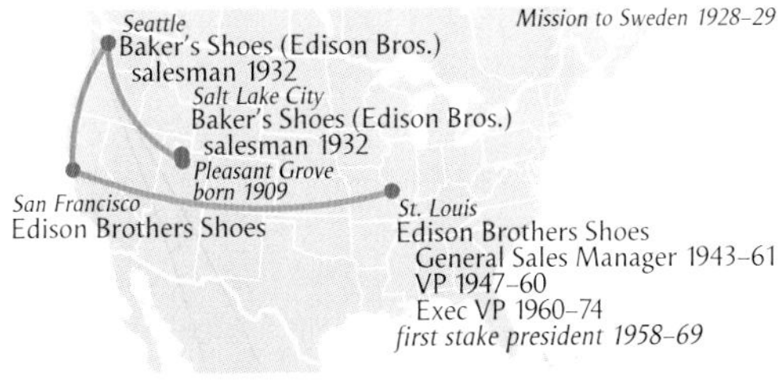

Businessman. Started as a shoe salesman, eventually becoming the executive vice president of Edison Brothers Shoes. Respected community leader and first president of the St. Louis Stake.

Welfare and Humanitarian Aid

1936–present

Latter-day Saints have taken care of the poor and needy from the very beginning. This desire springs from scriptural teachings such as "they did impart of their substance . . . to the poor" (Alma 1:27). Starting in 1931, bishops were tasked with redistributing tithing-in-kind (donations of farm products from members) to the poor, orphans, and widows through local bishop's storehouses. During the late nineteenth century, the Relief Society (see p. 102) also took on the responsibility for providing charitable aid, including the storage of grain and the building of hospitals.

During the 1930s, the suffering of the Great Depression led many bishops and stake presidents to institute more extensive programs in their own congregations. In the Salt Lake Valley, the Pioneer, Liberty, Granite, Grant, and Cottonwood stakes all created independent activities to assist their needy members. Drawing upon the experiences of these stake presidents, the Church formally organized the Church Security Plan for the entire membership in 1936.

The Plan (soon renamed the Welfare Program) initially focused on basic survival, providing food, clothing, and shelter. Members donated cash through monthly fast offerings and time working on farms owned by local congregations (thus providing the food that had earlier been donated directly). During the early years, welfare efforts (both contributions of labor and money, and disbursements of money and goods) were concentrated in the Intermountain West, where there were sufficient resources and needs. Soon the scope of the Welfare Program expanded to include broader goals, such as education, employment, health, and mental and spiritual strength. These goals were accomplished through the disbursement of money to needy members by their local leaders, but also through an expanding network of welfare-related facilities, including bishops' storehouses, Deseret Industries thrift stores, social services offices, and hospitals. Throughout this evolution the emphasis was on self-reliance, encouraging LDS families to prepare themselves for unforeseen troubles so they would not be dependent on long-term aid. In fact, during the New Deal era, the Church often proudly reported the number of members who had stopped receiving government aid.

continued on page 150

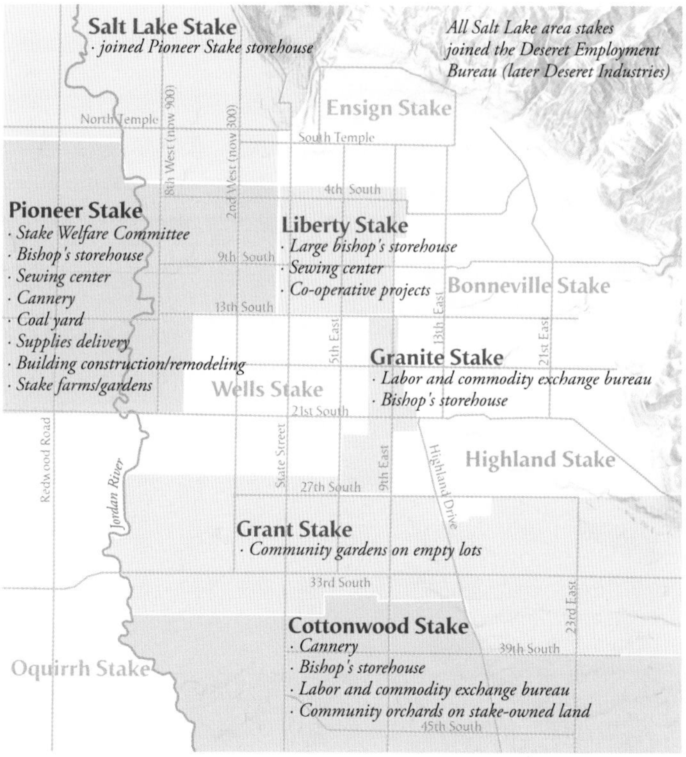

Pre-1936 Welfare Efforts

As the Great Depression left thousands of Church members in need, several stakes in Salt Lake County developed programs to aid their poorest members. Unemployed members and volunteer neighbors worked together to raise and prepare food, build and maintain homes, distribute fuel, and redistribute donated clothing and other goods. The most extensive and fully developed effort was in Pioneer Stake in Salt Lake City. Harold B. Lee, its stake president who would later become President of the Church, led this very successful program during the Great Depression, and in 1936, was asked to implement its best aspects Churchwide.

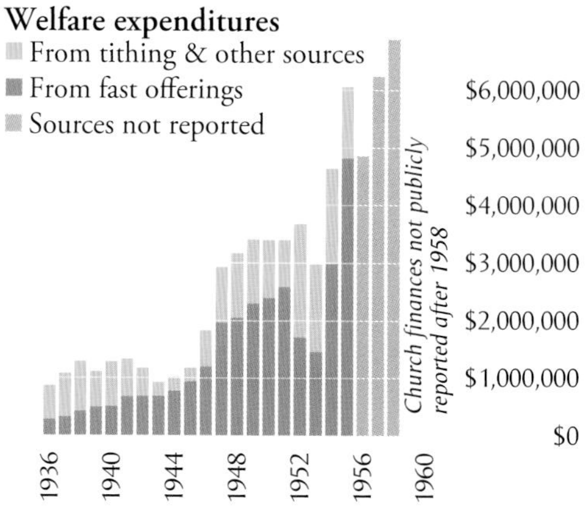

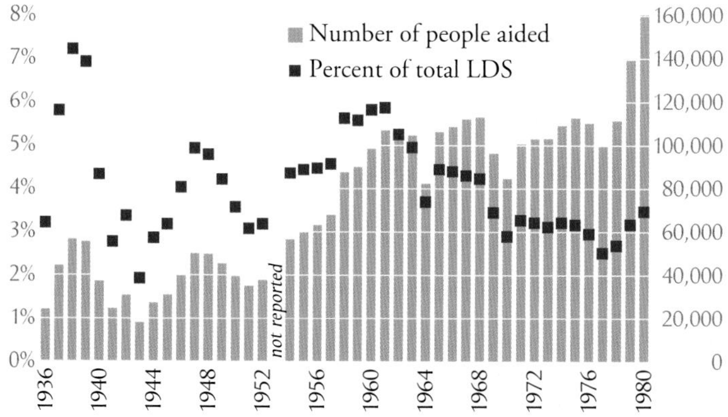

Welfare Operations in the Early Years

Over the years, the amount of assistance provided by the Welfare Program has varied significantly. Major increases came at the beginning, as the program's resources caught up with the needs of members, and after World War II when massive aid was provided to Europe. Fast offerings, donations given by members while fasting on the first Sunday of the month, were intended to fund the program, but during the early years, it was always subsidized by tithing funds. As the Church has grown, so have the needs and resources of the Welfare Program, although the proportion of the members receiving assistance declined from 1960 until the Church stopped publicly reporting welfare statistics in 1981.

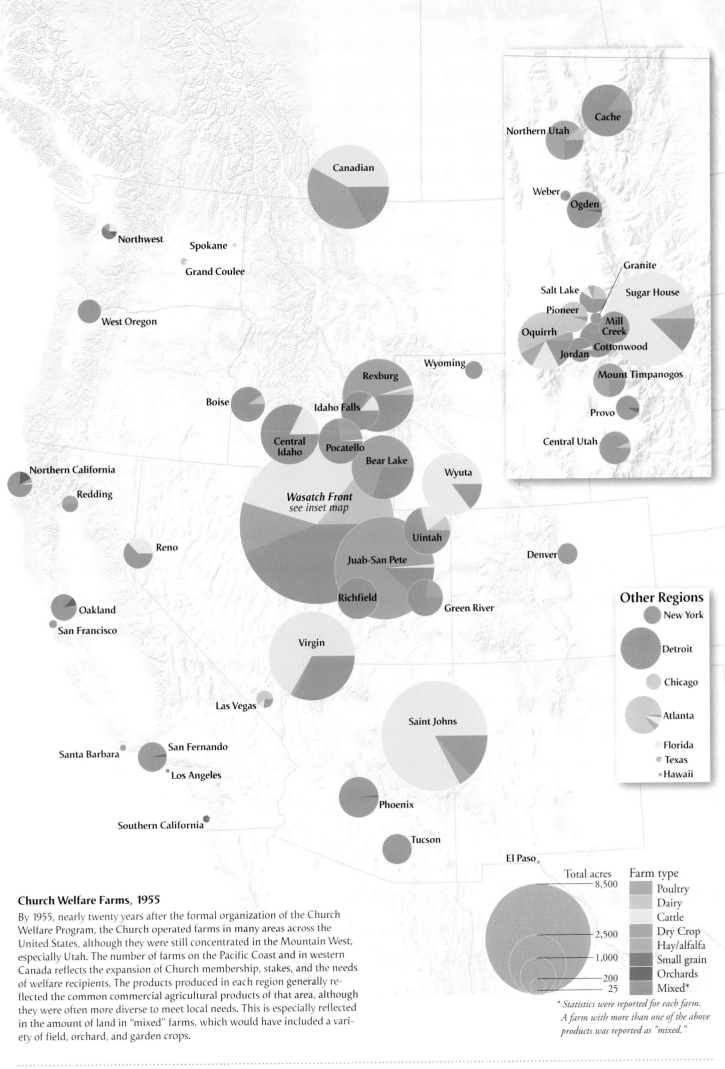

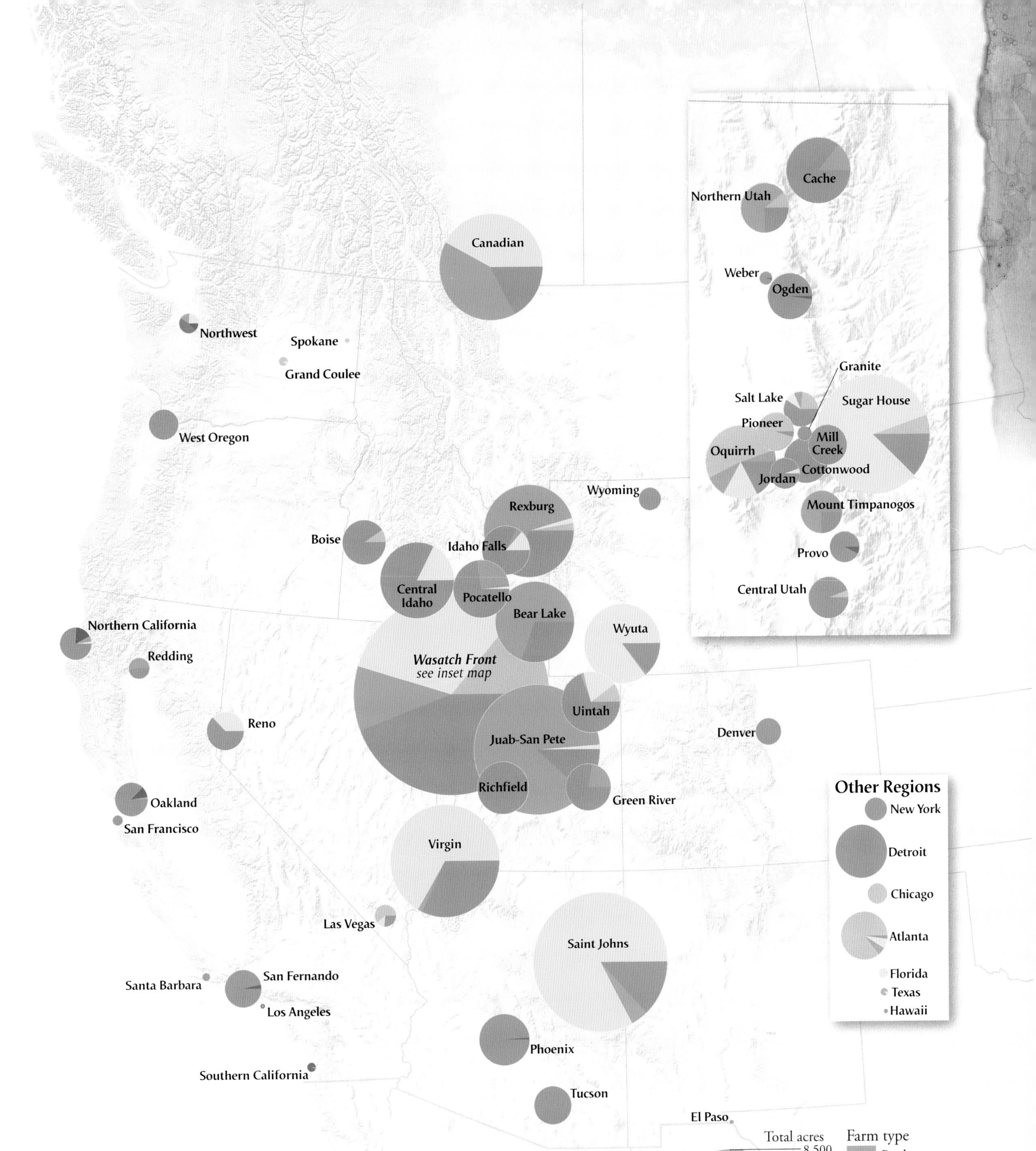

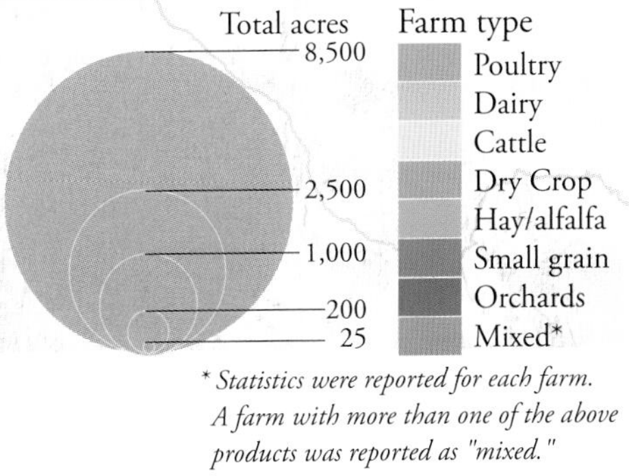

Church Welfare Farms, 1955

By 1955, nearly twenty years after the formal organization of the Church Welfare Program, the Church operated farms in many areas across the United States, although they were still concentrated in the Mountain West, especially Utah. The number of farms on the Pacific Coast and in western Canada reflects the expansion of Church membership, stakes, and the needs of welfare recipients. The products produced in each region generally reflected the common commercial agricultural products of that area, although they were often more diverse to meet local needs. This is especially reflected in the amount of land in "mixed" farms, which would have included a variety of field, orchard, and garden crops.

Welfare and Humanitarian Aid

continued

As the incomes of members increased during the postwar economic boom, so did charitable donations. These increasing resources enabled the Church to expand its aid efforts around the world, well beyond its own membership, by creating the Humanitarian Services Division. This organization has facilitated the distribution of emergency supplies to disaster-stricken countries throughout the world, to LDS members and others alike. Temporary shelters, food, water and medical supplies have been provided in rapid response. In transporting this aid, the Church has often entered into partnerships with other aid organizations such as the Red Cross, Catholic Relief Services, and Islamic Relief. Humanitarian aid has also been provided by service missionaries who assist with projects to meet sanitary, agricultural, and medical needs in the poorest countries of the world, helping them to become self-reliant as well.

Donald Q. Cannon and James B. Mayfield

Hospitals

The Church began building hospitals for two reasons: an act of charity to take care of the sick who could not afford health care, especially the elderly and children who needed long-term care; and because the governments and the economy of Utah did not have sufficient resources to provide secular public health services. Thus, it was initially seen (and funded) as part of the Welfare Program. Early efforts were not centrally organized: some facilities were built by the Relief Society (see p. 102) or the Primary, but gradually a coordinated system emerged. By the 1970s, the Health Services Corporation was a large, self-sufficient organization, when the Church decided it could serve its international membership better through humanitarian aid and service missionaries than physical hospitals. In 1975, the 15 hospitals were divested into a new, independent nonprofit company called Intermountain Health Care (IHC).

■ before 1900
■ ● 1905–1924
■ ● 1943–1953
● 1959–1973
purchased or managed
built by the Church
○ Divested before 1975

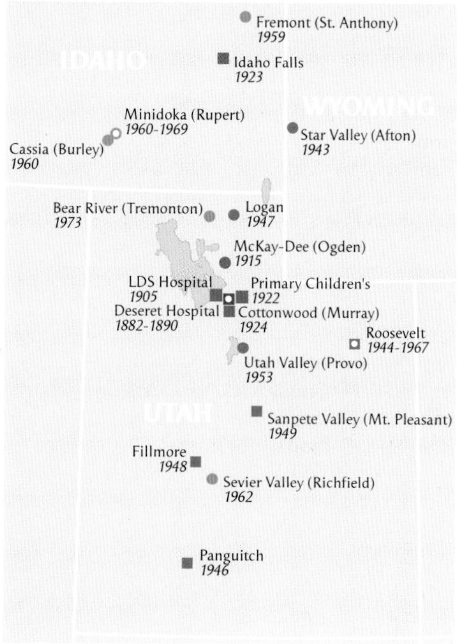

Church Humanitarian Aid projects have aided people around the world without regard for religious affiliation. In cases of natural disasters such as earthquakes, tsunamis, floods, hurricanes, etc., the Church has provided emergency relief including food, clothing, blankets, tents, medical supplies, water, and other basic survival supplies. Humanitarian aid missionaries have also helped people in poor countries better provide for their critical needs, such as water infrastructure and improved agricultural practices. Projects tend to be concentrated in areas with significant numbers of members who can volunteer, in regions where the Church wants to improve its image, or in areas where the Church can easily partner with other aid organizations.

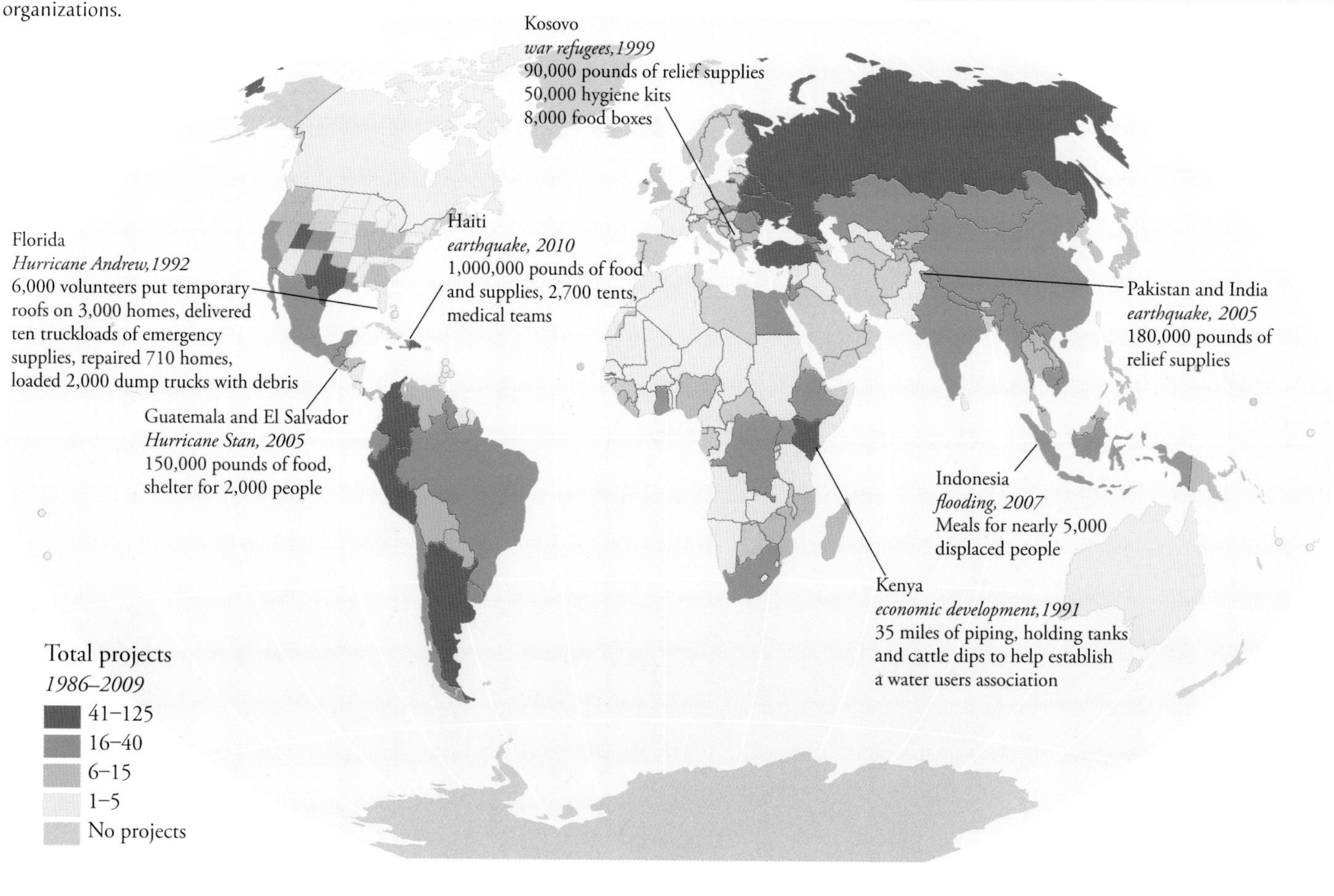

Welfare Farms in Utah County

In 1974, at about the height of traditional welfare farm operations, Utah County had extensive welfare farmlands. In fact, many stakes in the Salt Lake Valley had their stake farms here. Most of the farms were small plots scattered throughout the urban area. The most common products were alfalfa, dairy, orchards, and livestock.

As the population grew, the Church realized that the real estate value of the smaller properties was much higher than their agricultural value, and has systematically sold them to developers (reserving needed space for meetinghouses, of course). These profits could then be used to purchase properties adjacent to larger farms that could be run more efficiently with professional farmers (especially as new generations of local members had no farming skills). For the same reason, much of the Church's welfare properties are now leased to private farmers, and the proceeds are used to purchase bulk food for the Welfare Program. This increase in efficiency has allowed the Church to serve more people worldwide.

- 1979 Church lands sold by 2010
- 1979 Church lands still owned in 2010
- Land acquired 1979–2010

- 40 acres
- 160 acres
- 640 acres (1 sq mi)

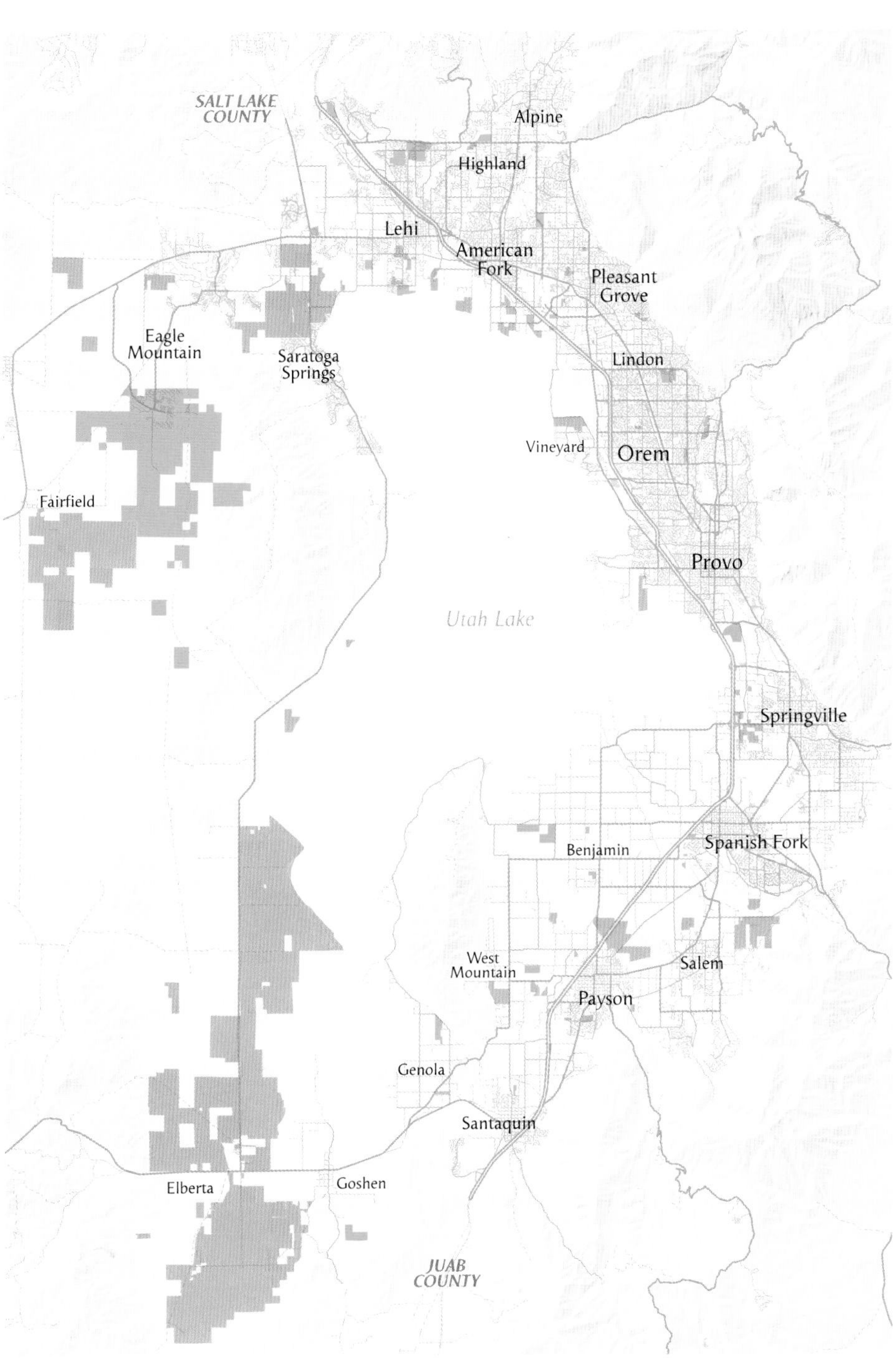

Church Welfare Timeline

1831 Edward Partridge called as first bishop, not to preside over a congregation but to administer the Law of Consecration

1831 First Bishop's Storehouse established in Independence, Missouri

1842 Relief Society organized; a major part of its mission is to care for the poor

1849 Church Public Works Department employs members in building Utah infrastructure

1850–1923 Tithing yards in each settlement redistribute tithing-in-kind to the poor

1882–90 Relief Society runs the Deseret Hospital

1890s Deseret Employment Bureau created

1914–18 Relief Society grain storage donated to the war effort

1919 Relief Society Social Services Committee created; now LDS Family Services, a semi-independent organization

1932–1936 Independent efforts by wards and stakes to mitigate effects of the Great Depression

1936 Church Security Plan established

1938 Renamed Church Welfare Program; Welfare Square constructed; Deseret Industries created to provide employment and training

1946 Apostle Ezra Taft Benson oversees massive aid distribution in postwar Europe

1959 Welfare Department organized

1971 Welfare Service Missionaries (humanitarian aid)

1975 Church divests its hospital system

1985 Humanitarian Services created to provide aid beyond Church membership

1996 Latter-day Saint Charities formed as an independent nonprofit organization

1830 1845 1860 1875 1890 1905 1920 1935 1950 1965 1980 1995 2010

Genealogy

1894–present

Anciently, the Assyrians, Chinese, Egyptians, Greeks, Romans, Pacific Islanders, and many others have been interested in tracing their lineage. It has also been popular among Americans since Benjamin Franklin and George Washington. Starting with the New England Historic Genealogical Society (NEHGS), many genealogical societies were organized in the United States during the nineteenth century, which typically focused on particular regions, events, or ethnic groups. One of the largest of these has been the Genealogical Society of Utah (GSU), founded by The Church of Jesus Christ of Latter-day Saints in Salt Lake City in 1894. The Church saw the Society and the Genealogical Library it created as crucial parts of its mission because members desired to perform saving ordinances on behalf of their ancestors.

Although the initial collections of the library included mostly books, the growth of the materials expanded in the 1930s when the GSU began using the new technology of microfilming. Beginning in the eastern United States, this project expanded internationally to include not only microfilming but also digitizing genealogical records. The GSU began microfilming records in England in 1945 and continued filming records in other European countries.

Now under the jurisdiction of the Family History Department (commonly known as FamilySearch), the Family History Library is the largest genealogical research library in the world. The present building was dedicated in 1985. In addition, the Church has established over 4,500 satellite family history centers in more than 88 countries, typically located in local meetinghouses. These small centers have limited collections of loaned microfilm copies but full access to the library's digital resources.

Starting in the 1990s, the Family History Department increasingly focused on digital databases, which can be distributed and accessed much more easily than microfilm. First distributed on CD-ROM, then via the Internet using the FamilySearch.org website, the digital collections of the Family History Library (including both scanned images of original documents and databases of information extracted therefrom) reference hundreds of millions of deceased individuals; when the microfilm collection is fully digitized, that number is expected to top 3 billion people.

Today, more people are interested in tracing their ancestry than ever before. Greater advancements in computer technology and the Internet make research easier, more widely available, and more rewarding. The Genealogical Society of Utah, FamilySearch, and Family History Library in Salt Lake City are helping people to achieve their family history goals.

Kip Sperry

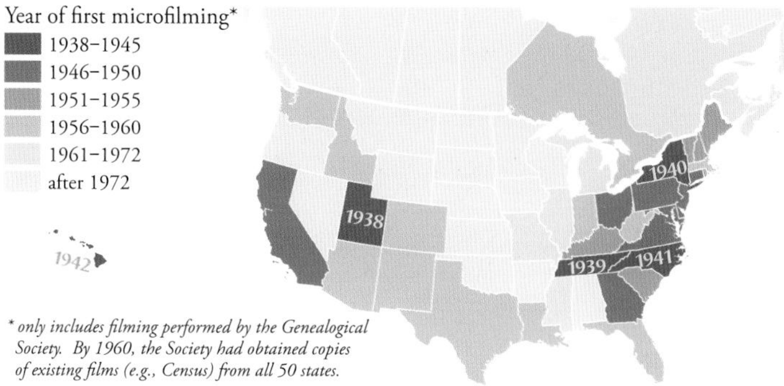

Early Microfilming

With the emphasis for Latter-day Saints to search out their own ancestors, the Genealogical Society of Utah realized that it was not practical for members to visit every locality and foreign country where their ancestors lived. James M. Black championed the new technology of microfilming as a means for one library to contain the information of many libraries. After some initial experiments, the Society began microfilming genealogical and historical records, starting with the Church's own records, then focusing on states that were amenable to copying and states that were the ancestral homes of many Church members (mostly in the eastern United States). Churches and local governments were the most common sources of records, often under agreements for the Society to give them copies of the films. The microfilm collection quickly grew to several thousand rolls.

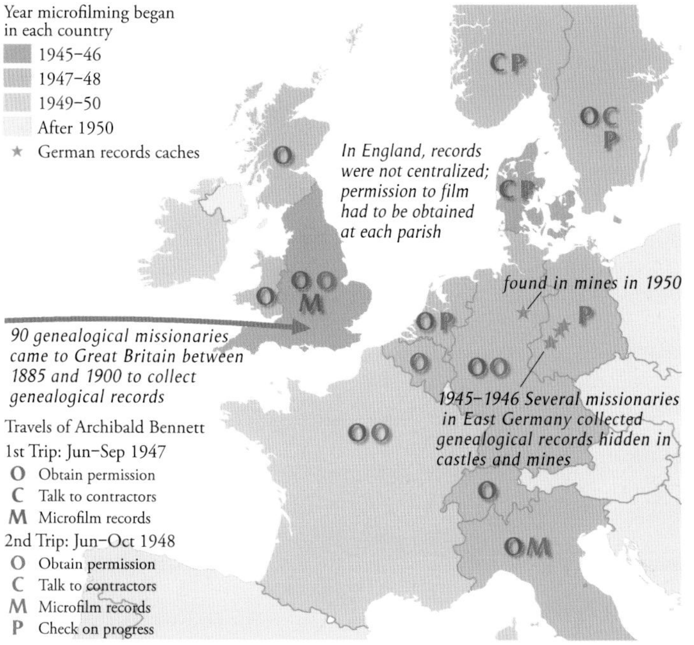

Preserving European Records

After the success of microfilming in the United States, the focus turned to records in foreign countries. After World War II, Archibald Bennett of the Genealogical Society of Utah led a cadre of missionaries into Europe to locate records and secure permission to film them. They found an abundance of records as well as officials understandably interested in preserving their history from destruction. Ironically, Adolf Hitler, in his obsession with ethnic purity, had required German churches to send copies of their records to Berlin; hidden in mines and castles, they were spared the ravages of war that destroyed many of the churches and their original records. An emphasis was first placed on church records, such as parish registers and civil registrations (births, marriages, and deaths), but many other record types have also been filmed. The initial focus was on regions from which many Mormon converts had emigrated, such as Switzerland, the British Isles, the Netherlands, and Scandinavia; gradually, focus has spread to the rest of Europe.

Worldwide Expansion of Microfilming

The Genealogical Society gradually expanded its microfilming efforts into Latin America (Mexico, 1952), the Pacific (Australia and New Zealand, 1959), and more recently, Asia and Africa. This expansion mirrored the global expansion of the Church, with its members eager to discover their ancestors to perform temple ordinances for them. As before, microfilming focused on Church records (parish registers) and civil registration (births, marriages, and deaths) but also other available records. Microfilming was largely carried out by specifically called missionaries, mostly couples. For the last several years, microfilm has been replaced by digital cameras for acquiring new records (and microfilm records are being scanned), since digital images are more easily accessible on the Internet. To make the names on these images searchable, the Church has recruited hundreds of thousands of volunteer indexers (including both Mormons and non-Mormons) to read and record the information on the images into a massive database.

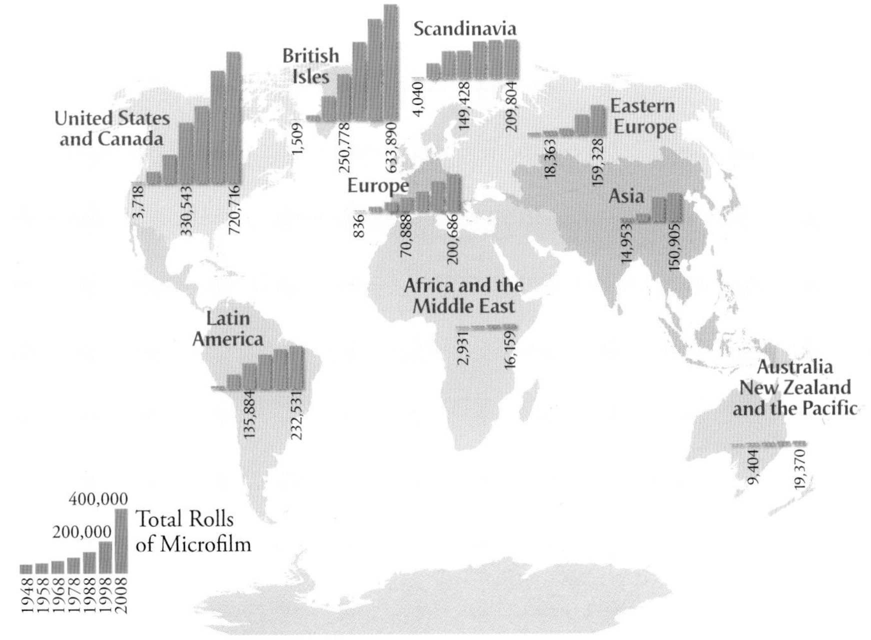

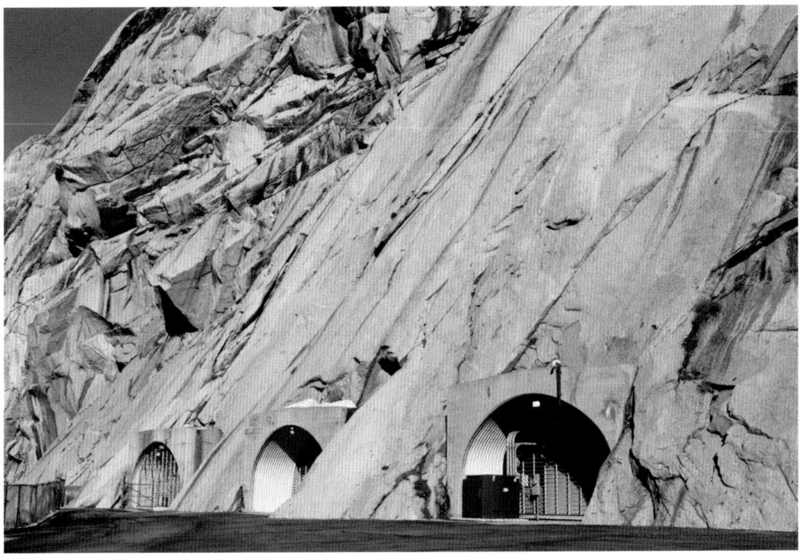

Granite Mountain Records Vault

Built into a cliff near Salt Lake City in 1965, the Granite Mountain Records Vault provides an extremely safe, climate-controlled environment for long-term storage of almost 3 million rolls of microfilm, microfiche, and other records.

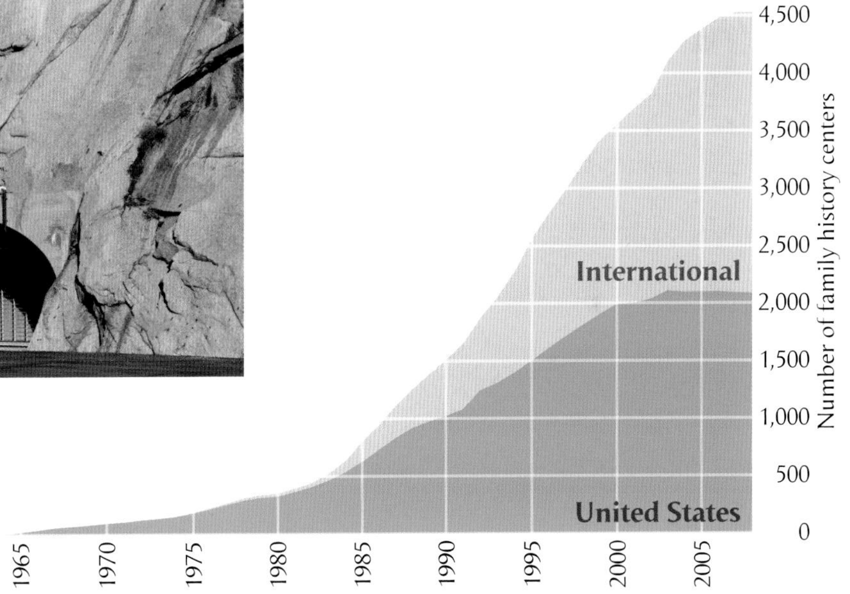

Family History Centers

Aware that many people could not travel to Salt Lake City to search for their ancestors, the LDS Church created branch genealogical libraries to bring library services to members and friends elsewhere, the first being in the Harold B. Lee Library at Brigham Young University, Provo, Utah. Later renamed family history centers, over 4,500 facilities are now located throughout the United States and in over 80 countries, typically housed within LDS meetinghouses.

Recently, smaller branch libraries have been combined into larger regional FamilySearch Centers in places like Riverton, St. George, Ogden, and Logan, Utah; Los Angeles, California; and Mesa, Arizona.

These centers were most valuable for the microfilm copies patrons could loan from the massive collection, but since 1990, services have expanded to digital resources (first on CD-ROM and now online) and education.

Genealogy and the Church

1894 Genealogical Society of Utah formed as a semi-independent auxiliary organization with a small research library

1933 Genealogical Library opens in former LDS University in downtown Salt Lake City

1938 Microfilming begins with LDS records

1963 First (and still largest) branch genealogical library opened in Provo

1965 Granite Mountain Records Vault opened in Little Cottonwood Canyon near Salt Lake City

1975 Genealogical Department folded into Church administration

1985 Family History Library

1987 Renamed Family History Department

2000 FamilySearch website

2000 Family History Dept. merges with Church History Dept.

1890 1910 1930 1950 1970 1990 2010

Specialized Congregations

1947–present

CONGREGATIONS IN The Church of Jesus Christ of Latter-day Saints have strict geographical boundaries to which members are assigned. However, some members have challenges worshiping with the general congregation, typically due to differences in language, marital status, and culture. Under certain circumstances, specialized wards, branches, and even stakes have been created for these groups to worship together. However, separation has its disadvantages, so Church policies governing their creation have changed over the years.

Special units started in the mid-nineteenth century, including German-speaking congregations in Nauvoo and London, but were rare. At the height of immigration during 1890–1910, a number of foreign-language branches and newspapers were created in Salt Lake City, but by the 1940s, all but a Mexican branch had been discontinued as international converts were encouraged to build the Church in their homelands rather than immigrate.

Specialization increased elsewhere in the middle of the century. Missionary efforts in the western United States were expanding to Native Americans and Latinos, resulting in new language-based branches in several states. At Brigham Young University, the massive influx of post-war students overwhelmed local wards, leading to the formation of the first student branches that promoted leadership and participation.

However, by the early 1970s, many Church leaders questioned the policy of providing specialized wards and missions. Specialized wards provided better opportunities for leadership and community-building (and for singles, marriage), but hampered their integration into the larger Church, and some saw it as a stigma on those not part of the "ideal Mormon family." Many ethnic, language, and non-student singles units were consolidated into general wards that were asked to support their needs.

Unfortunately, many non-English speakers in the United States simply stopped attending Church. Since 1980, there has thus been a renewed increase in specialized units. One difficulty has been dealing with ethnic groups that originally spoke other languages, especially Polynesians and Native Americans, but are now predominantly English-speaking. Despite the Church's desire to not separate members on ethnicity alone, and despite the elimination of many of these units in the 1990s, some congregations have survived.

Recognizing the desire of the increasingly mobile members to worship in their native language, the Church has created branches for minority languages throughout the world. Since the 1960s, English-speaking wards and stakes have been created for American servicemen, students, and business executives stationed overseas, even in China and the Middle East.

Policies for singles wards have also changed back and forth at times. The first non-student singles ward was created in Salt Lake City in 1973. During the 1980s, a stake could create a ward for "Young Single Adults" (YSA, age 18–30) if it had 200 single members. Members returned to regular wards after they married or turned 31. These wards have become very common throughout the United States, as many as 10 percent of all congregations in some areas, possibly reflecting long-term shifts in the demographics of the Church. Starting in 2010, the student ward system has been gradually merged into the YSA wards to reduce confusion in cities where both types existed.

Dealing with multicultural groups creates a dilemma for the Church. While revelation states that "every man shall hear the fullness of the gospel in his own tongue, and in his own language," (D&C 90:11) the Church has encouraged integration so that members can become "fellow citizens with the saints" (Ephesians 2:19). These contrasting ideals have led to the changing policies concerning specialized wards.

Jessie L. Embry and A. LeGrand Richards

Special Congregations

- **1852** Danish and German Utah immigrants hold Church meetings in their native languages
- **1860** Karl G. Maeser called to preside over German meetings in Salt Lake City
- **1877** Non-English branches become part of the Salt Lake Stake
- **1892** First sunday school for the deaf started in Ogden, Utah
- **1917** First deaf branch created in Ogden
- **1918** Non-English wards in Salt Lake City discontinued during World War I
- **1925** Mexican Branch (later the Lucero Ward) created in Salt Lake City
- **1935** Creation of the Spanish American (Spanish-speaking) Mission in the American Southwest
- **1942** Dissolving of non-English speaking wards in Utah during World War II except the Mexican Branch
- **1943** Creation of the Navajo-Zuni Mission (later the Southwest Indian Mission)
- **1947** First student branches created at BYU
- **1956** First student stake created at BYU
- **1960–62** Creation of Japanese, German, Dutch, Swedish, Danish, two new Spanish-speaking, and two Native American wards and French, Mandarin, and Cantonese Sunday Schools in Salt Lake City
- **1970** End of Spanish-speaking missions in the United States, foreign-language missionaries part of general missions
- **1972** Dissolving of the Southwest Indian Mission and First Presidency letters to stake, ward, and branch leaders to be conscious of "racial, language, and cultural groups"
- **1973** First non-student singles ward created in Salt Lake City
- **1977** Basic Unit Plan facilitates small language and cultural branches

1850 1860 1870 1880 1890 1900 1910 1920 1930 1940 1950 1960 1970

Special Congregations in the United States

Determining the number of specialized units in the United States and the world is difficult since a separate count is not readily available to researchers, and specialized wards have not always been clearly identified in Church directories. That said, it is clear that the number of specialized/minority groups in the United States has grown during the 1980s, 1990s, and 2000s. While the largest concentrations are in Utah, the number has grown throughout the United States, especially as the Spanish-speaking population has grown. There were at least 500 foreign-language wards and branches in the United States by 1997, and at least two-thirds were Spanish-speaking. In several places there were also foreign-language stakes, among others, the five Spanish-speaking stakes in the Los Angeles area (see p. 184).

During the 1980s, Young Single Adult (YSA) wards appeared throughout the United States; due to 1990s policies, almost half of them disappeared (not including student wards). However, in recent years there has been a remarkable growth in YSA wards.

Spanish | Students, singles
Other languages* | Other specialties
esp. Polynesian, Asian | *deaf, military, care centers, prisons*

* *includes Native American congregations only in areas where the general wards speak English, not general wards on reservations that may speak native languages.*

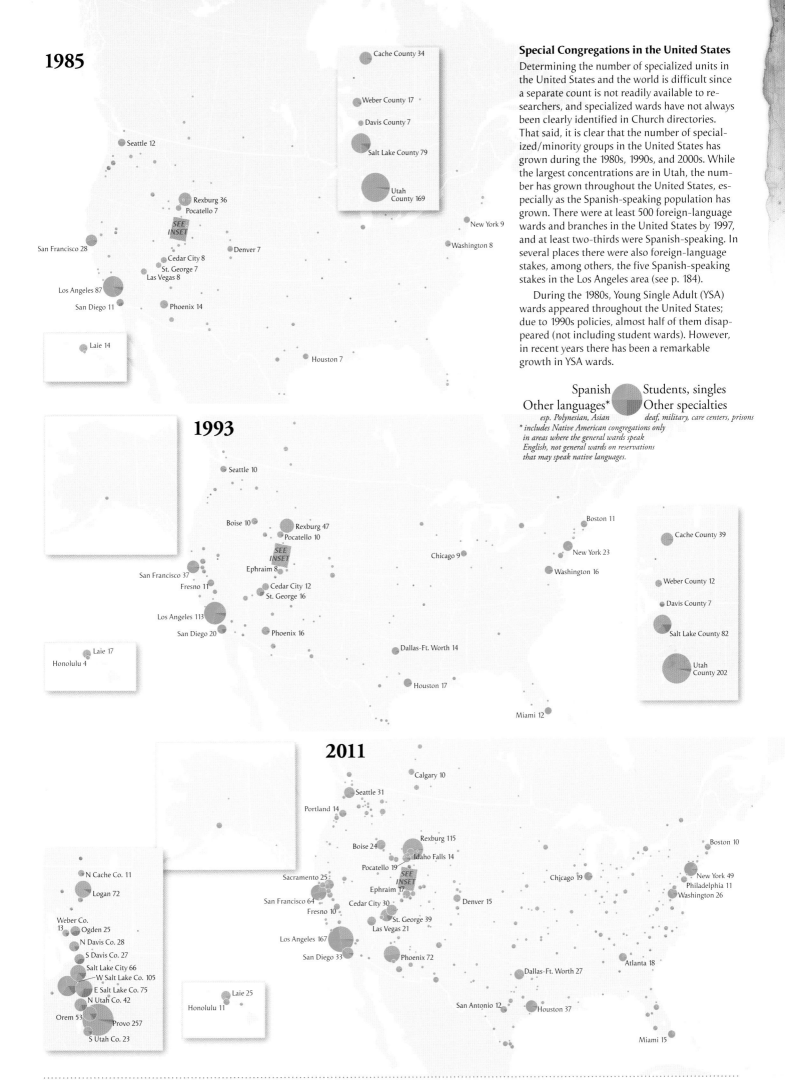

The Church in 1950

The LDS Church was in a major transition in 1950. Heber J. Grant and George Albert Smith, the first Presidents born in Utah, had focused most of their attention on the Intermountain West, even as members were migrating across the United States for education and employment. By the 100th anniversary of the pioneer trek in 1947, Church membership reached one million members, and growth was occurring as missionaries returned to Europe, Latin America, and the Pacific. World War II had led to a new presence for the Church in many countries, where American Mormon soldiers were stationed, even as members in Eastern Europe were cut off from communication with the Church behind the Iron Curtain. However, 92% of the members lived in the United States (an all-time high). President David O. McKay would soon change that by discouraging converts from immigrating to Utah, and focusing his attention on strengthening the presence of the Church around the world, both spiritually, through increased travel by him and the other General Authorities; and physically, through the construction of meetinghouses, stakes, and temples.

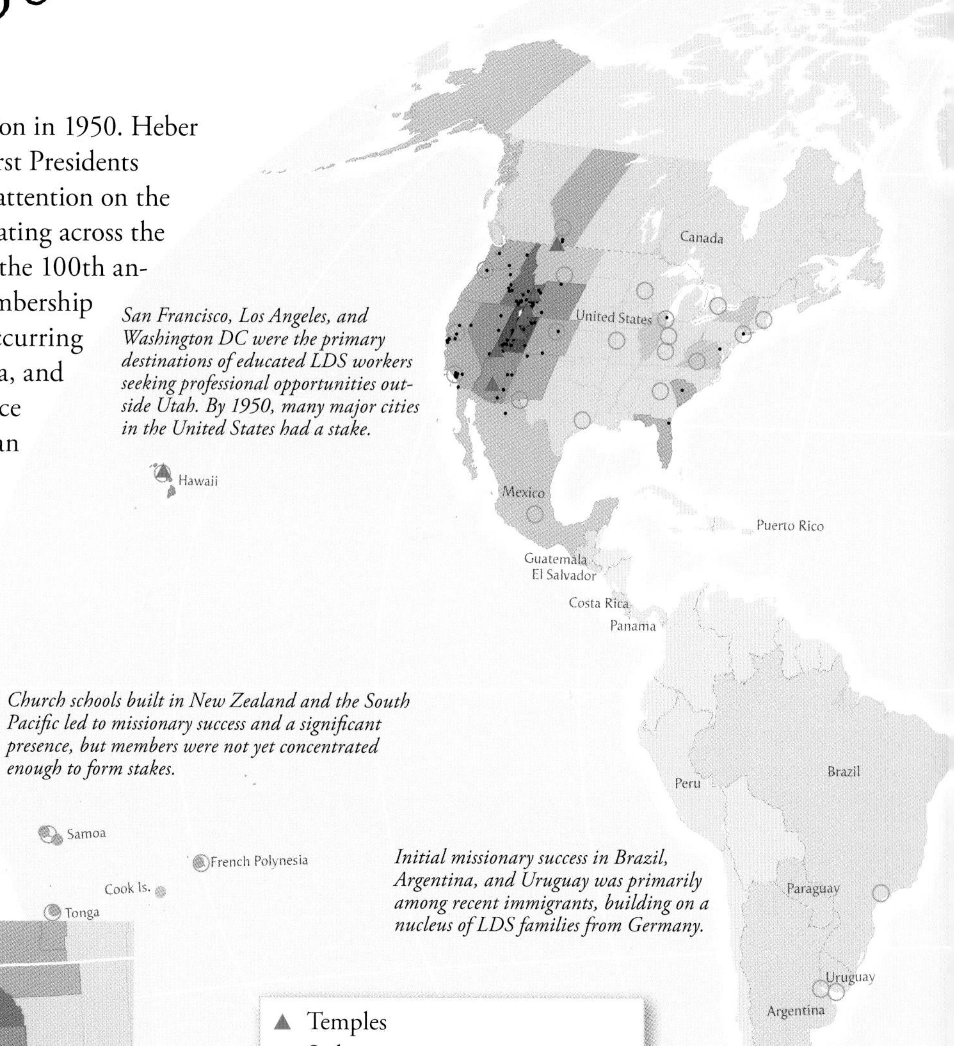

Canada
United States
Mexico
Hawaii
Puerto Rico
Guatemala
El Salvador
Costa Rica
Panama
Peru
Brazil
Samoa
French Polynesia
Cook Is.
Tonga
Paraguay
Uruguay
Argentina
San Francisco, Los Angeles, and Washington DC were the primary destinations of educated LDS workers seeking professional opportunities outside Utah. By 1950, many major cities in the United States had a stake.
Church schools built in New Zealand and the South Pacific led to missionary success and a significant presence, but members were not yet concentrated enough to form stakes.
Initial missionary success in Brazil, Argentina, and Uruguay was primarily among recent immigrants, building on a nucleus of LDS families from Germany.

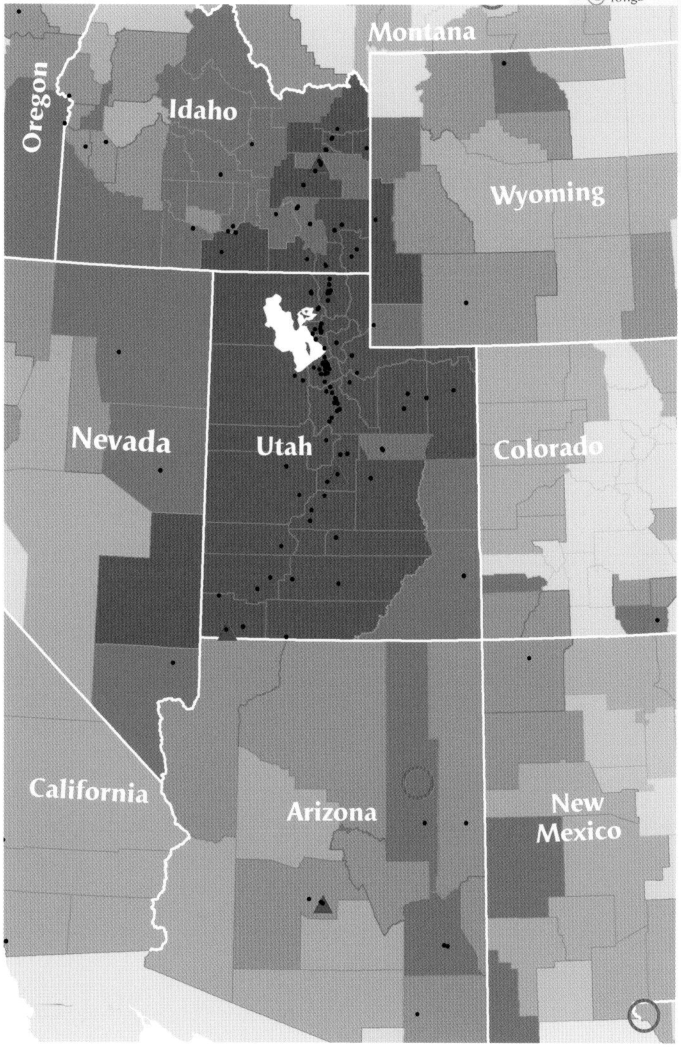

Montana
Oregon
Idaho
Wyoming
Nevada
Utah
Colorado
California
Arizona
New Mexico

▲ Temples
· Stakes
○ Missions

Membership
- Stage VI: Dominance
  The Church is the dominant cultural power, stakes in small villages, at least 50% LDS
- Stage V: Plurality
  LDS probably the largest denomination, a major influence, at least 1 LDS in 10
- Stage IV: Pervasive
  Most people personally know a Mormon, stakes cover the country, at least 1 LDS in 50
- Stage III: Widespread
  Wards and stakes in most cities, most people have heard of Mormons, at least 1 LDS in 500
- Stage II: Established
  Significant, permanent presence; has a stake in the largest cities, at least 1 LDS in 5,000
- Stage I: Pioneering
  Few members; branches but not stakes; legally open to missionaries
- Stage 0: Restricted
  Very few members, mostly expatriates; no proselytizing, usually restricted by law
- no Church presence

The Church Spreads

The Outmigration that had started in the 1920s included many families who moved from the traditional Mormon Cultural Region to non-Mormon cities throughout the Intermountain West, including Boise, Denver, and Phoenix. At the same time, missionaries finally found success in the region, leading to an established minority presence in both urban and rural areas throughout the West.

Iceland
Norway
Sweden
Finland
United Kingdom
Denmark
Ireland
Netherlands
East Germany
Poland
Belgium
West Germany
Czechoslovakia
France
Austria
Switzerland
Hungary
Italy
Greece
Syria
Lebanon
Israel
Japan
Hong Kong
Philippines
Northern Rhodesia
Southern Rhodesia
Southwest Africa
South Africa
Basutoland
Australia
New Zealand
Fiji
Many Eastern European members, primarily German, lost contact with the Church with the beginning of the Cold War in the late 1940s.
David O. McKay ended LDS emigration from Western Europe by building temples, meetinghouses, and stakes to create a lasting, visible establishment.
After World War II, missionaries returned to Japan (after a 24 year hiatus) and Hong Kong (after 96 years). This time they were more successful.

Growth in the mid-Twentieth Century

1918 Heber J. Grant, 7th President of the Church

1919 Hawaii Temple dedicated

1923 Cardston Alberta Temple dedicated
First stake outside Mormon cultural area, Los Angeles

1925 Missionary work officially begins in South America

1927 Mesa Temple dedicated
Membership reaches 500,000

1933 Last of academies sold, closed, or converted to colleges

1934 First modern stake in eastern U.S., New York

1935 First stake outside North America, Laie Hawaii

Idaho Falls Temple dedicated **1945**
George Albert Smith, 8th President of the Church

Church membership reaches 1 million **1947**

Missionaries return to Hong Kong for first time since 1853 **1950**

1951 David O. McKay, 9th President of the Church

1955 Swiss Temple dedicated

1958 New Zealand & London Temples dedicated

1960–62 Surge in baptisms in Europe

1961 First non-English stake, The Hague, Netherlands
First Latin American stake, Mexico City, Mexico

1963 Membership reaches 2 million

First stake in South America, São Paulo, Brazil **1966**

First regional representatives called **1967**

1915 1920 1925 1930 1935 1940 1945 1950 1955 1960 1965

David O. McKay

1880–1970

NEAR THE END OF HIS LIFE David O. McKay was asked by a reporter what he felt his most important accomplishment had been as Church President. He replied, "The making of the Church a world-wide organization." President McKay began several initiatives to acheive this mission shortly after he became President in 1951, but the seeds were planted over the decades during which he became the most-traveled General Authority to date.

Until his call to serve a full-time mission to Scotland in 1897, McKay had not ventured outside his home state of Utah. Two years in a foreign country exposed him to harsh realities that he had never encountered previously: weak local leadership; infighting within fledgling congregations; rented, often shoddy meeting facilities; and overt hostility toward the Church. He experienced the same conditions in his 1920–21 voyage around the world as an Apostle, and again as European Mission president. The lessons never left him, and over a half-century later, upon becoming Church President, he addressed each.

As President, he was able to take many journeys to strengthen the far-flung areas of the Church. Perhaps the most important trip was in 1954. Responding to pleas from the president of the South African Mission, who noted that in the century since the mission was founded not a single General Authority had ever visited it, McKay embarked on a journey to Europe, Africa, and South America. He was particularly concerned about the lack of local leadership in South Africa, a condition brought about by the Church's recent tightening of a policy that required documentation of exclusively European (i.e., non-black-African) ancestry of local men prior to priesthood ordination. Speaking to a conference of missionaries he said, "To observe conditions as they are was one of the reasons that I wished to take this trip." He abolished the requirement of genealogical documentation, while leaving intact the overall policy forbidding ordination of men whose black African ancestry was not in doubt. Even that policy came under scrutiny; eventually, McKay came to a realization that it had little doctrinal support, but awaited a direct revelation to change it; this revelation came eight years after his death, but its antecedents clearly reside in the 1954 trip to South Africa.

The importance of his travels was enormous, leading to temples in Switzerland, England, and New Zealand, the first constructed by the Church outside North America; the Church College of Hawaii (now BYU–Hawaii) and secondary schools in the South Pacific (see p. 140); the Polynesian Cultural Center, which became the leading tourist attraction in the Hawaiian Islands; a worldwide program of chapel construction (see p. 160); and an initiative of personal and institutional diplomacy that largely erased the negative image in which the international Church had been cast for over a century. He did not exaggerate in noting that "the making of the Church a world-wide organization" was the hallmark of his administration.

Gregory A. Prince

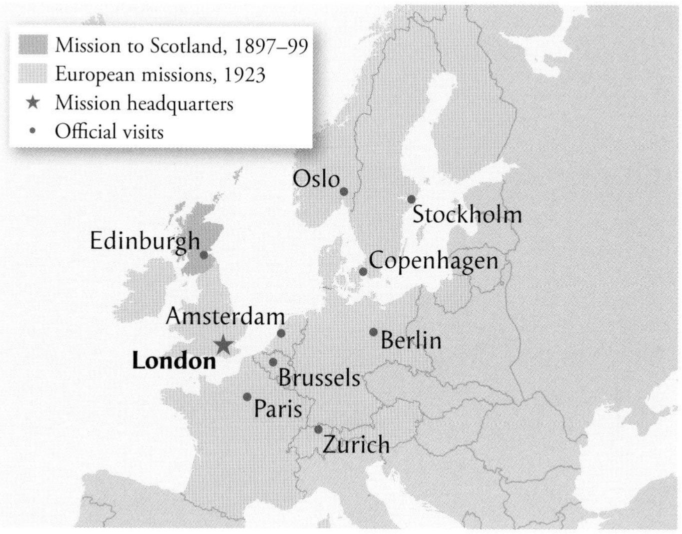
Mission to Scotland, 1897–99
European missions, 1923
★ Mission headquarters
• Official visits
Oslo
Stockholm
Edinburgh
Copenhagen
Amsterdam
Berlin
London
Brussels
Paris
Zurich

European Mission

One year after completing his around-the-world trip, McKay was assigned to preside over the European Mission. During the two years he spent in Europe, he held over 500 meetings with missionaries and local members throughout most of western Europe. In the process, he gained a deep understanding of the conditions holding back the development of a mature Church. Meeting facilities continued to be deplorable. Senator Smoot, accompanying McKay to meetings in Copenhagen, noted the poor conditions: "Headquarters back of a saloon . . . why do we also get in such poor locations and undesirable parts of the cities[?] . . . Some day this present policy will be exchanged and the sooner the better." Several weeks later McKay conveyed the same sentiment in a letter to the First Presidency: "The crying need of this mission is more respectable buildings in which to hold services." In addition, he saw a level of vitriol towards the Church that exceeded what he had experienced a quarter-century earlier, and that would require direct attention to reverse.

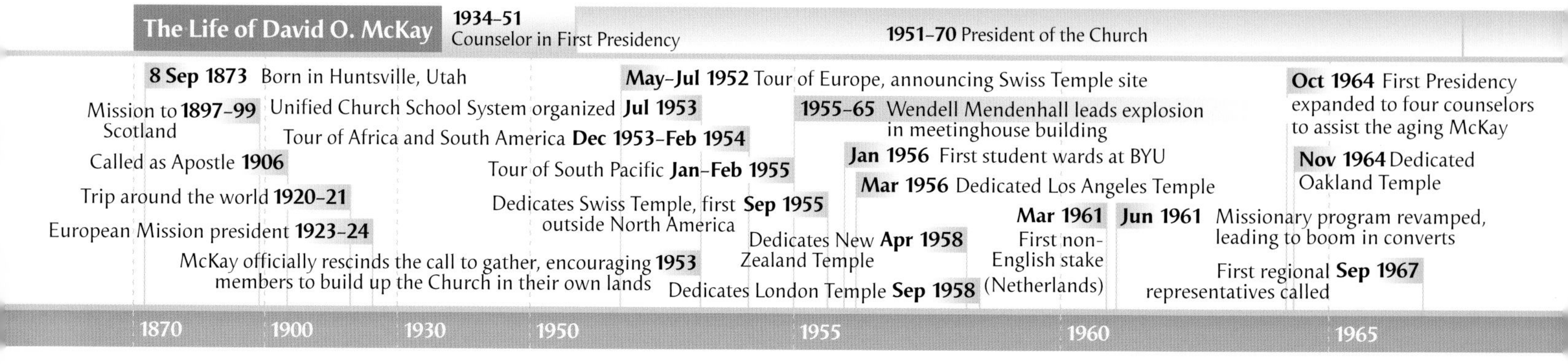
The Life of David O. McKay
1934–51 Counselor in First Presidency
1951–70 President of the Church
8 Sep 1873 Born in Huntsville, Utah
Mission to Scotland 1897–99
Called as Apostle 1906
Trip around the world 1920–21
European Mission president 1923–24
Unified Church School System organized Jul 1953
Tour of Africa and South America Dec 1953–Feb 1954
Tour of South Pacific Jan–Feb 1955
Dedicates Swiss Temple, first outside North America Sep 1955
McKay officially rescinds the call to gather, encouraging members to build up the Church in their own lands 1953
May–Jul 1952 Tour of Europe, announcing Swiss Temple site
1955–65 Wendell Mendenhall leads explosion in meetinghouse building
Jan 1956 First student wards at BYU
Mar 1956 Dedicated Los Angeles Temple
Dedicates New Zealand Temple Apr 1958
Dedicates London Temple Sep 1958
Mar 1961 First non-English stake (Netherlands)
Jun 1961 Missionary program revamped, leading to boom in converts
First regional representatives called Sep 1967
Oct 1964 First Presidency expanded to four counselors to assist the aging McKay
Nov 1964 Dedicated Oakland Temple
1870
1900
1930
1950
1955
1960
1965

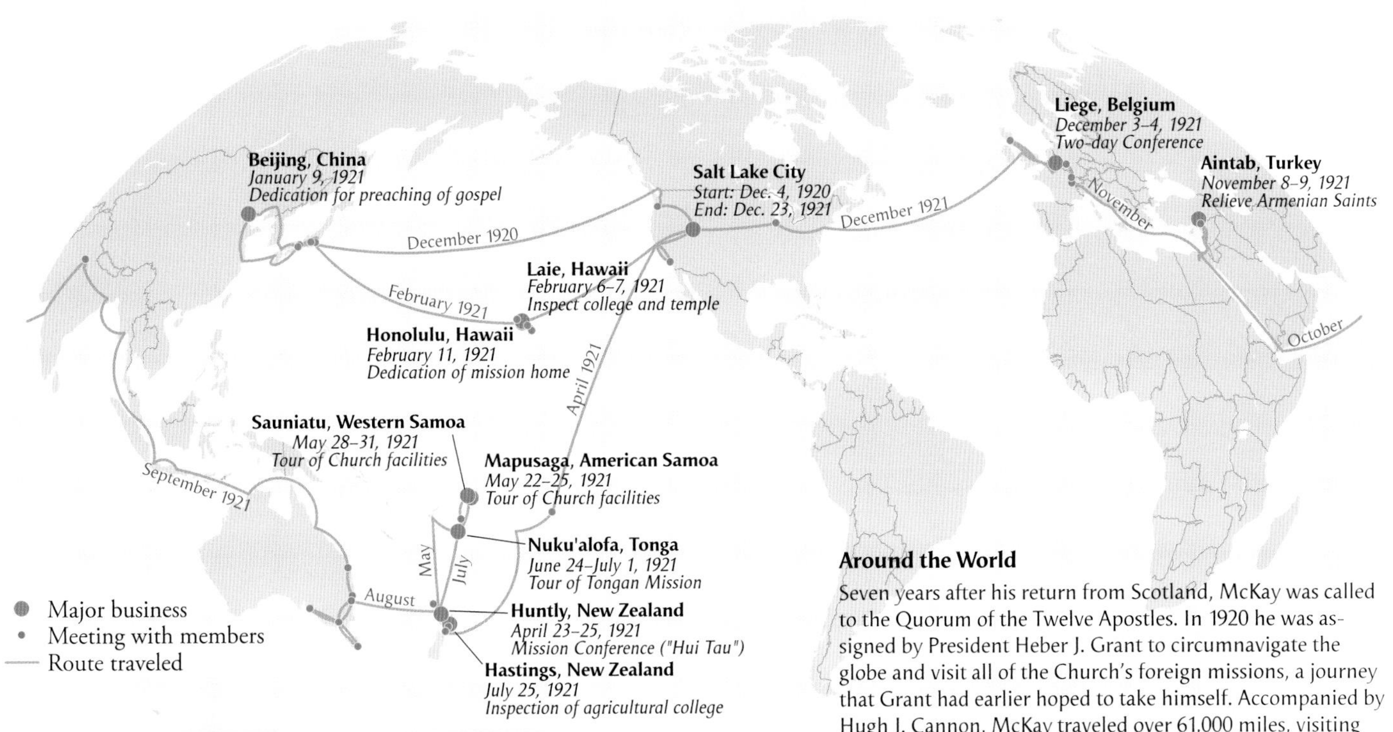

61,646 miles; 366 days 23,777 on land 37,869 on sea	
Ship	37,305
Railroad	22,444
Automobile	675
Camel	36
Horseback	11
Other land travel	611
Other water travel	573

Around the World

Seven years after his return from Scotland, McKay was called to the Quorum of the Twelve Apostles. In 1920 he was assigned by President Heber J. Grant to circumnavigate the globe and visit all of the Church's foreign missions, a journey that Grant had earlier hoped to take himself. Accompanied by Hugh J. Cannon, McKay traveled over 61,000 miles, visiting five continents and every foreign mission except the South African. All of the problems he experienced in Scotland were reinforced, and he encountered new challenges. Traveling throughout Hawaii and the South Pacific, areas in which the Church had seen significant proselytizing success for more than a century, he lamented the poor status of public education and promised to improve it. In addition, he confronted for the first time non-Christian and non-Western cultures. Writing from China to fellow Apostle and U.S. senator Reed Smoot, he noted, "Our visit here, as in Japan, has been one constant round of interest and surprises, and the best means of education in the world. The only right way to learn a people is to visit them in their own land and in their own homes."

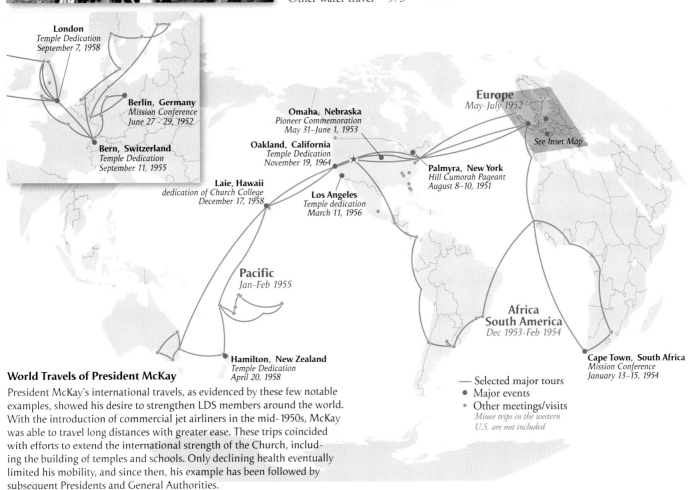

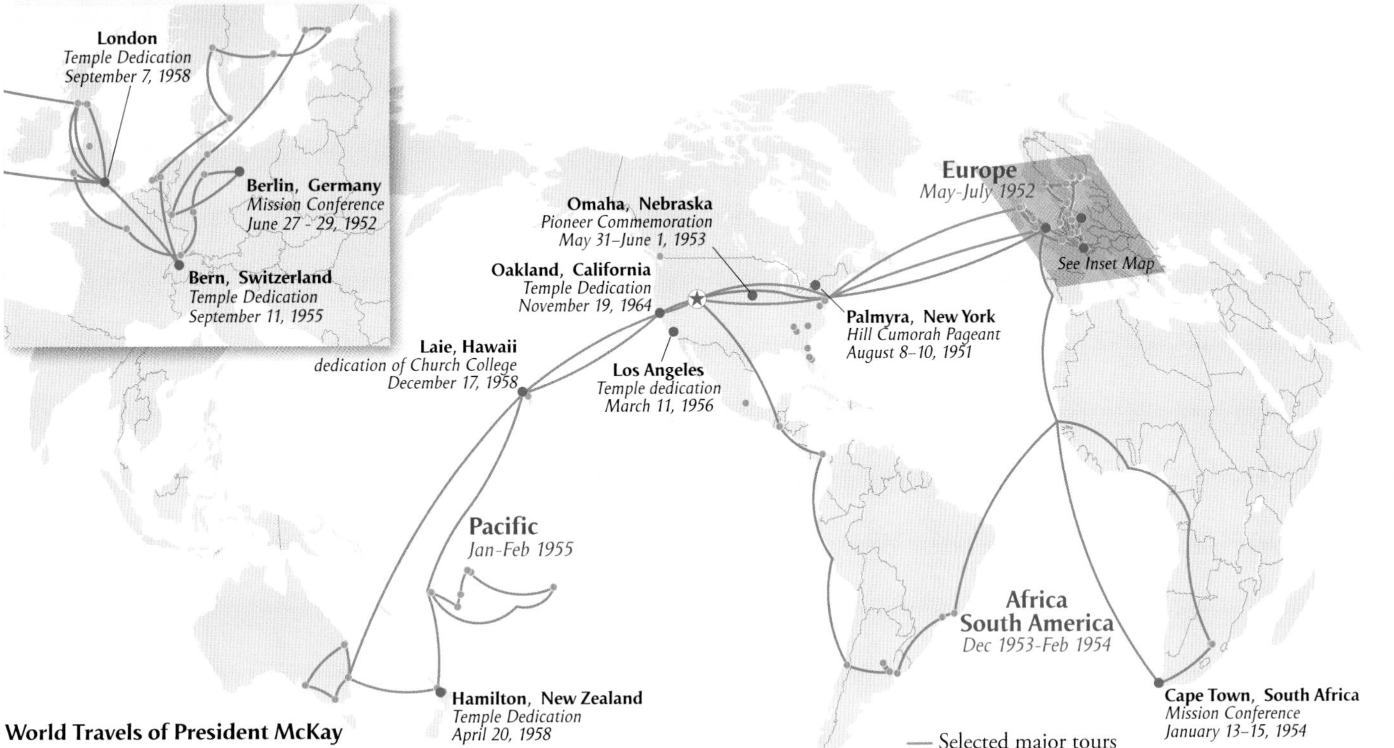

World Travels of President McKay

President McKay's international travels, as evidenced by these few notable examples, showed his desire to strengthen LDS members around the world. With the introduction of commercial jet airliners in the mid-1950s, McKay was able to travel long distances with greater ease. These trips coincided with efforts to extend the international strength of the Church, including the building of temples and schools. Only declining health eventually limited his mobility, and since then, his example has been followed by subsequent Presidents and General Authorities.

Building Meetinghouses

1952–present

Latter-day Saint meetinghouses are among the most familiar landmarks of the Mormon cultural landscape. In Utah and Idaho they stand in nearly every neighborhood, and where Mormon congregations are sparser they are easily recognized outposts of the Church.

Before the Church's move to the West in 1847, there were no ward meetinghouses. The Kirtland and Nauvoo Temples were built for public worship, and a variety of schoolhouses, homes, and other structures also served this need. Members also built a few small chapels for worship in areas of early missionary success.

The first ward meetinghouses in pioneer Utah usually served both as schools and churches. Modest rectangular structures without towers, few of these buildings remain today. In the later nineteenth century, schools and churches separated, and many meetinghouses acquired the characteristics of religious architecture: spires, Gothic and Classical windows, elaborate cornices, impressive doorways, and interior embellishments. Sometimes Mormon wards and stakes had multiple adjacent buildings, such as separate amusement halls, Relief Society buildings, tithing offices, and stake office buildings.

Impressive tabernacles in larger settlements included stake offices and a large assembly room for stake conferences and a wide variety of other religious, civic, and cultural activities. Tabernacles became prominent regional landmarks throughout the West. They continued to be built into the 1950s when they were superseded by multi-use stake centers.

continued on page 162

Custom plans / Standard plans

- ● 1867–1929
- ● ■ 1930–1950
- ● ■ 1951–1960
- ● ■ 1961–1970
- ■ 1971–1980
- ■ 1981–1990
- ■ 1991–2000
- ■ 2001–2009
- ○ Buildings no longer in use

Numbered locations correspond to the models below.

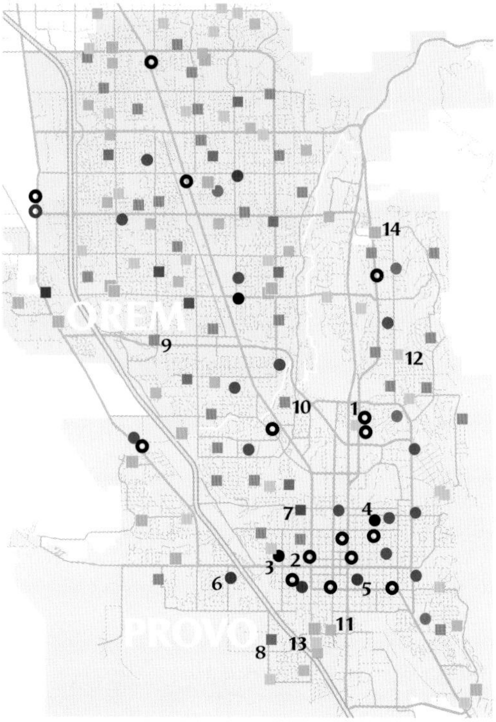

Meetinghouses in Provo and Orem

In areas of the western United States where Latter-day Saints are a significant part of the population, meetinghouses can be found in nearly every neighborhood. Meetinghouses are spread rather evenly across Provo and Orem, Utah, the densest concentration in the world (eight per square mile in places). The dates of construction, reflected in the changing architectural styles of the buildings, present a historical record of the growth of LDS communities. The earliest buildings are clustered in Provo's central area, with a few meetinghouses in the centers of former small rural communities. The red, orange, and yellow dots reflect the suburban expansion of the area beginning in the 1960s and continuing today.

Provo Tabernacle *1883–2010*
One of many magnificent tabernacles in major Mormon towns (see p. 96) that accommodated large stake conferences and a wide variety of other civic and cultural activities; burned in December 2010, but being rebuilt as a temple

Note: transparent sections are later additions

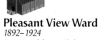

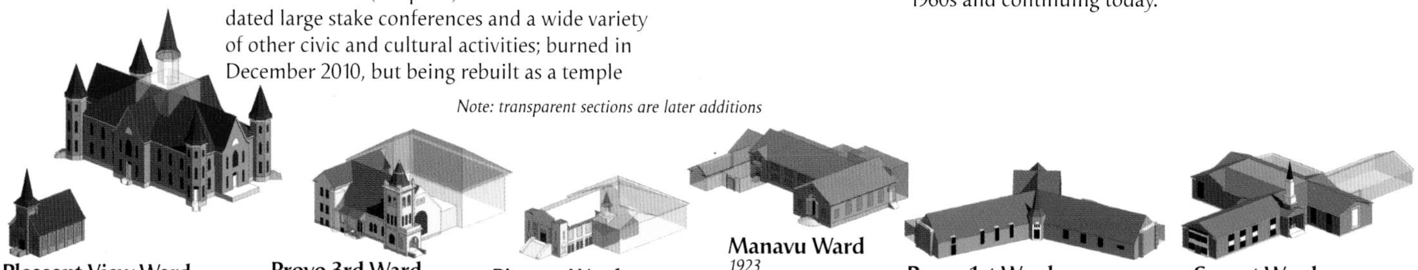

Pleasant View Ward *1892–1924*
A typical late-19th century vernacular meetinghouse with a small chapel and classrooms in the basement
1 *on Provo/Orem map*

Provo 3rd Ward *1901–1979*
Gothic Revival building typical of Protestant churches of the day; now a school
2

Pioneer Ward *1918*
Modern design reflecting the influence of Frank Lloyd Wright and other modernists; most Prairie Style details removed in later addition/remodel
3

Manavu Ward *1923*
Georgian Revival building typical of those drawn by the Church Building Department
4

Provo 1st Ward *1930*
Unusual custom-designed meetinghouse with separate wings for the chapel, classrooms, and amusement hall
5

Sunset Ward *1950*
One of hundreds of post-War meetinghouses that combined Colonial and Modern influences in similar layouts
6

COMMON ARCHITECTURAL STYLES

- Gothic & Romanesque Revival
- Prairie Style (F.L. Wright)
- Colonial & Georgian Revival
- Mormon Moderne
- Modernized Colonial

Periods of central oversight of building design

- 1900–20 *Little central control over design leads to a variety of classic and modern architectural designs*
- 1921–33 *Church Architectural Bureau provides custom plans for about half of meetinghouses*
- 1933–45 *Bureau hires all projects to private architects*

- **1905** Amusement Halls first built as separate buildings near meetinghouses
- **1921** Relief Societies given meetinghouse space rather than separate buildings
- **1925** First standard plans by Joseph D.C. Young
- **1937** The Church assumes 50% of building costs, easing the burden on wards
- **1946** Standards issued for room needs and sizes, but not design
- **1946** "Stake centers" begin to replace tabernacles

1890 | 1900 | 1910 | 1920 | 1930 | 1940

Washington, D.C., Chapel

The ornate chapel in Washington, D.C., dedicated in 1935 while the city still only had a branch, represents the height of custom meetinghouse design prior to World War II. Evoking the architecture of the Salt Lake Temple, including a statue of the angel Moroni on the tower (unique among meetinghouses), the building was intended as a symbol of a permanent Mormon presence in the nation's capital.

Unfortunately, the building materials aged more quickly than expected, and most of the local membership shifted to the suburbs. The building was sold to another church in 1975, and the angel Moroni statue is now displayed in the Church History Museum in Salt Lake City.

In this 1948 picture, Church President George Albert Smith (center) is joined by Apostle John A. Widtsoe (second from left), Thomas E. McKay (second from right), an Assistant to the Twelve, and local leaders.

Standard Plans

The buildings shown below are typical of the standardized meetinghouse designs developed at Church headquarters; with rapid membership growth, building plans have focused on facilitating construction, traffic flow during meetings, and energy efficiency rather than architectural aesthetics.

During the 1950s and 1960s, several elements of meetinghouse design emerged that have survived to the present: only a single story, a cultural hall behind the chapel to also serve as overflow seating, one to four classroom "wings" that facilitate expansion, and hallways wrapping around the rear (and during the 1980s, the front) of the chapel and cultural hall to enable multiple wards to use the building simultaneously.

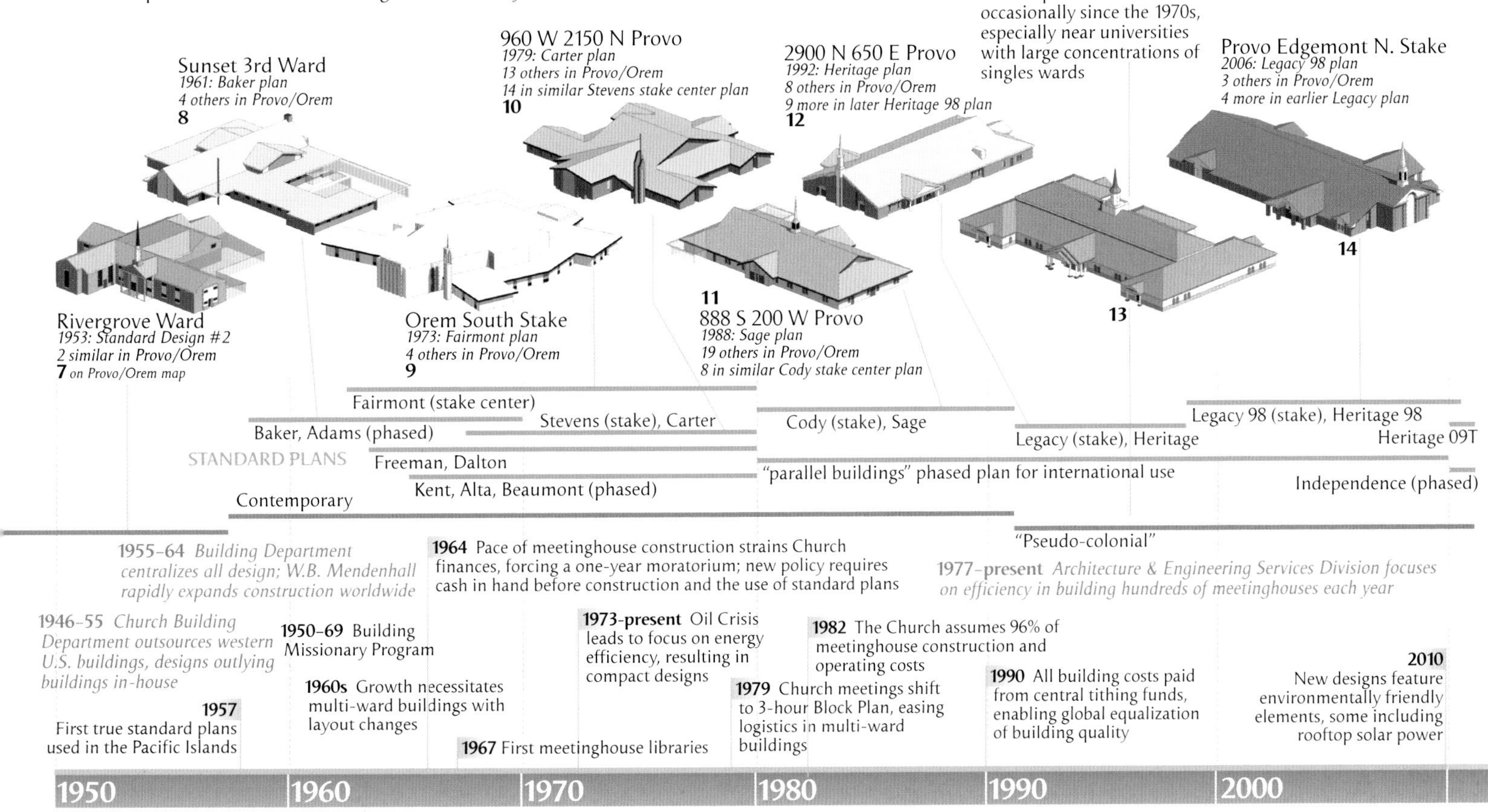

Building Meetinghouses

continued

By the beginning of the twentieth century, LDS meetinghouses were constructed in a wide variety of sizes and styles, often including recreation halls, Relief Society rooms, and many classrooms. LDS buildings were built in Gothic and Classical styles much like Protestant Churches of the period. In the 1910s and 1930s, many LDS buildings reflected more progressive "Prairie Style" and Art Deco influences.

A central Church Architectural Department provided plans for red brick Colonial-style meetinghouses, mostly without towers, from 1923 to 1933 at no cost to local congregations. About 350 meetinghouses were built from these plans, while many other congregations chose to hire their own architects to develop individualized plans. Responsibility to design and build meetinghouses returned to local units during the Depression and war years of the 1930s and early 1940s.

In the decades following World War II, the demographic shift of membership and rapid growth created a constantly expanding need for new meetinghouses. The Church Building Department, established in 1946, oversaw the preparation of plans and the construction process in coordination with local Church leaders. It also paid a portion of building costs; local congregations raised the rest through donations and labor. More than 630 meetinghouses were built under this system from 1945 to 1955. In most areas of the United States and Canada, these were red brick Colonial-style buildings with white steeples, although other styles were occasionally used.

Although American LDS meetinghouses were built with a variety of designs and styles in the decade following 1955, by 1965 standardized meetinghouse plans in modern style created at Church headquarters became almost universal. These plans evolved over the years, ranging from small expandable structures to fully equipped ward buildings with a chapel, cultural hall, offices, kitchen, Relief Society room, children's meeting room, and more than a dozen classrooms. Many meetinghouses were constructed to accommodate multiple congregations. Stake centers had similar facilities plus offices for stake leaders and larger cultural halls attached to chapels for stake conferences. In 1978, the Department of Physical Facilities was organized to include the Real Estate, Building, and Operations and Maintenance divisions. The Church's building program has been one of its largest and most expensive operations, providing well over 10,000 meetinghouses all over the world between 1948 and 2000.

Paul L. Anderson

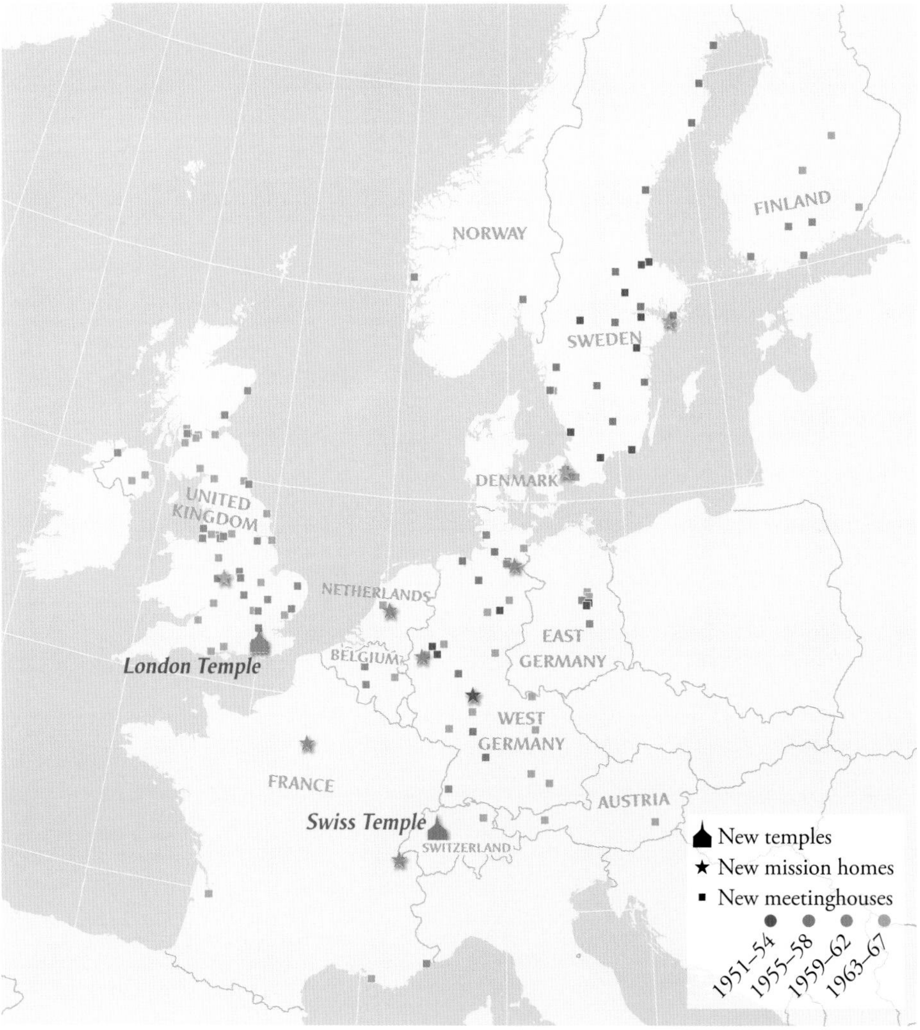

Buildings in Europe, 1951–67

Before World War II, nearly all European LDS branches met in rented facilities or buildings purchased and modified for religious use. However, in the sixteen years illustrated on this map, the Church embarked on an ambitious program of meetinghouse construction, beginning in Scandinavia and Germany, and expanding into the British Isles, with a few buildings in other countries. The Building Missionary Program was introduced in Europe in 1961 to enable more rapid construction. Even more dramatic growth would follow missionary success in many more European nations over the next few decades.

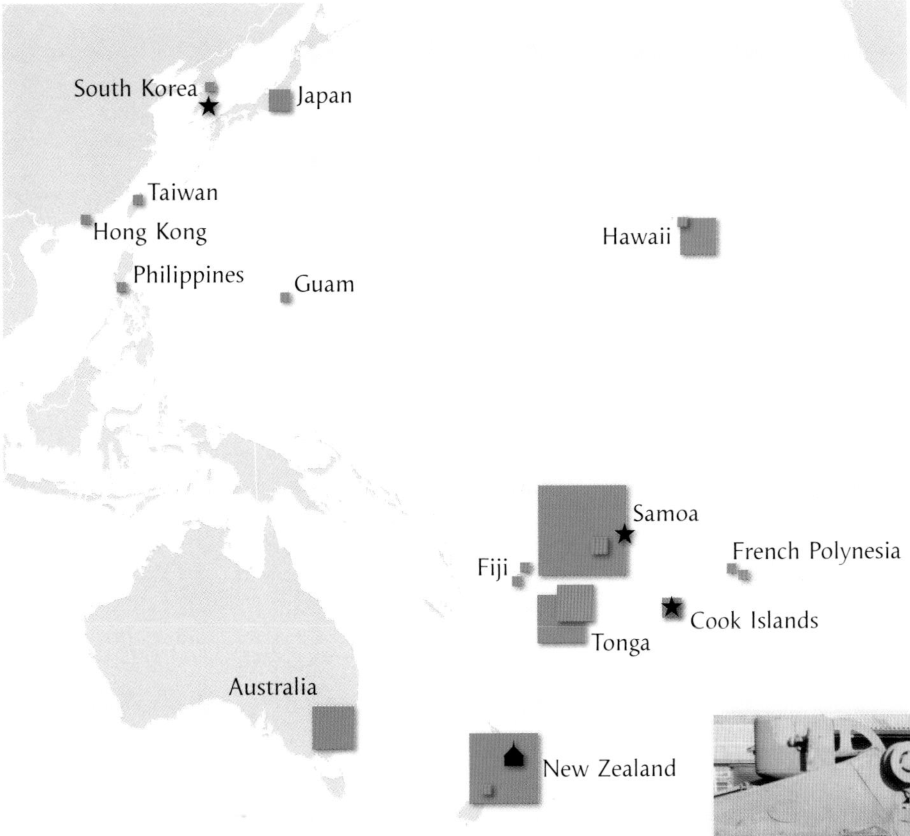

The Building Missionary Program

In the 1950s, the need for new meetinghouses and schools was particularly great in the Pacific Islands, Australia, and Europe. In 1953, the Building Missionary Program was organized in these areas. Members with construction skills were called to supervise young building missionaries and other local volunteers, who gained valuable job skills as well as serving in the Church. More than 2,000 buildings were constructed in this program before its last projects were completed in 1969, including a few in Asia, Latin America, the United States, and Canada. Building missionaries also assisted in constructing the New Zealand Temple.

In 2012, the Church is beginning to experiment with the concept again in Africa.

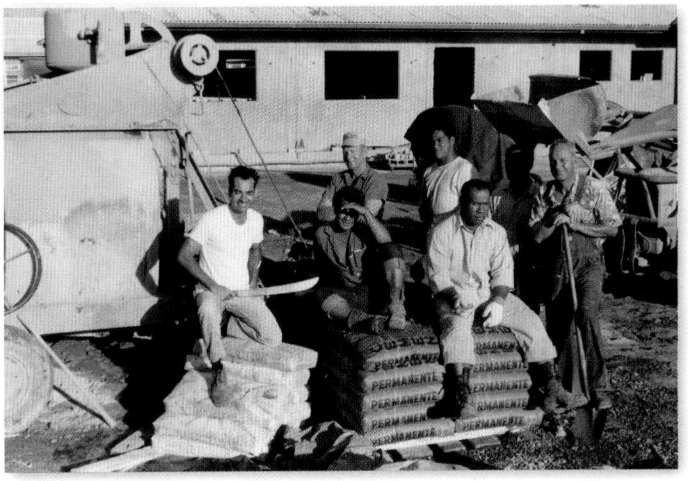

CCH Missionaries

At the height of the building missionary program in 1955, men were called from many countries, especially Tonga, to build the Church College of Hawaii (now BYU-Hawaii).

Phased Meetinghouses

Some of the first standard plans introduced by the Church Building Department were *phased meetinghouses*, expandable buildings designed to efficiently meet the needs of growing congregations in the mission fields of the Church. The Kent Plan at right was commonly used from 1965 to 1979. Starting with a small inexpensive chapel/multi-purpose room and a few classrooms, the building could grow in three more phases as attendance and activity increased into a full two-ward meetinghouse or even a stake center.

During the 1980s and 90s, phased buildings in the United States were typically sections of the large, complex plans, while international buildings were very simple. In 2011, the new Independence plan (shown above), replacing both domestic and international plans, reintroduced the earlier wing concept. This very flexible design can be built or expanded in six sizes from 2,500 square feet (for a small branch) to 21,000 square feet (a multi-ward stake center).

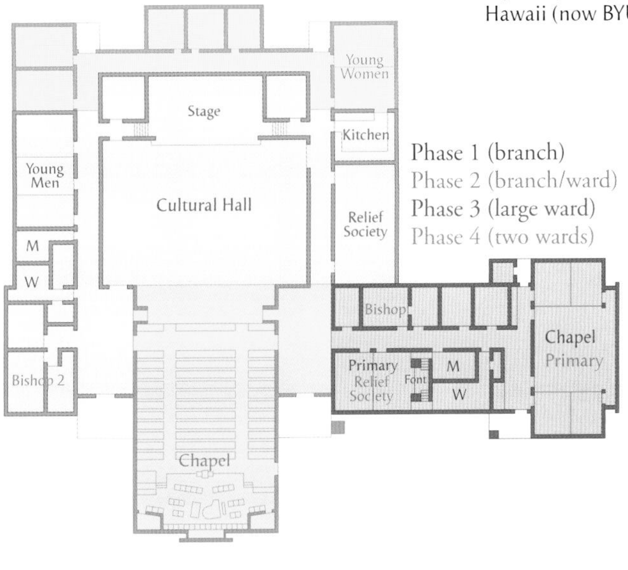

Phase 1 (branch)	3,380 sq ft	built 199 times
Phase 2 (branch/ward)	+3,620 sq ft	built 145 times
Phase 3 (large ward)	+7,370 sq ft	built 156 times
Phase 4 (two wards)	+1,900 sq ft	built 4 times

Administering the Worldwide Church

1960–present

COMMUNICATION between general and local leaders has always been an issue for the growing Church. During the mid-twentieth century, as the membership beyond the Intermountain West grew exponentially, it became infeasible for the First Presidency and the Twelve Apostles to directly supervise the members, stakes, and missions worldwide.

Since 1854, the European Mission had guided the missions and members in Europe, especially to oversee emigration, but it was closed in 1950. In 1941, Assistants to the Twelve were called to serve as intermediaries, but by 1960 a more substantial system was needed for facilitating general–local cooperation.

The solution has generally been a series of two-tiered systems of regional (4–5 stakes) and area (state to continent scale) supervision that facilitated communication between local and general authorities, trained leaders, and resolved local issues. Executive authority traditionally vested in Apostles was gradually distributed to regional and area leaders, especially after the First Quorum of the Seventy was reconstituted.

The present system of areas, first instituted in 1984, has lasted longer than previous approaches, but it too has changed as maturing local leadership and improving communication technology have allowed for further decentralization of decision-making authority. Regional administration is likely to continue to evolve as the growing Church presents new opportunities and challenges.

Brandon S. Plewe

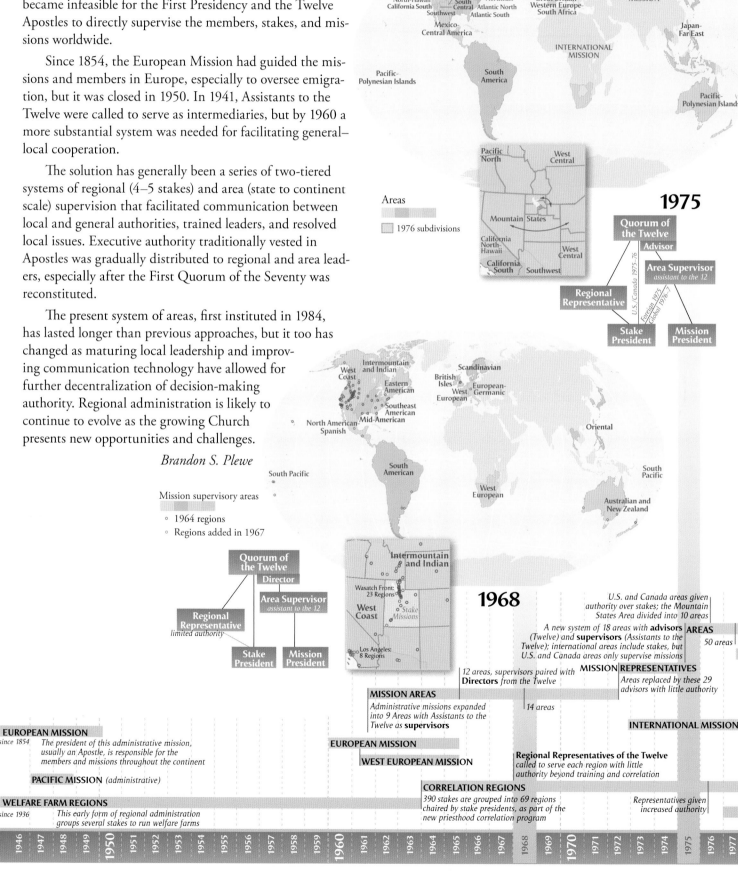

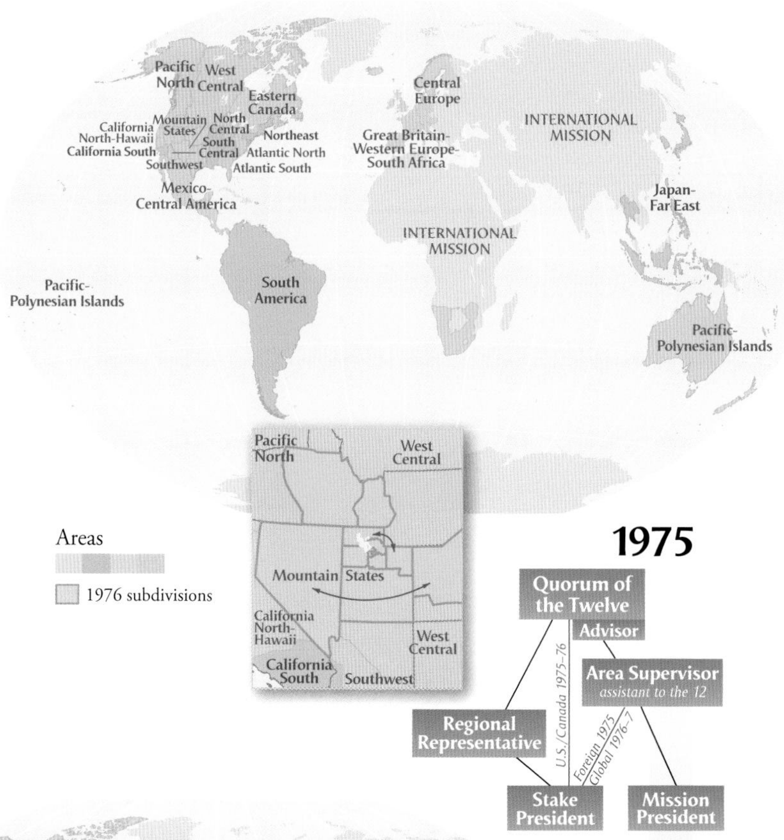

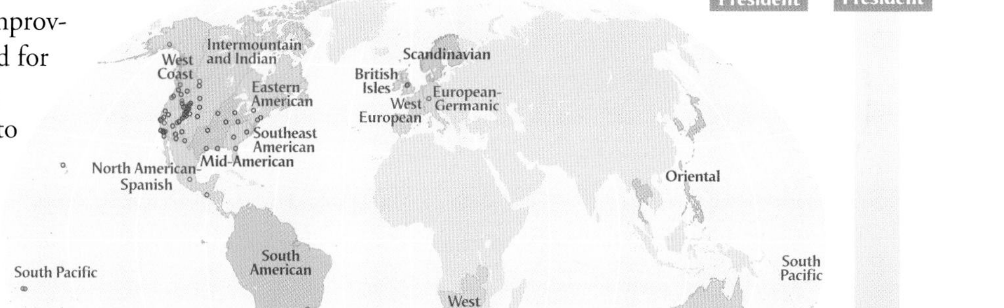

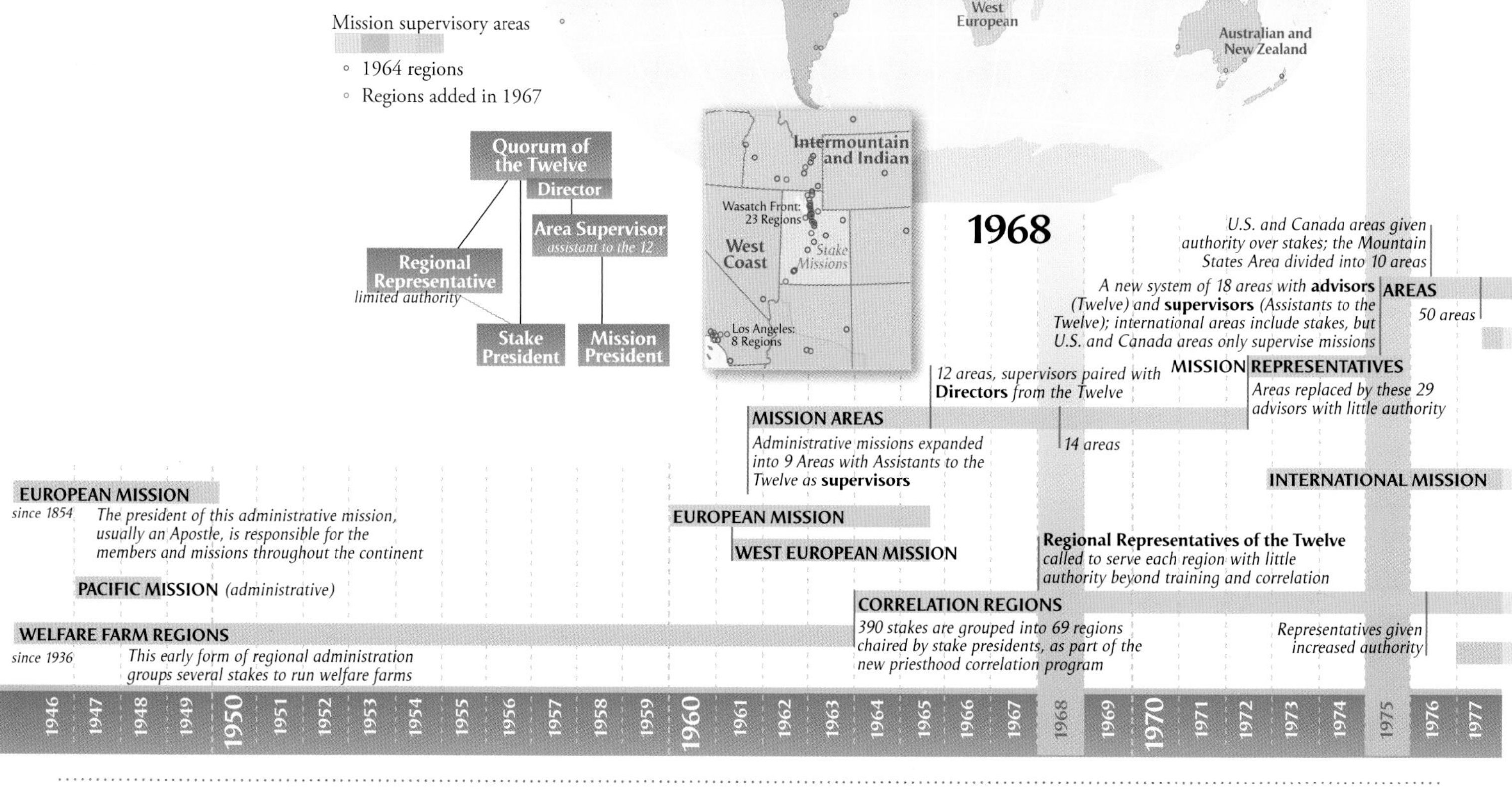

In the present area system, first instituted in 1984, areas are led by presidencies called from the Quorums of the Seventy. As stakes and missions multiplied, areas were subdivided to keep the work of area presidencies manageable (typically about 400,000 members per area), reaching a maximum of 31 areas in 2006. Realignments have also been common, especially in Utah (1988, 1994, 2003) and Europe (1987, 1991, 1995, 2000, 2003, 2008).

In recent years, maturing leadership in stakes and wards have reduced the need for direct supervision by General Authorities. Satellite broadcasting, then the Internet, have facilitated remote training and correlation. The regional representatives have been disbanded, as have area presidencies in the United States and Canada, replaced by direct (but limited) supervision by the Presidency of the Seventy. Elsewhere, many areas have been consolidated, as further autonomy is delegated to stake and mission presidents, and greater authority (including ecclesiastical, temporal, and educational affairs) has been delegated from the General Authorities to area presidencies.

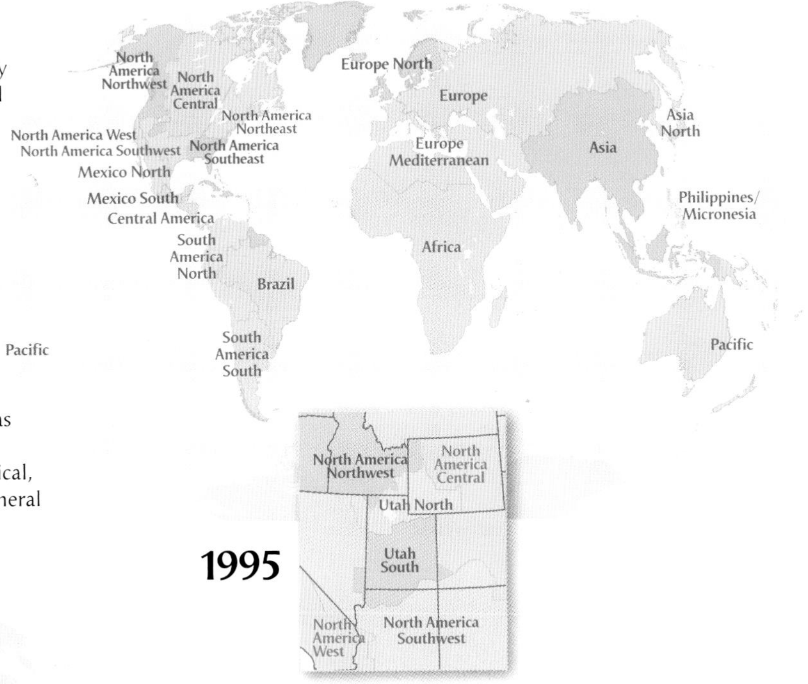

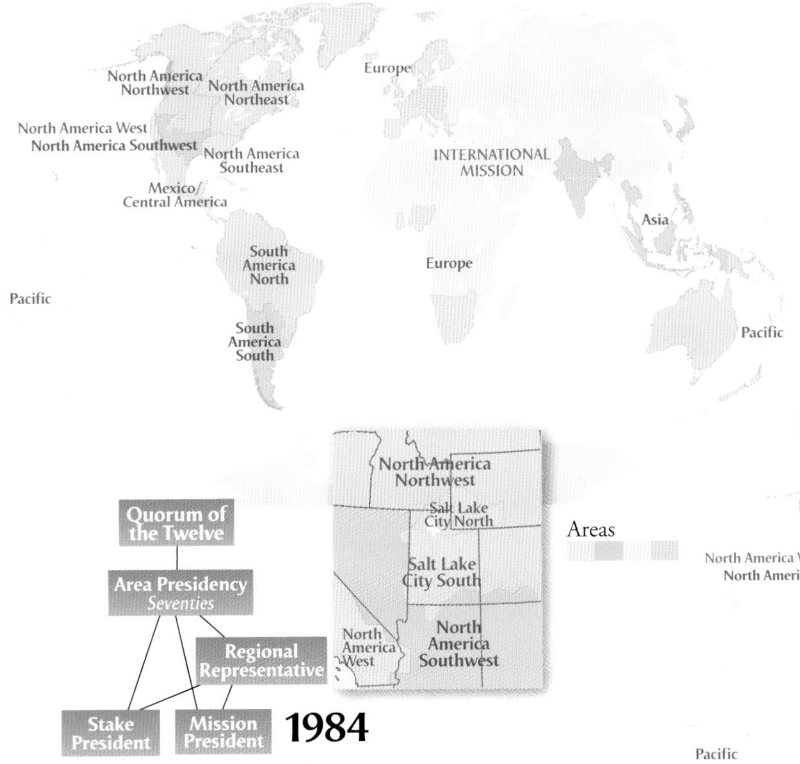

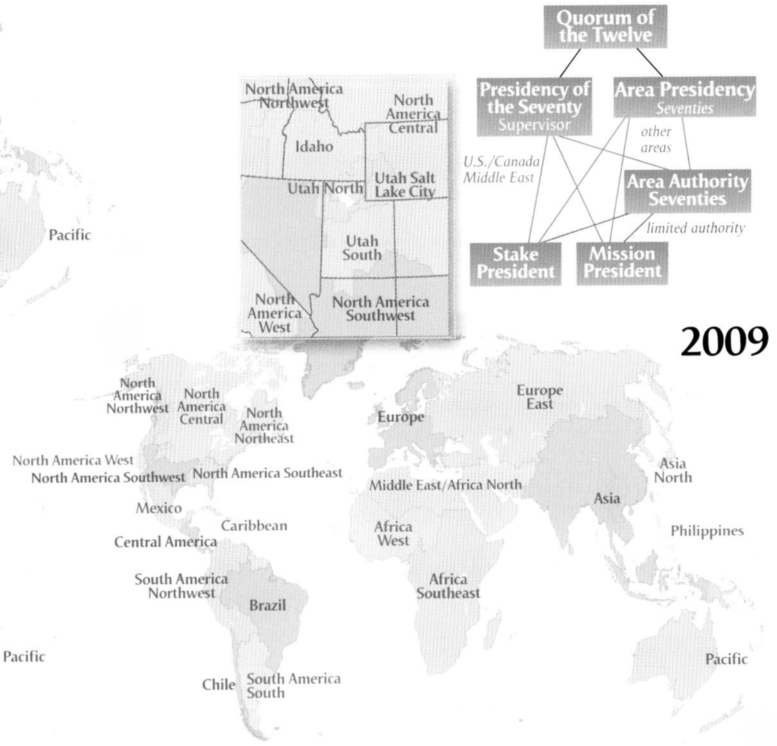

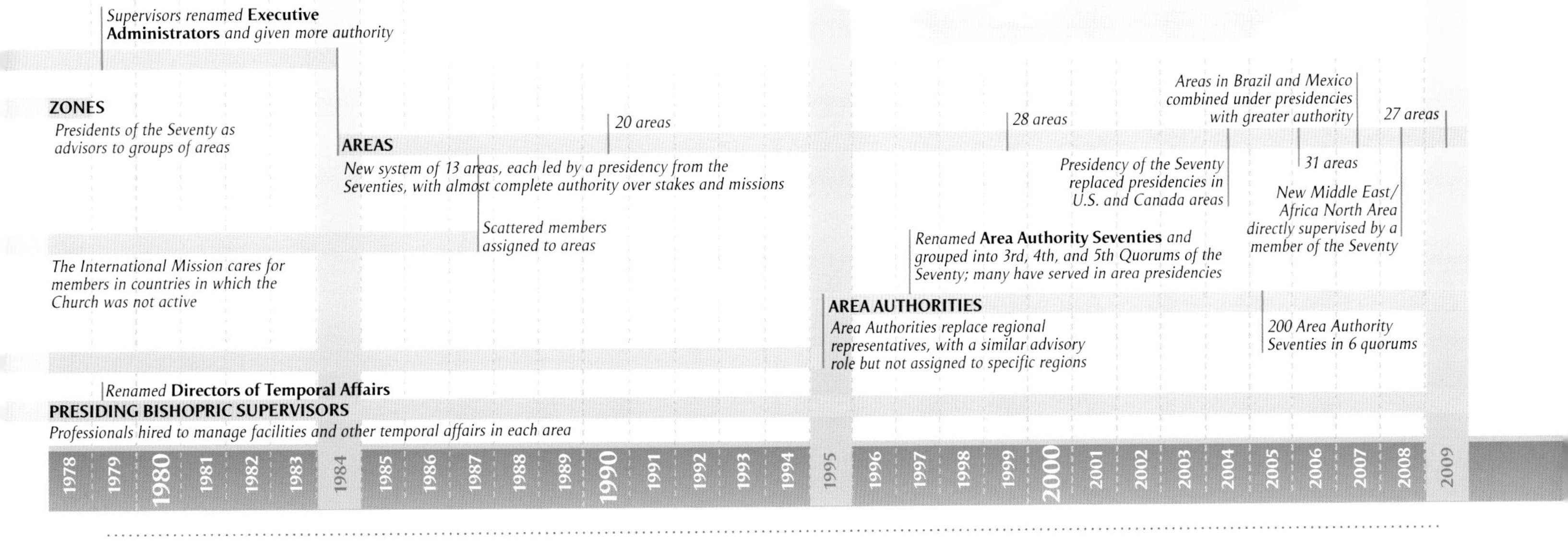

Spencer W. Kimball

1895–1985

President Kimball's boyhood in rural Arizona was a time of horse and wagon. His presidency years were a time of jet airplanes. He once crossed the Atlantic on a Concorde in three and a half hours, faster than the speed of sound. These developments in transportation made it possible for him to travel the world, reaching out to Church members, projecting his deep love for them by his presence.

A major characteristic of the Kimball presidency was an effort to take the Church to the people, as exemplified by the holding of area conferences, gatherings of thousands of members in their homelands. Area conferences had begun three years before he became President in 1973; a conference was already scheduled for Stockholm in 1974. However, he quickly escalated the program, scheduling seven conferences for 1975 in South America and the Orient. Between 1975 and 1981, when his health did not allow such travel, fifty-nine more area conferences were convened, bringing the general Church leaders to tens of thousands who would never be able to attend a general conference.

As he traveled, President Kimball sought opportunities to meet with heads of state or other high government officials to emphasize that the Latter-day Saints in the country were loyal and productive citizens. The same desire to reach out was to be seen in the holding of sixty or more solemn assemblies, meetings limited to local Church leaders for candid instruction, especially across the United States.

The move to globalize the Church led to a great burst of temple-building, making temple participation available to more and more members and thus increasing the strength temple-going Mormons tend to give back to the Church. During the twelve years of the Kimball administration, the number of dedicated temples rose from fifteen to thirty-six, with construction begun on five more and another six temples announced. President Kimball usually personally announced the decision to build a temple, and when he could he attended the groundbreaking and formal dedication of temples.

Edward L. Kimball

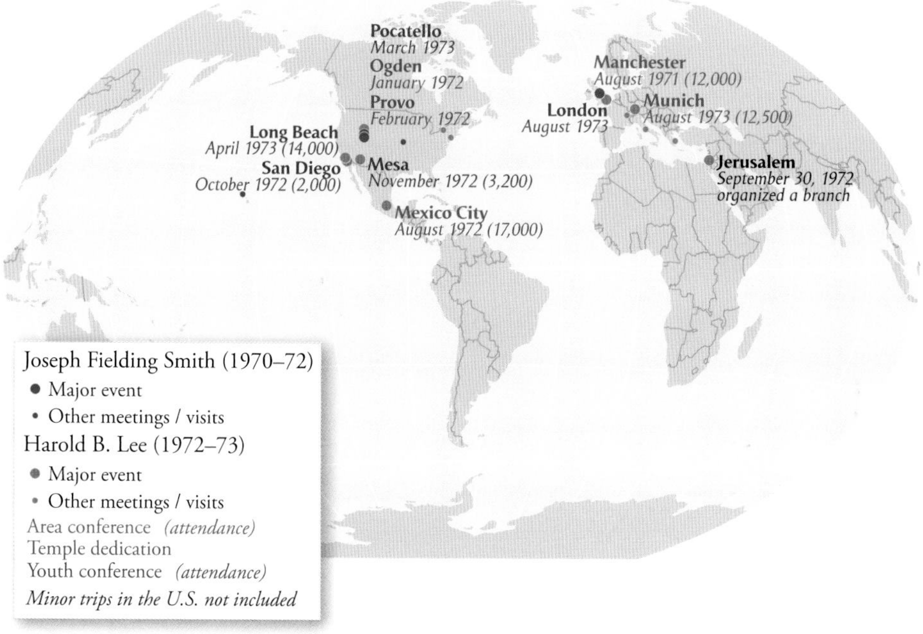

Joseph Fielding Smith and Harold B. Lee

Joseph Fielding Smith and Harold B. Lee each presided only eighteen months, but they started the pattern of area conferences later continued by President Kimball. At first, they were held once a year, in England (1971), Mexico (1972), and Germany (1973). To give the feel of a general conference, the traveling party seldom numbered fewer than thirty, and sometimes as many as fifty persons, including General Authorities, their spouses, technicians, security, and others. There were usually five meetings over two days. In 1972, President Lee also made the first trip to the Holy Land by a Church President.

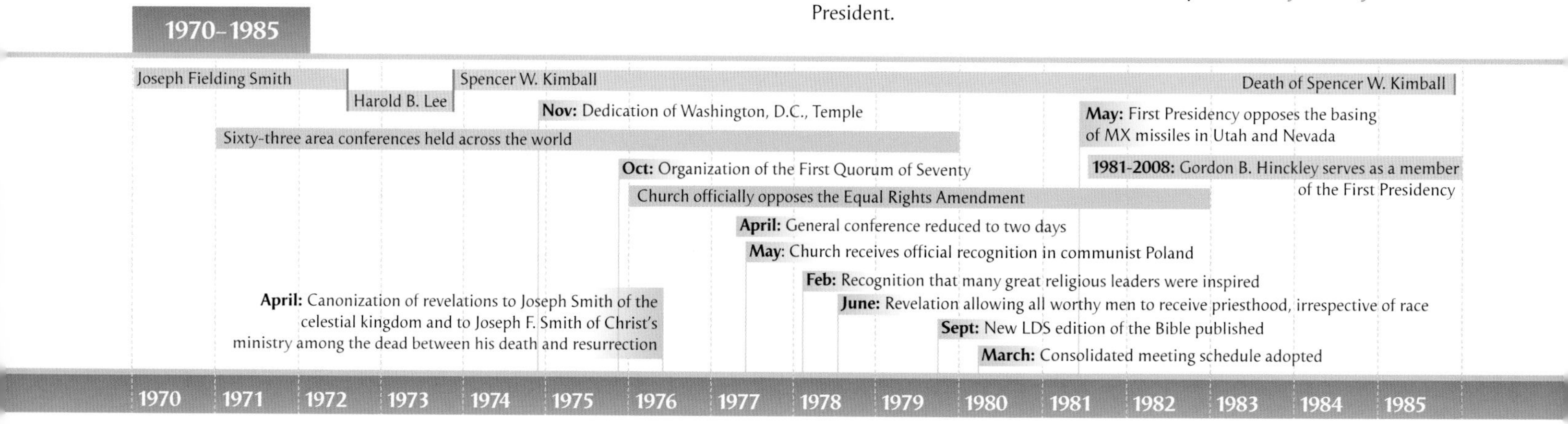

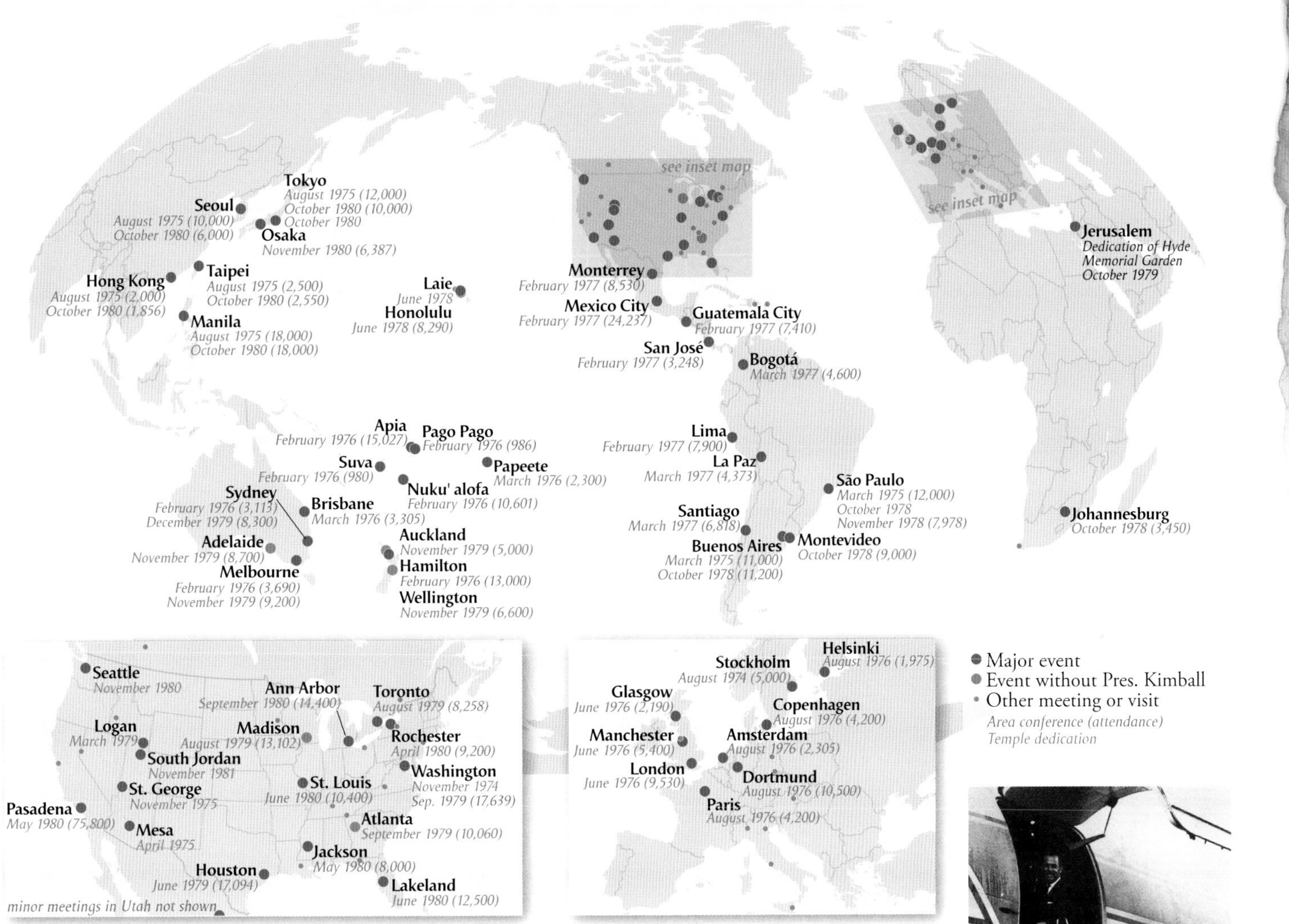

President Kimball's World Travels

Spencer W. Kimball travelled far more than any of his predecessors during his 12-year administration. President Kimball and his entourage typically flew on commercial airlines. Kimball felt that area conferences and solemn assemblies (special meetings with local priesthood leaders) were crucial venues for meeting closely with Church members, and he attended over 60 of each. Only Gordon B. Hinckley would travel more, often using a private jet owned by a member (see p. 170).

Special Ambassador for the Church

In 1974, David M. Kennedy was one of the Church's most prominent and respected members, when he was asked to be a special ambassador for the Church, with a mission to open new doors for the Church. Kennedy had been the U.S. Secretary of the Treasury and a U.S. Ambassador (see p. 146), and these experiences helped him make contacts that were difficult for ecclesiastical leaders. His greatest successes were opening Portugal to missionaries in 1974 and gaining official recognition for the Church in communist Poland in 1977. He continued to serve until 1990.

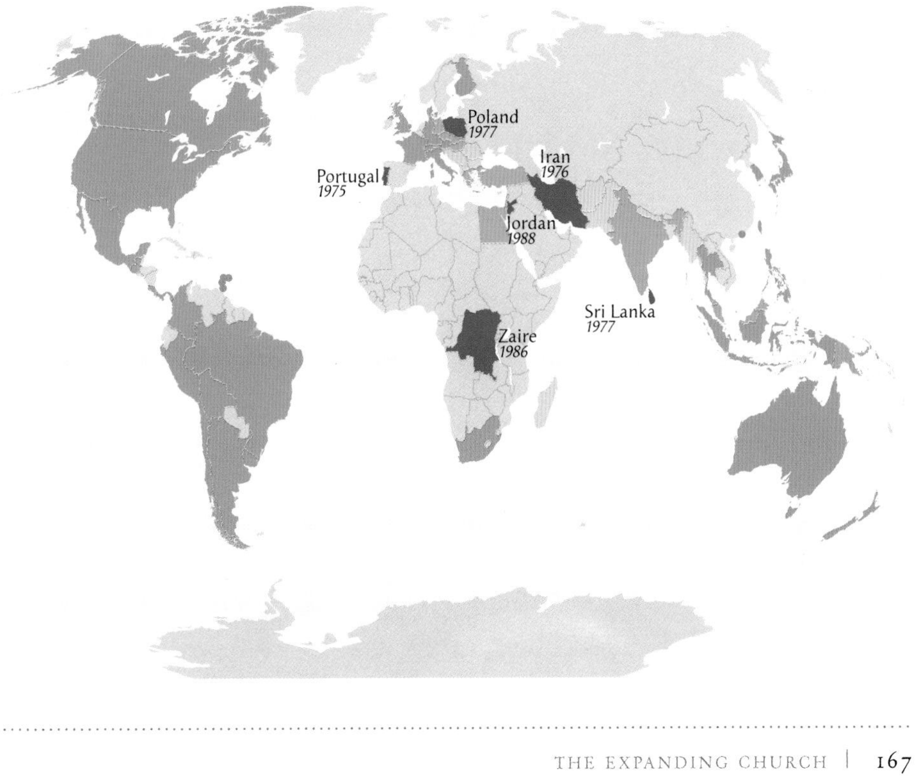

Status of the Church at time of visit
- Fully established Church presence
- Few members, restricted Church presence
- Little or no Church presence
- Status substantially improved by Kennedy

The Church in 1980

Under the leadership of David O. McKay and Spencer W. Kimball, the Church gained a permanent, established presence around the globe, although the majority of members still lived in the western United States. The Church was in the midst of a period of exponential membership growth, averaging about 5–6% growth every year, doubling every 15 years. During the 1970s and 1980s, growth was especially strong in Latin America, but members' attention was drawn to the many new countries opening each year. After the 1978 revelation giving the priesthood to blacks, missionary work rapidly spread into Africa and the Caribbean (and exploded in Brazil). Through the work of Church diplomats like David M. Kennedy and local members, restrictions in Eastern Europe gradually eased, until the fall of the Iron Curtain opened the region to missionaries. To keep up with this growth, the Church built an unprecedented number of temples during the mid-1980s (not to be surpassed until 1999). Administering this far-flung organization called for creative solutions in organization (e.g., area supervision, regional conferences) and technology (e.g., satellite broadcast of general conference).

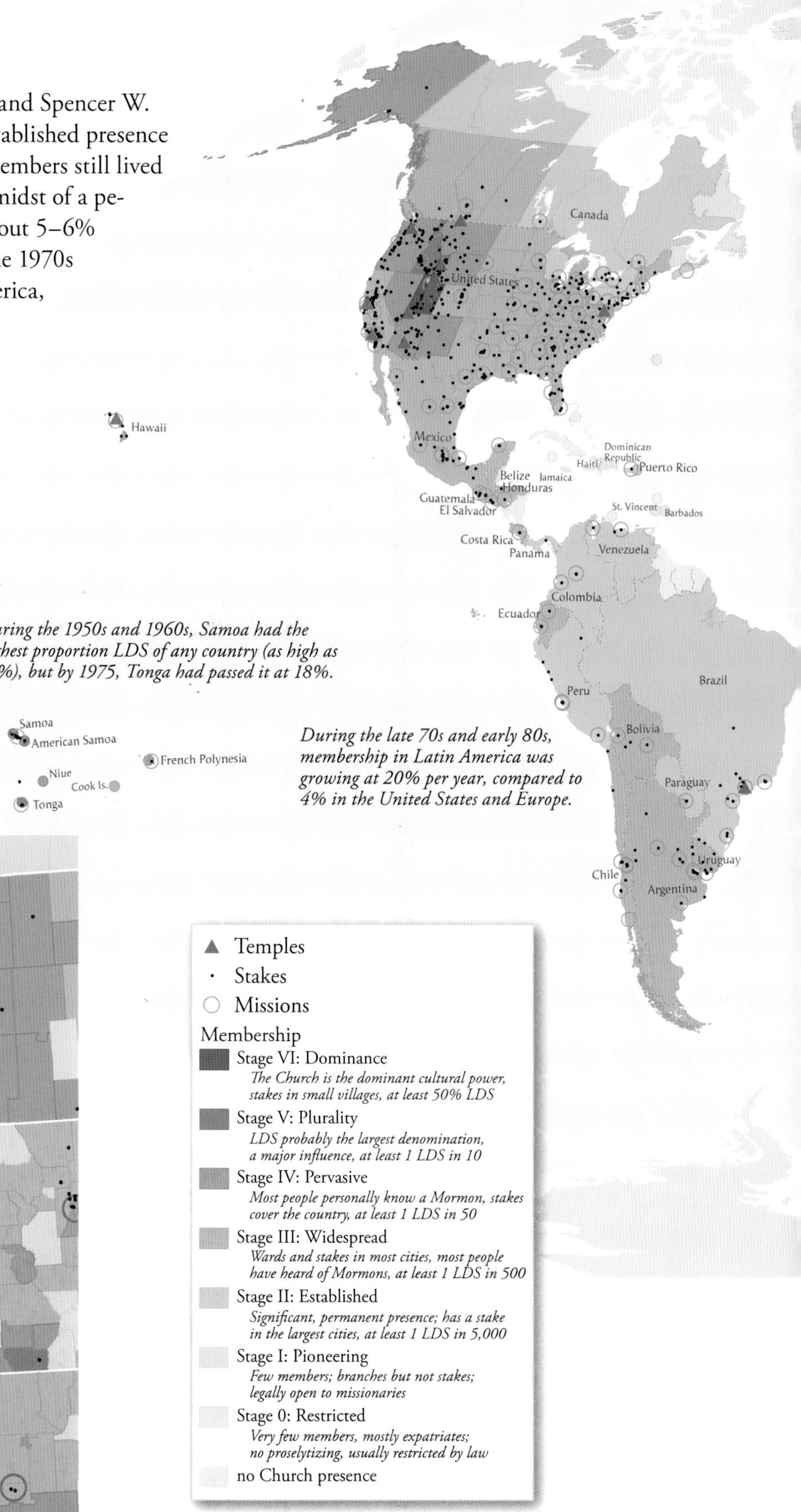
Canada
United States
Hawaii
Mexico
Belize
Jamaica
Honduras
Guatemala
El Salvador
Haiti
Dominican Republic
Puerto Rico
St. Vincent
Barbados
Costa Rica
Panama
Venezuela
Colombia
Ecuador
Peru
Brazil
Bolivia
Paraguay
Uruguay
Chile
Argentina
Samoa
American Samoa
French Polynesia
Niue
Cook Is.
Tonga
Temples
Stakes
Missions
Membership
Stage VI: Dominance
The Church is the dominant cultural power, stakes in small villages, at least 50% LDS
Stage V: Plurality
LDS probably the largest denomination, a major influence, at least 1 LDS in 10
Stage IV: Pervasive
Most people personally know a Mormon, stakes cover the country, at least 1 LDS in 50
Stage III: Widespread
Wards and stakes in most cities, most people have heard of Mormons, at least 1 LDS in 500
Stage II: Established
Significant, permanent presence; has a stake in the largest cities, at least 1 LDS in 5,000
Stage I: Pioneering
Few members; branches but not stakes; legally open to missionaries
Stage 0: Restricted
Very few members, mostly expatriates; no proselytizing, usually restricted by law
no Church presence

During the 1950s and 1960s, Samoa had the highest proportion LDS of any country (as high as 16%), but by 1975, Tonga had passed it at 18%.

During the late 70s and early 80s, membership in Latin America was growing at 20% per year, compared to 4% in the United States and Europe.

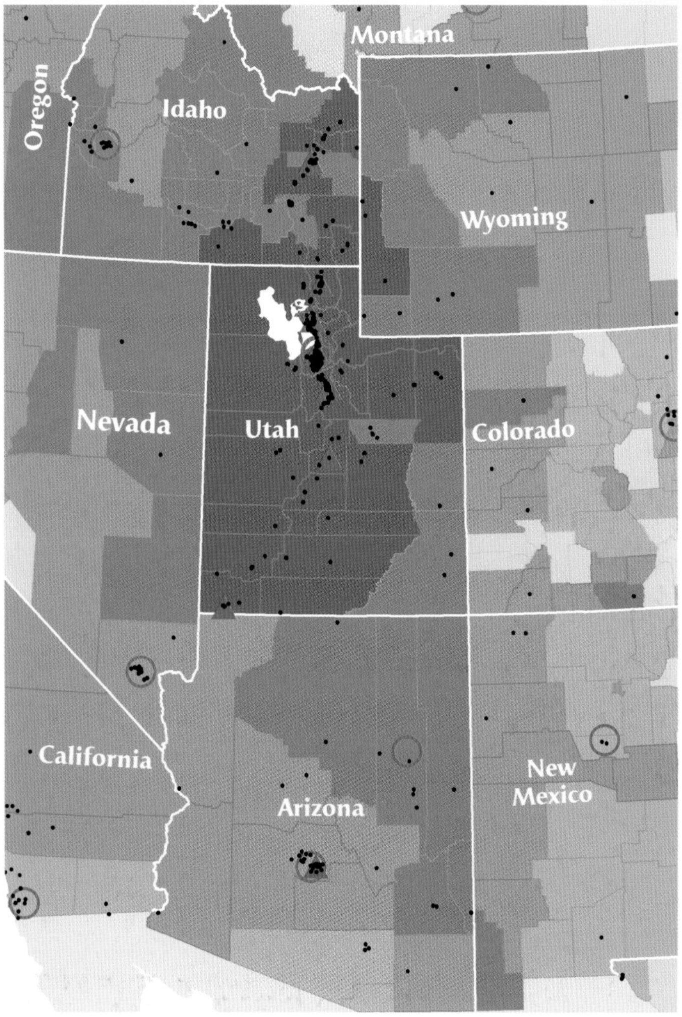
Montana
Oregon
Idaho
Wyoming
Nevada
Utah
Colorado
California
Arizona
New Mexico

By 1980, the Church had an established presence throughout the West, due to LDS migration, missionary work, and suburbanization. Stakes were widespread, and most westerners could say they personally knew a Mormon.

Church Milestones, 1970–1995

1970 Joseph Fielding Smith, 10th President

1972 Harold B. Lee, 11th President

1973 Spencer W. Kimball, 12th President; International Mission created

1975 Membership reaches three million; First Quorum of the Seventy instituted

Revelation giving priesthood **1978** to all worthy males; Rapid Church growth begins in West Africa

1982 Membership reaches five million

1983 Six temples dedicated in one year

1984 Area presidencies instituted

Ezra Taft Benson, 13th President **1985**

Membership reaches six million **1986**

1989 Second Quorum of the Seventy

1990 Eastern Europe opened to the Church; Membership reaches seven million

Howard W. Hunter, 14th President; **1994** Membership reaches eight million

Gordon B. Hinckley, **1995** 15th President

1970 1975 1980 1985 1990

Travels of Gordon B. Hinckley

1910–2008

"WHEN I WAS A YOUNG MAN, a mere boy of 11, I received a patriarchal blessing from a man I had never seen before and never saw thereafter. It is a remarkable document, a prophetic document. It is personal, and I will not read extensively from it. However, it contains this statement: 'The nations of the earth shall hear thy voice and be brought to a knowledge of the truth by the wonderful testimony which thou shalt bear.'

"When I was released from my mission in England, I took a short trip on the continent. I had borne my testimony in London; I did so in Berlin and again in Paris and later in Washington, D.C. I said to myself that I had borne my testimony in these great capitals of the world and had fulfilled that part of my blessing" (April 2006 conference address).

No one could have imagined the lifelong fulfillment of that prophetic patriarch's blessing on the head of a skinny 11-year-old boy. The 15th President of The Church of Jesus Christ of Latter-day Saints, Gordon B. Hinckley, traveled more miles and bore testimony in more places than any Church president.

His historic around-the-world trip in 2005 (at the age of 95) was a first for a President of the Church: David O. McKay's voyage around the world as an Apostle in 1920–21 took 384 days, while President Hinckley visited members in eight cities in nine days. As he reported in general conference the following October,

> I recently traveled around the world, more than 25,000 miles, visiting Alaska, Russia, Korea, Taiwan, Hong Kong, India, Kenya, and Nigeria, where in this last place we dedicated a new temple. We then dedicated the Newport Beach California Temple. I have just been to Samoa for another temple dedication, another 10,000 miles. I do not enjoy travel, but it is my wish to get out among our people to extend appreciation and encouragement, and to bear testimony of the divinity of the Lord's work.

While his circumnavigation made history, his itinerary was similar to his many trips. A trip made to northern Mexico in 1988 (while 2nd Counselor) is typical:

- Monday: Leave Salt Lake City, fly to Hermosillo for member meeting (2,917 in attendance); fly to Ciudad Obregon, dinner at hotel, then member meeting (3,329 in attendance)
- Tuesday: Fly to Culiacán for member meeting (4,100 in attendance); fly to Guadalajara, dinner at hotel, then member meeting (6,123 in attendance)
- Wednesday: Fly to Torreón for member meeting (5,320 in attendance); fly to Leon, dinner at hotel, then member meeting (5,845 in attendance)
- Thursday: Fly to Ciudad Victoria for member meeting (4,333 in attendance); fly to Monterrey, dinner at hotel, then member meeting (12,900 in attendance)
- Friday: Visit possible temple sites in Monterrey; lunch at hotel; fly to Chihuahua, dinner at hotel, then member meeting (3,705 in attendance)
- Saturday: Fly to Ciudad Juárez, meet with stake president, lunch at hotel, regional conference leadership meeting (581 in attendance)
- Sunday: Regional conference meeting in Ciudad Juárez (4,356 in attendance); fly to Salt Lake City following conference

In seven days, President Hinckley held meetings in ten different cities with 53,404 people, traveling 3,979 miles. This was typical of his travel schedules. Once, while traveling from Salt Lake City to meetings in South America, his party arrived at a layover in Costa Rica earlier than expected, and President Hinckley observed that there might be time to meet with members in San Jose before retiring. A 7:00 meeting was quickly arranged at a local stake center, where President Hinckley met an overflow crowd of thousands. "Rest days" were simply not part of his vocabulary.

"I do not enjoy travel," he once said, "I weary of it. Jet lag, for me, is a very real thing. But I do enjoy looking into the faces and shaking the hands of faithful Latter-day Saints" (October 1996 conference address).

Clark B. Hinckley

The Travels of Gordon B. Hinckley

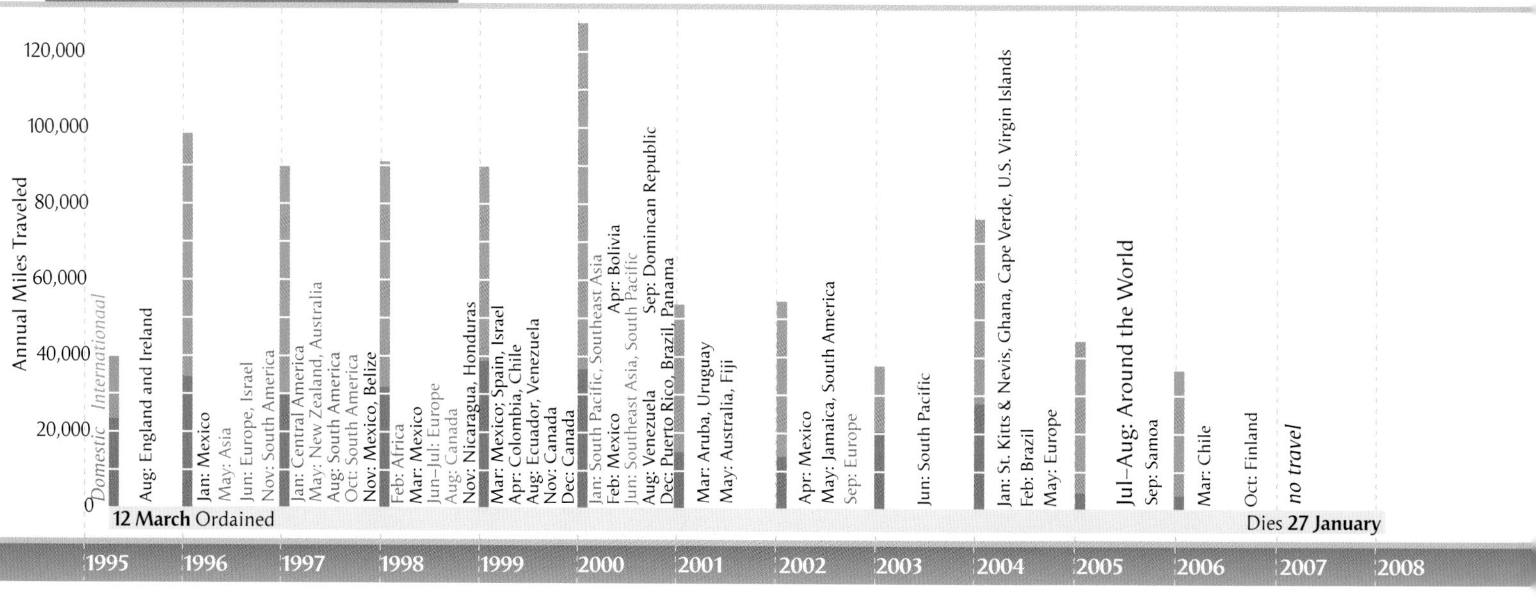

First Presidency Travels, 1981–1995

Gordon B. Hinckley served as counselor to three Presidents: Spencer W. Kimball, Ezra Taft Benson, and Howard W. Hunter. During much of this time, their health limited their travel. Long before he became President, Hinckley was essentially the public face of the Church, conducting conferences, giving press conferences, and dedicating temples.

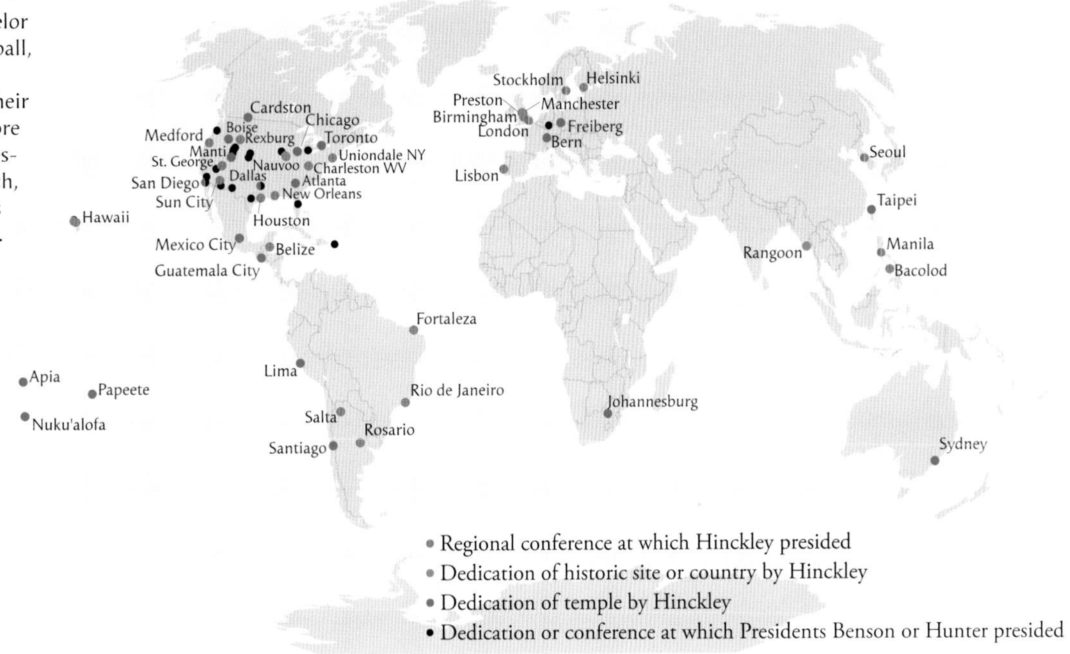

International Travels, 1995–2008

As President, Gordon B. Hinckley visited 68 countries beyond the United States, including 12 never before visited by a President of the Church; he traveled over 830,000 miles. Only a few of his dozens of multi-city tours are shown here, including his 2005 circumnavigation of the globe (the first time any President did so, at the age of 95). He traveled most during the early years of his presidency, but continued to visit Church members all over the world until health problems limited his mobility for the last year or two of his life.

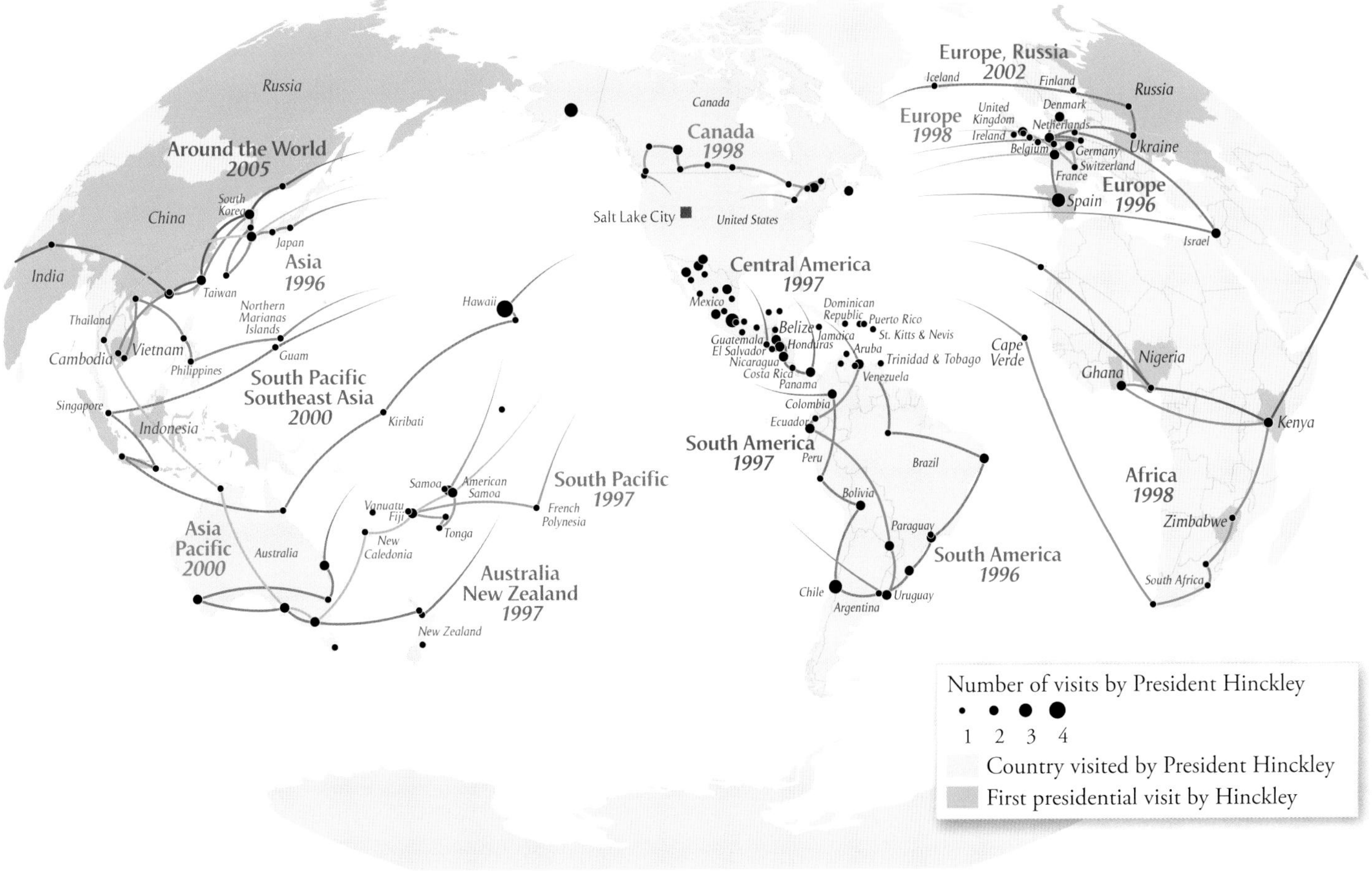

The Church in 2012

During the presidency of Gordon B. Hinckley, the LDS Church expanded globally to an extent that there is independent strength in most countries, rather than the "colonial" dependence on Utah during most of the previous century. This is exemplified by several recent milestones:

- Fewer than half of the members of the Church speak English, and fewer than half live in the United States.
- Mexico and Brazil each have more than 1,000,000 members.
- The Church is more prevalent in much of Latin America than it is in the eastern United States.
- Immigration to the Intermountain West is reducing the traditional dominance of the Church there.
- For the first time, an Apostle was called from outside the U.S. and Canada (earlier foreign-born Apostles had immigrated previously).

That said, the Church is still far stronger in the Western Hemisphere than in the Eastern Hemisphere. Large parts of Asia and Africa remain unreached by the Latter-day Saints.

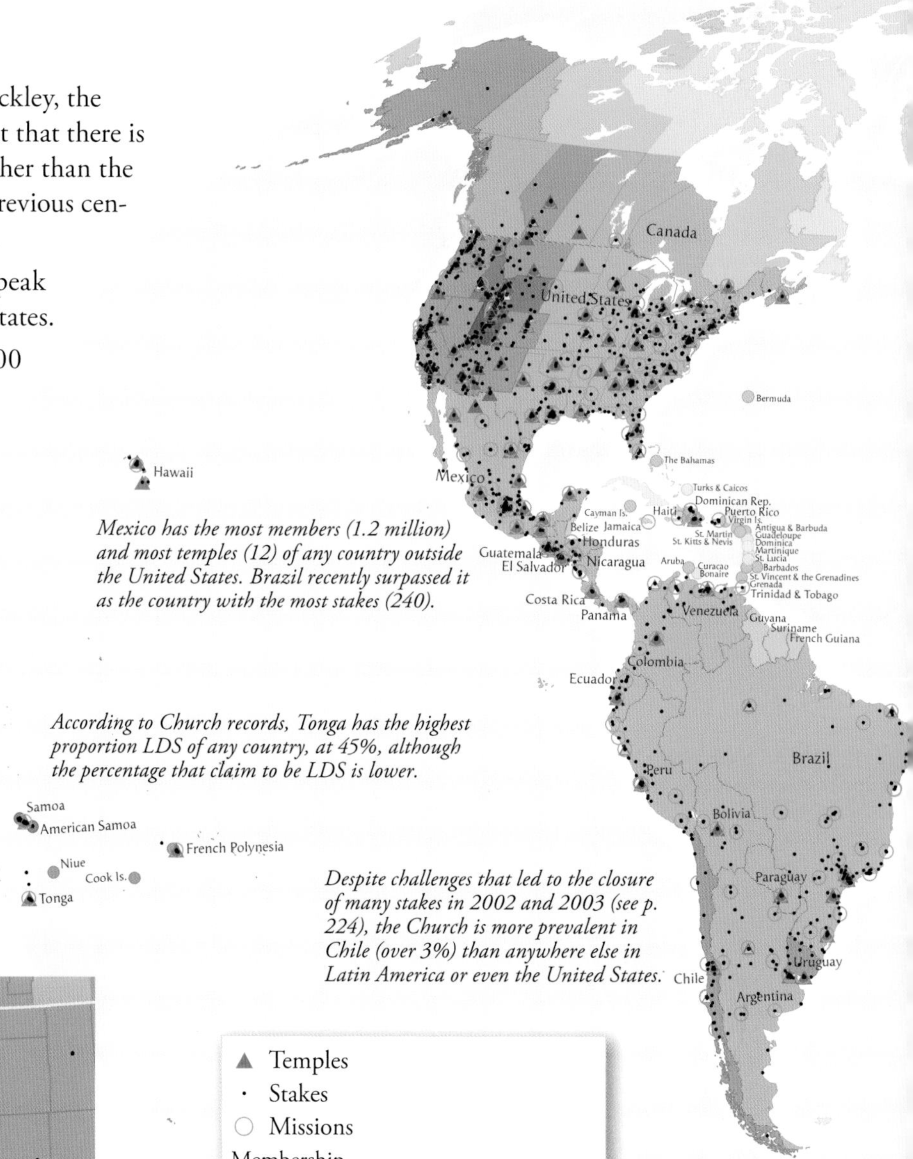

Mexico has the most members (1.2 million) and most temples (12) of any country outside the United States. Brazil recently surpassed it as the country with the most stakes (240).

According to Church records, Tonga has the highest proportion LDS of any country, at 45%, although the percentage that claim to be LDS is lower.

Despite challenges that led to the closure of many stakes in 2002 and 2003 (see p. 224), the Church is more prevalent in Chile (over 3%) than anywhere else in Latin America or even the United States.

▲ Temples
• Stakes
○ Missions

Membership

- Stage VI: Dominance — *The Church is the dominant cultural power, stakes in small villages, at least 50% LDS*
- Stage V: Plurality — *LDS probably the largest denomination, a major influence, at least 1 LDS in 10*
- Stage IV: Pervasive — *Most people personally know a Mormon, stakes cover the country, at least 1 LDS in 50*
- Stage III: Widespread — *Wards and stakes in most cities, most people have heard of Mormons, at least 1 LDS in 500*
- Stage II: Established — *Significant, permanent presence; has a stake in the largest cities, at least 1 LDS in 5,000*
- Stage I: Pioneering — *Few members; branches but not stakes; legally open to missionaries*
- Stage 0: Restricted — *Very few members, mostly expatriates; no proselytizing, usually restricted by law*
- no Church presence

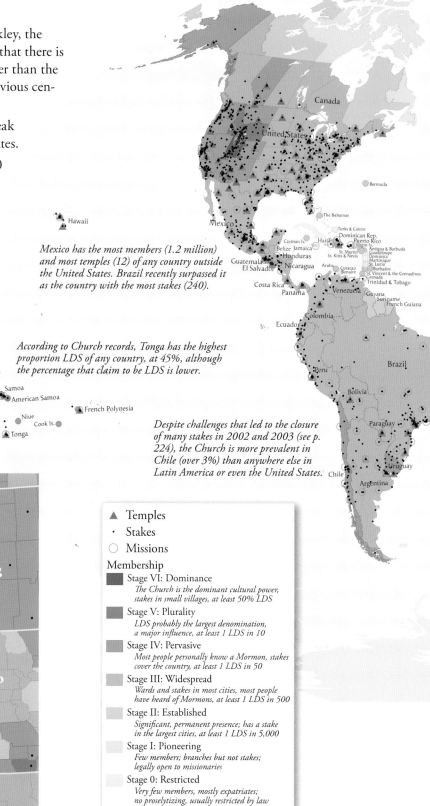

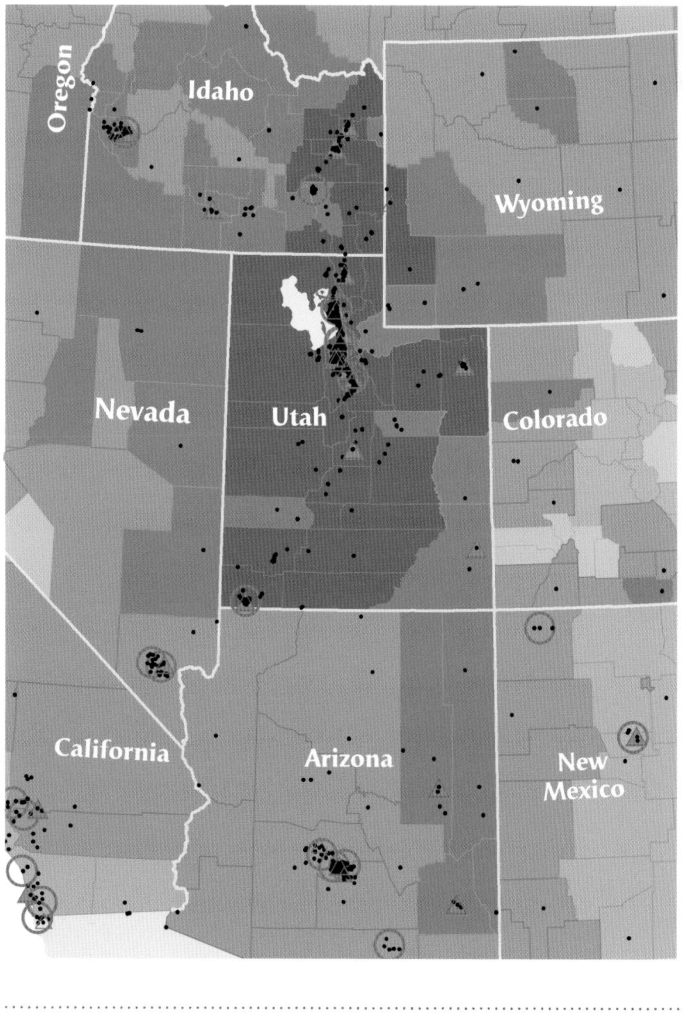

As large numbers of people of various backgrounds move to the Intermountain West, the predominance of the LDS Church has diminished in many areas, reducing the area of the "Mormon Culture Region." Some have even predicted that in 30 years, fewer than half of Utahns will be LDS. That said, the Church continues to become more prevalent in areas beyond the traditional core.

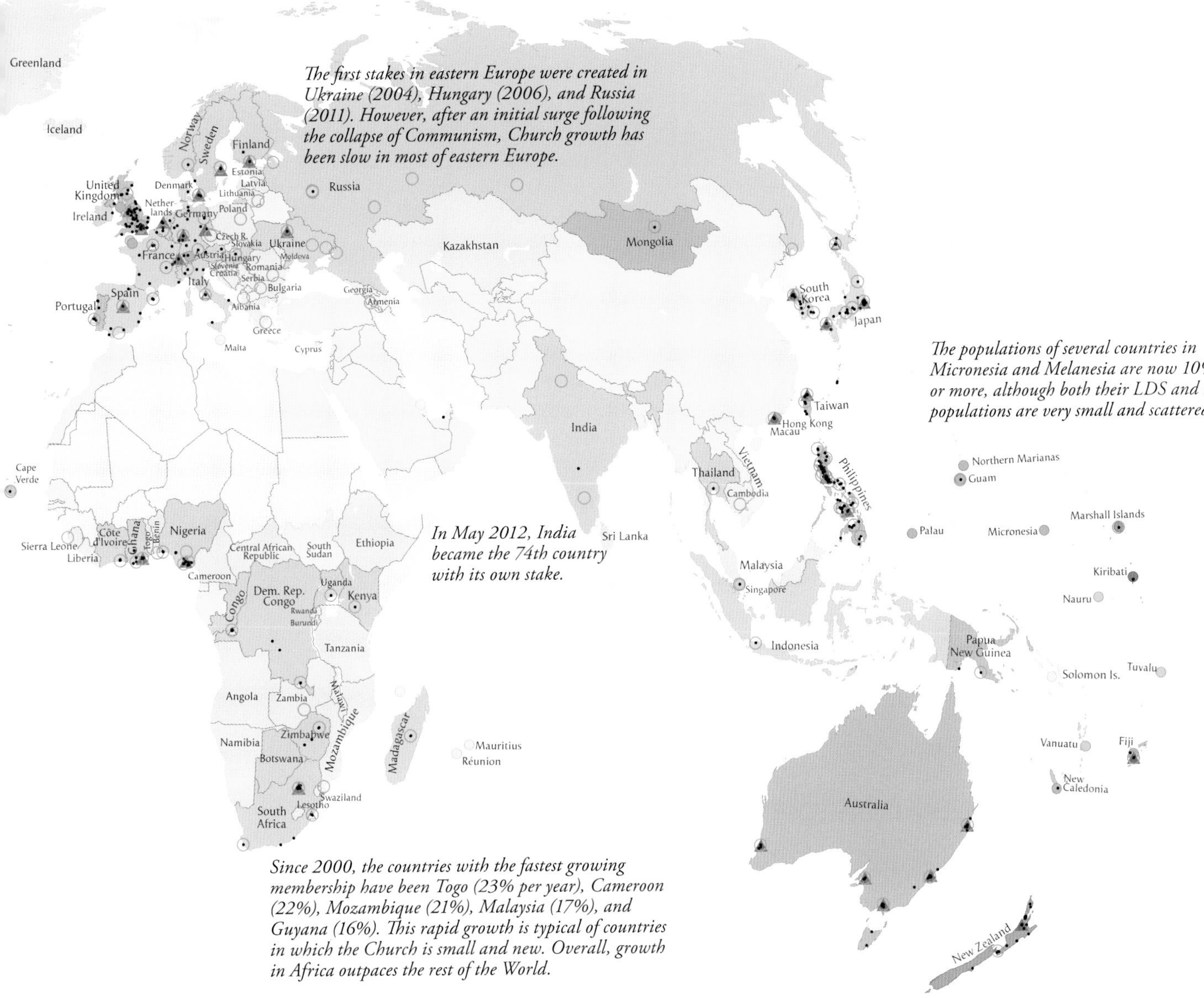

Timeline

1995 Gordon B. Hinckley becomes the 15th President of the Church; Area authorities replace regional representatives

1996 More than half of members live outside the U.S.

1998 ten million members

1999 First of more than 40 smaller temples built

2000 LDS Conference Center dedicated; 11 million members 100th temple dedicated; More than half of members speak languages other than English

2001 Perpetual Education Fund started

2004 12 million members; one million members in Mexico

2007 13 million members; one million members in Brazil

2008 Thomas S. Monson becomes the 16th President

2010 14 million members

1995 1997 1999 2001 2003 2005 2007 2009 2011 2013

Membership Distribution

1850–present

THE CHURCH OF JESUS CHRIST OF LATTER-DAY SAINTS has worked to spread its beliefs internationally from almost the moment of its founding in 1830. Today, Mormonism is present in virtually every country where Christian proselytizing is allowed. Worldwide growth accelerated rapidly after World War II, reaching new areas, rapidly moving the Church from a largely insular Intermountain West community to one which now has members in countries across the world. As evidence of this change, on February 28, 1996, the Church announced that it had more members living outside of the United States than within it—4.720 million Mormons in foreign countries compared with 4.719 million in the United States.

That said, the Church has grown in various countries and regions of the world at very different rates, and has a drastically different presence from one region to another. Explanations for this pattern include proximity to Utah, religious heritage, openness to religious change, political relationships with the United States, and level of economic development.

The Church has a long history in Polynesia (see p. 238) and has had a significant acceptance level in several countries there. In fact, the small island nations of Tonga and Samoa have the highest percentage of Mormons of any country in the world (approximately 45 and 31 percent respectively). LDS adherents in Oceania overall are similar in number to those found in Europe, even though the general population of Oceania is much smaller. Western Europe, despite its long Church history (see p. 228), has only grown in numbers since immigration ended in the 1950s and now must compete with a low level of religiosity and openness to change, among other factors, so recent Church growth there has been much slower than in most other world regions.

The Church began to record noticeable gains in Latin America after 1960 (see p. 218, p. 224), and this trend has continued. Indeed, more than 71 percent of the Church's non-U.S. membership now lives in the Americas south of the U.S. border. When Mormon numbers in the United States and Canada are added to those of the rest of the Americas, it becomes apparent that The Church of Jesus Christ of Latter-day Saints is now dominantly (85%) an "American" Church in the broad sense of the term.

Many countries in Asia also saw their first sustained Church presence after World War II, largely due to the increased American activity there (see p. 236), most notably in the Philippines, which is already Christian. Although the Church has only recently made a major effort in Africa (see p. 232), it is currently the most rapidly growing region of the world. On the other hand, Eastern Europe, Russia, and most of mainland Asia comprise an emerging region of still sparse Mormon populations, where missionary work was sporadic before the 1990s. They are just beginning to register substantial congregations. The closed religious and political conditions of most Muslim nations in the Middle East and North Africa explain the fact that these subregions of Asia and Africa have the fewest Mormons of any part of the world (see p. 231). In many cases, the Church is not officially recognized or allowed there.

The current pattern of international membership reflects a fascinating intersection of worldwide historical, political, and religious realities with the timing, relative size, and resources of the missionary efforts of the Church.

Samuel M. Otterstrom

Worldwide Membership Distribution

The relative distribution of LDS members worldwide has changed significantly over the past few decades. No longer does Utah and the rest of the United States dominate. Where North America was home to the vast majority of the LDS people fifty years ago, it now makes up less than half of the members in the world. The growing importance of Middle and South America indicates the shift south in the Church's membership base. Instead of the Church of Jesus Christ of Latter-day Saints being primarily a North American Church it is now very much a North and South America faith with over 80 percent of its members residing on these two continents.

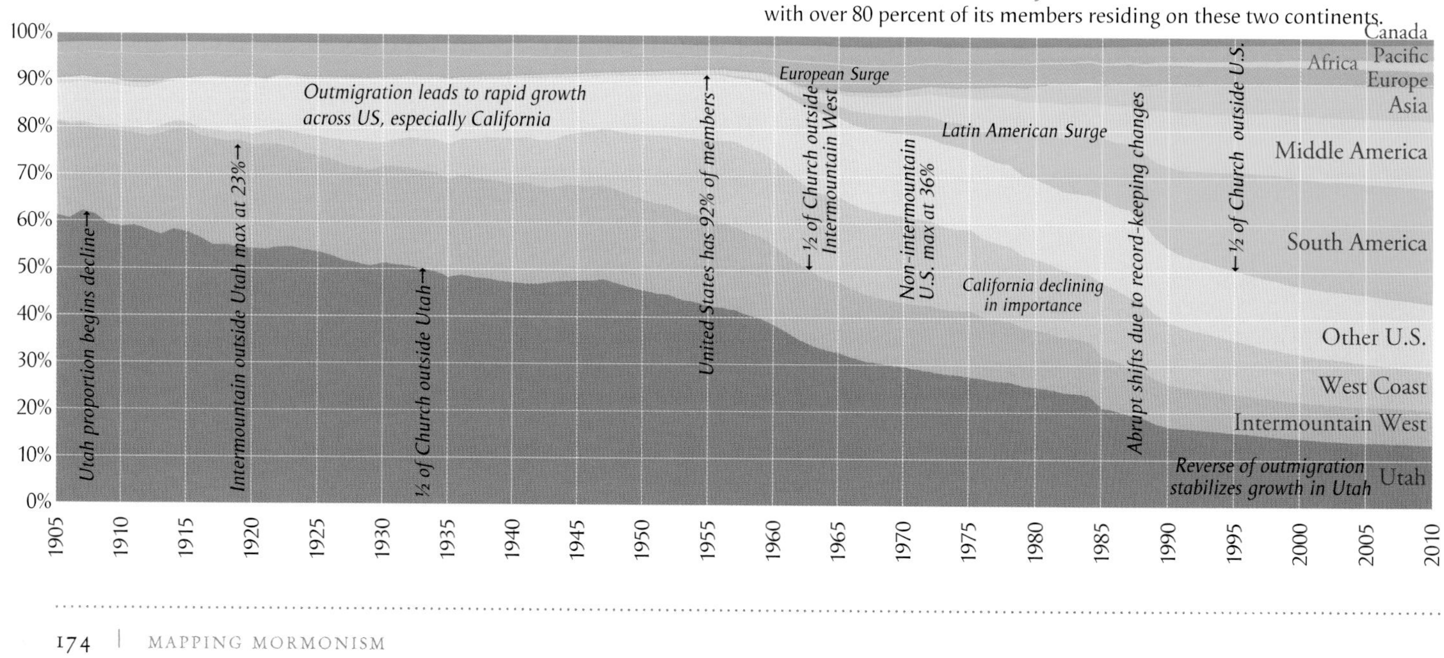

Membership and Annual Growth

In this cartogram, the size of each country depends on the number of LDS members, not its true size. Colors represent the annual rate of growth.

Church growth has varied throughout the modern period in different parts of the world. Latin America grew particularly fast from the 1960s through the 1980s and has slowed noticeably since then, although it still is adding members more rapidly than most other parts of the world. Africa started to grow rapidly in the 1980s, after the priesthood was extended to all male members regardless of race in 1978. Membership is still relatively small in Africa, but it was increasing most rapidly of any world region from 1995 to 2005.

In contrast, membership in many countries of Western Europe has been growing very slowly over the past decades, and Germany even registered a small decline in the 1990s when large numbers of American Mormons left the country as the U.S. military cut back its presence. Eastern Europe and Spain have been increasing more rapidly recently, but the overall trend of Europe from 1995 to 2005 is steady growth at about the growth rate of Utah. Additionally, in the United States, the Pacific states showed slower growth than all the American regions to the east of it from 1990 to 2004; and the eastern states, in particular, have added new Mormons to their local congregations faster than the growth of the general population through immigration, natural increase, and conversions.

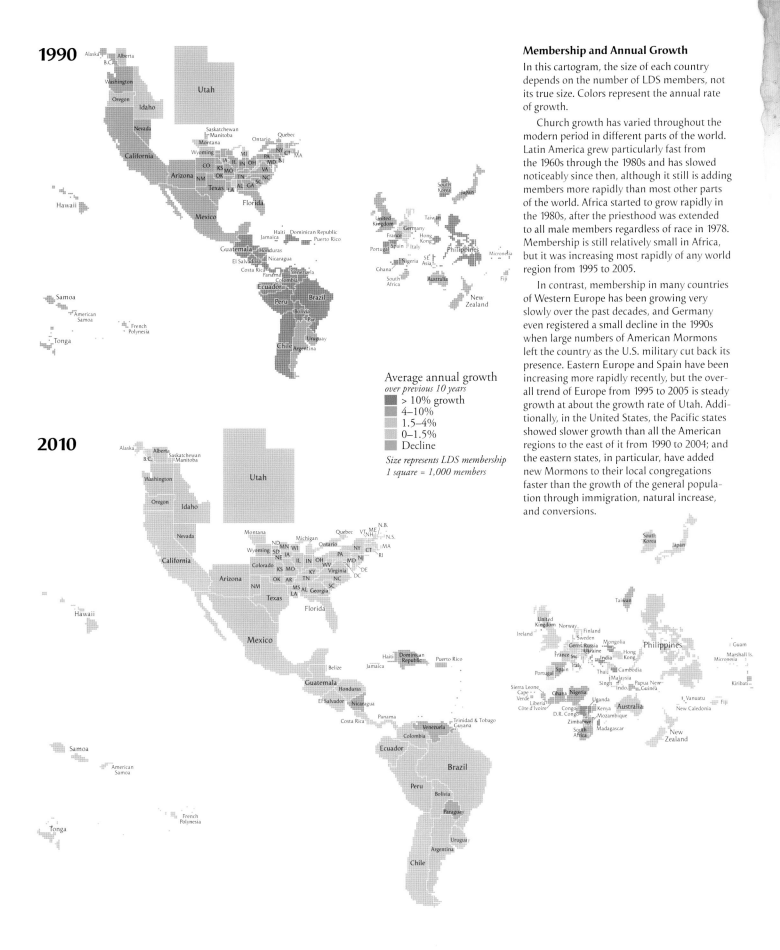

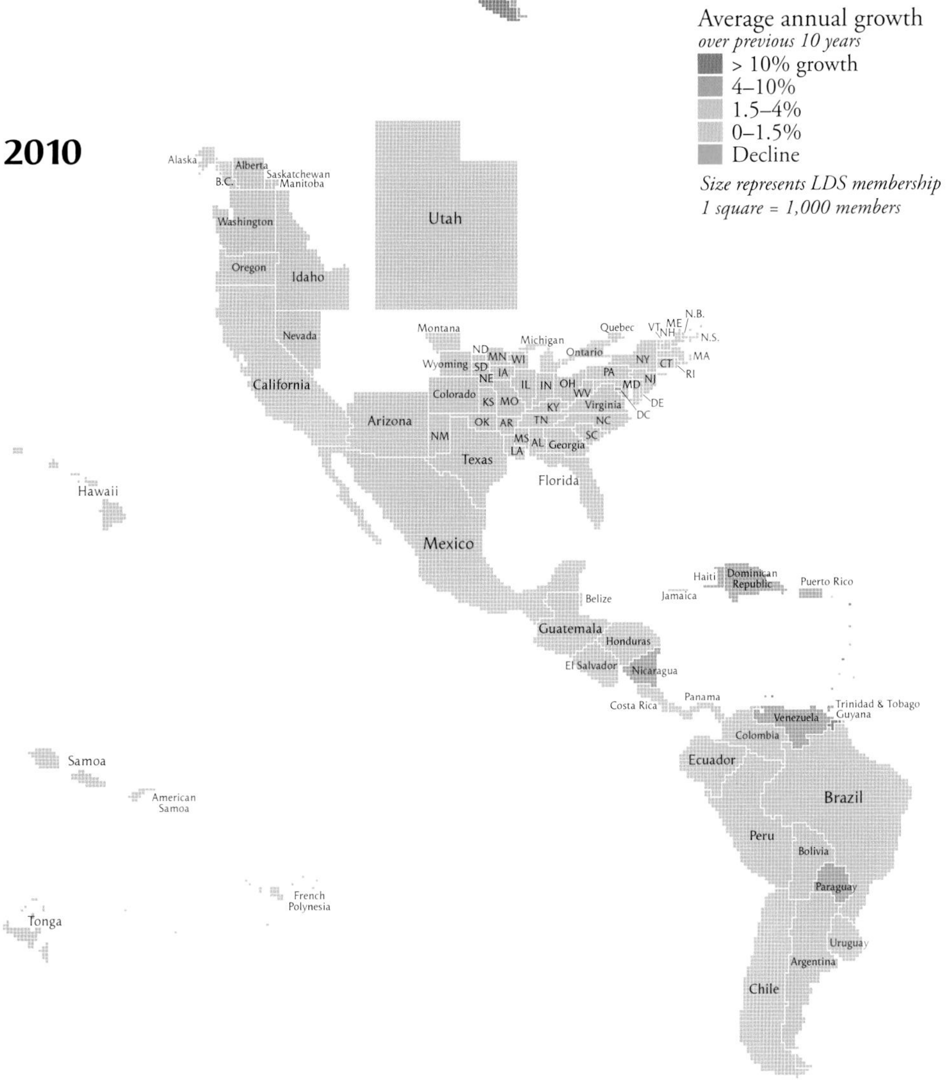

Church Leadership

1830–present

THE GENERAL AUTHORITIES form the upper echelon of priesthood leadership in The Church of Jesus Christ of Latter-day Saints, possessing authority and stewardship over the general membership of the Church, in contrast to local leaders who direct specific congregations. The concept of general leadership evolved considerably during the life of Joseph Smith (see pp. 38, 46, 58]), but the overall pattern was eventually established in Doctrine and Covenants section 107: First Presidency, Quorum of Twelve Apostles, Presidency of the Seventy, and Presiding Bishopric. Other general offices, such as the Patriarch, Assistants to the Twelve, and the First and Second Quorums of the Seventy, have come and gone (see p. 164), but the general trend has been one of increasing numbers of leaders to manage a growing Church.

Many wonder to what degree the General Authorities should be representative of the membership of the Church in general. Is the geographic and ethnic composition of the body of General Authorities similar to the distribution of the members? Is the group too homogeneous? Too Utah-centric? Because the Church is not a democracy, and General Authorities are neither representatives of their home countries nor members of a legislative body, these questions are not entirely relevant. Church members believe that God calls whom he needs to run the Church, regardless of geographic background.

However, there is a clear discrepancy between the geographic distribution of members and that of General Authorities, despite the fact that people all over the world have the capability to be effective leaders. This difference is apparently less due to bigotry than to the time required to prepare lay leaders for greater responsibilities. The best Church leaders not only need strong personal traits, but need experiences in a mature Church environment that can sometimes take generations to develop. Thus, the calling of General Authorities from a particular country or region is a sign of the strength of the Church there. Another issue is that General Authorities serve full time (usually living in Salt Lake City), forcing them to leave their careers (with a small living stipend if needed); this makes it more difficult for capable leaders from poorer countries to serve. That said, the gap has narrowed in recent years, as the distribution of the home countries of General Authorities has widened, and the leadership has become increasingly diverse.

Brandon S. Plewe

When Dieter F. Uchtdorf was called as an Apostle in 2004 and then into the First Presidency in 2008, many Church members hailed it as a singular event in the globalization of the Church, but this was not a recent innovation. From 1880–1931, one or both of the counselors in the First Presidency were native Europeans, including Joseph F. Smith's counselors from 1901 to 1910, John R. Winder (England, left) and Anthon H. Lund (Denmark, right).

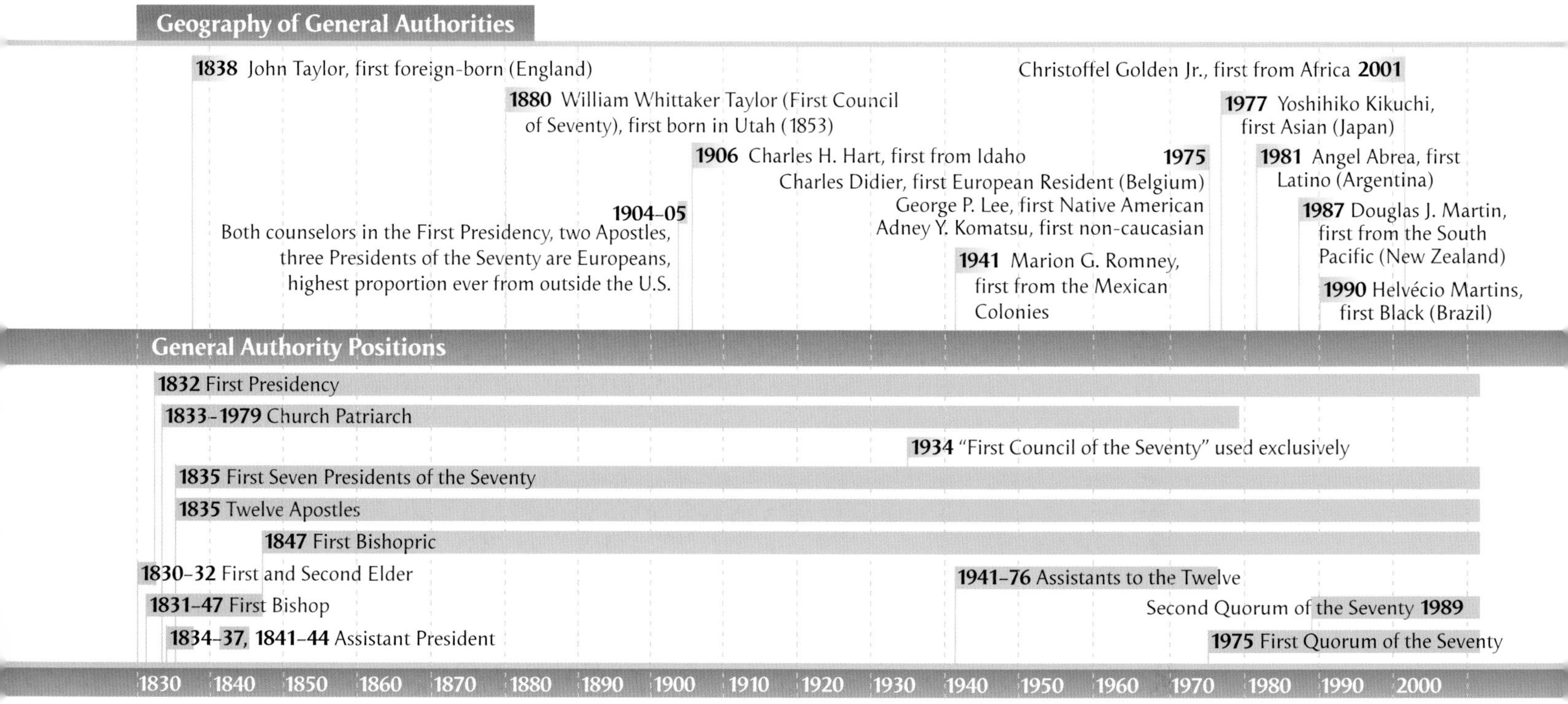

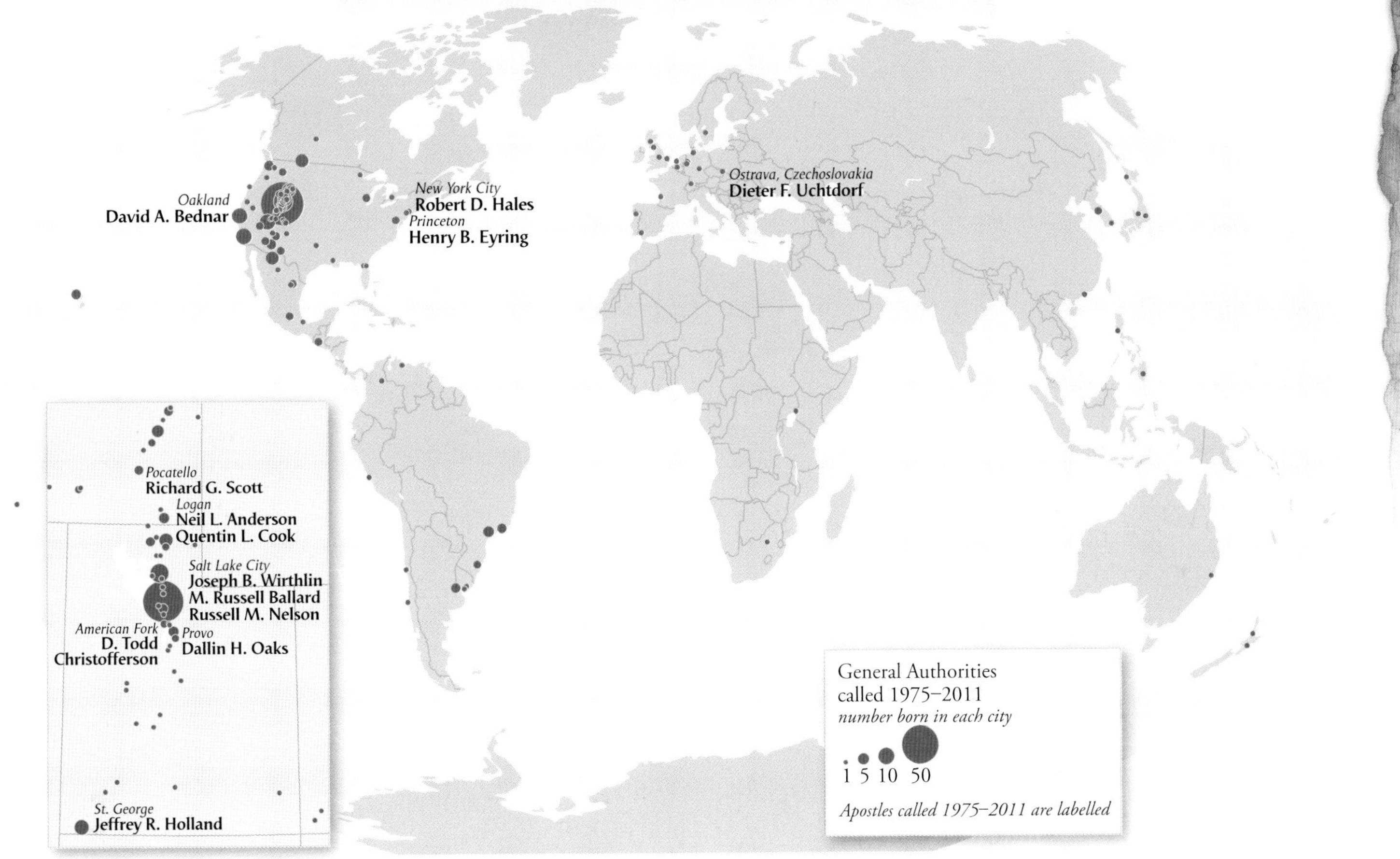

Birthplaces of Recent General Authorities

The geographic makeup of the body of General Authorities has clearly changed over time, falling into three periods: the first generation of Church leaders (and members) was overwhelmingly from the eastern United States. During the late nineteenth and early twentieth centuries, most leaders were second-generation members born in Utah, but there were also several General Authorities who were European convert-immigrants.

Since then, the distribution has shown a gradual trend toward greater diversity. Comparing this graph to the historical distribution of Church membership (see p. 174), it is apparent that the distribution of General Authorities is similar to the distribution of Church members many years earlier. This lag could be viewed as a slow reaction to geographic realities by conservative Church leaders but is more likely due to the time needed to develop strong leadership (often requiring a local Church presence of multiple generations). The gap is steadily decreasing, though, from about 60 years during the 1980s, to 35 years during the 1990s, to 25 years during the past decade. This acceleration of diversity is likely due to improved environments for developing new leaders.

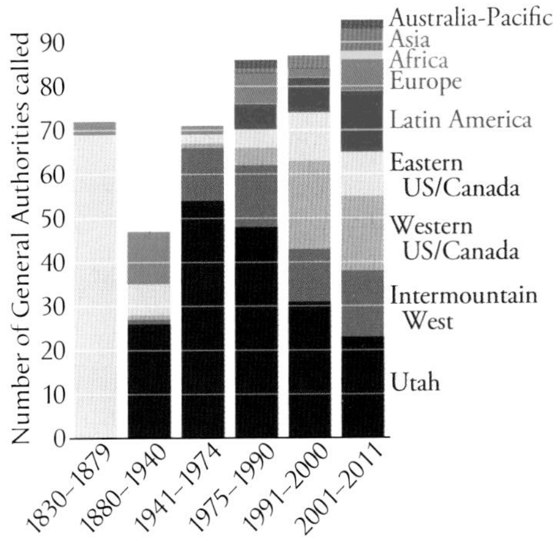

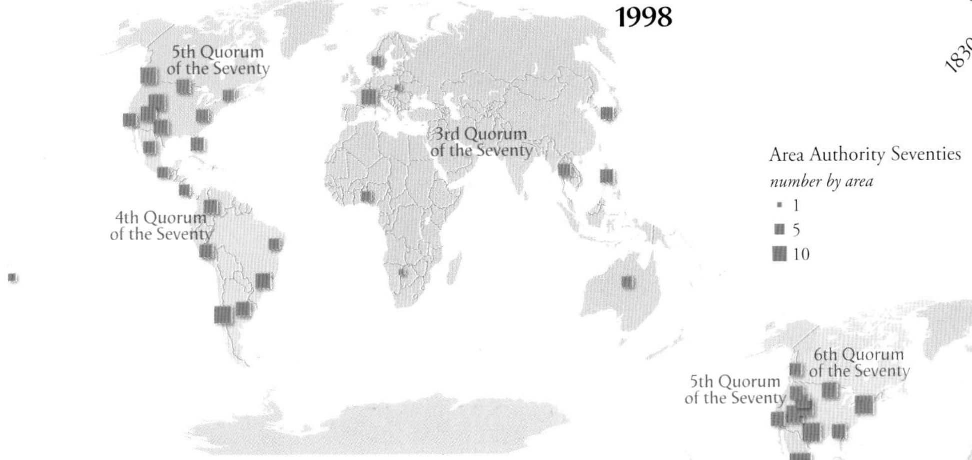

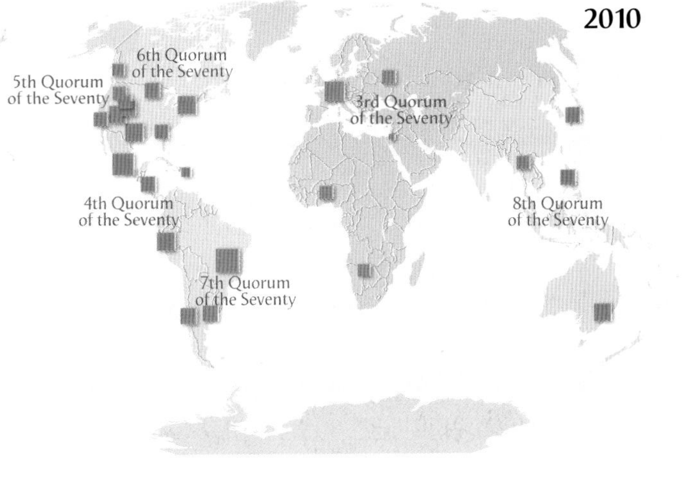

Area Authority Seventies

Area Authority Seventies were first called in 1995, replacing regional representatives as a form of "middle management" in the Church (see p. 164). Although they do not have direct authority over local stakes and missions, they communicate local and regional issues to the General Authorities, and carry instruction from the general to the local. Their distribution is more similar to the current geography of the Church than the top levels of leadership, even improving between 1998 and 2010. These Seventies also receive valuable "advanced training" in Church leadership; in recent years, most new General Authorities have previously served as area authorities.

Missionary Work

1900–present

Missionary work is the lifeblood of The Church of Jesus Christ of Latter-day Saints. Every member, even if not a convert, has ancestors who came into the Church as a consequence of the Church's missionary program. Patterns of missionary service and organization varied considerably during the nineteenth Century (see pp. 40, 94), but in the early 1900s, the program gradually standardized into the form we see now. Today, a mission is an administrative region of the world where missionary activity is conducted by Latter-day Saints. In each mission, a presidency is given authority over many missionaries (generally 50–200) and over the members who do not reside in stakes (see p. 184). Young men ages 19–25 typically serve missions for 24 months, single women 21 years and older may serve for 18 months, and senior couples (husbands and wives) typically serve from 12 to 24 months.

During the mid- to late-nineteenth century, missionary work had been hampered by negative public opinions of the Church (largely due to the practice of plural marriage) and by restrictions by many governments. After the Manifesto (see p. 122), the Church greatly increased the number and distribution of missionaries, who not only made new converts but also improved the public image of the Church.

As the Church has grown in numerical strength and social acceptance, the commitment to missionary work has likewise increased. As the call to gather to Utah was eliminated (see p. 158), new converts typically remained at home and became missionaries themselves because of their excitement in their newfound faith. Thus the addition of converts to the Church has perpetuated a continual growth and expansion of Church membership and hence a continuing spread of the gospel throughout the world. As mission branches and districts matured and strengthened, they eventually became wards and stakes (see p. 184) with less reliance on missionary leadership and greater ability to send their own missionaries elsewhere.

President Spencer W. Kimball was a champion of the spread of missionary work. In 1978, he said that "it seems clear to me—indeed, this impression weighs upon me, that the Church is at a point in its growth and maturity when we are at last ready to move forward in a major way. . . . We have paused on some plateaus long enough. Let us resume our

continued on page 180

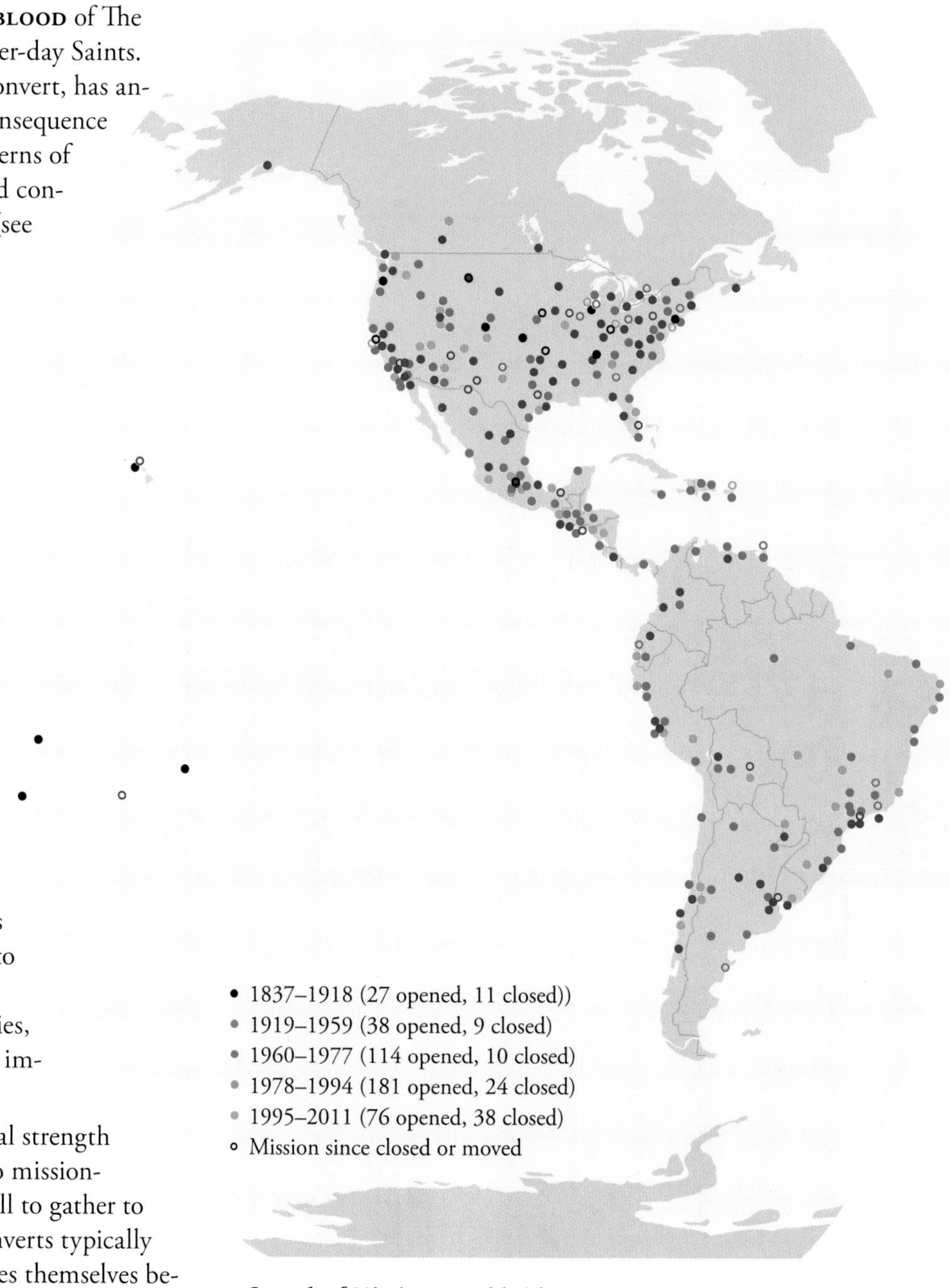

Growth of Missions Worldwide

The spread of missions worldwide has reflected the focus of the Church during each time period. In the middle of the twentieth century, pioneering missions were opened in Latin America and Asia, the latter especially after World War II (see p. 236). When the number of missionaries suddenly doubled in the early 1960s, missions throughout Europe and the United States were divided (many were reconsolidated when the boom slowed a few years later). After the revelation on priesthood (1978), missions opened in Africa and the Caribbean, but even more were created in Latin America as missionary success exploded there (see p. 218). After 1990, the work opened throughout Eastern Europe (see p. 230), but an increasing force of missionaries led to new missions all over the world. As of December 31, 2011, there were 340 missions of the Church in more than 146 of the world's nations and territories, with 55,410 full-time missionaries. Missions are present everywhere except in countries that have restrictions on Christian religious activity, such as in the Muslim world and China. In recent years, there has been a significant re-allotment of missionaries, with less successful missions in Europe, Japan, and North America being consolidated as new missions are being opened in more promising areas of Africa, Latin America, and Asia.

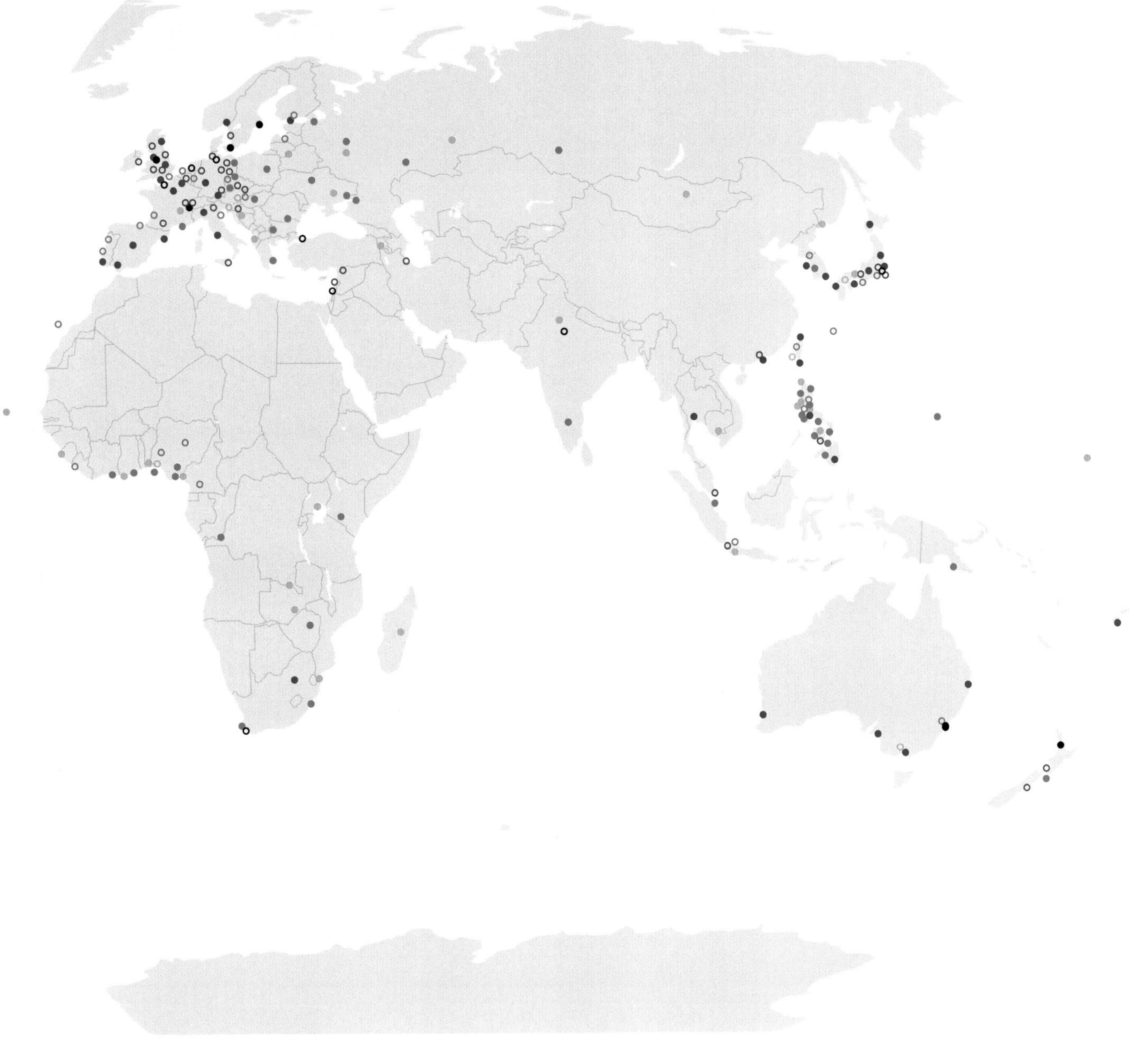

Missionary Work, 1920–Present

1920 European missions reopen after World War I

1925 Salt Lake Mission Home opens to prepare outgoing missionaries for a few days

Dec 1925 South American Mission opens

Missionaries **Aug 1939** withdrawn from Germany

Almost all missionaries **Mar 1942–45** withdrawn, and most missions vacated, during World War II

Married men replace most young **1951–1953** elders on missions during Korean War

1952 First standardized lesson plans for missionaries

Language Training **Nov 1961** Institute opens at BYU

Mission calls reduced **1965** during Vietnam War

Jul 1960 Age for elders to serve missions reduced from 20 to 19

1961–1964 Explosion in baptisms, due to advent of baby boom missionaries, overhaul of missionary program, and some questionable practices

1976 Missionary Training Center opens in Provo

"Preach My Gospel" lesson plan introduced **Oct 2004** (the 5th since 1952), coinciding with stricter standards for convert baptisms

Jul 1978 Revelation on priesthood leads to expansion of work in Africa, Brazil, and the Caribbean

Elders' missions **Apr 1982–Jan 1985** reduced to 18 months

Oct 2002 "Raising the Bar" initiative increases standards for outgoing missionaries

1920 | 1930 | 1940 | 1950 | 1960 | 1970 | 1980 | 1990 | 2000

Missionary Work
continued

journey forward and upward." Two years later, he followed this up, saying, "We have already asked you and we now repeat that request, that every family, every night and every morning, in family prayer and in secret prayers, too, pray to the Lord to open the doors of other nations so that their people, too, may have the Gospel of Jesus Christ." Since these declarations, well over one hundred new missions have been organized worldwide. A third of the new missions were created in South and Central America, more than 18 percent were organized in Asian countries, and a significant percentage of its missions were organized in other, non-U.S. countries.

David F. Boone

Missionary Training Centers

The earliest missionaries for the Church had little formal training except what they might have received from parents, extended family, or Church leaders. Most went to their assigned missions without sufficient financial support, depending on the hospitality of the local citizens, and preached in homes, on the streets, or wherever they could be heard. The School of the Prophets, established in 1833 in the Newel K. Whitney Store in Kirtland, was the first formal attempt to train men to better preach the gospel. Similar schools were established in subsequent Church centers, joining temples as places for the preparation and instruction for potential missionaries.

In 1925, the Mission Home opened in downtown Salt Lake City. Its location changed over the next 50 years (see p.114), but it was crucial in providing a brief (usually one week) initiation to full-time missionary service for thousands of missionaries. However, during the 1960s, the number of missionaries rose from approximately 5,000 to over 13,000, necessitating a more significant service. In 1961, a Missionary Institute was established at Brigham Young University to teach Spanish; its success led to expansion in 1963 to become the Language Training Mission, teaching a variety of languages on the BYU campus. Church schools in Rexburg, Idaho, and Laie, Hawaii, were likewise utilized, the latter specializing in Polynesian and Asian languages.

In September 1976, a new facility opened adjacent to the BYU campus. The Missionary Training Center (MTC) continued to leverage the strong international and foreign language programs at the university, especially the large number of students who spoke foreign languages (many returned missionaries themselves) who could help teach the young American missionaries. The facilities in Salt Lake City, Idaho, and Hawaii were soon closed to consolidate all training at the MTC. As the number of American missionaries continued to rise, the MTC was enlarged. However, the 1970s also saw a massive increase in the number of missionaries from other countries, and the Church recognized that the most efficient way to train them was to construct regional Mission Training Centers closer to their homes. These centers, much smaller than the Provo site, typically had less need for language training but more need for doctrinal education, hence they were often built next to temples. In 1993, fifteen training centers were in operation worldwide.

In recent years, the costs of maintaining these facilities have increased far faster than transportation costs, such that, in countries such as South Korea and Japan, it has become more efficient to fly local missionaries to Provo for training. These and a few other MTCs are being closed or moved as needs continue to change. Although the process, scale, and locations of missionary preparation may change and expansion is expected, it is a certainty that the Church remains committed to its missionary emphasis.

Jonathan Napela led one of the earliest efforts to train missionaries for service beyond their native land. A recent convert in Hawaii, Napela felt that he could assist the missionaries arriving from Utah. In 1852, he began teaching them Hawaiian language and culture, providing them with housing and food if they would do their part and study. Although it was a considerable personal sacrifice for Brother Napela, these efforts proved to be greatly beneficial to the proselytizing success of the missionaries in Hawaii, predating official efforts by the Church by over one hundred years.

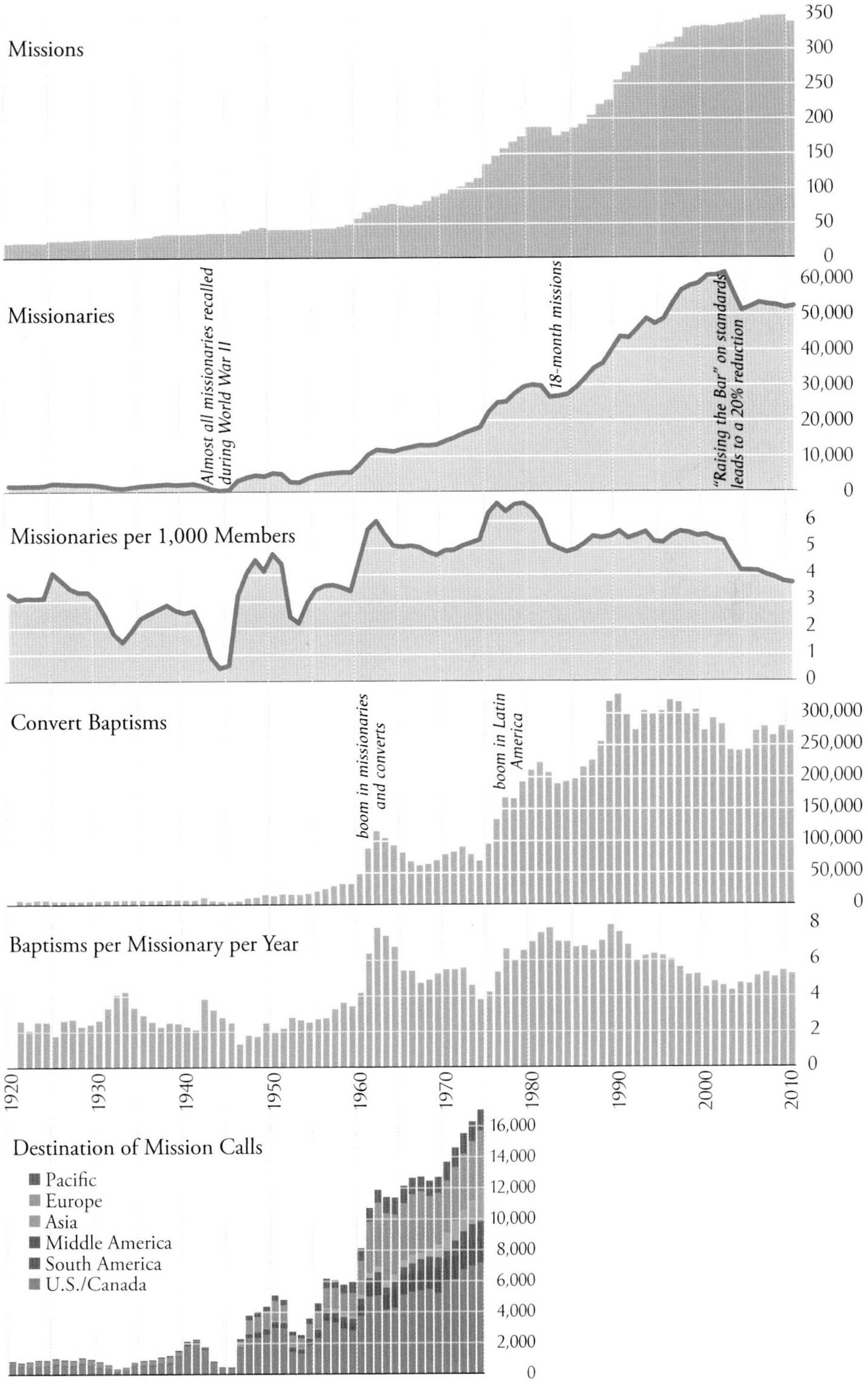

Missionary Work by the Numbers

The numerical success of the LDS Missionary Program has waxed and waned during the twentieth and twenty first centuries, in response to a variety of factors. Declines in the numbers of missionaries during the Great Depression and major wars were offset by an explosion in the number of missionaries in the early 1960s (due to the onset of the Baby Boom and the establishment of the standard age of 19 for young men to serve missions). This wave of missionaries was very successful in terms of baptisms, due to improved training and standardized teaching practices, as well as questionable practices such as using sports to recruit youth into the Church. Although growth slowed over the next decade, it accelerated again during the 1980s, especially as Latin America became the dominant source of converts as well as a growing source of missionaries. Since then, the program has slowed significantly, due to a variety of factors: long-term demographic shifts leading to a lower proportion of young men and women in the Church, rising eligibility standards for both missionaries and their prospective converts, and the increasing secularization of the world. However, the Church still recognizes the importance of spreading its message around the world, and looks for every opportunity to expand that effort.

Temples

1836–present

LATTER-DAY SAINTS REGARD THE TEMPLE as the "House of the Lord," serving two major functions—places where God communes with man (Exodus 25:8, 22) and where sacred priesthood ordinances are performed (D&C 124:38), including: baptism on behalf of deceased ancestors (introduced in 1840); the endowment, in which members learn of their potential eternal destiny and enter into covenants with God (introduced in 1842); and sealings of husbands, wives, and children for eternity (introduced in 1843). These roles emerged gradually; the two temples built during Joseph Smith's lifetime at Kirtland (see p. 30) and Nauvoo (see p. 56) were primarily meetinghouses, but they were also the sites of visions, revelations, and new ordinances.

During the second half of the nineteenth century, Latter-day Saints built four temples in Utah, including the great temple at Salt Lake City. The Logan and Manti temples introduced beautiful rooms with murals on their walls for presenting the endowment. Four more temples were built during the first half of the twentieth century—in Hawaii, Alberta, Arizona, and Idaho—reflecting the Church's expansion beyond Utah. These smaller temples incorporated a modern design and omitted the large assembly halls, completing the transition from Kirtland's meetinghouse design to a focus on temple ordinances.

The second half of the twentieth century brought the first "overseas temples"—in Switzerland, New Zealand, and England. These smaller temples introduced motion pictures to facilitate presenting the endowment in multiple languages. Other temples followed in the Pacific, Asia, Europe, Africa, and South America. A temple was even dedicated behind the "Iron Curtain" in East Germany. Forty-seven temples were in service when Gordon B. Hinckley became President of the Church in 1995. For at least two decades he had been concerned with making temple blessings more readily available to the scattered international Saints. A 1997 visit to the Mormon colonies in Mexico inspired him to build over fifty very small temples around the world.

As the twenty-first century dawned, some larger temples once again were built in centers of significant Latter-day Saint population. Thus temples of varying sizes and designs were meeting the spiritual needs of a worldwide Church.

Richard O. Cowan

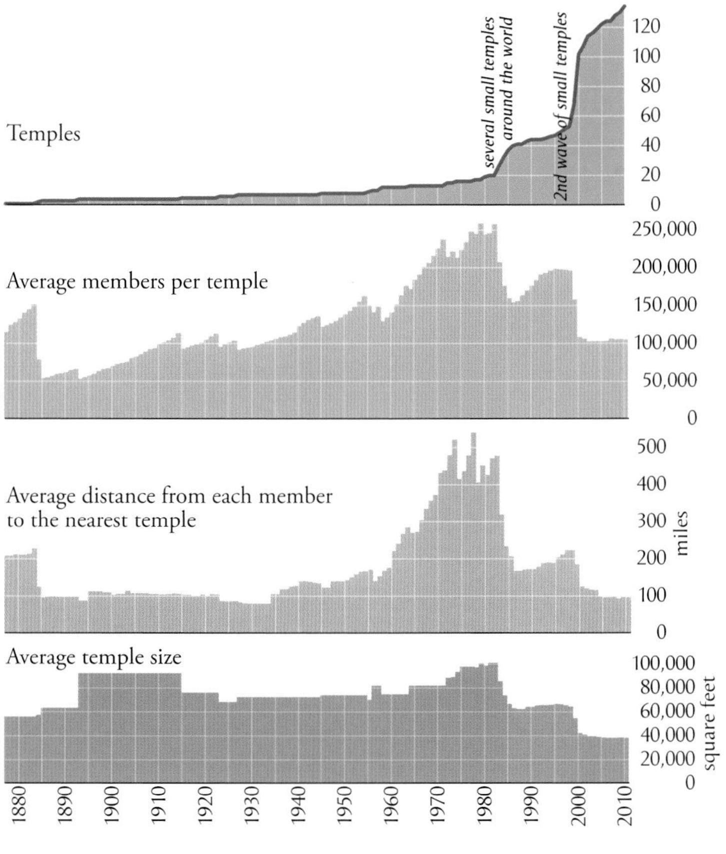

several small temples around the world
2nd wave of small temples
Temples
0
20
40
60
80
100
120
Average members per temple
0
50,000
100,000
150,000
200,000
250,000
Average distance from each member to the nearest temple
0
100
200
300
400
500
miles
Average temple size
0
20,000
40,000
60,000
80,000
100,000
square feet
1880
1890
1900
1910
1920
1930
1940
1950
1960
1970
1980
1990
2000
2010

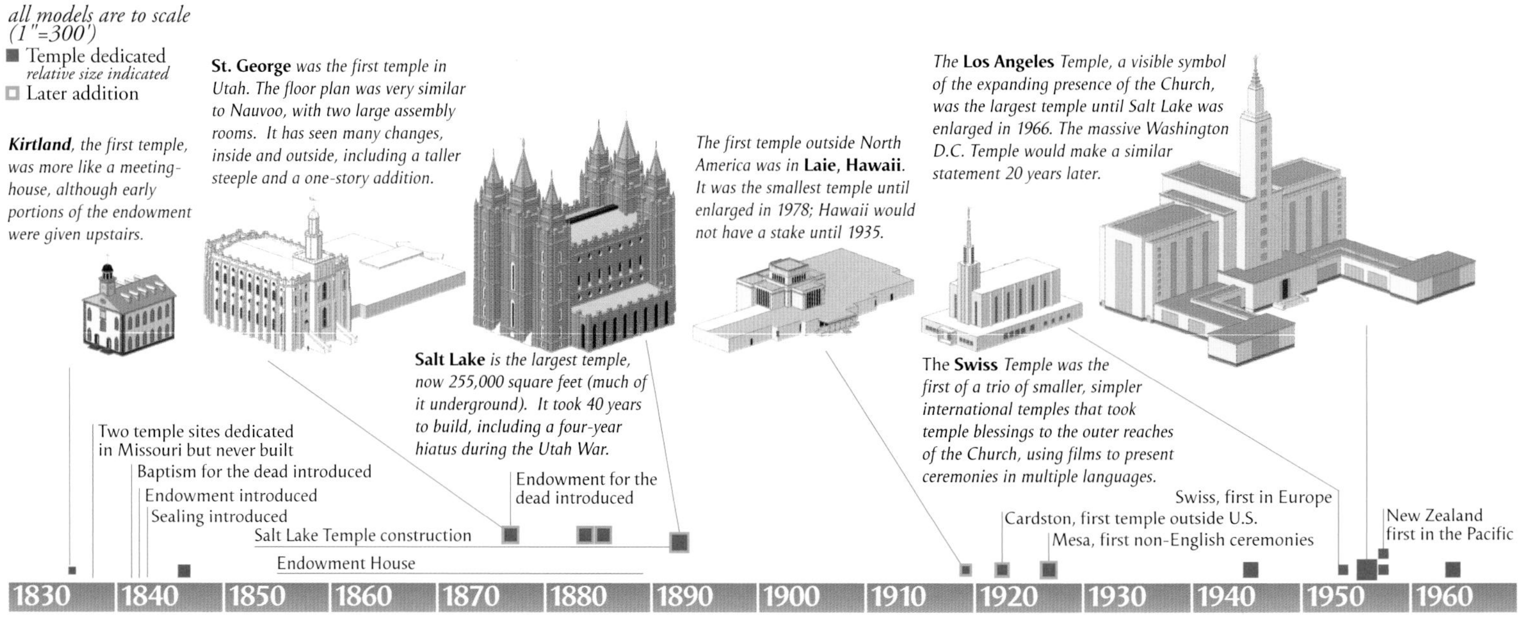

all models are to scale (1"=300')
Temple dedicated relative size indicated
Later addition
Kirtland, the first temple, was more like a meeting-house, although early portions of the endowment were given upstairs.
St. George was the first temple in Utah. The floor plan was very similar to Nauvoo, with two large assembly rooms. It has seen many changes, inside and outside, including a taller steeple and a one-story addition.
Salt Lake is the largest temple, now 255,000 square feet (much of it underground). It took 40 years to build, including a four-year hiatus during the Utah War.
The first temple outside North America was in Laie, Hawaii. It was the smallest temple until enlarged in 1978; Hawaii would not have a stake until 1935.
The Los Angeles Temple, a visible symbol of the expanding presence of the Church, was the largest temple until Salt Lake was enlarged in 1966. The massive Washington D.C. Temple would make a similar statement 20 years later.
The Swiss Temple was the first of a trio of smaller, simpler international temples that took temple blessings to the outer reaches of the Church, using films to present ceremonies in multiple languages.
Two temple sites dedicated in Missouri but never built
Baptism for the dead introduced
Endowment introduced
Sealing introduced
Salt Lake Temple construction
Endowment House
Endowment for the dead introduced
Swiss, first in Europe
Cardston, first temple outside U.S.
Mesa, first non-English ceremonies
New Zealand first in the Pacific
1830
1840
1850
1860
1870
1880
1890
1900
1910
1920
1930
1940
1950
1960

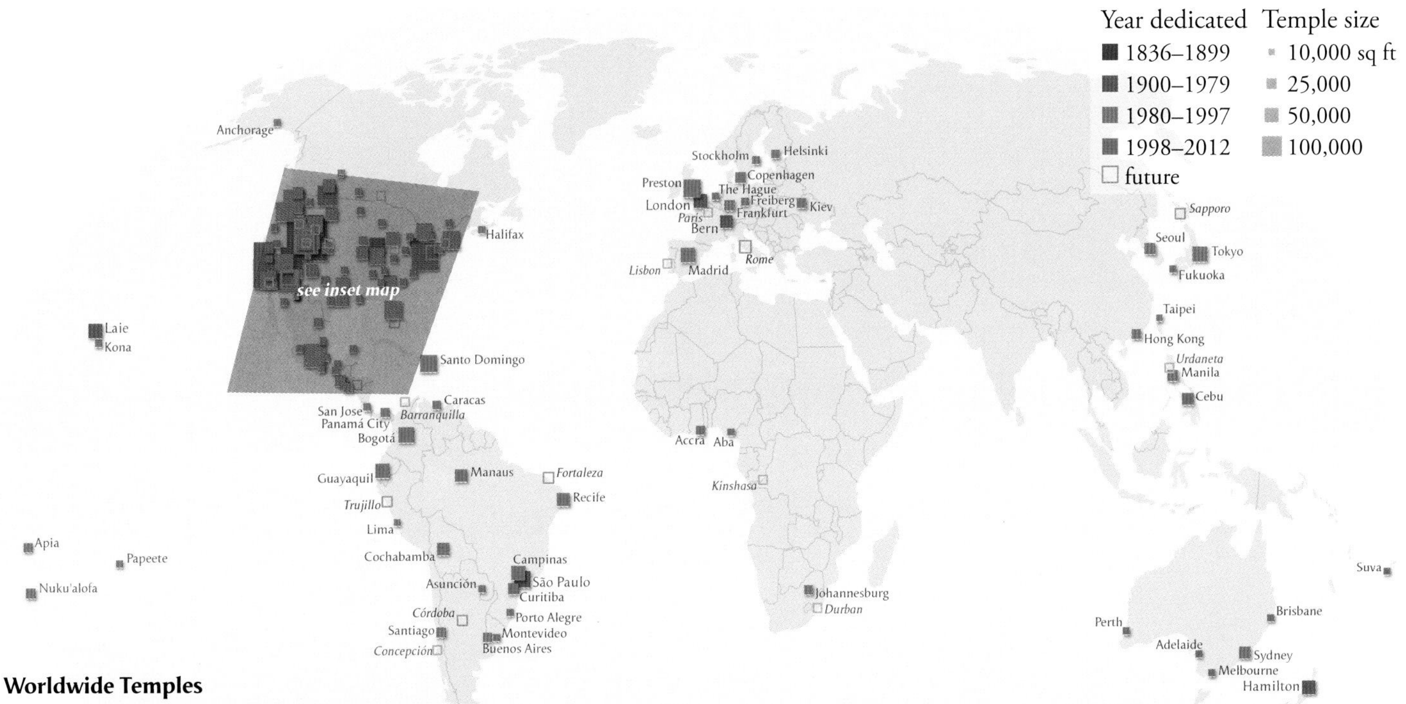

Worldwide Temples

In 1900, all of the functioning temples were in Utah. The first half of the twentieth century saw three temples built in other parts of western North America, and one in Hawaii. Since that time, temples have spread around the world, particularly after President Hinckley received the inspiration in 1997 to build much smaller temples. Temples have been built in a variety of sizes, typically depending on the number of members in the local area. The Church's five largest temples are located in Salt Lake City (1893), Los Angeles (1956), Washington, D.C. (1974), South Jordan Utah (1981), and Mexico City (1983), while the smallest is in the Mormon village of Colonia Juarez, Mexico (6,800 square feet).

◀ More Temples Closer to Members

Before 1980, the growth in Church membership was generally faster than the growth in the number of temples. Since that time, the construction of new temples has generally been at a greater rate. As the growth in membership became more international, the average distance to temples increased, but with the increased construction of temples, the average distance decreased. The recent rapid increase in the number of temples was possible in part because smaller temples have been built to be near smaller concentrations of members.

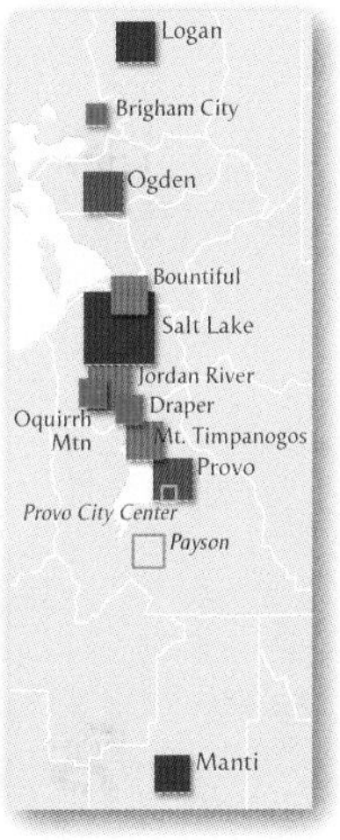

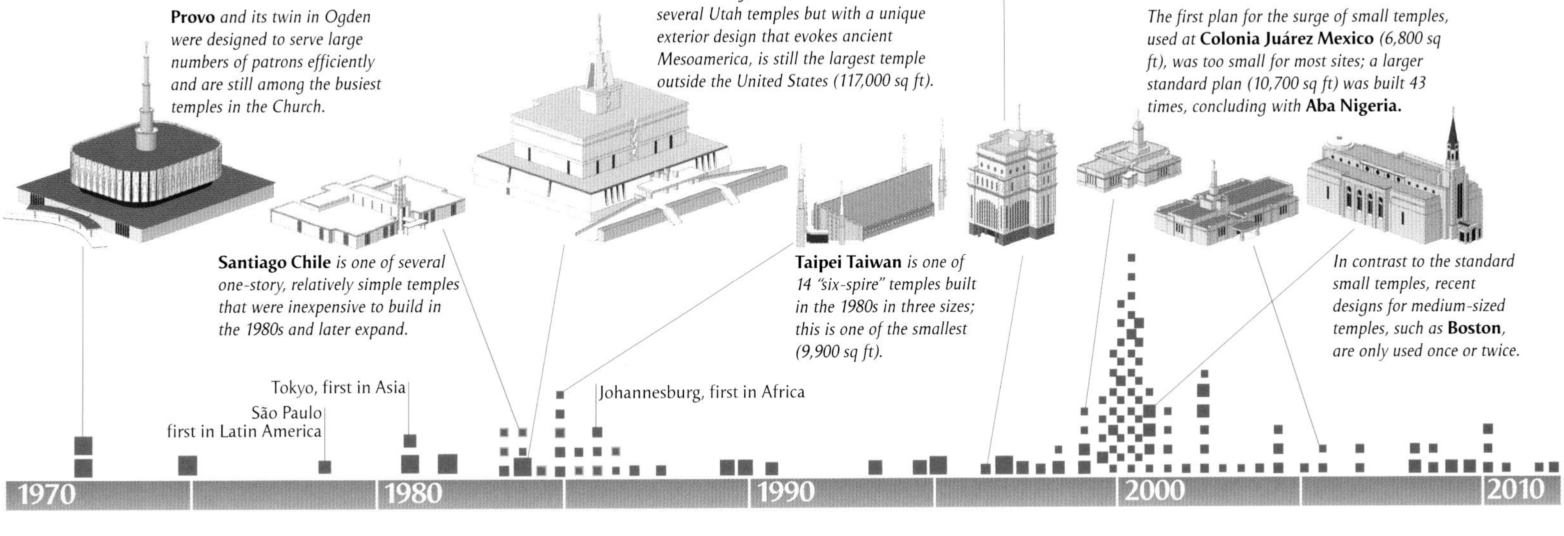

***Provo** and its twin in Ogden were designed to serve large numbers of patrons efficiently and are still among the busiest temples in the Church.*

***Santiago Chile** is one of several one-story, relatively simple temples that were inexpensive to build in the 1980s and later expand.*

***Mexico City**, somewhat similar to several Utah temples but with a unique exterior design that evokes ancient Mesoamerica, is still the largest temple outside the United States (117,000 sq ft).*

***Taipei Taiwan** is one of 14 "six-spire" temples built in the 1980s in three sizes; this is one of the smallest (9,900 sq ft).*

***Hong Kong** and Manhattan are urban temples, part of a multi-story, multi-use Church building.*

*The first plan for the surge of small temples, used at **Colonia Juárez Mexico** (6,800 sq ft), was too small for most sites; a larger standard plan (10,700 sq ft) was built 43 times, concluding with **Aba Nigeria.***

*In contrast to the standard small temples, recent designs for medium-sized temples, such as **Boston**, are only used once or twice.*

Stakes

1910–present

THE PROPHET ISAIAH, seeing the latter-day glory of Zion, wrote figuratively about her preparation for rejoicing: "Enlarge the place of thy tent, and let them stretch forth the curtains of thine habitations: spare not, lengthen thy cords, and strengthen thy stakes" (Isaiah 54:2). Latter-day revelations identify "stakes" as sources of spiritual strength and refuge (see D&C 82:14; 115:5–6; 133:9). In contrast to a mission district, which generally must *receive* strength and leadership *from* the Church, a stake is able to give strength and stability *to* the Church, just as stakes support a tent. Hence, the formation of new stakes is a measure of maturity and development in a region, better than a mere increase in membership because it takes activity and leadership into account.

The growth of the Church since 1900 is well illustrated by the creation of new stakes in diverse parts of the world. Before 1923, all stakes were located in traditional areas of Latter-day Saint settlement in the Intermountain West (see p. 128). As the members have expanded beyond this core (by conversion and migration) and local leadership has matured, "pioneer" stakes have been created in new realms: California in the 1920s, then the rest of the United States; then internationally to the Pacific in the 1950s, Europe and Latin America in the 1960s, and Asia and Africa in the 1970s.

The pace of organizing stakes has quickened over the years, in keeping with the growth of membership. In the first half of the twentieth century, one or two stakes were formed each year. During the late 1970s and again in the mid-1990s, over 100 stakes were organized each year. The first decade of the twenty-first century has seen a more cautious growth, with no more than 50 stakes organized during any single year.

The ideal is to have the more complete stake programs available to all Church members. During the twentieth century, wards and stakes became significantly smaller to better serve members, although in some cases they were too small to remain stable (see p. 224). By 2011, the total number of stakes exceeded 2,900.

Richard O. Cowan

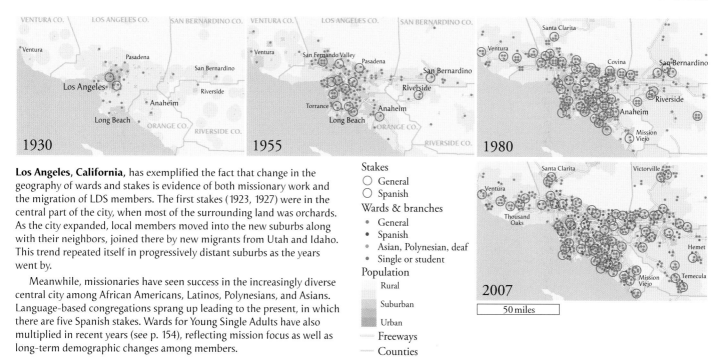

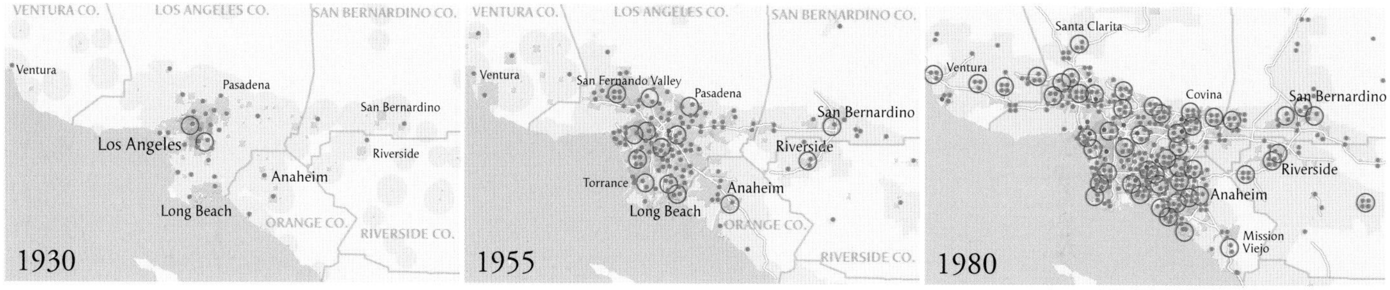

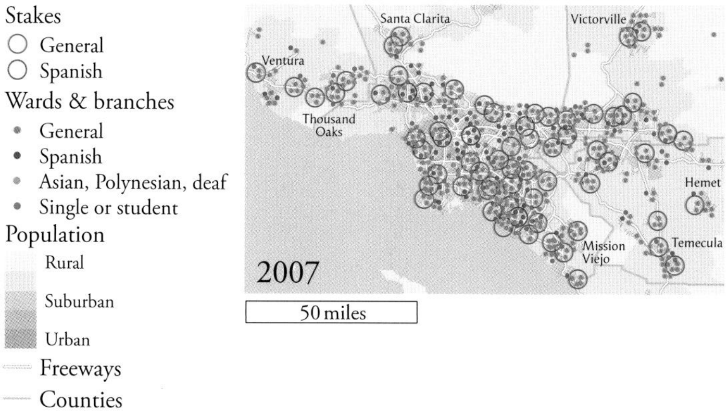

Los Angeles, California, has exemplified the fact that change in the geography of wards and stakes is evidence of both missionary work and the migration of LDS members. The first stakes (1923, 1927) were in the central part of the city, when most of the surrounding land was orchards. As the city expanded, local members moved into the new suburbs along with their neighbors, joined there by new migrants from Utah and Idaho. This trend repeated itself in progressively distant suburbs as the years went by.

Meanwhile, missionaries have seen success in the increasingly diverse central city among African Americans, Latinos, Polynesians, and Asians. Language-based congregations sprang up leading to the present, in which there are five Spanish stakes. Wards for Young Single Adults have also multiplied in recent years (see p. 154), reflecting mission focus as well as long-term demographic changes among members.

Stake Milestones

- **1834** First stake organized: Kirtland, Ohio
- First stake outside US: Cardston, Alberta **1895**
- First modern stake beyond Mormon Corridor: Los Angeles **1923**
- 100th stake formed: Lehi, Utah **1928**
- First stake outside of North America: Honolulu, Hawaii **1935**
- First stake outside of U.S. and Canada: Auckland, New Zealand **1958**
- First stake in Europe: Manchester, England **1960**
- First non-English speaking stake: The Hague, Netherlands **1961**
- First stake in South America: São Paulo, Brazil **1966**
- 500th stake formed: Fallon, Nevada **1970**
- First stake in Asia: **1970** Tokyo, Japan
- **1970** First stake in Africa: Johannesburg, South Africa
- **1979** 1000th stake formed: Nauvoo, Illinois
- **1989** Mexico has 100 stakes
- **1994** 2000th stake: Mexico City
- **1996** A record 146 stakes created in one year
- **2001–3** 56 undersized stakes closed, including 39 in Chile alone

1830 1850 1870 1890 1910 1930 1950 1970 1990 2010

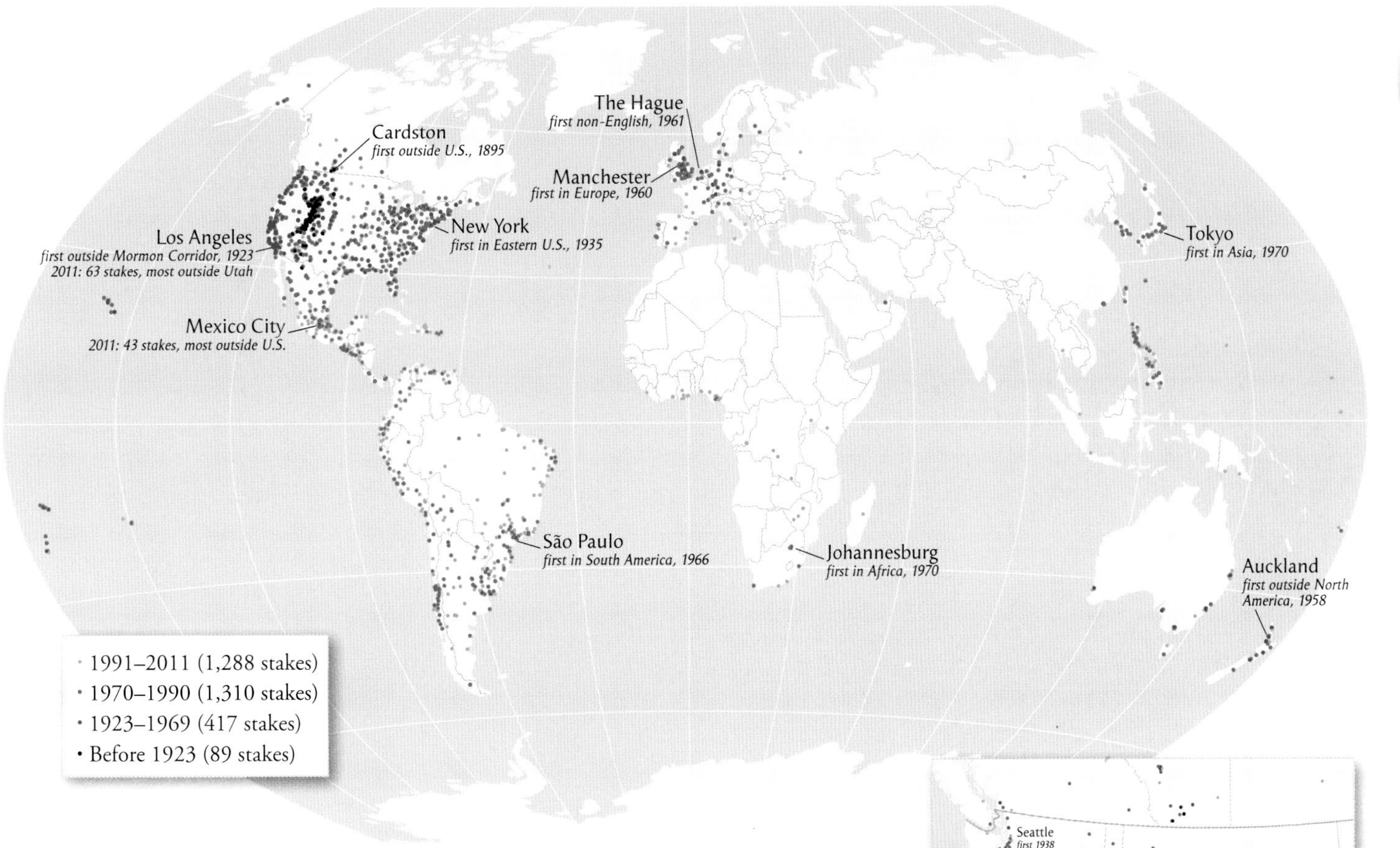

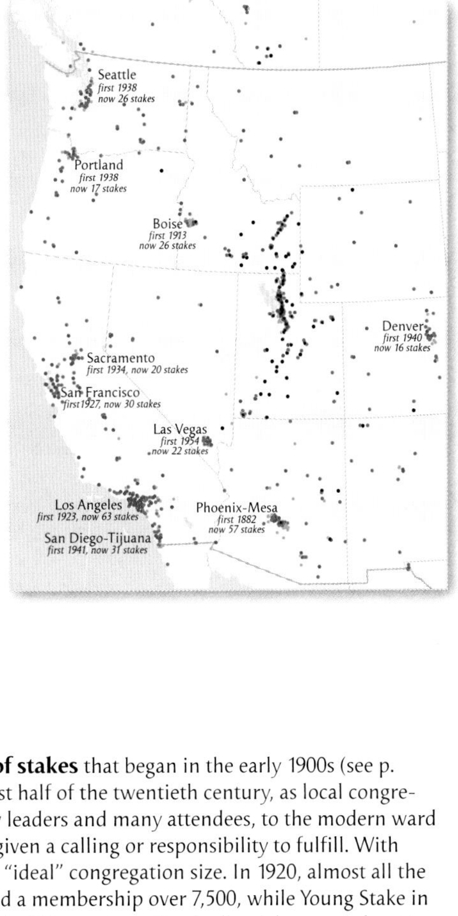

Stake Growth in the Twentieth Century

As late as 1920 all of the Church's stakes were located in traditional areas of Latter-day Saint colonization in the Intermountain West. During the 1920s, however, the first stakes were organized in California at Los Angeles and San Francisco. Over the next 20 years, stakes were established throughout California as membership surged there, and were established in many major cities such as New York, Chicago, Denver, Portland, and Seattle.

One of the major goals of President David O. McKay (see p. 158) was to build independent strength of Church members around the world; a major part of this plan was to spread the blessings of stake organization. Starting in New Zealand in 1958, the 1960s and early 70s saw pioneering stakes in major cities on every continent. Stakes in the eastern United States and Canada also multiplied rapidly during the 1970s and 1980s, but stake growth there has since slowed considerably. By 2010, most new stakes were being created in Latin America (especially Brazil) and Utah.

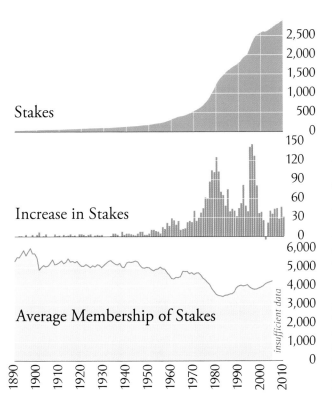

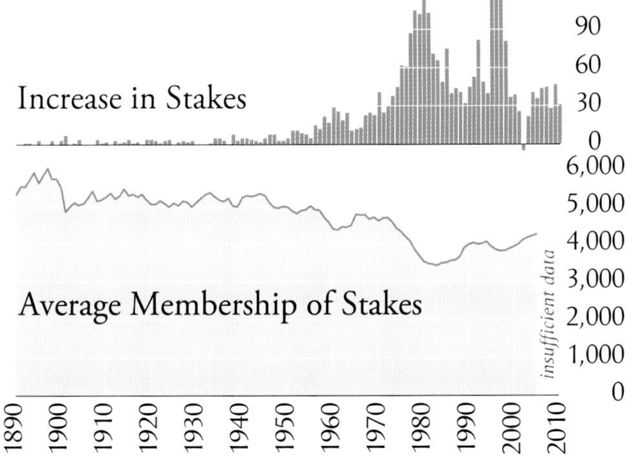

Major trends in the numbers of stakes that began in the early 1900s (see p. 128) continued throughout the first half of the twentieth century, as local congregations evolved from having a few leaders and many attendees, to the modern ward in which almost all members are given a calling or responsibility to fulfill. With this evolution came the idea of an "ideal" congregation size. In 1920, almost all the 16 stakes on the Wasatch Front had a membership over 7,500, while Young Stake in Colorado and New Mexico had only 950 members. Gradually, stakes evened out to about 4,000 members while wards averaged around 300–400 members (international wards and stakes tend to be smaller).

Growth in stakes was especially rapid during two periods, the late 1970s–early 1980s and the mid-1990s, when the Church made a concerted effort to make the strength of stakes available to as many members as possible. At the height of these waves, well over 90% of Church members lived in stakes (up from 80% during most of the twentieth century). In some cases, however, especially in Chile (see p. 222) and the Philippines in the late 1990s, the new very small stakes did not have enough qualified leaders, and dozens of stakes had to later be reconsolidated. In 2002, there was actually a net loss in the number of stakes, and since then, stake formation has been more cautious.

Cultural Ambassadors

1847–present

THROUGHOUT THEIR HISTORY, the Latter-day Saints have fostered the arts as a form of worship. In particular, the performing arts have served as a cultural outreach to the world, including the Mormon Tabernacle Choir, student performing groups at BYU and other Church schools, and entertainers such as the Osmond family. Church leaders have realized that these emissaries play a role in bringing the Church out of relative obscurity in the world. A visit from a Church performing arts group to a place has often brought greater respect and acceptance for the Church, reaching individuals who may not have had interest or opportunity before.

The best example of these groups is the Mormon Tabernacle Choir, which traces its roots to the small choir at the Church Conference held in August 1847 in the hastily erected bowery on Temple Square soon after the vanguard pioneer company arrived in the Salt Lake Valley. In 1867, the current dome-shaped Tabernacle was completed on Temple Square (see p. 114); its unique acoustics and beautiful organ give the 360-voice Choir its signature sound.

Although the Choir's primary role is to provide music for Church conferences, it has become one of the most recognized entities of The Church of Jesus Christ of Latter-day Saints through its weekly broadcast, touring, and recordings.

The weekly broadcast of *Music and the Spoken Word* has given the Choir a widespread reputation since it began in 1929. The choir has received Grammy (1960) and Emmy (1987) awards, two platinum records (1991, 1992), the National Medal of Arts (2003), two Peabody awards (1943, 1961), and is in the National Association of Broadcasters Hall of Fame. They have performed at the inaugurations of five U.S. presidents and at the 2002 Winter Olympics in Salt Lake City. These grand achievements demonstrate the power of music and the dedication of many thousands of individuals who have contributed to the Choir's success.

The first Choir tour was to the Columbian Exposition in Chicago in 1893, where they received second place in the Eisteddfod music contest. Since then, the Choir has toured extensively in the United States, Canada, and Europe, and visited many other countries. With 500–700 individuals traveling together, each tour requires careful planning, including performance venues, hotels, transportation, and food, even for a weekend visit to Idaho.

Other groups sponsored directly or indirectly by the Church include orchestras and student companies at each of the three Church-owned universities. For example, Brigham Young University in Provo has 17 performing arts groups that tour extensively. In recent years, broadcast technology has furthered the reach of all these cultural ambassadors. Most notably, BYUtv (2000) and BYU Television International (2007) are carried on cable and satellite systems across the Americas and are available globally on the Internet, giving the Church further opportunities to spread its message through cultural exchange.

Cynthia Doxey Green

Church Cultural Groups – Tours and Other Milestones

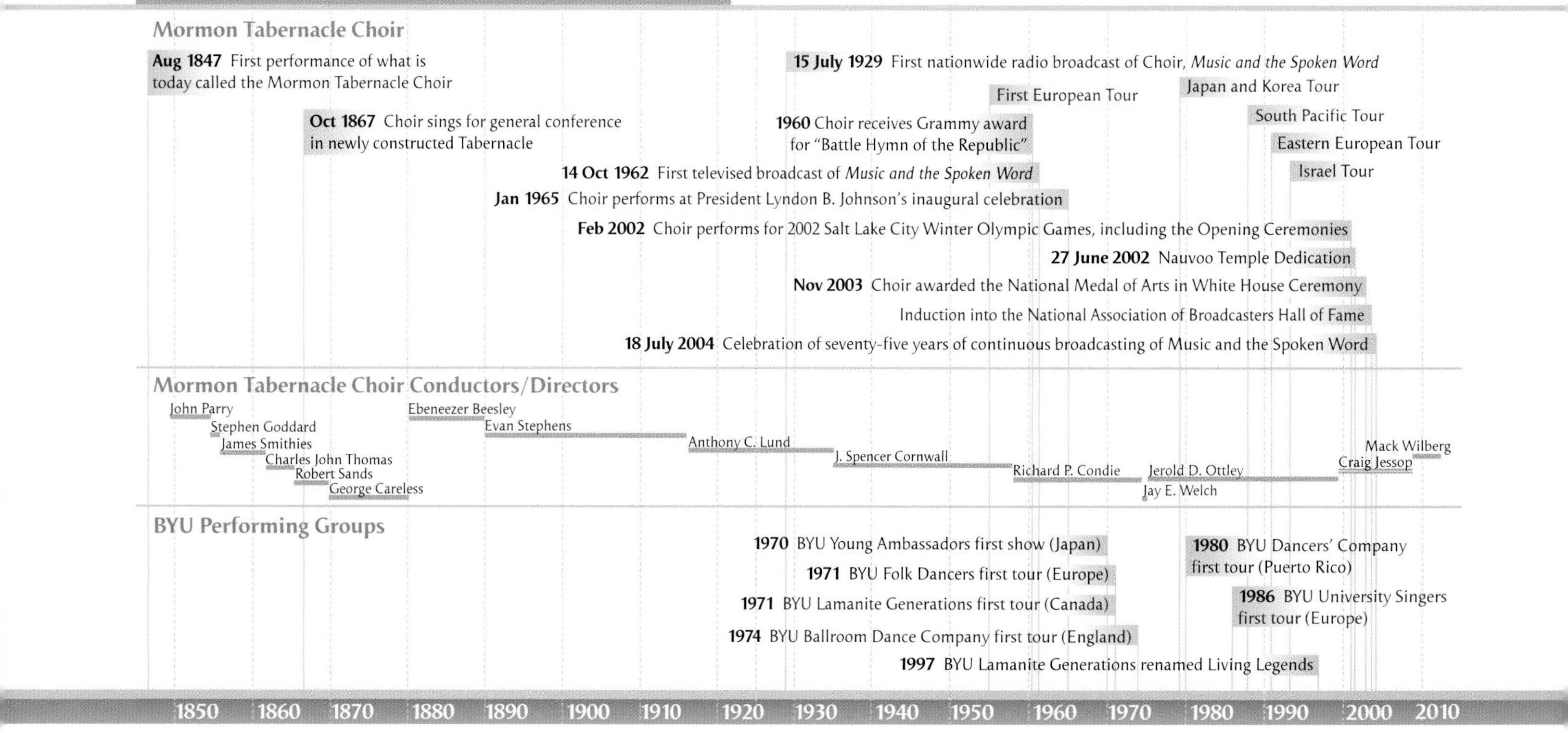

Mormon Tabernacle Choir
Aug 1847 First performance of what is today called the Mormon Tabernacle Choir
15 July 1929 First nationwide radio broadcast of Choir, Music and the Spoken Word
First European Tour
Japan and Korea Tour
Oct 1867 Choir sings for general conference in newly constructed Tabernacle
1960 Choir receives Grammy award for "Battle Hymn of the Republic"
South Pacific Tour
Eastern European Tour
Israel Tour
14 Oct 1962 First televised broadcast of Music and the Spoken Word
Jan 1965 Choir performs at President Lyndon B. Johnson's inaugural celebration
Feb 2002 Choir performs for 2002 Salt Lake City Winter Olympic Games, including the Opening Ceremonies
27 June 2002 Nauvoo Temple Dedication
Nov 2003 Choir awarded the National Medal of Arts in White House Ceremony
Induction into the National Association of Broadcasters Hall of Fame
18 July 2004 Celebration of seventy-five years of continuous broadcasting of Music and the Spoken Word
Mormon Tabernacle Choir Conductors/Directors
John Parry
Stephen Goddard
James Smithies
Charles John Thomas
Robert Sands
George Careless
Ebeneezer Beesley
Evan Stephens
Anthony C. Lund
J. Spencer Cornwall
Richard P. Condie
Jerold D. Ottley
Jay E. Welch
Craig Jessop
Mack Wilberg
BYU Performing Groups
1970 BYU Young Ambassadors first show (Japan)
1971 BYU Folk Dancers first tour (Europe)
1971 BYU Lamanite Generations first tour (Canada)
1974 BYU Ballroom Dance Company first tour (England)
1997 BYU Lamanite Generations renamed Living Legends
1980 BYU Dancers' Company first tour (Puerto Rico)
1986 BYU University Singers first tour (Europe)
1850 1860 1870 1880 1890 1900 1910 1920 1930 1940 1950 1960 1970 1980 1990 2000 2010

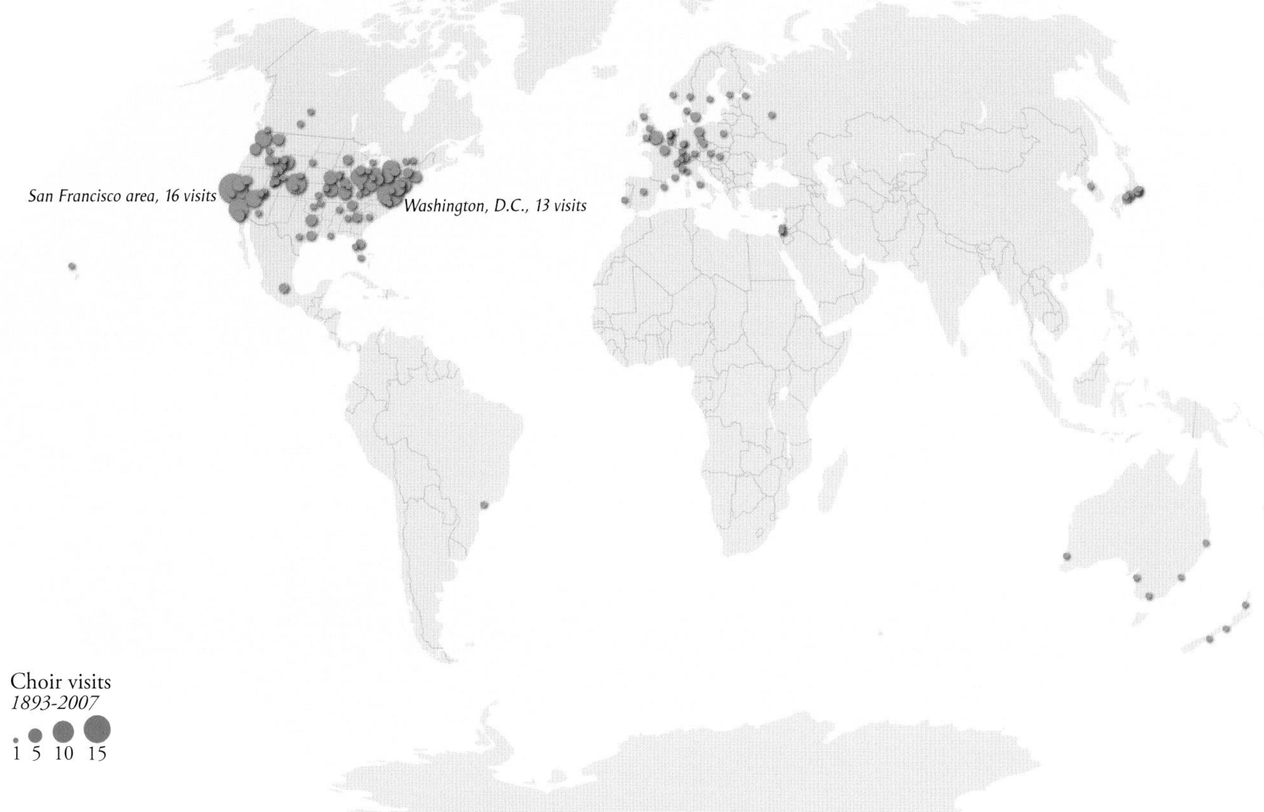

Mormon Tabernacle Choir Tours

Under the direction of the First Presidency, the Choir has toured frequently around the United States and the world. The major tours occur about every two years, with the shorter tours taking place more frequently, depending on invitations from specific groups or conventions. The Tabernacle Choir has traveled extensively in the United States, typically focusing on a region, such as the Northeastern tour of 2003 when the Choir held concerts in ten cities from Michigan to the Atlantic Coast, including music festivals at Interlochen, Chautauqua, Saratoga, Wolf Trap, and Tanglewood.

The first international tour took place in 1955 when the Choir spent nearly six weeks touring European cities such as Berlin, London, Paris, Amsterdam, and Copenhagen. Other international tours have touched cities in Asia, Europe, and the Pacific. Many tours have a specific purpose, such as the dedication of the Swiss Temple in 1955, or Australia's Bicentennial activities in 1988 (where they were the United States representative). In recent years, the Choir has added broadcasts and media coverage for the major tours, which allows many more people to see the Choir than can attend the concerts, and provides wider publicity for the Church in those areas.

BYU Performing Groups

Student performing groups from Brigham Young University have been a major force in building goodwill for the Church, as stated in part of their mission: "Performers whose lives are enlightened by the Spirit of the Lord and sustained by the moral virtues taught by living prophets will have power to further the worldwide work of the Church." These groups include the Young Ambassadors, who present music and dance variety shows; dance groups such as the Ballroom Dance Company who have won every national championship since 1982; and Living Legends, which showcases the performances of Native Americans, Latin Americans, and Polynesians. Starting in 1970, the various groups have toured extensively around the world, especially in Canada and Europe, and they have become especially popular in China, where they are frequently featured on national television.

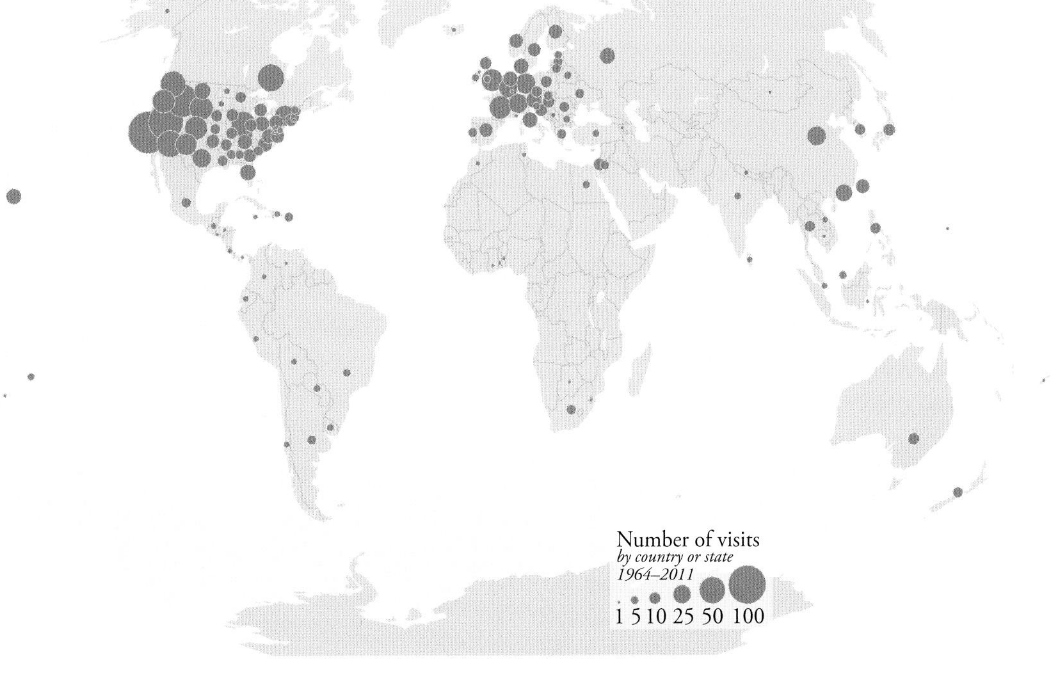

Political Affiliation

1900–present

For much of the nineteenth century, the LDS Church experienced persecution and hostility from state and national governments, including the 1838 extermination order from Missouri (see p. 50), the sending of the U.S. Army to Utah in 1857–58 to quell what some feared was a Mormon rebellion (see p. 110), and the repeated congressional repudiation of Utah's requests for statehood (see p. 92). Much has changed since then. In the century since statehood, there have been many changes in the political attitudes, behaviors, and influence of Latter-day Saints.

It is well known that Mormons presently tend to be more politically conservative and more likely to affiliate with the Republican Party than non-Mormons, but voting and polling data show that this trend has varied considerably. Party strength in Utah elections have shifted over the years, from sweeping Democratic victories in 1916, 1932–1944, and 1964, to near-total Republican dominance since the 1980s. Between these extremes, Utah has tended to vote moderately Republican.

There is also geographical variance in Mormon political attitudes. Mormons from eastern states are generally less conservative than in Utah. Within Utah, there is also significant variation in political behavior between urban and rural areas, which largely depends on the size of the local non-Mormon population.

Another trend in the last century is that the number of LDS officials nationwide has blossomed since statehood. Initially, there were challenges to the seating of Mormon representatives in the U.S. Congress, including Brigham H. Roberts (1900, eventually rejected) and Reed Smoot (1904, eventually seated). Since that time, Mormons have been elected to high office in 12 states and in several other countries. The number of LDS national officeholders in the United States peaked at 16 in 1999.

David Magleby and Jeff Fox

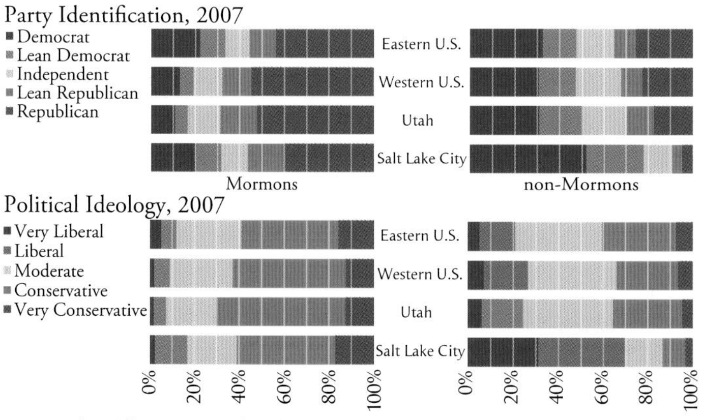

Party Identification and Political Ideology, 2007

Surveys and exit polls show the strong variations in partisanship among Mormons and non-Mormons in Utah, Salt Lake City, and the United States generally. In Utah and in the western United States, Mormons tend to be significantly more conservative (and significantly more Republican) than non-Mormons at large. In Salt Lake City and the eastern United States, this trend also exists but is less pronounced. The non-Mormon minority across Utah tends to be politically similar to the American population in general, but Salt Lake City (which may be less than 50% LDS) is considerably more liberal (and more Democratic). This may indicate that in the city, political affiliation is an important tool in building a collective non-Mormon identity, which was also the case in the nineteenth century (see p. 112).

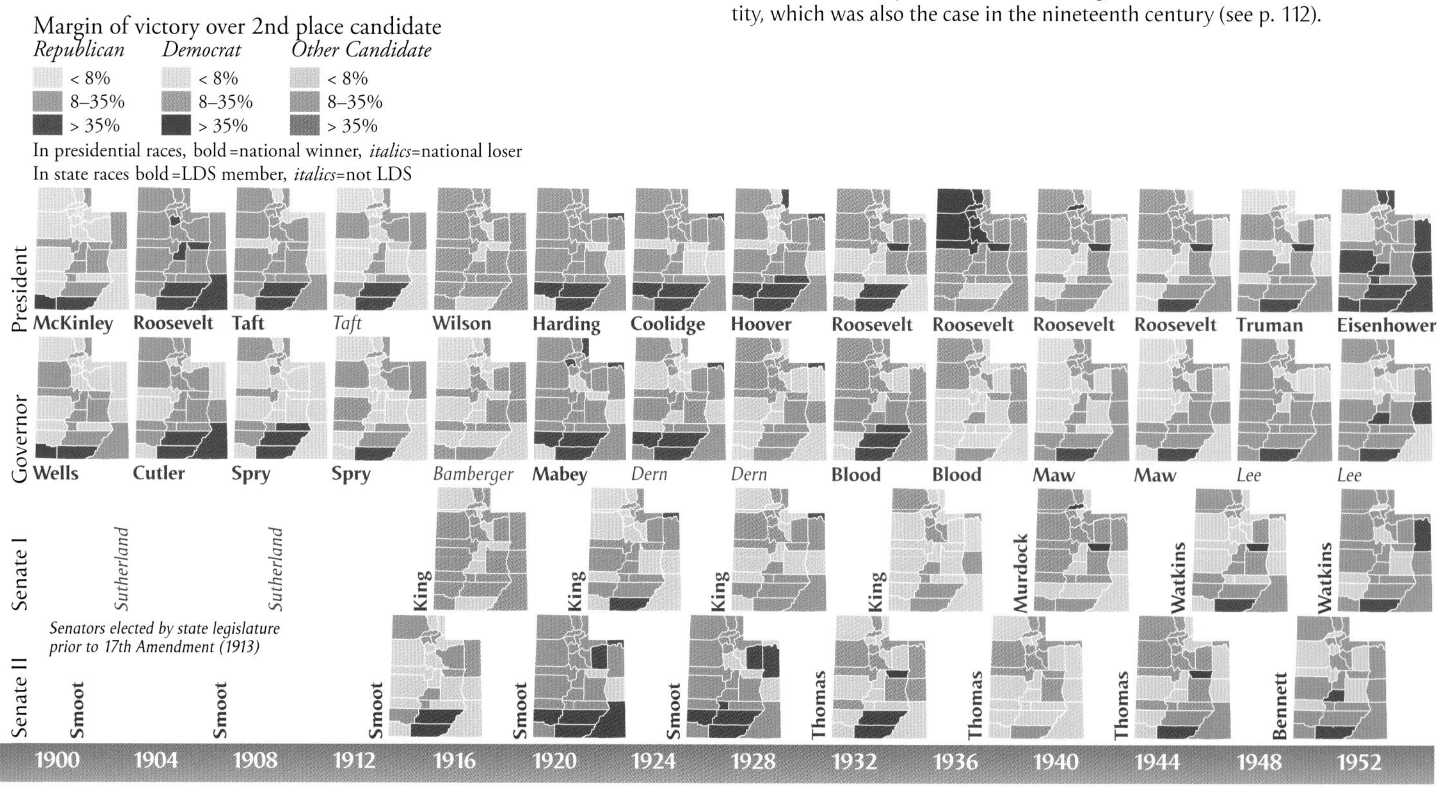

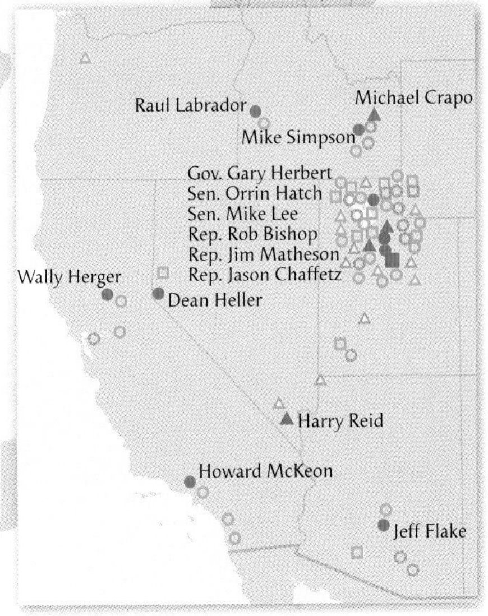

LDS Church Members in Political Office

Popular support for Mormon office holders was initially confined to Utah. Between 1940 and 1956, Mormons began to be elected to Congress from the other states in the Intermountain West. Berkeley Bunker was appointed to fill a Senate vacancy in Nevada in 1940 and was elected to a House seat in 1944. Mormons were elected to Congress from Idaho in 1950 and Arizona in 1954.

California became the first state outside of the Intermountain West to send Mormons to Congress in 1956, and it has done so consistently ever since. In 1976, a Mormon was elected to the House from Hawaii, and Paula Hawkins became the first LDS woman to serve in the U.S. Senate when she was elected to represent Florida in 1980. Mormons were elected to Congress from American Samoa in 1988, New Hampshire in 1990, Oklahoma in 1992, Oregon in 1996, and New Mexico in 1998.

As Mormon representation expanded geographically, it also grew numerically. In the 1940s, no more than five Mormons served in Congress in any given year. By the 1960s, nine Mormons were representing five different states. This leveled off during the 1970s and 1980s, but jumped to 13 in 1993 and peaked at 16 in 1999 (representing nine states). After the 2010 election, 14 Mormons from six states were serving in Congress. Mormons have also been elected as governor in five states and have served in the national legislatures of Brazil, Great Britain, Mexico, New Zealand, and Canada.

County-by-County Voting, 1900–2010

This county breakdown of Utah's voting in major races shows that preferences have varied significantly over the years. During the early state elections, there was a significant Democratic vote, likely a reaction to the extreme anti-Mormon hostility among the Republicans during the territorial period. In most years, Utah followed national trends, including the Democratic presidential landslides of 1916, 1932–1944, and 1964. Since 1964, the state has become increasingly Republican, far more so than the nation at large. Races for governor and senators show a combination of this recent trend, the coat tails of presidential elections (such as the Utah delegation being completely Democratic during the Roosevelt years), and personalities who were able to gain favor regardless of larger trends. For example, from 1964 to 1980, Democrats Calvin Rampton and Scott Matheson were very popular governors, even while Republicans dominated other races. Starting in 1984, Republicans (both Mormon and not) have had continuous success in contests for president, governor, and U.S. Senate, although Democrats have picked up some victories in U.S. House races (not shown here).

Within the state, there is some variation in partisanship. For example, Carbon, Grand, and, more recently, Summit counties (all of which have a lower LDS proportion than the rest of the state) are generally more Democratic, while Utah and Wasatch counties have been predictably Republican. Even more so is Kane County, which has only had a Democratic majority in three of the 89 races shown here.

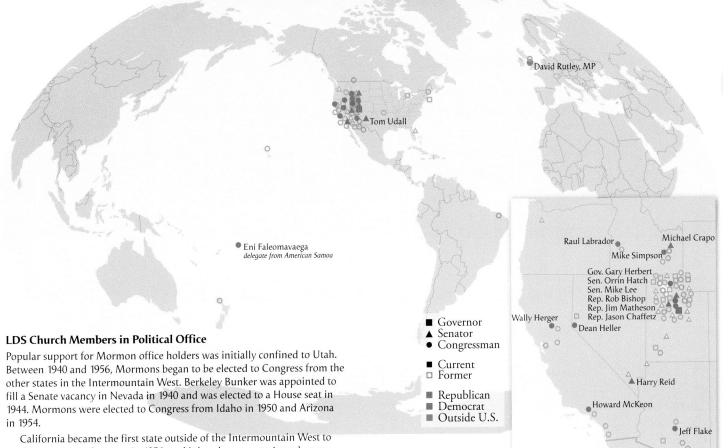

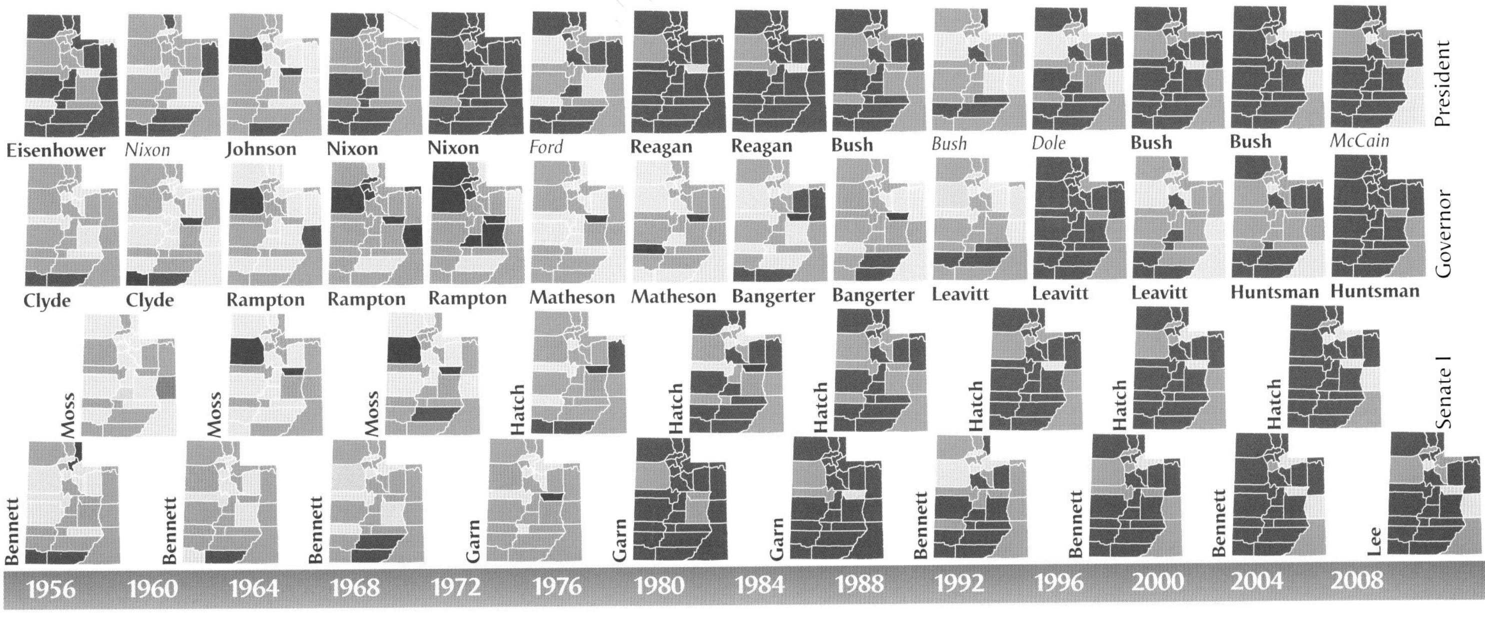

Book of Mormon Geographies

1842–present

THE BOOK OF MORMON was intended to be a spiritual work, to give readers a testimony of Jesus Christ, not a people's history and geography. However, for many scholars who believe in the book's literal truth, there is a natural curiosity to discover where the events in the book took place. Many believe that the historical and geographic context of the Book of Mormon can help readers better understand the spiritual message, as it does with the New Testament. Some hope for archaeological proof of the Book of Mormon.

A variety of professional scholars and passionate amateurs, both LDS and RLDS, have published at least 90 theories of the location of the places and events in the Book of Mormon. These theories include both external models, that attempt to correlate places in the text to actual places in the Americas; and internal models, that are based on geographical cues in the Book of Mormon itself with no attempt to tie them to real locations.

These models tend to follow a basic "hourglass" pattern, consisting of a "land northward" that contains the Hill Cumorah and is the setting for the book of Ether, and a "land southward" in which most of the Book of Mormon narrative takes place (containing cities such as Nephi, Zarahemla, and Bountiful); these are connected by a "narrow neck of land." However, some researchers have proposed other interpretations of the same scriptures, resulting in radically different geographies.

The introduction of new geographies has ebbed and flowed through the years, based on several factors: occasional statements by General Authorities supporting (unofficially) one theory or another, acceptance or rejection of ideas by the community of Book of Mormon scholars, and varying interest in the subject by the general membership. Since no theory can claim irrefutable proof of its truth, novel ideas will continue to appear.

Brandon S. Plewe

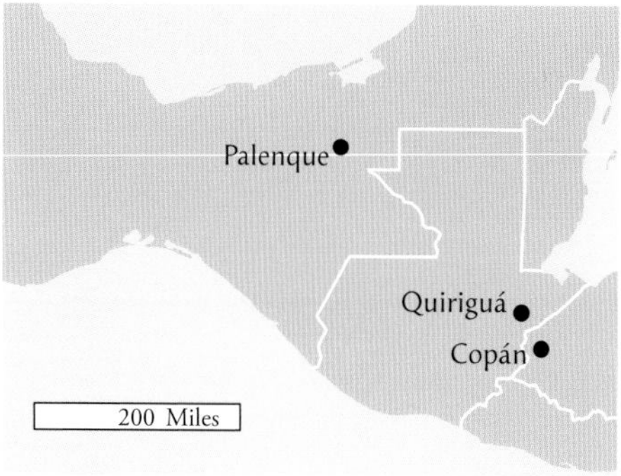

Early Saints, including Joseph Smith, frequently speculated about Book of Mormon lands and peoples based on the arrowheads, burial mounds, and other ancient artifacts they found around them. In 1842, Joseph received a copy of John Lloyd Stephens' *Incidents of Travel in Central America, Chiapas and Yucatan*, a best-selling sensation due in part to its beautiful illustrations of Mayan ruins. The Prophet and his editors published several articles in the *Times and Seasons* about the relationships they saw between Book of Mormon civilizations and Mesoamerica. They focused on three sites in particular that had been featured in Stephens' book, even suggesting that Quiriguá could be the Nephite capital Zarahemla.

During the nineteenth century, and much of the twentieth, most readers of the Book of Mormon assumed that its events covered the entire Western Hemisphere. Scholars such as George Reynolds (1880) and Joel Ricks developed specific theories of locations that restricted most of the narrative to a smaller area but keeping the Hill Cumorah as the final place of destruction.

This hemispheric approach, and the implication that all of today's Native Americans are Lamanites, was unofficially endorsed by some General Authorities during the early 1900s and still has a widespread acceptance, despite archaeological, ethnic, and genetic evidence to the contrary.

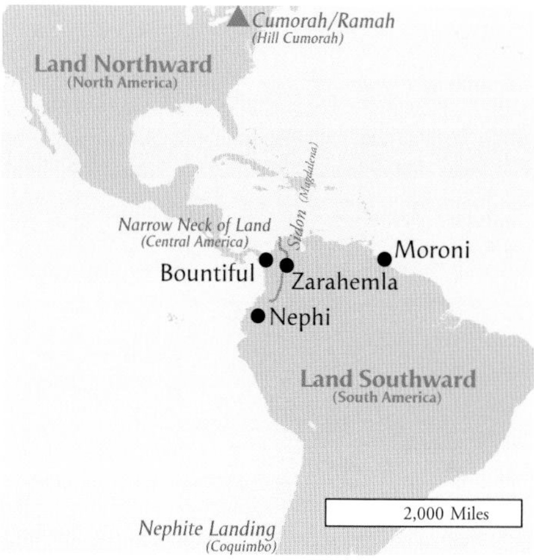

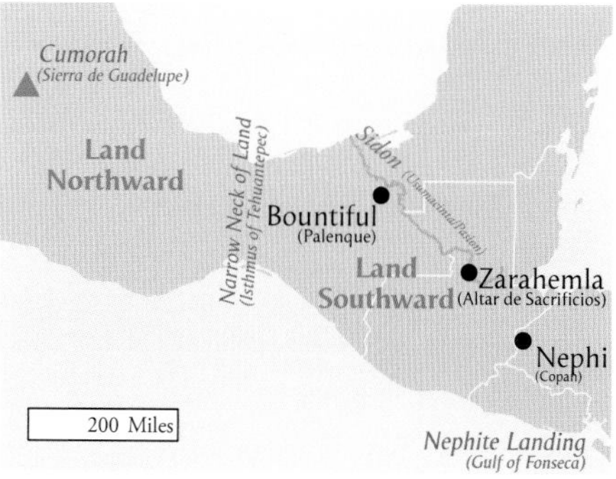

The 1917 model of Louis Hills (who was RLDS) was the first to respond to the issues of the hemispheric model by asserting that the Hill Cumorah where the Nephites and Jaredites were destroyed was not the hill where the plates were buried.

While the plausability and orthodoxy of this hypothesis were debated, dozens of similar limited mesoamerican theories were published, especially during a period of openness in the 1970s and 1980s. The 1985 model of John Sorenson has gained the widest acceptance by LDS scholars, despite the fact that archaeological support for a mesoamerican (or any other) setting is circumstantial.

Note: The maps shown here were selected to be representative of the variety of ideas and milestones in the history of this field of study, and are not necessarily the most likely nor the most widely accepted theories. The editors make no assertions of their scholarship, validity, or likelihood relative to models not shown here. The maps have been redrawn from original documents to facilitate comparisons.

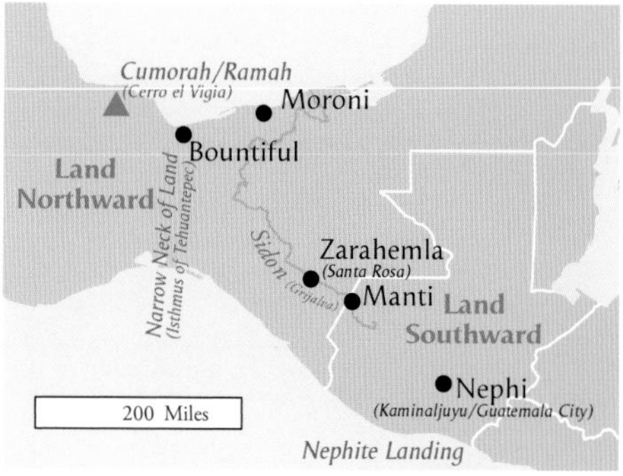

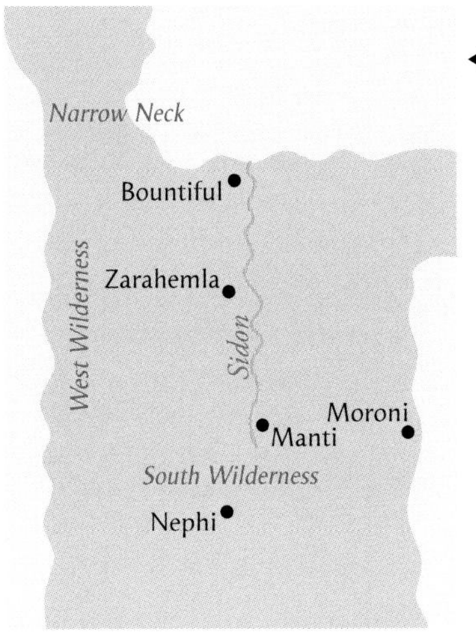

The first purely internal geography was published by Lynn Layton in 1938, avoiding archaeological challenges by not attempting to tie events to real locations. Authors have generally posited that such a correlation may eventually be possible as scientific evidence increases. Layton determined sites on his map based on statements of relative location (distances and directions) given in the Book of Mormon.

Internal geographies serve a variety of purposes. Some were a step in developing an external geography. John Clark's 1989 minimalist model was presented as a tool for validating other published models (internal and external). Others are marketed to a general audience of Book of Mormon readers hoping to better understand the narrative without taking an archaeological stance.

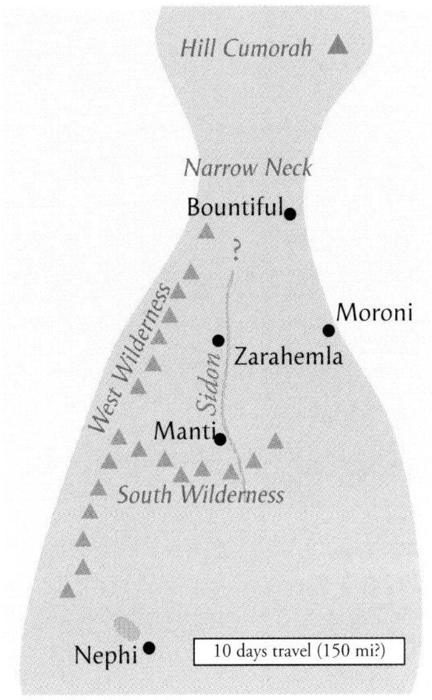

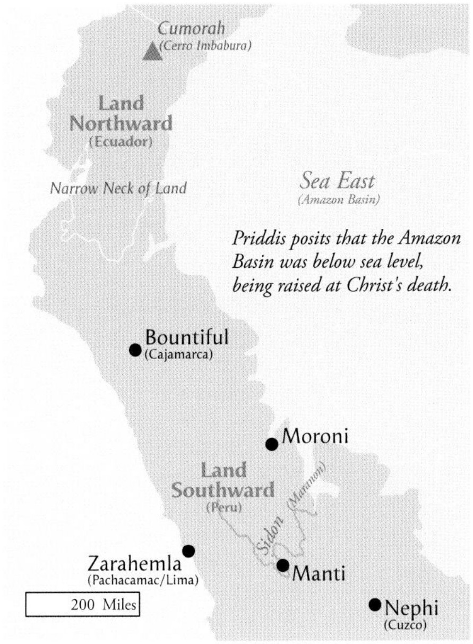

▲ Many authors have interpreted that when "the whole face of the land changed" (3 Nephi 8:12) at the death of Christ, the shoreline changed to today's configuration from something drastically different (often based on evidence of flooding in past geologic eras). This hypothesis has been used to identify lost "hourglasses" in South America (as suggested by Venice Priddis in 1975), Mesoamerica, and New York. Other scholars have cited scriptural and geologic evidence against such sweeping changes.

The widespread support for Sorenson's model largely subdued geographic research in the early 1990s, but many alternative geographies have been published recently. These include novel Mesoamerican theories (such as that of James Warr) and many attempts to locate the events in the book in New York (including the 1998 model of Duane Aston) and elsewhere in the United States. The latter have generally used innovative interpretations to avoid the classic "hourglass" model but have not gained wide acceptance.

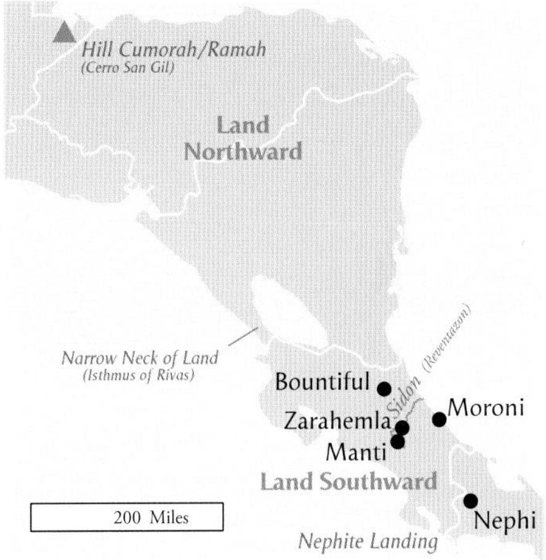

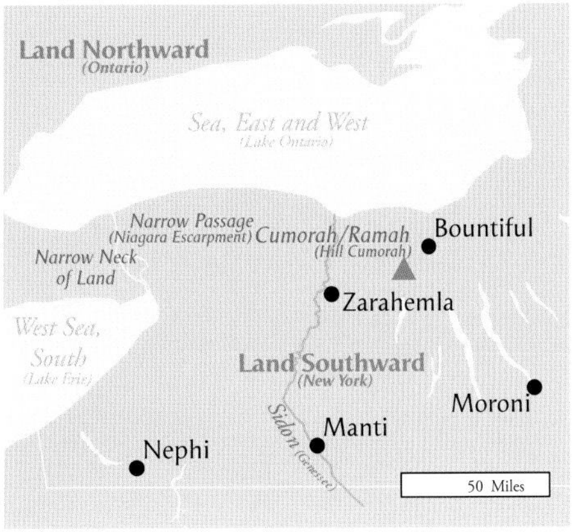

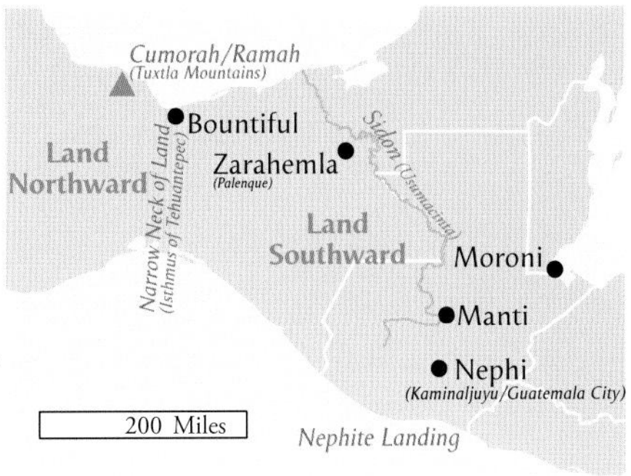

Although the variety of theories have increased, Mesoamerica remains the location that is most widely accepted among scholars. New theories, such as that of Garth Norman (2006), continue to place the Nephites and Lamanites in the Mayan region, and guided group tours to "the lands of the Book of Mormon" are very popular.

Almost 90 theories of Book of Mormon geography have been published over the past 170 years. General locations have gone in and out of favor, and most authors have resorted to minor publishing houses or self-publishing to get their ideas in print.

Location
- Western Hemisphere
- Mesoamerica
- South America or Panama
- United States / New York
- Other location
- Internal Model

Publisher
- Major
  Church magazine, Deseret Book, etc.
- Minor publisher or journal
- Self-published

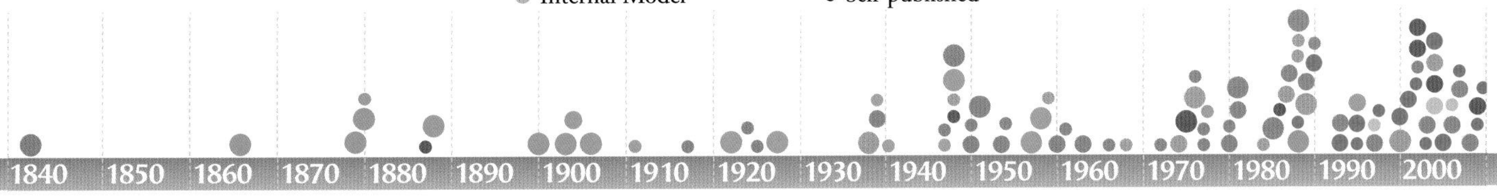

Community of Christ

1860–present

THE REORGANIZED CHURCH of Jesus Christ of Latter Day Saints (RLDS Church) emerged during the 1850s from the conflict and schism that arose after the assassination of Joseph Smith Jr. in 1844 (see p. 64). Many recollected that he had designated his son Joseph Smith III (1832–1914) to succeed him but had not indicated anyone to lead until his son should be old enough to preside. A nucleus of Saints in Wisconsin and southern Illinois began to create what they felt to be a continuation of the original Church. They adamantly objected to the practice of polygamy and began pressing for an interim organization to await the availability of a son of the founding prophet to lead them.

The "New Organization," as the Church was called for a time, sent representatives in 1856 to Joseph Smith III in Nauvoo, Illinois, to officially invite him to head the Church. Smith firmly declined, but after several spiritual experiences, he accepted in early 1860. On April 6, 1860, Joseph Smith III was ordained the prophet-president of the Church of Jesus Christ of Latter Day Saints (renamed the Reorganized Church of Jesus Christ of Latter Day Saints in 1872 to avoid confusion with the Church in Utah) at its conference at Amboy, Illinois. Smith was both strongly opposed to polygamy and was deeply convinced that his father could have had nothing to do with its inception. He convinced other RLDS leaders, writers, missionaries, and members, who fought for decades to uphold this conviction. They also disagreed with other doctrines emerging in the Church in Utah, such as absolute theocracy, baptism for the dead, plural gods, and the exclusion of blacks from priesthood offices.

Because of the success of RLDS missionaries in southwest Iowa, the center of Church population shifted westward, and early in the 1880s Church headquarters moved from Plano, Illinois, to the new settlement of Lamoni, Iowa. Herald Publishing House, printer of the *Saints Herald* and all RLDS publications, soon followed. Graceland College was founded in 1895 in Lamoni.

Unlike the Church in Utah, the power base of the Reorganized Church has generally been vested in the branches. World Conferences are as much legislative sessions of delegates as spiritual gatherings. Joseph's son Frederick M. Smith sought to centralize more administrative control at Church headquarters, leading to much disputation and many

continued on page 194

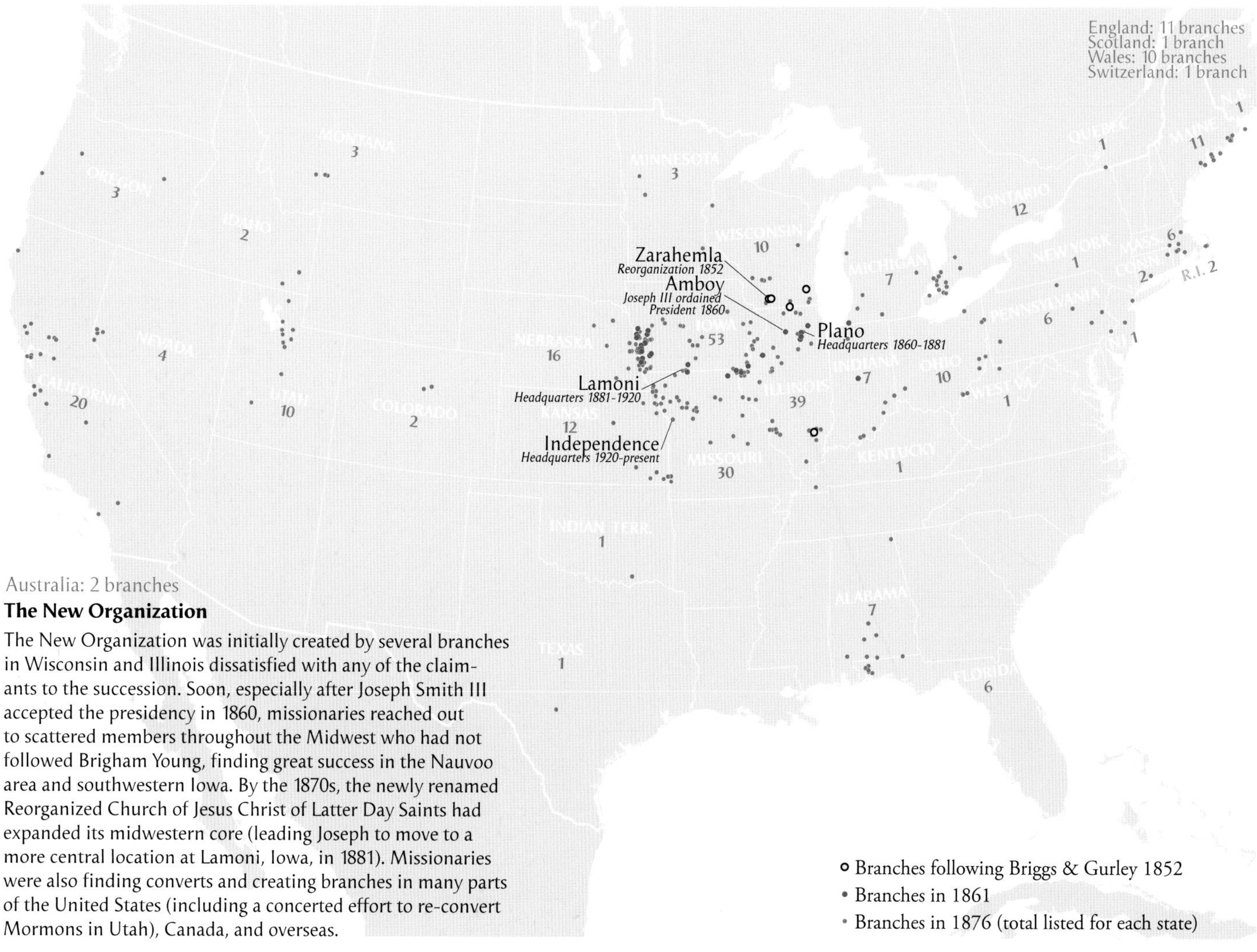

The New Organization

The New Organization was initially created by several branches in Wisconsin and Illinois dissatisfied with any of the claimants to the succession. Soon, especially after Joseph Smith III accepted the presidency in 1860, missionaries reached out to scattered members throughout the Midwest who had not followed Brigham Young, finding great success in the Nauvoo area and southwestern Iowa. By the 1870s, the newly renamed Reorganized Church of Jesus Christ of Latter Day Saints had expanded its midwestern core (leading Joseph to move to a more central location at Lamoni, Iowa, in 1881). Missionaries were also finding converts and creating branches in many parts of the United States (including a concerted effort to re-convert Mormons in Utah), Canada, and overseas.

Joseph Smith III
1860–1914

On April 6, 1860, Joseph Smith III became prophet-president of the Church at its conference at Amboy, Illinois. About 20 years later, he moved his headquarters to Lamoni, Iowa. His ministry focused on bringing unity to a disparate collection of congregations and leaders.

received RLDS D&C sections 114–131

Frederick M. Smith
1914–1946

The primary emphases of his thirty-one-year presidency were centralization of administrative control into a more theocratic mode; practical theological training for the Church's ministry; expansion of missionary efforts; and development of the "Center Place" (Independence, Jackson County, Missouri). Church headquarters officially moved there in early 1920.

received D&C sections 132–138

Israel A. Smith
1946–1958

Younger brother of Frederick M. Smith, during his twelve-year tenure the Church built financial reserves and greatly expanded the missionary forces, along with increasing the number of branches and missions outside the United States.

received D&C sections 139–144

W. Wallace Smith
1958–1978

The third son of Joseph Smith III to serve as prophet-president, he further expanded the Church worldwide and promoted ecumenism and interfaith relations. He presided over a reworking of the Church's foundational theology and expression of mission. Unlike earlier prophet-presidents who had served until their deaths, W. Wallace publicly designated his son as successor in 1976 and retired in 1978.

received D&C sections 145–152

Wallace B. Smith
1978–1996

The last member of the Smith family to hold the office of prophet-president oversaw major changes in the Church, including a doubling of the nations in which the Church operated, the ordination of women, and the building of the temple. He broke with tradition by naming one of his counselors as successor.

received D&C sections 153–160

W. Grant McMurray
1996–2004

The first prophet-president outside the Smith family saw the renaming of the Church to Community of Christ, further expansion of missionary work, and further alignment with the Christian community before resigning as president.

received D&C sections 161, 162

Steven M. Veazey
2005–present

Veazey, one of the Twelve Apostles, was designated the new prophet-president at a special conference in 2005. He has emphasized the Christian character of the Community of Christ, the discipleship of members, and the mission of the Church.

received D&C sections 163, 164

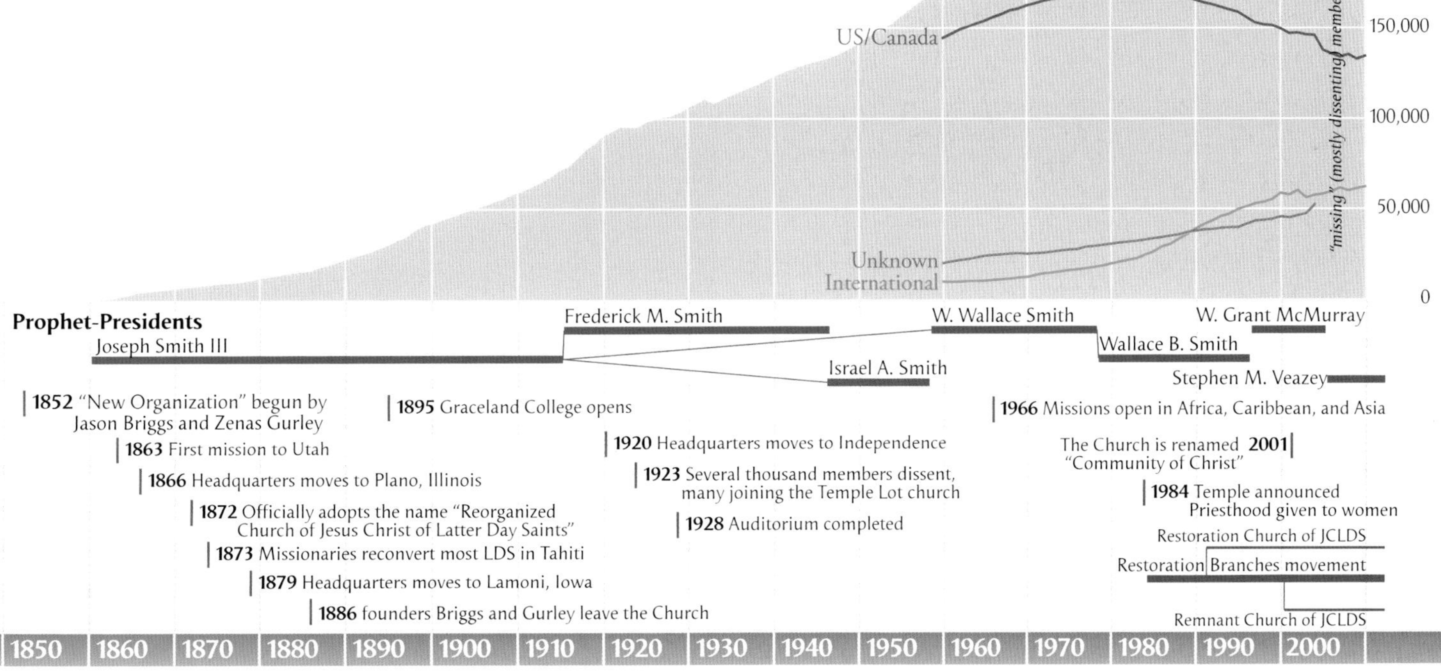

Community of Christ

continued

defections to the Church of Christ (Temple Lot) (see p. 196). Since then, decision-making authority has been relatively balanced between central and local authorities.

Under brothers Frederick M., Israel A., and William Wallace Smith, the Church greatly expanded its missionary force, focusing on worldwide outreach to Europe, the Caribbean, Asia, Africa, and the Pacific.

In 1968, William Wallace brought to the Church a document that called for starting to plan for a temple to be built in Independence. However, it would take a revelation to his son Wallace B. Smith, accepted in 1984 (as D&C Section 156), to build the Temple, which was completed in 1994 and dedicated to the pursuit of peace where daily prayers for peace are offered 365 days a year.

The same 1984 revelation called for opening priesthood ordination to women as well as men. This was a change from the 150-year tradition, and there was both strong agreement and strong disagreement among members. Many chose to leave the Church, but many more found new opportunities for service and new life in their congregations.

In 1995, Wallace B. Smith indicated that W. Grant McMurray was to be his successor upon his retirement. The first president who was not a Smith descendant, McMurray continued the long-term trends of expanding global mission outreach and of closer ecumenism with other Christian churches. In 2001, the Church changed its name to Community of Christ, a name that more adequately represented the Church's theology and mission.

Grant McMurray resigned leadership in November 2004, and the two remaining members of the First Presidency presided over the Church until the special conference in June 2005, when Stephen M. Veazey was ordained to the office of prophet-president of the Community of Christ. Doctrine and practices have continued to evolve: in the most recent revelation (D&C 164, accepted in 2010), converts were accepted with their previous baptisms in other Christian churches, and the door was opened to greater tolerance of same-sex relationships.

Barbara Hands Bernauer

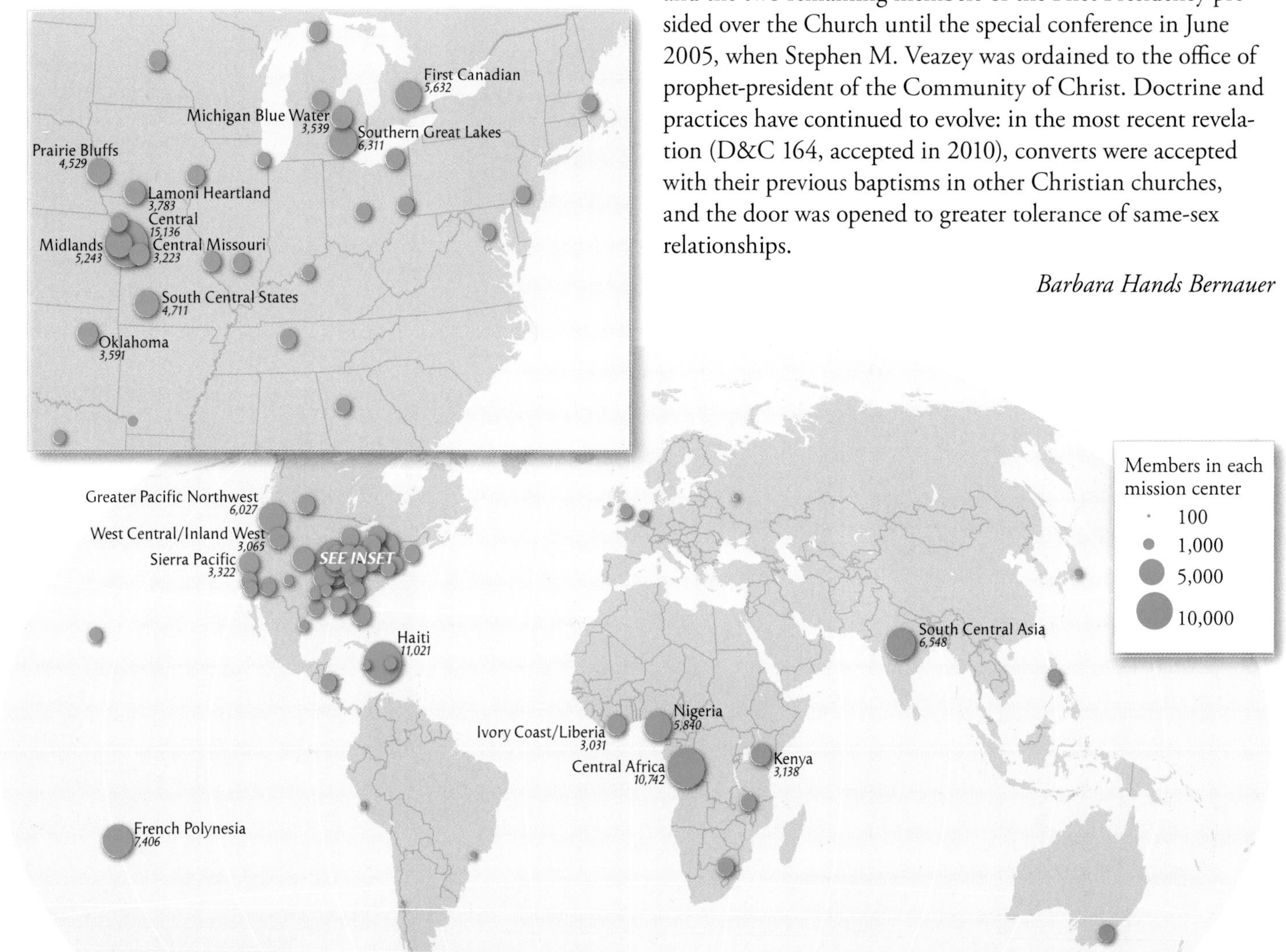

Community of Christ in 2009

2009 membership of Community of Christ, so named since 2001, still shows a major concentration around "the Center Place" of Independence, Missouri, and the midwestern United States. However, international missions have been a major focus in the past 30 years, and now about 25% of the membership lives outside the United States. The most significant countries are Haiti (11,000 members), Democratic Republic of the Congo (10,700), French Polynesia (7,400), India (6,500), and Nigeria (5,800).

Note: only one circle is shown for each mission center, although some mission centers include several countries.

The Restoration Branches Movement

For most of its history, the RLDS Church adhered fairly closely to the theology that Joseph Smith articulated during the Kirtland period (1831-1838). However, in the last half of the twentieth century, the Church began to move in new directions. One factor was the secularizing influence of the increasing wealth of its members. Second, a significant number of members were attending Protestant seminaries, causing many of them to rethink the distinctive doctrines of the Church. A third factor was the growing international missionary effort, led by Apostle Charles Neff, who was concerned that the Church's traditional message reflected American culture rather than universal religious principles, and encouraged missionaries to focus more on Christian themes and less on RLDS "distinctives."

By the 1960s, a new generation was taking positions of leadership at Church headquarters and at Church-sponsored Graceland College, where they published articles and books that reflected the new scholarship, influencing the members and the general officers of the Church. Tension mounted as it became clear that some leaders no longer believed many of the traditional teachings of the Church.

The growing fundamental-liberal tension came to a head at the 1984 World Conference when a revelation was presented that called for the ordination of women and the construction of a temple dedicated to the "pursuit of peace, reconciliation, and healing of the spirit." Conference delegates voted to accept it as D&C Section 156, but about 20 percent of the delegates voted against it.

Soon many of these delegates, and perhaps one-fourth of the active members, left the Church and organized independent "restoration branches," congregations that did not follow the RLDS hierarchy, but preached the traditional teachings of the Church. Most of these branches have remained independent, considering themselves to be "branches in exile," waiting for the Church to return to orthodoxy. Loose associations, such as the Conference of Restoration Elders, give them a chance to collaborate without reorganizing. Others have decided to form entirely new churches, the most prominent being the Remnant Church of Jesus Christ of Latter Day Saints, whose president is a direct descendant of Joseph Smith through his mother. Other men have also stepped forward as a prophet whom God has called to lead the Church back onto the right path.

Generally these groups have garnered the most support in places where there is a higher concentration of members, especially Missouri, Iowa, and Michigan; elsewhere it has been more difficult for dissenters to find enough like-minded members to join with them and start a separate group. Oklahoma and Texas also have significant schismatic groups, partly from a reasonable concentration of members and partly due to the more conservative nature of the region. Outside the United States, only a very few branches have been organized.

William Russell

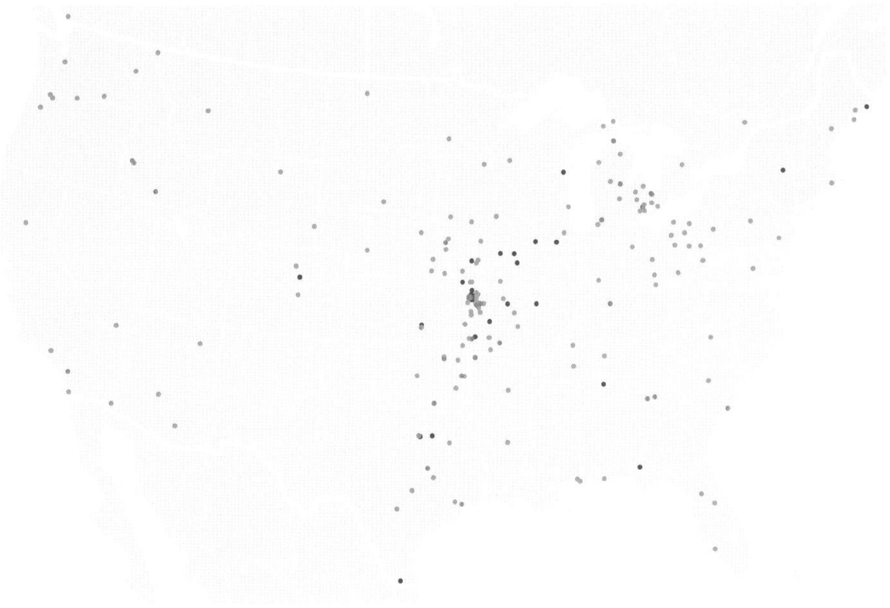

Restoration churches in the Kansas City area

- Community of Christ
- Restoration Branches
- Church of Christ (Temple Lot)
- Church of Christ with the Elijah Message
- Church of Jesus Christ of Latter-day Saints
- Church of Christ (Cutlerites)
- ■ Church headquarters

See p. 136 for more detail of churches in downtown Independence

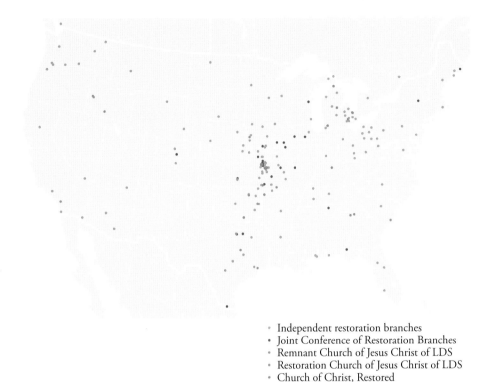

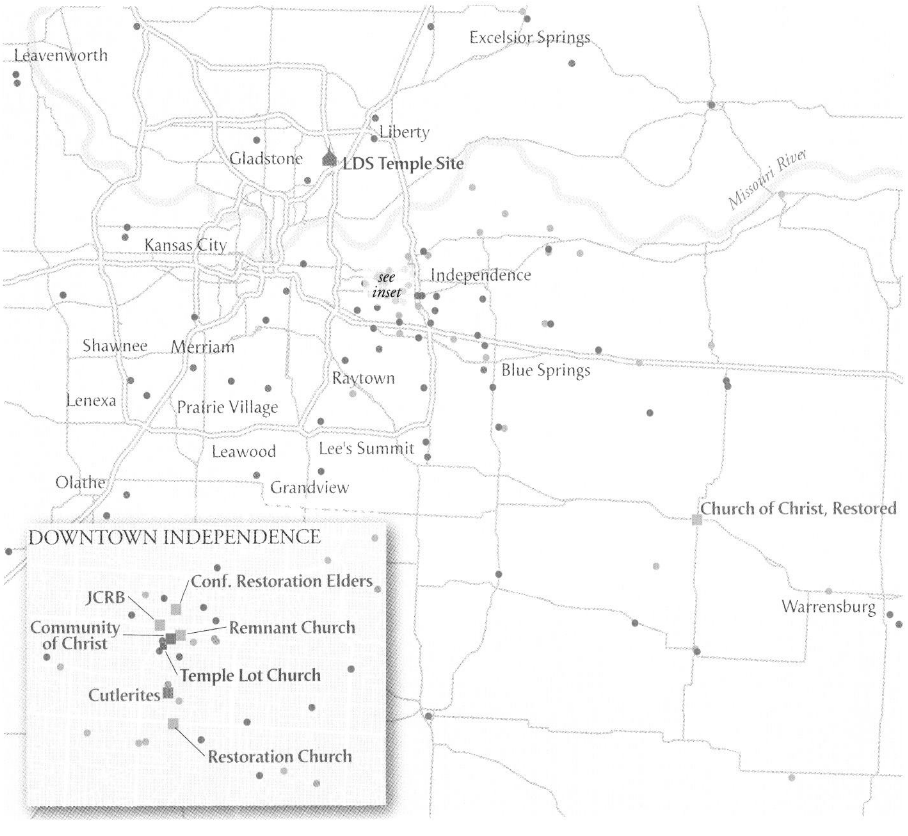

The Restored Church(es)

1844–present

THE REVELATORY NATURE OF THE RESTORATION movement started by Joseph Smith has been a major factor in its longevity, but it has also been a source of dissension and schism. For believers, the presence of a prophet provides constancy and stability of fundamental doctrines despite a changing world but also opportunity for new revelation from God when change is warranted. However, some are concerned that the Church is changing too much and needs to be returned to purity (who may be termed "fundamentalists") or not changing enough and needs to keep up with changing times ("reformers"). Power struggles and cries of "false prophet" or "fallen prophet" frequently lead to the creation of new churches. This happened several times during Joseph Smith's lifetime (see p. 64), although the schismatic Churches created before 1844 did not last long.

From the competing movements following Joseph's death, four primary churches have endured to the present: The Church of Jesus Christ of Latter-day Saints (LDS) in Salt Lake City (following Brigham Young), by far the largest; The Reorganized Church of Jesus Christ of Latter Day Saints, now Community of Christ, in Independence, Missouri (following Joseph Smith III; see p. 192); the Church of Jesus Christ in Monongahela, Pennsylvania (following William Bickerton); and the Church of Christ (Temple Lot) in Independence, Missouri (following Granville Hedrick). Each of these churches has experienced its own schisms, often coming in times of succession between prophets.

Today, there may be as many as 75 Churches with more than a few members, beyond the primary four, claiming Joseph Smith as their founding prophet. Some have been rather successful at converting (or re-converting) thousands of members; some consist of one or two loyal congregations; many are only a lone prophet with a website.

Although most of the early doctrines of Joseph's day (through the early Kirtland period, at least) are fairly consistent throughout the many branches of the movement, each has evolved along its own path, leading to a great diversity in belief and practice. For example, The Church of Christ (Temple Lot) and The Church of Jesus Christ accept the Book of Mormon, but both claim that Joseph Smith began to go astray soon after the Church was organized, and do not accept the Doctrine and Covenants (and thus the new doctrines introduced therein) as scripture.

Brandon S. Plewe

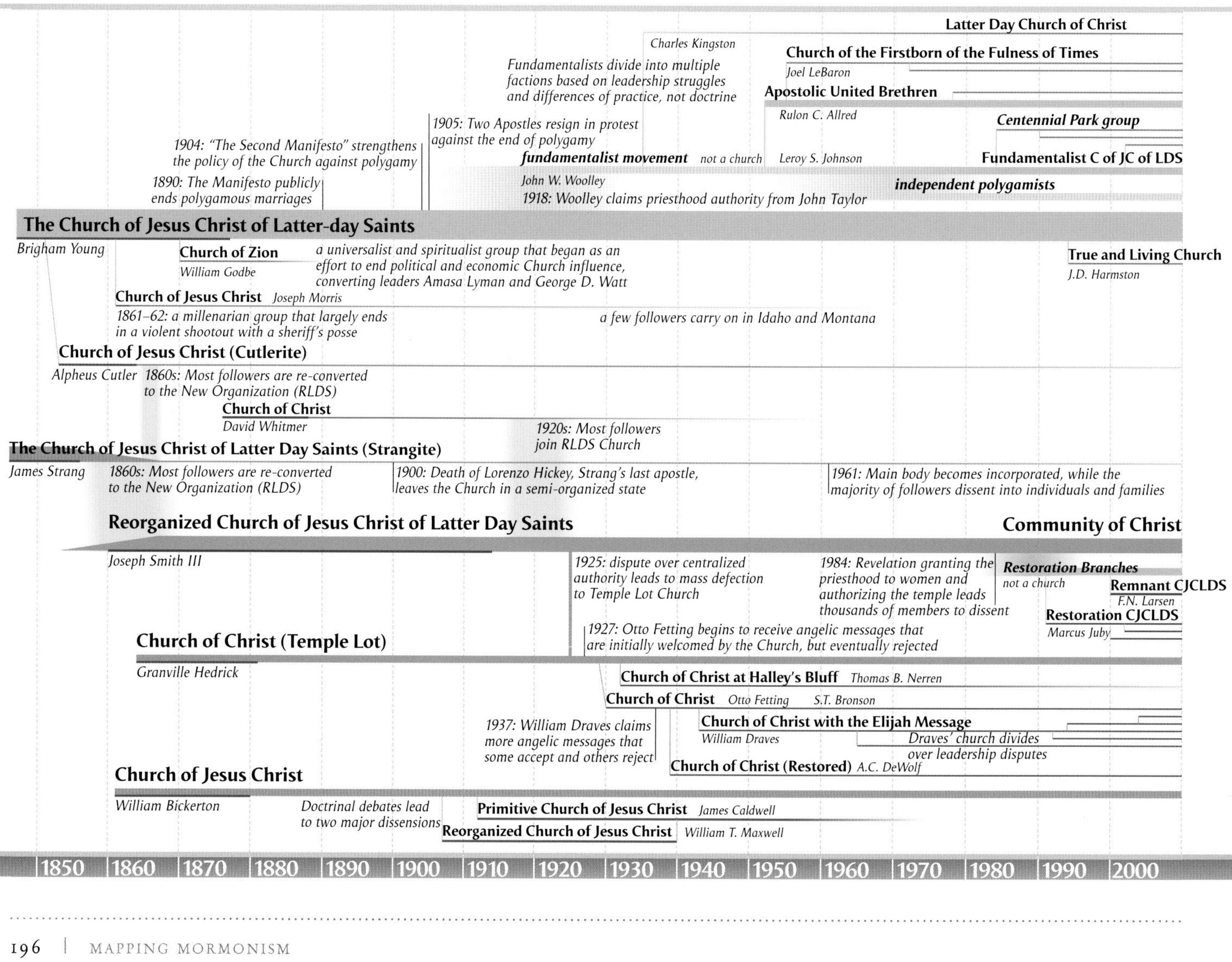

Otto Fetting (center), praying at the ground breaking for the Temple in Independence, Missouri, April 6, 1929. Here he was at the height of his influence in the Church of Christ (Temple Lot), before he was officially "silenced" that October and formed his own church with perhaps half of the members of the Church of Christ. The Great Depression strained the finances of the Church, and the Temple was never built.

Churches of the Restoration in 2010

For the Church in Utah, the primary cause of dissension was the abandonment of polygamy in the 1890s and a contemporary Americanization of Mormon culture and standardization of Church doctrine. Some called President Woodruff a fallen prophet when he delivered the Manifesto ending polygamy in 1890, claimed proof of revelations received by John Taylor that polygamy would never be abandoned, and maintained that Taylor had made secret ordinations of successors should the Church go astray. Since then, several polygamous Churches have emerged, in addition to as many as 15,000 polygamists who are not affiliated with any organized Church; this collection generally refer to themselves as fundamentalist Mormons. Liberal reformist branches of the LDS Church started in 1870 with William Godbe's Church of Zion, but have tended to be sporadic and only loosely organized.

In contrast, reform-minded theologians had greater influence on the Reorganized Church of Jesus Christ of Latter Day Saints (now Community of Christ), leading to major changes in doctrine and practice and to the fundamantalist Restoration Branches movement (see p. 194).

Although the early schisms among William Bickerton's followers either died out or reconciled with the main body, branches from the Temple Lot Church have continued, perhaps (together) having as many members as the original Church. Most of these are the result of Otto Fetting, who, after dissenting from the RLDS Church to join the Church of Christ (Temple Lot) in the 1920s with thousands of others, claimed 30 or more visitations by John the Baptist giving revelations to the Church. He was initially revered as a prophet and apostle but was eventually rejected as the revelations became more radical. Fetting created his own church, which has continued to divide, as recently as 2004, as members either accept or reject leaders claiming further angelic visitations.

Not shown are dozens of very small denominations, unaffiliated fundamentalists (15,000?), unaffiliated Restoration Branches (15,000–30,000?), and unaffiliated Strang followers (300–2,000?). Some members may be claimed by multiple denominations.

Three American Churches

1830–present

THE CHURCH OF JESUS CHRIST OF LATTER-DAY SAINTS is often described as a rapidly growing international Church. As one evaluates the growth of the Church and the relative distribution of members around the world, it is helpful to compare Mormonism to other churches in similar circumstances: is the map of the Church typical or unique? Two other religious organizations are especially useful: the Seventh-day Adventist Church and the Jehovah's Witnesses. All three denominations have their roots in the northeastern United States of the nineteenth century. All three have a centralized, hierarchical structure that emphasizes global proselytizing activities and keeps detailed records. All three experienced dynamic membership growth (in numbers and geographic extent) during the twentieth century. In addition, all three have their own unique doctrine, which sets them apart from each other and from other Christian denominations (and are thus usually branded as "non-mainstream Christian" and often accused of not being Christian at all), and all three have built a strong sense of religious identity and community. These general similarities set the backdrop for very interesting comparisons concerning international growth and diffusion.

Of course, statistical comparisons should be made with caution. Each Church uses its own methodology for keeping and publishing membership statistics. The total membership of the Church of Jesus Christ of Latter-day Saints, reported each April in General Conference, is of "members of record," which includes all baptized members and children who have been blessed (usually, soon after birth). Thus, LDS statistics include members who lapse into inactivity, unless they specifically request to have their names removed from the records, and members with whom the Church has lost complete contact (the so-called "lost file"), which is estimated to be about 15% of the total membership.

The Seventh-day Adventist Church reports baptized members; youth are usually baptized as teenagers. This includes inactive members, but long-term inactive members are regularly removed from the records of the Church; for example, although more than one million baptisms were recorded for 2008, Church membership reportedly increased only by some 260,000 Adventists.

The Jehovah's Witnesses do not report a grand total of baptized "members," as the other two do. Instead, they report "peak witnesses," those who regularly report their time spent "witnessing" door to door. A comparable statistic in the LDS Church would be the number of members who attend Church weekly and hold callings, which is not reported to the public, but has been estimated to be a quarter to a third of the total reported membership. Thus, the LDS Church is probably the least conservative of the three in the total membership it reports.

Daniel Reeves

Growth Rates of Three American Churches

While one should not directly compare the total membership of each church due to differences in reporting (see above), it is helpful to compare their relative growth rates. All saw a period of rapid, exponential growth between 1945 and 2000, with the Latter-day Saints growing most rapidly early on but the Seventh-day Adventists growing more rapidly recently. The Jehovah's Witnesses experienced a major increase in the early 1970s, partially due to their religious exemption from the U.S. military draft and excitement about a predicted date for the Second Coming of Jesus Christ. The growth of all three has slowed somewhat in the twenty-first century.

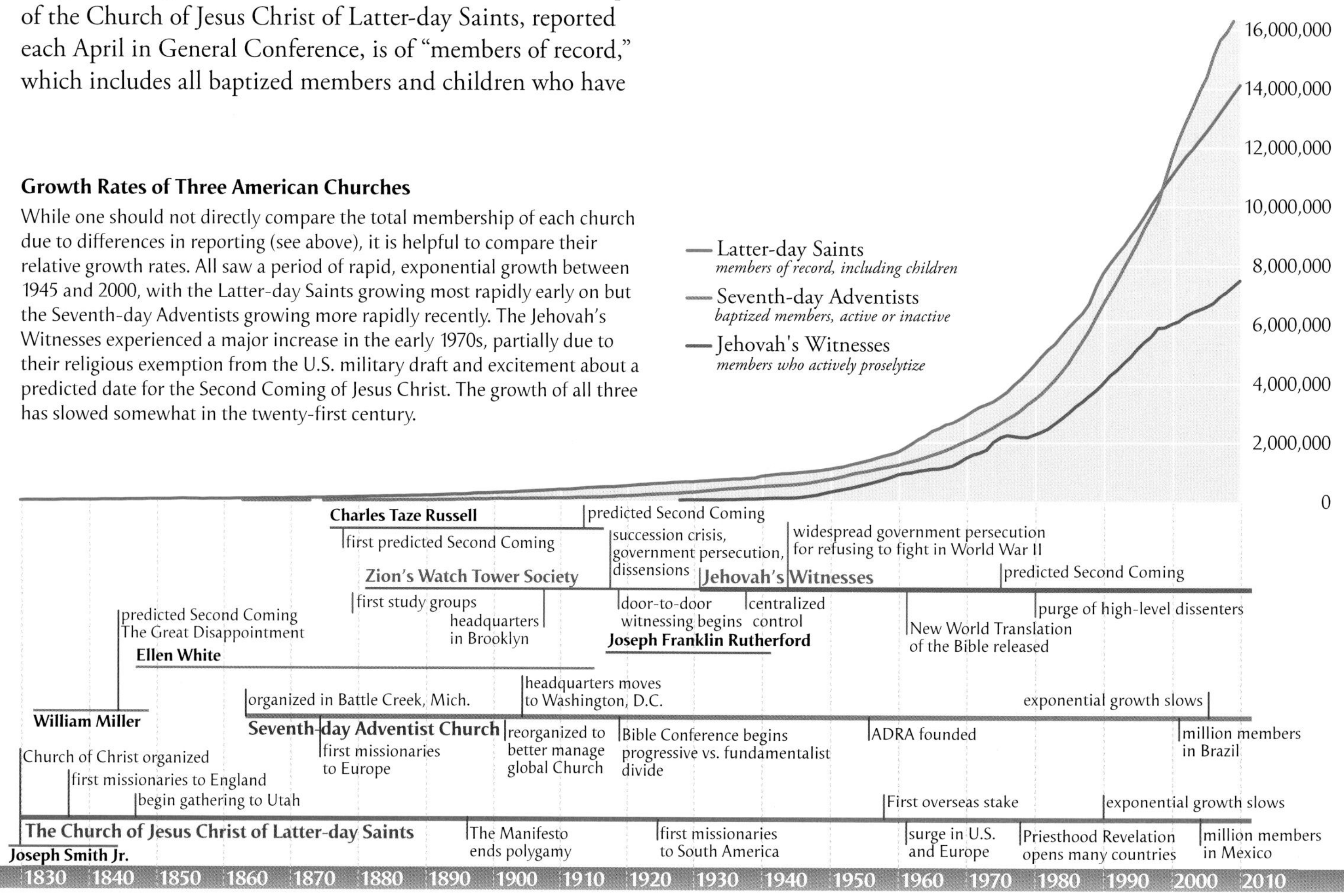

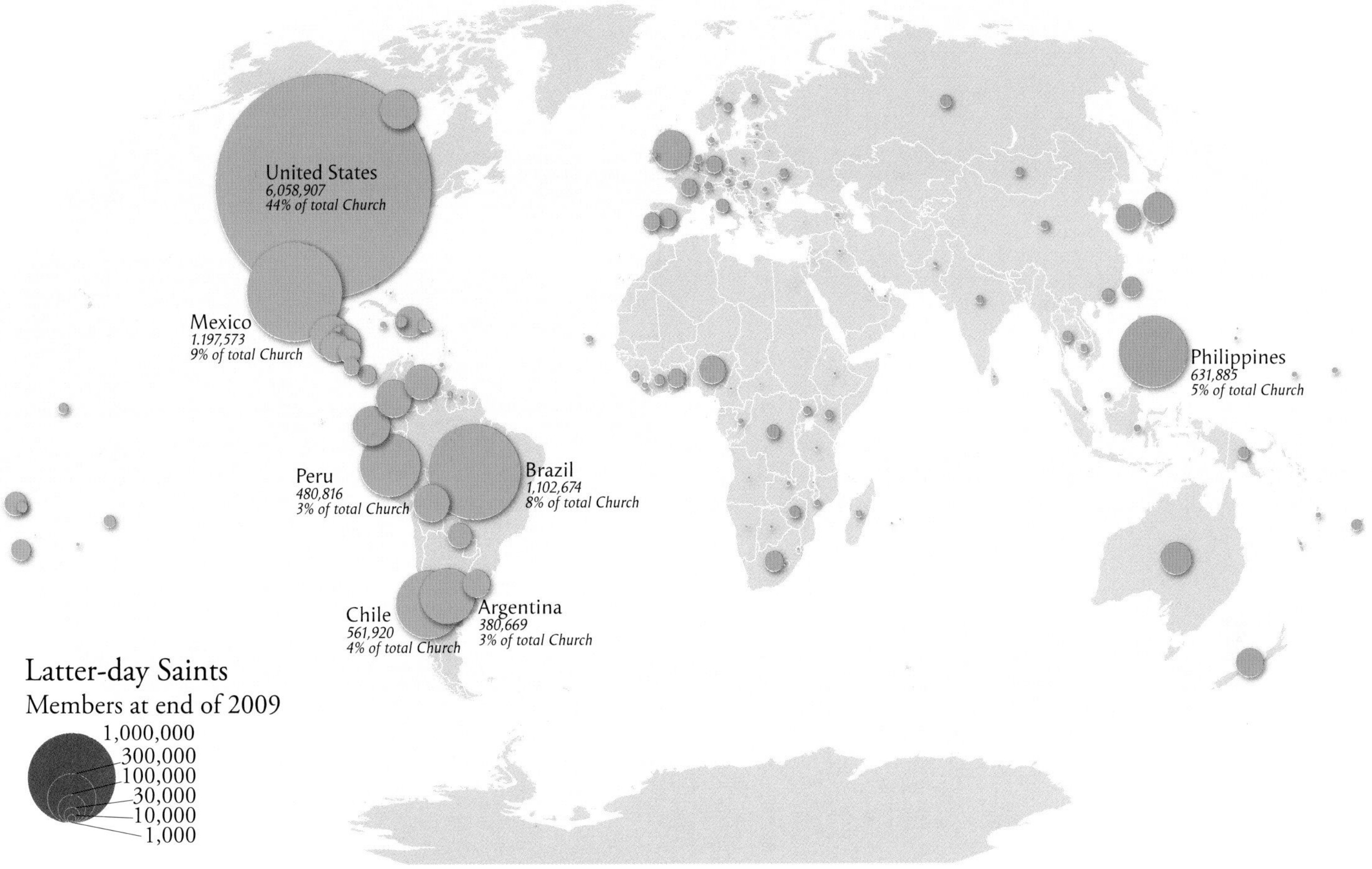

LDS Church Distribution

The Mormon "gathering," the practice of immigrating to join with the core membership of the Church (see p. 104), helps to explain the current distribution of members of The Church of Jesus Christ of Latter-day Saints. Very few of the tens of thousands of European converts in the 1800s remained in their homelands, even after the First Presidency announced in 1911 that Church members should remain in their native lands and build the foundation for stronger local congregations. This local development only began in earnest in the 1950s (see p. 228). As a result, the United States clearly dominates the Church; only recently did it drop below half of the total membership. In general, a concentric distribution surrounding the western United States, is evident with large Mormon populations throughout Latin America (see p. 174). Much of the rapid twentieth century growth in Latin America can be attributed to Mormon tradition that the indigenous people of the Americas are descendants of the people in the Book of Mormon, which has focused missionary efforts there, and provided a message to which Latinos have been receptive.

Beyond the Americas, the long-term missionary effort in western Europe (especially Great Britain) and the Pacific has resulted in higher membership than elsewhere. At the other extreme, previous to a fairly recent administrative change (Official Declaration 2, 1978) that extended the privilege of holding the priesthood to all worthy male members of the Church, Mormon missionaries were slow to enter most African countries, and membership there is relatively small but rapidly growing. The Church in Asia is concentrated in the Philippines, which is largely Christian and thus more receptive to the general focus of missionaries on the restoration of early Christianity.

The Church Office Building in Salt Lake City has been the administrative headquarters of the Church of Jesus Christ of Latter-day Saints since it was completed in 1972 (see p. 116), although the offices of the President and most ecclesiastical leaders are in the Church Administration Building (1917) to the right.

Three American Churches

continued

The headquarters complex of the Jehovah's Witnesses has a prominent position in Brooklyn, New York, facing the East River, the Brooklyn Bridge, and Lower Manhattan. In fact, Charles Russell moved his operations there in 1909 to increase visibility. Recently, as the church has outgrown this location, new facilities have been built in several rural towns further up the Hudson River.

Jehovah's Witnesses Distribution

The organization of Jehovah's Witnesses, as we know it today, grew out of the Bible Student movement established by Charles Russell in Pennsylvania in 1881. After Russell's death in 1917, Joseph Rutherford took control of the society and implemented significant organizational and doctrinal changes, eventually leading to the adoption of the name Jehovah's Witnesses in 1931.

A denominational office was established in London in 1900, and by 1949, Jehovah's Witnesses were operating in more than one hundred different countries. The legacy of this early focus on Europe is clearly evident in the current distribution of Witnesses. Of the three denominations, Jehovah's Witnesses have by far the strongest relative position in Europe, which is home to nearly 19% of their membership. Italy, Germany, and Russia rank among the top ten national populations of Jehovah's Witnesses, and several other European countries are home to very large Witness communities. Jehovah's Witnesses first entered central and southern Africa in 1908 and have been quite successful in these regions, particularly in Nigeria, Zambia, and the Democratic Republic of Congo.

A major factor in the growth of this Church has been the active involvement of lay members in proselytizing efforts. All members, including youth, are expected to spend several hours a month witnessing.

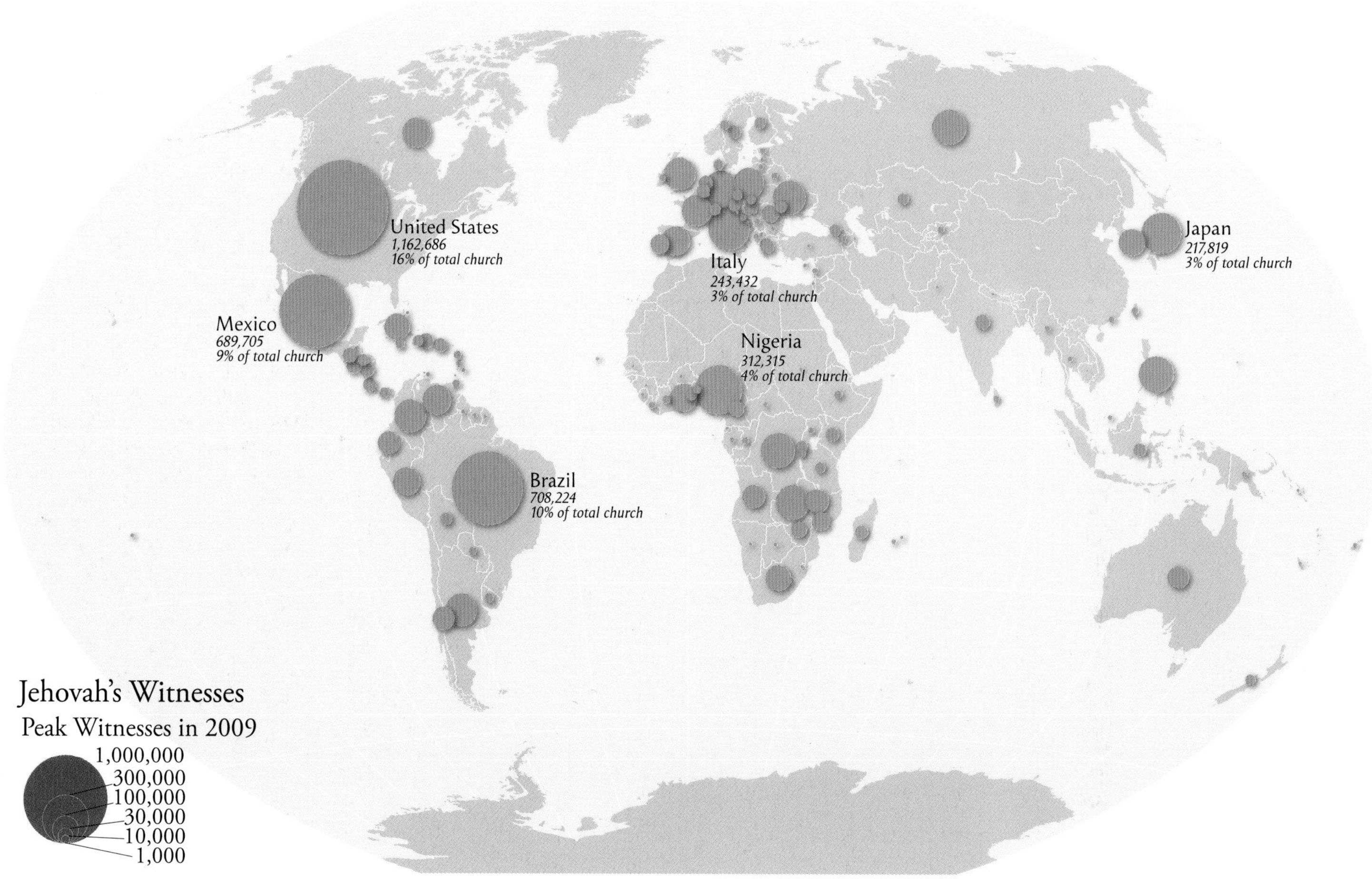

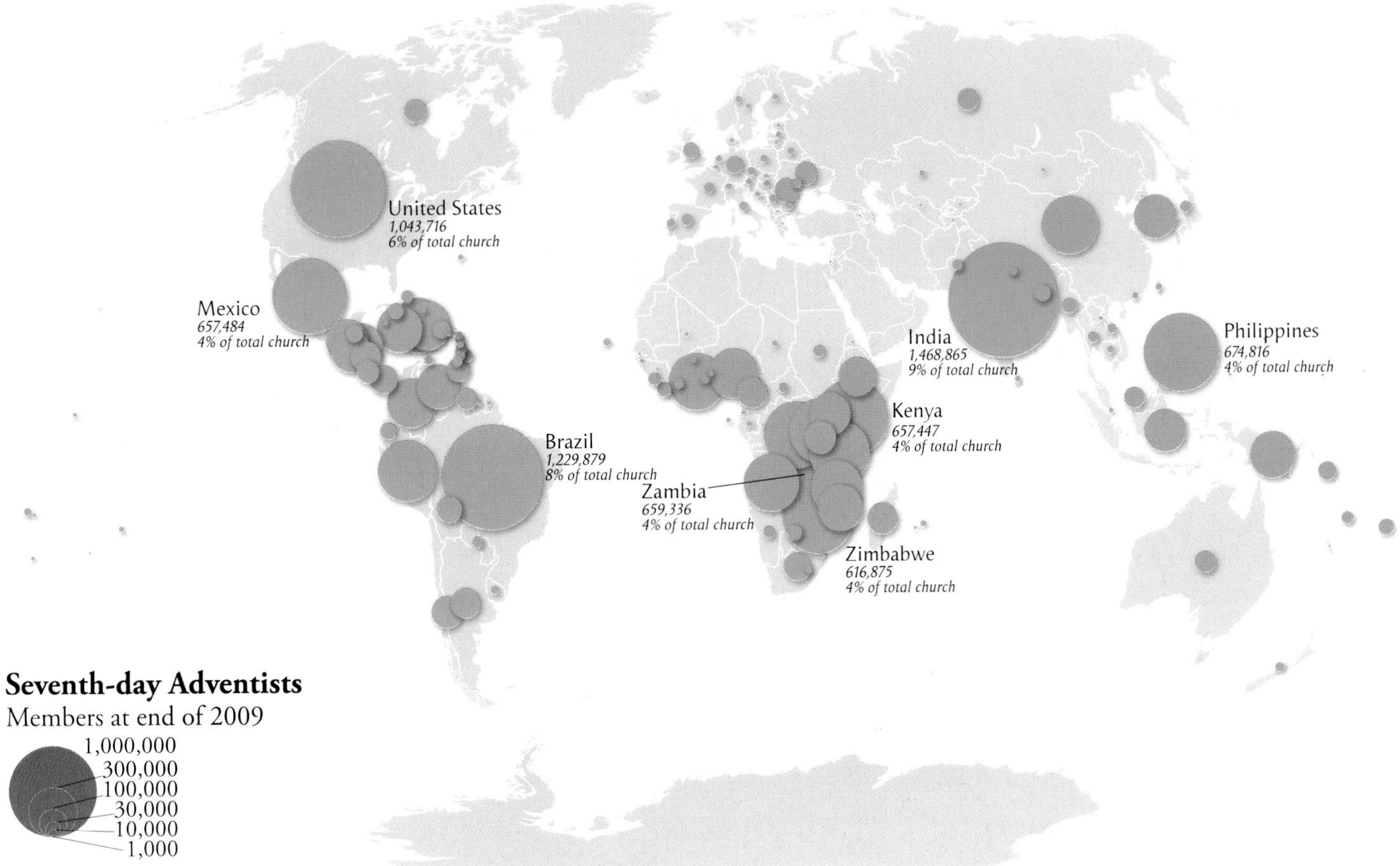

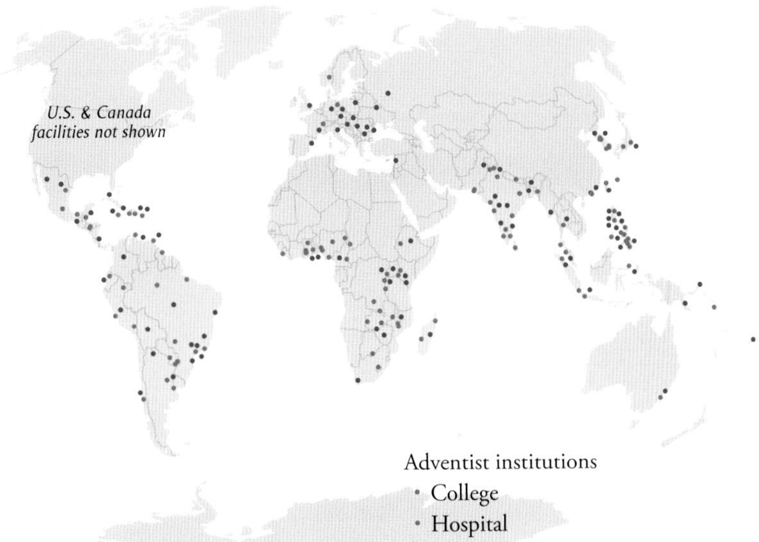

Seventh-day Adventist Distribution

The Seventh-day Adventist Church emerged out of a number of smaller Church groups in the Adventist and Millerite movements (1840s, New York and New Hampshire) and was officially established in 1863 in Battle Creek, Michigan. Adventist missionaries quickly set out for the "four corners of the Earth," entering continental Europe during the 1870s, Russia in 1886, the South Pacific in 1890, India in 1893, western and southern Africa and South America in 1894, and China and Japan in 1896. In China, eastern Europe, and India, Adventists had strong communities in place before significant government changes made further missionary work difficult; this allowed them to continue to operate, although perhaps less freely, in all of these countries. Humanitarian aid through the Adventist Development and Relief Agency (ADRA) and the establishment of schools and hospitals in developing areas (shown at left) make up an important component of Adventist missionary efforts and help explain the relatively high numbers of Seventh-day Adventists in Africa, south and southeast Asia, eastern Europe, and the Caribbean. The significant presence of the Seventh-day Adventist Church in India and its dominance of the Caribbean are quite impressive. Of the three Churches presented, Seventh-day Adventists have the most balanced international membership; no single country accounts for more than 9% of total Church membership (India is home to 8.9%).

The headquarters of the Seventh-day Adventist Church in the suburbs of Washington, D.C., built in 1989.

The Future of the Church

2010–2040

How many members of the Church will there be in five, ten, or thirty years? This question arises frequently but is very difficult to answer. The growth of the Church, like that of any population, is a complex interaction of factors that increase membership (conversion, births, immigration) or decrease it (deaths, emigration, disaffection). Each of these factors changes over time in both expected and unexpected ways, making accurate prediction impossible. However, estimates can be a useful way to judge how the current activities of the Church may influence the future and encourage members to do their best to make the "Kingdom of God" improve and advance.

When asked to predict the growth of a population, sociologists, demographers, and geographers typically look for long-term and short-term patterns in recent growth statistics, then extrapolate those patterns into the future. In the most simple cases, we might assume that the population will add the same number of people each year that it has in recent years (known as linear or arithmetic growth) or that it will increase by the same percentage each year (exponential or geometric growth); the latter typically projects much larger populations than the former.

Church members have frequently been intrigued by glowing predictions of the Church growing exponentially until it becomes a major world religion (typically announced during periods of rapid numerical growth, such as the 1980s), but the trend since 1990 has been of slower growth, attributed to factors such as declining missionary success in some areias and intentional controls on growth so as to not outpace leadership development. This has led to recent models being more restrained. So we may ask, will slow yet sustained growth continue? Could it accelerate to an exponential rate again, as it did in the 1970s? Could it slow even further, until LDS membership begins to decline? Social scientists, as well as proponents and opponents of the Church, have posited all of these scenarios.

One approach to refining projections of Church growth is to look at patterns within each region or country. Membership has grown at different rates in different parts of the world (see p. 174). Rapidly growing regions like Latin America are largely influenced by conversions, while places like Western Europe and Canada are seeing much slower growth due to fewer conversions, but most are still growing faster than the non-LDS population, possibly due to the tendency of Mormons to have larger families than the general population.

While growth tends to follow long-term trends as expected, unforeseen events can have profound effects, at least in certain regions, such as the outmigration from Utah to the western and eastern United States (see p. 144) and the effect of the 1978 Priesthood Revelation on Brazil and Africa (see pp. 222, 232). If large countries that currently have limited or no active LDS missionary presence are opened for Church missionaries, such as China, then these numbers could change substantially (although this would be tempered if the recent tendency continues of mission leaders to control growth so as to not outpace leadership development). Also, the Church has recently begun to consolidate missions in less promising areas such as Europe and shift missionaries to countries where growth is already rapid (especially in Africa); if this trend continues, then those regions will grow at a greater rate than currently predicted.

The most significant change in these trends could come if the Church improves the rate of retention of its converts (increasing the base strength of growing areas) and its youth (thus increasing the pool of missionaries from its current stagnation; see p. 178), or if the members of the Church take on a significantly greater role in proselytizing than they have in the recent past.

Samuel M. Otterstrom and Brandon S. Plewe

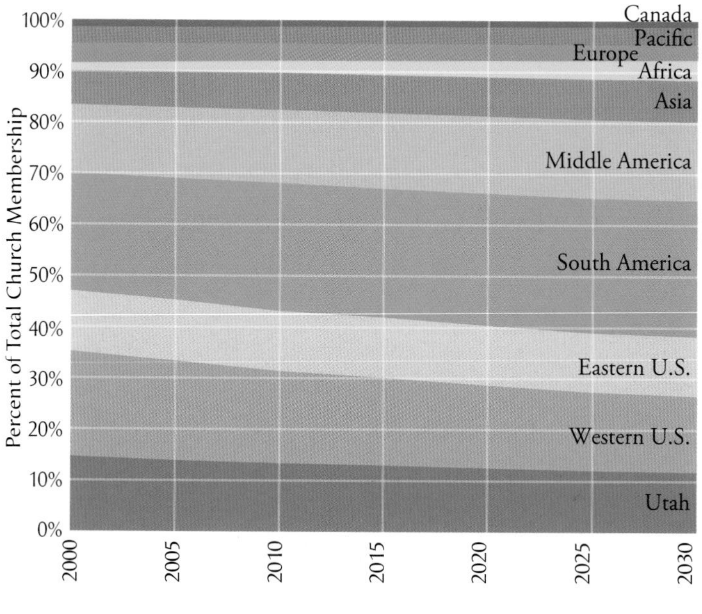

Proportional Growth by Region

The possible future scenario shown on this chart continues the long-term regional trends over the past few decades (see p. 174) using the Linear Regression of %LDS per Region model discussed on the facing page. The Church in Latin America and Africa will probably continue to grow rapidly (but somewhat more slowly than in recent years). By 2020, Africa is likely to have more members than Europe, and Latin America more members than the United States. The overall proportion of the Church in the western United States will likely continue to decline significantly, although this trend could be drastically different as interstate migration patterns change one way or the other.

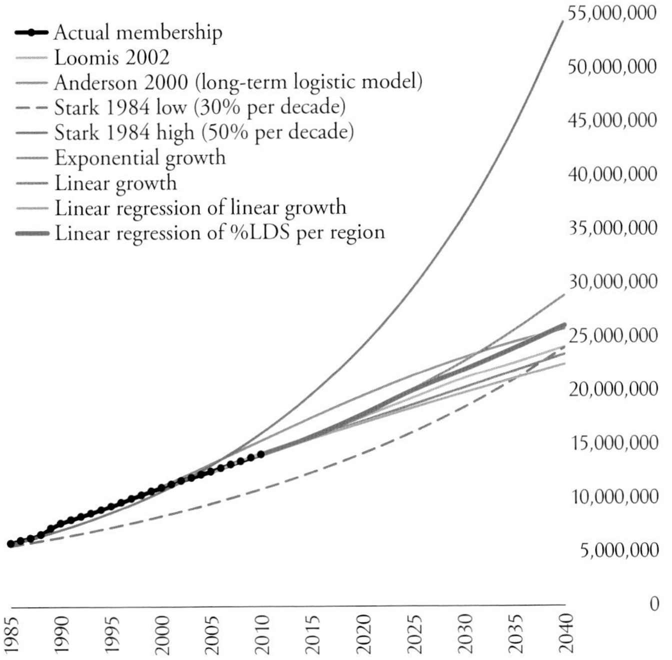

Membership Growth Projections Through 2040

Various models of future growth have been proposed by researchers, and more may be based on the latest statistics. The exponential growth model of Stark (1984) was based on the phenomenal numerical growth seen in the 1970s and 1980s. Although the unforeseen spike in total membership in 1989–1990 (the result of improved recordkeeping, not sudden mass conversions; see p. 220) temporarily pushed actual membership above even his most optimistic estimates, the trend has clearly been closer to a linear rather than exponential rate in recent years. Several more realistic recent models posit a 2040 membership between 22 and 29 million.

For this atlas, Samuel Otterstrom and Brandon Plewe developed a new model they call "Linear Regression of Percent LDS per Region," based on the observation that even at its slowest (in places like Western Europe, Canada, and the Eastern U.S.), LDS membership tends to grow slightly faster than the population as a whole. Rapidly growing regions (Latin America and Africa) have slowed in recent years, but we predict they will continue to outpace their populations as well. Therefore, we looked for patterns in the proportion of the population that is LDS, rather than total membership. Our model, a linear regression of these proportions for each region, applied to future population projections from the Population Resource Bureau, results in a prediction that growth will be somewhere between linear and exponential, with a 2040 membership of about 26 million. However, this too is merely an estimate, and a multitude of factors could make it quite inaccurate in 30 years.

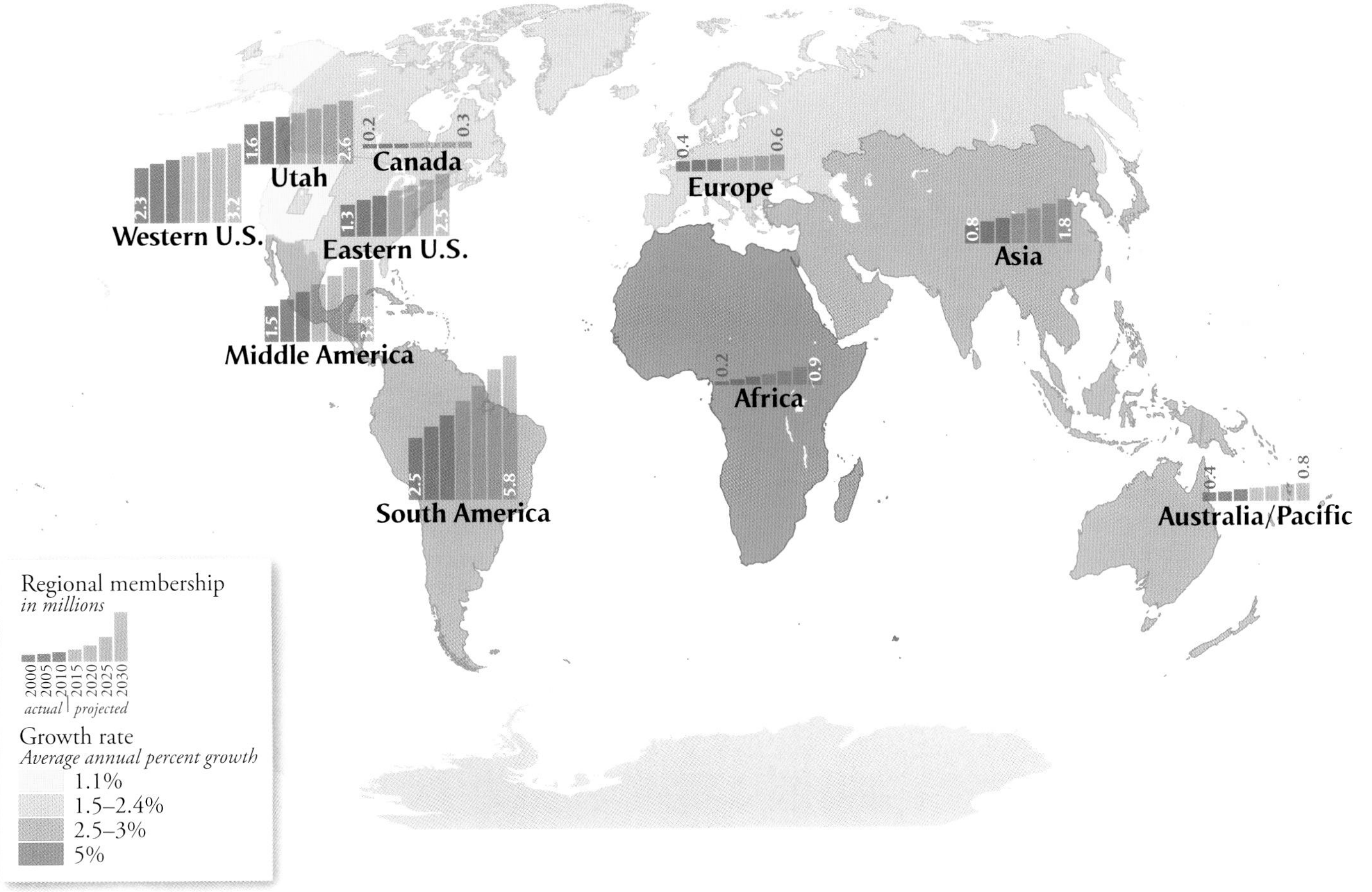

Projected LDS Growth by Region

In terms of total members, the Church will likely continue to grow in every region and nearly every country. In Africa, growth in the countries with the largest membership (e.g., Nigeria, South Africa) will likely slow, newer countries will likely continue to grow rapidly, and several countries with no current Church presence could easily be opened to missionaries in the next few years. Latin America is gradually slowing, but will still likely increase until 2020, when there could be more members in South America than in the United States (other than Utah). Growth in Asia is probably the most unpredictable, with a large number of countries currently closed to the Church, such as China and the Middle East that may or may not become more open in the next 20 years. The western United States is also rather unpredictable, because LDS membership there is heavily influenced by shifting migration patterns. Europe's growth may appear unimpressive, but it is encouraging given that the overall population of the region is expected to be stagnant or even declining by 2030.

SECTION 4

Regional History

THE CHURCH OF JESUS CHRIST OF LATTER-DAY SAINTS is today a global religion, with members in almost every part of the world. However, its introduction and growth has taken a unique path in each region, due to differences in local history and human geography.

Beyond the United States and Canada, the first major mission field was Europe. Although millions of Mormons are the descendants of European converts, the Gathering (see p. 104) kept membership in Europe very small until the 1960s.

Missionaries entered Australia and the South Pacific in the mid-1850s, and Mormonism has since reached a larger share of the population there than anywhere else in the world.

Recent missionary success has been most striking in Middle and South America, even though growth was very slow there after the first forays into Mexico in 1876. Mexico and Brazil each has more than a million members, where in 1960 there were fewer than 16,000 LDS total between those two countries. In comparison, Germany numbered 16,656 LDS in 1960 but grew to only about 40,000 by 2007. Chile has become even more "Mormon" (per capita) than the United States—about 3 percent of Chileans belong to the Church.

Early attempts to preach in Asia were largely unsuccessful, until increased U.S. presence after World War II brought Americans in closer contact with Asians. Success there has been most profound in the Philippines.

Africa is still in the early stages of LDS growth, and many countries do not have established LDS congregations. Africa has less than a tenth of the members that South America has and has the fewest members of all the world regions. However, Africa is growing faster overall than any other region.

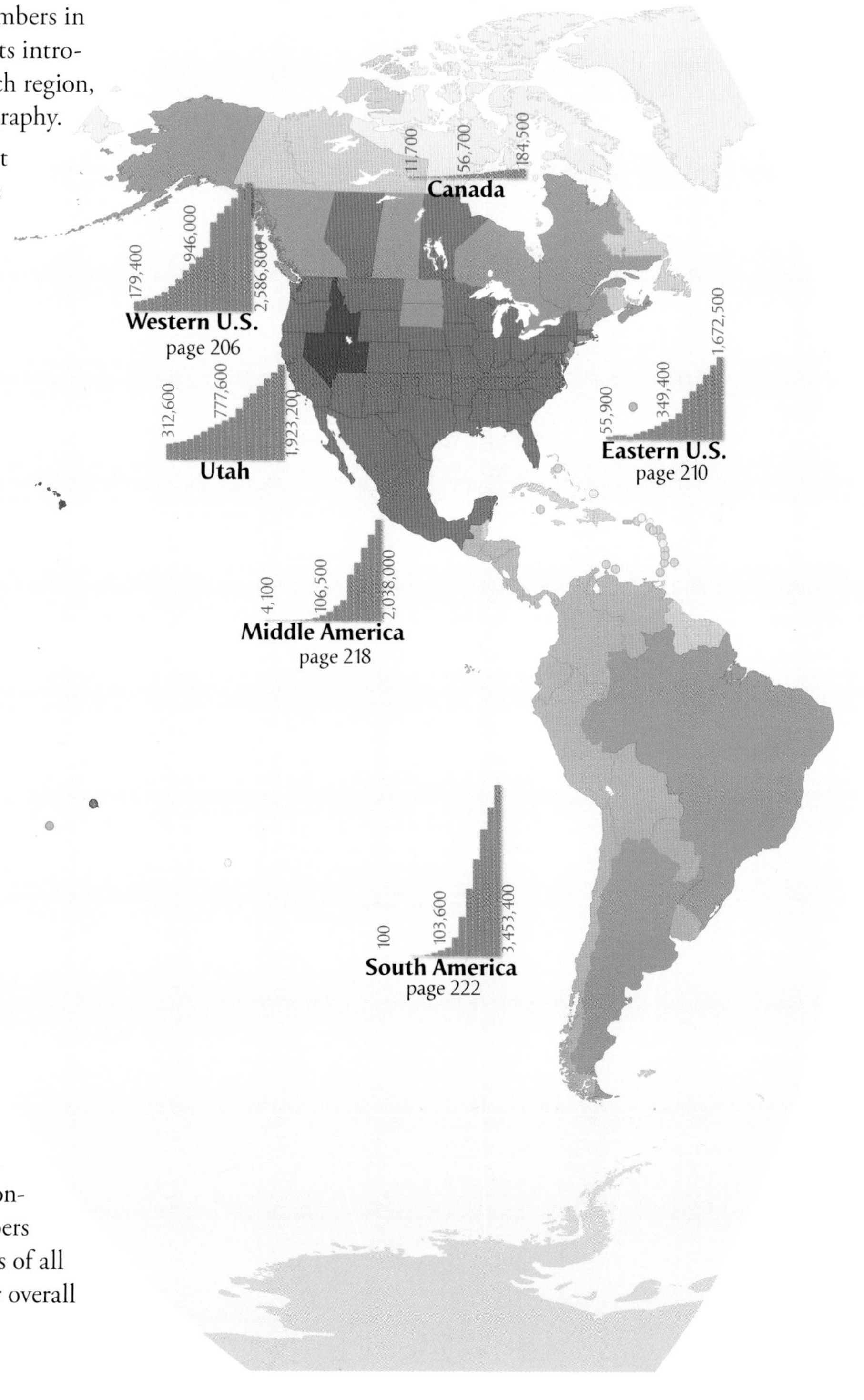

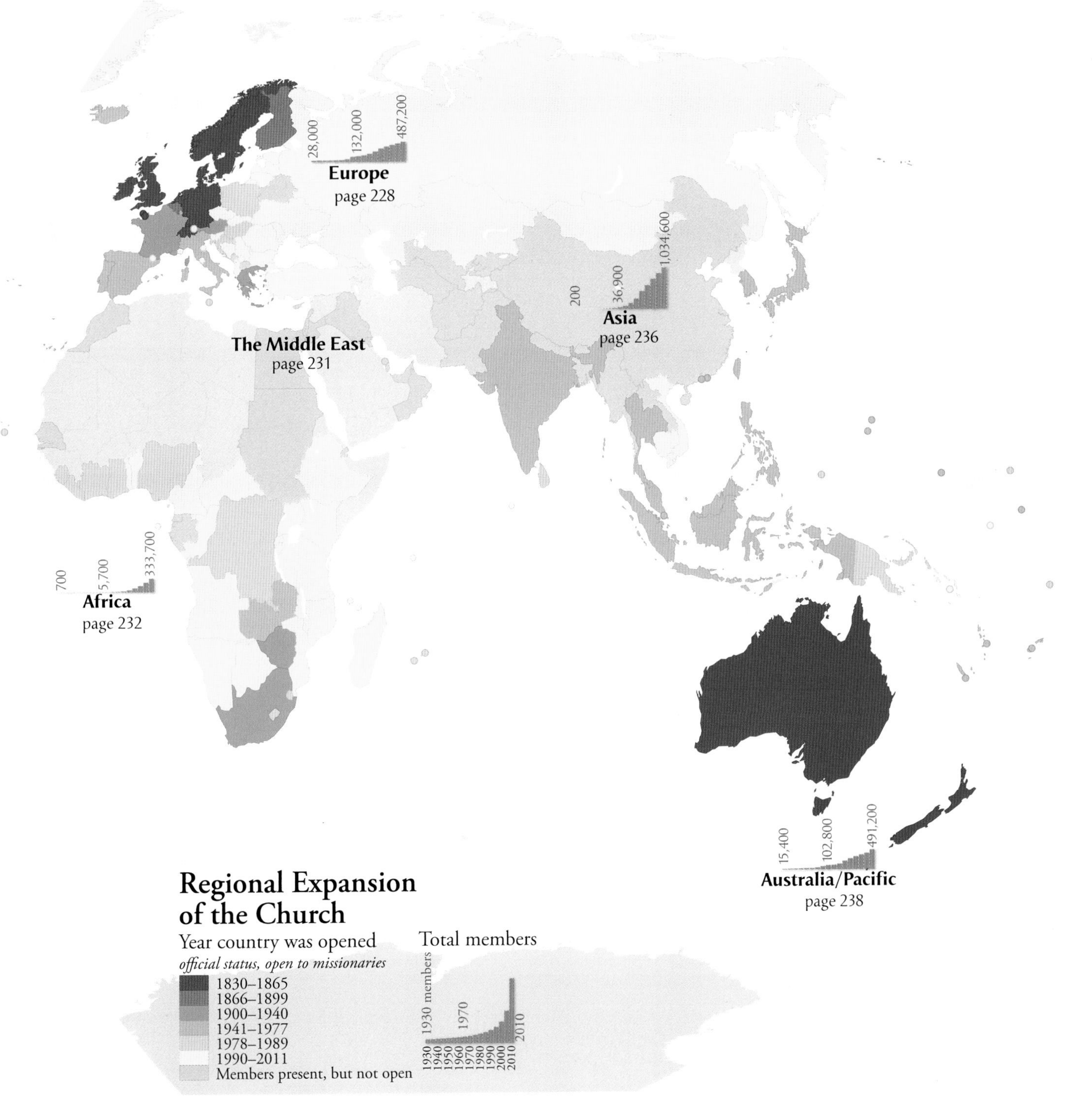
28,000
132,000
487,200
Europe
page 228
200
36,900
1,034,600
Asia
page 236
The Middle East
page 231
700
5,700
333,700
Africa
page 232
15,400
102,800
491,200
Australia/Pacific
page 238
Regional Expansion of the Church
Year country was opened
official status, open to missionaries
1830–1865
1866–1899
1900–1940
1941–1977
1978–1989
1990–2011
Members present, but not open
Total members
1930 members
1970
2010
1930
1940
1950
1960
1970
1980
1990
2000
2010

Western United States and Canada

1890–present

The role of the Church's presiding leadership in organizing the Mormon exploration and colonization of the Intermountain West had essentially ended by 1890 with the last centrally directed settlements in Canada and Mexico (see p. 96), and only the most marginal sites for possible settlement in the vicinity remained. Expansion of the Church would continue unabated after 1890, but now it consisted of the independent migration of Mormon families in response to economic, political, and social events originating far from Salt Lake City as the Mormons became ever more drawn into national events.

Federal laws and massive irrigation projects encouraged the agricultural development of formerly marginal lands, which expanded farmland in Utah but also attracted Mormon farmers to form new communities in surrounding states without a calling from their leaders, continuing a trend begun in eastern Idaho in the 1880s. The Church role in development became more indirect but important nonetheless. For example, Church leadership was instrumental in funding the establishment of the Utah Sugar Company in the 1890s, expanding well beyond Utah by the time the Church gradually divested itself in the 1920s (see p. 118). This and other Church-initiated companies resulted directly from Church leaders attempting to provide nonfarm jobs for the growing population of the region. Ultimately, however, the population growth in the Mormon West exceeded the ability of the region to provide a livelihood for the children and grandchildren of earlier settlers. Other corporations also entered the area with large-scale agricultural projects that drew Mormons and others to new settlements in Idaho, Wyoming, Oregon, New Mexico, and Alberta. At the same time, this industrial-scale production provided nonfarm jobs for the continually growing population unable to obtain land to farm within Utah.

National and foreign corporations funded mining across the region, providing jobs near existing centers and boomtowns that drew Mormon labor and provided markets for Mormon farmers. Mormon-owned businesses also expanded into other states, such as the timber empire of David Eccles in eastern Oregon and elsewhere.

After World War I, new migration patterns began that have impacted the Church in the West to the present. While

continued on page 208

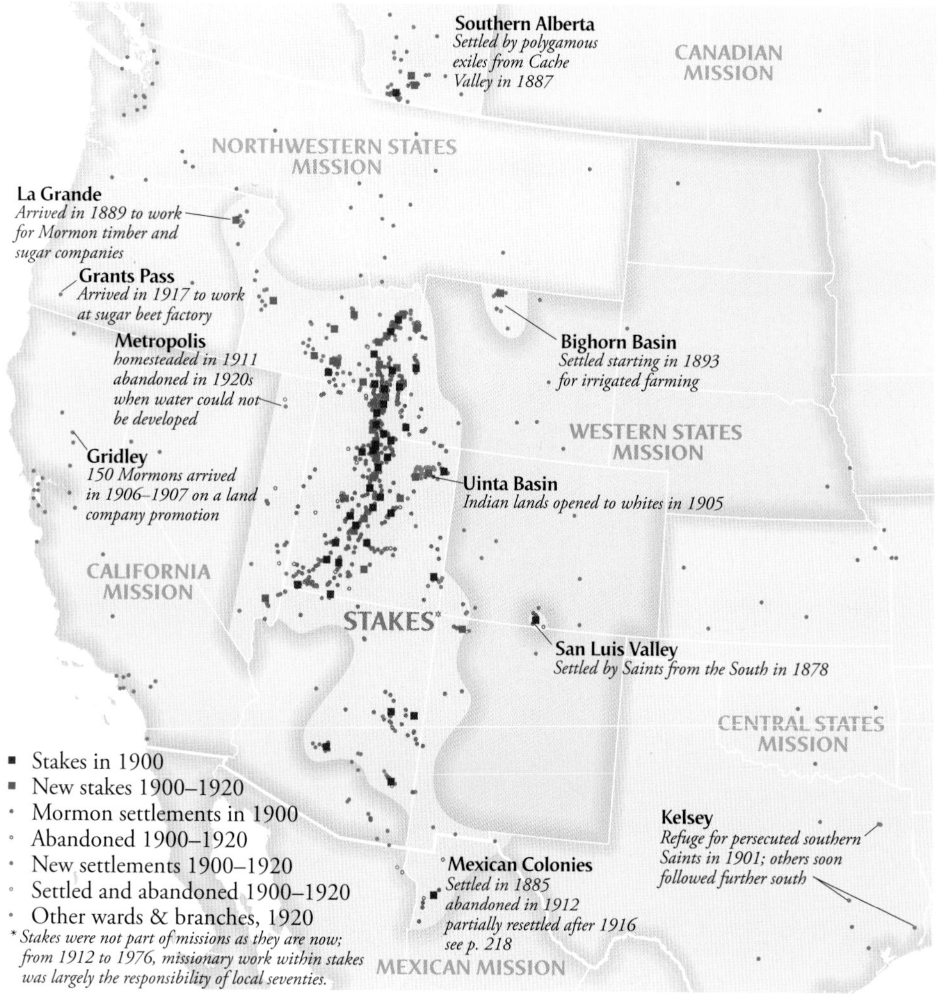

LDS Settlements beyond Utah after 1890

Agriculture was the basis of the pioneer period of settlement directed by the Church, but after 1890 new lands were opened by the federal government. The Newlands Reclamation Act of 1902 opened the way for large-scale irrigation projects that far exceeded the earlier efforts in Utah. Some of these developed cultivation of more land in areas already occupied by Mormons, such as the Strawberry Project, one of the earliest, which brought water from the Colorado River drainage to Utah County. Others, such as reservoirs along the Snake River in Idaho, provided jobs and land for growing Mormon settlements. Projects elsewhere in the West attracted Mormon farmers to new settlements they would share with others. The first stakes outside the traditional Mormon Cultural Region were thus in these new rural communities: San Luis (southern Colorado 1883), Alberta (Cardston 1895), Union (La Grande, Oregon, 1901), Bighorn (northern Wyoming 1901), Raymond (Alberta, 1903), Young (Farmington, New Mexico, 1912), and Boise, Idaho (1913).

As mechanization automated much of the labor in agriculture, fewer farmers could manage larger farms, and Mormons as well as farmers across the country began to migrate into the city; by 1920, more than half of the U.S. population resided in urban areas, and this trend was reflected among Mormons, both in Utah (see p. 88) and in the destinations for the waves of people leaving Utah in the twentieth century.

The growth of Latter-day Saints in the states and provinces of western North America reflects their earlier colonization and expansion. The five states with the largest LDS populations account for almost 80 percent of total membership in the United States and Canada. Growth in total numbers continues in most states, although California's historic rapid growth from the 1920s to the 1970s has leveled off; it is the only state in the country that has declined in membership since 2005. That said, the percentage of the population that is LDS is declining in most western states, as non-LDS migration continues into the West.

The late 1970s and early 1980s saw a boom in stake creation around the world (see p. 184), including this region; since then, stake growth has been slowed in most states, except in growing LDS communities in Utah and Arizona.

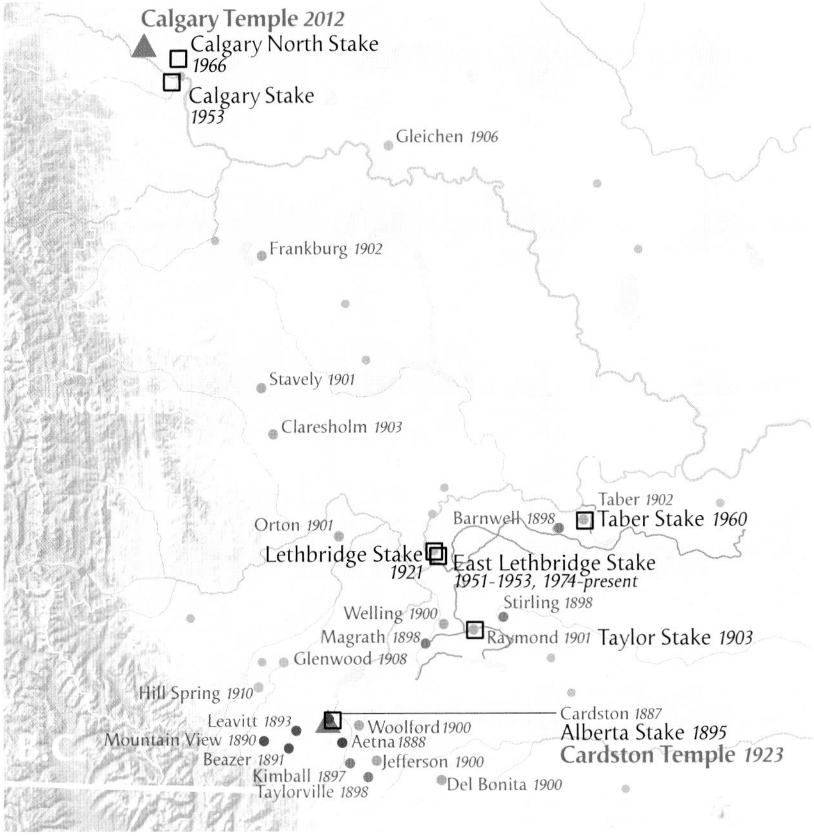

Southern Alberta became a significant colonization destination in the mid-1880s as the persecution of Mormon polygamists became intense in Utah. Charles O. Card was dispatched from Logan to look for suitable settlement sites, and on June 3, 1887, he and 41 Utah Mormons established what later became Cardston. Others followed, especially after 1897, when Card and other local leaders contracted to construct a 100-kilometer irrigation canal from the Saint Mary River near Cardston to Lethbridge. Thousands of acres were opened to farming, and Mormons established new settlements there in 1898 at Magrath and Sterling. In 1901, Jesse Knight, a Mormon mining magnate in Provo, purchased land for farming sugar beets and established Raymond (named after his son). By 1905, Mormons had built twenty or more settlements, but they were only part of a great land boom in western Canada that attracted thousands of American immigrants.

By 1921, Alberta had almost 10,000 Mormons, compared to only a few hundred in the rest of Canada. As in Utah, the two world wars, the Great Depression, and the increasing mechanization of agriculture fueled a mass migration of the southern Alberta Mormons to cities, especially to Calgary but also to Edmonton, Vancouver, Toronto, and elsewhere, strengthening the Church across the country.

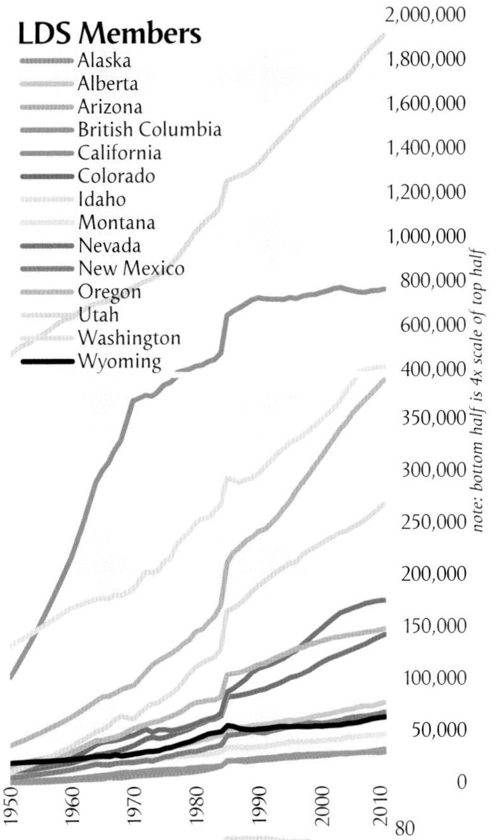

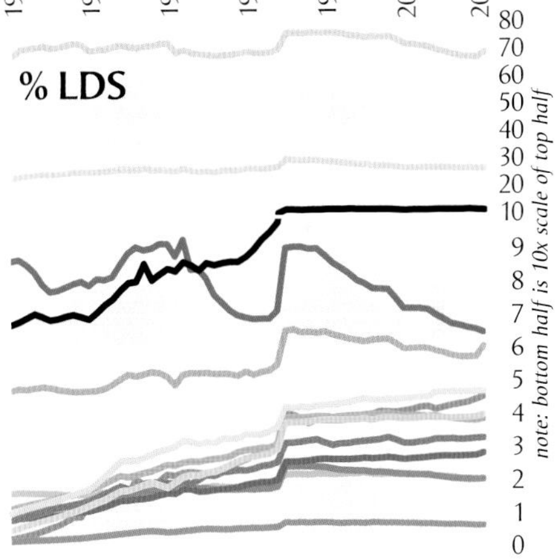

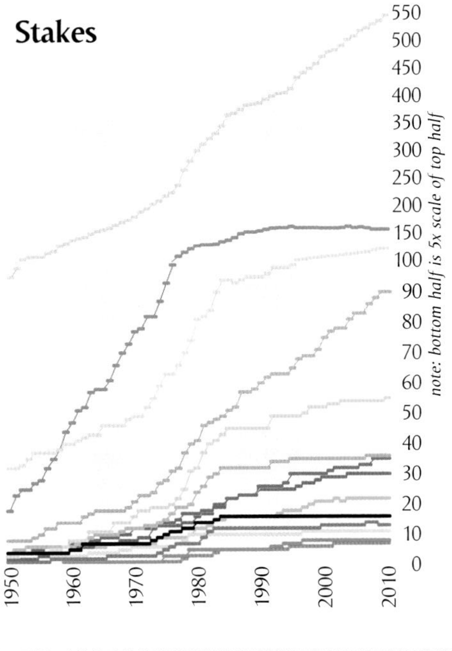

Western United States and Canada

continued

thousands of Mormons left the core region in search of educational and career opportunities, especially in California (see p. 144), people from across the country continued to move to the West, eventually including the mountain states. These trends, along with the growth of the Church worldwide, have reduced the dominance of the Intermountain West as the home of the Mormons.

Richard H. Jackson

Stakes and Early Branches in California

After the Utah War forced the abandonment of the Mormon colony in San Bernardino, the Church had very little presence in California. Even after the California Mission opened in 1892, growth was rather slow, but by 1914, there were branches in most major cities and a Mormon farming colony at Gridley.

Then World War I spurred industrial growth on the West Coast, initiating a great outmigration (see p. 144). Shipbuilding in San Diego and job opportunities in the Los Angeles region drew Mormons from Utah to Southern California. Although they were just one strand in the great population movement to the West Coast, the effect on the Church was profound. From 1919 to 1925, LDS membership in California tripled from 5,000 to 15,000 (growing 20 percent per year), and a stake was formed in Los Angeles. By 1930, it had more than doubled again to 34,000, with three stakes. By then the Mormon population was becoming a recognizable and important minority. LDS growth in California cities continued unabated until it slowed abruptly in 1970, as the economic boom of the 1950s and '60s ended. By then, California had almost 400,000 members. Since then there has been a small but gradually increasing reverse flow to Utah.

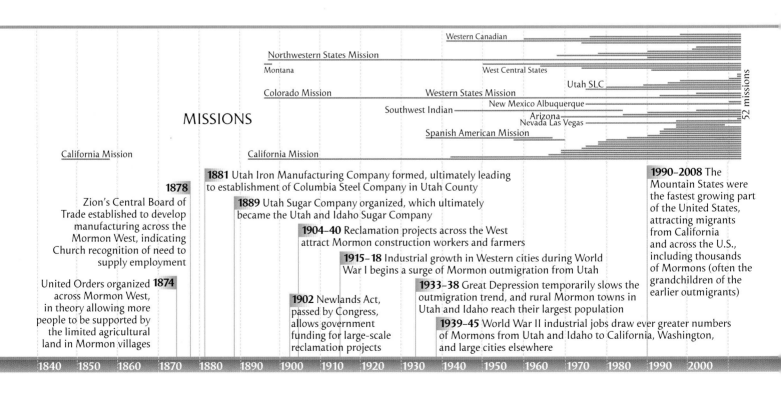

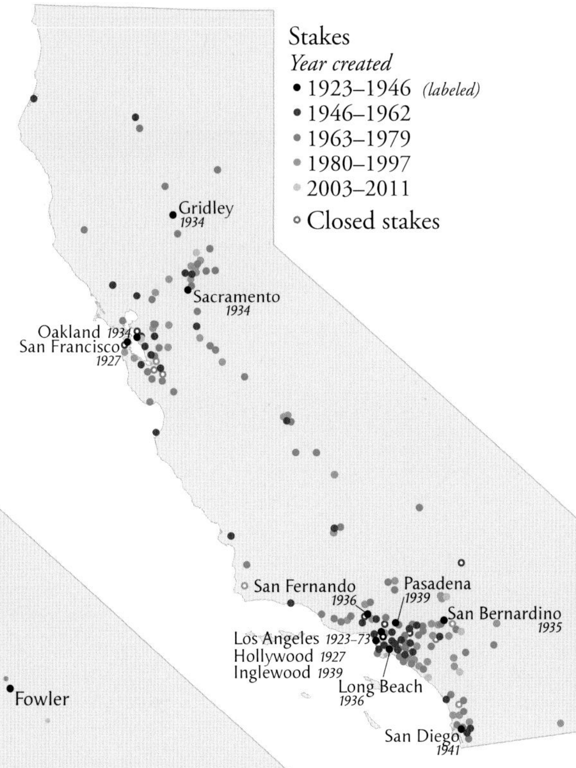

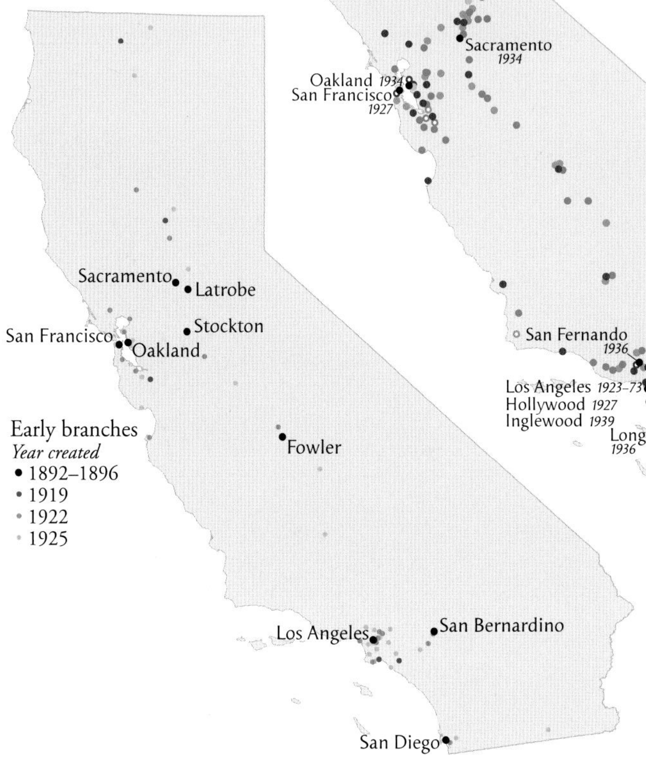

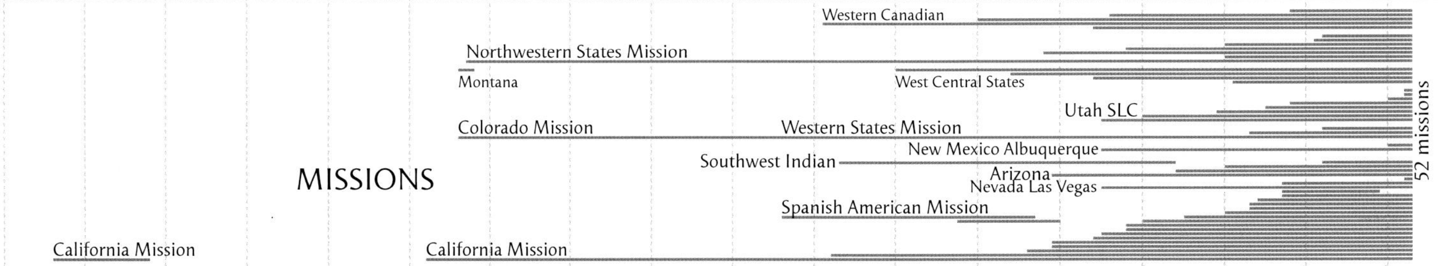

1874 United Orders organized across Mormon West, in theory allowing more people to be supported by the limited agricultural land in Mormon villages

1878 Zion's Central Board of Trade established to develop manufacturing across the Mormon West, indicating Church recognition of need to supply employment

1881 Utah Iron Manufacturing Company formed, ultimately leading to establishment of Columbia Steel Company in Utah County

1889 Utah Sugar Company organized, which ultimately became the Utah and Idaho Sugar Company

1902 Newlands Act, passed by Congress, allows government funding for large-scale reclamation projects

1904–40 Reclamation projects across the West attract Mormon construction workers and farmers

1915–18 Industrial growth in Western cities during World War I begins a surge of Mormon outmigration from Utah

1933–38 Great Depression temporarily slows the outmigration trend, and rural Mormon towns in Utah and Idaho reach their largest population

1939–45 World War II industrial jobs draw ever greater numbers of Mormons from Utah and Idaho to California, Washington, and large cities elsewhere

1990–2008 The Mountain States were the fastest growing part of the United States, attracting migrants from California and across the U.S., including thousands of Mormons (often the grandchildren of the earlier outmigrants)

1840 1850 1860 1870 1880 1890 1900 1910 1920 1930 1940 1950 1960 1970 1980 1990 2000

LDS Membership in the Western U.S. and Canada

The changing distribution of Mormonism in the West is highlighted in this series of maps. Counties where Mormons have been dominant (more than 50 percent of the population) are primarily in Utah and southeastern Idaho throughout the century, but the fringe of this core area has changed over the years. Some counties in Utah have been less than 50 percent LDS at times, especially where mining or agriculture has attracted non-Mormon workers, where American Indian populations have been significant, or where world-class recreation (especially Park City) has attracted wealthy residents. Just beyond this core is a fringe of dozens of counties that have seen an increasing Mormon presence; Mormons have continued to move outward as they did in the nineteenth century (see p. 96) but now mix with other people rather than living in separate settlements. In fact, although it is a minority of the total population, Mormonism is the largest single denomination in many parts of Nevada, Wyoming, Arizona, and Idaho.

Eastern United States and Canada

1875–present

THE GATHERING OF THE LATTER-DAY SAINTS to the Rocky Mountains in the last half of the nineteenth century strengthened the core of the LDS Church at a crucial time, but it came at a steep price, weakening it everywhere else. The lost presence took decades to restore, but eventually the Church gained a strong presence in all regions of the world. This trend is probably strongest in the eastern part of North America, the cradle of the Restoration. Here, the history of the Church after the pioneer exodus (see p. 80) can be divided into four phases:

- **Gathering the Scattered Saints, 1852–74.** In 1852, Brigham Young issued a call to the members across the United States who were still loyal to him (perhaps 10,000 east of the Rocky Mountains) to gather to Utah or risk losing contact with the Church, due to the need for leaders to build up the new communities in the West rather than to administer to far-flung branches; many heeded the call, many drifted away from the Church, and a few stayed put but remained loyal. This emptying of the East was accelerated by the Utah War of 1857 (see p. 110), during which almost all missionaries were called home; by the Civil War (1861–65); and by the negative publicity generated by the practice of plural marriage, first announced in 1852 (see p. 122). Tens of thousands of European Mormon emigrants passed through New York and other eastern cities but did not stay. By 1867, one could count no more than 395 active Mormons in all the northeastern United States and Canada, with a comparable number in the South.
- **A Tentative Return to the East, 1875–1929.** In the last years of his life, Brigham Young began to call missionaries to serve in the East. While they met with great persecution (especially in the South), they found enough success to establish permanent branches (also especially in the South). The discontinuation of plural marriage had an impact on the success of missionary work, especially after the Reed Smoot hearings (1900–07) laid the issue to rest. The integration of Mormon and non-Mormon soldiers in World War I, a growing pool of missionaries (transitioning from calling family men to calling young

continued on page 212

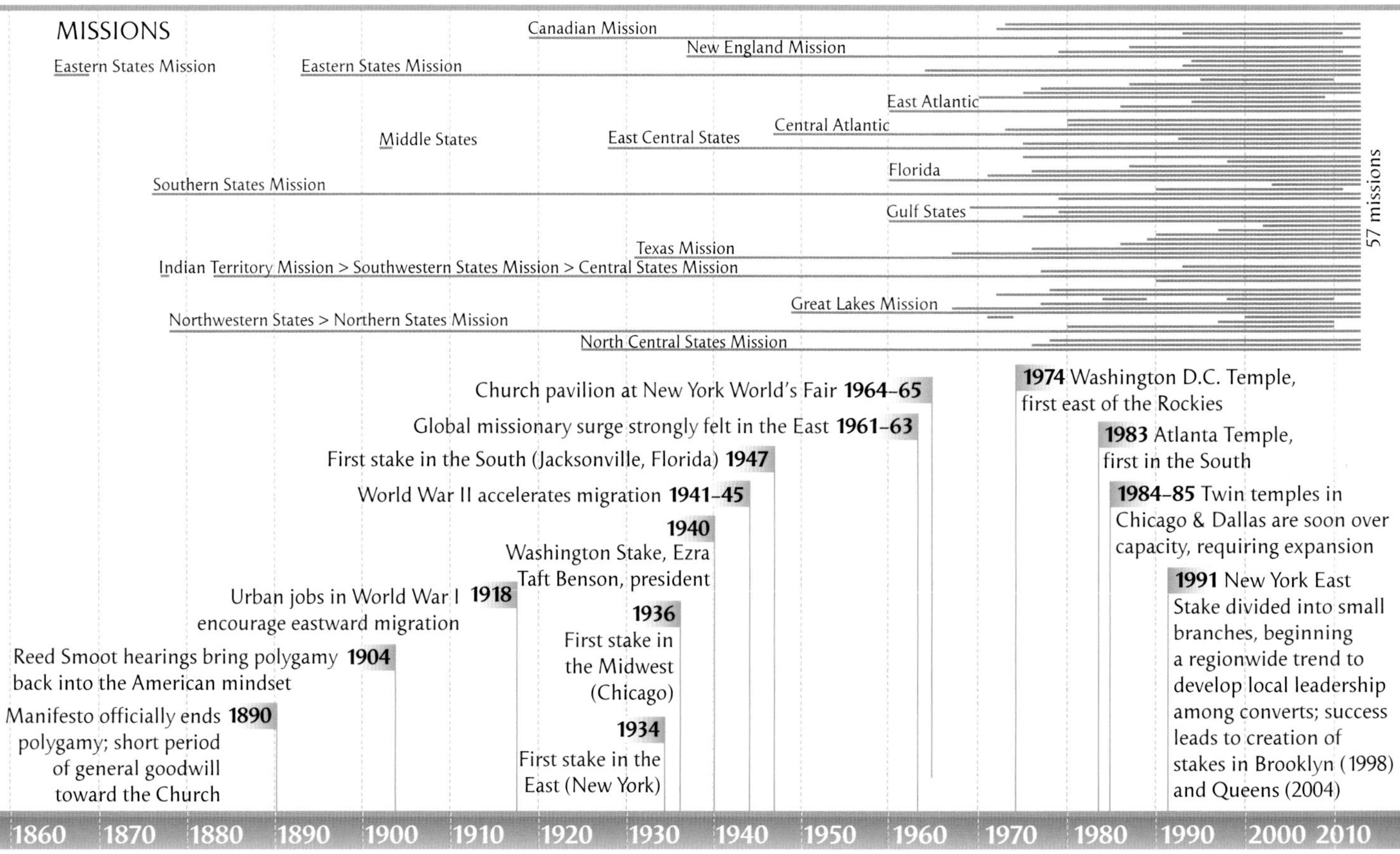

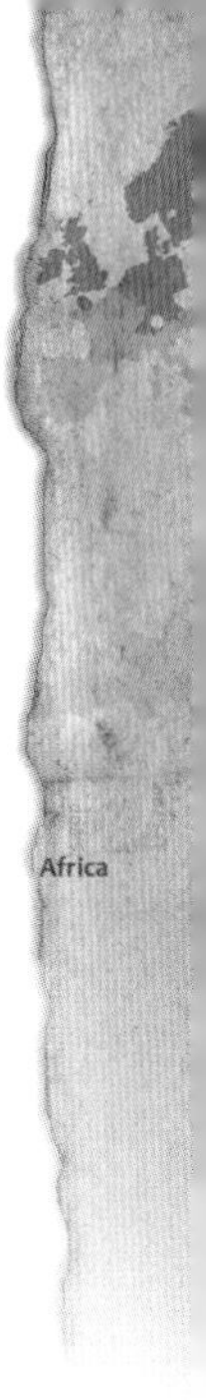

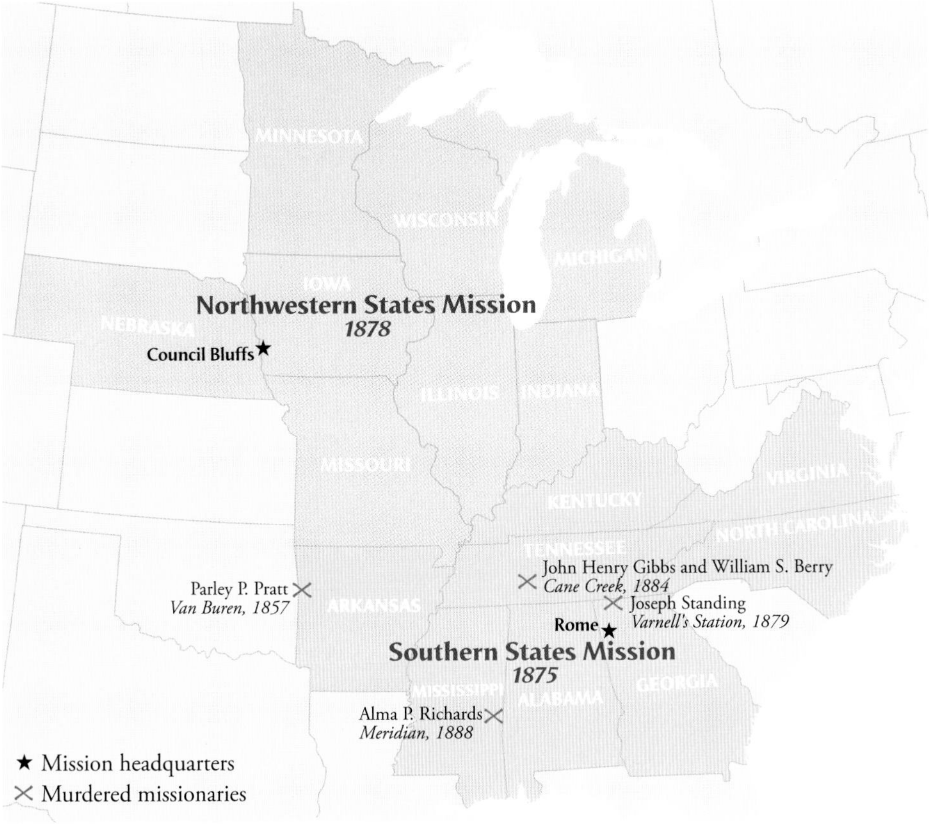

Missionaries Return East, 1875–1889

During the Church's most isolated era (1857–75), missionaries occasionally preached in eastern towns on their way to or from Europe, but branches were rare and fleeting until the last years of Brigham Young's life, when he began to call missionaries to serve in the United States. They were rather ineffectual until the formal creation of the Southern States Mission under Henry G. Boyle and the Northwestern States Mission under Cyrus H. Wheelock (soon renamed Northern States). Missionaries were able to find converts and create a few branches, despite rampant persecution due to the practice of plural marriage and (especially in the South) the memory of Mountain Meadows (see p. 110). In the South, missionaries found minor success in rural areas, focusing on friends and families of existing members, despite the murder of several missionaries and converts.

Permanent Establishment

Large numbers of missionaries were called to the eastern United States in the late 1870s (see p. 94), where they soon visited almost every state. In some, they were able to convert enough people to create permanent branches, while less successful states were abandoned (or saw only sporadic visits) until the 1890s. At that time, growth began to accelerate as the number of missionaries grew sharply, the Church abandoned plural marriage (see p. 122), and missions concentrated their efforts in the cities, especially after the creation of the Eastern States Mission in 1893 at Brooklyn under Job Pingree (the primary purpose of which President Wilford Woodruff stated was "to try to locate and revive the scattered saints") and the Canadian Mission after World War I in 1919 under Nephi Jensen. Sustained growth, however, was still offset by emigration to the West, including settlements established in southern Colorado and eastern Texas specifically for southern Saints (see p. 206).

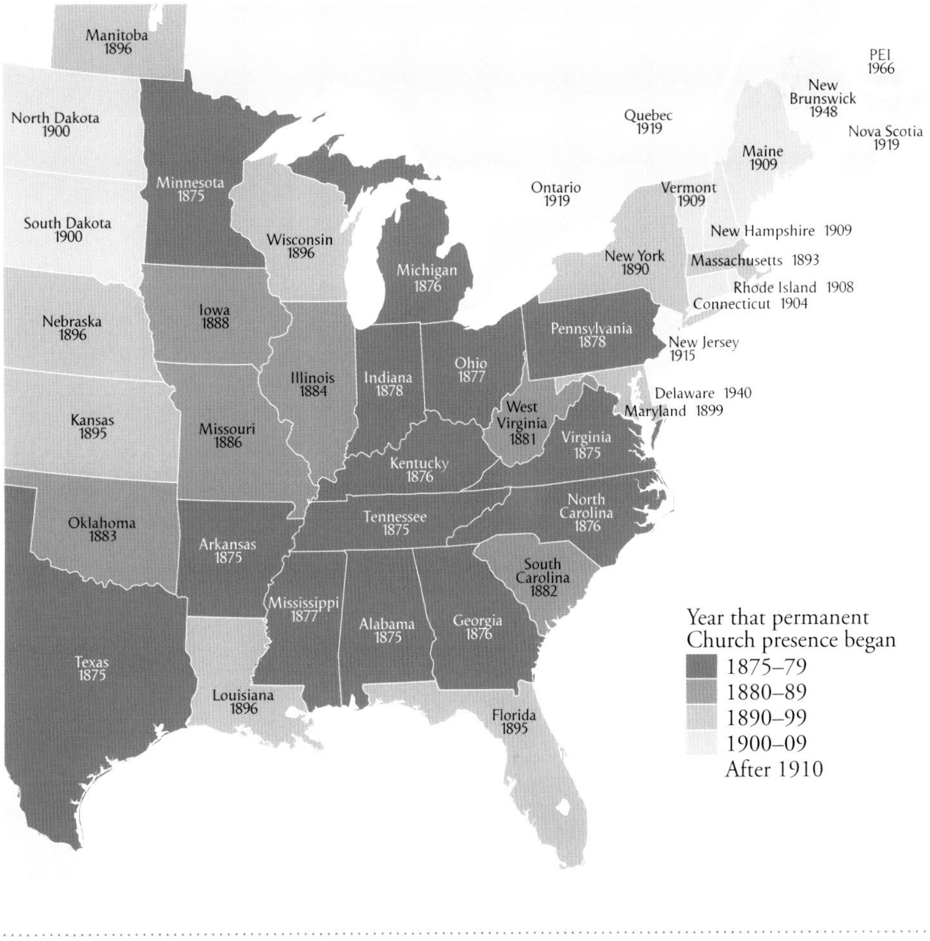

Eastern United States and Canada

continued

single adults), and the development of Church historical sites also laid the foundation for growth, although public opinion remained generally antagonistic. Also, the gathering was still a powerful force; of the 2,238 converts who joined the Church in the Southern States between 1880 and 1888, over half moved to Utah before the end of the century. By 1930, missionaries and about 40,000 members were scattered across almost every state and province in the region.

- **Proliferation, 1930–79.** Although the Great Depression reduced the number of missionaries who could afford to serve in the East, it strengthened the impetus for western members to migrate to the eastern cities for education and work (see p. 144). This accelerating migration, combined with continued calls from Salt Lake City for eastern Saints not to gather but to build up the Church locally, led to increased growth, especially during the economic boom of the 1950s.
- **Stable Growth, 1980–present.** As the outmigration slowed and was balanced by return migration to the West, sustained growth was increasingly reliant on missionary work and the development of local leaders. The Church has continued to grow across the East at a pace slightly faster than the population as a whole.

Richard E. Bennett

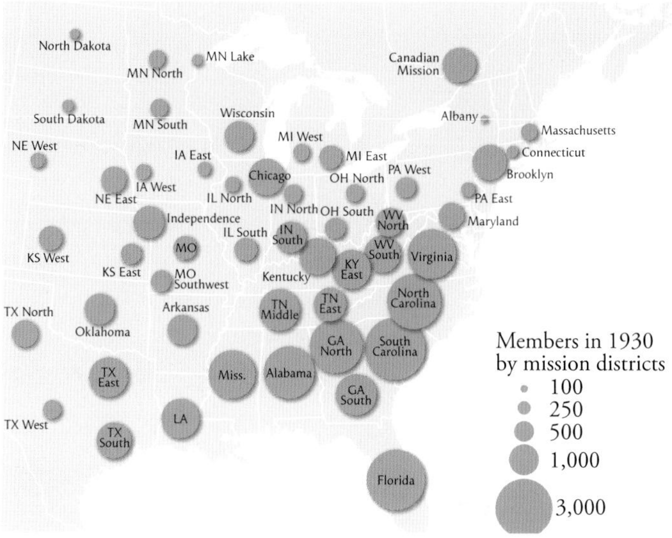

Church Membership in 1930

By the time Church Historian Andrew Jenson surveyed the state of the Church for the *Encyclopedic History of the Church* (1930), missionaries were serving throughout eastern North America, and branches were scattered among most states and provinces. In the South, continued proselytizing efforts had led to slow, sustained growth. This region had the largest membership (15,454), consisting almost entirely of converts, but it was still too scattered to support stakes. In contrast, the Church in the Northeast was largely concentrated in the major cities, where the first eastern stakes would be created in New York (1934), Chicago (1936), and Washington, D.C. (1940); even in 1930, a large proportion of the membership there, and almost all of the leadership, consisted of transplants from the Intermountain West, including many Mormon students attending prestigious colleges such as Columbia and Harvard (see p. 144).

The New York World's Fair of 1964 was a watershed event for the Church in the East. The prominent pavilion attracted over a million visitors and tens of thousands of referrals resulting in hundreds of local area baptisms—a highly successful effort of the Church to improve its image and establish a permanent foothold in the East.

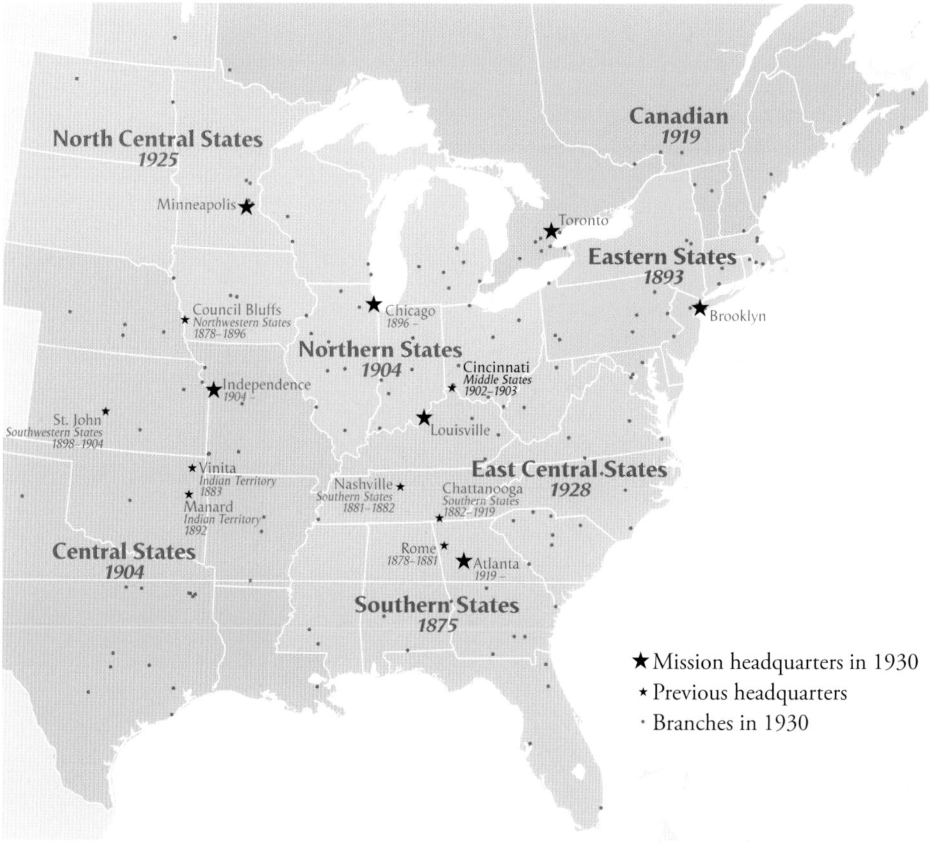

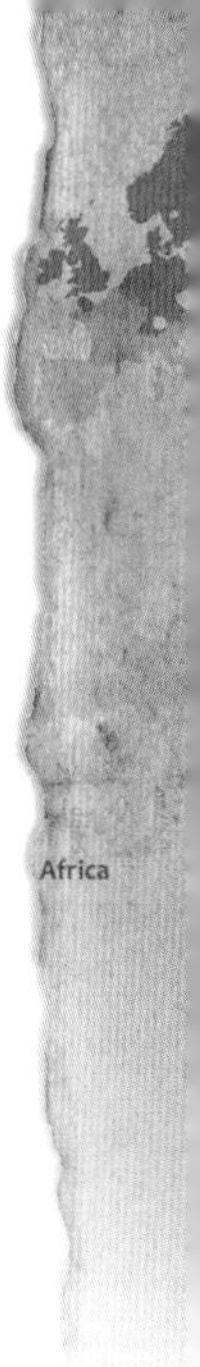

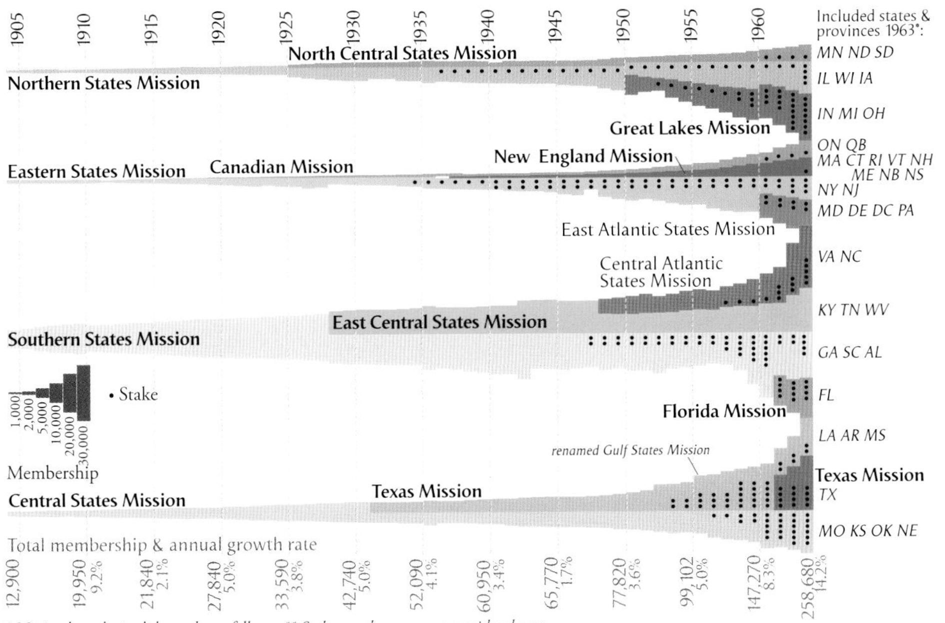

** Mission boundaries did not always follow state/province boundaries, often including a few branches in neighboring states*

*** Stake members were not considered part of missions but are here counted within the mission in which they would likely be included*

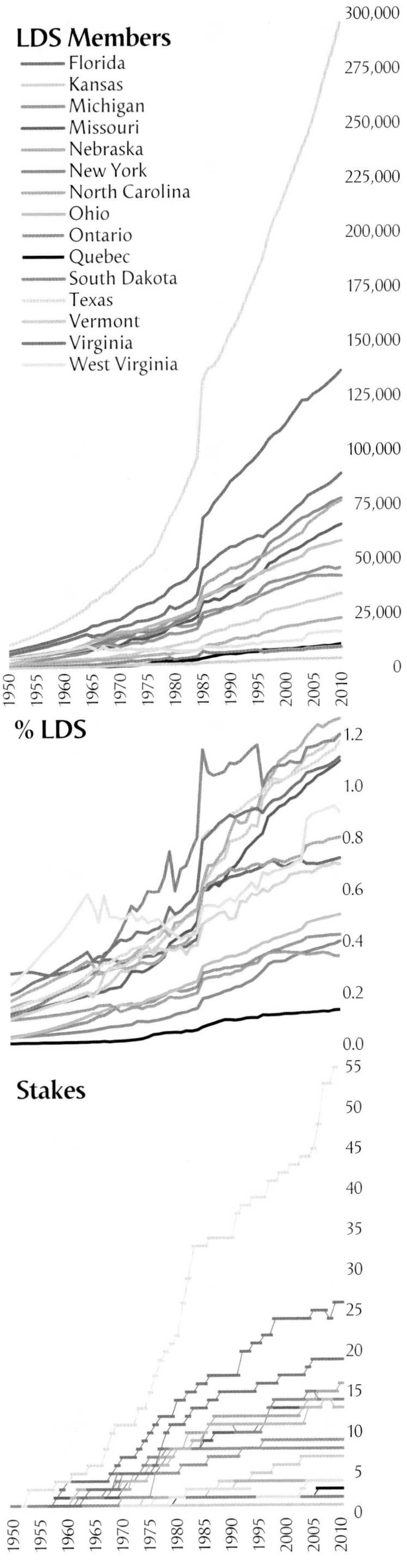

Missions in the Mid-twentieth Century

Membership growth in each mission was slow but sustained until World War II, when thousands of LDS servicemen were relocated to military training bases all over the South and East. The war and the subsequent economic boom brought thousands of Mormon students, scientists, business leaders, government workers, and other job-seekers from the West. This influx expanded to places like Detroit, Pittsburgh, St. Louis, Boston, and Toronto (coming from Alberta). The wave of migration came later to the South (the first stakes in Florida and South Carolina were almost entirely local members) but was just as influential, especially in Texas, Florida, and Atlanta. These newcomers bolstered missionary efforts, formed the core membership of the new wards and stakes, and provided most of the leadership. In fact, developing local leadership among the converts has been a difficult issue in many of these cities ever since.

Meanwhile, the numbers of full-time young missionaries spiked from a few hundred in 1945 to over 16,000 by 1966. During the 1960s, the number of new Mormon converts multiplied, aided by an ambitious Church-wide chapel-building program (an overt effort by the Church to discourage converts from gathering to Utah, see p. 160) and new and more effective missionary preparation and teaching efforts.

Recent Growth Trends

Since the 1960s, growth in most Eastern states and provinces has continued, especially in economically dynamic states such as Texas, Florida, and Virginia that continue to attract Mormons from elsewhere. In every state, LDS membership is growing a little faster than the population at large (unlike the West, where the LDS proportion is declining, see p. 206). The Church is generally most predominant in the Midwest, averaging over one percent LDS, and weakest in Quebec and the Maritimes, with LDS proportions similar to Europe. The East saw a remarkable increase in stakes in the late 1970s, when all but a few remote branches became part of a stake, but stake growth has slowed substantially since then; Michigan, for example, saw four new stakes between 1975 and 1979, but none since then (despite membership doubling). This trend may be due to challenges in retaining converts or developing local leadership, issues felt throughout the East.

The apparent spike in membership in most states in 1985 was due to a change in how the Church reported state and province statistics (members with unknown addresses began to be counted in their last known region), not to an actual surge in members.

United States and Canada in 2012

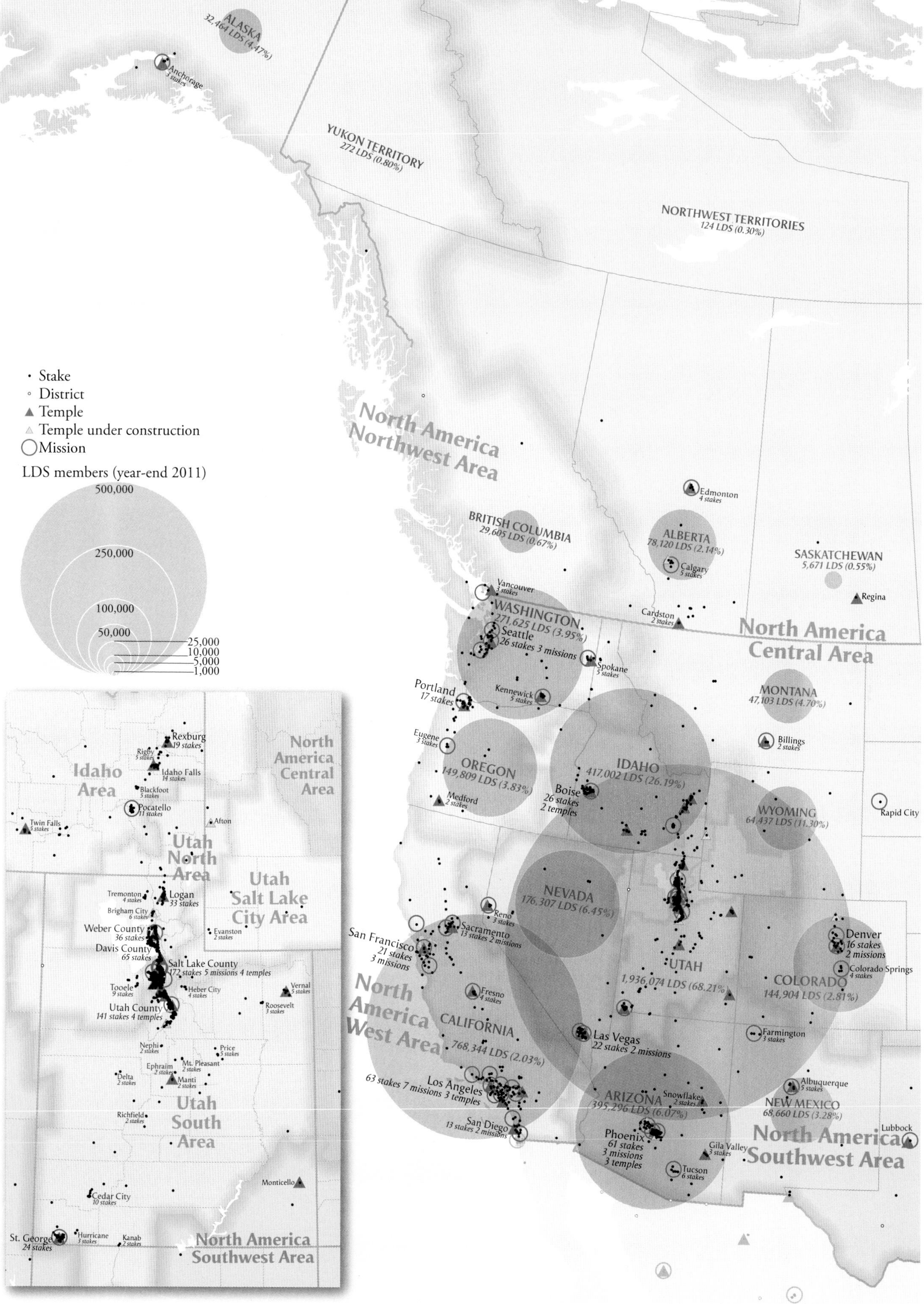
3 stakes

YUKON TERRITORY
272 LDS (0.80%)

NORTHWEST TERRITORIES
124 LDS (0.30%)

North America
Northwest Area

Edmonton
4 stakes

BRITISH COLUMBIA
29,605 LDS (0.67%)

ALBERTA
78,120 LDS (2.14%)

Calgary
5 stakes

SASKATCHEWAN
5,671 LDS (0.55%)

Regina

Vancouver
3 stakes

WASHINGTON
271,625 LDS (3.95%)

Seattle
26 stakes 3 missions

Cardston
2 stakes

North America
Central Area

Spokane
5 stakes

Portland
17 stakes

Kennewick
5 stakes

MONTANA
47,103 LDS (4.70%)

Eugene
3 stakes

OREGON
149,809 LDS (3.83%)

IDAHO
417,002 LDS (26.19%)

Boise
26 stakes
2 temples

WYOMING
64,437 LDS (11.30%)

Billings
2 stakes

Medford
2 stakes

Rapid City

Reno
5 stakes

Sacramento
13 stakes 2 missions

NEVADA
176,307 LDS (6.45%)

Denver
16 stakes
2 missions

San Francisco
21 stakes
3 missions

UTAH
1,936,074 LDS (68.21%)

COLORADO
144,904 LDS (2.81%)

Colorado Springs
4 stakes

Fresno
4 stakes

North
America
West Area

CALIFORNIA
768,344 LDS (2.03%)

Las Vegas
22 stakes 2 missions

Farmington
3 stakes

Los Angeles
63 stakes 7 missions 3 temples

San Diego
13 stakes 2 missions

ARIZONA
395,296 LDS (6.07%)

Snowflake
2 stakes

Albuquerque
5 stakes

NEW MEXICO
68,660 LDS (3.28%)

Lubbock

Phoenix
61 stakes
3 missions
3 temples

Gila Valley
3 stakes

North America
Southwest Area

Tucson
6 stakes

Inset Map

Rexburg
19 stakes

Rigby
5 stakes

Idaho
Area

Idaho Falls
14 stakes

Blackfoot
5 stakes

North
America
Central
Area

Twin Falls
3 stakes

Pocatello
11 stakes

Afton

Tremonton
4 stakes

Logan
33 stakes

Utah
North
Area

Brigham City
6 stakes

Utah
Salt Lake
City Area

Weber County
36 stakes

Evanston
2 stakes

Davis County
65 stakes

Salt Lake County
172 stakes 5 missions 4 temples

Vernal
5 stakes

Tooele
9 stakes

Heber City
4 stakes

Roosevelt
3 stakes

Utah County
141 stakes 4 temples

Nephi
2 stakes

Price
5 stakes

Delta
2 stakes

Ephraim
2 stakes

Mt. Pleasant
2 stakes

Manti
2 stakes

Richfield
2 stakes

Utah
South
Area

Monticello

Cedar City
10 stakes

St. George
24 stakes

Hurricane
3 stakes

Kanab
2 stakes

North America
Southwest Area

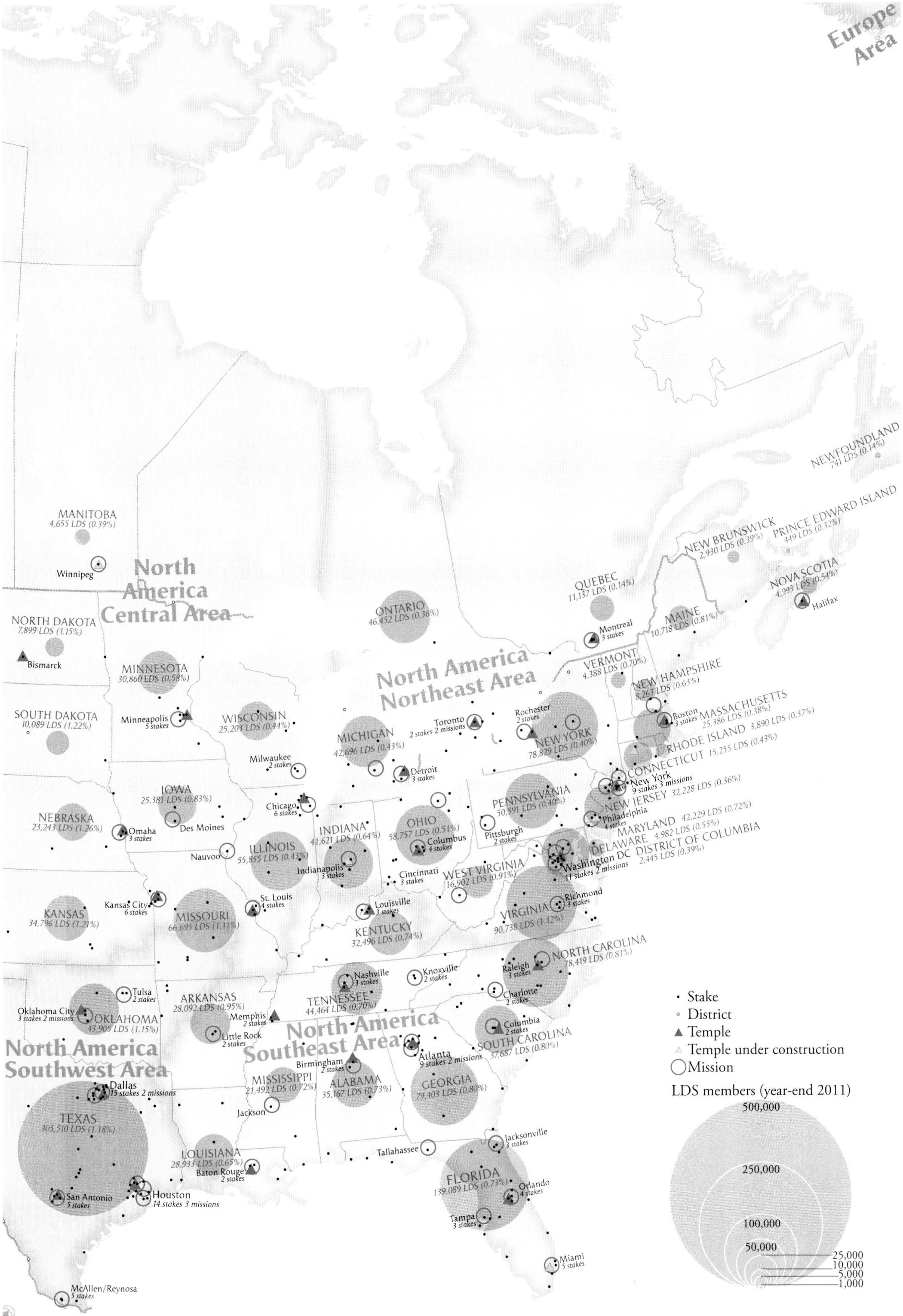
Europe Area
North America Central Area
North America Northeast Area
North America Southeast Area
North America Southwest Area
MANITOBA
4,655 LDS (0.39%)
Winnipeg
NORTH DAKOTA
7,899 LDS (1.15%)
Bismarck
SOUTH DAKOTA
10,089 LDS (1.22%)
MINNESOTA
30,860 LDS (0.58%)
Minneapolis
5 stakes
WISCONSIN
25,203 LDS (0.44%)
Milwaukee
2 stakes
IOWA
25,381 LDS (0.83%)
Des Moines
NEBRASKA
23,243 LDS (1.26%)
Omaha
3 stakes
Nauvoo
Chicago
6 stakes
ILLINOIS
55,855 LDS (0.43%)
KANSAS
34,796 LDS (1.21%)
Kansas City
6 stakes
MISSOURI
66,695 LDS (1.11%)
St. Louis
4 stakes
ONTARIO
46,452 LDS (0.36%)
MICHIGAN
42,696 LDS (0.43%)
Toronto
2 stakes 2 missions
Detroit
3 stakes
INDIANA
41,621 LDS (0.64%)
Indianapolis
3 stakes
OHIO
58,757 LDS (0.51%)
Columbus
4 stakes
Cincinnati
3 stakes
Louisville
3 stakes
KENTUCKY
32,496 LDS (0.74%)
WEST VIRGINIA
16,902 LDS (0.91%)
Pittsburgh
2 stakes
PENNSYLVANIA
50,591 LDS (0.40%)
QUEBEC
11,137 LDS (0.14%)
Montreal
3 stakes
Rochester
2 stakes
NEW YORK
78,829 LDS (0.40%)
VERMONT
4,388 LDS (0.70%)
NEW HAMPSHIRE
8,263 LDS (0.63%)
MAINE
10,718 LDS (0.81%)
Boston
3 stakes
MASSACHUSETTS
25,386 LDS (0.38%)
RHODE ISLAND 3,890 LDS (0.37%)
CONNECTICUT 15,255 LDS (0.43%)
New York
9 stakes 3 missions
NEW JERSEY 32,228 LDS (0.36%)
Philadelphia
4 stakes
MARYLAND 42,229 LDS (0.72%)
DELAWARE 4,982 LDS (0.55%)
Washington DC
11 stakes 2 missions
DISTRICT OF COLUMBIA
2,445 LDS (0.39%)
NEW BRUNSWICK
2,930 LDS (0.39%)
PRINCE EDWARD ISLAND
449 LDS (0.32%)
NOVA SCOTIA
4,993 LDS (0.54%)
Halifax
NEWFOUNDLAND
741 LDS (0.14%)
VIRGINIA
90,738 LDS (1.12%)
Richmond
3 stakes
NORTH CAROLINA
78,419 LDS (0.81%)
Raleigh
3 stakes
Charlotte
2 stakes
Knoxville
2 stakes
Nashville
3 stakes
TENNESSEE
44,464 LDS (0.70%)
Memphis
2 stakes
ARKANSAS
28,092 LDS (0.95%)
Little Rock
2 stakes
Tulsa
2 stakes
Oklahoma City
3 stakes 2 missions
OKLAHOMA
43,905 LDS (1.15%)
Columbia
2 stakes
SOUTH CAROLINA
37,687 LDS (0.80%)
Atlanta
9 stakes 2 missions
GEORGIA
79,403 LDS (0.80%)
Birmingham
2 stakes
ALABAMA
35,167 LDS (0.73%)
MISSISSIPPI
21,492 LDS (0.72%)
Jackson
Dallas
15 stakes 2 missions
TEXAS
305,510 LDS (1.18%)
San Antonio
5 stakes
Houston
14 stakes 3 missions
LOUISIANA
28,933 LDS (0.65%)
Baton Rouge
2 stakes
Tallahassee
Jacksonville
3 stakes
FLORIDA
139,089 LDS (0.73%)
Orlando
4 stakes
Tampa
3 stakes
Miami
5 stakes
McAllen/Reynosa
5 stakes
• Stake
◦ District
▲ Temple
△ Temple under construction
◯ Mission
LDS members (year-end 2011)
500,000
250,000
100,000
50,000
25,000
10,000
5,000
1,000

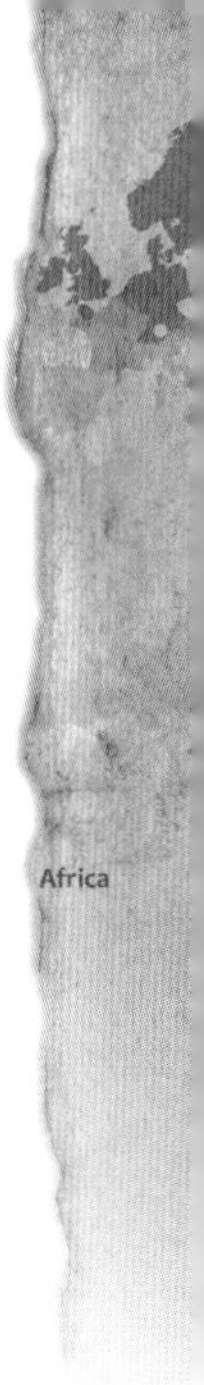
Africa

Western United States Cities in 2012

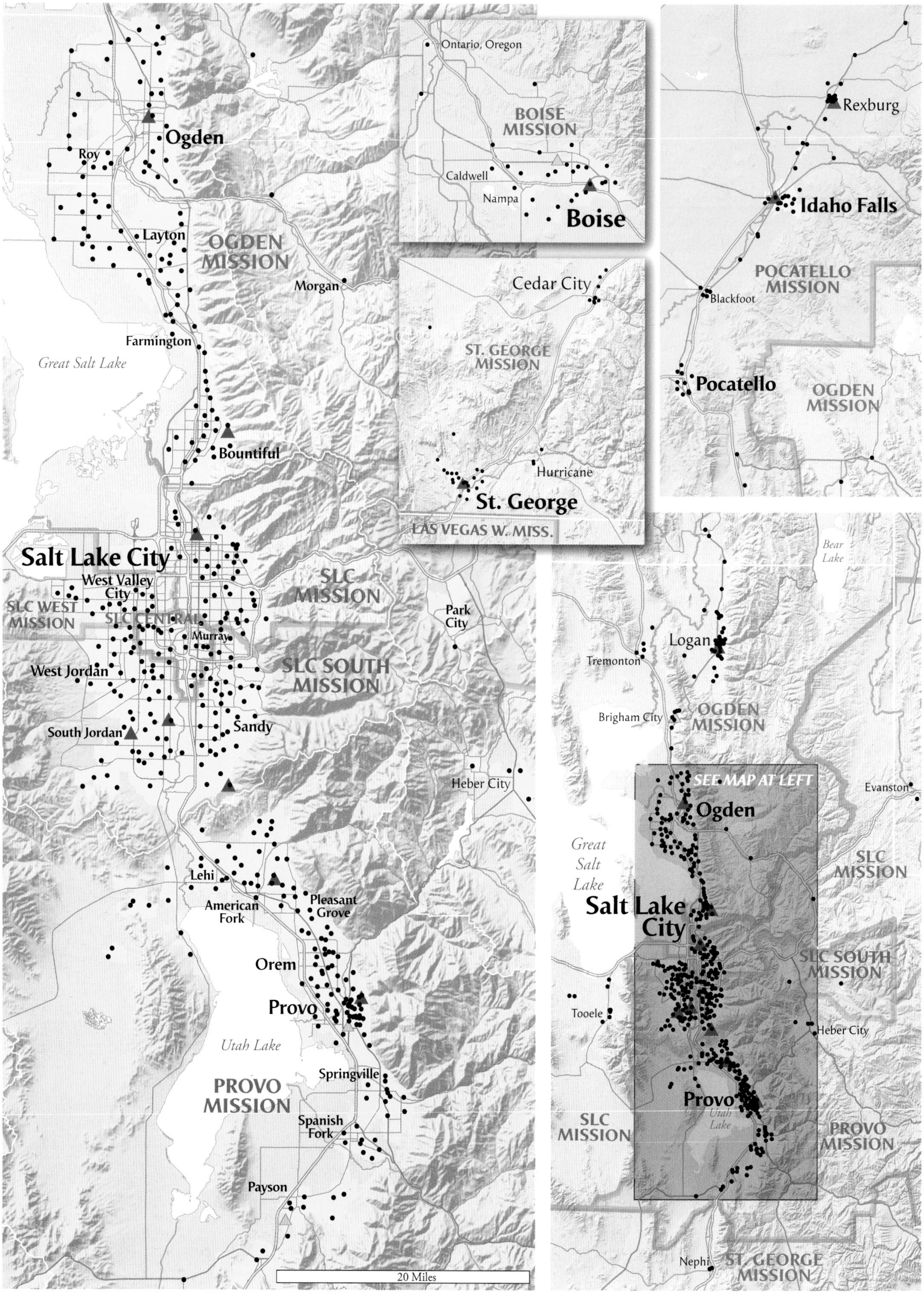

Ogden
Roy
Layton
OGDEN MISSION
Morgan
Farmington
Great Salt Lake
Bountiful
Salt Lake City
West Valley City
SLC WEST MISSION
SLC CENTRAL
Murray
SLC MISSION
Park City
SLC SOUTH MISSION
West Jordan
South Jordan
Sandy
Heber City
Lehi
American Fork
Pleasant Grove
Orem
Provo
Utah Lake
PROVO MISSION
Springville
Spanish Fork
Payson
20 Miles
Ontario, Oregon
BOISE MISSION
Caldwell
Nampa
Boise
Cedar City
ST. GEORGE MISSION
Hurricane
St. George
LAS VEGAS W. MISS.
Rexburg
Idaho Falls
POCATELLO MISSION
Blackfoot
Pocatello
OGDEN MISSION
Bear Lake
Logan
Tremonton
Brigham City
OGDEN MISSION
SEE MAP AT LEFT
Evanston
Ogden
Great Salt Lake
SLC MISSION
Salt Lake City
SLC SOUTH MISSION
Tooele
Heber City
Provo
Utah Lake
SLC MISSION
PROVO MISSION
Nephi
ST. GEORGE MISSION

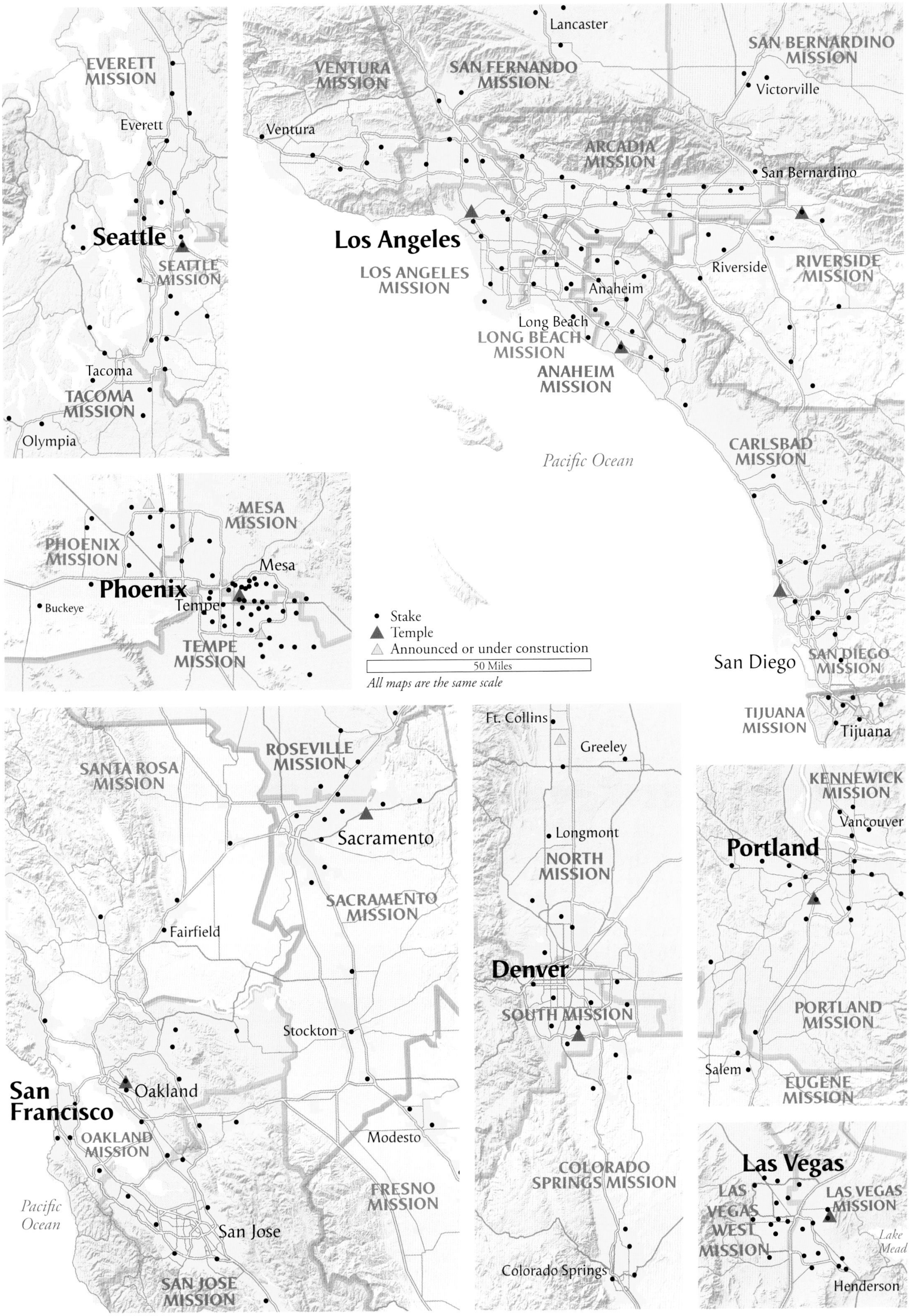

Seattle
EVERETT MISSION
Everett
SEATTLE MISSION
Tacoma
TACOMA MISSION
Olympia
Los Angeles
Lancaster
VENTURA MISSION
SAN FERNANDO MISSION
SAN BERNARDINO MISSION
Victorville
Ventura
ARCADIA MISSION
San Bernardino
LOS ANGELES MISSION
Riverside
RIVERSIDE MISSION
Anaheim
Long Beach
LONG BEACH MISSION
ANAHEIM MISSION
Pacific Ocean
CARLSBAD MISSION
San Diego
SAN DIEGO MISSION
TIJUANA MISSION
Tijuana
Phoenix
MESA MISSION
PHOENIX MISSION
Mesa
Tempe
Buckeye
TEMPE MISSION
Stake
Temple
Announced or under construction
50 Miles
All maps are the same scale
San Francisco
SANTA ROSA MISSION
ROSEVILLE MISSION
Sacramento
SACRAMENTO MISSION
Fairfield
Stockton
Oakland
OAKLAND MISSION
Modesto
Pacific Ocean
FRESNO MISSION
San Jose
SAN JOSE MISSION
Denver
Ft. Collins
Greeley
Longmont
NORTH MISSION
SOUTH MISSION
COLORADO SPRINGS MISSION
Colorado Springs
Portland
KENNEWICK MISSION
Vancouver
PORTLAND MISSION
Salem
EUGENE MISSION
Las Vegas
LAS VEGAS WEST MISSION
LAS VEGAS MISSION
Lake Mead
Henderson

Middle America

1875–present

MIDDLE AMERICA, the area between the United States and South America, consists of three distinct regions that each have a unique history of the presence of the LDS Church: Mexico, Central America, and the Caribbean Islands. Historically, each was populated by a large variety of native American groups. European colonization by the Spanish began in the sixteenth century, and other European colonists brought African slaves to the Caribbean during the seventeenth. These three groups have mixed together in different parts of the area, creating several distinct ethnic regions that have influenced the success of LDS missionaries and the spread of the Church. LDS interest in Mexico and Central America has been strong due to the belief that the indigenous Americans are the descendants of the peoples of the Book of Mormon (see p. 190).

Although Joseph Smith called a missionary to Jamaica in the 1840s (who apparently did not go there), the Church did not make inroads into this region until the late nineteenth century. The first exploratory missionaries in 1875–76 recognized the great potential of Mexico for both colonization and proselytizing. Starting in 1885, Mormon families created several successful colonies in northern Mexico; meanwhile, missionaries were having some success in the villages around Mexico City. During the early twentieth century, Church organizations and missionary work in Mexico struggled due to political conflict, war, and internal discord in the branches. Despite these trials, members emerged with greater spiritual strength, and the first Latin American stake was organized in Mexico City in 1961.

The success of the Church in Mexico expanded into the small countries of Central America (and Puerto Rico) during the mid-twentieth century, starting with American members working there for the U.S. government. Significant growth occurred during the 1960s and 1970s, leading to the first Central American stake in Guatemala City in 1967. Unfortunately, war and political disruptions, particularly in Guatemala, Nicaragua, and El Salvador, negatively affected the Church, with members of the Church on both sides of the conflicts. Most extreme was the anti-American communist regime of Daniel Ortega in Nicaragua, in which the LDS Church was singled out and persecuted by the government, including confiscating several LDS chapels.

The residents of most Caribbean islands (other than Puerto Rico) are predominantly of African descent. The Church's policy on race resulted in limited activities in the region until the priesthood restriction was lifted in 1978.

continued on page 220

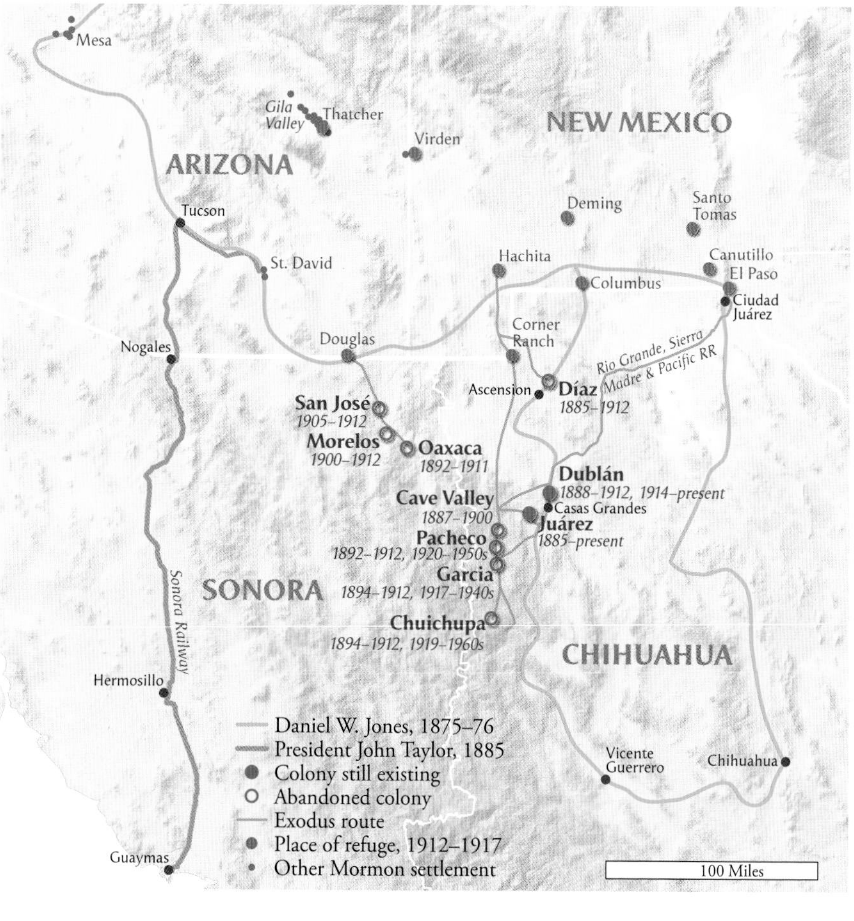

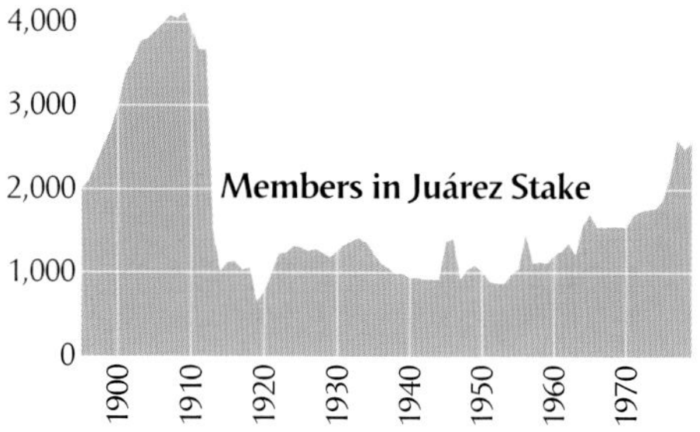

The Mexican Colonies

Daniel W. Jones, called by Church leaders to explore southern sites for Mormon settlement, founded Lehi (now Mesa), Arizona, then continued into northern Mexico. His party reported good prospects for both settlement and preaching to the Mexican Indians, but further action was not taken for a decade. Soon after Church President John Taylor visited Guaymas to discuss settlement plans with government officials, the first settlers arrived. Eventually, at least ten settlements were founded in the steppes and mountain valleys of the states of Chihuahua and Sonora, an environment very similar to Utah. The Juárez Stake was organized in 1895 with a ward in each colony. During the Mexican Civil War, Mormons were harassed by both government forces and revolutionaries. Forced to leave, they temporarily settled north of the border.

After the war, some stayed in New Mexico and El Paso, Texas, some moved to other Mormon settlements in Arizona and New Mexico, and some returned to Mexico. Colonia Juárez and Colonia Dublán soon returned to their previous size, but the resettled villages to the south did not last long. The number of American descendants who live in the colonies has slowly dwindled, but the stake grew when nearby Spanish-speaking congregations were eventually integrated. That said, several families from the colonies have achieved prominence in the Church and the world, with names like Pratt, Eyring, and Romney (see pp. 144, 176).

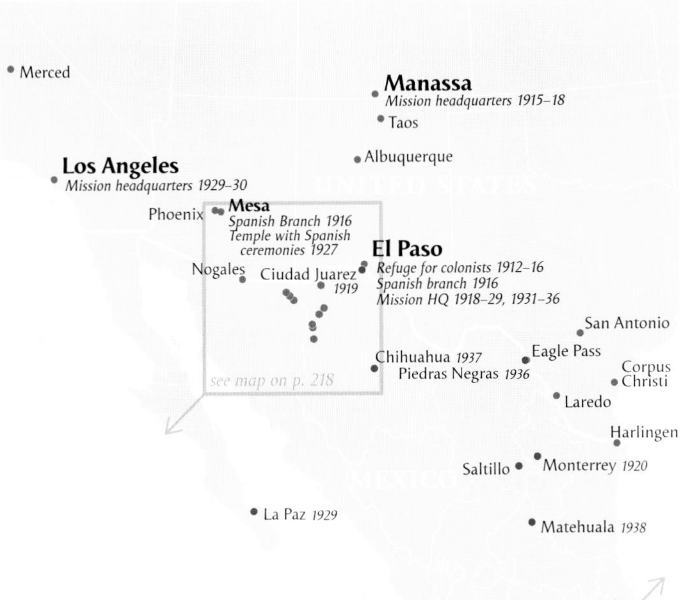

The Early Mexican Mission
- Mexico branches (1879–1936)
- U.S. branches (1915–1936)
- Mormon colonies (1885–1912)

Early branches in central Mexico
- Created during first mission (1879–1885)
- Created by 1938
- Significant influence of Third Convention (1936–1946)

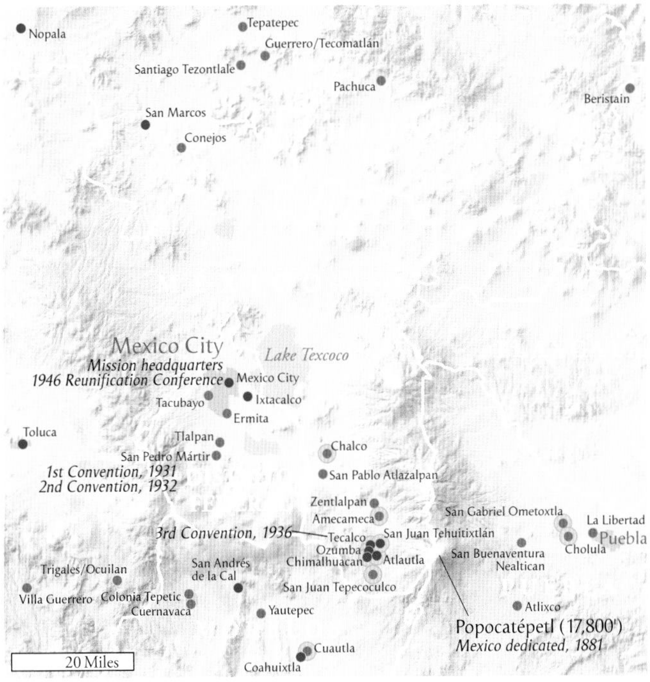

The Church in Mexico

Armed with the new Spanish translation of the Book of Mormon, the first major missionary effort was in central Mexico in 1879. Rejection in Mexico City led the missionaries to rural villages in nearby valleys, where they found many converts, until events in Utah forced the closure of the mission in 1888. Meanwhile, Mormon colonists established nine new settlements in Northern Mexico between 1885 and 1900. For decades, the "Colonias" were an important source of experienced Church leaders who were also Spanish-speaking Mexican citizens.

The mission reopened in 1901, with many of the missionaries and presidents coming from the northern colonies (thus avoiding government restrictions on foreign clergy). When civil war erupted in 1910, the mission was closed once again. The Mexican Mission-in-exile started preaching to Spanish speakers in the United States, raising branches in several southwestern cities. Mexico was briefly opened again from 1922 to 1926; the sporadic mission presence forced local members to become self-reliant. Even though the Mexican part of the mission was reopened, the efforts continued to focus on the United States, and the local members petitioned the First Presidency for a Mexican mission president who would give continuity to the work while complying with laws restricting foreign clergy.

The lack of understanding between the Mexican Saints and the leaders of the Church and the mission led about 800 of the 2,400 members in central Mexico to create a parallel group called the Third Convention in 1936. Although they claimed loyalty to the Church and its Prophet, the "convencionistas" functioned as a separate church, with their own branches, buildings, publications, and missionaries. In 1946, mission president Arwell L. Pierce and President George Albert Smith were able to reconcile with the disaffected Saints with promises of amnesty rather than retribution; almost all soon returned to full fellowship and worked together toward stakehood (achieved in 1961).

This episode was a major turning point in how the Church dealt with its increasingly diverse international membership. After this, mission branches and districts were increasingly thought of as wards and stakes in embryo, in which local strength and leadership was nurtured and developed, diminishing the reliance on leaders from Utah and the pressure to emigrate.

The 1946 Reunification Conference

Abel Páez, a local leader of the Third Convention, speaks at the conference at which Church President George Albert Smith (seated behind and to the left of Páez) personally presided. Mission president Arwell L. Pierce (to the left of President Smith) had convinced him that the convencionistas were still loyal to the Prophet, and that only he could bring them back by coming to Mexico. After President Smith spoke of his love for all of the Saints and encouraged them to return, local member Agricol Lozano recorded the moment captured in this photograph:

> "I was deeply impressed because I saw and heard him, when Brother Abel Páez all of a sudden got up from his seat and went to the podium and declared to the congregation that George Albert Smith was truly a prophet of God. It was a very significant moment, our bodies trembled from the emotion, and the reconciliation took effect."

Middle America

continued

The Church was established in most of the islands within ten years of that date. Growth has been greatest in the Spanish-speaking islands of Puerto Rico and Dominican Republic, with growth also occurring in French-speaking Haiti. The spread of the Church in the other islands has been slow but methodical, in part due to small populations and opposition from other churches (see p. 198).

Today, the Church is stronger in Mexico and Central America than anywhere outside the United States and the Pacific. In fact, in areas of indigenous Mayan populations like western Guatemala, Mormon concentrations are similar to the West Coast of the United States. As of 2010, the region as a whole has 40 missions, 333 stakes, and 20 temples that have been constructed or announced.

Mark Grover and Fernando R. Gomez

Church Expansion in Middle America

From 1875 to 1947, the Church in Middle America was limited to northern and central Mexico. Rare exceptions beyond that included Paul Henning, a Mesoamerican archeologist who lived in Guatemala and served as a missionary in Mexico. After World War II, members of the Church were among many United States government workers sent to aid development efforts in Central America, creating English-speaking groups and occasionally baptizing local citizens. After sporadic missionaries from the Mexican Mission found success, the Central American Mission was organized in 1952 and Church growth escalated. Meanwhile, mission presidents in Florida were exploring the opportunities of preaching in the Caribbean islands, but outside of Puerto Rico, the islanders (including the residents of British Honduras, later Belize) were predominantly of African descent; priesthood restrictions limited their interest in the Church. After the 1978 revelation (Official Declaration 2), missionaries were sent from Florida throughout the West Indies; within eight years almost every island had an official Church presence. Missionaries were especially successful in the Dominican Republic, which has since become one of the dominant centers of Church strength in all of Latin America.

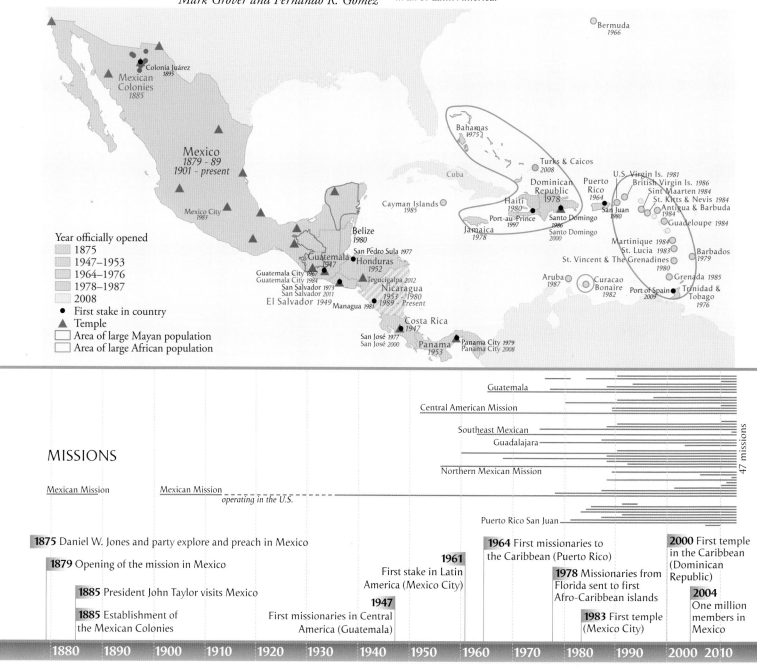

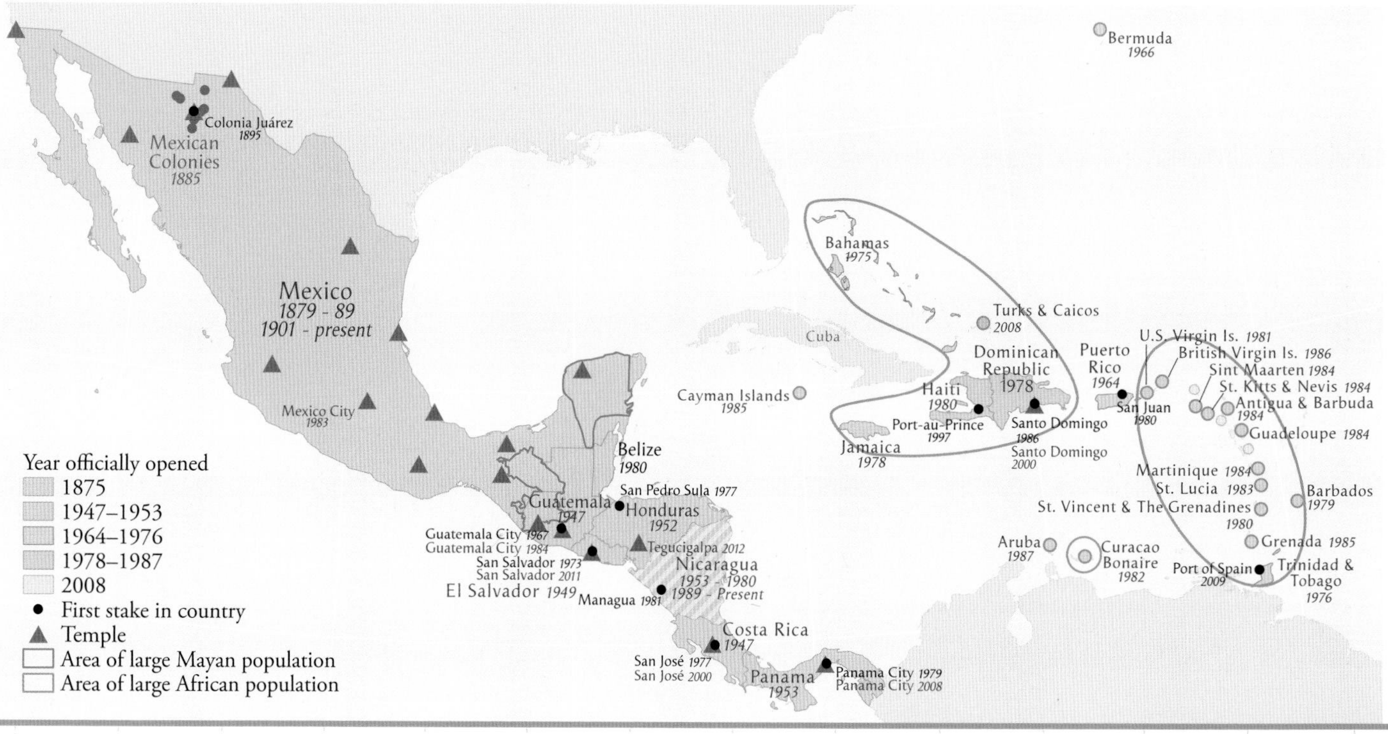

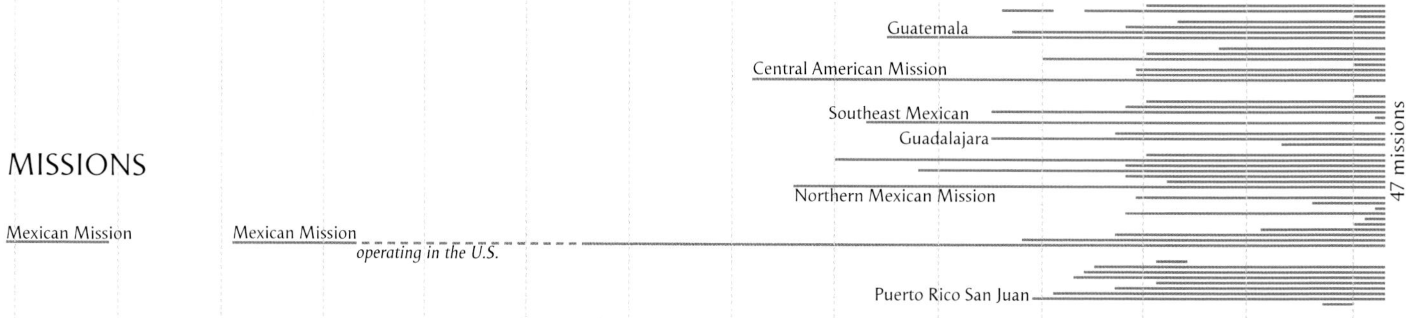

1875 Daniel W. Jones and party explore and preach in Mexico

1879 Opening of the mission in Mexico

1885 President John Taylor visits Mexico

1885 Establishment of the Mexican Colonies

1947 First missionaries in Central America (Guatemala)

1961 First stake in Latin America (Mexico City)

1964 First missionaries to the Caribbean (Puerto Rico)

1978 Missionaries from Florida sent to first Afro-Caribbean islands

1983 First temple (Mexico City)

2000 First temple in the Caribbean (Dominican Republic)

2004 One million members in Mexico

1880 1890 1900 1910 1920 1930 1940 1950 1960 1970 1980 1990 2000 2010

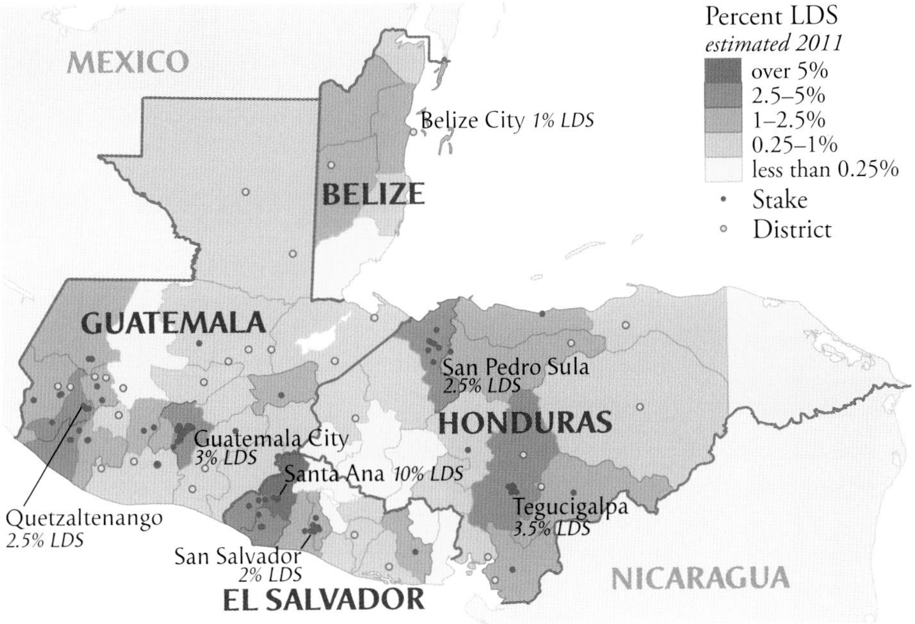

Northern Central America

The expansion of the Church in most of Latin America has centered in the urban areas, with selected exceptions. That is to be expected since missionary work tends to spread outward from areas of strength and almost all missionary work started in the capital cities. This map shows the concentration of members in the capital cities of northern Central America: Guatemala City, San Salvador, and Tegucigalpa and then in the second or third largest cities in the country. Exceptions to this pattern are in western Guatemala and western El Salvador, where missionaries, influenced by Book of Mormon beliefs related to the indigenous populations, have been successful in small indigenous villages, and the city of Quetzaltenango, which is only the sixth largest city in the country but has its own temple.

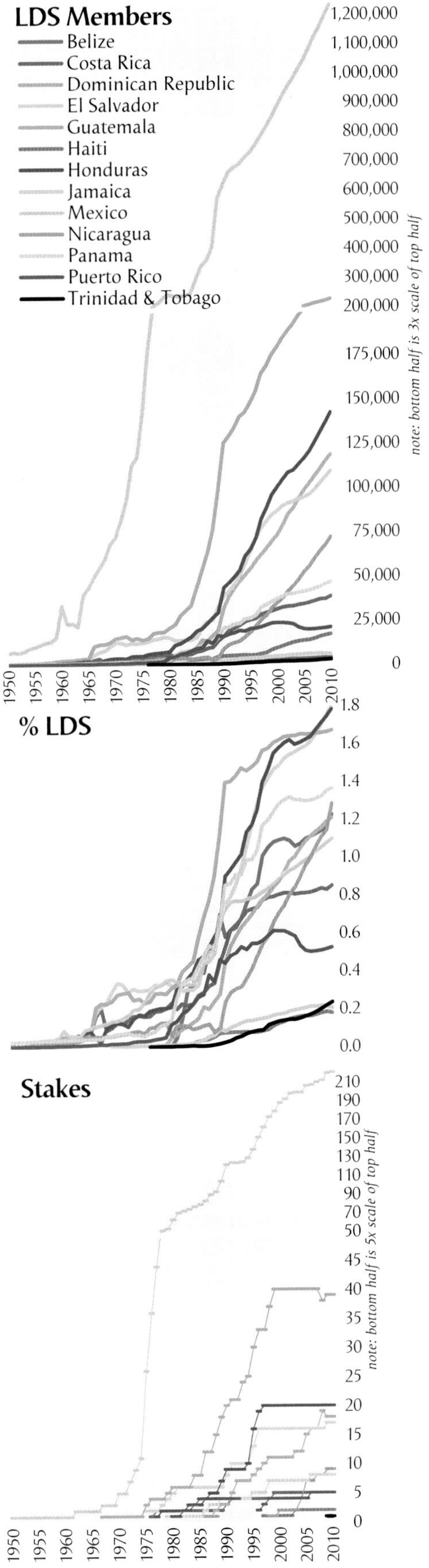

Recent Church Growth

The Church has been growing very rapidly in Mexico since the 1960s, but in most of Central America, dynamic growth did not begin until the 1980s. The Mormon presence in Nicaragua was very small during the anti-American regime in the 1980s but has grown rapidly since. The Church was not established in the Caribbean until after the revelation on priesthood and even since then has grown relatively slowly, due to the small island populations and the major presence of other churches, such as the Seventh-day Adventists (see p. 198); the Dominican Republic is a notable exception. The apparent surge in the late 1980s was due to the process of digitizing membership records, during which process hundreds of thousands of unreported baptisms were found from previous years.

South America

1925–present

THE FOURTEEN COUNTRIES OF SOUTH AMERICA consist of native Americans, Europeans, Africans brought to the continent as slaves, and various mixtures of the three groups, with groups of Asians in some cities. Early LDS interest in the continent was sparked by the desire to make contact with and convert the indigenous population, believed to be descendants of Book of Mormon peoples. Apostle Parley P. Pratt, his wife, and Rufus Allen went to Chile in 1851–52 as the first missionaries to South America. They returned after five months having had no success.

In 1925, the immigration of several German members to Argentina encouraged Church leadership to send three General Authorities to Buenos Aires: Apostle Melvin J. Ballard along with Rey L. Pratt and Rulon W. Wells of the First Council of the Seventy. They stayed six months and had seven baptisms. Reinhold Stoof, a German immigrant to Utah, served nine years as president of the South American Mission (1926–35). After two failed attempts to establish the Church among the native populations of northern Argentina, the missionaries concentrated on the immigrant population, primarily Germans, expanding to German communities in southern Brazil.

Growth was slow in all of South America until the 1960s, with only a small number of missionaries sent to South America, possibly due to a lingering semiofficial doctrine that the descendants of Israel were found primarily among northern Europeans rather than the southern European heritage of most immigrants to South America. However, the Church gradually expanded beyond Argentina and Brazil into neighboring countries and to the West Coast during the 1950s and 1960s. The Church was typically introduced into these new countries by American LDS expatriates working for multinational corporations.

During the 1960s, David O. McKay's desire for growth worldwide deemphasized the focus on northern Europe, and he assigned A. Theodore Tuttle of the First Council of the Seventy to move with his family to Montevideo, Uruguay, in 1961 to direct the Church regionally. His leadership resulted in an increase in missions, missionaries, and baptisms, and the organization of numerous additional congregations. Elder Tuttle encouraged the local members and the leaders in Salt Lake City to change their thinking, suggesting that South America was no longer just a distant outpost but an integral part of the Church that deserved to participate fully in all the programs of the Church. That change was demonstrated in the 1960s and 1970s, with the organization of stakes in major cities, then temples in the 1970s and 1980s.

Another major change came with the priesthood revelation in 1978, which eliminated a Church-imposed barrier to growth, especially in Brazil (45 percent of its population is of African descent) and the three Guianan countries. The organization of Area Presidencies in the mid-1980s decentralized Church administration, enabling the development of local leaders. Between 1980 and 2000, there

continued on page 224

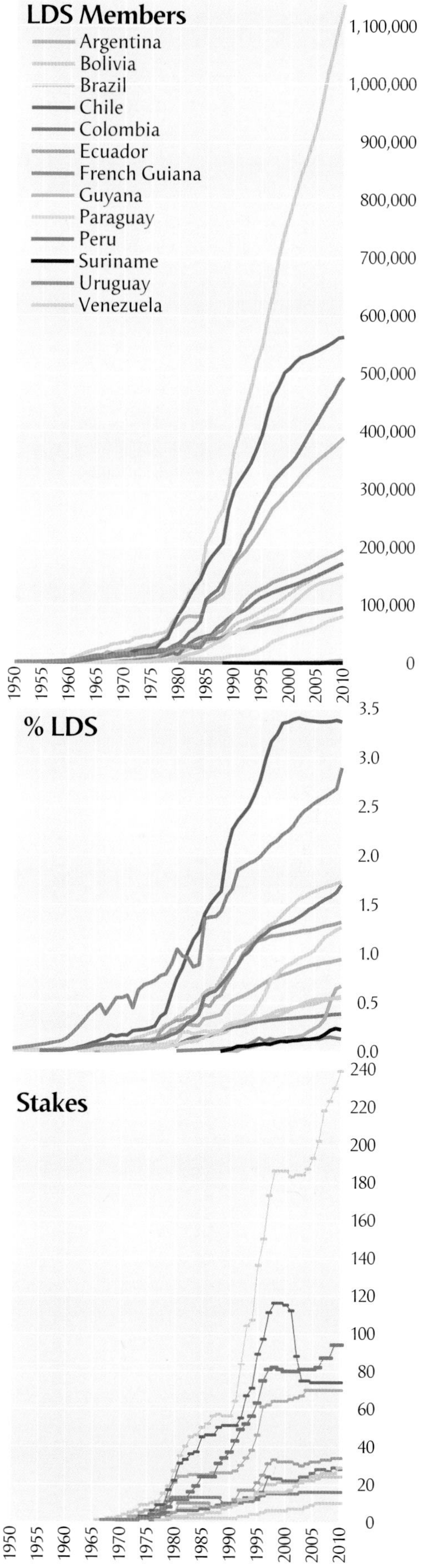

Church Membership in South America
Membership in South America grew slowly and steadily until the late 1970s, when it suddenly exploded (due to the priesthood revelation and other factors), beginning a 20-year period of phenomenal growth. As a result, Brazil and Chile have the highest number of members in the region, while Chile and Uruguay have the highest LDS percentage of the population.

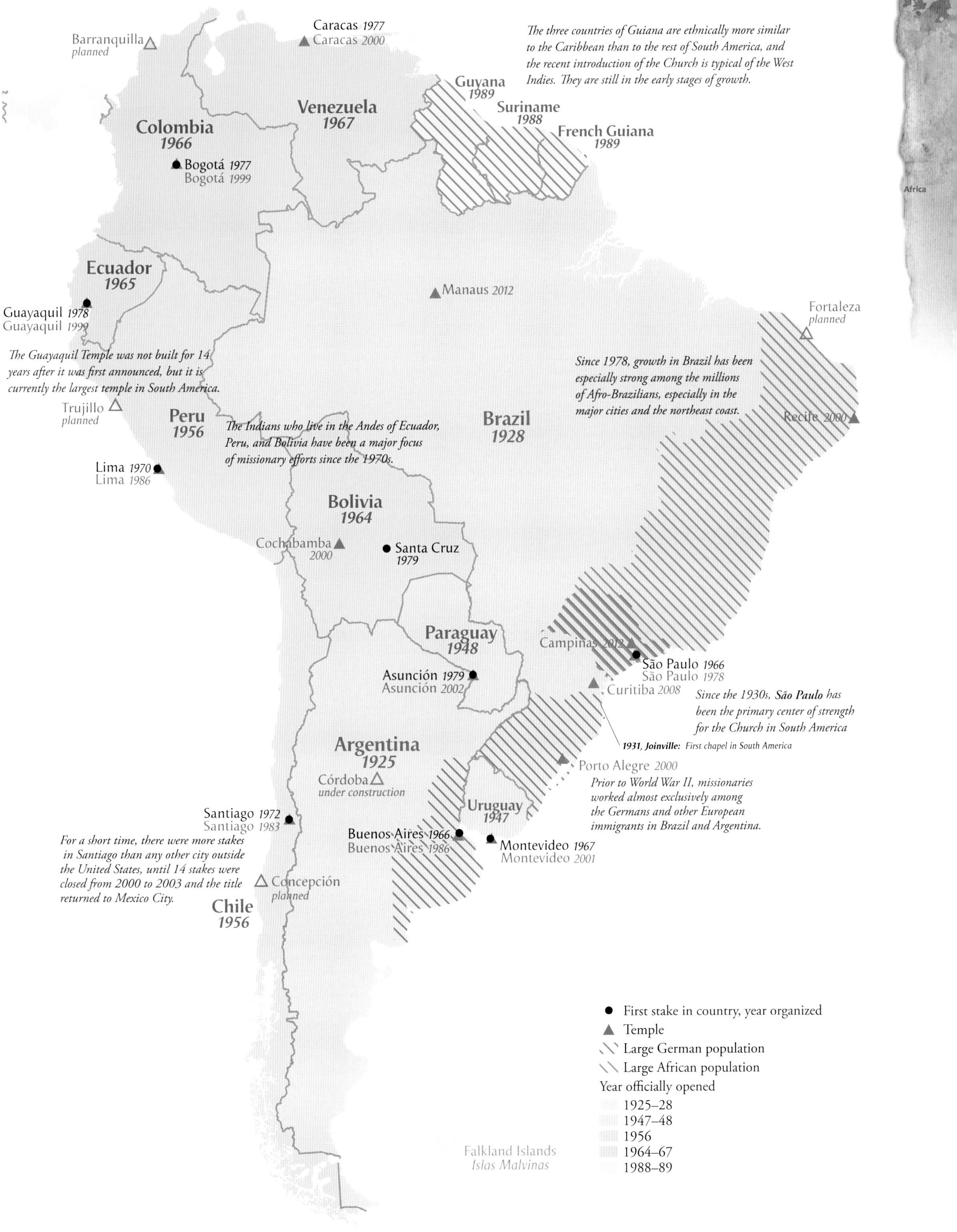
Barranquilla
planned
Caracas 1977
Caracas 2000
The three countries of Guiana are ethnically more similar to the Caribbean than to the rest of South America, and the recent introduction of the Church is typical of the West Indies. They are still in the early stages of growth.
Guyana
1989
Suriname
1988
French Guiana
1989
Venezuela
1967
Colombia
1966
Bogotá 1977
Bogotá 1999
Ecuador
1965
Manaus 2012
Guayaquil 1978
Guayaquil 1999
Fortaleza
planned
The Guayaquil Temple was not built for 14 years after it was first announced, but it is currently the largest temple in South America.
Since 1978, growth in Brazil has been especially strong among the millions of Afro-Brazilians, especially in the major cities and the northeast coast.
Trujillo
planned
Peru
1956
The Indians who live in the Andes of Ecuador, Peru, and Bolivia have been a major focus of missionary efforts since the 1970s.
Brazil
1928
Recife 2000
Lima 1970
Lima 1986
Bolivia
1964
Cochabamba
2000
Santa Cruz
1979
Paraguay
1948
Campinas 2012
São Paulo 1966
São Paulo 1978
Asunción 1979
Asunción 2002
Curitiba 2008
Since the 1930s, São Paulo has been the primary center of strength for the Church in South America
1931, Joinville: First chapel in South America
Argentina
1925
Córdoba
under construction
Porto Alegre 2000
Prior to World War II, missionaries worked almost exclusively among the Germans and other European immigrants in Brazil and Argentina.
Santiago 1972
Santiago 1983
Uruguay
1947
Buenos Aires 1966
Buenos Aires 1986
Montevideo 1967
Montevideo 2001
For a short time, there were more stakes in Santiago than any other city outside the United States, until 14 stakes were closed from 2000 to 2003 and the title returned to Mexico City.
Concepción
planned
Chile
1956
First stake in country, year organized
Temple
Large German population
Large African population
Year officially opened
1925–28
1947–48
1956
1964–67
1988–89
Falkland Islands
Islas Malvinas
Africa

South America

continued

occurred a growth in the number of baptisms almost unparalleled in the history of the Church. This growth was aided by general social, economic, and political changes in most South American countries that changed the political climate, decreased the influence of the Catholic Church, and allowed and encouraged cultural change (other churches also experienced phenomenal growth during this time). The membership of the Church residing in South America went from 0.8 percent of the entire Church in 1960 to 24 percent in 2010. Unfortunately, in the beginning of the twenty-first century leaders recognized that these masses of converts were not all staying active: in Chile and Brazil, only about 20–25 percent of baptized members list themselves as LDS in the national census.

By the beginning of 2012, the LDS Church was established in all the countries of South America, with a baptized membership of 3,549,839. There were 74 missions, 641 stakes, and 20 functioning or planned temples.

Mark Grover

Chile

The most significant expansion of the Church in Latin America occurred in the last twenty years of the twentieth century. That expansion is evident when we look at the growth of stakes in Chile. To keep up with the rapid growth in membership, a program was carried out during the 1990s to organize wards and stakes that were smaller than normal, in order to encourage more active participation by converts and to provide more leadership opportunities. This philosophy was successful in many cases but also led to problems with poorly prepared and overburdened leaders and poor convert retention (especially among the youth). In the beginning of the twenty-first century, the Church was forced to consolidate its strength by recombining or eliminating dozens of stakes and wards. In 2002, Apostle Jeffrey R. Holland was assigned to live in Chile for a year to reorganize the Church and institute a greater focus on convert retention.

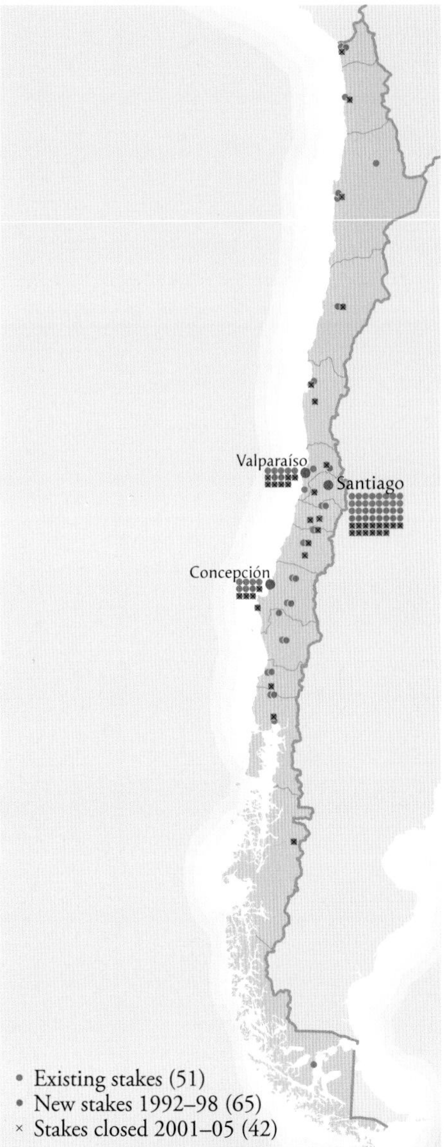

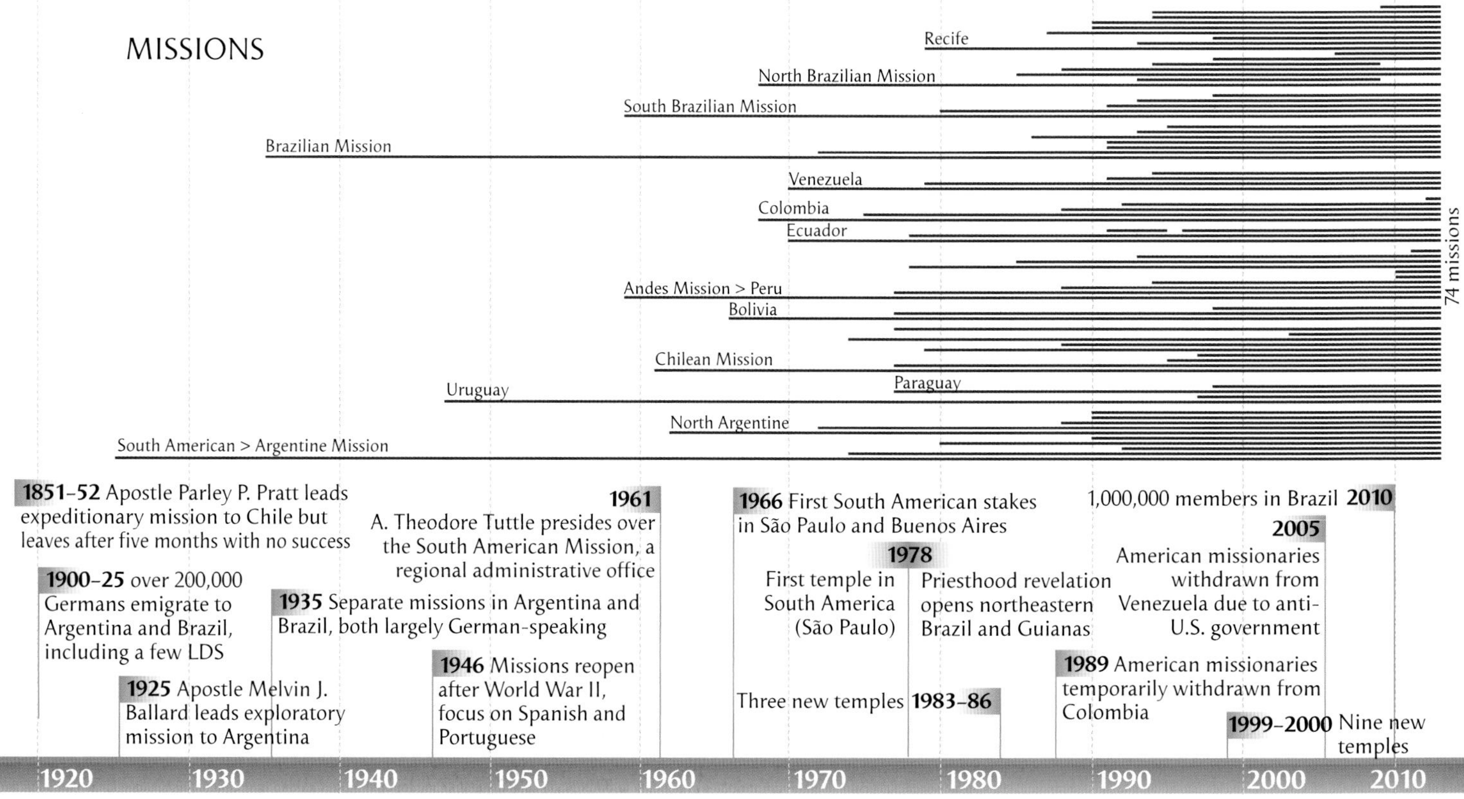

1851–52 Apostle Parley P. Pratt leads expeditionary mission to Chile but leaves after five months with no success

1900–25 over 200,000 Germans emigrate to Argentina and Brazil, including a few LDS

1925 Apostle Melvin J. Ballard leads exploratory mission to Argentina

1935 Separate missions in Argentina and Brazil, both largely German-speaking

1946 Missions reopen after World War II, focus on Spanish and Portuguese

1961 A. Theodore Tuttle presides over the South American Mission, a regional administrative office

1966 First South American stakes in São Paulo and Buenos Aires

1978 First temple in South America (São Paulo)

1978 Priesthood revelation opens northeastern Brazil and Guianas

Three new temples **1983–86**

1989 American missionaries temporarily withdrawn from Colombia

1999–2000 Nine new temples

2005 American missionaries withdrawn from Venezuela due to anti-U.S. government

1,000,000 members in Brazil **2010**

Expansion of the Church in Brazil

1950–1964

This period of limited though steady growth still focused on European immigrants, especially in São Paulo. The mission was split in 1959 when the Brazil South Mission was organized, encompassing the three southern states. Expansion into the north to the city of Recife occurred in 1961.

1995–2010

The fortifying of the Church throughout the entire country. Membership surpassed the one million mark.

1980–1994

Expansion occurred primarily in the north and central regions of the country, especially the northeastern coast where most Afro-Brazilians live.

1965–1979

A period of stabilization, particularly in São Paulo and Rio de Janeiro. The first stake was organized in 1966. The most important event of this period was the priesthood revelation in 1978, which opened all of Brazil for missionary work. The construction of the São Paulo Temple brought all the aspects of Mormonism to Brazil.

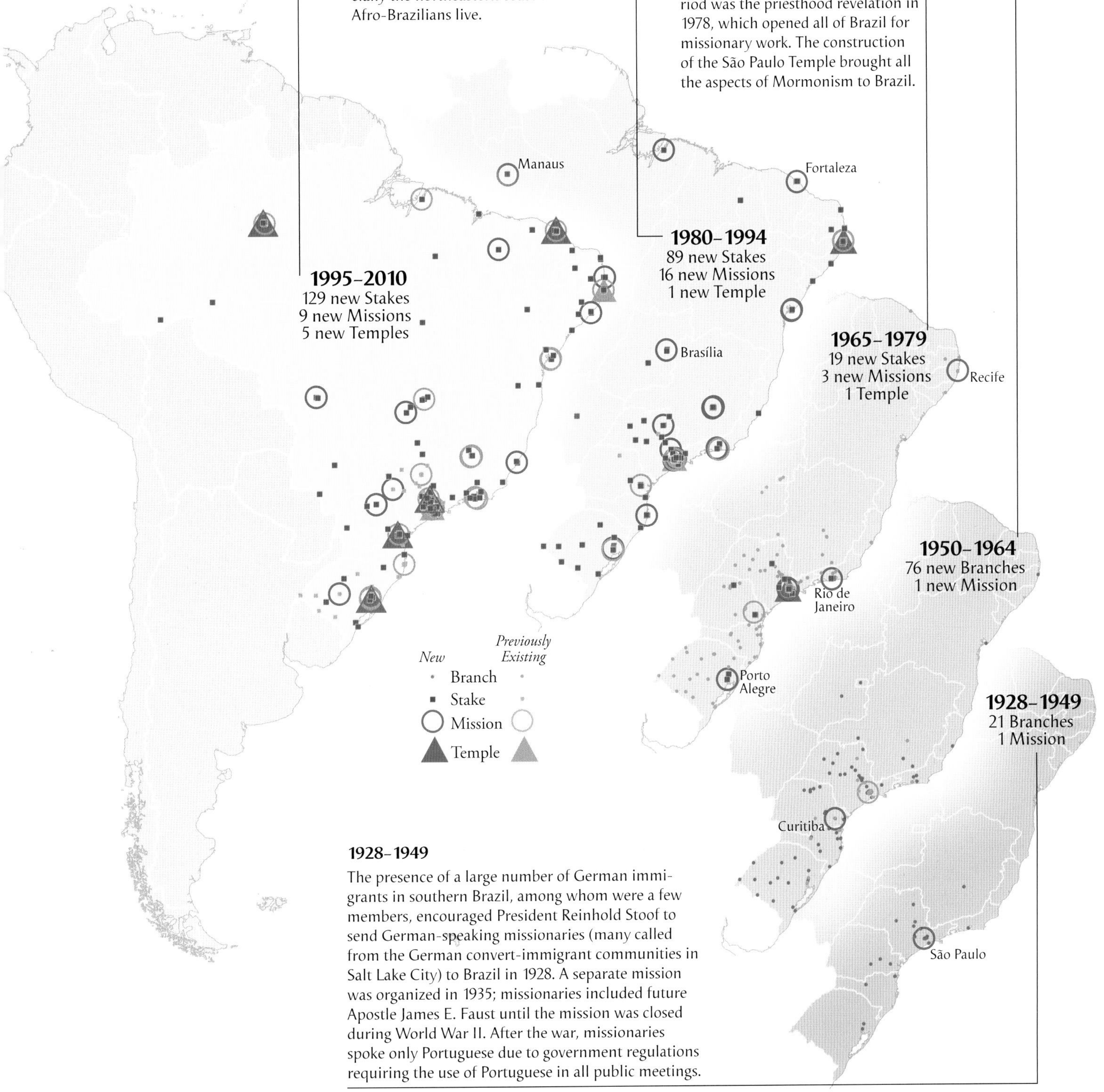

1928–1949

The presence of a large number of German immigrants in southern Brazil, among whom were a few members, encouraged President Reinhold Stoof to send German-speaking missionaries (many called from the German convert-immigrant communities in Salt Lake City) to Brazil in 1928. A separate mission was organized in 1935; missionaries included future Apostle James E. Faust until the mission was closed during World War II. After the war, missionaries spoke only Portuguese due to government regulations requiring the use of Portuguese in all public meetings.

Latin America in 2012

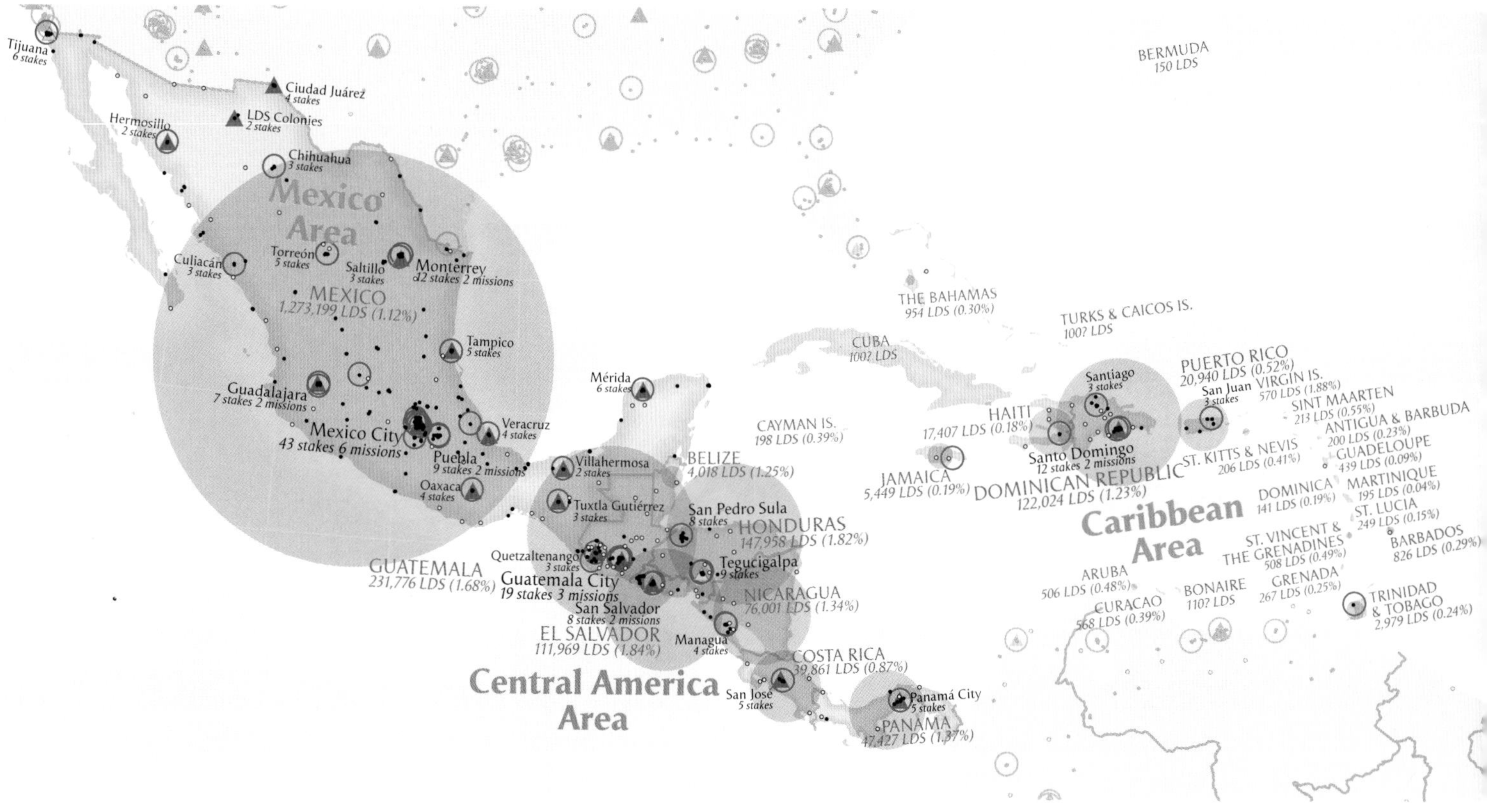

Tijuana
6 stakes
Ciudad Juárez
4 stakes
LDS Colonies
2 stakes
Hermosillo
2 stakes
Chihuahua
3 stakes
Mexico Area
Culiacán
3 stakes
Torreón
5 stakes
Saltillo
3 stakes
Monterrey
12 stakes 2 missions
MEXICO
1,273,199 LDS (1.12%)
Tampico
5 stakes
Guadalajara
7 stakes 2 missions
Mexico City
43 stakes 6 missions
Veracruz
4 stakes
Puebla
9 stakes 2 missions
Oaxaca
4 stakes
Mérida
6 stakes
Villahermosa
2 stakes
Tuxtla Gutiérrez
3 stakes
BELIZE
4,018 LDS (1.25%)
San Pedro Sula
8 stakes
HONDURAS
147,958 LDS (1.82%)
Quetzaltenango
3 stakes
GUATEMALA
231,776 LDS (1.68%)
Guatemala City
19 stakes 3 missions
Tegucigalpa
9 stakes
San Salvador
8 stakes 2 missions
EL SALVADOR
111,969 LDS (1.84%)
NICARAGUA
76,001 LDS (1.34%)
Managua
4 stakes
COSTA RICA
39,861 LDS (0.87%)
San José
5 stakes
Central America Area
Panamá City
5 stakes
PANAMA
47,427 LDS (1.37%)
BERMUDA
150 LDS
THE BAHAMAS
954 LDS (0.30%)
TURKS & CAICOS IS.
100? LDS
CUBA
100? LDS
CAYMAN IS.
198 LDS (0.39%)
JAMAICA
5,449 LDS (0.19%)
HAITI
17,407 LDS (0.18%)
Santiago
3 stakes
Santo Domingo
12 stakes 2 missions
DOMINICAN REPUBLIC
122,024 LDS (1.23%)
PUERTO RICO
20,940 LDS (0.52%)
San Juan
3 stakes
VIRGIN IS.
570 LDS (1.88%)
SINT MAARTEN
213 LDS (0.55%)
ANTIGUA & BARBUDA
200 LDS (0.23%)
ST. KITTS & NEVIS
206 LDS (0.41%)
GUADELOUPE
439 LDS (0.09%)
DOMINICA
141 LDS (0.19%)
MARTINIQUE
195 LDS (0.04%)
ST. LUCIA
249 LDS (0.15%)
Caribbean Area
ST. VINCENT & THE GRENADINES
508 LDS (0.49%)
BARBADOS
826 LDS (0.29%)
ARUBA
506 LDS (0.48%)
BONAIRE
110? LDS
GRENADA
267 LDS (0.25%)
CURAÇAO
568 LDS (0.39%)
TRINIDAD & TOBAGO
2,979 LDS (0.24%)

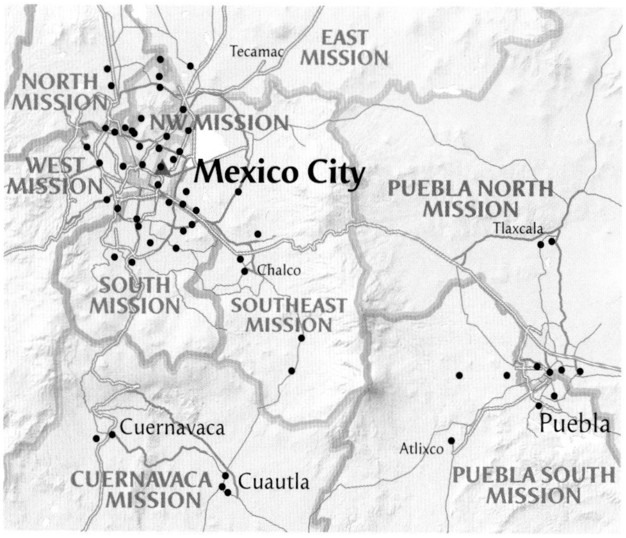

Tecamac
EAST MISSION
NORTH MISSION
NW MISSION
WEST MISSION
Mexico City
PUEBLA NORTH MISSION
Tlaxcala
Chalco
SOUTH MISSION
SOUTHEAST MISSION
Cuernavaca
Puebla
Atlixco
CUERNAVACA MISSION
Cuautla
PUEBLA SOUTH MISSION

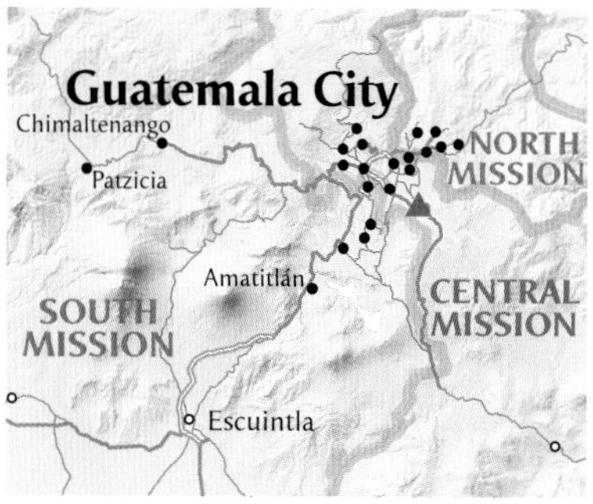

Guatemala City
Chimaltenango
NORTH MISSION
Patzicia
Amatitlán
SOUTH MISSION
CENTRAL MISSION
Escuintla

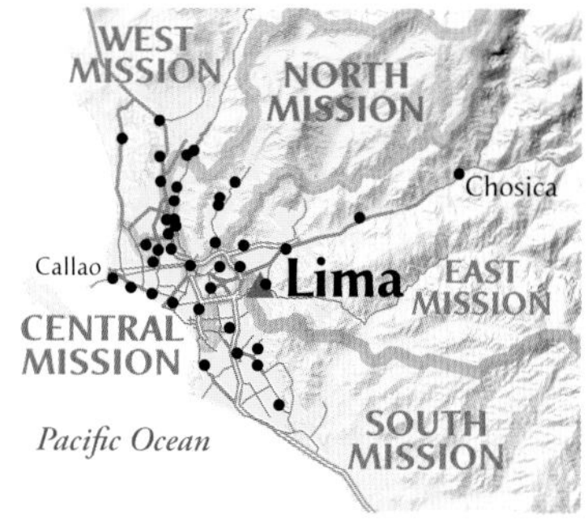

WEST MISSION
NORTH MISSION
Chosica
Callao
Lima
EAST MISSION
CENTRAL MISSION
Pacific Ocean
SOUTH MISSION

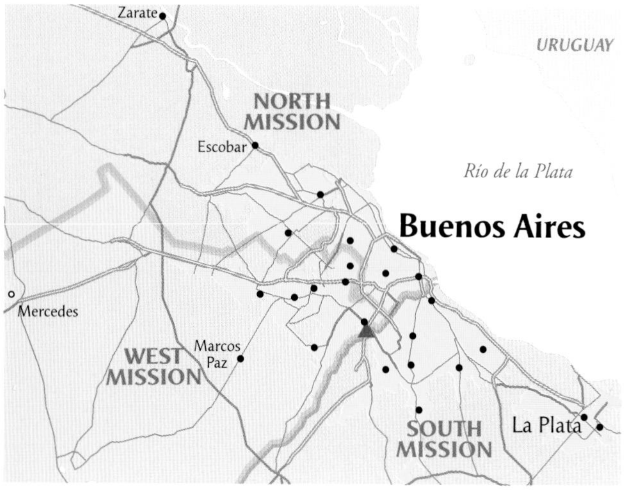

Zarate
URUGUAY
NORTH MISSION
Escobar
Río de la Plata
Buenos Aires
Mercedes
WEST MISSION
Marcos Paz
SOUTH MISSION
La Plata

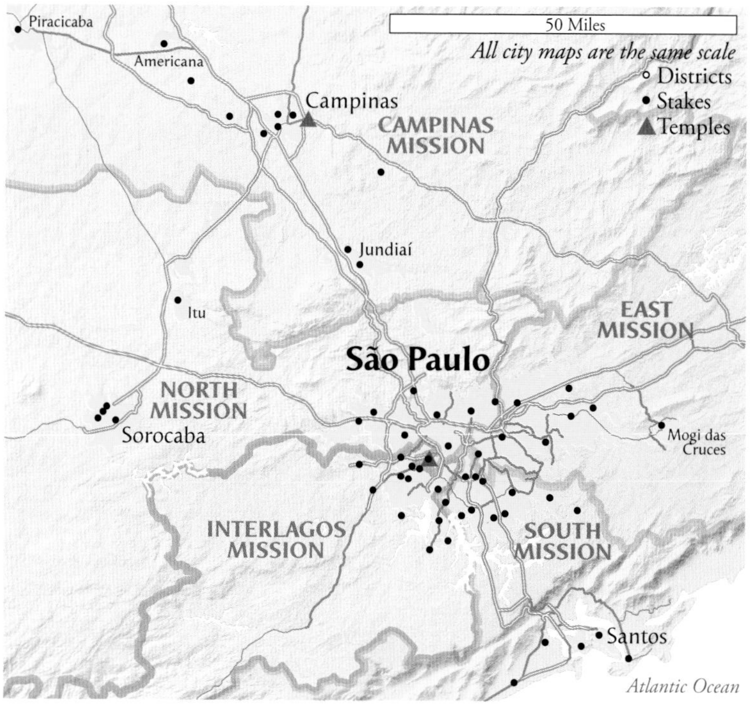

Piracicaba
50 Miles
All city maps are the same scale
Americana
Districts
Stakes
Temples
Campinas
CAMPINAS MISSION
Jundiaí
Itu
EAST MISSION
São Paulo
NORTH MISSION
Sorocaba
Mogi das Cruces
INTERLAGOS MISSION
SOUTH MISSION
Santos
Atlantic Ocean

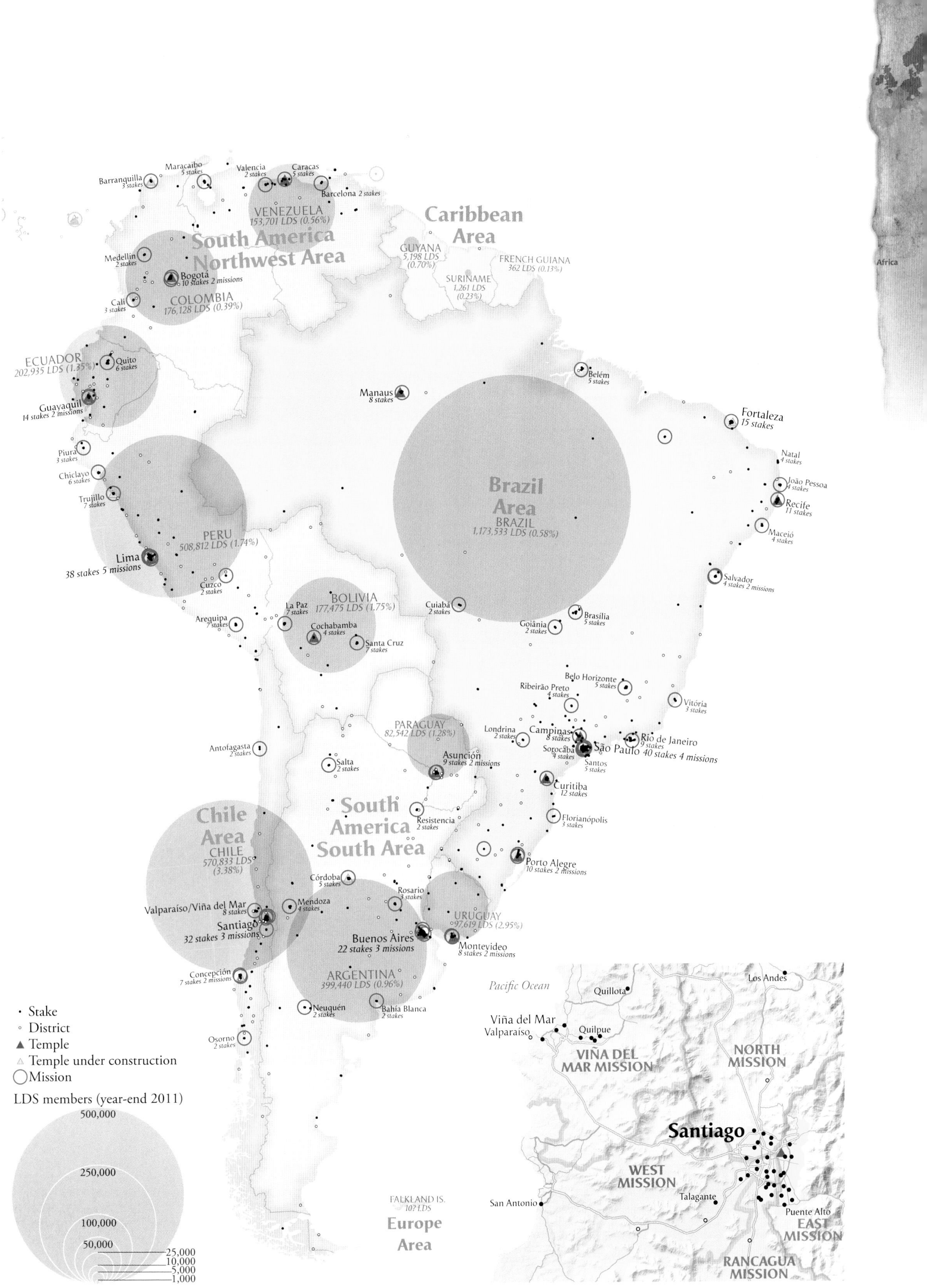

Maracaibo
5 stakes
Barranquilla
3 stakes
Valencia
2 stakes
Caracas
5 stakes
Barcelona 2 stakes
VENEZUELA
153,701 LDS (0.56%)
South America
Northwest Area
Caribbean
Area
GUYANA
5,198 LDS
(0.70%)
FRENCH GUIANA
362 LDS (0.13%)
SURINAME
1,261 LDS
(0.23%)
Medellín
2 stakes
Bogotá
10 stakes 2 missions
Cali
3 stakes
COLOMBIA
176,128 LDS (0.39%)
ECUADOR
202,935 LDS (1.35%)
Quito
6 stakes
Guayaquil
14 stakes 2 missions
Belém
5 stakes
Manaus
8 stakes
Fortaleza
15 stakes
Piura
3 stakes
Natal
4 stakes
Chiclayo
6 stakes
João Pessoa
4 stakes
Trujillo
7 stakes
Recife
11 stakes
Brazil
Area
BRAZIL
1,173,533 LDS (0.58%)
Maceió
4 stakes
PERU
508,812 LDS (1.74%)
Lima
38 stakes 5 missions
Cuzco
2 stakes
Salvador
4 stakes 2 missions
BOLIVIA
177,475 LDS (1.75%)
La Paz
7 stakes
Cuiabá
2 stakes
Brasília
5 stakes
Arequipa
7 stakes
Cochabamba
4 stakes
Santa Cruz
7 stakes
Goiânia
2 stakes
Belo Horizonte
5 stakes
Ribeirão Preto
4 stakes
Vitória
3 stakes
PARAGUAY
82,542 LDS (1.28%)
Londrina
2 stakes
Campinas
8 stakes
Rio de Janeiro
9 stakes
Sorocaba
4 stakes
São Paulo 40 stakes 4 missions
Santos
5 stakes
Antofagasta
2 stakes
Asunción
9 stakes 2 missions
Salta
2 stakes
Curitiba
12 stakes
South
America
South Area
Resistencia
2 stakes
Florianópolis
3 stakes
Chile
Area
CHILE
570,833 LDS
(3.38%)
Porto Alegre
10 stakes 2 missions
Córdoba
5 stakes
Rosario
3 stakes
Mendoza
4 stakes
Valparaíso/Viña del Mar
8 stakes
Santiago
32 stakes 3 missions
URUGUAY
97,619 LDS (2.95%)
Buenos Aires
22 stakes 3 missions
Montevideo
8 stakes 2 missions
Concepción
7 stakes 2 missions
ARGENTINA
399,440 LDS (0.96%)
Neuquén
2 stakes
Bahía Blanca
2 stakes
Osorno
2 stakes
• Stake
◦ District
▲ Temple
△ Temple under construction
◯ Mission
LDS members (year-end 2011)
500,000
250,000
100,000
50,000
25,000
10,000
5,000
1,000
FALKLAND IS.
107 LDS
Europe
Area
Africa
Pacific Ocean
Los Andes
Quillota
Viña del Mar
Valparaíso
Quilpue
VIÑA DEL
MAR MISSION
NORTH
MISSION
Santiago
WEST
MISSION
Talagante
San Antonio
Puente Alto
EAST
MISSION
RANCAGUA
MISSION

Europe

1837–present

PAINSTAKINGLY, INCREMENTALLY, over more than a century and a half, The Church of Jesus Christ of Latter-day Saints has penetrated the European continent in its effort to spread the news of the Restoration. Apostles directed the first wave of nineteenth century missionaries, mounting efforts in western Europe and Scandinavia (see pp. 46, 94). Some countries (generally Protestant) saw thousands of converts, most of whom emigrated to America, while other countries (generally Catholic) saw only a small, short-lived presence. Later in the century and at the dawn of the next, a few intrepid expeditionary missionaries preached in Finland, Czech Bohemia, Hungary, Serbia, Romania, Bulgaria, and Russia with limited success.

The incursion of this new religion from America incurred the opposition of religious authorities. Their sponsoring governments routinely harassed and evicted missionaries. This opposition stunted growth where the Church was established and blighted it elsewhere. The departure of many members to America also weakened the growth of the Church in Europe.

During the twentieth century two world wars and the growth of secular societies diminished the control of the civil and ecclesiastical authorities over the religious lives of western Europeans. France, Germany, the Netherlands, and Austria all granted the Church legal recognition in the 1950s, though congregations had existed there as much as a century earlier. Also, the Church increasingly discouraged emigration to Utah and encouraged European members to stay and build local congregations. To emphasize this, the Church built high-profile chapels, mission homes, and temples (see p. 160). By the early 1960s, stakes were being created in several countries. The early 1960s also saw an explosion in growth (with membership doubling between 1959 and 1962) due to an increase in the number of missionaries when the sending of 19-year-olds became standard practice, in better training and teaching materials, and, unfortunately, in some dubious practices (such as baptizing youth interested in playing American sports).

Between the world wars, missionaries saw some success in eastern Europe, but much of this area fell behind the Iron Curtain during the Cold War, and communication with members in East Germany, Czechoslovakia, and Hungary was tenuous at best. Later in the twentieth century,

continued on page 230

Europe in the Nineteenth Century

In the nineteenth century, missionaries were often sent to the lands of their heritage because they had learned the native tongue in the homes of immigrant parents and were already accustomed to the culture. Starting in Great Britain, missionaries found sustained success in Scandinavia, Switzerland, Germany, and the Netherlands, while lack of success in France, Italy, Iceland, Austria, and Belgium temporarily ended the work there. Thus the early pattern was a church foundation in the Protestant countries of the United Kingdom, northern Europe, and Switzerland, a lone beacon in the center of the continent. The latter (which officially granted the Church legal recognition in 1864) provided a safe haven from which missionaries proceeded to reestablish the work in Germany, France, Belgium, the Netherlands, Austria, and Italy.

Europe in the Twentieth Century

After World War I, new missionary efforts were mounted in Greece, France, Hungary, and Czechoslovakia, although members in the latter two countries (and East Germany) were left behind the Iron Curtain after World War II. The work then spread throughout postwar western Europe, where members stayed and built local stakes rather than moving to Utah. As Soviet control faded, missionaries reentered Hungary, Poland, Croatia, and Serbia. After the breaching of the Berlin Wall, Church emissaries, in quick succession, crossed the borders of Estonia, Russia, Czechoslovakia (for the third time), Romania and Bulgaria (for the second time), Ukraine, Slovenia, Albania, Lithuania, Belarus, and Moldova. The last European countries to open to the Church are the war-torn lands of the former Yugoslavia, which are in the early stages of opening in 2012.

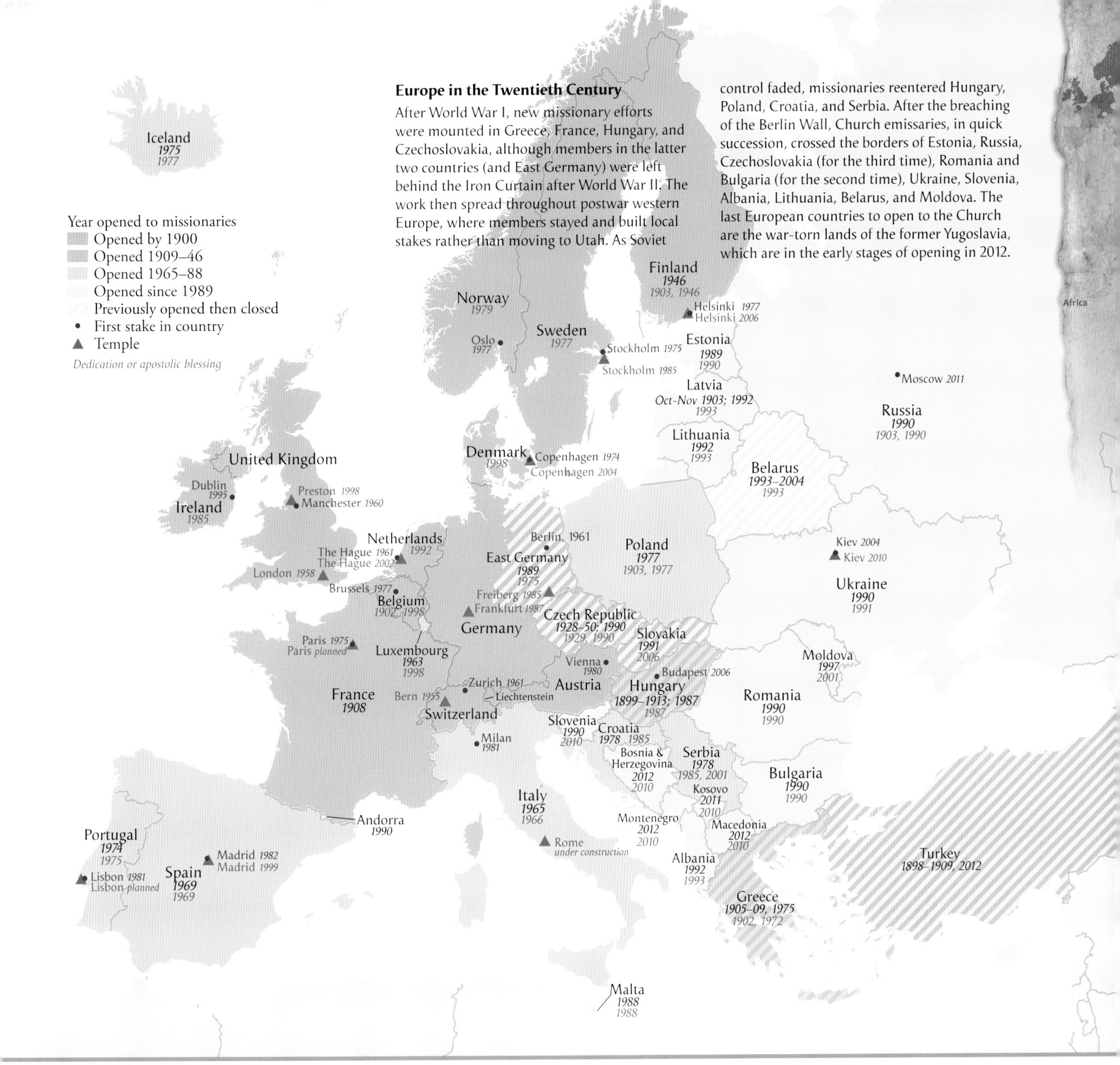

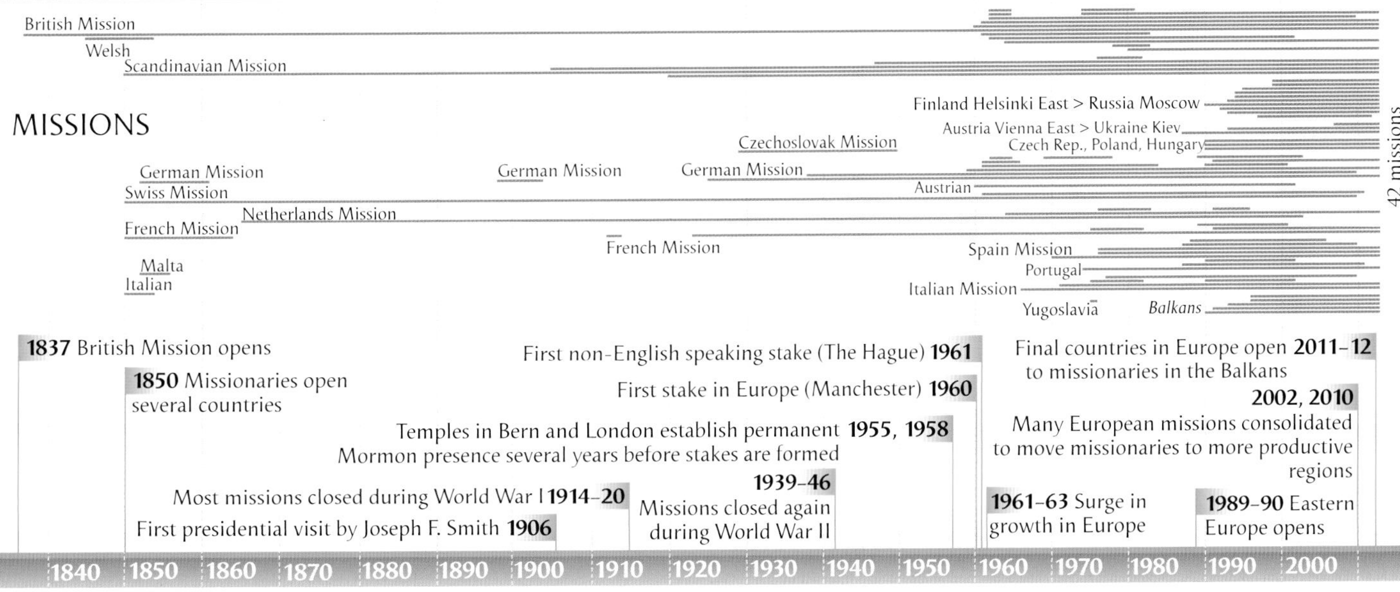

Europe

continued

the scope of the Church's proselytizing effort moved south into the Catholic countries of Italy, Spain, and Portugal, which saw rapid growth during the 1980s and 1990s. With the demise of Soviet power, the Church then spread eastward into the former communist realm. Starting in 1989, eastern Europe was reopened, and missionaries found some initial success. Since the early years, growth has been slow but has outpaced the overall population (which is actually declining in much of eastern Europe). Today, 42 percent of European membership resides in southern and eastern Europe.

The commencement of the work in a country has often been heralded by a blessing by an Apostle, generally referred to as "dedicatory prayer" for the preaching of the gospel. The practice seems to have been sporadic in the nineteenth century, with only a few recorded dedications, but it was a routine practice in the twentieth century. In 1902–1903, European Mission President Francis M. Lyman blessed Belgium, Greece, Finland, and Russia. A few new countries were blessed in midcentury as Marion G. Romney blessed Spain in 1969 and Thomas S. Monson blessed Portugal in 1975. Some western European countries were blessed long after missionary work had commenced. After religious freedom was granted in eastern Europe, multiple Apostles blessed the various countries, most recently in the previously war-torn new nation-states of the former Yugoslavia.

Among the signs of Church maturation is the creation of stakes and the erection of temples. In 1960, the United Kingdom was the first European country to receive a stake. The drain of members to America precluded this happening earlier. Later in the century, the Church established stakes in western Europe, Scandinavia, and southern Europe in that sequence. To date, three eastern European countries have stakes.

Membership growth today is very slow across Europe. The main reason is that the increasing secularism that brought religious freedom has also limited the interest of western Europeans in the Church. Most converts today are immigrants from Africa and elsewhere. Europe has a relatively small but strong and mature membership. This is exemplified by the fact that although it constitutes only 3.5 percent of global Church members, it has 4 percent of the stakes, 8 percent of the temples, and is the homeland of a member of the First Presidency.

Kahlile Mehr

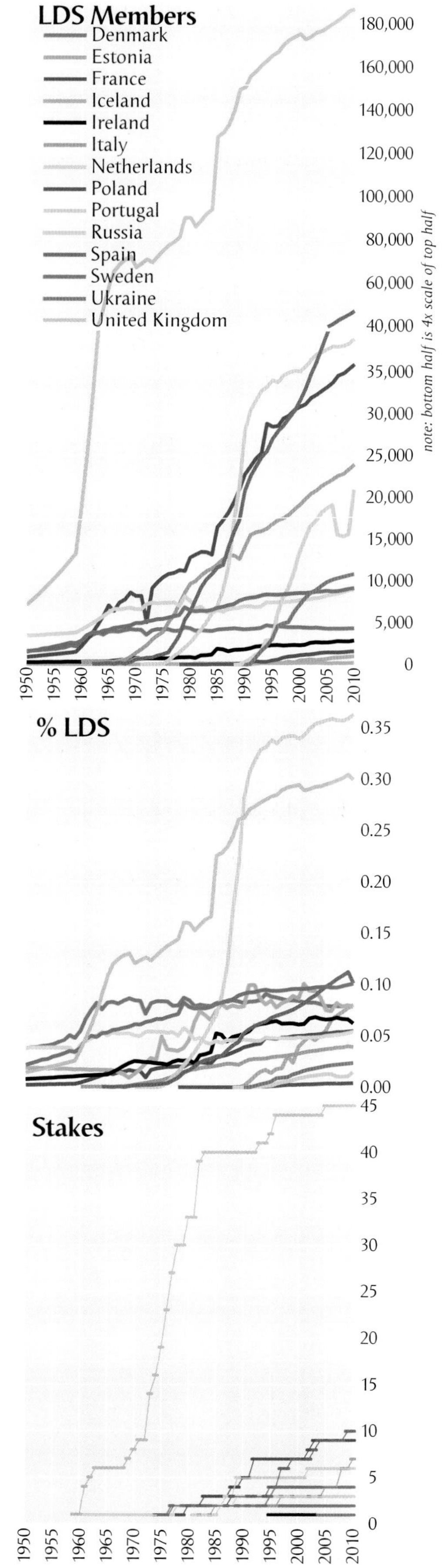

Church Growth in Selected European Countries

The selected countries shown are representative of various patterns evident across Europe. The twentieth-century growth in the United Kingdom shows the maturing of the Church in a society where there is no official governmental opposition, where the missionary force has grown and become more sophisticated in their teaching techniques, and where there is a foundation of experienced local leadership and a well-established community of members to welcome and sustain new converts. In northern Europe, the Church has seen very slow growth or even decline in membership for decades, but the total population there is even more stagnant. Spain and Portugal saw rapid early growth during the 1980s and 1990s, but it has slowed somewhat. The countries of eastern Europe saw an initial surge in the early 1990s followed by slow growth thereafter.

The Middle East

1840–present

THE MIDDLE EAST (southwestern Asia and northern Africa) has been a land of interest for Mormons since the day the Church was organized. In addition to having a widespread millenarian interest in the gathering of Israel, Latter-day Saints have come to this region to study, to work, to fight, and to preach. The first LDS visitor was Orson Hyde, who arrived in Jerusalem on October 21, 1841, later climbing the Mount of Olives to first dedicate the land for the gathering of "Abraham's children."

The first LDS missionary in the region was Jacob Spori, who arrived in Constantinople in January 1885 to open the Turkish Mission. In this and most subsequent missions in the Middle East, the focus was on converting Christians, not Muslims or Jews, especially the Armenians of what is now eastern Turkey and northern Syria and the sizable Christian populations of Lebanon and Palestine. Despite some success, each mission was eventually closed due to political turmoil, ethnic and religious clashes, or persecution by the majority religions. Later mission attempts included the Iran Tehran Mission, which after three years closed on the eve of the Islamic fundamentalist revolution, and the current Armenia Yerevan Mission, the only mission to see some lasting success.

After World War II, the U.S. and Europe established a military presence in the region, first in NATO ally Turkey, and more recently in Kuwait, Iraq, and Afghanistan. Latter-day Saint servicemen have held meetings in small groups or as organized branches on larger bases. During the most recent conflicts, the LDS military presence in Iraq and Afghanistan was large enough to form military districts.

Since the 1950s, expatriate Latter-day Saints (primarily from the United States, but with significant numbers from Europe and the Philippines) have lived and worked in the Middle East, primarily in developing the petroleum industry. Many of these members brought leadership experience as well as their families. In the 1970s and 1980s, groups and branches of foreigners operated under the direction of the International Mission, culminating in the first (and currently only) stake in the region being created by Elder Boyd K. Packer in 1983, consisting of wards and branches scattered all over the Persian Gulf area. Mormons in the region are typically under strict government restrictions on preaching, especially to native Muslims. In 2008, the Middle East/Africa North Area was created to serve the members in the region.

Latter-day Saints, including archaeologists, linguists, theologians, historians, and students, have also come to the region to study. Their work has led to strong friendships with scholars and leaders of other Christian, Jewish, and Muslim religions; to branches in Egypt, Israel, and Jordan; and to the satellite center of Brigham Young University in Jerusalem.

The standing of the Church in the Middle East has been strengthened by the tolerance it preaches for other faiths, such as Judaism and Islam, as taught in the eleventh article of faith. As Church President Howard W. Hunter said, "Both the Jews and the Arabs are children of our Father. They are both children of promise, and as a Church, we do not take sides. We have love for and an interest in each."

Matthew Heiss

See timeline on page 233

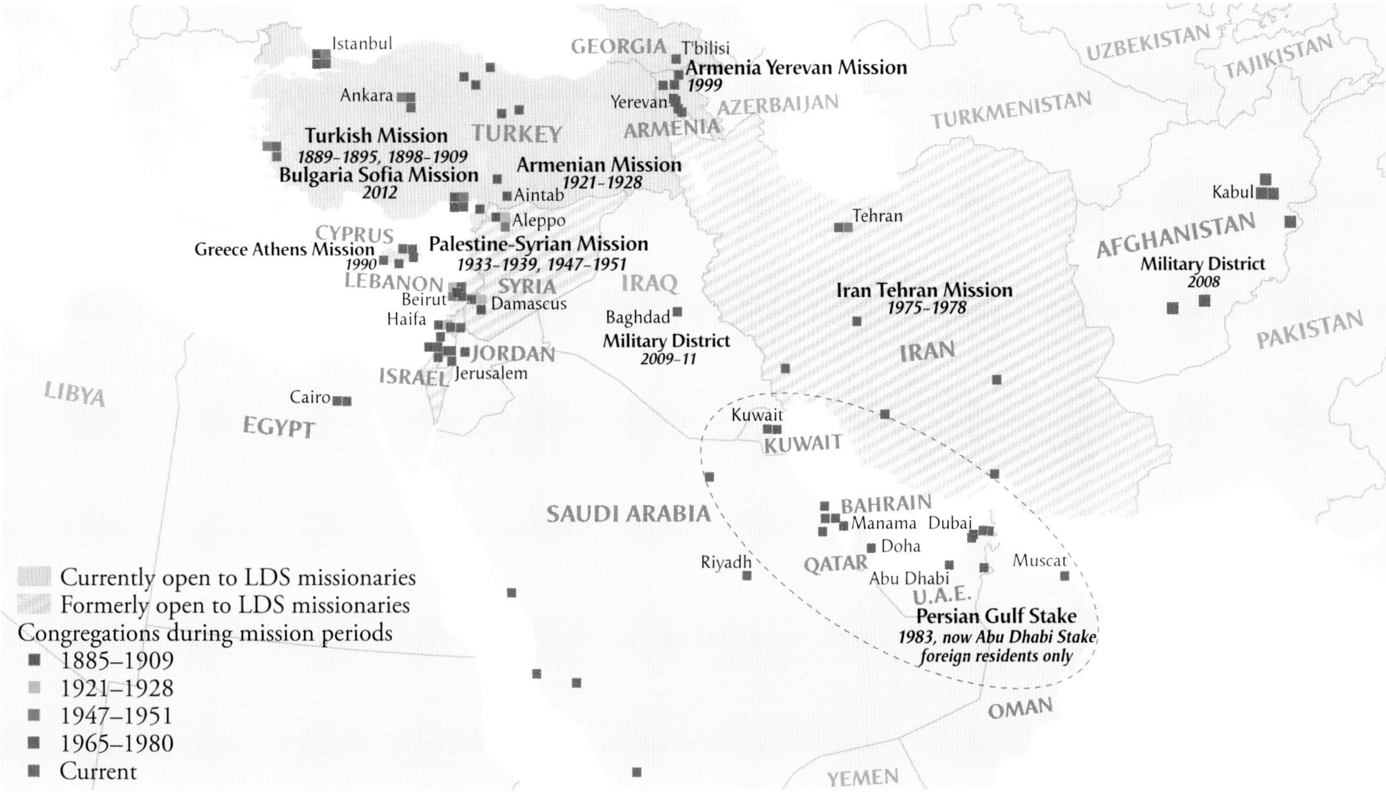

Africa

1851–present

Over its history, the Church in Africa has seen starts and stops, periods of slow and steady growth, as well as significant growth spurts. At times, Church members were isolated from the Church due to war, political oppression, and distance. As the African Latter-day Saints remained faithful, they were blessed with missions, stakes, areas, and ultimately temples.

The first LDS missionaries arrived in South Africa on April 19, 1853. There were many converts, but their emigration to Utah left the Church weak, and the mission was closed in 1865.

After the South African Mission was reestablished in 1903, work expanded throughout the area that is now South Africa, Zambia (then Northern Rhodesia), and Zimbabwe (then Southern Rhodesia). However, the spread of the gospel was hampered by the two world wars, government restrictions on foreign nationals entering South Africa, an inability to communicate with Afrikaans-speaking citizens, the immense size of the mission, and race relations.

Beyond the reach of the mission, individuals were converted to Mormonism on their own, due to travel to the United States and Europe, or after finding the Book of Mormon or other literature. Frequent requests for missionaries came from many places, especially Nigeria, but attempts to open a new mission were not successful until the 1978 revelation granting the priesthood to all worthy males.

The first missionaries to Ghana and Nigeria found entire (unofficial) congregations ready for baptism. Within ten years of the revelation, Africa grew from one stake in one mission to six stakes, six missions, and a temple. Throughout the 1980s and 1990s, new countries were opened on a regular basis. A sign of the continuing growth of the Church in Africa is the 2011 announcement of temples to be built in Durban, South Africa, and Kinshasa, Democratic Republic of the Congo.

The Church in Africa has also seen difficulty, such as "The Freeze" of 1989–1990, during which the Church was banned by the government of Ghana. The civil wars that are rampant in many African countries have made missionary work and church construction next to impossible at times, and in places where missionaries can preach, mass baptisms have often overwhelmed the development of new leaders.

These challenges, however, have forged a strong force of native missionaries and leaders that have made Africa a bastion of sustainable Church growth.

Matthew Heiss

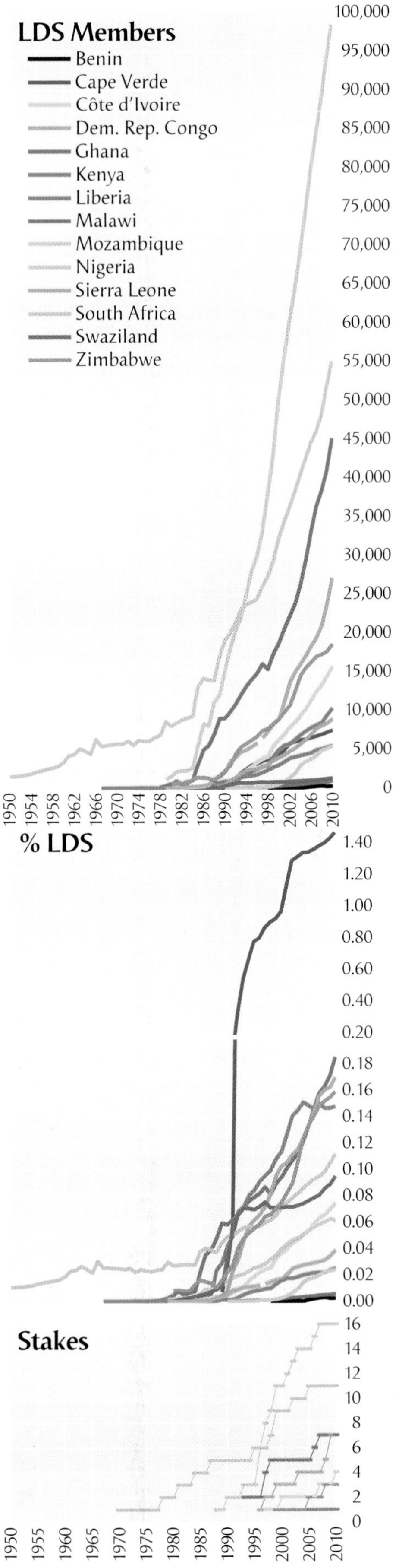

Elder Edwin Q. "Ted" Cannon and his wife were one of the first missionary couples to preach in Nigeria in 1978. Here they found independent churches run by people who had self-converted to Mormonism after encountering the Book of Mormon and other Church literature, and were able to baptize hundreds at a time. Since then, independent "Mormon" churches have been found in many other newly-opened countries as well, but in recent years the Church has been cautious about mass baptisms like the one shown here, instead emphasizing personal, individual conversion.

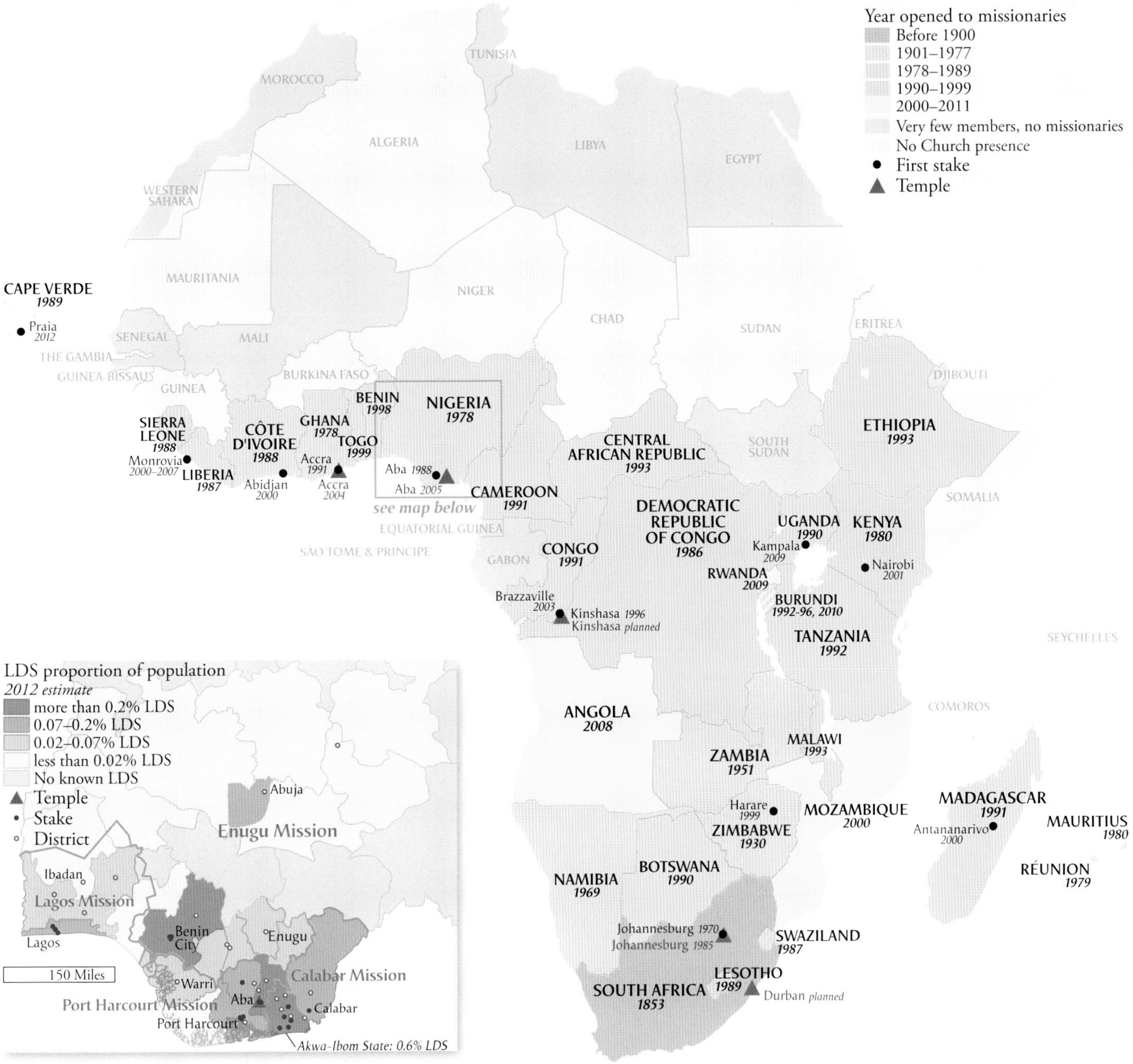

Southern Nigeria is where the Church has spread most strongly, reaching relatively rural areas as well as cities. The strength of the Church in the towns of Akwa Ibom and surrounding states dates back to the founding of the Church in Nigeria in 1979, when they were able to convert entire churches at a time. Even with this success, the Church is still in its infancy in Africa, and these strongest areas have a tenth the membership of similarly populated areas in Latin America (see p. 220).

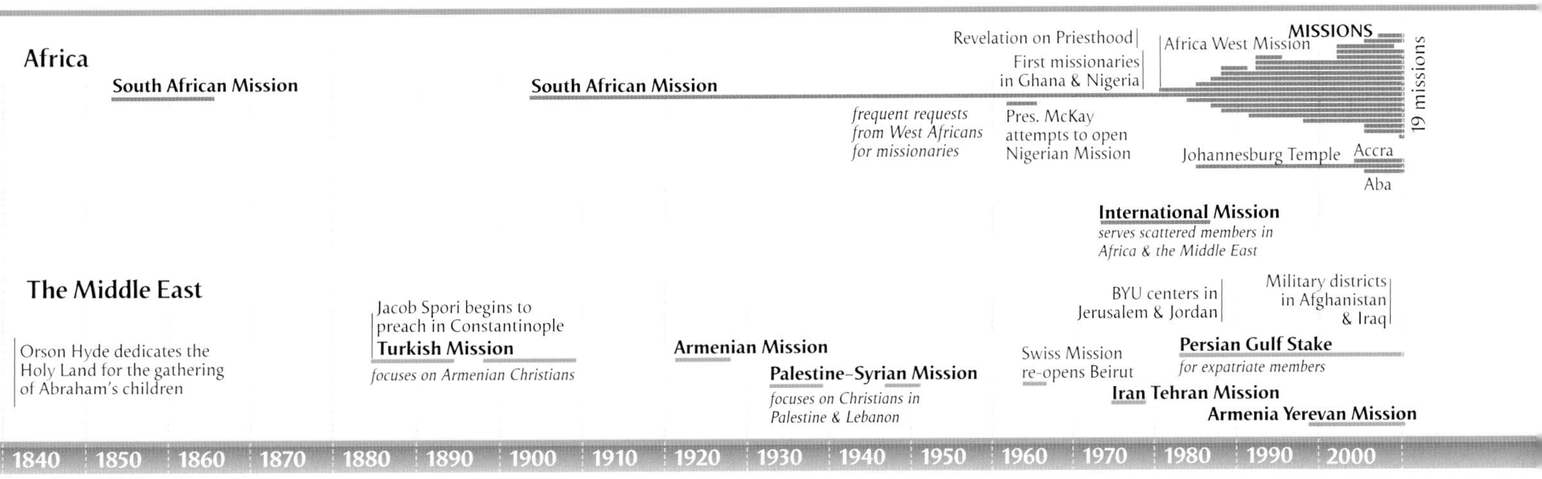

Europe and Africa in 2012

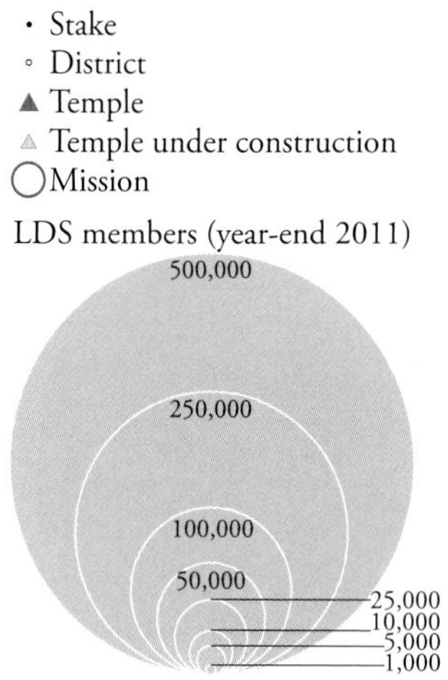

Stake
District
Temple
Temple under construction
Mission
LDS members (year-end 2011)
500,000
250,000
100,000
50,000
25,000
10,000
5,000
1,000

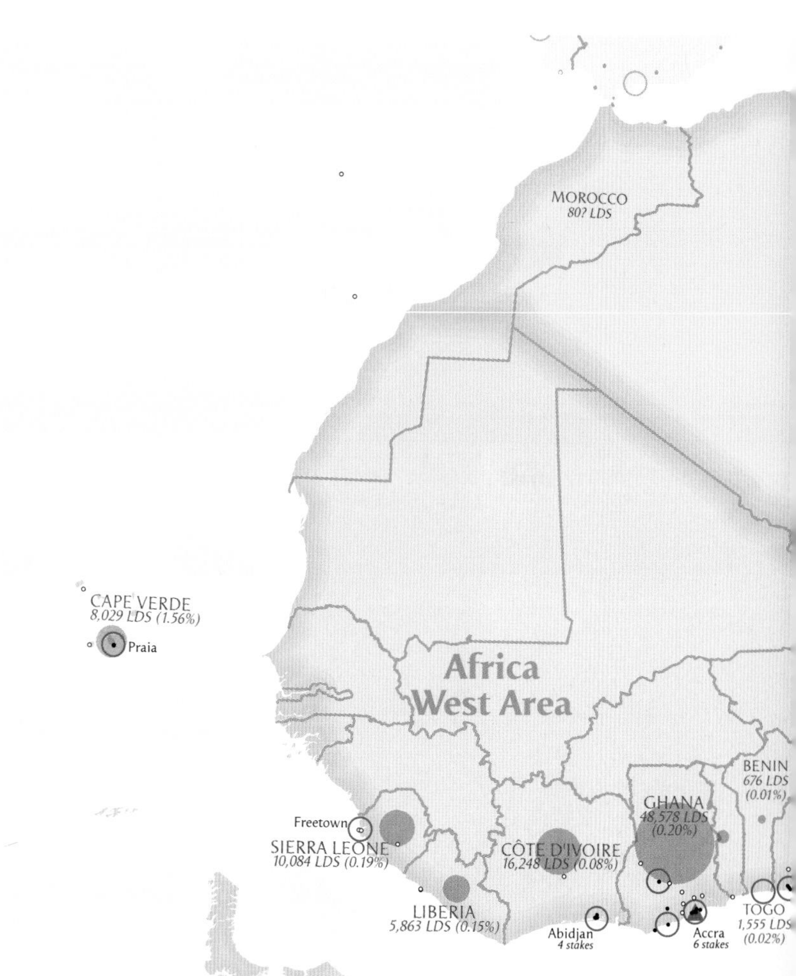

MOROCCO
80? LDS
CAPE VERDE
8,029 LDS (1.56%)
Praia
Africa West Area
BENIN
676 LDS
(0.01%)
GHANA
48,578 LDS
(0.20%)
Freetown
SIERRA LEONE
10,084 LDS (0.19%)
CÔTE D'IVOIRE
16,248 LDS (0.08%)
LIBERIA
5,863 LDS (0.15%)
Abidjan
4 stakes
Accra
6 stakes
TOGO
1,555 LDS
(0.02%)

Europe Area
GREENLAND
15 LDS (0.03%)
ICELAND
257 LDS (0.08%)
Europe Area
NORWAY
4,438 LDS (0.09%)
SWEDEN
9,344 LDS (0.10%)
FINLAND
4,715 LDS (0.09%)
Oslo
2 stakes
Stockholm
2 stakes
Helsinki
St. Petersburg
Yekaterinburg
RUSSIA
21,418 LDS (0.02%)
ISLE OF MAN
291 LDS (0.34%)
UNITED KINGDOM
188,029 LDS
(0.30%)
IRELAND
2,915 LDS (0.06%)
Preston
2 stakes
DENMARK
4,388 LDS (0.08%)
Copenhagen
ESTONIA
1,065 LDS (0.08%)
LATVIA
1,145 LDS (0.05%)
LITHUANIA
895 LDS (0.03%)
Vilnius
Moscow
Samara
NETHERLANDS
9,164 LDS
(0.06%)
Rotterdam
2 stakes
7 stakes 2 missions
London
Berlin
BELARUS
500? LDS
Europe East Area
GUERNSEY
47 LDS (0.07%)
JERSEY
299 LDS (0.32%)
LUXEMBOURG
312 LDS (0.06%)
BELGIUM
6,100 LDS (0.06%)
Brussels
GERMANY
38,668 LDS (0.05%)
Warsaw
POLAND
1,716 LDS (0.00%)
Kiev
Frankfurt
Prague
CZECH REPUBLIC
2,312 LDS (0.02%)
UKRAINE
11,015 LDS (0.02%)
Paris
2 stakes
SWITZERLAND
8,342 LDS
(0.11%)
SLOVAKIA
203 LDS
Rostov
FRANCE
36,403 LDS (0.06%)
Bern
AUSTRIA
4,334 LDS (0.05%)
Budapest
MOLDOVA
341 LDS (0.01%)
HUNGARY
4,844 LDS (0.05%)
SLOVENIA
396 LDS
CROATIA
552 LDS
ROMANIA
2,972 LDS (0.01%)
Porto
2 stakes
PORTUGAL
39,760 LDS
(0.37%)
SPAIN
48,675 LDS (0.10%)
BOSNIA & HERZEGOVINA
50? LDS
SERBIA
304 LDS
GEORGIA
204 LDS
ANDORRA
66 LDS (0.08%)
Madrid
2 stakes
Lisbon
3 stakes
Barcelona
2 stakes
MONTENEGRO
257 LDS
KOSOVO
50? LDS
BULGARIA
2,251 LDS (0.03%)
ARMENIA
2,965 LDS (0.1%)
Yerevan
Rome
MACEDONIA
25? LDS
ITALY
24,443 LDS (0.04%)
ALBANIA
2,093 LDS
(0.07%)
TURKEY
293 LDS
GREECE
740 LDS (0.01%)
MALTA
151 LDS (0.04%)
CYPRUS
407 LDS (0.04%)

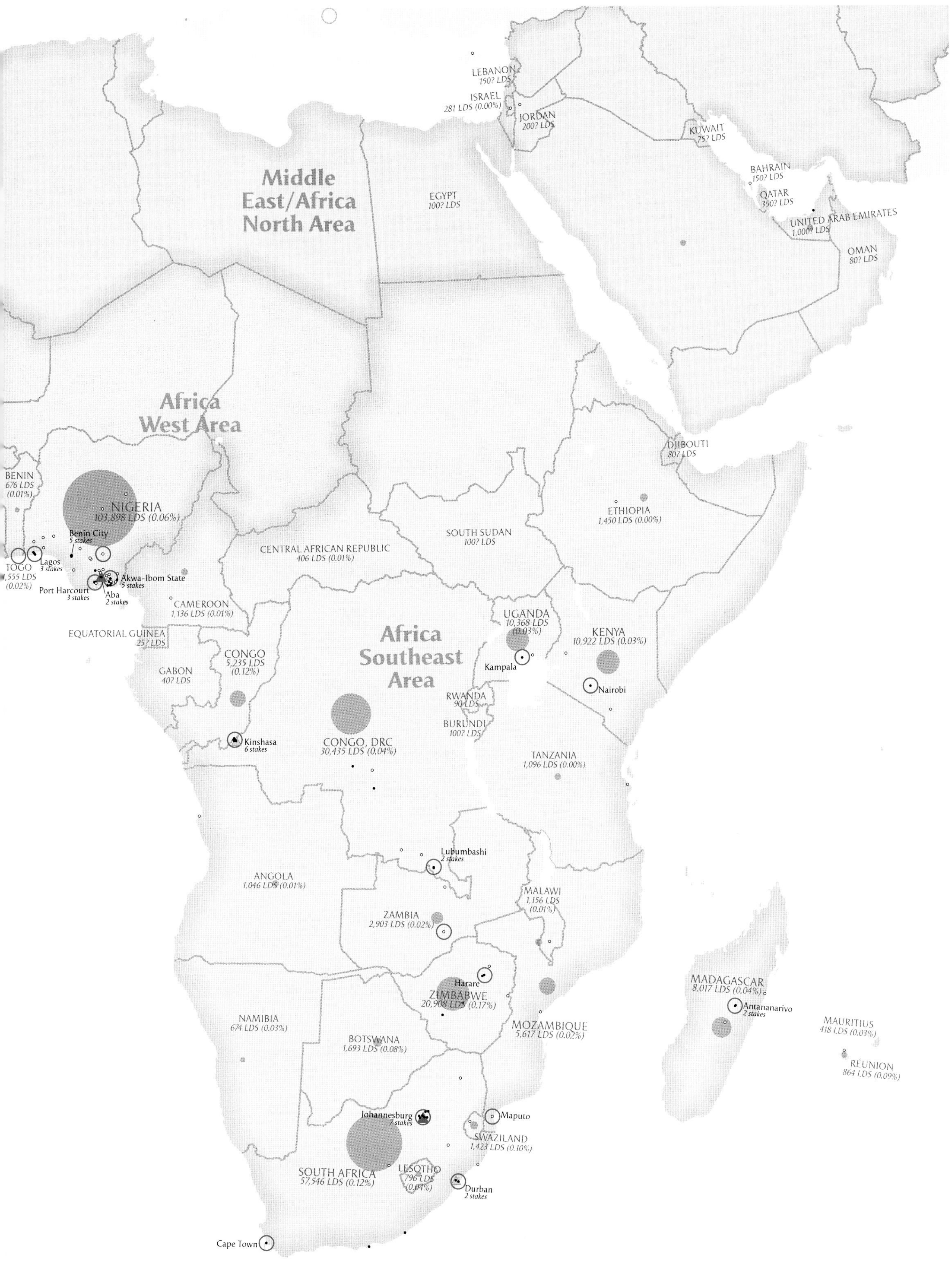
LEBANON
150? LDS
ISRAEL
281 LDS (0.00%)
JORDAN
200? LDS
KUWAIT
75? LDS
BAHRAIN
150? LDS
QATAR
350? LDS
UNITED ARAB EMIRATES
1,000? LDS
OMAN
80? LDS
Middle East/Africa North Area
EGYPT
100? LDS
Africa West Area
DJIBOUTI
80? LDS
BENIN
676 LDS
(0.01%)
NIGERIA
103,898 LDS (0.06%)
Benin City
5 stakes
Lagos
3 stakes
TOGO
,555 LDS
(0.02%)
Port Harcourt
3 stakes
Akwa-Ibom State
5 stakes
Aba
2 stakes
ETHIOPIA
1,450 LDS (0.00%)
SOUTH SUDAN
100? LDS
CENTRAL AFRICAN REPUBLIC
406 LDS (0.01%)
CAMEROON
1,136 LDS (0.01%)
EQUATORIAL GUINEA
25? LDS
UGANDA
10,368 LDS
(0.03%)
Kampala
KENYA
10,922 LDS (0.03%)
Nairobi
CONGO
5,235 LDS
(0.12%)
GABON
40? LDS
Africa Southeast Area
RWANDA
90 LDS
BURUNDI
100? LDS
Kinshasa
6 stakes
CONGO, DRC
30,435 LDS (0.04%)
TANZANIA
1,096 LDS (0.00%)
Lubumbashi
2 stakes
ANGOLA
1,046 LDS (0.01%)
MALAWI
1,156 LDS
(0.01%)
ZAMBIA
2,903 LDS (0.02%)
Harare
ZIMBABWE
20,908 LDS (0.17%)
MOZAMBIQUE
5,617 LDS (0.02%)
MADAGASCAR
8,017 LDS (0.04%)
Antananarivo
2 stakes
MAURITIUS
418 LDS (0.03%)
RÉUNION
864 LDS (0.09%)
NAMIBIA
674 LDS (0.03%)
BOTSWANA
1,693 LDS (0.08%)
Johannesburg
7 stakes
Maputo
SWAZILAND
1,423 LDS (0.10%)
SOUTH AFRICA
57,546 LDS (0.12%)
LESOTHO
796 LDS
(0.04%)
Durban
2 stakes
Cape Town

Asia

1854–present

ASIA IS BY FAR THE MOST POPULOUS REGION of the world; it includes more than half of the Earth's inhabitants. However, during most of the history of the LDS Church, it has been a relatively minor focus of missionary work. There are several reasons for this lack, and overcoming these obstacles is crucial to enabling future Church growth in Asia.

The major obstacle for the Church in Asia has always been cultural and religious differences. While most Christian missionaries during the colonial era focused their message on converting non-Christians to the gospel of Jesus Christ, the restorationist message of the LDS Church is tailor-made to existing Christians. Missionaries have tended to build relationships on a common belief in Christ, and adapting their message to other world religions has been challenging. This distinction is most visible in the Philippines, the only largely Christian nation in Asia, with four times more LDS than any other country in the region.

A second reason is that the dominant religions of Asia—Buddhism, Hinduism, and Islam—are more than just a personal belief; they are dominant cultural influences on national identities. Converts are often forced to relinquish family, friends, cultural norms, and part of who they are for their testimonies.

Third, governments have often viewed the LDS Church skeptically, as with other Western churches, as an element of American influence and a relic of colonialism. In many Asian countries, the Church operates under legal restrictions that limit the entry of foreign missionaries. Fortunately, these restrictions create opportunities for local members to lead and to preach.

During the nineteenth century, LDS General Authorities allocated less than one percent of their missionary force to Asia (see p. 94). Even this minor focus was merely an outgrowth of the Church in Europe, as missionaries preached primarily to British colonists. When outside factors limited the available missionary force, Asia was the first area to be abandoned.

The greatest growth of the Church in Asia came during the Cold War (1945–90), as LDS soldiers built cores of membership at U.S. military bases and as the American sphere of influence opened doors for LDS missionaries. Growth was especially strong in U.S.-allied countries such as Japan, South Korea, Taiwan, and the Philippines. By the end of the first decade of the twenty-first century, there were nearly one million members in Asia.

Although growth has slowed somewhat in recent years, opportunities have arisen as new countries have been opened beyond the traditional American sphere of influence, such as Mongolia and Cambodia. Even restricted nations such as China are seeing increasing membership from citizens being converted abroad and local members sharing their faith with their family members. Overall, however, Mormonism has barely scratched the surface of Asia.

Reid L. Neilson

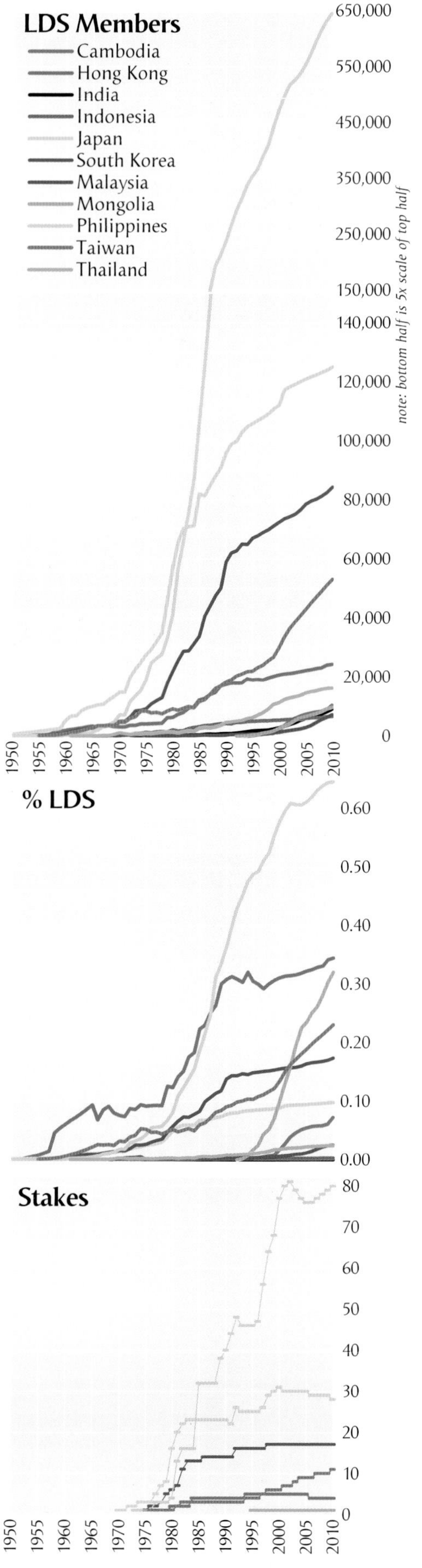

The Church was planted in Asia after World War II, but growth in many Asian nations has been very impressive since the mid-1970s. However, Mormonism still remains a small minority in all Asian nations: even in the Philippines, less than one percent of the population is LDS. Growth in Japan, Korea, and Hong Kong has leveled off recently, due to the typical challenges of missionary work in Asia combined with the secularizing effects of economic success also seen in western Europe. Growth is most dynamic in countries where the Church is relatively new and small, such as Mongolia, Malaysia, and Cambodia. Nevertheless, there are now dozens of stakes in Asia, including about 80 in the Philippines and many others in northern and southeastern Asia, along with temples in Japan, South Korea, Taiwan, Hong Kong, and the Philippines.

Early Missionary Work

When the Saints moved into the western United States, Asia suddenly became more accessible, and leaders discussed sending missionaries to Asia via California. In August 1852, President Brigham Young called more than 100 missionaries to evangelize throughout the world (see p. 94), including the Asian nations of India, Siam (Thailand), and China. They were able to convert a few people (almost exclusively European colonists) but struggled in their missionary efforts before abandoning their posts. In 1853, Hosea Stout, James Lewis, and Chapman Duncan sailed from San Francisco to Hong Kong, where they attempted to establish a branch of the Church, but the ongoing Taiping Rebellion, lack of money, and stifling heat discouraged them, and they returned to Utah after several disappointing weeks. Mormon missionaries did not evangelize in Japan until 1901 and closed the mission in 1924, after two decades of disappointing results.

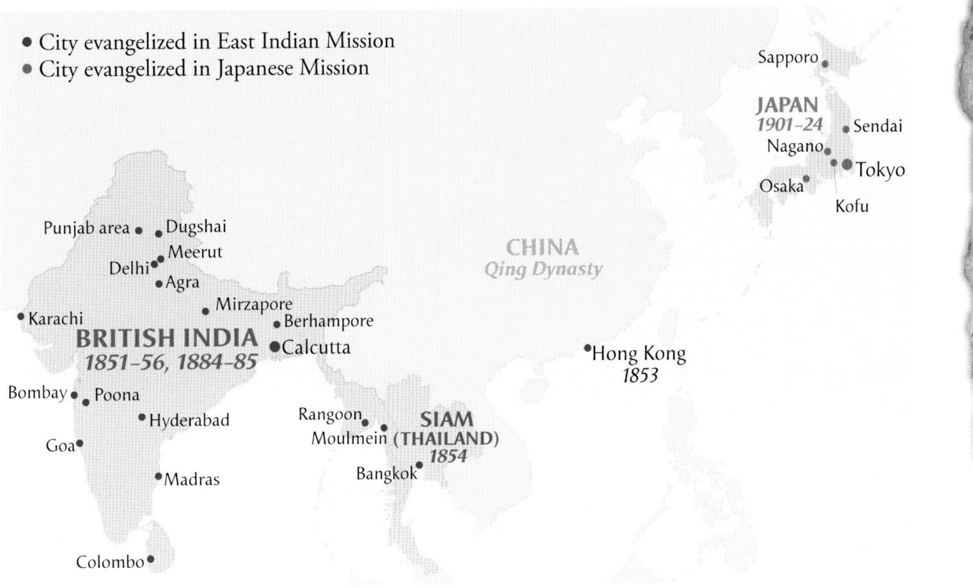

Spreading the Gospel in Asia

The end of World War II marked a new beginning for Mormonism in Asia. Pleased with the ecclesiastical success of LDS American servicemen in Japan, Church leaders reopened the Japan Mission in 1948. A year later missionaries returned to Hong Kong, almost 100 years after the first mission there. The Korean War, which brought such misery to the Korean populace, also allowed LDS servicemen stationed in Asia during the conflict to begin meeting in Church groups in Korea, Japan, Taiwan, and the Philippines. In 1955 Elder Joseph Fielding Smith split the Far East Mission, headquartered in Japan, into the Northern and Southern Far East missions, headquartered in Japan and Hong Kong, respectively. Once things stabilized on the Korean Peninsula, missionaries were sent from Japan to South Korea in 1956, where they enjoyed great success in subsequent decades. Five years later, missionary work began in the Philippines, which in time became the most fertile field for Mormonism in all of Asia. During the 1960s, Mormon representatives opened the work in Southeast Asia in the countries of Thailand, Vietnam, India, Singapore, Indonesia, and Malaysia. In more recent decades, the Church has gained a foothold in Sri Lanka, Cambodia, Mongolia, Nepal, and Pakistan.

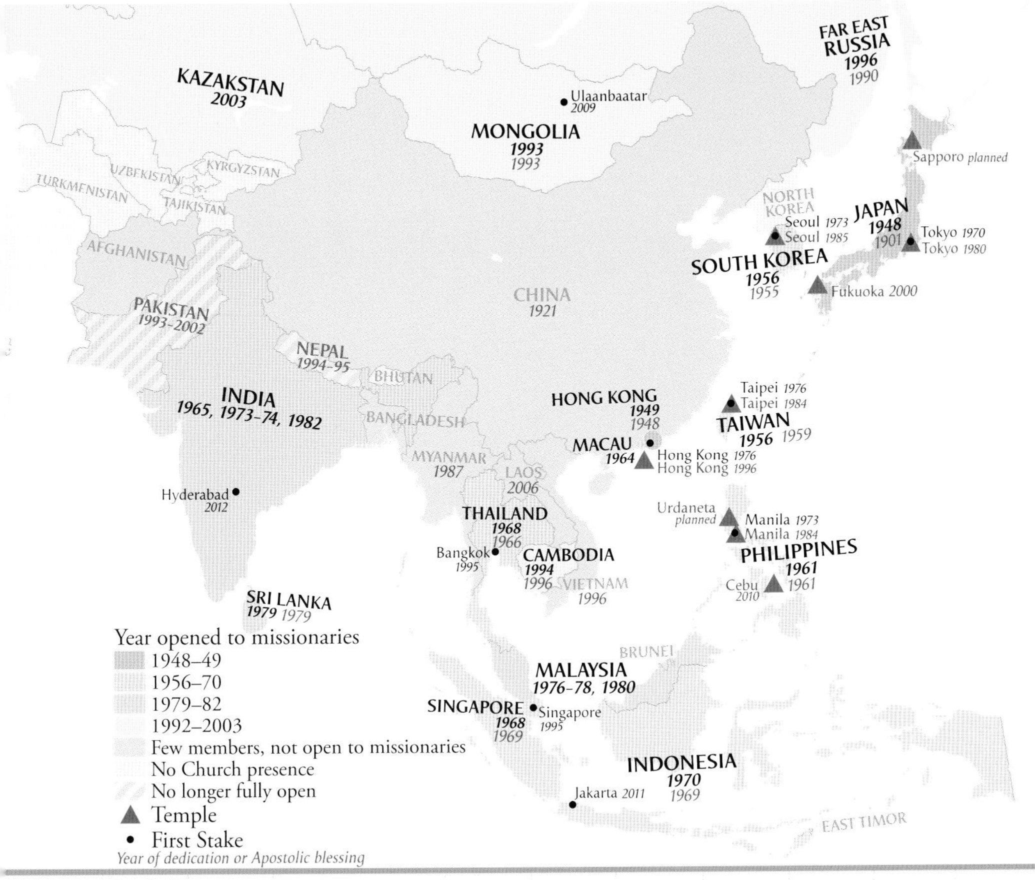

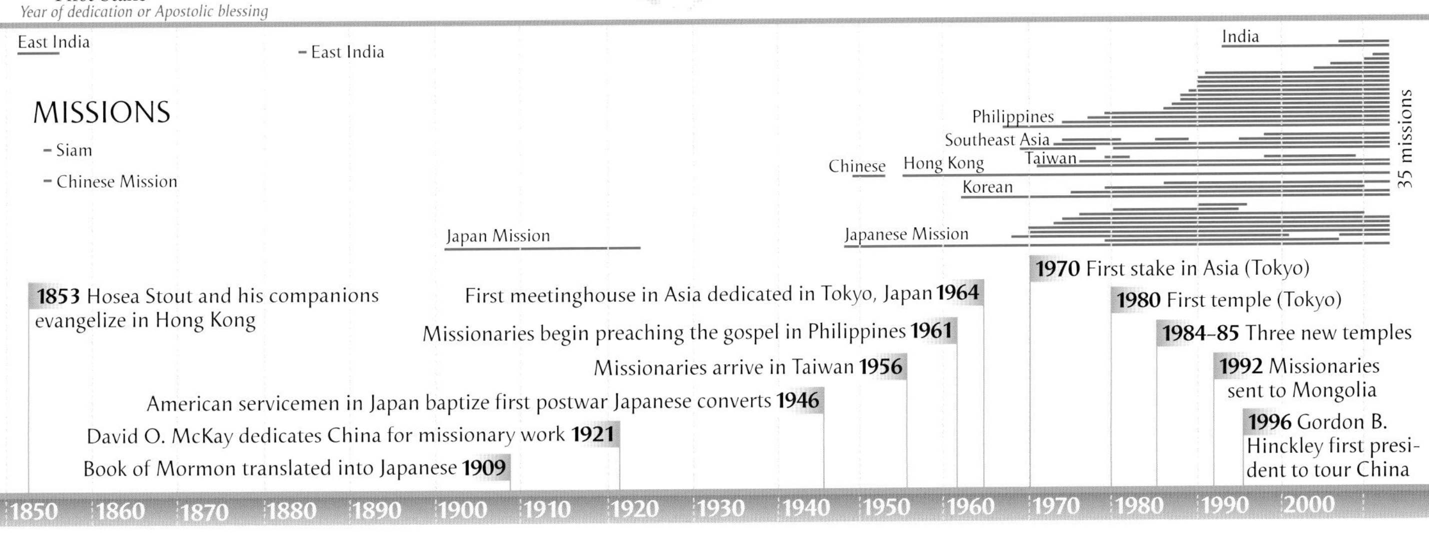

Australia and the Pacific

1854–present

DESPITE THEIR RELATIVELY SMALL POPULATIONS, the island nations of the Pacific are major centers of strength for Mormonism. Since missionaries first preached the gospel in Polynesia in the 1840s, the Church has taken root across the Pacific and continues to grow in the twenty-first century.

The success of the Church in the Pacific has been phenomenal. For example, nearly half of Tongans are LDS, and almost all island groups have a higher proportion LDS than the United States does. A variety of reasons have been suggested for this success. One is that island cultures, especially their focus on families, fit well with Church doctrines. Another is the common belief, preached by missionaries since 1851, that the people of the Pacific are Israelites, possibly descended from people who left the Americas during the time of the Book of Mormon.

The Church in the Pacific has seen its share of challenges. Missionaries were largely absent from the time of their withdrawal during the Utah War until the 1880s (see p. 94). During this time, an apostate leader temporarily gained control of the Church in Hawaii, while RLDS missionaries to Australia and French Polynesia convinced many local members of the legitimacy of Joseph Smith III as prophet. The competition between the LDS and RLDS churches in Tahiti caused confusion well into the twentieth century. While most members are very faithful, many have taken their conversion lightly and are counted as members of multiple denominations. As the Church has recently expanded to reach smaller islands, it can be a challenge to build a critical mass of members to sustain a viable Church presence. For example, the tiny country of Niue is 20 percent LDS, but this amounts to fewer than 300 members.

Polynesian members have had an influence well beyond their home countries. LDS Tongans and Samoans have been part of a general migration to wealthier places like New Zealand, Hawaii, California, and Salt Lake City, where they form a significant cultural minority. During the 1970s, the Brigham Young University football team began recruiting in these enclaves, a trend that soon spread to many other colleges and the NFL, where Mormon Polynesians are visible role models.

Reid L. Neilson

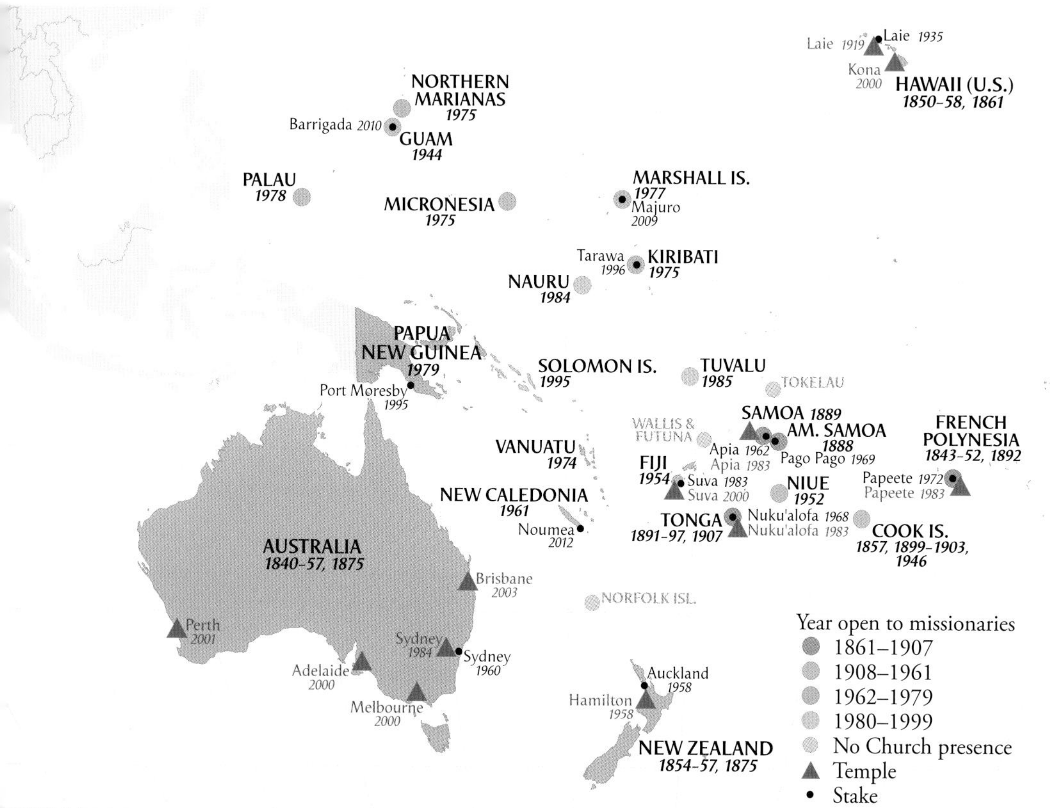

Church Expansion in Pacific

The first missionaries in this region were British converts immigrating to Australia who saw very limited success. Meanwhile, sailor-turned-missionary Addison Pratt and others reported astounding success in French Polynesia (see p. 40). When Parley P. Pratt was called to preside over missionaries in the Pacific in 1850 (see p. 94), he focused efforts on Hawaii and Australia, where great success was found. By 1854 the Church could boast of more than four thousand Hawaiian Church members, and dynamic growth in Australia had spread to the *pakeha* (British) population in New Zealand. Hawaii also acted as a springboard for the spread of Mormonism in Polynesia. Hawaiian Church leader Walter Murray Gibson (who was an apostate at the time) sent two faithful members to their native Samoa, where they planted seeds for a future Church presence. During the 1880s, large numbers of missionaries returned to the Pacific, reopening some countries and entering others for the first time. Following the example of other churches, LDS schools became a valuable tool for preaching the gospel and improving the well-being of members (see p. 142). After World War II, the Church spread west into Melanesia and Micronesia, due to an increased American presence and the freedoms gained through a wave of independence in the 1970s.

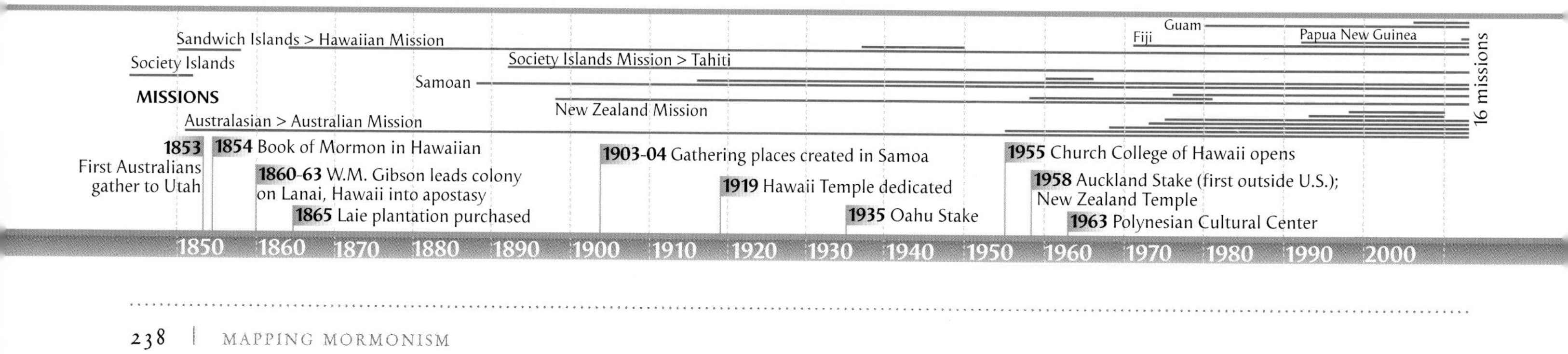

Church Growth in Pacific Countries

By 2010 Church membership in both Australia and New Zealand had exceeded 100,000 members each, while Samoa and Tonga each had over 50,000 Latter-day Saints, which is noteworthy given their small populations. While the number of Church members in small Pacific countries like French Polynesia, Fiji, and Kiribati remain relatively tiny, they are likewise experiencing impressive growth. In fact, the nations of Tonga, Samoa, and American Samoa continue to have the highest percentage of Church members in a country anywhere in the world. Kiribati, French Polynesia, and the Marshall Islands likewise have much higher ratios of Mormons to non-Mormons than any other nation. As the number of stakes typically tracks the number of Latter-day Saints, there are now dozens of stakes in Australia, New Zealand, Tonga, and Samoa. And most Pacific nations now have at least one stake, moving beyond the mission districts that were common even two decades ago, signaling the maturity of Mormonism as both a people and a religious organization.

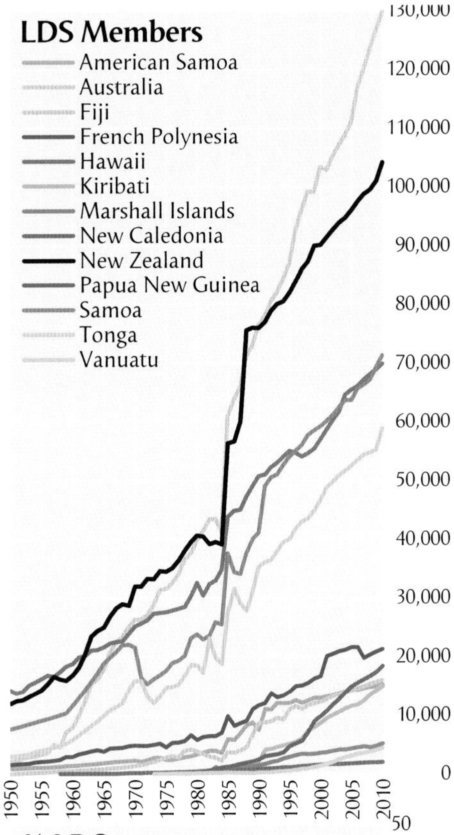

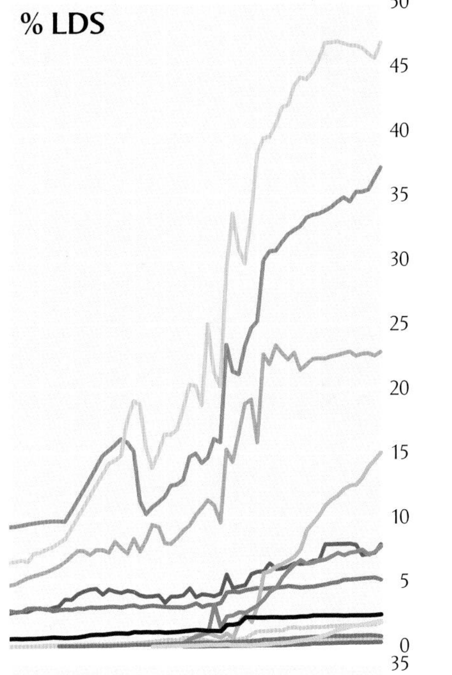

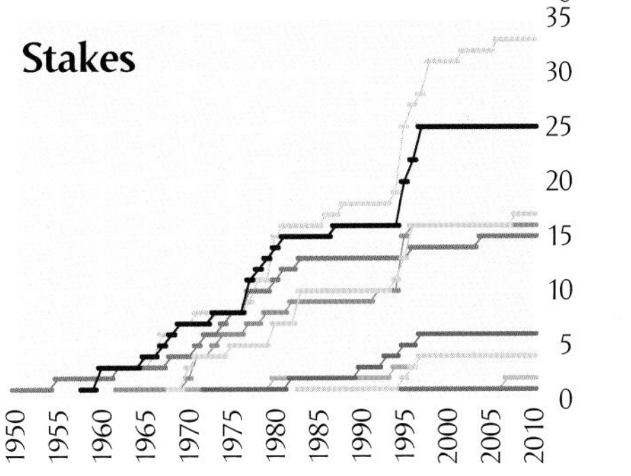

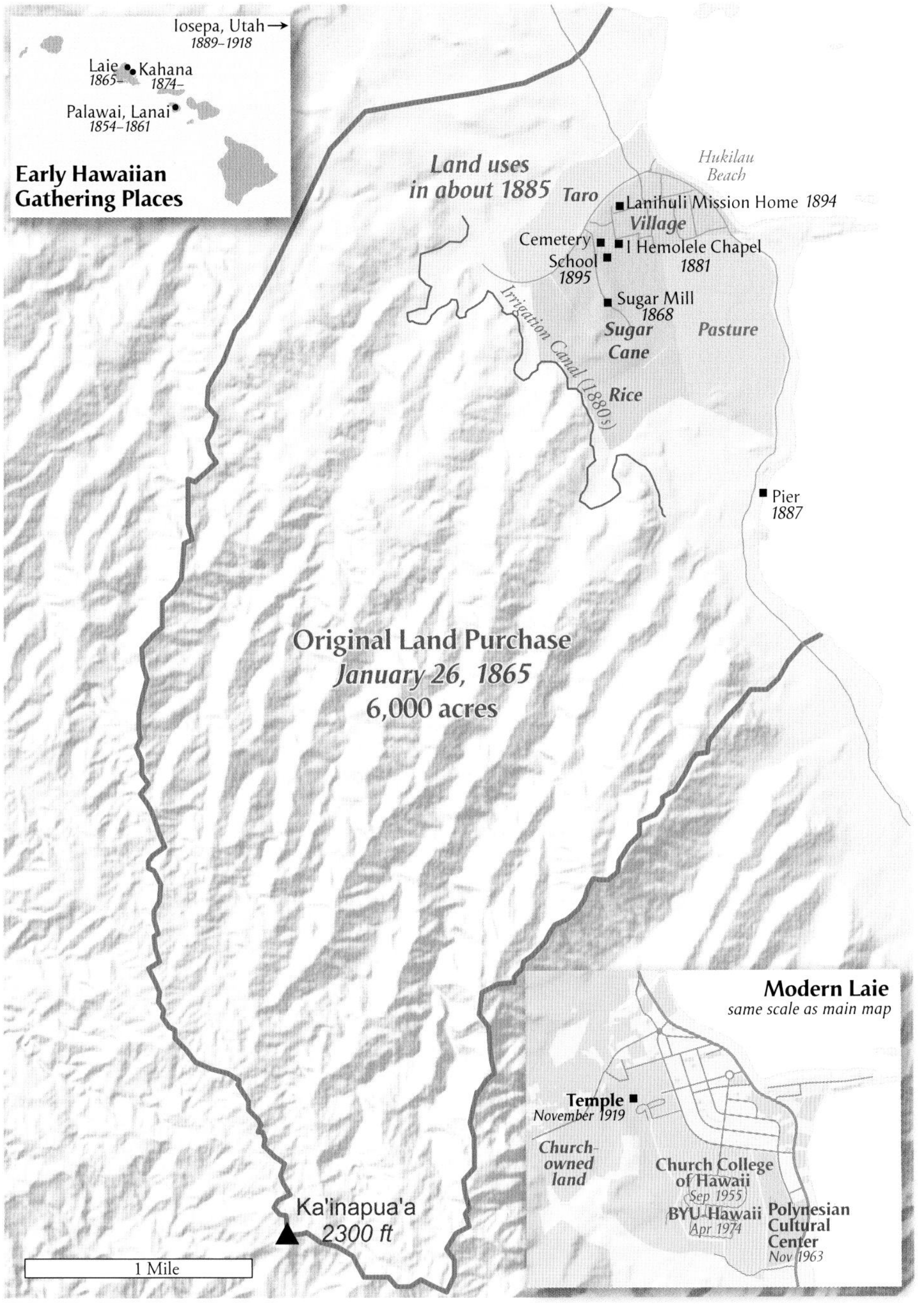

Development of Laie, Hawaii

Determined to create a Mormon stronghold in the Pacific, Church leaders set out to create a gathering place for the Hawaiian Saints, first on the island of Lanai in the 1850s and, when that failed, on the island of Oahu. Church agents paid $14,000 for the Laie plantation in January 1864, which included 6,000 acres on the northeastern shore of Oahu. Church leaders, missionaries, and local members worked side by side to cultivate the land, teaching the Hawaiian Saints to be financially self-sufficient. A variety of crops were grown, but sugar cane became the most profitable, even though the plantation never succeeded financially. Laie remained the headquarters of the Hawaiian Mission until 1919, when the mission home was moved to Honolulu. That same year Church leaders dedicated the Hawaii Temple for the use of Saints throughout the Pacific and Asia, cementing its status as the spiritual gathering place for Latter-day Saints in the Pacific Basin. Laie eventually became the home of the Church College of Hawaii, dedicated by President David O. McKay in 1955 (see p. 142), later renamed BYU–Hawaii, and the Polynesian Cultural Center, which opened its doors to tourists in 1963. This model of a local gathering place for Polynesian Saints was successfully followed on a smaller scale in American Samoa (Mapusaga), Western Samoa (Sauniatu), Tonga (Liahona), and New Zealand (Hamilton).

Asia and the Pacific in 2012

· Stake
◦ District
▲ Temple
△ Temple under construction
◯ Mission
LDS members (year-end 2011)
500,000
250,000
100,000
50,000
25,000
10,000
5,000
1,000
RUSSIA
21,418 LDS (0.02%)
Europe East Area
Yekaterinburg
Novosibirsk
KAZAKHSTAN
193 LDS (0.00%)
Ulaanbaatar
MONGOLIA
10,217 LDS (0.33%)
Sapporo
2 stakes
Asia North Area
Seoul
10 stakes
SOUTH KOREA
85,041 LDS (0.17%)
Tokyo
9 stakes
Osaka
5 stakes
JAPAN
125,744 LDS
(0.10%)
Fukuoka
AFGHANISTAN
600? LDS
Middle East Africa North Area
PAKISTAN
3,200? LDS
Asia Area
CHINA
9,500? LDS
New Delhi
NEPAL
150? LDS
Taipei
4 stakes
Taichung
2 stakes
TAIWAN
54,529 LDS (0.24%)
INDIA
9,964 LDS (0.00%)
BANGLADESH
100? LDS
MYANMAR
150? LDS
VIETNAM
1,000? LDS
MACAU
1,308 LDS
(0.23%)
HONG KONG
23,992 LDS (0.34%)
4 stakes
LAOS
150? LDS
Philippines Area
Manila
20 stakes 3 missions
661,598 LDS
(0.65%)
THAILAND
16,871 LDS (0.03%)
Bangalore
Bangkok
CAMBODIA
10,999 LDS
(0.07%)
Phnom Penh
Cebu
5 stakes
Bacolod
4 stakes
Cagayan de Oro
3 stakes
SRI LANKA
1,301 LDS (0.01%)
ANGELES MISSION
QUEZON CITY NORTH MISSION
Malolos
Manila Bay
Quezon City
Q.C. SOUTH MISSION
Manila
Cavite
Laguna de Bay
MANILA MISSION
Cabuyao
SAN PABLO MISSION
MALAYSIA
7,926 LDS (0.03%)
SINGAPORE
3,573 LDS (0.07%)
INDONESIA
6,812 LDS (0.00%)
Jakarta

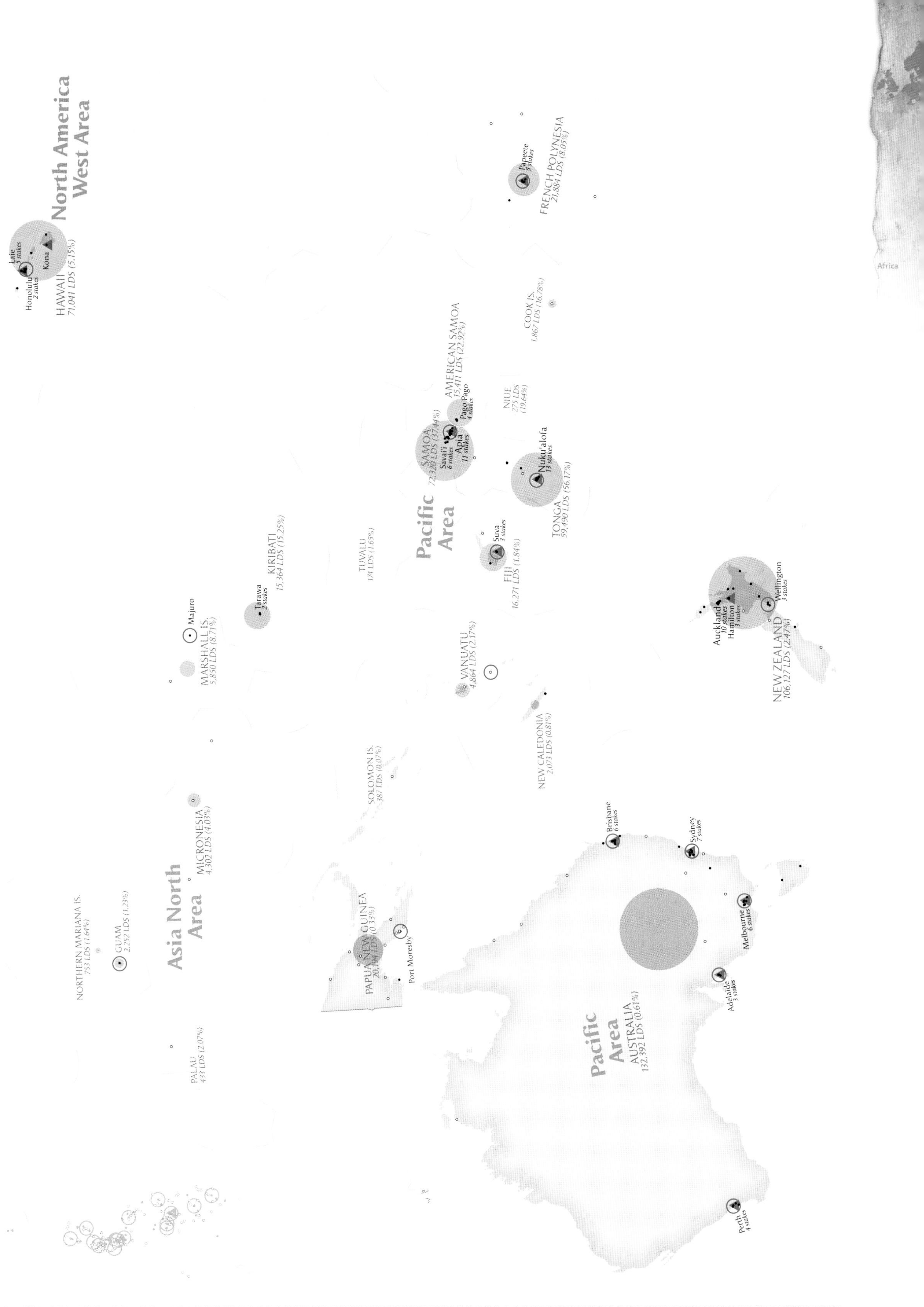
North America West Area
HAWAII
71,041 LDS (5.15%)
Honolulu
2 stakes
Laie
5 stakes
Kona
FRENCH POLYNESIA
21,884 LDS (8.05%)
Papeete
5 stakes
COOK IS.
1,867 LDS (16.78%)
AMERICAN SAMOA
15,411 LDS (22.92%)
Pago Pago
4 stakes
NIUE
275 LDS
(19.64%)
SAMOA
72,320 LDS (37.44%)
Savai'i
6 stakes
Apia
11 stakes
Nuku'alofa
13 stakes
TONGA
59,490 LDS (56.17%)
Pacific Area
Suva
3 stakes
FIJI
16,271 LDS (1.84%)
TUVALU
174 LDS (1.65%)
KIRIBATI
15,364 LDS (15.25%)
Tarawa
2 stakes
Majuro
MARSHALL IS.
5,850 LDS (8.71%)
VANUATU
4,864 LDS (2.17%)
Auckland
10 stakes
Hamilton
3 stakes
Wellington
3 stakes
NEW ZEALAND
106,127 LDS (2.47%)
NEW CALEDONIA
2,073 LDS (0.81%)
SOLOMON IS.
387 LDS (0.07%)
MICRONESIA
4,302 LDS (4.03%)
Asia North Area
NORTHERN MARIANA IS.
753 LDS (1.64%)
GUAM
2,252 LDS (1.23%)
PAPUA NEW GUINEA
20,104 LDS (0.33%)
Port Moresby
PALAU
433 LDS (2.07%)
Brisbane
6 stakes
Sydney
7 stakes
Melbourne
6 stakes
Adelaide
3 stakes
Pacific Area
AUSTRALIA
132,392 LDS (0.61%)
Perth
4 stakes
Africa

Glossary

This is not a complete dictionary of terms relevant to The Church of Jesus Christ of Latter-day Saints but focuses on terms used frequently in this work. For simplicity, the definitions and claims below are from a Mormon perspective.

Apostle: Beginning in 1835, this position is the highest priesthood office of the Church; an Apostle is designated as a special witness of Jesus Christ to all the world. The First Presidency and the Quorum of the Twelve (and others in rare circumstances) are ordained Apostles.

Area: Since 1984 (with earlier precedents), it is the largest geographical administrative subdivision of the Church and presided over by an Area Presidency consisting of three members of the quorums of the Seventy.

Assistants to the Twelve: A General Authority office created in 1941 to help the Quorum of the Twelve carry out administrative work; the office was eliminated in favor of the First Quorum of the Seventy in 1976.

Auxiliary: An organization that serves a specific group of members other than the priesthood quorums, currently including Relief Society (adult women), Young Men and Young Women (ages 12–17), Primary (ages 1–11), and Sunday School (all members ages 12 and over).

Baptism: An ordinance performed through immersion in water by a priesthood holder, by which a person officially becomes a member of the Church.

Bishop: Originally called only to manage the economic welfare of the Church and its members, since the 1870s they are the erscclesiastical leaders, both pastorally and administratively, of an LDS ward; this position is similar to a priest, minister, or pastor of other churches, but in the LDS Church it is a lay, not professional, office.

Book of Mormon: One of the core books of scripture canonized by the Church, it contains the religious history of an ancient group that lived somewhere in the Americas for 1,000 years, as translated by Joseph Smith Jr.

Branch: The original name for organized congregations of the Church, led by a branch presidency. Since the advent of wards, only smaller, more simply organized congregations are called branches.

Conference: An early term for regional groupings of branches in outlying regions of the Church; conferences were gradually replaced by districts in the early twentieth century.

Dedication: An official blessing given by a priesthood holder, typically marking the opening of a sacred building or program.

Deseret: A word, meaning honey bee, found in the Book of Mormon. As a symbol of industriousness, it was proposed as the name of the territory that became Utah and continues to be a common name for many institutions in the region.

District: A regional unit similar to a stake but much smaller in membership (typically consisting of two or three branches) and simpler in organization, presided over by a district president; the term replaced conference in the early twentieth century. It is meant to be transitional, a "stake in embryo."

Doctrine and Covenants (D&C): One of the books canonized as scripture, this book is a collection of important revelations received chiefly by Joseph Smith Jr. for the governance of the Church and for clarifying doctrine.

Elder: A priesthood office available to worthy male members of the Church ages eighteen and older. The title of elder is used as a general title for all bearers of the Melchizedek Priesthood and is commonly used as a title for missionaries, members of the quorums of the Seventy, and the Twelve Apostles.

First Vision: The original visitation of God and Jesus Christ to Joseph Smith Jr. in 1830, near Palmyra, New York.

First Presidency: The governing quorum of the Church since 1832, consisting of the President and his counselors (typically two but occasionally more if necessary).

General Authority: A priesthood holder with ecclesiastical authority over the entire Church. At present, General Authorities include the First Presidency, the Quorum of the Twelve, the First and Second Quorums of the Seventy, and the Presiding Bishopric.

General Conference: Churchwide meetings that are now held every April and October, consisting of at least five sessions of discourses by General Authorities and other leaders.

Gentiles: During the nineteenth century, this term was often used to refer to someone who is not a member of the LDS Church.

Gospel: Latter-day Saints use this term in many ways, but typically it encapsulates all of the core doctrines of the Church, especially those regarding the atonement of Jesus Christ.

Mission: A geographical area in which full-time missionaries (typically 50–200 per mission) proselytize to the local residents, directed by a mission president.

Missionary: A member of the Church who temporarily (for 1–2 years) volunteers to preach about Christ and the Church in a mission selected by General Authorities; typically includes young men ages 19–21, young women ages 21–22, and retired couples.

Moroni: The last prophet recorded in the Book of Mormon, who buried the gold plates in New York around AD 430; he visited Joseph Smith Jr. in 1823 as an angel, directing him to the plates. The spire of almost every LDS temple is topped with a gold-clad representation of Moroni.

Ordinance: A sacred rite that brings spiritual blessings to a recipient, set forth in scripture and performed by members of the priesthood.

Pioneer: A Latter-day Saint who crossed the plains to Utah prior to the building of the transcontinental railroad in 1869.

President: The highest position of authority in the Church on earth, sustained by the Church members as prophet, seer, and revelator.

Presiding Bishop: A General Authority responsible for much of the temporal affairs of the Church, including responsibilities such as buildings, land holdings, membership records, and the welfare program.

Priesthood: The power and authority by which the Church is organized and directed. Worthy males in the Church may receive the priesthood to be able to act in the name of God, perform ordinances, and give blessings.

Quorum of the Twelve: Twelve men ordained to the office of Apostle; the second ranking quorum over the Church.

Relief Society: The official adult women's organization of the Church.

Revelation: Direct communication from God to man. Prophets have described many forms, including visions, dreams, vocal pronouncements, and spiritual feelings.

Seminary: A weekday religious instruction for youth of high school age.

Seventy: A priesthood office denoted in scripture as having responsibility for missionary work. Until the 1980s there were quorums in every stake, but now quorums exist only at the general and area level.

Stake: A regional grouping of several (usually 5–12) wards and branches, led by a president with two counselors and a twelve-member high council. Since the 1950s, each stake has offices and holds semiannual conferences in a large meetinghouse called a stake center.

Temple: A sacred building, often referred to as "the house of the Lord," where ordinances are performed that grant recipients divine blessings and covenants that are not available elsewhere.

Tithing: Cash or in-kind contributions made by Latter-day Saints. These contributions fund the Church.

Ward: Since the 1850s, a geographically defined congregation of Church members, usually consisting of between 300 and 600 people, presided over by a bishop. Smaller congregations are called branches.

Zion: A term for the utopian ideal of the Church, variously applied to a place of gathering (most commonly referring to Independence, Missouri; Utah; and North and South America), the ideal society of believers wherever they live, or the awaited Kingdom of God after Christ's return.

Bibliography

General Works

Berrett, L. C. (1999–2007). *Sacred places: A comprehensive guide to early LDS historical sites* (6 vols.). Salt Lake City: Bookcraft, Deseret Book.

Brown, S. K., Cannon, D. Q., & Jackson, R. (1994). *Historical atlas of Mormonism*. New York: Simon & Schuster.

Jenson, A. (1830–1972). *Journal history of The Church of Jesus Christ of Latter-day Saints*. Salt Lake City: Historical Department, The Church of Jesus Christ of Latter-day Saints.

Jenson, A. (1941). *Encyclopedic history of The Church of Jesus Christ of Latter-day Saints*. Salt Lake City: Deseret Book. Retrieved April 16, 2012, from http://contentdm.lib.byu.edu/cdm/ref/collection/BYUIBooks/id/2694

U.S. Bureau of the Census (1840–2010). *Decennial census of population and housing*. Minneapolis, MN: National Historical Geographic Information System (summary statistics). Retrieved April 20, 2012, from https://www.nhgis.org/ (summary data), http://www.census.gov/prod/www/abs/decennial/index.html (statistical reports)

Section 1: The Restoration

Bushman, R. L. (2005). *Joseph Smith: Rough stone rolling*. New York: Alfred A. Knopf.

The Church of Jesus Christ of Latter-day Saints. (1981). *Doctrine and covenants*. Salt Lake City: The Church of Jesus Christ of Latter-day Saints. Retrieved April 15, 2012, from http://www.lds.org/scriptures/dc-testament?lang=eng

Smith, J., Jr. (1949). *History of The Church of Jesus Christ of Latter-day Saints*, Ed. B. H. Roberts (7 vols.). Salt Lake City: Deseret News Press.

Smith, J., Jr. (2012). *Histories*. Published as K. L. Davidson, D. J. Whittaker, M. Ashurst-McGee, & R. L. Jensen (Eds.). *The Joseph Smith papers* (Vol. 1, 2). Salt Lake City: The Church Historian's Press.

Smith, L. M. (2001) *Memoir*. Published as L. F. Anderson (Ed.). *Lucy's book: A critical edition of Lucy Mack Smith's family memoir*. Salt Lake City: Signature Books.

Origins of Early Church Leaders

Anderson, R. L. (2003). *Joseph Smith's New England heritage: Influences of grandfathers Solomon Mack and Asael Smith*. Salt Lake City: Deseret Book.

Gaustad, E. S., & Barlow, P. L. (2001). *New historical atlas of religion in America*. New York: Oxford University Press.

Howe, D. W. (2007). *What hath God wrought: The transformation of America, 1815–1848*. New York: Oxford University Press.

Noll, M. A. (2002). *America's God: From Jonathan Edwards to Abraham Lincoln*. New York: Oxford University Press.

Quinn, D. M. (1994). *The Mormon hierarchy: Origins of power*. Salt Lake City: Signature Books & Smith Research Associates.

The Joseph and Lucy Mack Smith Family

Anderson, R. L. (2003). *Joseph Smith's New England heritage: Influences of grandfathers Solomon Mack and Asael Smith*. Salt Lake City: Deseret Book.

Cannon, D. Q. (1973). Topsfield, Massachusetts: Ancestral home of the Prophet Joseph Smith. *BYU Studies*, 14(1), 56–76. Retrieved April 15, 2012, from https://byustudies.byu.edu/showTitle.aspx?title=5097

Porter, L. C. (1971). *A study of the origins of The Church of Jesus Christ of Latter-day Saints in the states of New York and Pennsylvania, 1816–1831*. Ph.D. dissertation, Brigham Young University, Provo, UT.

Stillwell, L. D. (1948). *Migration from Vermont*. Montpelier, VT: Vermont Historical Society.

Stommel, H., & Stommel, E. (1979). *Volcano weather: The story of 1816, the year without a summer*. Newport, RI: Seven Seas Press.

Palmyra & Manchester

Porter, L. C. (1971). *A study of the origins of The Church of Jesus Christ of Latter-day Saints in the states of New York and Pennsylvania, 1816–1831*. Ph.D. dissertation, Brigham Young University, Provo, UT.

Turner, O. (1851). *History of the pioneer settlement of Phelps and Gorham's purchase, and Morris' reserve*. Rochester, NY: William Alling. Retrieved April 15, 2012, from http://books.google.com/books?id=TUX698v8KGkC

The Spiritual Environment of the Restoration

Allen, I. M. (1833, 1836). *Baptist triennial register*. Philadelphia: T. W. Ustick. Retrieved April 20, 2012, from http://archive.org/details/unitedstatesbapt00alle, http://archive.org/details/baptisttriennial00sln

Allen, R. (1911). *A century of the Genesee annual conference of the Methodist Episcopal Church, 1810–1910*. Rochester, NY: the author. Retrieved April 15, 2012, from http://books.google.com/books?id=sWbUAAAAMAAJ

Asplund, J. (1794). *The universal register of the Baptist denomination in North America*. Boston: John W. Folsom. Retrieved April 21, 2012, from http://books.google.com/books?id=zM4CAAAAQAAJ

Butler, J. (1992). *Awash in a sea of faith: Christianizing the American people*. Cambridge, MA: Harvard University Press.

Cross, W. R. (1950). *The burned-over district: The social and intellectual history of enthusiastic religion in western New York, 1800–1850*. Ithaca, NY: Cornell University Press.

Gaustad, E. S., & Barlow, P. L. (2001). *New historical atlas of religion in America*. New York: Oxford University Press.

Hotchkin, J. H. (1848). *A history of the purchase and settlement of western New York and of the rise, progress, and present state of the Presbyterian Church in that section*. New York: M. W. Dodd. Retrieved April 15, 2012, from http://books.google.com/books?id=zQ5KAAAAMAAJ

Howe, D. W. (2007). *What hath God wrought: The transformation of America, 1815–1848*. New York: Oxford University Press.

Methodist Episcopal Church (1840). *Minutes of the annual conferences of the Methodist Episcopal Church, for the years 1773–1881*. New York: Mason & Lane. Retrieved April 15, 2012, from http://books.google.com/books?id=vj4mAQAAIAAJ

Noll, M. A. (2002). *America's God: From Jonathan Edwards to Abraham Lincoln*. New York: Oxford University Press.

Presbyterian Church in the U.S.A. (1808). *Minutes of the general assembly of the Presbyterian Church in the U.S.A.* Philadelphia: Thomas & William Bradford. Retrieved April 15, 2012, from http://books.google.com/books?id=BmbUAAAAMAAJ

Wigger, J. H. (1998). *Taking heaven by storm: Methodism and the rise of popular Christianity in America*. New York: Oxford University Press.

Cradle of the Restoration

Burr, D. H., & De Witt, S. (1829). *An atlas of the state of New York: Containing a map of the state and of the several counties, projected and drawn by a uniform scale from documents deposited in the public offices of the state and other original & authentic information, under the superintendence & direction of Simeon DeWitt, surveyor general, pursuant to an act of the legislature and also the physical geography of the state & of the several counties & statistical tables of the same*. New York: Rawdon, Clark & Co., Rawdon, Wright & Co. Retrieved April 15, 2012, from http://www.davidrumsey.com/luna/servlet/s/6xovp9

Bushman, R. L. (1984). *Joseph Smith and the beginnings of Mormonism*. Urbana: University of Illinois Press.

Largey, D. L. (Ed.). (2003). *Book of Mormon reference companion*. Salt Lake City: Deseret Book.

Porter, L. C. (1971). *A study of the origins of The Church of Jesus Christ of Latter-day Saints in the states of New York and Pennsylvania, 1816–1831*. Ph.D. dissertation, Brigham Young University, Provo, UT.

Turley, R. E., & Slaughter, W. W. (2011). *How we got the Book of Mormon*. Salt Lake City: Deseret Book.

Vance, D. H. (cartographer). (1825). *Map of the western part of the state of New York*. Albany, NY: John Ogden Dey. Retrieved April 7, 2012, from http://www.davidrumsey.com/luna/servlet/s/8unqy8

Latter-day Scriptures

Flake, C. J., & Draper, L. W. (Eds.). (2004). *A Mormon bibliography, 1830–1930* (2nd ed.). Provo, UT: Religious Studies Center, Brigham Young University.

Largey, D. L. (Ed.). (2003). *Book of Mormon reference companion*. Salt Lake City: Deseret Book.

Skousen, R. (2004). *Analysis of textual variants of the Book of Mormon* (6 vols.). Provo, UT: Foundation for Ancient Research and Mormon Studies.

Staker, M. (2009). *Hearken, O ye people: The historical setting for Joseph Smith's Ohio revelations*. Salt Lake City: Greg Kofford Books.

Turley, R. E., Jr., & Slaughter, W. W. (2011). *How we got the Book of Mormon*. Salt Lake City: Deseret Book.

Woodford, R. J. (1984). The doctrine and covenants: A historical overview. In R. L. Millet & K. P. Jackson (Eds.), *Studies in scripture: The doctrine and covenants* (pp. 3–22). Sandy, UT: Randall Book Co.

The First Year of The Church of Christ

Bushman, R. L. (1984). *Joseph Smith and the beginnings of Mormonism*. Urbana: University of Illinois Press.

Porter, L. C. (1971). *A study of the origins of The Church of Jesus Christ of Latter-day Saints in the states of New York and Pennsylvania, 1816–1831*. Ph.D. dissertation, Brigham Young University, Provo, UT.

Romig, R. E. (1994). The Lamanite mission. *John Whitmer Historical Association Journal, 14*, 25–33.

Williams, R. S. (1969). *The missionary movements of the LDS Church in New England, 1830–1850*. Master's thesis, Brigham Young University, Provo, UT. Retrieved from http://contentdm.lib.byu.edu/cdm/ref/collection/MTNZ/id/31071

The Travels of Joseph Smith Jr.

Conkling, J. C. (1979). *A Joseph Smith Chronology*. Salt Lake City: Deseret Book Company.

Smith, J., Jr. (2008). *Journals*. Published as D. C. Jessee, M. Ashurst-McGee & R. L. Jensen (Eds.). *The Joseph Smith papers* (2 vols.). Salt Lake City: Church Historian's Press.

The Western Reserve

Anderson, K. R. (1989). *Joseph Smith's Kirtland: Eyewitness accounts*. Salt Lake City: Deseret Book.

Backman, M. V. (1983). *The heavens resound : A history of the Latter-day Saints in Ohio, 1830–1838*. Salt Lake City: Desert Book.

Cowdery, O. (Ed.). (1834–37). *The Latter Day Saints' messenger and advocate* (3 vols.). Kirtland, OH: F. G. Williams & Co. Retrieved 2012 from http://lib.byu.edu/digital/mpntc/az/L.php#latter-advocate (transcription at http://www.centerplace.org/history/ma/)

Phelps, W. W. (Ed.). (1832–1834). *The evening and morning star* (2 Volumes). Independence, MO: W. W. Phelps & Co. Retrieved 2012 from http://contentdm.lib.byu.edu/cdm/ref/collection/NCMP1820-1846/id/5919 (transcription at http://www.centerplace.org/history/ems/).

Romig, R. E. (1994). The Lamanite mission. *John Whitmer Historical Association Journal, 14*, 25–33.

Savory, W., & Sumner, W. (cartographers). (1833). *Map of the western reserve, including the fire lands of Ohio*. Nelson, OH: Allen Taylor. Retrieved 2012, from http://www.davidrumsey.com/luna/servlet/s/fl895p

Staker, M. (2009). *Hearken, O ye people: The historical setting for Joseph Smith's Ohio revelations*. Salt Lake City: Greg Kofford Books.

Kirtland, Ohio

Anderson, K. R. (1989). *Joseph Smith's Kirtland: Eyewitness accounts*. Salt Lake City, Utah: Deseret Book.

Backman, M. V. Jr. (1983). *The heavens resound: A history of the Latter-day Saints in Ohio, 1830–1838*. Salt Lake City: Desert Book.

Beals, W. W. (cartographer). (1837). *A map of Kirtland city*. Kirtland: Geauga County.

Briggs, L. *Transcription of LDS Land Transactions in Kirtland, Ohio*. Church History Library, Salt Lake City.

Geauga County Recorder. (1820–1840). *Deeds*. (Mormon-related records transcribed by Lyle Briggs, in Church History Library). Chardon, OH.

Hill, M. S., Rooker, C. K., & Wimmer, L. T. (1977). The Kirtland economy revisited: A market critique of sectarian economics. *BYU Studies, 17*(4), 389–475. Retrieved April 15, 2012, from https://byustudies.byu.edu/showTitle.aspx?title=5302

Holzapfel, R. N. (1991). *Old Mormon Kirtland and Missouri: Historic photographs and guide*. Santa Ana, CA: Fieldbook Productions.

Layton, R. L. (1971). Kirtland: A perspective on time and place. *BYU Studies, 11*(4), 423–438. Retrieved April 15, 2012, from https://byustudies.byu.edu/showTitle.aspx?title=4975

Staker, M. (2009). *Hearken, O ye people: The historical setting for Joseph Smith's Ohio revelations*. Salt Lake City: Greg Kofford Books.

The Settlement of Zion

Cannon, D. Q., & Cook, L. W. (1983). *Far West record*. Salt Lake City: Deseret Book.

Garr, A. K., & Johnson, C. V. (Eds.). (1994). *Regional studies in Latter-day Saint Church history: Missouri*. Provo, UT: Brigham Young University Department of Church History and Doctrine.

Holzapfel, R. N. (1991). *Old Mormon Kirtland and Missouri: Historic photographs and guide*. Santa Ana, CA: Fieldbook Productions.

Johnson, C. V. (1992). *Mormon redress petitions: Documents of the 1833–1838 Missouri conflict*. Provo, Utah: Religious Studies Center, Brigham Young University. Retrieved April 15, 2012, from http://contentdm.lib.byu.edu/cdm/ref/collection/rsc/id/44782

Ouellette, R. D. (2005). Zion's gallows: The cultural geography of the Mormon temple lot site. *John Whitmer Historical Association Journal, 25*, 161–174.

Parkin, M. H., & Berrett, L. C. (2004). *Sacred places: Missouri*. Salt Lake City: Deseret Book.

Phelps, W. W. (Ed.). (1832–1834). *The evening and morning star* (2 vols.). Independence, MO: W. W. Phelps & Co. Retrieved 2012, from http://contentdm.lib.byu.edu/cdm/ref/collection/NCMP1820-1846/id/5919 (transcription at http://www.centerplace.org/history/ems/)

Porter, L. C., & Romig, R. E. (2007). The prairie branch, Jackson County, Missouri. *Mormon Historical Studies, 8*(1–2), 1–36. Retrieved April 15, 2012, from http://mormonhistoricsitesfoundation.org/publications/studies_2007/2007.htm

Union Historical Company. (1881). *The history of Jackson County, Missouri*. Kansas City: Birsall, Williams & Co.

The Church in the Kirtland-Missouri Era

Cowdery, O. (Ed.). (1834–37). *The Latter Day Saints' messenger and advocate* (3 vols.). Kirtland, OH: F. G. Williams & Co. Retrieved 2012, from http://lib.byu.edu/digital/mpntc/az/L.php#latter-advocate (transcription at http://www.centerplace.org/history/ma/)

Crawford, M. A. (2007). *Branches of The Church of Jesus Christ of Latter-day Saints, 1830–1834*. Master's thesis, Brigham Young University, Provo, UT.

Phelps, W. W. (Ed.). (1832–1834). *The evening and morning star* (2 vols.). Independence, MO: W. W. Phelps & Co. Retrieved 2012 from http://contentdm.lib.byu.edu/cdm/ref/collection/NCMP1820-1846/id/5919 (transcription at http://www.centerplace.org/history/ems/)

Platt, L. D. (1991). Early branches of The Church of Jesus Christ of Latter-day Saints 1830–1850. *Nauvoo Journal, 3*(1), 3–50. Retrieved April 15, 2012, from http://mormonhistoricsitesfoundation.org/publications/nj_1991/1991.htm

Travel Between Ohio and Missouri

Baugh, A. L. (2005). Joseph Smith and Zion's Camp. *Ensign, 35*(6), 42–47.

Darowski, J. F. (2010). Seeking after the ancient order: Conferences and councils in early Church governance. *Mormon Historical Studies, 11*(1), 27–39.

Hunter, L. C. (1969). *Steamboats on the western rivers: An economic and technological history*. New York: Octagon Books.

Jenson, A. (1888). Kirtland camp. *The Historical Record, 7*(7), 593–603. Retrieved April 15, 2012, from http://archive.org/stream/historicalrecord01jens#page/592/mode/2up

Launius, R. D. (1984). *Zion's Camp: Expedition to Missouri, 1834*. Independence, MO: Herald House.

Manscill, C. K. (2000). "Journal of the branch of the Church in Pontiac, 1834": Hyrum Smith's division of Zion's Camp. *BYU Studies, 39*(1), 167–188. Retrieved April 15, 2012, from https://byustudies.byu.edu/showTitle.aspx?title=6637

Murdock, J. (1830–1867). *Journal and autobiography*. L. Tom Perry Special Collections, BYU Harold B. Lee Library. Provo, UT.

Parkin, M. H., & Berrett, L. C. (2004). *Sacred places: Missouri*. Salt Lake City: Deseret Book.

Quinn, D. M. (1994). *The Mormon hierarchy: Origins of power*. Salt Lake City: Signature Books & Smith Research Associates.

Romig, R. E. (1994). The Lamanite mission. *John Whitmer Historical Association Journal,* 14, 25–33.

Early Missions

Baumgarten, J. N. (1960). *The role and function of the Seventies in LDS Church history*. Master's thesis, Brigham Young University, Provo, UT. Retrieved from http://contentdm.lib.byu.edu/cdm/ref/collection/MTAF/id/15545

Bitton, D. (1971). Kirtland as a center of missionary activity. *BYU Studies,* 11(4), 497–516. Retrieved April 15, 2012, from https://byustudies.byu.edu/showTitle.aspx?title=4978

Brannon, S., & Pratt, P. P. (Ed.). (1844–1845). *The prophet/the New York messenger* (2 vols.). New York City: Samuel Brannan.

British Mission (1840–1970). *Latter-day Saints' millennial star* (132 vols.). Manchester, Liverpool, and London, England: British Mission. Retrieved April 21, 2012, from http://lib.byu.edu/digital/mpntc/az/M.php#latter-star

Cowdery, O. (Ed.). (1834–37). *The Latter Day Saints' messenger and advocate* (3 vols.). Kirtland, OH: F. G. Williams & Co. Retrieved 2012 from http://lib.byu.edu/digital/mpntc/az/L.php#latter-advocate (transcription at http://www.centerplace.org/history/ma/)

Ellsworth, S. G. (1951). *A history of Mormon missions in the United States and Canada, 1830–1860*. Ph.D. dissertation, University of California, Berkeley.

Ellsworth, S. G. (Ed.). (1990). *The journals of Addison Pratt*. Salt Lake City: University of Utah Press.

Irving, G. (1975). Numerical strength and geographical distribution of the LDS missionary force, 1830–1974. *Vol. 1. Task Papers in LDS History.* Salt Lake City: Historical Department, Church of Jesus Christ of Latter-day Saints.

McFarlane, B. (1961). *The role of preaching in the early Mormon Church, 1830–1846*. Ph.D. dissertation, University of Missouri, Columbia.

Robinson, E., & Smith, D. C. (Ed.). (1839–1846). *Times and seasons* (6 Volumes). Nauvoo, IL: Robinson & Smith. Retrieved 2012 from http://lib.byu.edu/digital/mpntc/az/T.php#times-seasons (transcription at http://www.centerplace.org/history/ts/)

Smith, G. A. (1869). *Rise, progress and travels of The Church of Jesus Christ of Latter-day Saints*. Salt Lake City: Deseret News. Retrieved April 15, 2012, from http://books.google.com/books?id=pFhNAAAAYAAJ

Whittaker, D. J. (2000). Mormon missiology: An introduction and guide to the sources. In S. D. Ricks, D. W. Parry & A. H. Hedges (Eds.), *The disciple as witness: Essays on Latter-day Saint history and doctrine in honor of Richard Lloyd Anderson* (pp. 459–538). Provo, UT: Foundation for Ancient Research and Mormon Studies.

Williams, R. S. (1969). *The missionary movements of the LDS Church in New England, 1830–1850*. Master's thesis, Brigham Young University, Provo, UT. Retrieved from http://contentdm.lib.byu.edu/cdm/ref/collection/MTNZ/id/31071

Woodruff, W. (1983). *Journal*. Published as S. G. Kenney (Ed.). *Wilford Woodruff's journal, 1833–1898 Typescript*. Midvale, UT: Signature Books.

The City of Zion Plat

Baum, J. H. (1967). *Geographical characteristics of early Mormon settlements*. Master's thesis, Brigham Young University, Provo, UT. Retrieved from http://contentdm.lib.byu.edu/cdm/ref/collection/MTAF/id/15544

Bushman, J. K. (1997). *Prophets, planning, and politics: Utah's planning heritage and its significance today and tomorrow*. Master's thesis, Brigham Young University, Provo, UT. Retrieved from http://contentdm.lib.byu.edu/cdm/ref/collection/MTAF/id/15590

Bushman, R. L. (1997). *Making space for the Mormons: Ideas of sacred geography in Joseph Smith's America*. Logan, UT: Utah State University Press.

Jackson, R. H. (1976). The Mormon village: Analysis of a settlement type. *Professional Geographer,* 28(2), 136–141.

Jackson, R. H. (1993). Sacred space and city planning: The Mormon example. *Architecture et Comportement/Architecture and Behaviour,* 9(2), 251–259. Retrieved April 19, 2012, from http://lasur.epfl.ch/files/content/sites/lasur/files/A&C%20Vol.9%20No.2/JACKSON.pdf

Unknown. (1838). *Plat map of Far West, Missouri*. Vault MSS 303, L. Tom Perry Special Collections. Harold B. Lee Library, Brigham Young University, Provo, UT.

Williams, F. G. (cartographer). (1833). *Plat of the city of Zion*. Kirtland, OH. Retrieved April 15, 2012, from http://contentdm.lib.byu.edu/cdm/ref/collection/RelEd/id/5665

The Twelve Apostles

Allen, J. B., Esplin, R. K., & Whittaker, D. J. (1992). *Men with a mission: the Quorum of the Twelve Apostles in the British Isles, 1837–41*. Salt Lake City: Deseret Book.

British Mission (1840–1970). *Latter-day Saints' millennial star* (132 vols.). Manchester, Liverpool, and London, England: British Mission. Retrieved April 21, 2012, from http://lib.byu.edu/digital/mpntc/az/M.php#latter-star

Ellsworth, S. G. (1951). *A history of Mormon missions in the United States and Canada, 1830–1860*. Ph.D. dissertation, University of California, Berkeley.

Esplin, R. K. (1981). *The emergence of Brigham Young and the Twelve to Mormon leadership, 1830–1841*. Ph.D. dissertation, Brigham Young University, Provo, UT.

Esplin, R. K. (1996). Brigham Young and the transformation of the "first" Quorum of the Twelve. In S. E. Black & L. C. Porter (Eds.), *Lion of the Lord, essays on the life and service of Brigham Young*. Salt Lake City: Deseret Book.

Settling Northern Missouri

Baugh, A. L. (2000). *A call to arms: The 1838 Mormon defense of northern Missouri*. Provo, UT: Joseph Fielding Smith Institute for Latter-day Saint History; BYU Studies.

Cannon, D. Q., & Cook, L. W. (1983). *Far West record*. Salt Lake City: Deseret Book.

Garr, A. K., & Johnson, C. V. (Eds.). (1994). *Regional studies in Latter-day Saint Church history: Missouri*. Provo, UT: Brigham Young University Department of Church History and Doctrine.

Gentry, L. H. (2000). *A history of the Latter-day Saints in northern Missouri from 1836 to 1839*. Provo, UT: Joseph Fielding Smith Institute for Latter-day Saint History; BYU Studies.

Hamer, J. (2004). *Northeast of Eden: A historical atlas of Missouri's Mormon country*. Mirabile, MO: Far West Cultural Center.

Holzapfel, R. N. (1991). *Old Mormon Kirtland and Missouri: Historic photographs and guide*. Santa Ana, CA: Fieldbook Productions.

Johnson, C. V., & Romig, R. E. (2005). *An index to early Caldwell County, Missouri land records* (revised ed.). Independence, MO: Missouri Mormon Frontier Foundation.

Lewis, W. J. (1981). *Mormon land ownership as a factor in evaluating the extent of Mormon settlements and influence in Missouri 1831–1841*. Master's thesis, Brigham Young University, Provo, UT. Retrieved from http://contentdm.lib.byu.edu/cdm/ref/collection/MTGM/id/23529

Parkin, M. H., & Berrett, L. C. (2004). *Sacred places: Missouri*. Salt Lake City: Deseret Book.

The Mormon-Missouri War

Baugh, A. L. (2000). *A call to arms: The 1838 Mormon defense of northern Missouri*. Provo, UT: Joseph Fielding Smith Institute for Latter-day Saint History; BYU Studies.

Garr, A. K., & Johnson, C. V. (Eds.). (1994). *Regional studies in Latter-day Saint Church history: Missouri*. Provo, UT: Brigham Young University Department of Church History and Doctrine.

Gentry, L. H. (2000). *A history of the Latter-day Saints in northern Missouri from 1836 to 1839*. Provo, UT: Joseph Fielding Smith Institute for Latter-day Saint History; BYU Studies.

Hartley, W. G. (2001). Missouri's 1838 extermination order and the Mormons' forced removal to Illinois. *Mormon Historical Studies,* 2(1), 5–27. Retrieved April 21, 2012, from http://mormonhistoricsitesfoundation.org/publications/studies_spring_01/spring_01.htm

Johnson, C. V. (1992). *Mormon redress petitions: Documents of the 1833–1838 Missouri conflict*. Provo, Utah: Religious Studies Center, Brigham Young University. Retrieved April 15, 2012, from http://contentdm.lib.byu.edu/cdm/ref/collection/rsc/id/44782

LeSueur, S. C. (1987). *The 1838 Mormon war in Missouri*. Columbia: University of Missouri Press.

LeSueur, S. C. (2004). The Mormon experience in Missouri. In N. G. Bringhurst & L. F. Anderson (Eds.), *Excavating Mormon pasts: The new historiography of the last half century* (pp. 87–112). Salt Lake City: Greg Kofford Books.

Parkin, M. H., & Berrett, L. C. (2004). *Sacred places: Missouri*. Salt Lake City: Deseret Book.

Pratt, P. P. (1839). *History of the late persecution inflicted by the state of Missouri upon the Mormons, in which ten thousand American citizens were robbed, plundered, and driven from the state, and many others imprisoned, martyred, &c. for their religion, and all this by military force, by order of the executive*. Detroit, MI: Dawson & Bates, Printers. Retrieved April 15, 2012, from http://archive.org/details/historyoflateperooprat

Commerce, Illinois

Cannon, J. R. (1991). *Nauvoo panorama: Views of Nauvoo before, during, and after its rise, fall, and restoration*. Nauvoo, IL: Nauvoo Restoration Inc.

Cook, L. W. (1979). Isaac Galland: Mormon benefactor. *BYU Studies,* 19(3), 261–284. Retrieved April 15, 2012, from https://byustudies.byu.edu/showTitle.aspx?title=5376

General Land Office. (1816). *Public lands survey plats, Illinois*. Illinois State Archives. Retrieved April 20, 2012, from http://landplats.ilsos.net/

General Land Office. (1816–1840). *Land patents, Hancock County, Illinois*. Bureau of Land Management. Retrieved April 20, 2012, from http://glorecords.blm.gov/

General Land Office. (1836–1852). *Public lands survey plats, Iowa*. Iowa Geographic Map Server. Retrieved April 20, 2012, from http://ortho.gis.iastate.edu/

Hancock County Recorder's Office. (1830–1850). *Deeds*. Carthage, IL.

Hancock County Recorder's Office. (1830–1850). *Plats*. Carthage, IL.

Leonard, G. M. (2002). *Nauvoo: A place of peace, a people of promise*. Salt Lake City: Deseret Book.

Miller, D. E., & Miller, D. S. (1974). *Nauvoo: The city of Joseph*. Bountiful, UT: Utah History Atlas.

Buying Nauvoo

Cook, L. W. (1979). Isaac Galland: Mormon benefactor. *BYU Studies,* 19(3), 261–284. Retrieved April 15, 2012, from https://byustudies.byu.edu/showTitle.aspx?title=5376

Hancock County Recorder's Office. (1830–1850). *Deeds.* Carthage, IL.

Hancock County Recorder's Office. (1830–1850). *Plats.* Carthage, IL.

Leonard, G. M. (2002). *Nauvoo: A place of peace, a people of promise.* Salt Lake City: Deseret Book.

Building Nauvoo

Cannon, J. R. (1991). *Nauvoo panorama: Views of Nauvoo before, during, and after its rise, fall, and restoration.* Nauvoo, IL: Nauvoo Restoration Inc.

Colvin, D. F. (2002). *Nauvoo temple: A story of faith.* Salt Lake City: Covenant Communications. Retrieved April 15, 2012, from http://contentdm.lib.byu.edu/cdm/ref/collection/rsc/id/13032

Ehat, A. (1982). *Joseph Smith's introduction of temple ordinances and the 1844 Mormon succession question.* Master's thesis, Brigham Young University, Provo, UT.

Leonard, G. M. (2002). *Nauvoo: A place of peace, a people of promise.* Salt Lake City: Deseret Book.

Miller, D. E., & Miller, D. S. (1974). *Nauvoo: The city of Joseph.* Bountiful, UT: Utah History Atlas.

Greater Nauvoo Region

Esplin, R. K. (1981). *The emergence of Brigham Young and the Twelve to Mormon leadership, 1830–1841.* Ph.D. dissertation, Brigham Young University, Provo, UT.

Esplin, R. K. (1996). Brigham Young and the transformation of the "first" Quorum of the Twelve. In S. E. Black & L. C. Porter (Eds.), *Lion of the Lord, essays on the life and service of Brigham Young.* Salt Lake City: Deseret Book.

Hancock County Recorder's Office. (1830–1850). *Deeds.* Carthage, IL.

Hancock County Recorder's Office. (1830–1850). *Plats.* Carthage, IL.

Platt, L. D. (1991). Early branches of The Church of Jesus Christ of Latter-day Saints 1830–1850. *Nauvoo Journal,* 3(1), 3–50. Retrieved April 15, 2012, from http://mormonhistoricsitesfoundation.org/publications/nj_1991/1991.htm

The Church in the Nauvoo Era

British Mission (1840–1970). *Latter-day Saints' millennial star* (132 vols.). Manchester, Liverpool, and London, England: British Mission. Retrieved April 21, 2012, from http://lib.byu.edu/digital/mpntc/az/M.php#latter-star

Platt, L. D. (1991). Early branches of The Church of Jesus Christ of Latter-day Saints 1830–1850. *Nauvoo Journal,* 3(1), 3–50. Retrieved April 15, 2012, from http://mormonhistoricsitesfoundation.org/publications/nj_1991/1991.htm

Robinson, E., & Smith, D. C. (Ed.). (1839–1846). *Times and seasons* (6 vols.). Nauvoo, IL: Robinson & Smith. Retrieved 2012 from http://lib.byu.edu/digital/mpntc/az/T.php#times-seasons (transcription at http://www.centerplace.org/history/ts/)

Conflict in Hancock County

Godfrey, K. W. (2002). *The battle of Nauvoo revisited.* Paper presented at the John Whitmer Historical Association Conference, Nauvoo, Illinois.

Hampshire, A. P. (1982). The triumph of mobocracy in Hancock County, 1844–46. *Western Illinois Regional Studies,* 5(17), 2–37.

Leonard, G. M. (2002). *Nauvoo: A place of peace, a people of promise.* Salt Lake City: Deseret Book.

The Succession Crisis

Bringhurst, N. G., & Hamer, J. (Eds.). (2007). *Scattering of the Saints: Schism within Mormonism.* Independence, MO: John Whitmer Books.

Davis, I. S. (1981). *The story of the Church* (2nd ed.). Independence, MO: Herald House. Retrieved April 15, 2012 from http://www.centerplace.org/history/misc/soc/

Ehat, A. (1982). *Joseph Smith's introduction of temple ordinances and the 1844 Mormon succession question.* Master's thesis, Brigham Young University, Provo, UT.

Entz, G. R. (2001). Zion valley: The Mormon origins of St. John, Kansas. *Kansas History,* 24(2), 98–117. Retrieved April 21, 2012, from http://www.kshs.org/p/kansas-history-summer-2001/12410

Gregory, T. J. (1981). Sidney Rigdon: Post Nauvoo. *BYU Studies,* 21(1), 51–67. Retrieved April 21, 2012, from https://byustudies.byu.edu/showTitle.aspx?title=5450

Jensen, R. S. (2005). *Gleaning the harvest: Strangite missionary work, 1846–1850.* Master's thesis, Brigham Young University, Provo, UT. Retrieved from http://contentdm.lib.byu.edu/cdm/ref/collection/ETD/id/411

Jorgensen, D. L. (1995). Dissent and schism in the early Church: Explaining Mormon fissiparousness. *Dialogue: A Journal of Mormon Thought,* 28(3), 15–39. Retrieved April 15, 2012, from https://www.dialoguejournal.com/wp-content/uploads/sbi/articles/Dialogue_V28N03_29.pdf

Leonard, G. M. (2002). *Nauvoo: A place of peace, a people of promise.* Salt Lake City: Deseret Book.

Norton, W. (2003). Competing identities and contested places: Mormons in Nauvoo and Voree. *Journal of Cultural Geography,* 21(1), 95–119.

Quinn, D. M. (1976). The Mormon succession crisis of 1844. *BYU Studies,* 16(2), 187–234. Retrieved April 15, 2012, from https://byustudies.byu.edu/showtitle.aspx?title=5216

Saunders, R. L. (1989). *Francis Gladden Bishop and Gladdenism: A study in the culture of a Mormon dissenter and his movement.* Master's thesis, Utah State University, Logan. Retrieved from http://scholarship.utm.edu/9/

Shields, S. L. (1990). *Divergent paths of the restoration* (4th ed.). Los Angeles: Restoration Research.

Smith, J., III, & Smith, H. C. (1897). *History of The Church of Jesus Christ of Latter Day Saints* (4 vols.). Lamoni, IA: Board of Publication of the Reorganized Church of Jesus Christ of Latter Day Saints. Retrieved April 15, 2012, from http://galenet.galegroup.com.erl.lib.byu.edu/servlet/Sabin?af=RN&ae=CY105223063&srchtp=a&ste=14 (transcription at http://www.centerplace.org/history/ch/)

Planning the Exodus

Christian, L. C. (1972). *A study of Mormon knowledge of the American far west prior to the exodus.* Master's thesis, Brigham Young University, Provo, UT. Retrieved from http://contentdm.lib.byu.edu/cdm/ref/collection/MTAF/id/24554

Frémont, J. C. (1970). *The expeditions of John Charles Frémont.* Published as D. Jackson & M. L. Spence (Eds.), (3 vols.). Urbana: University of Illinois Press.

Frémont, J. C., & Preuss, C. (1845). *Map of an exploring expedition to the Rocky Mountains in the year 1842 and to Oregon & north California in the years 1843–44.* Washington, D.C.: Blair and Rives. Retrieved April 15, 2012, from http://www.davidrumsey.com/luna/servlet/s/i371s8

Leonard, G. M. (2002). *Nauvoo: A place of peace, a people of promise.* Salt Lake City: Deseret Book.

Mitchell, S. A. (1846). *A new map of Texas, Oregon, and California with the regions adjoining.* Philadelphia, PA: S. A. Mitchell. Retrieved April 15, 2012, from http://www.davidrumsey.com/luna/servlet/s/3da8s6

Section 2: The Empire of Deseret

Alexander, T. G. (2003). *Utah, the right place: The official centennial history* (2nd ed.). Salt Lake City: Gibbs Smith.

Arrington, L. J. (1958). *Great basin kingdom: An economic history of the Latter-day Saints, 1830–1900.* Cambridge, MA: Harvard University Press.

Jackson, R. H. (Ed.). (1978). *The Mormon role in settlement of the West.* Provo, UT: Brigham Young University Press.

Poll, R. D., Alexander, T., Campbell, E. E., & Miller, D. E. (1989). *Utah's history.* Provo, UT: Brigham Young University Press.

Roberts, B. H. (1910). *Comprehensive history of the Church* (6 vols.). Salt Lake City: Deseret News Press.

Various wards, stakes, branches, and missions. (1830–present). *Manuscript histories.* Church History Library, Salt Lake City.

The Exodus Begins

Bagley, W. (1997). *The pioneer camp of the Saints: the 1846 and 1847 Mormon trail journals of Thomas Bullock.* Norman, OK: Arthur H. Clark Co.

Bennett, R. E. (1987). *Mormons at the Missouri 1846–1852.* Norman: University of Oklahoma Press.

Black, S. E., & Hartley, W. G. (Eds.). (1997). *The Iowa Mormon trail.* Orem, UT: Helix Publishing.

Brown, J. (1941). *Autobiography.* Published as J. Z. Brown (Ed.). *Autobiography of pioneer John Brown, 1820–1896.* Salt Lake City: Steven & Wallis.

Bullock, R. H. (2009). *Ship Brooklyn Saints: Their journey and early endeavors in California.* Sandy, UT: the Author.

Crockett, D. R. (1996). *Saints in exile: A day by day pioneer experience, Nauvoo to Council Bluffs.* Tucson, AZ: LDS-Gems Press.

Hartley, W. G. (1993). *My best for the kingdom: History and autobiography of John Lowe Butler, a Mormon frontiersman.* Salt Lake City: Aspen Books.

Leonard, G. M. (2002). *Nauvoo: A place of peace, a people of promise.* Salt Lake City: Deseret Book.

Peterson, B. L. (1941). *A geographic study of the Mormon migration from Nauvoo, Illinois, to the Great Salt Lake Valley (1846–1847).* Master's thesis, University of California, Los Angeles.

The Middle Missouri Valley

Bennett, R. E. (1987). *Mormons at the Missouri 1846–1852.* Norman: University of Oklahoma Press.

General Land Office. (1836–1852). *Public lands survey plats, Iowa.* Iowa Geographic Map Server. Retrieved April 20, 2012, from http://ortho.gis.iastate.edu/

General Land Office. (1853–1855). *Land patents, Iowa.* Bureau of Land Management. Retrieved April 20, 2012, from http://glorecords.blm.gov/

Hyde, O. (Ed.). (1849–1852) *Frontier guardian* (2 vols.). Kanesville, Iowa.

Shumway, E. W. (1953). *History of Winter Quarters, Nebraska, 1846–1848.* Master's thesis, Brigham Young University, Provo, UT. Retrieved from http://contentdm.lib.byu.edu/cdm/ref/collection/MTNZ/id/22809

State of Iowa. (1852). *State census.* Iowa GenWeb Project (transcription). Retrieved April 20, 2012, from http://iagenweb.org/pottawattamie/census-1852.htm

Watt, R. G. (1991). *Iowa branch index: 1839–1859.* Church History Library, Salt Lake City.

The Mormon Battalion

Bigler, H. W. (1963). *Diaries.* Published as E. G. Gudde (Ed.) *Chronicle of the West: the conquest of California, discovery of gold, and Mormon settlement, as reflected in Henry William Bigler's diaries.* Berkeley: University of California Press.

Frazier, D. S. (1998). *The United States and Mexico at war: Nineteenth-century expansionism and conflict.* New York: Simon & Schuster and Prentice Hall International.

Golder, F. A. (1928). *The march of the Mormon Battalion, from Council Bluffs to California: Taken from the journal of Henry Standage.* New York: The Century Company.

Ricketts, N. B. (1996). *The Mormon Battalion: U.S. army of the West, 1846–48.* Logan: Utah State University Press.

Tyler, S. D. (1969). *A concise history of the Mormon Battalion in the Mexican War, 1846–1847.* Glorieta, NM: The Rio Grande Press, Inc.

Pioneer Trails

Aird, P. (2002). Bound for Zion: The ten- and thirteen-pound emigrating companies, 1853–54. *Utah Historical Quarterly,* 70(4), 300–325. Retrieved April 19, 2012, from http://utah.ptfs.com/awweb/guest.jsp?smd=1&cl=all_lib&lb_document_id=11930

Bagley, W. (1997). *The pioneer camp of the Saints: The 1846 and 1847 Mormon trail journals of Thomas Bullock.* Norman, OK: Arthur H. Clark Co.

Church History Library. (2008). Mormon pioneer overland travel, 1847–1868. *Church History.* Retrieved April 15, 2012, from http://lds.org/churchhistory/library/pioneercompanysearch/

Hulmston, J. K. (1990). Mormon immigration in the 1860s: The story of the Church trains. *Utah Historical Quarterly,* 58(1), 32–48. Retrieved April 19, 2012, from http://utah.ptfs.com/awweb/guest.jsp?smd=1&cl=all_lib&lb_document_id=35221

Jackson, R. H. (1978). The overland journey to Zion. In R. H. Jackson (Ed.), *The Mormon role in the settlement of the West.* (vol. 9, pp. 1–27). Provo, UT: Brigham Young University Press.

Kimball, S. B. (1988). *Historic sites and markers along the Mormon and other western trails.* Urbana: University of Illinois Press.

Kimball, S. B. (1997). *Mormon trail 1997 official guide: The Mormon pioneer trail.* Layton, UT: Mormon Trail Association, Gibbs Smith Publishers.

Peterson, B. L. (1941). *A geographic study of the Mormon migration from Nauvoo, Illinois, to the Great Salt Lake Valley (1846–1847).* Master's thesis, University of California, Los Angeles.

Settling the Salt Lake Valley

Boyce, R. R. (1957). *An historical geography of greater Salt Lake City, Utah.* Master's thesis, University of Utah, Salt Lake City.

General Land Office. (1856). *Public lands survey plats, Utah.* Utah State Office, Bureau of Land Management. Retrieved April 20, 2012, from http://www.ut.blm.gov/LandRecords/Land_Records.html

Jackson, R. H. (1978). Mormon perception and settlement. *Annals of the Association of American Geographers,* 68(3), 317–334.

Jackson, R. H. (1992). The Mormon experience: The plains as Sinai, the Great Salt Lake as the Dead Sea, and the Great Basin as Desert-cum-Promised Land. *Journal of Historical Geography,* 18(1), 41–58.

Jackson, R. H. (1993). Sacred space and city planning: The Mormon example. *Architecture et Comportement/Architecture and Behaviour,* 9(2), 251–259. Retrieved April 19, 2012, from http://lasur.epfl.ch/files/content/sites/lasur/files/A&C%20Vol.9%20No.2/JACKSON.pdf

Jackson, R. H. (1994). Geography and settlement in the Intermountain West: Creating an American Mecca. *Journal of the West,* 33(3), 22–34.

Koch, A. (cartographer). (1870). *Bird's eye view of Salt Lake City, Utah Territory, 1870.* Chicago: Chicago Lithographers Co. Retrieved April 21, 2012, from http://memory.loc.gov/cgi-bin/query/D?gmd:6:./temp/~ammem_Wut6::@@@mdb

Mitchell, M. (1997). Gentile impressions of Salt Lake City, Utah, 1849–1870. *Geographical Review,* 87(3), 334–352.

Salt Lake County Recorder. (1852–1888). *Plat records.* Family History Library, Salt Lake City.

Seeman, A. L. (1938). Communities in the Salt Lake Basin. *Economic Geography,* 14(3), 300–308. Retrieved April 23, 2012, from http://www.jstor.org/stable/141347

Speth, W. W. (1967). Environment, culture and the Mormon in early Utah: A study in cultural adaptation. *Yearbook of the Association of Pacific Coast Geographers,* 29, 53–67. Retrieved April 18, 2012, from http://pao.chadwyck.com.erl.lib.byu.edu/articles/displayItem.do?QueryType=articles&QueryIndex=journal&ItemNumber=4&QueryType=journals|ItemID=v070|issue=29%20(1967)

Exploring Utah

Frémont, J. C. (1970). *The expeditions of John Charles Fremont.* Published as D. Jackson & M. L. Spence (Eds.), (3 vols.). Urbana: University of Illinois Press.

Goetzmann, W. H. (1966). *Exploration and empire: The explorer and the scientist in the winning of the American West* (1st ed.). New York: Knopf.

Rogers, J. S. (2005). "One vast contiguity of waste": Documents from an early attempt to expand the Mormon kingdom into the Uinta Basin, 1861. *Utah Historical Quarterly,* 73(3), 249–264. Retrieved April 21, 2012, from http://utah.ptfs.com/awweb/guest.jsp?smd=1&cl=all_lib&lb_document_id=11944

Smart, W. B., & Smart, D. T. (1999). *Over the rim: The Parley P. Pratt exploring expedition to southern Utah, 1849–1850.* Logan: Utah State University Press.

Stansbury, H. (1852). *An expedition to the valley of the Great Salt Lake of Utah.* Philadelphia: Lippincott, Grambo, & Co. Retrieved April 15, 2012, from http://books.google.com/books?id=D3dCAAAAcAAJ

Stott, C. L. (1984). *Search for sanctuary: Brigham Young and the White Mountain expedition.* Salt Lake City: University of Utah Press.

U.S. War Department. (1855). *Reports of explorations and surveys, to ascertain the most practicable and economical route for a railroad from the Mississippi River to the Pacific Ocean, made under the direction of the secretary of war, in 1853–4* (Vol. 2). Washington D.C.: U.S. War Department. Retrieved April 20, 2012, from http://memory.loc.gov/ammem/ndlpcoop/moahtml/afk4383.html

Settling the Wasatch Front

General Land Office. (1856). *Public lands survey plats, Utah.* Utah State Office, Bureau of Land Management. Retrieved April 20, 2012, from http://www.ut.blm.gov/LandRecords/Land_Records.html

Griffin, R. D. (1965). *The Wasatch Front in 1869: A geographical description.* Master's thesis, Brigham Young University, Provo, UT. Retrieved from http://contentdm.lib.byu.edu/cdm/ref/collection/MTGM/id/3325

Harper, K. C. (1974). *The Mormon role in irrigation beginnings and diffusions in the western states: An historical geography.* Master's thesis, Brigham Young University, Provo, UT. Retrieved from http://contentdm.lib.byu.edu/cdm/ref/collection/MTGM/id/13964

Hunter, M. R. (1945). *Brigham Young the colonizer* (3rd ed.). Independence, MO: Zion's Printing & Publishing Company. Retrieved April 15, 2012, from http://books.google.com/books?id=OFerCXMR_JoC (incomplete)

Seeman, A. L. (1938). Communities in the Salt Lake Basin. *Economic Geography,* 14(3), 300–308. Retrieved April 23, 2012, from http://www.jstor.org/stable/141347

White, C. L. (1925). *The agricultural geography of the Salt Lake oasis.* Ph.D. dissertation, Clark University, Worcester, MA.

White, C. L. (1928). Distribution of population in the Salt Lake oasis. *Journal of Geography,* 27(1), 1–14.

President Brigham Young

Arrington, L. J. (1985). *Brigham Young: American Moses.* New York: Alfred A. Knopf.

Arrington, L. J., & Esplin, R. K. (1977). Building a commonwealth: The secular leadership of Brigham Young. *Utah Historical Quarterly,* 45(3), 216–232. Retrieved April 19, 2012, from http://utah.ptfs.com/awweb/guest.jsp?smd=1&cl=all_lib&lb_document_id=34924

Church Historian's Office. (1844–1879). *Journal.* Church History Library, Salt Lake City.

Irving, G. (1977). Encouraging the Saints: Brigham Young's annual tours of the Mormon settlements. *Utah Historical Quarterly,* 45(3), 233–251. Retrieved April 19, 2012, from http://utah.ptfs.com/awweb/guest.jsp?smd=1&cl=all_lib&lb_document_id=34924

Deseret and Utah Territory

Leonard, G. M. (1992). The Mormon boundary question in the 1849–50 statehood debates. *Journal of Mormon History,* 18(1), 114–136. Retrieved April 15, 2012, from http://digitalcommons.usu.edu/mormonhistory/vol18/iss1/1

Lyman, E. L. (1986). *Political deliverance: The Mormon quest for Utah statehood.* Urbana: University of Illinois Press.

MacKinnon, W. P. (2003). "Like splitting a man up his backbone": The territorial dismemberment of Utah, 1850–1896. *Utah Historical Quarterly,* 71(2), 100–124. Retrieved April 19, 2012, from http://utah.ptfs.com/awweb/guest.jsp?smd=1&cl=all_lib&lb_document_id=35439

Madsen, M. H. (1999). *The Mormon influence on the political geography of the West.* Master's thesis, Brigham Young University, Provo, UT. Retrieved from http://contentdm.lib.byu.edu/cdm/ref/collection/MTGM/id/33224

Meinig, D. W. (1996). The Mormon nation and the American empire. *Journal of Mormon History,* 22(1), 33–51. Retrieved April 15, 2012, from http://digitalcommons.usu.edu/mormonhistory/vol22/iss1/1

U.S. Congress. (1849–1872). *Bills and resolutions.* Washington, D.C.: Government Printing Office. Retrieved April 22, 2012, from http://memory.loc.gov/ammem/amlaw/lwhbsb.html

U.S. House of Representatives (1849–1872). *House journal.* Washington, D.C.: Government Printing Office. Retrieved April 22, 2012, from http://memory.loc.gov/ammem/amlaw/lwhj.html

U.S. Senate (1849–1872). *Senate journal.* Washington, D.C.: Government Printing Office. Retrieved April 22, 2012, from http://memory.loc.gov/ammem/amlaw/lwsj.html

Missions of the 19th Century

Ellsworth, S. G. (1951). *A history of Mormon missions in the United States and Canada, 1830–1860.* Ph.D. dissertation, University of California, Berkeley.

Irving, G. (1975). Numerical strength and geographical distribution of the LDS missionary force, 1830–1974. *Vol. 1. Task Papers in LDS History.* Salt Lake City: Historical Department, Church of Jesus Christ of Latter-day Saints.

Price, R. T., Jr. (1991). *The Mormon missionary of the nineteenth century.* Ph.D. dissertation, University of Wisconsin, Madison.

Whittaker, D. J. (1995). Brigham Young and the missionary enterprise. In S. E. Black & L. C. Porter

(Eds.), *Lion of the Lord: Essays on the life and service of Brigham Young* (pp. 85–106). Salt Lake City: Deseret Book.

Whittaker, D. J. (2000). Mormon missiology: An introduction and guide to the sources. In S. D. Ricks, D. W. Parry & A. H. Hedges (Eds.), *The disciple as witness: Essays on Latter-day Saint history and doctrine in honor of Richard Lloyd Anderson* (pp. 459–538). Provo, UT: Foundation for Ancient Research and Mormon Studies.

Intermountain Colonization

Arrington, L. J. (1985). *Brigham Young: American Moses.* New York: Alfred A. Knopf.

Baum, J. H. (1967). *Geographical characteristics of early Mormon settlements.* Master's thesis, Brigham Young University, Provo, UT. Retrieved from http://contentdm.lib.byu.edu/cdm/ref/collection/MTAF/id/15544

Bennion, L. C. (1995). Meinig's "Mormon culture region" revisited. *Historical Geography,* 24(1 & 2), 22–33.

Hunter, M. R. (1945). *Brigham Young the colonizer* (3rd ed.). Independence, MO: Zion's Printing & Publishing Company. Retrieved April 15, 2012, from http://books.google.com/books?id=OFerCXMR_JoC (incomplete)

Jackson, R. H. (1978). Mormon perception and settlement. *Annals of the Association of American Geographers,* 68(3), 317–334.

Jackson, R. H. (1981). Utah's harsh lands, hearth of greatness. *Utah Historical Quarterly,* 49(1), 4–25. Retrieved April 19, 2012, from http://utah.ptfs.com/awweb/guest.jsp?smd=1&cl=all_lib&lb_document_id=35439

Jackson, R. W. (2003). *Places of worship: 150 years of Latter-day Saint architecture.* Provo, UT: Religious Studies Center, Brigham Young University. Retrieved April 15, 2012, from http://contentdm.lib.byu.edu/cdm/ref/collection/rsc/id/53490

Lehr, J. C. (1972). Mormon settlement morphology in southern Alberta. *Albertan Geographer,* 8, 6–13.

Meinig, D. W. (1965). The Mormon culture region: Strategies and patterns in the geography of the American West, 1847–1964. *Annals of the Association of American Geographers,* 55(2), 191–220.

Wilcox, A. G. (1950). *Founding of the Mormon community in Alberta.* Master's thesis, University of Alberta, Calgary.

Mormon-Indian Relations

Christy, H. A. (1978). Open hand and mailed fist: Mormon-Indian relations in Utah, 1847–1852. *Utah Historical Quarterly,* 46(3), 216–235. Retrieved April 19, 2012, from http://utah.ptfs.com/awweb/guest.jsp?smd=1&cl=all_lib&lb_document_id=34973

Christy, H. A. (1979). The Walker War: Defense and conciliation as strategy. *Utah Historical Quarterly,* 47(4), 395–420. Retrieved April 19, 2012, from http://utah.ptfs.com/awweb/guest.jsp?smd=1&cl=all_lib&lb_document_id=34978

Christy, H. A. (1991). "What virtue there is in stone" and other pungent talk on the early Utah frontier. *Utah Historical Quarterly,* 59(3), 300–319. Retrieved April 19, 2012, from http://utah.ptfs.com/awweb/guest.jsp?smd=1&cl=all_lib&lb_document_id=35219

Peterson, J. A. (1998). *Utah's Black Hawk War.* Salt Lake City: University of Utah Press.

The Relief Society

Derr, J. M., Cannon, J. R., & Beecher, M. U. (1992). *Women of covenant: The story of Relief Society.* Salt Lake City: Deseret Book.

Empy, E. Y. (1870). Resolutions, adopted by the first young ladies' department of the Ladies' Cooperative Retrenchment Association, Salt Lake City. *Deseret News Weekly,* 19(21), 249. Retrieved April 15, 2012, from http://news.google.com/newspapers?id=Xa4UAAAAIBAJ&sjid=_rUDAAAAIBAJ&pg=4541%2C6893496

Female Relief Society. (Ed.). (1872–1914). *Woman's exponent* (41 vols.). Salt Lake City: Relief Society. Retrieved April 16, 2012, from http://lib.byu.edu/digital/mpntc/az/W.php#womans-exponent

Female Relief Society of Nauvoo. (1842–44). *A book of records containing the proceedings of the female Relief Society of Nauvoo.* Church History Library, Salt Lake City. Retrieved April 15, 2012, from http://josephsmithpapers.org/paperSummary/nauvoo-relief-society-minute-book#1

Gates, S. Y. (1922). Relief Society beginnings in Utah. *Relief Society Magazine*, 9, 1922, p. 184–196.

Horne, M. I., & Kimball, S. M. (1870). Minutes of Ladies' Cooperative Retrenchment meeting . . . Feb. 10th 1870. *Deseret Evening News,* 3(72), 2. Retrieved April 15, 2012, from http://news.google.com/newspapers?id=TbwjAAAAIBAJ&sjid=5jADAAAAIBAJ&pg=2742%2C1525162

Jensen, R. L. (1983). Forgotten relief societies, 1844–67. *Dialogue: A Journal of Mormon Thought,* 16, 105–125. Retrieved April 15, 2012, from https://www.dialoguejournal.com/wp-content/uploads/sbi/articles/Dialogue_V16N01_107.pdf

Kimball, S. M. (1883). Auto-biography. *Woman's Exponent,* 12(7), 51. Retrieved April 15, 2012, from http://contentdm.lib.byu.edu/cdm/ref/collection/WomansExp/id/10872

Relief Society. (1880–1892). *Relief Society record.* Church History Library, Salt Lake City.

Relief Society. (Ed.). (1914–1970). *Relief Society magazine.* Church History Library, Salt Lake City.

Relief Society. (ca. 1884). *Relief Society: Names of stake and branch presidents of the Relief Society of Latter-day Saints, in the valleys of the mountains.* [broadsheet]. Church History Library, Salt Lake City.

Rogers, A. S. (1898). *Life sketches of Orson Spencer and others and history of primary work.* Salt Lake City: George Q. Cannon & Sons.

Snow, E. R. (1995). *Sketch of my life.* Published as M. U. Beecher (Ed.). *The personal writings of Eliza Roxcy Snow.* Salt Lake City: University of Utah Press.

Wells, E. B. (1903). History of the Relief Society. *Woman's Exponent,* 31–32 (published in series throughout 1903). Retrieved April 15, 2012, from http://contentdm.lib.byu.edu/cdm/ref/collection/WomansExp/id/34272

Gathering to Zion

Bushman, R. L. (1997). *Making space for the Mormons: Ideas of sacred geography in Joseph Smith's America.* Logan, UT: Utah State University Press.

Church History Library. (2008). Mormon pioneer overland travel, 1847–1868. *Church History.* Retrieved April 15, 2012, from http://lds.org/churchhistory/library/pioneercompanysearch/

Howard, H. F. (2008). *An economic analysis of the perpetual emigrating fund.* Ph.D. dissertation, Cornell University, Ithaca, NY.

Mulder, W. B. (2000). *Homeward to Zion: The Mormon migration from Scandinavia*. Minneapolis: University of Minnesota Press.

Sonne, C. B. (1983). *Saints on the seas: A maritime history of Mormon migration, 1830–90.* Salt Lake City: University of Utah Press.

Sonne, C. B. (1987). *Ships, saints, and mariners: A maritime encyclopedia of Mormon migration, 1830–1890.* Salt Lake City: University of Utah Press.

Taylor, P. A. M. (1965). *Expectations westward: The Mormons and the emigration of their British converts in the nineteenth century.* Ithaca, NY: Cornell University Press.

Woods, F. E. (2001). *Gathering to Nauvoo.* American Fork, UT: Covenant Communications.

Woods, F. E. (2012). *Mormon migration database.* Retrieved April 15, 2012, from Harold B. Lee Library, Brigham Young University http://lib.byu.edu/mormonmigration/

Handcart Pioneers

Carter, L. M. (2006). Handcarts across Iowa: Trial runs for the Willie, Haven, and Martin handcart companies. *Annals of Iowa,* 65(2/3), 190–225.

Hafen, L. R. & Hafen, A. W. (1992). *Handcarts to Zion: the story of a unique westerm migration, 1856–1860.* Spokane, WA: University of Nebraska Press.

Jackson, R. H. (1978). The overland journey to Zion. In R. H. Jackson (Ed.), *The Mormon role in the settlement of the West.* (vol. 9, pp. 1–27). Provo, UT: Brigham Young University Press.

Rescuing the Martin and Willie Companies

Long, G. D. (2009). *The journey of the James G. Willie handcart company, October, 1956.* Cheyenne, WY: the Author.

Lyman, P. D. (2006). *The Willie handcart company.* Provo, UT: BYU Studies. Retrieved from http://www.loc.gov/catdir/toc/ecip072/2006031962.html

Olsen, A. D. (2006). *The price we paid: The extraordinary story of the Willie and Martin handcart pioneers.* Salt Lake City, UT: Deseret Book. Retrieved from http://www.loc.gov/catdir/toc/ecip0615/2006018246.html

Utah War

Eldredge, J. (2008). *The Utah War: A guide to the historic sites, South Pass to Camp Floyd.* Riverton, UT: Trailbuff.com Press.

Hafen, L.R. (1958). *The Utah Expedition, 1857–58.* Glendale, CA: Arthur H. Clark.

McKinnon, W. P. (2008). *At sword's point: A documentary history of the Utah War to 1858.* Norman, OK: Arthur H. Clark.

Walker, R. W., Turley, R. E., Jr., & Leonard, G. M. (2008). *Massacre at Mountain Meadows: An American tragedy.* New York: Oxford University Press.

The Gentiles

Alexander, T., & Allen, J. B. (1984). *Mormons & Gentiles: A history of Salt Lake City.* Boulder, CO: Pruett Publishing Co.

Dwyer, R. J. (1941). *The Gentile comes to Utah.* Washington, D.C.: Catholic University of America Press.

Ferguson, M., & Topping, G. (2009). *Salt Lake City, 1890–1930.* San Francisco: Arcadia Publishing.

Madsen, B. D. (1980). *Corinne: The Gentile capital of Utah.* Salt Lake City: University of Utah Press.

Meinig, D. W. (1965). The Mormon culture region: Strategies and patterns in the geography of the American West, 1847–1964. *Annals of the Association of American Geographers,* 55(2), 191–220.

Meinig, D. W. (1996). The Mormon nation and the American empire. *Journal of Mormon History,* 22(1), 33–51. Retrieved April 15, 2012, from http://digitalcommons.usu.edu/mormonhistory/vol22/iss1/1

Mitchell, M. (1997). Gentile impressions of Salt Lake City, Utah, 1849–1870. *Geographical Review,* 87(3), 334–352.

Mooney, B. M., & Fitzgerald, J. T., Msgr. (2008). *Salt of the earth: The history of the Catholic Church in Utah.* Salt Lake City: University of Utah Press.

R. L. Polk & Co. (1902). *Salt Lake City directory.* Salt Lake City: R. L. Polk & Co.

Smith, S. (2008). *The wasp in the beehive: Non-Mormon presence in 1880s Utah.* Master's thesis, Pennsylvania State University, State College. Retrieved from https://etda.libraries.psu.edu/paper/8769/

Walker, R. W. (1998). *Wayward Saints: The Godbeites and Brigham Young.* Urbana: University of Illinois Press.

Yorgason, E. R. (1999). *The transformation of the Mormon culture region and the creation of new regional citizens.* Ph.D. dissertation, University of Iowa, Iowa City.

Church Headquarters

Arrington, L. J., & Swinton, H. S. (1986). *The hotel: Salt Lake City's classy lady, the Hotel Utah, 1911–1986.* Salt Lake City: The Westin Hotel Utah.

Halverson, W. D. (2000). *Building history—history building: The LDS Conference Center and its history.* Salt Lake City: Heritage Associates.

Jackson, R. H. (1993). Sacred space and city planning: The Mormon example. *Architecture et Comportement/Architecture and Behaviour,* 9(2), 251–259. Retrieved April 19, 2012, from http://lasur.epfl.ch/files/content/sites/lasur/files/A&C%20Vol.9%20No.2/JACKSON.pdf

Legacy Constructors. (2000). *The Conference Center, The Church of Jesus Christ of Latter-day Saints: The story of its construction.* Salt Lake City: Legacy Constructors.

Romney, E. J. (1972). *History of General Church Office Building.* Church History Library, Salt Lake City.

Economic Development

Alexander, T. G. (Ed.). (1991). *Great Basin kingdom revisited.* Logan, UT: Utah State University Press.

Arrington, L. J., & Alexander, T. (1974). *A dependent commonwealth: Utah's economy from statehood to the Great Depression.* Provo, UT: Charles Redd Center for Western Studies, Brigham Young University.

Arrington, L. J., Fox, F. A., & May, D. L. (1976). *Building the city of God: Community and cooperation among the Mormons.* Salt Lake City: Deseret Book.

Kearl, J. R., Pope, C., & Wimmer, L. T. (1980). Household wealth in a settlement economy: Utah, 1850–1870. *Journal of Economic History,* 40(3), 477–496.

Pope, C. (1989). Households on the frontier: The distribution of income and wealth in Utah, 1850–1900. In D. W. Galenson (Ed.), *Markets in history: Economic studies of the past.* New York: Cambridge University Press.

The Church in 1870

British Mission (1840–1970). *Latter-day Saints' Millennial Star* (132 Volumes). Manchester, Liverpool, and London, England: British Mission. Retrieved April 21, 2012, from http://lib.byu.edu/digital/mpntc/az/M.php#latter-star

Plural Marriage

Bennion, L. C., & Carter, T. R. (2010). Touring polygamous Utah with Elizabeth W. Kane, winter 1872–73. In D. J. Whittaker (Ed.), *Colonel Thomas L. Kane and the Mormons, 1846–1883* (pp. 158–192). Provo, UT: BYU Studies & University of Utah Press.

Bennion, L. C., Morrell, A. L., & Carter, T. (2005). *Polygamy in Lorenzo Snow's Brigham City: An architectural tour.* Salt Lake City: University of Utah College of Architecture & Planning.

Daynes, K. M. (2001). *More wives than one: Transformation of the Mormon marriage system, 1840–1910.* Urbana: University of Illinois Press.

Embry, J. L. (2007). *Mormons & polygamy.* Orem, UT: Millennial Press.

Flake, K. (2004). *The politics of American religious identity: The seating of Senator Reed Smoot, Mormon Apostle.* Chapel Hill: University of North Carolina Press.

Hardy, B. C. (2007). *Doing the works of Abraham: Mormon polygamy, its origin, practice, and demise.* Norman, OK: The Arthur H. Clark Co.

Whitley, C., & Brimhall, S. D. (Eds.). (2002). *Brigham Young's homes.* Logan: Utah State University Press.

Church Academies

Alexander, T. G. (1986). *Mormonism in transition: A history of the Latter-day Saints, 1890–1930.* Urbana: University of Illinois Press.

Bennion, M. L. (1939). *Mormonism and education.* Salt Lake City: Department of Education, Church of Jesus Christ of Latter-day Saints.

Berrett, W. E. (1988). *A miracle in weekday religious education.* Salt Lake City: Salt Lake Printing Center.

Esplin, S. C. (2006). *Education in transition: Church and state relationships in Utah education, 1888–1893.* Ph.D. dissertation, Brigham Young University, Provo, UT. Retrieved from http://contentdm.lib.byu.edu/cdm/ref/collection/ETD/id/627

Garr, A. K. (1973). *A history of Brigham Young College, Logan, Utah.* Master's thesis, Utah State University, Logan, UT.

The Emergence of Modern Stakes and Wards

Alexander, T. G. (1986). *Mormonism in transition: A history of the Latter-day Saints, 1890–1930.* Urbana: University of Illinois Press.

Salt Lake County Surveyor (cartographer). (1908). *Map of election districts & precincts of Salt Lake County Utah.* Salt Lake City: Salt Lake County.

The Pioneer Presidents

Holzapfel, R. N. (2000). *Joseph F. Smith: Portrait of a prophet.* Salt Lake City: Deseret Book.

Woodruff, W. (1983). *Journal.* Published as S. G. Kenney (Ed.). *Wilford Woodruff's journal, 1833–1898 Typescript.* Midvale, UT: Signature Books.

The Church in 1910

U.S. Bureau of the Census. (1910). *Census of religious bodies, 1906.* Washington, D.C.: Government Printing Office. Retrieved April 20, 2012, from http://www.thearda.com/Archive/Files/Descriptions/1906CENSCT.asp

U.S. Bureau of the Census. (1920). *Census of religious bodies, 1916.* Washington, D.C.: Government Printing Office. Retrieved April 20, 2012, from http://www.thearda.com/Archive/Files/Descriptions/1916CENSCT.asp

Section 3: The Expanding Church

Church of Jesus Christ of Latter-day Saints. (Ed.). (1892–present). *Directory of General Authorities and officers.* Salt Lake City: Church of Jesus Christ of Latter-day Saints. Retrieved April 15, 2012, from http://archive.org/details/directoryofgeneroounse (only a few early years online)

Church of Jesus Christ of Latter-day Saints. (Ed.). (1899–present). *General conference reports.* Salt Lake City: The Church of Jesus Christ of Latter-day Saints. Retrieved April 15, 2012, from http://archive.org/details/conferencereport

Cowan, R. O. (1985). *The Church in the twentieth century.* Salt Lake City: Bookcraft.

Deseret News. (1974–present). *Church almanac.* Salt Lake City, UT: Deseret News.

Various wards, stakes, branches, and missions. (1830–present). *Manuscript histories.* Church History Library, Salt Lake City.

Historical Sites

Cannon, J. R. (1991). *Nauvoo panorama: Views of Nauvoo before, during, and after its rise, fall, and restoration.* Nauvoo, IL: Nauvoo Restoration Inc.

Davis, J. A., & Jackson, R. H. (2003). LDS heritage sites. In M. W. Jackson (Ed.), *Geography, culture and change in the Mormon West: 1847–2003.* (pp. 65–78). Jacksonville, AL: National Council for Geographic Education.

Givens, G., & Givens, S. (2000). *Nauvoo fact book: Questions and answers for Nauvoo enthusiasts.* Lynchburg, VA: Parley Street Publishers.

Jackson, R. H., Rinschede, G., & Knapp, J. W. (1990). Pilgrimage in the Mormon Church. In G. Rinschede & S. M. Bhardwaj (Eds.), *Pilgrimage in the United States.* (pp. 26–61). Berlin, Germany: Dietrich Reimer Verlag.

Madsen, M. H. (2003). *Mormon Meccas: The spiritual transformation of Mormon historical sites from points of interest to sacred space.* Ph.D. dissertation, Syracuse University, Syracuse, NY.

Mormon Historic Sites Foundation. (2012). *Mormon historic sites registry.* Retrieved 2012, from http://www.mormonhistoricsitesregistry.org/

Ouellette, R. D. (2005). Zion's gallows: The cultural geography of the Mormon temple lot site. *John Whitmer Historical Association Journal,* 25, 161–174.

The Church Educational System

Alexander, T. G. (1986). *Mormonism in transition: A history of the Latter-day Saints, 1890–1930.* Urbana: University of Illinois Press.

Berrett, W. E. (1988). *A miracle in weekday religious education.* Salt Lake City: Salt Lake Printing Center.

Hatch, E. (2005). *Brigham Young University: A pictorial history of physical facilities, 1875–2005.* Provo, UT: Physical Facilities Division, Brigham Young University. Retrieved April 18, 2012, from http://plantwo.byu.edu/main/history/

Seminaries & Institutes. (1950–present). Seminaries and institutes of religion annual report. Salt Lake City: Church Educational System.

Wilkinson, E. L., & Arrington, L. J. (1976). *Brigham Young University: The first one hundred years* (4 vols.). Provo, UT: Brigham Young University Press.

The Mormon Outmigration

Arrington, L. J. (1992). *Harold F. Silver: Western inventor, businessman, and civic leader.* Logan: Utah State University Press.

Cowan, R. O., & Homer, W. E. (1996). *California Saints: A 150-year legacy in the Golden State.* Provo, UT: Religious Studies Center, Brigham Young University. Retrieved April 15, 2012, from http://contentdm.lib.byu.edu/cdm/ref/collection/rsc/id/50249

Eyring, H. J. (2007). *Mormon scientist: The life and faith of Henry Eyring.* Salt Lake City: Deseret Book.

Hickman, M. B. (1987). *David Matthew Kennedy: Banker, statesman, churchman.* Salt Lake City: Deseret Book and David M. Kennedy Center for International Studies, Brigham Young University.

O'Brien, R. (1977). *Marriott: The J. Willard Marriott story.* Salt Lake City: Deseret Book.

Poll, R. D. *Howard J. Stoddard: Founder, Michigan National Bank.* East Lansing: Michigan State University Press.

Quinn, D. M. (2001). *Elder statesman: A biography of J. Reuben Clark.* Salt Lake City: Signature Books.

Welfare and Humanitarian Aid

The Church of Jesus Christ of Latter-day Saints. (1936–1958). Financial statement. In *Conference reports.* Salt Lake City: The Church of Jesus Christ of Latter-day Saints. Retrieved April 22, 2012, from http://archive.org/details/conferencereport

LDS Humanitarian Services. (2011). Humanitarian activities worldwide. *Provident Living.* Retrieved 2012, from http://www.providentliving.org/project/0,13501,4607-1-2009,00.html

Rathjen, M. R. (1969). *Evolution and development of the Mormon welfare farms.* Ph.D. dissertation, Michigan State University, East Lansing.

Recorder, U. C. (1979, 2010). *Parcel ownership maps.* Provo, UT: Utah County.

Robison, L. J. (1992). *Becoming a Zion people.* Salt Lake City: Hawkes Publishing.

Rudd, G. L. (1995). *Pure religion: The story of Church welfare since 1930.* Salt Lake City: The Church of Jesus Christ of Latter-day Saints.

Taylor, H. D. (1984). *The Church welfare plan.* Salt Lake City: the Author.

Genealogy

Allen, J. B. (1995). The LDS family history library. In D. J. Whittaker (Ed.), *Mormon Americana: A guide to sources and collections in the United States* (pp. 135–153). Provo, UT: BYU Studies.

Allen, J. B., Embry, J. L., & Mehr, K. B. (1995). *Hearts turned to the fathers: A history of the Genealogical Society of Utah, 1894–1994.* Provo, UT: BYU Studies.

Family History Department. (2010). *FamilySearch.* Retrieved 2010, from http://www.familysearch.org/

Mehr, K. B. (1985). *Preserving the source: Early microfilming efforts of the Genealogical Society of Utah, 1938–1950.* Master's thesis, Brigham Young University, Provo, UT. Retrieved from http://contentdm.lib.byu.edu/cdm/ref/collection/MTGM/id/41488

Sperry, K. (2007). *A guide to Mormon family history sources.* Provo, UT: Ancestry Publishing.

Specialized Congregations

Embry, J. L. (1997). *"In his own language": Mormon Spanish speaking congregations in the United States.* Provo, UT: Charles Redd Center for Western Studies.

Embry, J. L. (2001). *Mormon wards as community.* Binghamton, NY: Global Publications, State University of New York.

Jensen, R. L. (1987). Mother tongue: Use of the non-English languages in The Church of Jesus Christ of Latter-day Saints in the United States, 1850–1983. In D. Bitton & M. U. Beecher (Eds.), *New views of Mormon history: A collection of essays in honor of Leonard J. Arrington.* Salt Lake City: University of Utah Press.

The Church in 1950

National Council of Churches. (1952). *Churches and Church membership in the United States: An enumeration and analysis by counties, states, and regions.* Association of Religion Data Archives. Retrieved April 21, 2012, from http://www.thearda.com/Archive/Files/Descriptions/CMS52CNT.asp

David O. McKay

Cannon, H. J. (2005). *David O. McKay around the world: An apostolic mission.* Provo, UT: Spring Creek Book Co.

McKay, D. L. (1989). *My father, David O. McKay.* Salt Lake City: Deseret Book.

McKay, D. O. (1999). *Journals.* Published as S. Larson & P. Larson (Eds.), *What e'er thou art, act well thy part: The missionary diaries of David O. McKay.* Salt Lake City: Blue Ribbon Books.

Prince, G. A. (2005). *David O. McKay and the rise of modern Mormonism.* Salt Lake City: University of Utah Press.

Building Meetinghouses

Bradley, M. S. (1981). *"The Church and Colonel Saunders": Mormon standard plan architecture.* Master's thesis, Brigham Young University, Provo, UT. Retrieved from http://contentdm.lib.byu.edu/cdm/ref/collection/MTAF/id/35726

Jackson, R. W. (2003). *Places of worship: 150 years of Latter-day Saint architecture.* Provo, UT: Religious Studies Center, Brigham Young University. Retrieved April 15, 2012, from http://contentdm.lib.byu.edu/cdm/ref/collection/rsc/id/53490

Administering the Worldwide Church

Church News. (1961, July 1). New program to intensify supervision of world-wide church missions: Nine authorities to have direct charge of areas. *Church News*, p. 6. Retrieved April 23, 2012, from http://news.google.com/newspapers?id=48EzAAAAIBAJ&sjid=OkgDAAAAIBAJ&pg=6013%2C138568

Church News. (1967, October 7). Regional representatives: 69 receive calls. *Church News*, p. 4.

Church News. (1972, July 1). Keeping pace with the growth: 29 mission representatives expand proselyting program. *Church News*, p. 3, 5. Retrieved April 23, 2012, from http://news.google.com/newspapers?id=ZAEPAAAAIBAJ&sjid=8noDAAAAIBAJ&pg=5777%2C175627

Church News. (1975, May 17). New mission program. *Church News*, p. 3. Retrieved April 23, 2012, from http://news.google.com/newspapers?id=DyVVAAAAIBAJ&sjid=7n8DAAAAIBAJ&pg=3827%2C4562785

Church News. (1977, May 7). 11 zones set up worldwide. *Church News*, p. 3.

Church News. (1984, August). Area presidencies called as Church modifies geographical administration. *Ensign* 14(8), p. 75. Retrieved April 23, 2012, from http://www.lds.org/ensign/1984/08/news-of-the-church

Church News. (1995, April 8). New position is announced. *Church News*, p. 14. Retrieved April 23, 2012, from http://www.ldschurchnews.com/articles/25719/New-position-is-announced.html

Mehr, K. B. (2001). Area supervision: Administration of the worldwide Church, 1960–2000. *Journal of Mormon History,* 27(1), 192–214. Retrieved April 22, 2012, from http://digitalcommons.usu.edu/mormonhistory/vol27/iss1/1/

Spencer W. Kimball

Gibbons, F. M. (1995). *Spencer W. Kimball: Resolute disciple, prophet of God.* Salt Lake City: Deseret Book.

Hickman, M. B. (1987). *David Matthew Kennedy: Banker, statesman, churchman.* Salt Lake City: Deseret Book and David M. Kennedy Center for International Studies, Brigham Young University.

Kimball, E. L. (1977). *Spencer W. Kimball.* Salt Lake City: Bookcraft.

Kimball, E. L. (2005). *Lengthen your stride: The presidency of Spencer W. Kimball.* Salt Lake City: Deseret Book.

The Church in 1980

Glenmary Research Center. (1980). *Churches and Church membership in the United States.* Association of Religion Data Archives. Retrieved April 20, 2012, from http://www.thearda.com/Archive/Files/Descriptions/CMS80CNT.asp

Travels of Gordon B. Hinckley

Dew, S. L. (1996). *Go forward with faith: The biography of Gordon B. Hinckley.* Salt Lake City: Deseret Book.

The Church in 2012

Association of Statisticians of American Religious Bodies. (2000). *Religious congregations and membership in the United States.* Association of Religion Data Archives. Retrieved April 21, 2012, from http://www.thearda.com/Archive/Files/Descriptions/RCMSCY.asp

Martinich, M. (2012). *LDS Church growth.* Retrieved 2012, from http://ldschurchgrowth.blogspot.com/

Stewart, D., & Martinich, M. (2011). Taking the gospel to the nations: Challenges and opportunities for international LDS growth. *Cumorah.com: International Resources for Latter-day Saints.* Retrieved April 15, 2012, from http://cumorah.com/index.php?target=missiology_articles

Membership Distribution

Bennion, L. C. (1995). The geographic dynamics of Mormondom, 1965–1995. *Sunstone* 18, 21–32.

Bennion, L. C., & Young, L. A. (1996). The uncertain dynamics of LDS expansion. *Dialogue: A Journal of Mormon Thought,* 29(1), 8–32. Retrieved April 15, 2012, from https://www.dialoguejournal.com/wp-content/uploads/sbi/articles/Dialogue_V29N01_14.pdf

Missionary Work

Cowan, R. O. (1984). *Every man shall hear the gospel in his own language: A history of the missionary training center and its predecessors.* Provo, UT: Missionary Training Center.

Irving, G. (1975). Numerical strength and geographical distribution of the LDS missionary force, 1830–1974. *Vol. 1. Task papers in LDS history.* Salt Lake City: Historical Department, Church of Jesus Christ of Latter-day Saints.

Jensen, J. E. (1988). *The effect of initial mission field training on missionary proselyting skills.* Ed.D. dissertation, Brigham Young University, Provo, UT.

Kimball, S. W. (1979, May). Let us move forward and upward. *Ensign*, 9(5) p. 82. Retrieved April 18, 2011, from http://www.lds.org/ensign/1979/05/let-us-move-forward-and-upward

Whittaker, D. J. (2000). Mormon missiology: An introduction and guide to the sources. In S. D. Ricks, D. W. Parry & A. H. Hedges (Eds.), *The disciple as witness: Essays on Latter-day Saint history and doctrine in honor of Richard Lloyd Anderson* (pp. 459–538). Provo, UT: Foundation for Ancient Research and Mormon Studies.

Temples

Dew, S. L. (1996). *Go forward with faith: The biography of Gordon B. Hinckley.* Salt Lake City: Deseret Book.

Hinckley, G. B. (1997, November). Some thoughts on temples, retention of converts, and missionary service. *Ensign*, 27(11) p. 68. Retrieved April 18, 2012, from http://www.lds.org/ensign/1997/11/some-thoughts-on-temples-retention-of-converts-and-missionary-service

Satterfield, R. (2012). *LDSChurchTemples.com.* Retrieved 2012, from http://ldschurchtemples.com/

Talmage, J. (1912). *The house of the Lord: A study of holy sanctuaries, ancient and modern.* Salt Lake City: Deseret News. Retrieved April 15, 2012, from http://archive.org.erl.lib.byu.edu/details/houseoflordstudy00talm

Cultural Ambassadors

Calman, C. J. (1979). *The Mormon Tabernacle Choir.* New York: Harper & Row.

Doxey, C. (2000). International tours of the Tabernacle Choir. In S. E. Black (Ed.), *Out of obscurity: The LDS Church in the twentieth century.* Salt Lake City: Deseret Book.

Performing Arts Management. (2012). Past performances. *Performing Arts Management.* Retrieved April 18, 2012, from http://pam.byu.edu/maps.asp

Swinton, H. S. (2004). *America's choir: A commemorative portrait of the Mormon Tabernacle Choir.* Salt Lake City: Shadow Mountain Press and Mormon Tabernacle Choir.

Political Affiliation

Center for the Study of Elections and Democracy. (2007). *Utah colleges exit poll*. Provo, UT: Department of Political Science, Brigham Young University. Retrieved April 22, 2012, from http://exitpolldata.byu.edu/

Center for the Study of Elections and Democracy. (2011). *Center for the study of elections and democracy*. Retrieved 2011, from http://csed.byu.edu/

Cornwall, M., Heaton, T. B., & Young, L. A. (2001). *Contemporary Mormonism: Social science perspectives*. Urbana: University of Illinois Press.

Fox, J. C. (2006). *Latter-day political views*. Lanham, MD: Lexington Press.

Heaton, T. B., Bahr, S. J., & Jacobson, C. K. (2004). *A statistical profile of Mormons: Health, wealth, and social life*. Lewiston, NY: Edwin Mellen Press.

Inter-University Consortium for Political and Social Research. (1999). *United States historical election returns, 1824–1968*. Ann Arbor, MI: ICPSR. Retrieved April 22, 2012, from http://dx.doi.org/10.3886/ICPSR00001.v3

Lyman, E. L. (1986). *Political deliverance: The Mormon quest for Utah statehood*. Urbana: University of Illinois Press.

Mauss, A. L. (1994). *The angel and the beehive*. Chicago: University of Illinois Press.

Pew Forum on Religion & Public Life. (2007). *U.S. religious landscape survey*. Philadelphia: Pew Research Center.

Book of Mormon Geographies

Aston, D. R. (1998). *Return to Cumorah*. Sacramento, CA: American River Publications.

Clark, J. E. (1989). A key for evaluating Nephite geographies. *FARMS Review, 1*(1), 20–70. Retrieved April 22, 2012, from http://maxwellinstitute.byu.edu/publications/review/?vol=1&num=1&id=7

Hills, L. E. (1917). *A short work on the geography of Mexico and Central America: From 2234 BC to 421 AD*. Independence, MO: s.n.

Layton, L. C. (1938). An "ideal" Book of Mormon geography. *Improvement Era, 41*, 394–395.

Priddis, V. (1975). *The book and the map: New insights into Book of Mormon geography*. Salt Lake City: Bookcraft.

Reynolds, G. (1880). The lands of the Nephites. *The Juvenile Instructor, 15*(22), 261; 216(263), 226–227. Retrieved April 22, 2012, from http://archive.org/details/juvenileinstruct1522geor, http://archive.org/details/juvenileinstruct163geor

Sorenson, J. L. (1985). *An ancient American setting for the Book of Mormon*. Salt Lake City, UT: Deseret Book; Foundation for Ancient Research and Mormon Studies.

Sorenson, J. L. (1992). *The geography of Book of Mormon events: A source book*. Provo, UT: Foundation for Ancient Research and Mormon Studies.

Van Orden, B. A. (1982). George Reynolds and Janne M. Sjodahl on Book of Mormon geography. *The Thetean, 1982*(April), 60–79.

Warr, J. (2006). *Mormon's clues: A new look at Book of Mormon geography*. Herriman, UT: Circle W Books.

Community of Christ

Barlow, P. L. (2004). Space matters: A geographical context for the reorganization's great transformation. *John Whitmer Historical Association Journal, 24*, 21–39.

Community of Christ. (2010). History. *Community of Christ*. Retrieved April 23, 2012, from http://www.cofchrist.org/history/

Community of Christ. (2010). World conference enrollment data review. In *2010 World Conference Bulletin* (pp. B223–B224). Independence, MO: Community of Christ.

Conference of Restoration Elders. (2011). Directory of restoration branches. *CenterPlace*. Retrieved April 22, 2012, from http://www.centerplace.org/Branches/

Davis, I. S. (1981). *The story of the church* (2nd ed.). Independence, MO: Herald House. Retrieved April 15, 2012, from http://www.centerplace.org/history/misc/soc/

Remnant Church of Jesus Christ of Latter Day Saints. (2011). Locate a branch. *Remnant Church of Jesus Christ of Latter Day Saints*. Retrieved April 22, 2012, from http://www.theremnantchurch.com/Congregations/get_list.php

Reorganized Church of Jesus Christ of Latter-Day Saints. (1877). Annual conference report. *The Latter-day Saints Herald*, 24, May 1, 1877, p. 131–132.

Restoration Church of Jesus Christ of Latter Day Saints. (2011). Directory. *Restoration Church of Jesus Christ of Latter Day Saints*. Retrieved April 22, 2012, from http://www.restorationchurch.net/default2.asp?active_page_id=107

Sheen, I. (1860, October). Minutes of the semi-annual conference of the Church of Jesus Christ of Latter-Day Saints, held near Sandwich, Illinois, Oct. 6th to 9th, 1860. *The True Latter Day Saints' Herald*, 1, 1860, p. 238. Retrieved April 18, 2012, from http://books.google.com/books?id=UVwoAAAAYAAJ

Shields, S. L. (1990). *Divergent paths of the restoration* (4th ed.). Los Angeles: Restoration Research.

Smith, J., III, & Smith, H. C. (1897). *History of the Church of Jesus Christ of Latter Day Saints* (4 vols.). Lamoni, IA: Board of Publication of the Reorganized Church of Jesus Christ of Latter Day Saints. Retrieved April 15, 2012, from http://galenet.galegroup.com.erl.lib.byu.edu/servlet/Sabin?af=RN&ae=CY105223063&srchtp=a&ste=14 (transcription at http://www.centerplace.org/history/ch/)

The Restored Church(es)

Bringhurst, N. G., & Hamer, J. (Eds.). (2007). *Scattering of the Saints: Schism within Mormonism*. Independence, MO: John Whitmer Books.

Principle Voices. (2011). Fundamentalist Mormon FAQs. *Principle Voices: Power in Education, Advocacy and Communication for Equality*. Retrieved April 22, 2012, from http://principlevoices.org/diversity-of-fundamentalist-mormons

Shields, S. L. (1990). *Divergent paths of the restoration* (4th ed.). Los Angeles: Restoration Research.

Three American Churches

Jehovah's Witnesses. (2010). *2009 report of Jehovah's Witnesses worldwide*. New York, NY: Watch Tower Bible and Tract Society. Retrieved April 22, 2012, from http://www.watchtower.org/e/statistics/wholereport.htm

Office of Archives Statistics and Research. (2010). *Annual statistical report for 2009*. Silver Spring, MD: Seventh-day Adventist Church. Retrieved April 22, 2012, from http://www.adventistarchives.org/doc_info.asp?DocID=180512

The Future of the Church

Anderson, D. (2000). Estimates of the future membership of The Church of Jesus Christ of Latter-day Saints. *Mormonism and the LDS Church*. Retrieved 2010, from http://www.lds-mormon.com/churchgrowthrates.shtml

Bennion, L. C. (1995). The geographic dynamics of Mormondom, 1965–1995. *Sunstone* 18, 21–32.

Bennion, L. C., & Young, L. A. (1996). The uncertain dynamics of LDS expansion. *Dialogue: A Journal of Mormon Thought, 29*(1), 8–32. Retrieved April 15, 2012, from https://www.dialoguejournal.com/wp-content/uploads/sbi/articles/Dialogue_V29N01_14.pdf

Loomis, R. (2002). Mormon Church growth. *2002 Meetings*, Retrieved April 15, 2012 from http://www.lds4u.com/growth2/

Stark, R. (1984). The rise of a new world faith. *Review of Religious Research, 26*, 18–27.

Stark, R. (1998). The rise of a new world faith (with postscript). In J. T. Duke (Ed.), *Latter-day Saint Social Life* (pp. 9–27). Provo, UT: Religious Studies Center, Brigham Young University. Retrieved April 15, 2012, from http://contentdm.lib.byu.edu/cdm/ref/collection/rsc/id/1464

Section 4: Regional History

Cannon, D. Q., & Cowan, R. O. (2002). *Unto every nation: Gospel light reaches every land*. Salt Lake City: Deseret Book.

Church of Jesus Christ of Latter-day Saints (Ed.). (1892–present). *Directory of General Authorities and officers*. Salt Lake City: Church of Jesus Christ of Latter-day Saints. Retrieved April 15, 2012, from http://archive.org/details/directoryofgeneroounse (only a few early years online)

Deseret News. (1974–). *Church almanac*. Salt Lake City, UT: Deseret News.

Martinich, M. (2012). *LDS Church growth*. Retrieved 2012, from http://ldschurchgrowth.blogspot.com/

Noyce, G. H. (1985). *Church membership statistical summaries, 1850–1981*. Church History Library, Salt Lake City.

Satterfield, R. (2012). *LDSChurchTemples.com*. Retrieved 2012, from http://ldschurchtemples.com/

Stewart, D., & Martinich, M. (2011). Taking the gospel to the nations: Challenges and opportunities for international LDS growth. *Cumorah.com: International Resources for Latter-day Saints*. Retrieved April 15, 2012, from http://cumorah.com/index.php?target=missiology_articles

Western United States and Canada

Association of Statisticians of American Religious Bodies. (2000). *Religious congregations and membership in the United States*. Association of Religion Data Archives. Retrieved April 21, 2012, from http://www.thearda.com/Archive/Files/Descriptions/RCMSCY.asp

Bennion, L. C. (1995). Meinig's "Mormon culture region" revisited. *Historical Geography, 24*(1 & 2), 22–33.

Cowan, R. O., & Homer, W. E. (1996). *California Saints: A 150-year legacy in the Golden State*. Provo, UT: Religious Studies Center, Brigham Young University. Retrieved April 15, 2012, from http://contentdm.lib.byu.edu/cdm/ref/collection/rsc/id/50249

Glenmary Research Center. (1980). *Churches and Church membership in the United States*. Association of Religion Data Archives. Retrieved April 20, 2012, from http://www.thearda.com/Archive/Files/Descriptions/CMS80CNT.asp

Harper, K. C. (1974). *The Mormon role in irrigation beginnings and diffusions in the western states: An historical geography*. Master's thesis, Brigham Young University, Provo, UT. Retrieved from http://contentdm.lib.byu.edu/cdm/ref/collection/MTGM/id/13964

Jackson, M. W. (2003). *Geography, culture and change in the Mormon West: 1847–2003*. Jacksonville, AL: National Council for Geographic Education.

Lehr, J. C. (1972). Mormon settlement morphology in southern Alberta. *Albertan Geographer, 8*, 6–13.

Meinig, D. W. (1965). The Mormon culture region: Strategies and patterns in the geography of the American West, 1847–1964. *Annals of the Association of American Geographers, 55*(2), 191–220.

Muir, L. J. (1952). *A century of Mormon activities in California*. Salt Lake City: Deseret News Press. Retrieved

April 15, 2012, from http://contentdm.lib.byu.edu/cdm/ref/collection/FH29/id/78485

National Council of Churches. (1952). *Churches and Church membership in the United States: An enumeration and analysis by counties, states, and regions.* Association of Religion Data Archives. Retrieved April 21, 2012, from http://www.thearda.com/Archive/Files/Descriptions/CMS52CNT.asp

Rosenvall, L. A. (1982). The transfer of Mormon culture to Alberta. *American Review of Canadian Studies,* 12(2), 51–63.

Statistics Canada. (2000). *CANSIM table 051-0031: Components of population growth, census divisions and census metropolitan areas, 1976–1986.* Ottawa, ON: Statistics Canada. Retrieved April 22, 2012, from http://www5.statcan.gc.ca/cansim/a26

Statistics Canada. (2002). Profile of income of individuals, families, and households, social and economic characteristics of individuals, families and households, housing costs, and religion, for census divisions. *2001 Census of Canada.* Ottawa, ON: Statistics Canada.

Tagg, M. S. (Ed.). (1968). *A history of the Mormon Church in Canada.* Lethbridge, Alberta: Lethbridge Stake.

U.S. Bureau of the Census. (1910). *Census of religious bodies, 1906.* Washington, D.C.: Government Printing Office. Retrieved April 20, 2012, from http://www.thearda.com/Archive/Files/Descriptions/1906CENSCT.asp

U.S. Bureau of the Census. (1920). *Census of religious bodies, 1916.* Washington, D.C.: Government Printing Office. Retrieved April 20, 2012, from http://www.thearda.com/Archive/Files/Descriptions/1916CENSCT.asp

Wilcox, A. G. (1950). *Founding of the Mormon community in Alberta.* Master's thesis, University of Alberta, Calgary.

Wright, D. A. (Ed.). (2000). *Regional studies in Latter-day Saint Church history: Western Canada* (vol. 2). Provo, UT: Religious Studies Center, Brigham Young University. Retrieved April 15, 2012, from http://contentdm.lib.byu.edu/cdm/ref/collection/rsc/id/14549

Eastern United States and Canada

Seferovich, H. M. (1996). *History of the LDS Southern States Mission, 1875–1898.* Master's thesis, Brigham Young University, Provo, UT. Retrieved from http://contentdm.lib.byu.edu/cdm/ref/collection/MTNZ/id/22805

Tagg, M. S. (Ed.). (1968). *A history of the Mormon Church in Canada.* Lethbridge, Alberta: Lethbridge Stake.

Middle America

Dirección General de Estadística y Censos. (2010). Encuesta de hogares de propositos multiples [Annual multipurpose household survey]. *DIGESTYC.* Retrieved April 18, 2012, from http://www.digestyc.gob.sv/index.php?option=com_content&view=article&id=89&Itemid=119

Gómez Páez, F. R. (2004). *The Church of Jesus Christ of Latter-day Saints and the Lamanite conventions: From darkness to light.* Mexico City, D.F.: El Museo de Historia del Mormonismo en México.

Instituto Nacional de Estadística Guatemala. (2011). Población en Guatemala [estimated population by regional department]. *Instituto Nacional de Estadística Guatemala,* retrieved April 18, 2012, from http://www.ine.gob.gt/np/poblacion/

Instituto Nacional de Estadística Honduras. (2001). Censo nacional de población y vivienda [2001 census]. *Instituto Nacional de Estadística Guatemala.* Retrieved April 18, 2012, from http://www.ine.gob.hn/drupal/node/301

Irving, G. (1976). Mormonism and Latin America: A preliminary historical survey. *Vol. 10. Task Papers in LDS History.* Salt Lake City: Historical Department, Church of Jesus Christ of Latter-day Saints.

Romney, T. C. (1938). *The Mormon colonies in Mexico.* Salt Lake City: Deseret Book.

Smith, J. S., & White, B. N. (2004). Detached from their homeland: The Latter-day Saints of Chihuahua, Mexico. *Journal of Cultural Geography,* 21(2), 57–76.

Tullis, F. L. (1987). *Mormons in Mexico: The dynamics of faith and culture.* Logan: Utah State University Press.

South America

Acevedo A., R. A. (1991). *Los Mormones en Chile: 30 años de la Iglesia de Jesucristo de los Santos de los Ultimos Días (1956–1986).* Santiago, Chile: Impresos y Publicaciones Cumora.

Grover, M. L. (1985). *Mormonism in Brazil: Religion and dependency in Latin America.* Ph.D. dissertation, Indiana University, Bloomington.

Irving, G. (1976). Mormonism and Latin America: A preliminary historical survey. *Vol. 10. Task Papers in LDS History.* Salt Lake City: Historical Department, Church of Jesus Christ of Latter-day Saints.

Peterson, J. D. (1961). *History of the Mormon missionary movement in South America to 1940.* Master's thesis, University of Utah, Salt Lake City.

Williams, F. S., & Williams, F. G. (1987). *From acorn to oak tree: A personal history of the establishment and first quarter century development of the South American missions.* Fullerton, CA: Et Cetera Graphics.

Europe

Doxey, C., Freeman, R. C., Holzapfel, R. N., & Wright, D. A. (Eds.). (2007). *Regional studies in Latter-day Saint history: The British Isles* (Vol. 7). Provo, UT: Religious Studies Center, Brigham Young University. Retrieved April 15, 2012, from http://contentdm.lib.byu.edu/cdm/ref/collection/rsc/id/35133

Mehr, K. B. (2002). *Mormon missionaries enter Eastern Europe.* Provo, UT: Brigham Young University Press.

Morris, D. (2008). *MormonHistory.org: Dedicated to British Latter-day Saint history.* Retrieved April 18, 2012, from http://www.mormonhistory.org/

Van Orden, B. A. (1996). *Building Zion: The Latter-day Saints in Europe.* Salt Lake City: Deseret Book.

The Middle East

Balbridge, S. W., & Rona, M. M. (1989). *Grafting in: A history of the Latter-day Saints in the Holy Land.* Jerusalem: Jerusalem Branch, Church of Jesus Christ of Latter-day Saints.

Berrett, L. C., & Van Dyke, B. G. (2005). *Holy lands: A history of the Latter-day Saints in the Near East.* American Fork, UT: Covenant Communications.

Chatterly, M. (2009, March 7). Middle East Stake: 10 cities in 10 days. *Church News.* Retrieved April 15, 2012, from http://www.ldschurchnews.com/articles/56729/Middle-East-stake-10-cities-in-10-days.html

Haroldson, E. O. (1993, June 12). Branch in land of pyramids is "home away from home." *Church News.* Retrieved April 15, 2012, from http://www.ldschurchnews.com/articles/23629/Branch-in-land-of-pyramids-is-home-away-from-home.html

Hunter, H. W. (1979). All are alike unto God. In *BYU Speeches of the Year: 1979* (pp. 35–36). Provo, UT: Brigham Young University.

Lindsay, R. H. (1958). *A history of the missionary activities of The Church of Jesus Christ of Latter-day Saints in the Near East, 1884–1929.* Master's thesis, Brigham Young University, Provo, UT. Retrieved from http://contentdm.lib.byu.edu/cdm/ref/collection/MTGM/id/23531

Van Dyke, B. G., & Berrett, L. C. (2008). In the footsteps of Orson Hyde: Subsequent dedications of the Holy Land. *BYU Studies,* 47(1), 57–94. Retrieved April 15, 2012, from https://byustudies.byu.edu/showTitle.aspx?title=7875

Africa

Allen, J. B. (1991). Would-be Saints: West Africa before 1978. *Journal of Mormon History,* 17(1), 207–247. Retrieved April 15, 2012, from http://digitalcommons.usu.edu/mormonhistory/vol17/iss1/1

Kissi, E. A., & Heiss, M. K. (2004). *Walking in the sand: A history of The Church of Jesus Christ of Latter-day Saints in Ghana.* Provo, UT: Brigham Young University Press.

Morrison, A. B. (1990). *The dawning of a brighter day: The Church in black Africa.* Salt Lake City: Deseret Book.

National Population Commission of Nigeria. (2006). *Population by state and sex.* Lagos: National Population Commission of Nigeria. Retrieved April 22, 2012, from http://www.population.gov.ng/files/nationafinal.pdf

Orton, F., & Orton, P. (2003, May 17). Spreading the gospel in Africa. *Church News.* Retrieved April 15, 2012, from http://www.ldschurchnews.com/articles/43773/Spreading-the-gospel-in-Africa.html

Wright, E. P. (1977). *A history of the South African Mission* (3 vols.). s.l.: s.n.

Asia

Britsch, R. L. (1998). *From the East: The history of the Latter-day Saints in Asia, 1851–1996.* Salt Lake City: Deseret Book.

Neilson, R. L., & Gessel, V. C. (Eds.). (2006). *Taking the gospel to the Japanese, 1901–2001.* Provo, UT: Brigham Young University Press.

Palmer, S. J. (1970). *The Church encounters Asia.* Salt Lake City: Deseret Book.

Australia and the Pacific

Britsch, R. L. (1986). *Unto the isles of the sea: A history of the Latter-day Saints in the Pacific.* Salt Lake City: Deseret Book.

Ellsworth, S. G. (Ed.). (1990). *The journals of Addison Pratt.* Salt Lake City: University of Utah Press.

Moffat, R. M. (1997). *Historical sites around La'ie.* Laie, HI: Press & Design Center, Brigham Young University–Hawaii.

Neilson, R. L., Harper, S. C., Manscill, C. K., & Woodger, M. J. (2008). *Regional studies in Latter-day Saint Church history: The Pacific Isles.* Provo, UT: Religious Studies Center, Brigham Young University.

Newton, M. (1991). *Southern Cross Saints: The Mormons in Australia.* Laie, Hawaii: Institute for Polynesian Studies, Brigham Young University-Hawaii.

Wallace, W. K., III. (2002). La'ie: Land and people in transition. In *World communities: A multidisciplinary reader.* Boston, MA: Pearson Custom Publishing. Retrieved April 22, 2012, from http://library.byuh.edu/sites/library.byuh.edu/files/laie_history/WallaceLaie.pdf

Index

B

D

G

H

I

J

K

L

M

N

O

P

Q

R

S

T

Y

Z

Photo Credits

Cover Photos

Listed left to right as they appear on the open dust jacket (the first two and last two below do not appear on the bound cover)

Kirtland Temple. Photo by Bjorn Pendleton.

Grafton, Utah. Photo by Kenneth R. Mays. Courtesy L. Tom Perry Special Collections, Brigham Young University.

Kyiv Ukraine Temple. Courtesy The Church of Jesus Christ of Latter-day Saints. © Intellectual Reserve Inc.

The Saints Embark from Liverpool, England, painting by Ken Baxter. Oil on canvas, 1978. Courtesy Church History Museum, Salt Lake City. © Intellectual Reserve Inc.

Grandin Building, Palmyra, New York. Photo by Kenneth R. Mays. Courtesy L. Tom Perry Special Collections, Brigham Young University.

Peter Whitmer Cabin. Photo by Bjorn Pendleton.

Conference Center, Salt Lake City. Photo by Kenneth R. Mays. Courtesy L. Tom Perry Special Collections, Brigham Young University.

Hill Cumorah Monument, near Palmyra, New York. Photo by Bjorn Pendleton.

Sacred Grove, near Palmyra, New York. Photo by Kenneth R. Mays. Courtesy L. Tom Perry Special Collections, Brigham Young University.

Statue of Joseph and Hyrum Smith, Carthage, Illinois. Photo by Kenneth R. Mays. Courtesy L. Tom Perry Special Collections, Brigham Young University.

Salt Lake Temple. Courtesy The Church of Jesus Christ of Latter-day Saints. © Intellectual Reserve Inc.

Wagon train in Echo Canyon, Utah, 1866. Courtesy L. Tom Perry Special Collections, Brigham Young University.

Accra Ghana Temple. Courtesy The Church of Jesus Christ of Latter-day Saints. © Intellectual Reserve Inc.

Smith Family Log Home, Palmyra, New York. Photo by Bjorn Pendleton.

Nauvoo Illinois Temple. Courtesy The Church of Jesus Christ of Latter-day Saints. © Intellectual Reserve Inc.

Interior Photos

17 Hill Cumorah. Photo by George Edward Anderson. Public domain. Original in Church History Library.

27 Terminus of the Ohio and Erie Canal, 1832. The Western Reserve Historical Society, Cleveland, Ohio.

44 Plat of City of Zion. Church History Library. © Intellectual Reserve Inc.

45 Plat of Far West. Church Historical Library. Courtesy L. Tom Perry Special Collections, Brigham Young University.

53 Plat of Commerce, Illinois. Public domain. Hancock County Recorders' Office.

57 Nauvoo diorama in Nauvoo LDS Visitors' Center. Photo by Brandon Plewe.

66 House at Voree, Wisconsin, from the James Strang era. Courtesy John J. Hajicek.

67 Brigham Young with cane. Church History Library. © Intellectual Reserve Inc.

67 Joseph Smith III. Courtesy Community of Christ Archives.

67 Lyman Wight. Used by permission, Utah State Historical Society, all rights reserved.

67 Sidney Rigdon. Public domain. Church Historical Department.

67 William Bickerton. Stafford County Historical and Genealogical Society. Copy and reuse restrictions apply.

67 James J. Strang. Public domain.

68–69 Map of an exploring expedition to the Rocky Mountains in the year 1842 and to Oregon and north California in the years 1843–44. Library of Congress Geography and Map Division.

76 Winter Quarters diorama at LDS Visitors' Center at Winter Quarters, Nebraska. Photo by Brandon Plewe.

78 Page from diary of Henry William Bigler, January 24th, 1848. Gift of Henry William Bigler, 1890. The Society of California Pioneers.

91 Brigham Young and party at Colorado River. Photo by C. R. Savage, 1870. Courtesy L. Tom Perry Special Collections, Brigham Young University.

91 Brigham Young Travels, drawing. Used by permission, Utah State Historical Society, all rights reserved.

113 Boston and Newhouse Buildings, Salt Lake City. Used by permission, Utah State Historical Society, all rights reserved.

119 City Creek Center, Salt Lake City. Photo by Brandon Plewe.

124 Perrigrine Sessions family. Permission granted by Sessions Family Organization.

126 Emery Stake Academy. Courtesy L. Tom Perry Special Collections, Brigham Young University.

130 Wilford Woodruff: A visit to California. Used by permission, Utah State Historical Society, all rights reserved.

137 Mormon Battalion Visitors' Center, San Diego, California. Photo by Brandon Plewe.

138 Newel K. Whitney Store, Kirtland, Ohio. Photo by Brandon Plewe.

146 J. Reuben Clark. Used by permission, Utah State Historical Society, all rights reserved.

146 Edgar Brossard. Special Collections & Archives, Merrill-Cazier Lirary, Utah State University.

146 Ezra Taft Benson. © Intellectual Reserve Inc.

146 G. Stanley McAllister. *National Cyclopedia of American Biography* (Clifton, N.J.: James T. White and Co., 1975), volume 56, 380.

146 Reed Smoot. Public domain. Library of Congress. Bain News Service (photographer). Reed Smoot (ca1908). Photograph 31422 in Prints and Photographs Collection, G. G. Bain Collection. Washington, D.C.: Library of Congress.

146 Harvey Fletcher. Courtesy L. Tom Perry Special Collections, Brigham Young University.

146 Marriner S. Eccles. Special Collections Dept., J. Willard Marriott Library, University of Utah.

146 Ernest L. Wilkinson. Courtesy L. Tom Perry Special Collections, Brigham Young University.

146 J. Willard Marriott. Used by permission, Utah State Historical Society, all rights reserved.

147 John K. Edmunds. Courtesy William O. Swinyard.

147 Howard Stoddard. From Richard D. Poll, *Howard J. Stoddard, Founder, Michigan National Bank* (East Lansing: Michigan State University Press, 1980).

147 Harold F. Silver. Permission granted by Barnard Stewart Silver, Holladay, Utah.

147 George Albert Smith Jr. HBS Archives Photograph Collection: Faculty and Staff. Baker Library Historical Collections, Harvard Business School (olvwork377951).

147 Henry Eyring. Courtesy L. Tom Perry Special Collections, Brigham Young University.

147 George W. Romney. Used by permission, Utah State Historical Society, all rights reserved.

147 H. Taylor Peery. *National Cyclopedia of American Biography* (Clifton, N.J.: James T. White and Co., 1975), volume 53, 302.

147 David M. Kennedy. Courtesy L. Tom Perry Special Collections, Brigham Young University.

147 Esther Peterson. *Life* magazine photo archive hosted by Google. Photo by Francis Miller, published in *Life*, 1964.

147 Roy Oscarson. Courtesy Paul Oscarson.

153 Granite Mountain Records Vault, Utah. © Intellectual Reserve Inc.

159 World Mission Tour (Hugh J. Cannon and David O. McKay, in Giza, Egypt). Courtesy L. Tom Perry Special Collections, Brigham Young University.

161 Washington D.C. Chapel. *From left to right:* Unknown man; John A. Widstoe, Quorum of the Twelve; German Smith Ellsworth; George Albert Smith, Prophet and President of the L.D.S. Church; Thomas E. McKay, Assistant to the Twelve; Edgar Brossard, Stake President. Courtesy Richard German Ellsworth and Barbara E. Lowry.

163 Labor missionaries. Photo courtesy Brigham Young University–Hawaii Archives and Special Collections.

163 "Independence style meetinghouse," at Kansas City, Mo. © Intellectual Reserve Inc.

167 Spencer W. Kimball and Camilla Kimball on airplane. © Intellectual Reserve Inc.

176 LDS First Presidency, c. 1901 (*From left:* John R. Winder, Joseph F. Smith, Anthon H. Lund). Courtesy L. Tom Perry Special Collections, Brigham Young University.

181 Jonathan Napela. Church History Library, © Intellectual Reserve Inc.

193 Joseph Smith III. Courtesy Community of Christ Archives.

193 Frederick M. Smith. Courtesy Community of Christ Archives.

193 Israel A. Smith. Courtesy Community of Christ Archives.

193 W. Wallace Smith. Courtesy Community of Christ Archives.

193 Wallace B. Smith. Courtesy Community of Christ Archives.

193 W. Grant McMurray. Courtesy Community of Christ Archives.

193 Steven M. Veazey. Courtesy Community of Christ Archives.

197 Otto Fetting at ground breaking of temple in Independence, Mo., 1929. Courtesy Temple Lot Church, Independence, Mo.

199 Church Office Building. Photo by Brandon S. Plewe.

200 Watchtower building, Jehovah's Witness. Public domain.

201 Seventh-day Adventist headquarters. Courtesy of the Seventh-day Adventist Church.

213 Mormon Pavilion at New York World's Fair, 1964. Courtesy Stanley J. Plewe.

219 Abel Paez speaking to a conference in Mexico City, 1946, with President George Albert Smith. Courtesy Mexican Mormon History Museum.

232 Mass baptisms in Nigeria, 1978. Church History Library, © Intellectual Reserve Inc.